Community Policing

Community Policing

Contemporary Readings

Geoffrey P. Alpert
The University of South Carolina

Alex Piquero
Temple University

WAVELAND
PRESS, INC.
Prospect Heights, Illinois

For information about this book, write or call:
Waveland Press, Inc.
P.O. Box 400
Prospect Heights, Illinois 60070
(847) 634-0081

Contents

Part I

Historical and Conceptual Frameworks

Community policing has received increased attention in recent years at both the academic and practitioner levels. In addition, various aspects of community policing have received a great deal of attention within public policy circles. As a result, there is a growing literature that documents the history and bases on which community policing is built. The articles chosen for the first section of the book describe the historical and conceptual frameworks of community policing.

The first selection is from Professor Herman Goldstein. Commonly referred to as the pioneer of the community and problem-solving movement, Goldstein was an early advocate for these approaches to policing. In this selection, he discusses the impetus for community policing, as well as the potential benefits and pitfalls to such policing strategies.

The second selection is from another pioneer of the community policing movement, Professor Peter Manning. In this article, Manning reviews the meanings and assumptions of community policing. He closes the article by offering methods in which the community policing scheme can be successful and focuses on structural and legal changes both within the department and in society in general.

The next selection in this section is a second look at the "broken windows" notion presented originally by these authors in 1982. Professors Kelling and Wilson draw on successful case studies on the effectiveness of "fixing broken windows" in order to reduce crime and incidents of disorder. Kelling and Wilson suggest that the strategy of fixing neighborhood problems is more effective at crime prevention than conventional "incident-based" policing approaches.

In the fourth selection in this section, Professor Gary Cordner presents one of the most impressive assessments of community policing. This important contribution to community policing provides a needed look into the various dimensions of community policing: philosophical, strategic, tactical and organizational.

The fifth selection is written by John Eck and William Spelman. The authors highlight the main differences between the traditional incident-driven

1

approach that has marked policing for many years and the community-driven model of problem-oriented policing marked by the problem-solving process of scanning, analyzing, responding, and assessing.

The final selection in this section is written by William Pelfrey, who discusses the paradigmatic shift from traditional to community policing. He includes a brief discussion of the nature of paradigms, the eras of policing, and the research on police which influenced the move to community policing. He examines other critical factors which generated the shift, including court decisions and the evolving role of law enforcement.

1

Toward Community-Oriented Policing
Potential, Basic Requirements, and Threshold Questions

Herman Goldstein

The direction of change in policing has turned an important corner. Among progressive police administrators, the new knowledge and insights developed since interest in the police intensified in the 1960s are now taken for granted. It is assumed, for example, that the value of traditional policing methods intended to control crime is extremely limited. Likewise, it is accepted that the functions of the police inevitably involve more than just enforcing the law, and that some of these non-law enforcement functions are extremely important for the effect they have on the quality of life in a community. Rather than spend time challenging such conclusions, those on the cutting edge of policing are devoting their energy to experimenting with new forms of policing that are based upon the better understanding of the capacity and complexity of the police function that has been acquired in recent years. As the realities of politics and finances permit, changes are being implemented that are designed to be more responsive not only to crime, but to the fear of crime and, more broadly, to a wide range of problems that affect the quality of life in our urban areas.

The changes have been launched as new programs under an assortment of labels and acronyms, and take quite different forms. But many of them can be loosely grouped under the heading "community policing." This umbrella term has been used as descriptive of much of what is happening because the new programs often have one or more elements associated with the general concept of "community policing." Most common among these are the involvement of the community

Source: Reprinted by permission of Sage Publications from *Crime and Delinquency*, Vol. 33 No 1, pp. 6–30. Copyright 1987 by Sage Publications, Inc.

in getting the police job done; the permanent assignment of police officers to a neighborhood in order to cultivate better relationships; the setting of police priorities based on the specific needs and desires of the community; and the meeting of these needs by the allocation of police resources and personnel otherwise assigned to responding to calls for police assistance.

Cynics among us who have watched efforts to improve the police over the past several decades may dismiss the programs labeled "community policing" as simply another fad in a long series of proposals for improving policing that have been enthusiastically advanced, and shortly thereafter abandoned. Indeed, analysis of somewhat similar projects initiated in the past in this country (Sherman et al., 1973; Schwartz and Clarren, 1977; Mastrofski, 1984) provides ample basis for skepticism. In England, where much more experimentation has occurred over a longer period of time, community-policing projects have been criticized as largely nostalgic exercises, based upon questionable assumptions unsupported by research (Manning, 1984). It is claimed that they have had little impact because they were subverted by the strong occupational culture of those in the lower ranks (Holdaway, 1984). They pose serious questions about the political accountability of the police, with some arguing that they involve the police in politics in a way that is potentially dangerous in a democratic society (Short, 1983). And still another criticism is that they have been evaluated using methods that make the claims of their success of questionable validity (Weatheritt, 1983).

But there are some important distinctions between the older community-policing projects and those that have been launched within the past several years in this country. The newer projects have been started at the initiative of the police in an attempt to improve the quality of police service, rather than primarily as a means of giving the community more direct control over police operations. More important, however, they grow out of a more solid understanding of police operations and effectiveness than was available in the past (Mastrofski, 1984). These distinctions, alone, do not overcome the impediments encountered earlier. They do, however, significantly increase the potential for realizing the substantial benefits that have been held out for community policing (e.g., decreased tensions between the police and the community, more effective use of police resources, an increased quality of police service, increased effectiveness in dealing with community problems, increased job satisfaction for the police participating in the programs, and increased accountability to the community). Even the strongest critics of past efforts acknowledge these benefits are worth pursuing (Manning, 1984; Holdaway, 1984; Short, 1983; Mastrofski, 1984). I would go further. The recurring themes in the newest projects (more involvement of the community, greater accountability to the community, and improved service to the community) are so synonymous with the values inherent in the policing of a free society, one could argue that the label itself (i.e., community policing) is redundant. But it may be useful in giving needed emphasis to these very values. More substantively, however, if sufficient effort is invested in the move toward community policing and if the movement is seen not simply as a different way of labeling or packaging existing police services, but as a different way of thinking about the police, I would argue that a fully developed concept of what we now allude to by "community policing" could provide the umbrella under which a more integrated strategy for improving the quality of policing could be constructed.

In this article, I will (1) summarize briefly the most common characteristics of community policing; (2) identify the elements that are essential if a program of community policing is to succeed; and (3) raise some of the tough questions that must still be addressed if the concept is to be more fully developed and its maximum potential realized.

Common Characteristics of Community Policing

Among the most elementary programs that come under the community policing umbrella are those that demonstrate, for purposes of reducing fear and deterring crime, that the police have a presence in the community: that they are easily accessible, frequently visible, and caring in their relationships with citizens. This is often achieved by placing officers on foot, on motor scooters, or on motorcycles, thereby eliminating the psychological barrier created by a squad car. (In what I see as a gross oversimplification of the concept, community policing, in some quarters, has simply been equated to foot patrol, without exploration of what such patrol entails and how it ties into the more ambitious objectives of community policing.) Another dimension of these basic programs is crime prevention. The police educate citizens on how they can avoid becoming the victims of crime and enlist the eyes and ears of citizens in reporting suspicious circumstances. "Crime watch" programs, for example, serve this purpose. Community organization, in which the police officer serves as a coalescing force, is another method commonly employed in community policing. It is thought that increased neighborhood cohesion will both contribute to a reduction in fear and aid the police in dealing with the community's problems. (For a comprehensive review of the experiments and literature on community organization as it relates to crime prevention, see Greenberg et al., 1985. Also see Davis, 1985; Feins, 1983).

Officers are frequently expected not only to respond to the full range of problems that the public expects the police to handle, including peacekeeping (or order maintenance), but also to take the initiative to identify whatever community problems—beyond those within the widest definition of police functioning—that may affect the public's sense of well-being. And they may be urged to seek solutions to these problems, making full use of both their imagination and the various resources available in the community.

In most community-policing projects, it is implied—if not made explicit—that officers are to have much greater freedom and to exercise independence. It is also implied that the community will have some input into decisions made about the form of police services—especially the priority given to different problems.

More ambitious than these basic programs are those designed to enable the police to develop greater familiarity with both regular members of the community and those who in some way threaten the peace of the community. The ability of members of the community to know their community police officer by name is considered a measure of success. This requires that officers be assigned permanently to a given area, and devote much of their effort to outreach. Arrangements are made so that citizens can contact the assigned officer directly by telephone. The officer may work out of a site in the area or out of a newly established ministation. Officers may be encouraged to conduct door-to-door surveys in order to get to know residents and business people and to learn of their concerns. They will typically be provided with the information that the department has on the area to which they are assigned, and, in turn, will be encouraged to collect information that will not only help them in carrying out their duties, but that may also be helpful to other members of the department.

As police officers identify with an area, and become familiar with its residents and lifestyles, it is argued that the potential in community-oriented policing increases; that the work of the officer reinforces the informal social controls of the area (Wilson and Kelling, 1982). This argument has been criticized because it implies that communities are easily identifiable and homogeneous, and that the interests of the police and of the community can be fully harmonized (Walker, 1984; Mastrofski, 1984). If this can, in fact, be achieved (even partially), one could build up a substantial amount of goodwill among the citizens of the community. This, in turn, could lead to the ultimate potential in community policing—the development of a reservoir of respect and support that could greatly increase the capacity of police officers to deal with problems with less need to resort to the criminal process, or to the coercive force that officers derive from their uniform, their weapon, their badge, or the knowledge that they can summon reinforcements. As has repeatedly been pointed out, such an ideal set of circumstances—the British refer to it as policing by consent—would return us to the goals set out for the police in England in 1829, when it was assumed that police, who were unarmed and had limited authority, would rely on public approval for their needed power. It is a theme that is often reasserted in policing and that is among the distinguishing features of modern-day Japanese policing. Thus, community policing, in some of its major features, is clearly not a new concept. The question is whether it, or some combination of its features, can be made to work in a pluralistic society—in American cities with such racial and ethnic diversity in their populations and with such an intermingling of social norms.

Some Basic Requirements

Unlike many of the changes that have occurred in American policing over the years, community policing, if it is to realize its full potential, should not be viewed merely as a new project, method, or procedure that can simply be added, as an appendage of sorts, to an existing police organization. It can better be described as a way of thinking about policing—as an operating philosophy that, in order to succeed, must eventually have a pervasive influence on the operations of the entire agency. A number of key elements are needed to achieve this objective.

Integrating the Concept within the Organization of the Police Agency

Police agencies have to devote substantial resources to responding to emergencies, unpredictable calls for service, and serious crimes—matters that require a quick reactive response and that constitute what some have referred to as the "fire brigade" function of policing. No one would seriously suggest that these functions be abandoned. Not only are they essential tasks; the ability of the police to function in many other areas derives from the public's impression of how well they perform these crucial tasks, and the interest that officers have in their jobs is fed, in some measure, by the excitement and challenge presented by these emergency demands.

The problem, quite simply, is that these quick-response functions not only currently receive the bulk of police resources; they dictate the form and primary focus of police organizations. Preoccupation with reacting to calls for assistance dominates all aspects of police operations. Can a radically different, proactive form of policing be introduced into such a setting, with any confidence that it can survive?

Unless extraordinary measures are taken, officers assigned to perform community policing are likely to be ostracized and isolated in an organization with a heavily traditional orientation to reactive policing. They will not be viewed by the vast majority of officers as performing "real" police work. And depending on the arrangements under which they operate, they may be seen as not assuming their appropriate share of the routine work load and—worse yet—as not to be depended on should an officer need assistance in a dangerous situation. Flint, Michigan, has been among the pioneer cities in making a substantial commitment to community policing. Neighborhood officers are viewed as "full service" officers (Trojanowicz, 1982). But it appears to this observer that the city has created a department within a department, with much tension between the two. Baltimore County has been attempting to gain acceptance for the operating philosophy of its COPE (Community-Oriented Police Enforcement) unit by training its top command staff in COPE's objectives, and encouraging them to use the same techniques—with some indication that this has produced positive results (Taft, 1986). The Houston Police Department is reported as already having succeeded in developing a good relationship between officers assigned to working with the community out of storefront offices and those assigned to regular patrols in the same area (Skolnick and Bayley, 1986).

Some agencies have planned to deal with this problem—after the first introduction of community policing—by eventually splitting field services into two units—one to engage in community policing and the other to respond to emergencies, serious crimes, and calls requiring immediate investigation. This builds, to some degree, on the split-force experiment in Wilmington (Tien et al., 1977). Can the two units exist alongside each other, be mutually supportive, and to a degree integrated? Would the benefits that accrue to the police through careful development of community policing improve the capacity of the reactive force in getting its job done? Or would the work of the reactive unit (untrained in community policing and possibly engaging in such practices as aggressive stopping and questioning) reduce the effectiveness of the community-oriented police?

I sense a growing feeling among administrators committed to community policing that while it might be necessary, in an incubation period, to separate the officers engaged in community policing from the rest of the agency, separate units with different orientations are simply not workable in the long run. The concept of community policing, if it is to produce the desired results, must be the exclusive operating philosophy of the department. This means that the values and beliefs articulated by the administration must apply equally to the officer who responds to emergency calls and the officer permanently situated in a specific neighborhood. Ultimately, the organization of a police force and the allocation of personnel might be dictated primarily by the desire to serve, in a proactive fashion, the broad needs of neighborhoods. Officers assigned to assuring a quick response to emergency calls might be seen as functioning in a supportive role. Such a situation would reflect a complete inversion of present priorities.

Much of what constitutes traditional reactive policing is simply incompatible with the community-policing concept. Methods by which officers in the field have traditionally dealt with problems will have to be modified or abandoned. For example, a department could not long tolerate a situation in which officers in a residential area go out of their way to demonstrate that they are caring, service-oriented individuals, while other officers assigned to a roving task force make wholesale sweeps of loitering juveniles in that community. Such activities greatly diminish the credibility of officers who have invested heavily in developing rapport.

Creating a New Working Environment

Much more important than the organizational arrangements for assigning personnel are the steps that an administrator takes to incorporate new values into the management of the organization. The success of community policing initiatives will depend, to a great extent, on the degree to which they are supported by changes in the standards used in recruiting individuals into the agency, the training given new recruits, the expectations of supervisors, the manner in which productivity is measured, and the criteria for making rewards and promotions.

Numerous examples already are available of community-policing units that have been weakened because they were judged by traditional standards. A system that continues to reward exclusively those officers who make numerous arrests or who are especially heroic communicates clearly to community police officers that not much has changed; that they are indeed peripheral to the main mission. In some cities, joining the community policing project is currently viewed as ending one's chance for promotion. Community-policing officers may make a special effort to make large numbers of arrests and to make especially commendable arrests to legitimize themselves in the eyes of the officers assigned to traditional policing.

Traditional policing has created a style of management that is terribly negative. The success of sergeants, lieutenants, and captains is not measured by what they accomplish positively, but by the degree to which they control their subordinates and keep them out of trouble. The mere suggestion that police officers operate with greater flexibility and greater independence is viewed as an anathema by many of those in middle management. Indeed, they are at a loss as to how to supervise employees with such freedom. To be sure, one cannot dismiss the need for controls in a system in which armed employees exercise enormous authority without being easily observed. Correcting the situation will require a major reorientation of police middle management. It will require the adoption of new values, new management techniques, as well as an acknowledgment that errors in judgment will occasionally be made.

Reducing the Resistance of the Police Subculture

Ultimately, community policing will work only if rank-and-file police officers buy into the concept. Simon Holdaway (1984), in his penetrating study of the British police at work in Hilton, provides dramatic evidence of the capacity of rank-and-file officers to sabotage community-oriented policing policies that do not reflect their values. Their understanding of policing remained dominant, unaffected by the new policies formulated by top management. Although not directly related to the implementation of community-policing programs, several studies in this country demonstrate the enormous power of the police occupational culture (Van Maanen, 1974; Reuss-Ianni and Ianni, 1983).

One obvious way in which to begin to deal with this problem is to take greater cognizance, when designing new programs, of the conditions under which the police work—conditions that so directly affect their performance (e.g., conflicting pressures and demands, complex nature of problems with which they deal, hostile attitudes of those subject to their actions, unpredictable danger, rigid work rules, military-type supervision). Another is to arrange for greater involvement on the part of rank-and-file officers in the development of the community-policing concept. If properly coordinated, the changes contemplated in community policing can have great appeal to these officers. They welcome the modification of those current work rules that require mindless obedience to a higher authority. They value independence, which enables them to make greater use of their talents and expertise. They appreciate opportunities to develop more positive relationships with the community, to enhance their status, and to derive greater job satisfaction. The "common sense" aspects of community policing, which receive the enthusiastic endorsement of police officers, and the values an agency seeks to develop in implementing community policing often happily coincide.

One can also address the resistance of the occupational subculture by seeking, in a variety of ways, to alter the factors that contribute to the strength of that sub-culture. One can, for example, alter the extent to which the police feel defensive in their relationship with the community by giving greater visibility to their opera-tions—by acquainting the community with the limitations on their authority, by reducing community expectations, by recognizing the need for police to exercise discretion, and by acknowledging that the nature of policing is such that officers must take risks and will occasionally err. It would help if the function of the police was clarified, if appropriate alternatives were fashioned to enable them to deal effec-tively with the infinite variety of situations they are expected to handle, and if clearer guidance was provided for making the many on-the-spot decisions that must be made. Since community policing does incorporate many of these changes, the greatest need, it would appear, is to demonstrate convincingly to rank-and-file officers how these changes would serve their interests and how their interests coincide with those of the police organization and the community. (For elaboration, see Goldstein, 1977:264.)

Focusing on Substantive Problems

I would argue strongly that another basic prerequisite for realizing the potential in community policing is to develop a commitment to analyzing systematically the problems that the police are called upon to handle and to work for the development of more effective responses to these problems. This change in focus is perhaps the most radical of the several needs I have identified, in that it moves us from an emphasis on form to an emphasis on substance; from stressing process to stressing results. It seeks to get more directly at the end product of policing. Without a focus on substantive problems, community policing can be an empty shell.

A number of community-policing projects already encourage their officers to increase their effectiveness by viewing their role primarily as dealing with community problems. Officers are not precluded from using traditional police methods to solve these problems, but they are urged to resort to more than just the criminal justice system; to employ instead many different alternatives, such as counseling, mediation, referral to other agencies, and obtaining services from other municipal departments. The neighborhood foot-patrol project in Flint, the central-district project in Oakland, and the community patrol officer project in New York City are among the community-policing projects that incorporate this feature (Trojanowicz, 1982; Reiss, 1985; Vera Foundation, 1985).

These efforts in the context of community policing tie in with this author's prior work on "problem-oriented policing" (Goldstein, 1979). The concept has been implemented in the police departments of Baltimore County, Maryland (Taft, 1986) and Newport News, Virginia (Eck and Spelman, 1985) with the technical support of the Police Executive Research Forum, and also in the Madison, Wisconsin police department (Goldstein and Susmilch, 1982). London's Metropolitan Police have also experimented with it and incorporated the concept into a new statement of their operating philosophy (Newman, 1984:4).

Problem-oriented policing goes a step further than what is commonly conveyed in community policing by asserting up front that the police job is not simply law enforcement, but dealing with a wide range of community problems— only some of which constitute violations of the law. It further asserts that enforcement of the law is not an end in itself, but only one of several means by which the police can deal with the problems they are expected to handle.

Officers are encouraged to think in terms of *problems* rather than *incidents*. An officer permanently assigned to a community in a program that incorporates the problem approach is encouraged to pick up on the relationship between and among incidents occurring in the same family, in the same building, or in the same general neighborhood. The officer is encouraged to recognize related and recurring incidents as symptomatic of problems begging for solutions and to search for the solutions. The same concept applies to larger physical areas and to higher levels in the organization. Officers at all ranks are encouraged to group similar incidents that may constitute the same type of problem, and then to concentrate on thinking through the agency's response to the problem.

The analysis of the problem is critical to this approach. It may take various forms, from simple to complex. In the projects in Flint and in New York City, individual officers assigned to specific neighborhoods are encouraged, within the limits of their own resources, to gather facts about specific problems in the hope that careful analysis of them will lead to more effective solutions (Trojanowicz, 1982; Ward, 1985).

Baltimore County's COPE unit consists of 45 officers divided into three groups of 15, each of which is assigned to deal with specific problems that have generated fear. These units stay with each problem until it is resolved or reduced in magnitude. COPE officers are expected to probe deeply into each problem to which they are assigned. From the outset, the Baltimore County project has given high priority to conducting house-to-house surveys, which were initially designed to determine the level of fear and to identify community concerns. Officers also gather demographic data and other relevant information from appropriate government agencies, and turn to additional sources to learn as much as possible about the problem itself and those who may be responsible for it. Only after they have invested time in analyzing the problem and in synthesizing their data are they expected to diagnose it formally and begin the search for a solution (Taft, 1986).

In Newport News, a department task force identified two major problems that were then analyzed with the support of several full-time analysts. Now, individual officers, with varying degrees of support, are being encouraged to develop their own ability to analyze problems of concern to them on their beats. (See Eck and Spelman, article 5.)

After analyzing the problem, officers involved in these projects conduct an uninhibited search for alternative responses. They may settle on one of the responses identified above as commonly used in community policing, or they may go a step further, perhaps pressuring municipal agencies to carry out existing responsibilities or to invest new resources in an area. They may push for changes in the policies of other government agencies or advocate legislation that would enable police to deal more effectively with a problem that clearly warrants arrest and prosecution. The availability of a choice of well-designed responses, when combined with intimate familiarity with citizens in their area, gives police officers a much improved capacity to get their job done with minimal negative consequences. This whole process reflects a rather belated recognition that the police handle an incredibly wide variety of problems; that what may work for one problem may not work for another; that, using the medical analogy, some problems require no more than a band-aid or an aspirin, while others may require major surgery.

By drawing on the expertise of line officers and involving them in devising solutions, the problem-solving approach increases the potential for more effective police responses. It also challenges the officer's imagination and creativity, generating new enthusiasm for the job.

Some Fundamental Questions

If a conscious effort is made to meet the basic requirements set forth above, the current series of community projects could lead to a new and, in many respects, exciting strategy for improving police operations. But many perplexing questions remain to be settled. Four of the most important ones are examined here.

What Should Be the Outer Limits of the Police Function under the Community Policing Concept?

It was suggested earlier that it is helpful to think of policing as consisting primarily of dealing with community problems, but that image may appear too open-ended—especially when we want police officers to probe for the "root problem"—which, carried to the extreme, could lead to such large social problems as poverty, racism, unemployment, and lack of education. But is it wise in rethinking the police role in the context of community policing, to adopt limitations that might rule out what is clearly the most effective, direct response to a problem? While we should be apprehensive of an example drawn from such a radically different political environment as the People's Republic of China, a recent description of the police function in Beijing gives cause for reflection. The chief of the Erlong station in Beijing, emphasizing crime prevention as the prime police task, praised a 23-year-old officer for his outstanding performance in that he had, with the help of the public security committee on Wejia Street, his permanent assignment, found jobs for 17 youths with previous criminal records. The chief reported that no crime had occurred on the street in two years. The officer is reported as saying, "We should not keep watching those who are likely to make trouble. Instead we should ask ourselves what we can do to help them with their problems." He said it was not easy for a young man with a bad record to find a job, and that if the man is deserted by society he would most likely create problems for that society (Yun, 1985, p. 25).

Is the police role to be restricted to crime prevention, or should it extend to the sense of fear and insecurity in the community, or even more broadly, to the peace and tranquility of the community? Or, taken to the outer limit, should it extend to any problem that is appropriately a matter of concern to municipal government? It is essential that the limits of community policing be defined by some articulable criteria; otherwise, the limitless character of the role will make it extremely difficult to gain broad acceptance for the concept.

But even if the outer boundaries are spelled out, many questions will remain. The most obvious is one of volume. Once police officers demonstrate that they care about petty offenses, street disorders, environmental eyesores, and people who cannot help themselves, will the demands for assistance with these types of problems be overwhelming? Police officers, especially in large cities, are well aware of the massive volume of complex behavioral problems that are not receiving adequate attention, either because of lack of initiative on the part of the parties involved or because of inadequacies in the services of other government agencies. To assume responsibility for all of these unmet needs is unrealistic.

And how long should a community police officer remain involved in handling a given problem? Some community police officers currently counsel victims of spousal abuse in weekly sessions and meet regularly with troubled juveniles. The commitment is admirable, and the results are often impressive, but is there a limit to the time officers should spend in providing such individualized services? In like fashion, a decision on the part of a police officer to assist in dealing with a building-code violation or in getting rubbish collected should not result in the officer being viewed as the community's permanent building inspector or rubbish collector.

One of the distinctive roles that has emerged for community patrol officers is that of community ombudsman—the person who receives complaints and has the knowledge, contacts, and ability to pressure other public and private agencies to provide needed services. Initially, officers are not comfortable in this role. In their police training, they were usually taught to direct citizens to take such complaints to other departments, and if, for some compelling reason, they felt the need to see that something was done, they were trained to "work through channels."

If an officer is given permission to make such direct contacts, the results can be dramatic (Short, 1983; Taft, 1986). But if a community officer seeks to correct a specific problem that requires the attention of another municipal agency and gets no response, the officer's credibility and effectiveness are weakened in the eyes of the community. This is bound to happen in large cities if adequate prearrangements are not made and there is great competition for limited resources. A somewhat related problem, in large cities, is that so many of the problems an officer encounters are of a magnitude far beyond the capacity of the single officer to affect.

Among the most dramatic examples of community policing are those in which the police have joined with the community to advocate for a new program, redefine government policies, obtain a new piece of legislation, or pressure for the allocation of government resources. These "advocate-officers" can win enormous support for the police. But the mere suggestion that police assume the role of an advocate on behalf of community groups is offensive to many citizens because of the set of values that they assume police have. (For an interesting exploration of some of the problems raised, see Short, 1983.) Additionally, the police are bound to find themselves frequently in conflict with city hall, local political representatives, adjacent neighborhoods, various interest groups, and members of their own department. Somewhat similar questions are raised when community-policing officers are referred to as "agents of social change" (Brown, 1985). It is generally acknowledged that, in most contexts, this means that the police are committed to operating policies that facilitate, rather than impede, the social changes occurring in large cities. But since there is usually substantial disagreement within a community as to the appropriate direction, form, and speed of such change, the term is quite ambiguous and, for some individuals, the role of the police as agents of social change is worrisome.

Officers-as-advocates is a posture so fraught with potential problems that one's immediate reaction is to preclude it from any community policing scheme. But there is something fundamentally wrong with a government system in which the agency most acquainted with the bigotry, injustice, exploitation, and deprivation of the human condition is precluded from speaking out about these very problems. Sensitive police officers have lived for many years with people's sufferings, and yet conclude that they must "swallow hard" and accept them as part of their job. Ironically, when public interest eventually focuses on these problems, as it often does (e.g., spousal abuse, child abuse, rape victims), past handling by the police is frequently among the targets of criticism. The dilemma is well summarized by the sociologist, Maurice Punch (1979), when he observes that, "the police are always in danger of being left behind by social change but cannot, by their very nature, afford to march ahead of change."

How Does One Increase the Freedom and Independence of Individual Police Officers without Losing Accountability and Adding to the Likelihood of Corruption?

Police administrators devote an enormous amount of their total energy to controlling the actions of their subordinates, since the community judges the quality of policing on the number of complaints filed and exposures of wrongdoing or corruption. The task of controlling police officers is made difficult because, unlike workers on an assembly line, police carry out much of their job in private settings, where they cannot be observed by supervisors. Police managers therefore rely heavily on such devices as the filling out of many forms, the arrangements for checking in and out of service, and the frequent transfer of personnel to avoid the establishment of alliances. Even though their value is questionable, these devices are seen as creating some degree of accountability and as reducing the possibility for corruption. Holdaway (1984), in his study of unit-beat policing (a form of community policing) in Hilton, England, points out that one of the unanticipated consequences of granting greater freedom and independence to the officers assigned to specific areas was that they were less accountable to the community—though achieving accountability was one of the primary goals of the project.

In large cities in this country, with a prior or current history of corruption, the establishment of as close a working relationship between a police officer and a neighborhood as is contemplated in community policing is seen as a sure invitation to corrupt practices. It is a sad commentary on the state of policing in this country that the need to control corrupt practices stands in the way of more effective policing. Yet there is little question that, given the way in which the public judges the police, an administrator stands to lose more by facilitating corruption than by failing to take initiatives to achieve the benefits of community policing.

The New York City Police Department, which has had extensive experience with controlling corruption and is now experimenting with community policing, implemented a number of special steps to assure the integrity of the community-policing operation and they are reported, to date, as being effective (Farrell, 1986). As for some cities, however, in which police corruption or misuse of police authority is common, it may simply not be feasible to experiment with community policing. Stated more positively, a police administrator may be able to implement community policing only in those departments in which integrity and conformity with established legal requirements are the rule; where one can, with reasonable assurance, depend on self-discipline.

How Free Should Community Officers Be to Select Alternatives for Solving Problems?

Line officers have always made use of a wide range of alternatives for getting their job done. Yet officers are constantly aware that if any questions are raised about the propriety or legality of their actions, their conduct is judged by formally established standards. In community policing, officers are urged to employ openly a wide range of alternatives, and would be rewarded for their creativity. It is assumed that these officers will not act outside their legal authority. But what controls, if any, exist over their use of various alternatives and the propriety of their choices? Should this be a matter of concern?

Some alternatives, such as making physical changes (e.g., the installation of lights, the relocation of a bus stop, or changes in landscaping) may not be controversial or raise legal questions. The police may be widely acclaimed for their ingenuity in coming up with a solution to a long-standing problem. But most solutions are not likely to be uniformly supported, and some may create the potential for abuse.

As an illustration, community organizing is almost always listed as one of the tools available to community police officers. Not all problems require organizing the community, but many do. (A side issue is whether communities should be organized through packaged programs prepared by the police department, or only if it seems feasible to do so in order to deal with the problems identified by citizens.) If a problem, such as residential burglaries, is identified, it is admirable when a police officer can mobilize a neighborhood in ways that deal effectively with the problem. But what if the same organizational structure is subsequently used to lobby against a half-way house for the mentally ill, or is used to prevent a minority businessman from moving into the neighborhood, or is used to endorse candidates for public office? And can the police be selective in whom they organize within a neighborhood? Can they exclude those who are considered the problem in the neighborhood, such as juvenile gang members or "street people"? Interestingly, the more common problem experienced to date is not the lack of a representation for some groups or a runaway neighborhood organization, but rather the inability to sustain the interest of the assembled group over an extended period of time.

Police officers often find that informal actions (like warning a suspected drug dealer to stop selling or asking him to leave a neighborhood) may be the most effective and direct way of putting an end to a problem. What are the dangers in encouraging police officers to make greater use of informal authority? Wilson and Kelling (1982) raise the problem in their article, "Broken Windows," when they relate how the police, attempting to deal with gangs that terrorize residents of a housing project, are left with no alternative but to chase known gang members out of the projects. They quote a police officer describing the practice as, "We kick ass."

Should we encourage "kicking ass," which will, in many instances, win the applause of a given community, but which, in the long run, might undermine police efforts in the larger community to develop a more positive attitude toward the police? Or should we press police agencies to spell out and obtain appropriate authority to handle these situations? The police do not now have the authority to deal with many street situations they are expected to handle, because disorderly conduct, loitering, and vagrancy statutes, formerly used to cover such situations, have been declared constitutionally void because of their vagueness. In some cities, the vacuum has been filled by enactment of more specifically drawn statutes or ordinances. In the Oakland project, the department sought and obtained an ordinance prohibiting loitering for purposes of prostitution—not unlike that enacted in many locales (Reiss, 1985). In Madison, the department proposed and had enacted an ordinance that gets at the behavior of panhandlers who harass people but exempts street entertainers who collect coins from passersby. As ordinances, these efforts to proscribe specific forms of behavior take on more of the character of a regulation than a law (Reiss, 1984), giving officers alternatives to making a physical arrest. The issuance of a citation often suffices. But the use of this form of authority is nevertheless controlled in that the action of the officer is always subject to review if questioned by the alleged offender.

In the context of community policing, it is especially desirable that officers have the option, except when a serious offense is committed, to choose not to enforce the law if another alternative appears more effective. It is well established that the police exercise such discretion all of the time (Goldstein, 1977). But how can this use of discretion be formally encouraged at a time when a number of highly publicized court cases, holding the police liable for taking no enforcement action when they had evidence that an offense had been committed, remind us that there is no solid legal basis for the exercise of such discretion. Such cases include one in which a drunken driver was not arrested (*Irwin v. Ware*, 1984) and one in which a wife batterer was not arrested (*Thurman v. Torrington*, 1984). Despite these rather unusual and somewhat aggravated cases, selective enforcement of the law is gradually being recognized, but defending the practice requires that the police, at a minimum, spell out, in the form of policies, the criteria they employ in exercising their discretion. Should police simply continue to operate with current ambiguities until held to account, or should they press for a more solid legal foundation for the discretion that they must inevitably exercise—especially since community policing requires such discretion more than does traditional policing?

As for some large-volume problems, analysis may reveal that government regulation at a higher level can greatly reduce the incidents police must handle. The large number of shoplifters processed by the police can be decreased if some merchandising practices are prohibited. The number of thefts from automobiles can be greatly reduced if minimum operating standards are imposed on the owners of parking facilities. And the number of incidents the police must handle in premises that serve alcohol can be greatly reduced if a heavier responsibility is placed on the licensee. Obviously, merchants, parking facility operators, and dispensers of alcohol want to operate with few regulations. But at what point does the burden on the police and the problems created for the larger community warrant tighter regulations at the source of the problems? At issue are tough, close questions that require balancing the public's interest against the values placed on free enterprise and individual choice. The police rarely have the political power to bring about changes when aligned against the special interests that would be affected by them, unless supported by strong public sentiment. (The recent battle between the national police organizations, united in their stance, and the National Rifle Association over a proposed relaxation of gun controls is a dramatic example.)

This last illustration of the issues likely to arise in community policing regarding police use of their authority and other alternatives for dealing with problems points, once again, to the potential benefits of more careful study and analysis. Recommendations from a police agency for adoption of alternative responses will carry much more weight if the police, supported by independent research efforts, could more clearly demonstrate the effectiveness of one approach over another.

What Role Should the Community Have in Making
Policy Decisions within the Community-Policing Framework?

One of the major factors that distinguishes one form of community policing from another is the degree to which it is contemplated that the community—assuming we can first reach accord on what constitutes the community—will participate in making some of the important decisions. Some programs that police agencies have initiated operate in only one direction: they seek to engage the community by working with the citizenry and using their eyes and ears, but the agency retains all responsibility for making decisions. Other programs commit themselves to listening to the community and perhaps to consulting with it, making use, for example, of advisory councils, but with ultimate decisions made by the police. In contrast to these models, community policing in other jurisdictions has been advanced primarily as a method of giving citizens greater direct involvement in determining how they are policed. These projects stress the accountability of the police to the community being served.

From the preceding discussion, it should be clear that there are indeed many decisions to be made. Who, for example, is to decide what problems require police attention in a given neighborhood, and what priority should be given to them? And if a wide range of alternatives are to be used in responding to problems, who should choose from among them? Should the community have any say regarding the assignment of personnel—like the community police officer or the commander of a district? And what should be the relationship between community-oriented police and local legislative representatives (the city council member or alderperson)?

Questions about the degree of community involvement in determining the policies of police agencies are not as open-ended as the previous questions raised. Experience has taught us that, in carrying out some aspects of their functions, the police must be insulated from community influences. Some of their decision-making authority cannot be shared. The police cannot, for example, be responsive to community desires if doing so will violate the constitutional rights of any citizen or violate any other limitations on police authority. The standards of a neighborhood cannot be substituted for the rules of the state. Police administrators cannot surrender managerial controls over their agency (including the assignment of personnel) without significantly reducing their capacity to direct the agency. And partisan political interests of the type that contributed to corrupt practices in the past cannot be allowed to dictate police policies and practices.

But the range of decisions to be made in the policing of a community are sufficiently numerous that there remain a large number in which a community may participate without violating any of these limitations. The challenge is to identify them more clearly and to develop the procedures by which they can be made—including methods for dealing with conflicting demands from within the same community.

Some Concluding Observations

In attempting to put together an overview of the movement toward community policing and, in particular, to identify obvious needs and briefly raise some of the tough, unsolved questions, there is a risk that the magnitude of the task will be seriously understated and the problems that have to be addressed will be oversimplified. On a scale of one to ten, I would estimate that we have yet to reach one in development of our thinking and, most important, in the validation of some of our assumptions. One could, for example, greatly expand the list of fundamental questions raised above, and each of those raised should be explored in much greater detail than space and our limited experience at this time permit.

Research on the value of community policing, or any of its components, in this country is in its infancy. Trojanowicz (1982) has published his evaluation of the initial stages of the neighborhood foot patrol project in Flint. The Police Foundation has published their evaluation of the work aimed at reducing fear in Houston and Newark (Pate et al., 1986). The Vera Institute has been monitoring the community patrol officer program in New York City and will be conducting a more rigorous evaluation of the expansion of the project (Vera, 1985). It is natural to call for more rigorous research, especially since the percentage of funds we invest in evaluating the effectiveness of what we are doing in policing is such an infinitesimal percentage of the enormous total investment we make in the financing of police services in this country. But the effect of some of the changes being advocated may simply not be subject to evaluation. Too many changes are occurring at the same time. And there are enormous methodological problems—put aside cost—in conducting large-scale controlled experiments.

We may have to be satisfied with the results of less rigorous research. In their comprehensive description and analysis of police innovations in Oakland, Houston, Detroit, Newark, Denver, and Santa Ana, Jerome Skolnick and David Bayley (1986) note:

> We really can't advocate as strongly as we would like the developments described in this book. Our recommendations about the usefulness of community-oriented policing are based, like those of police administrators themselves, on arguments that such innovations "make sense" or on conclusions developed from field observations [p. 226].

And in his review of Oakland's experiment in the policing of its central district, Reiss (1985), noting that the time for experimentation was past when he was asked to review the project, nevertheless makes a convincing argument for the value of his report:

> Rather, what we can do is something like what the lawyer does in an adversary proceeding. We can present a number of facts and opinions, each of which provides evidence of how well it is working. We shall suggest that the preponderance of that evidence is that it is working well, at least in some ways. If we

are successful in that argument, then the burden of proof may shift to those who would argue otherwise [p. 38].

Interestingly, Skolnick and Bayley (1986) independently make almost the identical point:

> If some of the new we have praised is unproven, so too is the old. Rarely have traditional police practices been subjected to rigorous evaluation. When they have, they have usually been found wanting. Because doubts about traditional strategies are so widespread, the burden of proof should be on those who seek to maintain them. They, after all, account for the expenditure of vast sums of public money without reassuring results [p. 226].

What I believe is reflected in the work of these seasoned observers of policing—and what I strongly share—is the gut feeling that the projects they describe and that I have described more broadly under the heading of "community policing" are responsive to the most critical needs of the police field. They incorporate a number of important elements that we have not seen in previous efforts to improve policing: (1) a more realistic acknowledgment of police functions; (2) recognition of the interrelationship between and among police functions; (3) an acknowledgment of the limited capacity of the police to get their job done on their own and the importance, therefore, of an alliance between the police and the community; (4) less dependence on the criminal justice system, with emphasis, therefore, on developing new alternatives for responding to problems, (5) greatly increased use of the knowledge that police officers acquire about the areas to which they are assigned; (6) more effective use of personnel; and (7) a modest, but significant increase in the systematic analysis of community problems as a basis for designing more effective police responses.

Most striking, for me, have been my observations of the impact that community policing has had on the police officers involved in these programs. The officers with whom I have walked and talked express immense satisfaction in getting to know citizens more intimately, in following up on their initial contacts, and in seeing the results of their efforts. They like being helpful. They enjoy the freedom and independence they are given to be creative and imaginative, and to take the initiative in dealing with problems. And perhaps most important, they appreciate the trust that the programs place in them. An increase in job satisfaction could have an enormous influence on the quality of police service provided to the community.

This observation of the impact of community policing on the performance of individual police officers illustrates why all of these developments, taken together, are so significant. Like pieces in a puzzle, they fit nicely and are mutually supportive. Past efforts at reform in policing were often limited in their impact because they were not fully integrated into a coherent concept of policing. Thus, for example, a large investment has been made to attract more highly educated officers into policing. But without changes in the function and working environment of the police, the potential contribution that these officers could make to policing has not been fully realized. Furthermore, the very qualities we have sought in more educated officers have been smothered in the atmosphere of traditional policing.

If the overall concept of community policing is fully developed, including a concern with the substance of policing as well as its form, it could provide the integrated strategy for improving the quality of policing—and could thereby help to avoid the waste inherent in piecemeal and unrelated efforts. Progress toward this goal will depend heavily on strongly committed leadership. But it will also rely heavily on addressing the questions raised in this article—on producing a clearer and more coherent vision of community policing so that administrators and the citizenry can, with greater confidence, make the small, incremental changes they have the opportunity to make.

References

Brown, L. P. 1985. "Police-community power sharing." In *Police Leadership in America: Crisis and Opportunity*, edited by W. A. Geller. New York: Praeger.

Davis, R. C. 1985. "Organizing the community for improved policing." In *Police Leadership in America: Crisis and Opportunity*, edited by W. A. Geller. New York: Praeger.

Eck, J., and W. Spelman. 1985. *Crime Analysis Project Interim Report: Accomplishments During Phase One and Plans for Phase 2*. Washington, DC: Police Executive Research Forum.

Farrell, M. J. 1986. *The Community Patrol Officer Program: Interim Progress Report Number 2*. New York: Vera Institute of Justice.

Feins, J. D. 1983. *Partnerships for Neighborhood Crime Prevention*. Washington, DC: National Institute of Justice.

Goldstein, H. 1977. *Policing a Free Society*. Cambridge, MA: Ballinger.

_____. 1979. "Improving Policing: A Problem-Oriented Approach." *Crime and Delinquency* 25, 2:236–258.

Goldstein, H., and C. Susmilch. 1982. *Experimenting with the Problem-Oriented Approach to Improving Police Service: A Report and Some Reflections on Two Case Studies*. Madison: Univ. of Wisconsin Law School.

Greenberg, S. W., W. M. Rohe, and J. R. Williams. 1985. *Informal Citizen Action and Crime Prevention at the Neighborhood Level: Executive Summary*. Washington, DC: National Institute of Justice.

Holdaway, S. 1984. *Inside the British Police: A Force at Work*. New York: Basil Blackwell.

Irwin v. Ware. 1984. 467 NE2d 1292 Mass.

Manning, P. K. 1984. "Community Policing." *American Journal of Police* 3, 2:205-227.

Mastrofski, S. 1984. "Police Revitalization in its Second Decade: A Reflection on the Direction of Research-Based Reform." Paper presented at the American Society of Criminology, Cincinnati, OH, November.

Newman, K. 1984. *The Policing Principles of the Metropolitan Police*. London: Metropolitan Police Department.

Pate, A. M., M. A. Wycoff, W. G. Skogan, and L. W. Sjerman. 1986. *Reducing Fear of Crime in Houston and Newark: A Summary Report*. Washington, DC: Police Foundation.

Punch, M. 1979. "The Secret Social Services." In *The British Police,* edited by S. Holdaway, London.

Reiss, A. J., Jr. 1984. "Consequences of Compliance and Deterrence Models of Law Enforcement for the Exercise of Police Discretion." *Law and Contemporary Problems* 47, 3:83–122.

_____. 1985. *Policing a City's Central District: The Oakland Story.* Washington, DC: National Institute of Justice.

Reuss-Ianni, E. and F. A. J. Ianni. 1983. "Street Cops and Management Cops: The Two Cultures of Policing." In *Control in the Police Organization*, edited by M. Punch. Cambridge, MA: MIT Press.

Schwartz, A. I., and S. N. Clarren. 1977. *The Cincinnati Team Policing Experiment, A Summary Report.* Washington, DC: The Urban Institute and Police Foundation.

Sherman, L. W., C. H. Milton, and T. V. Kelly. 1973. *Team Policing: Seven Case Studies.* Washington, DC: Police Foundation.

Short, C. 1983. "Community Policing—Beyond Slogans." In *The Future of Policing*, edited by T. Bennett. Cambridge, England: Institute of Criminology.

Skolnick, J. H. and D. Bayley. 1986. *The New Blue Line: Police Innovation in Six American Cities.* New York: Free Press.

Taft, Philip B., Jr. 1986. *Fighting Fear—The Baltimore County COPE Project.* Washington, DC: Police Executive Research Forum.

Thurman v. Torrington. 1984. 595 F. Supp. 1521.

Tien, J. M., J. W. Simon, and R. C. Larson. 1977. *An Evaluation Report of an Alternative Approach in Police Patrol: The Wilmington Split Force Experiment.* Cambridge, MA: Public Systems Evaluation.

Trojanowicz, R. C. 1982. *An Evaluation of the Neighborhood Foot Patrol Program in Flint, Michigan.* East Lansing: Michigan State University.

Trojanowicz, R. C., and H. A. Harden. 1985. *The Status of Contemporary Community Policing Programs.* East Lansing, MI: National Neighborhood Foot Patrol Center.

Van Maanen, J. 1974. "Working the Street: A Developmental View of Police Behavior." In *The Potential for Reform of Criminal Justice*, edited by H. Jacob. Beverly Hills: Sage.

Vera Foundation. 1985. "The Community Patrol Officers Program: An Evaluation Plan." Proposal. New York.

Walker, S. 1983. *The Police in America: An Introduction.* New York: McGraw Hill.

_____. 1984. "Broken Windows and Fractured History: The Use and Misuse of History in Recent Police Patrol Analysis." *Justice Quarterly* 1, 1:75–90.

Ward, B. 1985. *The Community Patrol Officer Program.* New York: New York City Police Department.

Weatheritt, M. 1983. "Community Policing: Does it Work and How Do We Know?" In *The Future of Policing*, edited by T. Bennet. Cambridge, England: Institute of Criminology.

Wilson, J. Q., and G. L. Kelling. 1982. "The Police and Neighborhood Safety: Broken Windows." *Atlantic Monthly*, March: 29–38.

Yun, L. 1985. "A Day in the Life of the Police." *Beijing Review* 50 (December 16): 24.

2

Community-Based Policing

Peter K. Manning

Modern life is a concatenation of yearnings. Some of these are yearnings for lost lovers, for once-seen visions of the future, for the past, for dead heroes, for communities and associations that are as whole as one imagines they once were. A politics of nostalgia gains public respectability. Normative reactions to normlessness are the style of the day. Country and western singers moan for "Old Fashioned Love . . . like Mama and Daddy had . . . ," and people are heard requesting more police on the street. These trends are found in England as well. Although the tone of desperation is less, the degree to which people yearn for the past is greater, and here people are also heard requesting more police on the street. This represents the *Nostalgia Theme* in current times.

Yet another theme arises, not from a wish to recapture an imagined past, but from a wish to alter the current bureaucratic forms so that they might be more responsive to changes in social structure. Governmental lust for deregulation can be seen in part as an attempt to make markets more responsive to consumer demand and to limit the intrusion of the "welfare state" into ever larger parts of citizens' lives. The wish to deregulate markets and to reduce the size of government generally is both ideologically and economically motivated.

The theme of responsive bureaus which are less centralized and officious, and more concerned with individual needs, accessible and open (with respect to both services and records), resonates in modern American society. It is reflected in changes in and demands upon all professions, and the fragmentation and renting of their closed, self-serving and largely profit-making character. One can observe the growth of such things as do-it-yourself divorce kits, health maintenance organizations, self-help groups, on-demand abortions, and home computers. Cable

Source: *American Journal of Police* 3:205–227 (1984). Reprinted with permission of Anderson Publishing Company.

television has the remarkable capacity to bring to one's own screen virtually any imaginable human experience. This theme is that of *the personalization of service*. Police, like other occupations, now face new demands for personalization of their "service." Community policing is a devised answer to such demands.

This selection dissects the concept of "community policing," its levels of meaning and ideological character. Some evidence will be drawn from Great Britain; however, my interest is directed to developments in America. Community policing can be seen as a *metaphor* based on yearning and the wish for personalization of service which contrasts with bureaucratic/professional policing. It is a valid and important index of public sentiments. If community policing is to respond to the current political milieux, a whole series of unlikely changes within and outside of policing are required.

Community Policing

The concept of community policing has at least four meanings. On one level, it is an *ideological system* of beliefs which asserts that communities in previous times were more unitary, that police were a more legitimate and accepted part of communities, that crime and disorder were once better controlled through cooperative effort, and that social control on the whole was tighter, more coherent, and pervasive (see Alderson, 1979:1983). This view is quite consistent with the police notion that society is falling apart slowly like an apple rotting on the ground in the autumn, destroyed internally by its own sin, decadence and debauchery. This is the kind of Gibbonesque theory that can be heard in any police car in America during a slack time (see Skolnick, 1969:258-268; Stark, 1972).

Samuel Walker has recently summarized the historical evidence for close police-community relations in the late nineteenth and early twentieth century in America, and finds that police were in fact the center of continuing conflict. They were denied legitimacy, were corrupt and venial, and doubtless were engaged in ongoing adversarial relations with minorities (Walker, 1983; see Skolnick, 1969 and Monkonnen, 1981). These were the halcyon days captured in an ideology in the sense used by Mannheim, a defense of vested interests and a defense against change. It is also, it must be said, "utopian" when applied to policing because it yearns for a future which fits the rational, perfectible view of the liberal middle classes.

A second meaning of community policing is *programmatic*. As Alderson points out, police have created community programs as well as police strategies and have become political forces in a new fashion. This meaning for the concept of community policing entails *programs* with broad political aims intended to restore police "closeness" to the community (Broome, as quoted in Wetheritt, 1983), to assuage community fear, and to assure community members by police presence and accessibility. These programs are said to strengthen joint police and community responsibility for the security of neighborhoods (Kelling, 1983; Trojanowicz,

1982). These programs are *proactive activities* which seek to encourage the "common good" (Alderson, 1983:2) through involvement in the community at various levels and through diverse programs (community meetings, school liaison, sport programs, etc.).

A third meaning of community policing is *pragmatic.* It contrasts with current police practice. Wetheritt (1983), after a critical review of research on community policing in England, concludes that community policing as seen in British policing practice does not aim to react quickly and uniformly to all types of citizen demand ("fire brigade" policing), does not intend to arrogate all responsibility for crime control, and does not seek exclusive control of the definition(s) of crime. The new pragmatic police eschew one-way, top-down communication to citizens about the nature of the crime problems in a community. Programs are responses to perceived citizen discontent with police organizations that are bureaucratic, impersonal, focused on specific incidents, "professional," crime-focused and centralized. The wish to develop community responsibility for crime and to increase communicational processes and structures is emerging among prominent British police administrators (see Manning, 1983).

A fourth meaning of community policing is a set of programmatic elements and *organizational structures.* Sherman, Milton and Kelly (1973), in one of the earliest evaluation attempts of community policing, identified the elements shown in table 1. They are exemplary, not essential. Although these organizational and social elements specify features of the particular police departments studied, other elements could be derived from present community policing schemes.

Note that the emphasis is on working in a given area as a team, participating and communicating with community groups, and attempting to provide organizational and managerial support for the teams, especially by combining patrol and investigative functions. Butler, in a later evaluation (1979), found that the absence of rewards, the self-concept of officers which entailed a high value for crime-fighting, and absence of managerial commitment at the middle level made these programs short-lived and their success ambiguous.

It is important to note that there is *confusion* in the use of the term "community policing." It is used to describe programs such as "police community relations units," "team policing," "unit beat policing," "foot patrol" and the like. This confusion is not unintentional, for it would appear that police have made far too much of programs of this sort, have allowed the public to generalize from program to policy to the broad ideological context without clarification, and have played on public confusion. Researchers have done much the same thing by exaggerating the generality of findings and programs.

Perhaps the vague and misleading character of much of the discussion about community policing results because it is based upon unstated *assumptions* about its aims and objectives. It taps very basic political sentiments (yearning for the past and the wish for personalized treatment).

Table 1 *
Summary of Elements

(The following summarized the elements of team policing in each city.)

Operational Elements	Dayton	Detroit	New York	Syracuse	Holyoke	Los Angeles (Venice)	Richmond
Stable geographic assignment	+	+	−	+	+	+	
Intra-team interaction	−	+	−	−	+	+	+
Formal team conferences	−	+	−	−	+	+	+
Police community communication	+	+	−	−	+	+	
Formal community conferences	+			−	+	+	
Community participation in police work	+	+	+		+	+	
Systematic referals to social agencies	+	−	−	−			+
Organizational Supports							
Unity of supervision	+	+	−	+	+	+	+
Lower-level flexibility	−	−	−	+	+	+	+
Unified delivery of services	+	−	−	+	+	+	
Combined patrol and investigative functions	+	+		+	+	+	+

Key:
  + the element was planned and realized
  − the element was planned but not realized
    the element was not planned
*From Sherman, et al., 1973: 7.

Assumptions of Community Policing

There are at least ten assumptions which seem to lie behind the use of the term "community policing" and the arguments advocating its worth. These assumptions are largely untested and untestable; are unspoken yet matters of tacit agreement; reflect the political aims of policy; derive from some general sentiments or feelings about the nature of society, social relations, hierarchy and authority, and the nature of policing as a representation of state authority. These ideas arise from a political context.

Ten Assumptions

1. People desire to see police officers in their local areas of residence and business on a regular and casual basis.
2. The more police they see, the more they will be satisfied with police practices.
3. The more police they see (to some unknown limit), the more secure they will feel.
4. People yearn for personal contact of a nonadversial character with police.
5. The public is more concerned about crime than disorder.
6. There is a single public, a single public mood, and a "common good" that is known and coherently represented.
7. People are dissatisfied with current police practices.
8. Previous policing schemes have been shown to have failed.
9. Public satisfaction as measured in polls is a valid index of "public opinion."
10. The police are responsible for defending, defining, expanding, and shaping the common good of the community by active means.
11. Community policing best meets the above needs.

All such assumptions are factious. Evidence supporting them is at best mixed. It is perhaps useful to discuss them in order to establish their tentative factual status.

The desire of citizens to see officers seems related to whether the officer is there to serve a person in some indirect or direct fashion (e.g., by being present to symbolize authority such as entering a bank to sign the book—a practice in Washington, D.C.), by responding to a citizen's call, or whether the officer is seen as being engaged in crime control activities (see Wetheritt, 1983 for summary of these findings in Britain).

Some people do seem to want nonadversarial contact with the police if the Flint study of foot patrol is indicative (Trojanowicz, 1982). However, the amount, quality and character of these *contacts* is varied, and it is not clear which of the officer's activities were most salient in the opinion of the respondent (most did not know what the officer did or was supposed to do: tables 11, 12). Many groups either do not want to see the police, find them a threat, see them as representative of an alien force, or see police in an adversarial role (see Kettle and Hodges, 1982). The wish to have officers about is primarily an articulated demand of business. The nature of the "demand," in turn, depends on the social class composition, race, and age of the neighborhood (Mastrofski, 1983).

The evidence concerning whether "the public" actually observe the police is mixed. In the Kansas City preventative patrol study, a classic of its kind, *perception,* an assumed basis for deterrence and therefore of crime, fear of crime, and tendency to report crime, did not operate to discriminate between areas patrolled using reactive policing (responses only to calls), proactive policing (two to three times normal levels of patrol) or normal (control) beats when researchers examined measures of crime, reported crime, fear of crime, anti-crime protection, and attitudes of businesses toward crime and the police (Kelling, et al., 1974:1-4). In the Newark foot patrol study, seeing the police did make a difference in citizens' fears (they were very slightly reduced), but business people interviewed *did not perceive the conditions.* Business people were asked whether they saw police in their areas before and after the experiment began (foot patrols were dropped in some beats, added to others, and left at normal levels in others). Business people reported that they saw police much less frequently in all conditions. The most radical drop in reported sightings occurred in areas in which police were no longer patrolling (Police Foundation, 1982). If the argument is as I understand it—that the more people perceive the police to be in the area, the more secure they will feel, the less they will fear crime, and the fewer actions they will take to protect themselves— the data demand one conclusion: the experimental effects were not perceived. Therefore, one cannot attribute changes in dependent variables to differential effects of the experimental variable (levels of foot patrol).

There is no evidence, of course, that *more* police produce an additive effect on security; a reading of the Kansas City preventative patrol experiment suggests the opposite.

Crime waxes and wanes as a public issue. Reports from Flint, Newark and Birmingham, England suggests that "crime" *per se* is less important to citizens than "protection," "taking complaints" and the state of disorder that they experience. These studies however, are based on individual victimization reports or interviews rather than on studies of the social organization of communities. When Fred Dubow and Adam Podolefsky did this in several communities as a part of the Northwestern (LEAA sponsored) Fear of Crime Project, it was found that individual attitudes to crime varied with perceptions of the community and community visibility. In other words, if the community is seen as safe ("morally unitary" in Durkheim's terms), the fear of crime, whether high or low, was viewed as unimportant as was the actual crime rate. South Philadelphia, a socially integrated community, reported high rates of crime but low levels of fear.

These data and others suggest that there is no single "common good" defined in particular terms such as fear of crime or views of the police. Rather, this reflects one's sense of attachment to a given social order, community or neighborhood. If this logic is extended, one can appreciate that there cannot be a single sense of security in any community; that neighborhoods are immensely varied in what they expect of the police, what they receive from them, and their evaluations of police (Reiss, 1971:Ch. IV). Most notions about policing and its identification with the common good come from small communities where the sense of "community" is both more limited *and* more consensual (Jones, 1983).

There is no evidence that people on the whole are dissatisfied with the police, policing, or their experience with the police, if public opinion polls are to be accepted (Jones, 1983). That there is a falling off of confidence is accepted. Police continue to *overestimate* public confidence in them (Jones, 1983). Because people respond positively to foot patrol, for example, does not indicate that they feel other modes of policing have failed. The evidence on this is mixed (Comrie and Kings, 1975). It is perhaps safe to say that in both Britain and America public concern about policing has increased.

A case can be made that the police have indeed been very successful in developing very high public expectations of their effectiveness and have increased the legitimacy of these expectations when compared with nineteenth century urban police. They have succeeded in having their occupation viewed as an emerging profession (see Walker, 1983; Brown, 1981; Manning, 1977).

Finally, there is certainly considerable debate about the desired police role with respect to community intervention, shaping community structures, and participating in *community life* (see Short, 1983; Kettle and Hodges, 1982). The range of attempted projects, community contact and referrals remains amazing (see Short, 1983; Trojanowicz, 1982).

There is a certain arrogant contentiousness in claiming that the police know the informal control mechanisms found in a community, can accommodate them, and can in some fashion act to enhance them. This role for police is advocated by Wilson and Kelling: "The essence of the police role in maintaining order is to reinforce the informal control mechanisms of the community itself. The police cannot, without committing extraordinary resources, provide a substitute for that informal control. On the other hand, to reinforce those natural forces the police must accommodate them" (1982:34).

What is assumed here is that these informal mechanisms work to *complement* each other, rather than to produce conflict. This may be a false assumption since, for example, attempts to control drug traffic may bring with them retaliation and violence. There is evidence that many local cultures are in fact in persistent conflict with the police. Many local areas do not form moral and political wholes, but are a mere collection of letter boxes, telephone prefixes, addresses-in-order and parking places. Others are unified *against* the police and maintain a strong "self-help" tradition, vigilantes, or are patrolled by Guardian Angels (Black, 1983). Still other neighborhoods are divided and in conflict with some segments of the community. They are crime-dependent, while others are "good citizens." What norms will be strengthened here? What "common-good" is to be identified? What practices define policing? It seems rather obvious that the interests of the police become the basis for operational notions of "order" and individual officers the locus of prescriptive definitions. It is difficult to see how, in this context, the police can provide positive alternatives to informal social controls.

As many writers have pointed out, law and morality are in no way isomorphic; communities may be in internal conflict as well as in conflict with the police (Hagan, 1984:Ch. 1). Indeed, from a cultural point of view, the police symbolize the imposition of external authority in American society and at best they can act as mediators between the citizens and the state (Bayley, 1978:186). The ways in which this mediation has been accomplished in the past, according to Wilson and Kelling (1982), has had important consequences in communities:

> For centuries, the role of the police as watchmen has been judged primarily not in terms of its compliance with appropriate procedures but rather in terms of its attaining a desired objective. The objective was order, an inherently ambiguous term but a condition that people in a given community recognized when they saw it. The means were the same as those the community itself would employ, if its members were sufficiently determined, courageous, and authoritative. Detection and apprehending criminals, by contrast was a means to an end, not an end itself; a judicial determination of guilt or innocence was the hoped-for result of the law enforcement mode. From the first, the police were expected to follow rules defining that process, though states differed in how stringent the rules should be. The criminal-apprehension process was always understood to involve individual rights, the violation of which was unacceptable because it meant that the violating officer would be acting as a judge and jury—and that was not his job. Guilt or innocence was to be determined by universal standards under special procedures.

This mythical golden age of community consensus and delegation of accepted authority does not ring true with any published account of city life in the nineteenth century (their reference is vague, "For centuries . . ."). The notion that policing was once guided by respect for individual rights is wholly untenable. As Walker (1983:17) writes, ". . . This historical analysis is pure fantasy."

Comments on Assumptions

These ten assumptions are ideologically based and wishful extensions of a political and moral perspective. They represent a projected view of the world shared by police and reformers. This is an enacted environment (Weick, 1979). It is possible to further explicate the political and moral context of the wish for community policing by comparing it with current police organization and practice. The contrasting characteristics of two types of policing can be seen in table 2.

These features have further organization and social implications. In community policing, there is a concern for developing personalized forms of control, an extension of an informal, differentiated moral system in which the officer acts as if he or she were a member of the community and not as an officer of an external political system, an absolutist legal system, and an authoritative state. Such a policing system would rely upon decriminalization of certain laws and a del-

Table 2
Two Types of Policing

Community Policing	Bureaucratic Policing
Visible	Invisible
Available	Indirectly available
Personal	Impersonal
Generalist	Specialist
Moralist-in-residence	Strategic response held-in-ready
Crime = immorality	Crime = legal violation
Delicts = disorder	Delicts = nuisance jobs
Dedifferentiated social control	Differentiated, graded response

egation of authority in which the officer decides to create order on the basis of readings of community needs, informal norms, and "rules" *constructed* to maintain control (see Police Foundation, 1982; Wilson and Kelling, 1982:30, 38). Mediation and other forms of local justice would be required. Competition between local police and vigilante or community self-help groups would arise. Local contracts for law and order would be created. Enforcement, dispatching and allocation of resources would of necessity be localized, decentralized, locally-rooted and processed, bypassing central authority. Performance and rewards would be variable depending on neighborhood supervision and patrol duties as would promotion, transfer and salary. The management hierarchy would be flattened, yielding two or three ranks only—constable, sergeant and "other."

This pattern contrasts with current policing and community policing as presently organized and practiced in North America and Britain. Police are impersonal uniforms, badges and vehicles gliding by. They enforce the law, attack and murder competition, and seek to dominate informal and formal means of control. They argue that laws are equally enforced and that the penalties attached are fair. (These claims are tendentious and the police know it.) The dominant metaphor of police-community relations has been hierarchical, distant, and authoritative. The centralized management of policing, striving towards equity in enforcement and equal allocation of demands to all calls, is a critical part of modern bureaucratic policing. Performance is said to be evaluated by objective tests, performance evaluations, written exams, and boards. Transfers, promotions, raises and the like are, in theory, equally available to all officers. The paramilitary structure of policing dominates as a *symbol* of policing albeit a form of symbolic or mock bureaucracy. The crime focus is mythical, and unions and tradition, not crimes and work loads, determine patrol allocations.

Community policing urges equalitarian, intimate and nonauthoritarian communal relations. The further one pushes horizontal democratic relations, the more community policing appeals. Community policing would require a change in the uses of the law; in the standards used to apply the law and order enforcement; in the overall contracts governing police and the public and the degree of centralization, structure, hierarchy and formalization of such matters as recruitment, evaluation, promotion and rewards in police departments.

The implications of this argument are that, short of making changes in the direction indicated, much of the political rhetoric about community policing is ideology, yearning for the past, and a wish to respond to projected public "demands." The slow movement in this direction is perhaps most important, but it is inconsistent and uneven, and programs such as foot patrol are small and partial pragmatic adjustments to current trends. The halo effect associated with any new program is doubtless operating in the Newark and Flint experiments, and it is unlikely that the same findings could be reproduced in the same cities ten years later.

Conclusion

Several factors are conducive to the community policing movement. This article has suggested that there are at least four distinctive meanings of the term, "community policing." These include the ideological, programmatic, pragmatic and organizational meanings. Meanings attached to the term are based upon unstated assumptions about the aims and objectives of community policing and are embedded in current political sentiments. These assumptions are not supported by research. They contain some vague ideas about policing which are probably in themselves not testable. A number of groups have a vested interest in promoting the idea of closer police-community relations, including some segments of the police, police researchers and others. On the other hand, the sentiments are vague and are not easily associated with any particular political position (e.g., liberal, radical, conservative). Community policing schemes have been criticized from both left and right, and from both outside and within the police. Since the idea resonates of a period of societal harmony, an aim of both utopian and ideological thinking, it draws support and criticism from many persons in all sectors of public life. It is quite likely that the sort of social order envisaged by police-community relations schemes never existed in the past and will not exist in the future.

If a community policing scheme is to be successful it will require structural and legal change, changes in habits of dispute settlement and definition, in organizational structure, in performance evaluation, and in reward structures within the police. New definitions of crime control and crime prevention will be needed (see Wycoff and Manning, 1983 and Manning and Wycoff, forthcoming). This seems highly unlikely, but the crawl toward new forms of policing is inevitable and perhaps appropriate.

References

Alderson, J. 1979. *Policing Freedom*. Plymouth, UK: McDonald-Evans.
_____. 1983. "Community Policing," in T. Bennett (ed.) *The Future of Policing*. Cambridge: Institute of Criminology.
Bayley, D. 1978. *Forces of Order*. Berkeley: University of California Press.
Black, D. J. 1983. "Crime as Social Control." *American Sociological Review* 48:34-45.
Brown, M. 1981. *Working the Street*. New York: Russell Sage.
Butler, A. J. P. 1979. *A Study of the Occupation Perceptions of Police Officers*. Unpublished Ph.D. Dissertation. Faculty of Law, University of Birmingham.
Comrie, M. D. and E. J. Kings. 1975. *Study of Urban Workloads*. London: Home Office Police Research Services Unit.
Hagan, J. 1984. *Modern Criminology*. New York: McGraw Hill.
Jones, S. 1983. "Community Policing in Devon and Cornwall . . ." in T. Bennett (ed.) *The Future of Policing*. Cambridge: Institute of Criminology.
Kelling, G. 1983. *Reforming the Reformers*. Cambridge: Harvard University Press.
Kelling, G., T. Pate, D. Dieckman, and C. E. Brown. 1974. *The Kansas City Preventive Patrol Experiment: A Technical Report*. Washington, DC: Police Foundation.
Kettle, M. and L. Hodges. 1982. *Uprising*. London: Pan Books.
Manning, P. K. 1974. "Dramatic Aspects of Policing." *Sociology and Social Research* 59:283-306.
_____. 1977. *Police Work: The Social Organization of Policing*. Cambridge: MIT Press.
_____. 1983. "British Policing: Continuities and Changes." Paper presented to Howard League Conference. Criminal Justice in the 1980s. Pembroke College Oxford, September. [Published in *Howard Journal of Criminal Justice* 25 (November): 261-278.]
Manning, P. K. and M. A. Wycoff. 1984. *Crime Focused Policing*. Unpublished draft report to NIJ, Michigan State University.
Mastrofski, S. 1983. "The Police and Non-crime Services," in G. Whitaker and C. D. Phillips (eds.) *Evaluating Performance of Criminal Justice Agencies*. Beverly Hills: Sage.
Monkonnen, E. 1981. *Urban Policing*. Cambridge: Cambridge University Press.
Police Foundation. 1982. *The Newark Foot Patrol Experiment*. Washington, DC: Police Foundation.
Reiss, A. J., Jr. 1971. *The Police and the Public*. New Haven: Yale University Press.
Sherman, L. W., C. H. Milton, and T. V. Kelly. 1973. *Community Policing: Seven Case Studies*. Washington, DC: Police Foundation.
Short, C. 1983. "Community Policing—Beyond Slogans," in T. Bennett (ed.) *The Future of Policing*. Cambridge: Institute of Criminology.
Skolnick, J. 1969. *The Politics of Protest*. New York: Ballantine Books.
Stark, R. 1972. *Police Riots*. San Francisco: Wadsworth.
Trojanowicz, R. 1982. *An Evaluation of the Flint Foot Patrol Project*. East Lansing: Michigan State University.
Walker, S. 1983. "Broken Windows and Fractured History . . ." Paper presented at the annual meeting of the American Society of Criminology, Denver.
Weick, K. 1979. *The Social Psychology of Organizing, Second Edition*. Reading, MA: Addison-Wesley.

Wetheritt, M. 1983. "Community Policing: Does it work and how do we know?" in T. Bennett (ed.) *The Future of Policing.* Cambridge: Institute of Criminology.

Wilson, J. Q. and G. Kelling. 1982. "Broken Windows . . ." *Atlantic Magazine* 249 (March): 29-38.

Wycoff, M. A. and P. K. Manning. 1983. "The Police and Crime Control," in G. Whitaker and C. D. Phillips (eds.) *Evaluating Performance of Criminal Justice Agencies.* Beverly Hills: Sage.

3

Making Neighborhoods Safe

James Q. Wilson and *George L. Kelling*

New Briarfield apartments is an old, rundown collection of wooden buildings constructed in 1942 as temporary housing for shipyard workers in Newport News, Virginia. By the mid-1980s it was widely regarded as the worst housing project in the city. Many of its vacant units provided hiding places for drug users. It had the highest burglary rate in Newport News; nearly a quarter of its apartments were broken into at least once a year.

For decades the police had wearily answered calls for assistance and had investigated crimes in New Briarfield. Not much came of this police attentiveness—the buildings went on deteriorating, the burglaries went on occurring, the residents went on living in terror. Then, in 1984, Detective Tony Duke, assigned to a newly created police task force, decided to interview the residents of New Briarfield about their problems. Not surprisingly, he found that they were worried about the burglaries—but they were just as concerned about the physical deterioration of the project. Rather than investigating only the burglaries, Duke spent some of his time investigating the *buildings*. Soon he learned that many city agencies—the fire department, the public-works department, the housing department—regarded New Briarfield as a major headache. He also discovered that its owners were in default on a federal loan and that foreclosure was imminent.

The report he wrote to Darrel Stephens, then the police chief, led Stephens to recommend to the city manager that New Briarfield be demolished and its tenants relocated. The city manager agreed. Meanwhile, Barry Haddix, the patrol officer assigned to the area, began working with members of other city agencies to fix up the project, pending its eventual replacement. Trash was carted away, abandoned cars were removed, potholes were filled in, the streets were swept.

Source: *The Atlantic* 263(2): 46–52. Copyright 1989 by The Atlantic Monthly Company. Reprinted by permission of the publisher.

According to a study done by John E. Eck and William Spelman, of the Police Executive Research Forum (PERF), the burglary rate dropped by 35 percent after Duke and Haddix began their work.

Stephens, now the executive director of PERF, tells the story of the New Briarfield project as an example of "problem-oriented policing," a concept developed by Professor Herman Goldstein, of the University of Wisconsin Law School, and sometimes also called community-oriented policing. The conventional police strategy is "incident-oriented"—a citizen calls to report an incident, such as a burglary, and the police respond by recording information relevant to the crime and then trying to solve it. Obviously, when a crime occurs, the victim is entitled to a rapid, effective police response. But if responding to incidents is all that the police do, the community problems that cause or explain many of these incidents will never be addressed, and so the incidents will continue and their number will perhaps increase.

This will happen for two reasons. One is that a lot of serious crime is adventitious, not the result of inexorable social forces or personal failings. A rash of burglaries may occur because drug users have found a back alley or an abandoned building in which to hang out. In their spare time, and in order to get money to buy drugs, they steal from their neighbors. If the back alleys are cleaned up and the abandoned buildings torn down, the drug users will go away. They may even use fewer drugs, because they will have difficulty finding convenient dealers and soft burglary targets. By the same token, a neglected neighborhood may become the turf of a youth gang, whose members commit more crimes together in a group than they would if they were acting alone. If the gang is broken up, former members will still commit some crimes but probably not as many as before.

Most crime in most neighborhoods is local: the offenders live near their victims. Because of this, one should not assume that changing the environmental conditions conducive to crime in one area will displace the crime to other areas. For example, when the New York City police commissioner, Ben Ward, ordered Operation Pressure Point, a crackdown on drug dealing on the Lower East Side, dealing and the criminality associated with it were reduced in that neighborhood and apparently did not immediately reappear in other, contiguous neighborhoods. Suburban customers of the local drug dealers were frightened away by the sight of dozens of police officers on the streets where these customers had once shopped openly for drugs. They could not—at least not right away—find another neighborhood in which to buy drugs as easily as they once had on the Lower East Side. At the same time, the local population included some people who were willing to aid and abet the drug dealers. When the police presence made drug dealing unattractive, the dealers could not—again, at least not for the time being—find another neighborhood that provided an equivalent social infrastructure.

The second reason that incident-oriented police work fails to discourage neighborhood crime is that law-abiding citizens who are afraid to go out onto streets filled with graffiti, winos, and loitering youths yield control of these streets to people who are not frightened by these signs of urban decay. Those not frightened turn out to be the same people who created the problem in the first place. Law-abiding citizens, already fearful, see things occurring that make them even more fearful. A vicious cycle begins of fear-induced behavior increasing the sources of that fear.

A Los Angeles police sergeant put it this way: "When people in this district see that a gang has spray-painted its initials on all the stop signs, they decide that the gang, not the people or the police, controls the streets. When they discover that the Department of Transportation needs three months to replace the stop signs, they decide that the city isn't as powerful as the gang. These people want us to help them take back the streets." Painting gang symbols on a stop sign or a storefront is not, by itself, a serious crime. As an incident, it is trivial. But as the symptom of a problem, it is very serious.

In an earlier article in *The Atlantic* (March, 1982) we called this the problem of "broken windows": If the first broken window in a building is not repaired, then people who like breaking windows will assume that no one cares about the building and more windows will be broken. Soon the building will have no windows. Likewise, when disorderly behavior—say, rude remarks by loitering youths—is left unchallenged, the signal given is that no one cares. The disorder escalates, possibly to serious crime.

[handwritten marginal note: sign of weak informal social control]

The sort of police work practiced in Newport News is an effort to fix the broken windows. Similar projects are under way in cities all over America. This pattern constitutes the beginnings of the most significant redefinition of police work in the past half century. For example:

- When a gunfight occurred at Garden Village, a low-income housing project near Baltimore, the Baltimore County police responded by investigating both the shooting and the housing project. Chief Cornelius Behan directed the officers in his Community Oriented Police Enforcement (COPE) unit to find out what could be done to alleviate the fears of the project residents and the gang tensions that led to the shooting. COPE officers worked with members of other agencies to upgrade street lighting in the area, trim shrubbery, install door locks, repair the roads and alleys, and get money to build a playground. With police guidance, the tenants organized. At the same time, high-visibility patrols were started and gang members were questioned. When both a suspect in the shooting and a particularly troublesome parole violator were arrested, gang tensions eased. Crime rates dropped. In bringing about this change, the police dealt with eleven different public agencies.

[handwritten marginal note: Avoid people]

- When local merchants in a New York City neighborhood complained to the police about homeless persons who create a mess on the streets and whose presence frightened away customers, the officer who responded did not roust the vagrants but instead suggested that the merchants hire them to clean the streets in front of their stores every morning. The merchants agreed, and now the streets are clean all day and the customers find the stores more attractive.

- When people in a Los Angeles neighborhood complained to the police about graffiti on walls and gang symbols on stop signs, officers assigned to the Community Mobilization Project in the Wilshire station did more than just try to catch the gang youths who were wielding the spray cans; they also organized citizens' groups and Boy Scouts to paint over the graffiti as fast as they were put up.

- When residents of a Houston neighborhood became fearful about crime in their area, the police not only redoubled their efforts to solve the burglaries and thefts but also assigned some officers to talk with the citizens in their homes. During a nine-month period the officers visited more than a third of all the dwelling units in the area, introduced themselves, asked about any neighborhood problems, and left their business cards. When Antony Pate and Mary Ann Wycoff, researchers at the Police Foundation, evaluated the project, they found that the people in this area, unlike others living in a similar area where no citizen-contact project occurred, felt that social disorder had decreased and that the neighborhood had become a better place to live. Moreover, and quite unexpectedly, the amount of property crime was noticeably reduced.

These are all examples of community-oriented policing, whose current popularity among police chiefs is as great as the ambiguity of the idea. In a sense, the police have always been community-oriented. Every police officer knows that most crimes don't get solved if victims and witnesses do not cooperate. One way to encourage that cooperation is to cultivate the good will of both victims and witnesses. Similarly, police-citizen tensions, over racial incidents or allegations of brutality or hostility, can often be allayed, and sometimes prevented, if police officers stay in close touch with community groups. Accordingly, most departments have at least one community-relations officer, who arranges meetings between officers and citizens' groups in church basements and other neutral locales.

But these commonplace features of police work are add-ons, and rarely alter the traditional work of most patrol officers and detectives: responding to radio calls about specific incidents. The focus on incidents works against a focus on problems. If Detective Tony Duke had focused only on incidents in New Briarfield, he would still be investigating burglaries in that housing project; meanwhile, the community-relations officer would be telling outraged residents that the police were doing all they could and urging people to call in any useful leads. If a tenant at one of those meetings had complained about stopped-up drains, rotting floorboards, and abandoned refrigerators, the community-relations officer would have patiently explained that these were not "police matters."

And of course, they are not. They are the responsibility of the landlord, the tenants themselves, and city agencies other than the police. But landlords are sometimes indifferent, tenants rarely have the resources to make needed repairs, and other city agencies do not have a twenty-four-hour emergency service. Like it or not, the police are about the only city agency that makes house calls around the clock. And like it or not, the public defines broadly what it thinks of as public order, and holds the police responsible for maintaining order.

Community-oriented policing means changing the daily work of the police to include investigating problems as well as incidents. It means defining as a problem whatever a significant body of public opinion regards as a threat to community order. It means working with the good guys, and not just against the bad guys.

The link between incidents and problems can sometimes be measured. The police know from experience what research by Glenn Pierce, in Boston, and Lawrence Sherman, in Minneapolis, has established: fewer than 10 percent of the addresses from which the police receive calls account for more than 60 percent of those calls. Many of the calls involve domestic disputes. If each call is treated as a separate incident with neither a history nor a future, then each dispute will be handled by police officers anxious to pacify the complainants and get back on patrol as quickly as possible. All too often, however, the disputants move beyond shouting insults or throwing crockery at each other. A knife or a gun maybe produced, and somebody may die.

A very large proportion of all killings occur in these domestic settings. A study of domestic homicides in Kansas City showed that in eight out of ten cases the police had been called to the incident address at least once before; in half the cases they had been called *five times* or more. The police are familiar with this pattern, and they have learned how best to respond to it. An experiment in Minneapolis, conducted by the Police Foundation, showed that men who were arrested after assaulting their spouses were much less likely to commit new assaults than those who were merely pacified or asked to leave the house for a few hours. Research is now under way in other cities to test this finding. Arrest may prove always to be the best disposition, or we may learn that some kind of intervention by a social agency also helps. What is indisputable is that a domestic fight—like many other events to which the police respond—is less an "incident" than a problem likely to have serious, long-term consequences.

Another such problem, familiar to New Yorkers, is graffiti on subway cars. What to some aesthetes is folk art is to most people a sign that an important public place is no longer under public control. If graffiti painters can attack cars with impunity, then muggers may feel they can attack the people in those cars with equal impunity. When we first wrote in these pages about the problem of broken windows, we dwelt on the graffiti problem as an example of a minor crime creating a major crisis.

The police seemed powerless to do much about it. They could arrest youths with cans of spray paint, but for every one arrested ten more went undetected, and of those arrested, few were punished. The New York Transit Authority, led by its chairman, Robert Kiley, and its president, David Gunn, decided that graffiti-free cars were a major management goal. New, easier-to-clean cars were bought. More important, key people in the Authority were held accountable for cleaning the cars and keeping them clean. Whereas in the early 1980s two out of every three cars were covered with graffiti, today fewer than one in six is. The Transit Police have played their part by arresting those who paint the cars, but they have been more successful at keeping cars from being defaced in the first place than they were at chasing people who were spraying already defaced ones.

While the phrase "community-oriented policing" comes easily to the lips of police administrators, redefining the police mission is more difficult. To help the police become accustomed to fixing broken windows as well as arresting window-breakers requires doing things that are very hard for many administrators to do.

Authority over at least some patrol officers must be decentralized, so that they have a good deal of freedom to manage their time (including their paid over-time). This implies freeing them at least partly from the tyranny of the radio call. It means giving them a broad range of responsibilities: to find and understand the problems that create disorder and crime, and to deal with other public and private agencies that can help cope with these problems. It means assigning them to a neighborhood and leaving them there for an extended period of time. It means backing them up with department support and resources.

The reason these are not easy things for police chiefs to do is not simply that chiefs are slaves to tradition, though some impatient advocates of community-oriented policing like to say so. Consider for a moment how all these changes might sound to an experienced and intelligent police executive who must defend his department against media criticisms of officer misconduct, political pressure to cut budgets, and interest-group demands for more police protection everywhere. With decentralized authority, no one will know precisely how patrol officers spend their time. Moreover, decentralized authority means that patrol officers will spend time on things like schmoozing with citizens, instead of on quantifiable tasks like issuing tickets, making arrests, and clearing cases.

Making the community-oriented officers generalists means letting them deal with other city agencies, a responsibility for which few officers are well trained and which cuts across sensitive questions of turf and public expectations.

If officers are left in a neighborhood, some of them may start taking money from the dope dealers and after-hours joints. To prevent that, officers are frequently moved around. Moreover, the best people are usually kept in the detective squad that handles the really big cases. Few police executives want their best people settling into a neighborhood, walking around the bus stops and shopping malls.

The enthusiasts for community-oriented policing have answers for all these concerns, but sometimes in their zeal they forget that they are contending with more than mere bureaucratic foot-dragging—that the problems are real and require thoughtful solutions. Many police executives get in trouble not because the crime rate goes up but because cops are accused of graft, brutality, laziness, incivility, or indifference.

In short, police management is driven more by the constraints on the job than by the goals of the job. You cannot cope with those constraints without understanding them. This may be why some of the biggest changes toward community-oriented policing have occurred in cities where a new chief has come in from the outside with a mandate to shake up a moribund department. Lee Brown brought a community orientation to the Houston Police Department under precisely those circumstances—the reputation of the department was so bad that almost any change would have been regarded as an improvement.

What can we say to the worried police chief who is already running a pretty good department? Start with corruption: For decades police executives and reformers have believed that in order to prevent corruption, you have to centralize control over personnel and discourage intimacy between police officers and citizens. Maybe. But the price one pays for this is very high. For example, many neighborhoods are being destroyed by drug dealers, who hang out on every street corner. The best way to sweep them off the streets is to have patrol officers arrest them for selling drugs and intimidate their customers by parking police cars right next to suspected drug outlets. But some police chiefs forbid their patrol officers to work drug cases, for fear they will be corrupted. When the citizens in these cities see police cars drive past scenes of open drug dealing, they assume the police have been paid off. Efforts to prevent corruption have produced the appearance of corruption.

Police Commissioner Ben Ward, in New York, decided that the price of this kind of anti-corruption strategy was too high. His Operation Pressure Point put scores of police officers on the streets to break up the drug-dealing bazaar. Police corruption is no laughing matter, especially in New York, but some chiefs now believe that it will have to be fought in ways that do not require police officers to avoid contact with people.

Consider the problem of getting police resources and managing political pressures: resources can be justified with statistics, but statistics often become ends in themselves. One police captain we interviewed said that his department was preoccupied with "stacking widgets and counting beans." He asked his superior for permission to take officers out of radio cars and have them work on community problems. The superior agreed but warned that he would be watching to see what happened to "the stats." In the short run the stats—for example, calls answered, average response time—were likely to get worse, but if community problems were solved, they would get better as citizens had fewer incidents to report. The captain worried, however, that he would not be given enough time to achieve this and that the bean counters would cut off his program.

A better way to justify getting resources from the city is to stimulate popular demand for resources devoted to problem-solving. Properly handled, community-oriented policing does generate support for the department. When Newark police officers, under orders from Hubert Williams, then the police director, began stopping city buses and boarding them to enforce city ordinances against smoking, drinking, gambling, and playing loud music, the bus patrons often applauded. When Los Angeles police officers supervised the hauling away of abandoned cars, onlookers applauded. Later, when some of the officers had their time available for problem-solving work cut back, several hundred citizens attended a meeting to complain.

In Flint, Michigan, patrol officers were taken out of their cars and assigned to foot beats. Robert Trojanowicz, a professor at Michigan State University, analyzed the results and found big increases in citizen satisfaction and officer morale, and even a significant drop in crime (an earlier foot-patrol project in Newark had produced equivalent reductions in fear but no reductions in crime). Citizen support was not confined to statements made to pollsters, however. Voters in referenda twice approved tax increases to maintain the foot-patrol system, the second time by a two-to-one margin. New Briarfield tenants unquestionably found satisfaction in the role the police played in getting temporary improvements made on their housing project and getting a commitment for its ultimate replacement. Indeed, when a department experiments with a community-oriented project in one precinct, people in other precincts usually want one too.

Politicians, like police chiefs, hear these views and respond. But they hear other views as well. One widespread political mandate is to keep the tax rate down. Many police departments are already stretched thin by sharp reductions in spending that occurred in the lean years of the 1970s. Putting *one* additional patrol car on the streets around the clock can cost a quarter of a million dollars or more a year.

Change may seem easier when resources are abundant. Ben Ward could start Operation Pressure Point because he had at his disposal a large number of new officers who could be thrown into a crackdown on street-level drug dealing. Things look a bit different in Los Angeles, where no big increases in personnel are on the horizon. As a result, only eight officers are assigned to the problem-solving Community Mobilization Project in the Wilshire district—an economically and ethnically diverse area of nearly 300,000 residents.

But change does not necessarily require more resources, and the availability of new resources is no guarantee that change will be attempted. One temptation is to try to sell the public on the need for more policemen and decide later how to use them. Usually when that script is followed, either the public turns down the spending increase or the extra personnel are dumped into what one LAPD captain calls the "black hole" of existing commitments, leaving no trace and producing no effects.

What may have an effect is how the police are deployed and managed. An experiment jointly conducted by the Washington, D.C., Police Department and the Police Foundation showed that if a few experienced officers concentrate on known repeat offenders, the number of serious offenders taken off the streets grows substantially. The Flint and Newark experiences suggest that foot patrols in certain kinds of communities (but not all) can reduce fear. In Houston problem-oriented tactics seem clearly to have heightened a sense of citizen security.

The problem of interagency cooperation may, in the long run, be the most difficult of all. The police can bring problems to the attention of other city agencies, but the system is not always organized to respond. In his book *Neighborhood Services*, John Mudd calls it the "rat problem": "If a rat is found in an apartment, it is a housing inspection responsibility; if it runs into a restaurant, the health department has jurisdiction; if it goes outside and dies in an alley, public works takes over." A police officer who takes public complaints about rats seriously will go crazy trying to figure out what agency in the city has responsibility for rat control and then inducing it to kill the rats.

Matters are almost as bad if the public is complaining about abandoned houses or school-age children who are not in school. The housing department may prefer to concentrate on enforcing the housing code rather than go through the costly and time-consuming process of getting an abandoned house torn down. The school department may have expelled the truant children for making life miserable for the teachers and the other students; the last thing it wants is for the police to tell the school to take the kids back.

All city and county agencies have their own priorities and face their own pressures. Forcing them to cooperate by knocking heads together at the top rarely works; what department heads promise the mayor they will do may bear little relationship to what their rank-and-file employees actually do. From his experiences in New York City government Mudd discovered that if you want agencies to cooperate in solving neighborhood problems, you have to get the neighborhood-level supervisors from each agency together in a "district cabinet" that meets regularly and addresses common concerns. This is not an easy task (for one thing, police district lines often do not match the district boundaries of the school, housing, traffic, and public works departments), but where it has been tried it has made solving the "rat problem" a lot easier. For example, Mudd reports, such interagency issues as park safety and refuse-laden vacant lots got handled more effectively when the field supervisors met to talk about them than when memos went up the chain of command of one agency and then down the chain of command of another.

Community organizations along the lines of Neighborhood Watch programs may help reduce crime, but we cannot be certain. In particular, we do not know what kinds of communities are most likely to benefit from such programs. A Police Foundation study in Minneapolis found that getting effective community organizations started in the most troubled neighborhoods was very difficult. The costs and benefits of having patrol officers and sergeants influence the delivery of services from other city agencies has never been fully assessed. No way of wresting control of a neighborhood from a street gang has yet been proved effective.

And even if these questions are answered, a police department may still have difficulty accommodating two very different working cultures: the patrol officers and detectives who handle major crimes (murders, rapes, and robberies) and the cops who work on community problems and the seemingly minor incidents they generate. In every department we visited, some of the incident-oriented officers spoke disparagingly of the problem-oriented officers as "social workers," and some of the latter responded by calling the former "ghetto blasters." If a community-service officer seems to get too close to the community, he or she may be accused of "going native." The tension between the two cultures is heightened by the fact that in many departments becoming a detective is regarded as a major promotion, and detectives are often selected from among those officers who have the best record in making major arrests—in other words, from the ranks of the incident-oriented. But this pattern need not be permanent. Promotion tracks can be changed so that a patrol officer, especially one working on community problems, is no longer regarded as somebody who "hasn't made detective." Moreover, some police executives now believe that splitting the patrol force into two units—one oriented to incidents, the other to problems—is unwise. They are searching for ways to give all patrol officers the time and resources for problem-solving activities.

Because of the gaps in our knowledge about both the results and the difficulties of community-oriented policing, no chief should be urged to accept, uncritically, the community-oriented model. But the traditional model of police professionalism—devoting resources to quick radio-car response to calls about specific crime incidents—makes little sense at a time when the principal threats to public order and safety come from *collective*, not individual, sources, and from *problems*, not incidents; from well-organized gangs and drug traffickers, from uncared-for legions of the homeless, from boisterous teenagers taking advantage of their newfound freedom and affluence in congested urban settings.

Even if community-oriented policing does not produce the dramatic gains that some of its more ardent advocates expect, it has indisputably produced one that the officers who have been involved in it immediately acknowledge: it has changed their perceptions of the community. Officer Robin Kirk, of the Houston Police Department, had to be talked into becoming part of a neighborhood fear-reduction project. Once in it, he was converted. In his words, "Traditionally, police officers after about three years get to thinking that everybody's a loser. That's the only people you're dealing with. In community policing you're dealing with the good citizens, helping them solve problems."

4

Community Policing
Elements and Effects

Gary W. Cordner

In less than two decades, community policing has evolved from a few small foot patrol studies to the preeminent reform agenda of modern policing. With roots in such earlier developments as police-community relations, team policing, crime prevention, and the rediscovery of foot patrol, community policing has become, in the 1990s, the dominant strategy of policing—so much so that the 100,000 new police officers funded by the 1994 Crime Bill must be engaged, by law, in community policing.

Despite all this activity, four complicating factors have made it extremely difficult to determine the effectiveness of community policing:

- *Programmatic complexity*—There exists no single definition of community policing nor any universal set of program elements. Police agencies around the country (and around the world) have implemented a wide array of organizational and operational innovations under the label "community policing." Because community policing is not one consistent "thing," it is difficult to say whether "it" works.

- *Multiple effects*—The number of intended and unintended effects that might accrue to community policing is considerable. Community policing might affect crime, fear of crime, disorder, community relations, and/or police officer attitudes, to mention just a few plausible impacts. The reality of these multiple effects, as opposed to a single bottom-line criterion, severely reduces the likelihood of a simple yes or no answer to the question "Does community policing work?"

Source: *Critical Issues in Policing*, 3/E, edited by Roger G. Dunham and Geoffrey P. Alpert, pp. 451–468. Copyright 1997 by Waveland Press.

- *Variation in program scope*—The scope of community policing projects has varied from single-officer assignments to department-wide efforts. Some of the most positive results have come from projects that involved only a few specialist officers, small special units, or narrowly defined target areas. The generalizability of these positive results to full-scale department-wide implementation is problematic.

- *Research design limitations*—Despite heroic efforts by police officials and researchers, most community policing studies have had serious research design limitations. These include lack of control groups, failure to randomize treatments, and a tendency to measure only short-term effects. Consequently, the findings of many community policing studies do not have as much credibility as we might hope.

These complicating factors are offered not as excuses but rather to sensitize us to the very real difficulty of producing reliable knowledge about the effects of community policing. Additionally, they identify priority issues that need to be addressed in order to substantially improve what we know about the effectiveness of community policing.

What Is Community Policing?

Community policing remains many things to many people. A common refrain among proponents is "Community policing is a philosophy, not a program." An equally common refrain among police officers is "Just tell me exactly what you want me to do differently." Some critics, echoing concerns similar to those expressed by police officers, argue that if community policing is nothing more than a philosophy, it is merely an empty shell (Goldstein, 1987).

It would be easy to list dozens of common characteristics of community policing, starting with foot patrol and mountain bikes and ending with the police as organizers of, and advocates for, the poor and dispossessed. Instead, it may be more helpful to identify four major dimensions of community policing and some of the most common elements within each. These four dimensions of community policing are:

- The Philosophical Dimension
- The Strategic Dimension
- The Tactical Dimension
- The Organizational Dimension

The Philosophical Dimension

Many of its most thoughtful and forceful advocates emphasize that community policing is a new philosophy of policing, perhaps constituting even a paradigm shift away from professional-model policing. The philosophical dimension includes the central ideas and beliefs underlying community policing. Three of the most important of these are citizen input, broad function, and personalized service.

Citizen Input. Community policing takes the view that, in a free society, citizens should have open access to police organizations and input to police policies and decisions. Access and input through elected officials is considered necessary but not sufficient. Individual neighborhoods and communities should have the opportunity to influence how they are policed and legitimate interest groups in the community should be able to discuss their views and concerns directly with police officials. Police departments, like other agencies of government, should be responsive and accountable.

Mechanisms for achieving greater citizen input are varied. Some police agencies use systematic and periodic community surveys to elicit citizen input (Bureau of Justice Assistance, 1994a). Others rely on open forums, town meetings, radio and television call-in programs, and similar methods open to all residents. Some police officials meet regularly with citizen advisory boards, ministry alliances, minority group representatives, business leaders, and other formal groups. These techniques have been used by police chief executives, district commanders, and ordinary patrol officers; they can be focused as widely as the entire jurisdiction or as narrowly as a beat or a single neighborhood.

The techniques used to achieve citizen input should be less important than the end result. Community policing emphasizes that police departments should seek and carefully consider citizen input when making policies and decisions that affect the community. Any other alternative would be unthinkable in an agency that is part of a government "of the people, for the people, and by the people."

Broad Police Function. Community policing embraces a broad view of the police function rather than a narrow focus on crime fighting or law enforcement (Kelling and Moore, 1988). Historical evidence is often cited to show that the police function was originally quite broad and varied and that it only narrowed in recent decades, perhaps due to the influence of the professional model and popular media representations of police work. Social science data is also frequently cited to show that police officers actually spend relatively little of their time dealing with serious offenders or investigating violent crimes.

This broader view of the police function recognizes the kinds of non-enforcement tasks that police already perform and seeks to give them greater status and legitimacy. These include order maintenance, social service, and general assistance duties. They may also include greater responsibilities in protecting and enhancing "the lives of those who are most vulnerable—juveniles, the elderly, minorities, the poor, the disabled, the homeless" (Trojanowicz and Bucqueroux, 1990: xiv). In the bigger picture, the police mission is seen to include resolving conflict, helping victims, preventing accidents, solving problems, and reducing fear as well as reducing crime through apprehension and enforcement.

Personal Service. Community policing supports tailored policing based on local norms and values and individual needs. An argument is made that the criminal law is a very blunt instrument and that police officers inevitably exercise wide discretion when making decisions. Presently, individual officers make arrests and other decisions based on a combination of legal, bureaucratic, and idiosyncratic criteria, while the police department maintains the myth of full or at least uniform enforcement (Goldstein, 1977). Under community policing, officers are asked to consider the "will of the community" when deciding which laws to enforce under what circumstances, and police executives are asked to tolerate and even encourage such differential and personalized policing.

Such differential or tailored policing primarily affects police handling of minor criminal offenses, local ordinance violations, public disorder, and service issues. Some kinds of behavior proscribed by state and local law, and some levels of noise and disorder, may be seen as less bothersome in some neighborhoods than in others. Similarly, some police methods, including such aggressive tactics as roadblocks as well as more prevention-oriented programs such as landlord training, may coincide with norms and values in some neighborhoods but not others.

Even the strongest advocates of community policing recognize that a balance must be reached between differential neighborhood-level policing and uniform jurisdiction-wide policing. Striking a healthy and satisfactory balance between competing interests has always been one of the central concerns of policing and police administration. Community policing simply argues that neighborhood-level norms and values should be added to the mix of legal, professional, and organizational considerations that influences decision making about policies, programs, and resources at the executive level as well as enforcement-level decisions on the street.

This characteristic of community policing is also aimed at overcoming one of the most common complaints that the public has about government employees in general, including police officers—that they do not seem to care and that they are more interested in "going by the book" than in providing quality, personalized service. Many citizens seem to resent being subjected to "stranger policing" and would rather deal with officers who know them, and whom they know. Of course, not every police-citizen encounter can be amicable and friendly. But officers who generally deal with citizens in a friendly, open, and personal manner may be more likely to generate trust and confidence than officers who operate in a narrow, aloof, and/or bureaucratic manner.

The Strategic Dimension

The strategic dimension of community policing includes the key operational concepts that translate philosophy into action. These strategic concepts are the links between the broad ideas and beliefs that underlie community policing and the specific programs and practices by which it is implemented. They assure that agency policies, priorities, and resource allocation are consistent with a community-oriented philosophy. Three strategic elements of community policing are re-oriented operations, geographic focus, and prevention emphasis.

Re-oriented Operations. Community policing recommends less reliance on the patrol car and more emphasis on face-to-face interactions. One objective is to replace ineffective or isolating operational practices (e.g., motorized patrol and rapid response to low priority calls) with more effective and more interactive practices. A related objective is to find ways of performing necessary traditional functions (e.g., handling emergency calls and conducting follow-up investigations) more efficiently, in order to save time and resources that can then be devoted to more community-oriented activities.

Many police departments today have increased their use of foot patrol, directed patrol, door-to-door policing, and other alternatives to traditional motorized patrol (Cordner and Trojanowicz, 1992). Generally, these alternatives seek more targeted tactical effectiveness, more attention to minor offenses and "incivilities," a greater "felt presence" of police, and/or more police-citizen contact. Other police departments have simply reduced their commitment to any form of continuous patrolling, preferring instead to have their patrol officers engage in problem solving, crime prevention, and similar activities when not handling calls and emergencies.

Many police agencies have also adopted differential responses to calls for service (McEwen, Connors, and Cohen, 1986). Rather than attempting to immediately dispatch a sworn officer in response to each and every notification of a crime, disturbance, or other situation, these departments vary their responses depending upon the circumstances. Some crime reports may be taken over the telephone, some service requests may be referred to other government agencies, and some sworn officer responses may be delayed. A particularly interesting alternative is to ask complainants to go in person to a nearby police ministation or storefront office, where an officer, a civilian employee, or even a volunteer takes a report or provides other in-person assistance. Use of differential responses helps departments cope with the sometimes overwhelming burden of 911 calls and frees up patrol officer time for other activities, such as patrolling, problem solving, and crime prevention.

Traditional criminal investigation has also been reexamined in recent years (Eck, 1992). Some departments have de-specialized the activity, reducing the size of the detective unit and making patrol officers more responsible for follow-up investigations. Many have also eliminated the practice of conducting an extensive follow-up investigation of every reported crime, focusing instead on the more serious offenses and on more "solvable" cases. Investigative attention has also been expanded to include a focus on offenders as well as on offenses, especially in the form of repeat offender units that target high-frequency serious offenders. A few departments have taken the additional step of trying to get detectives to expand their case-by-case orientation to include problem solving and crime prevention. In this approach, a burglary detective would be as concerned with reducing burglaries through problem solving and crime prevention as s/he was with solving particular burglary cases.

Not all contemporary alternatives to motorized patrol, rapid response, and criminal investigation are closely allied with community policing. Those specific operational alternatives, and those uses of the freed-up time of patrol officers and detectives, that are consistent with the philosophical and strategic foundations of community policing can be distinguished from those that conform to other philosophies and strategies of policing (Moore and Trojanowicz, 1988).

Geographic Focus. Community policing strategy emphasizes the geographic basis of assignment and responsibility by shifting the fundamental unit of patrol accountability from time of day to place. That is, rather than holding patrol officers, supervisors, and shift commanders responsible for wide areas only during their eight- or ten-hour shifts, community policing seeks to establish 24-hour responsibility for smaller areas.

Of course, no single officer works 24 hours a day, seven days a week, week in and week out. Community policing usually deals with this limitation in one or a combination of three ways: (1) community police officers assigned to neighborhoods may be specialists, with most call handling relegated to a more traditional patrol unit; (2) each individual patrol officer may be held responsible for long-term problem solving in an assigned neighborhood, even though s/he handles calls in a much larger area and, of necessity, many of the calls in the assigned area are handled by other officers; or (3) small teams of officers share both call-handling and problem-solving responsibility in a beat-sized area.

A key ingredient of this geographic focus, however it is implemented, is permanency of assignment. Community policing recommends that patrol officers be assigned to the same areas for extended periods of time, to increase their familiarity with the community and the community's familiarity with them. Ideally, this familiarity will build trust, confidence, and cooperation on both sides of the police-citizen interaction. Also, officers will simply become more knowledgeable about the community and its residents, aiding early intervention and timely problem identification and avoiding conflict based on misperception or misunderstanding.

It is important to recognize that most police departments have long used geography as the basis for daily patrol assignment. Many of these departments, however, assign patrol officers to different beats from one day to the next, creating little continuity or permanency. Moreover, even in police agencies with fairly steady beat assignments, patrol officers are only held accountable for handling their calls and maintaining order (keeping things quiet) *during their shift.* The citizen's question, "Who in the police department is responsible for *my area,* my neighborhood?" can then only truthfully be answered "the chief" or, in large departments, "the precinct commander." Neither patrol officers nor the two or three levels of management above them can be held accountable for dealing with long-term problems in specific locations anywhere in the entire community. Thus, a crucial component of community policing strategy is to create some degree of geographic accountability at all levels in the police organization, but particularly at the level of the patrol officer who delivers basic police services and is in a position to identify and solve neighborhood problems.

Prevention Emphasis. Community policing strategy also emphasizes a more proactive and preventive orientation, in contrast to the reactive focus that has characterized much of policing under the professional model. This proactive, preventive orientation takes several forms. One is simply to encourage better use of police officers' time. In many police departments, patrol officers' time not committed to handling calls is either spent simply waiting for the next call or randomly driving around. Under community policing, this substantial resource of free patrol time is devoted to directed enforcement activities, specific crime prevention efforts, problem solving, community engagement, citizen interaction, or similar kinds of activities.

Another aspect of the preventive focus overlaps with the substantive orientation of community policing and problem-oriented operations. Officers are encouraged to look beyond the individual incidents that they encounter as calls for service and reported crimes in order to discover underlying problems and conditions (Eck and Spelman, 1987). If they can discover such underlying conditions and do something to improve them, officers can prevent the future recurrence of incidents and calls. While immediate response to in-progress emergencies and after-the-fact investigation of crimes will always remain important functions of policing, community policing seeks to elevate before-the-fact prevention and problem solving to comparable status.

Closely related to this line of thinking, but deserving of specific mention, is the desire to enhance the status of crime prevention within police organizations. Most police departments devote the vast majority of their personnel to patrol and investigations, primarily for the purposes of rapid response and follow-up investigation *after* something has happened. Granted, some prevention of crime through the visibility, omnipresence, and deterrence created by patrolling, rapid response, and investigating is expected, but the weight of research over the past two decades has greatly diminished these expectations (Kelling, Pate, Dieckman, and Brown, 1974; Greenwood and Petersilia, 1975; Spelman and Brown, 1982). Despite these lowered expectations, however, police departments still typically devote only a few officers specifically to crime prevention programming and do little to encourage patrol officers to engage in any kinds of crime prevention activity beyond routine riding around.

Moreover, within both informal and formal police cultures, crime solving and criminal apprehension are usually more highly valued than crime prevention. An individual officer is more likely to be commended for arresting a bank robber than for initiating actions that prevent such robberies. Detectives usually enjoy higher status than uniformed officers (especially in the eyes of the public), whereas, within many police agencies, crime prevention officers are seen as public relations functionaries, kiddie cops, or worse. To many police officers, crime prevention work is simply not real police work.

The preeminence of reactive crime fighting within police and popular cultures is understandable, given the dramatic nature of emergencies, crimes, and investigations. Much of police work is about responding to trouble and fixing it, about the contest between good and evil. Responding to emergencies and fighting crime have heroic elements that naturally appeal to both police officers and citizens. Given the choice, though, almost all citizens would prefer not being victimized in the first place to being dramatically rescued, to having the police successfully track down their assailant, or to having the police recover their stolen property. Most citizens would agree that "an ounce of prevention is worth a pound of cure." This is not to suggest that police should turn their backs on reactive handling of crimes and emergencies, but only that before-the-fact prevention should be given greater consideration.

A final element of community policing's preventive focus takes more of a social welfare orientation, particularly toward juveniles. An argument is made that police officers, by serving as mentors and role models, and by providing educational, recreational, and even counseling services, can affect people's behavior in positive ways that ultimately lead to reductions in crime and disorder. In essence, police are asked to support and augment the efforts of families, churches, schools, and other social service agencies. This kind of police activity is seen as particularly necessary by some in order to offset the deficiencies and correct the failures of these other social institutions in modern America.

The Tactical Dimension

The tactical dimension of community policing ultimately translates ideas, philosophies, and strategies into concrete programs, practices, and behaviors. Even those who insist that "community policing is a philosophy, not a program" must concede that unless community policing eventually leads to some action, some new or different behavior, it is all rhetoric and no reality (Greene and Mastrofski, 1988). Indeed, many commentators have taken the view that community policing is little more than a new police marketing strategy that has left the core elements of the police role untouched (see, e.g., Klockars, 1988; Manning, 1988; Weatheritt, 1988). Three of the most important tactical elements of community policing are positive interaction, partnerships, and problem solving.

Positive Interaction. Policing inevitably involves some negative contacts between officers and citizens—arrests, tickets, stops for suspicion, orders to desist in disruptive behavior, inability to make things much better for victims, etc. Community policing recognizes this fact and recommends that officers offset it as much as they can by engaging in positive interactions whenever possible. Positive interactions have further benefits as well, of course: they generally build familiarity, trust, and confidence on both sides; they remind officers that most citizens respect and support them; they make the officer more knowledgeable about people and conditions in the beat; they provide specific information for criminal investigations and problem solving; and they break up the monotony of motorized patrol.

Many opportunities for positive interaction arise in the course of call handling. Too many officers rush to clear their calls, however, often in response to workload concerns and pressure from their superiors, their peers, and dispatchers. As a result, they typically do a mediocre job of handling the immediate incident and make little or no attempt to identify underlying conditions, secure additional information, or create satisfied customers. The prime directive seems to be to do as little as possible in order to clear the call quickly and get back in the car and on the radio, ready to go and do little or nothing at the next call. Getting there rapidly and then clearing promptly take precedence over actually delivering much service or accomplishing anything. Community policing suggests, instead, that officers should look at calls as opportunities for positive interaction, quality service, and problem identification.

gendered emotion based activity conflicts w/ macho image

Even more opportunities for positive interaction can be seized during routine patrol, if officers are willing to exit their vehicles and take some initiative. Officers can go in and out of stores, in and out of schools, talk to people on the street, knock on doors, etc. They can take the initiative to talk not only with shopkeepers and their customers but also with teenagers, apartment dwellers, tavern patrons, and anybody else they run across in public spaces or who are approachable in private places. Police should insert themselves wherever people are and should talk to those people, not just watch them.

Partnerships. Participation of the community in its own protection is one of the central elements of community policing (Bureau of Justice Assistance, 1994c). This participation can run the gamut from watching neighbors' homes to reporting drug dealers to patrolling the streets. It can involve participation in problem identification and problem solving efforts, in crime prevention programs, in neighborhood revitalization, and in youth-oriented educational and recreational programs. Citizens may act individually or in groups, they may collaborate with the police, and they may even join the police department by donating their time as police department volunteers, reserves, or auxiliaries.

Under community policing, police agencies are expected not only to cooperate with citizens and communities but to actively solicit input and participation (Bureau of Justice Assistance, 1994b). The exact nature of this participation can and should vary from community to community and from situation to situation, in keeping with the problem-oriented approach. As a general rule, though, police should avoid claiming that they alone can handle crime, drug, or disorder problems, and they should encourage individual citizens and community groups to shoulder some responsibility for dealing with such problems.

Police have sometimes found it necessary to engage in community organizing as a means of accomplishing any degree of citizen participation in problem solving or crime prevention. In disorganized and transient neighborhoods, residents are often so distressed, fearful, and suspicious of each other (or just so unfamiliar with their neighbors) that police have literally had to set about creating a sense of community where none previously existed. As difficult as this kind of community organizing can be, and as far from the conventional police role as this may seem, these are often the very communities that most need both enhanced police protection and a greater degree of citizen involvement in crime prevention, order maintenance, and general watchfulness over public spaces.

One vexing aspect of community organizing and community engagement results from the pluralistic nature of our society. Differing and often conflicting interests are found in many communities, and they are sometimes represented by competing interest groups. Thus, the elders in a community may want the police to crack down on juveniles, while the youths themselves complain of few opportunities for recreation or entertainment. Tenants may seek police help in organizing a rent strike, while landlords want police assistance in screening or managing the same tenants. Finding common interests around which to rally entire communities, or just identifying common interests on which to base police practices, can be very challenging and, at times, impossible.

It is important to recognize that this inherent feature of pluralistic communities does not arise because of community policing. Police have long been caught in the middle between the interests of adults and juveniles, landlords and tenants, and similar groups. Sometimes the law has provided a convenient reference point for handling such conflicts, but just as often police have had to mediate, arbitrate, or just take the side of the party with the best case. Moreover, when the law has offered a solution, it has frequently been a temporary or unpopular one, and one that still resulted in the police taking sides, protestations of "we're just enforcing the law" notwithstanding.

Fortunately, nearly all citizens want to be safe from violence, want their property protected, and want some level of orderliness in their neighborhoods. Officers can usually find enough consensus in communities upon which to base cooperative efforts aimed at improving safety and public order. Sometimes, apparently deep conflicts between individuals or groups recede when attention is focused on how best to solve specific neighborhood problems. It would be naive to expect overwhelming community consensus in every situation, but it is equally mistaken to think that conflict is so endemic that widespread community support and participation cannot be achieved in many circumstances.

Problem Solving. Supporters of community policing are convinced that the very nature of police work must be altered from its present incident-by-incident, case-by-case orientation to one that is more problem-oriented (Goldstein, 1990). Certainly, incidents must still be handled and cases must still be investigated. Whenever possible, however, attention should be directed toward underlying problems and conditions. Following the medical analogy, policing should address causes as well as symptoms, and should adopt the epidemiological public health approach as much as the individual doctor's clinical approach.

This problem-solving approach should be characterized by several important features: (1) it should be the standard operating method of policing, not an occasional special project; (2) it should be practiced by personnel throughout the ranks, not just by specialists or managers; (3) it should be empirical, in the sense that decisions are made on the basis of information that is gathered systematically; (4) it should involve, whenever possible, collaboration between police and other agencies and institutions; and (5) it should incorporate, whenever possible, community input and participation, so that it is the community's problems that are addressed (not just the police department's) and so that the community shares in the responsibility for its own protection.

The problem-solving process consists of four steps: (1) careful identification of the problem; (2) careful analysis of the problem; (3) a search for alternative solutions to the problem; and (4) implementation and assessment of a response to the problem. Community input can be incorporated within any or all of the steps in the process. Identification, analysis, and assessment should rely on information from multiple sources. A variety of alternative solutions should be considered, including, but not limited to, traditional enforcement methods. Typically, the most effective solutions are those that combine several different responses, including some that draw on more than just the police department's authority and resources.

A crucial characteristic of the problem-oriented approach is that it seeks tailored solutions to specific community problems. Arrests and law enforcement are *not* abandoned—rather, an effort is made in each situation to determine which alternative responses best fit the problem. Use of the criminal law is always considered, as are civil law enforcement, mediation, community mobilization, referral, collaboration, alteration of the physical environment, public education, and a host of other possibilities. The commonsense notion of choosing the tool that best fits the problem, instead of simply grabbing the most convenient or familiar tool in the tool box, lies close to the heart of the problem-solving method.

The Organizational Dimension

It is important to recognize an organizational dimension that surrounds community policing and greatly affects its implementation. In order to support and facilitate community policing, police departments often consider a variety of changes in organization, administration, management, and supervision. The elements of the organizational dimension are not really part of community policing *per se*, but they are frequently crucial to its successful implementation. Three important organizational elements of COP are structure, management, and information.

Structure. Advocates of community policing often look at various ways of restructuring police agencies in order to facilitate and support implementation of the philosophical, strategic, and tactical elements described above. Any organization's structure should correspond with its mission and the nature of the work performed by its members. Some aspects of traditional police organization structure seem more suited to routine, bureaucratic work than to the discretion and creativity required for COP.

The types of restructuring often associated with community policing include:

- *Decentralization*—Authority and responsibility can sometimes be delegated more widely so that commanders, supervisors, and officers can act more independently and be more responsive.

- *Flattening*—The number of layers of hierarchy in the police organization can sometimes be reduced in order to improve communications and reduce waste, rigidity and bureaucracy.

- *De-specialization*—The number of specialized units and personnel can sometimes be reduced, with more resources devoted to the direct delivery of police services (including COP) to the general public.

- *Teams*—Efficiency and effectiveness can sometimes be improved by getting employees working together as teams to perform work, solve problems, or look for ways of improving quality.

- *Civilianization*—Positions currently held by sworn personnel can sometimes be reclassified or redesigned for non-sworn personnel, allowing both cost savings and better utilization of sworn personnel.

Management. Community policing is often associated with styles of leadership, management, and supervision that give more emphasis to organizational culture and values and less emphasis to written rules and formal discipline. The general argument is that when employees are guided by a set of officially sanctioned values they will usually make good decisions and take appropriate actions. Although many formal rules will still probably be necessary, managers will need to resort to them much less often in order to maintain control over subordinates.

Management practices consistent with this emphasis on organizational culture and values include:

- *Mission*—Agencies should develop concise statements of their mission and values and use them consistently in making decisions, guiding employees, and training new recruits.

- *Strategic Planning*—Agencies should engage in continuous strategic planning aimed at ensuring that resources and energy are focused on mission accomplishment and adherence to core values; otherwise, organizations tend to get off track, confused about their mission and about what really matters.

- *Coaching*—Supervisors should coach and guide their subordinates more, instead of restricting their roles to review of paperwork and enforcement of rules and regulations.

- *Mentoring*—Young employees need mentoring from managers, supervisors, and/or peers—not just to learn how to do the job right but also to learn what constitutes the right job; in other words, to learn about ethics and values and what it means to be a good police officer.

- *Empowerment*—Under COP, employees are encouraged to be risk-takers who demonstrate imagination and creativity in their work—this kind of empowerment can only succeed, however, when employees are thoroughly familiar with the organization's core values and firmly committed to them. *& rewarded*

- *Selective Discipline*—In their disciplinary processes, agencies should make distinctions between intentional and unintentional errors made by employees and between employee actions that violate core values versus those that merely violate technical rules.

Information. Doing community policing and managing it effectively require certain types of information that have not traditionally been available in all police departments. In the never-ending quality vs. quantity debate, for example, community policing tends to emphasize quality. This emphasis on quality shows up in many areas: avoidance of traditional bean-counting (arrests, tickets) to measure success, more concern for how well calls are handled than merely for how quickly they are handled, etc. Also, the geographic focus of community policing increases the need for detailed information based on neighborhoods as the unit of analysis. The emphasis on problem solving highlights the need for information systems that aid in identifying and analyzing community-level problems. And so on.

Several aspects of police administration under community policing that have implications for information are:

- *Performance Appraisal*—Individual officers can be evaluated on the quality of their community policing and problem-solving activities, and perhaps on results achieved, instead of on traditional performance indicators (tickets, arrests, calls handled, etc.).

- *Program Evaluation*—Police programs and strategies can be evaluated more on the basis of their effectiveness (outcomes, results, quality) than just on their efficiency (effort, outputs, quantity).

- *Departmental Assessment*—The police agency's overall performance can be measured and assessed on the basis of a wide variety of indicators (including customer satisfaction, fear levels, problem solving, etc.) instead of a narrow band of traditional indicators (reported crime, response time, etc.).

- *Information Systems*—An agency's information systems need to collect and produce information on the whole range of the police function, not just on enforcement and call-handling activities, in order to support more quality-oriented appraisal, evaluation, and assessment efforts.

- *Crime Analysis*—Individual officers need more timely and complete crime analysis information pertaining to their specific geographic areas of responsibility to facilitate problem identification, analysis, fear reduction, etc.

- *Geographic Information Systems* (GIS)—Sophisticated and user-friendly computerized mapping software available today makes it possible for officers and citizens to obtain customized maps that graphically identify "hot spots" and help them picture the geographic locations and distribution of crime and related problems.

What Do We Know?

Despite the programmatic and evaluation complexities discussed earlier, we do have a substantial amount of information from empirical studies of community policing. Table 1 summarizes the "preponderance of the evidence" on the effects of community policing based on a review of over 60 such studies (recent reviews have also been completed by Normandeau, 1993; Bennett, 1994; Leighton, 1994; and Skogan, 1994).

The first thing to note in table 1 is that almost three-fourths of the 28 cells are blank, indicating that the effects are unknown (completely or substantially untested). Nearly all of the evaluations conducted to-date have focused on the tactical dimension of community policing, leaving us with little or no information on the effects of philosophical, strategic, and organizational changes. This gap in community policing research is undoubtedly caused by a combination of two factors: (1) most community policing efforts, at least until recently, have been limited programmatic and street-level initiatives rather than large-scale strategic or organizational-change initiatives; and (2) evaluation of narrowly focused programmatic initiatives is much easier and more feasible than evaluation of philosophical and organization-wide change.

The most useful way to summarize the evidence on the effects of community policing is to scan the tactical row of table 1.

Crime

The evidence is mixed. Only a few studies have used experimental designs and victimization surveys to test the effects of community policing on crime; many others have relied on simple before-after comparisons of reported crime or single-item victimization questions drawn from community surveys. Overall, a slight majority of the studies have detected crime decreases, giving reason for optimism, but evaluation design limitations prevent us from drawing any authoritative conclusions.

Table 1
Preponderance of the Evidence on Community Policing

Effects/ Dimensions	Crime	Fear	Disorder	Calls for Service	Community Relations	Police Officer Attitudes	Police Officer Behavior
Philosophical: Citizen Input Broad Police function Personal Service							
Strategic: Re-oriented Operations Geographic Focus Preventive Emphasis							
Tactical: Positive Interaction Partnerships Problem Solving	MIX	MIX	POS	MIX	POS	POS	MIX
Organizational: Structure Management Information						POS	

POS=positive effects (beneficial effects)
NEG=negative effects
MIX=mixed effects
blank=unknown (completely or substantially untested)

Fear of Crime

Again the evidence is mixed, but it leans more heavily in the positive direction. A number of studies have employed community surveys to make before-after comparisons of fear and related perceptions, some with experimental designs. Fear has typically been measured using a variety of survey items, lending the studies more credibility. The now widely-accepted view that community policing helps reduce levels of fear of crime and increases perceptions of safety seems reasonably well-founded, although some efforts have failed to accomplish fear reductions.

Disorder

The impact of community policing on disorder, minor crime, incivilities, and signs of crime has not been subjected to careful testing as frequently as its impact on crime and fear. The available evidence suggests, though, that community policing, and especially foot patrol and problem solving, helps reduce levels of disorder, lending partial support to the "broken windows" thesis (Wilson and Kelling, 1982).

Calls for Service

Community policing might reduce calls for service in several ways: problem solving might address underlying issues that generate calls; collaboration might increase call referrals to other government agencies; foot patrols and ministations might receive citizen requests directly, thus heading off calls to central dispatch; and workload management might find alternative responses for some types of calls. Although the ability of the last approach (workload management) to reduce the volume of calls dispatched to sworn units for immediate response has clearly been demonstrated (McEwen et al., 1986), the rest of the evidence on the effects of community policing on calls for service is mixed. Several studies have found positive effects but several others have not.

Community Relations

The vast majority of the studies that have looked at the impact of community policing on citizens' attitudes toward the police have uncovered positive effects. Clearly, citizens generally appreciate ministations in their neighborhoods, foot patrols, problem-solving efforts, and other forms of community policing. These very consistent findings are all the more remarkable because baseline measures of citizen satisfaction with, and support for, their police are frequently quite positive to begin with, thus offering relatively little room for improvement.

Police Officer Attitudes

A clear majority of the studies that have investigated the effects of community policing on officers' job satisfaction, perceptions of the community, and other related attitudes have discovered beneficial effects. Officers involved in community policing, especially if they are volunteers or members of special units, typically thrive on their new duties and responsibilities. Also, there is some evidence that organizing and managing officers differently (the so-called "inside-out" approach) can have positive effects on their morale and related attitudes (Wycoff and Skogan, 1993).

What is somewhat less certain, however, is (1) whether the positive effects of community policing on officers will survive the long term and (2) whether these benefits are as universal when *all* officers are required to engage in community policing. Whenever community policing is practiced only by specialists, as has generally been the case until recently in most departments, one condition that *is* nearly universal is conflict between the specialists and other members of the agency, frequently reflected in derogatory remarks about "the grin and wave squad."

Police Officer Behavior

Significant anecdotal evidence suggests that foot patrol, problem solving, permanent assignment, ministations, and other features of community policing lead to changes in some police officers' behavior, but these behavioral effects have only been lightly documented thus far (Mastrofski, Worden, and Snipes, 1995). Evidence also suggests that many officers resist changing their behavior, out of opposition to the philosophical underpinnings of community policing, doubts that community policing really works, or just plain habit.

Conclusion

A great deal of energy has been invested since 1980 in determining the nature of community policing and its effects. These efforts have paid off to the extent that the scope and variation of community policing is much better understood today and some of its effects have been fairly well documented. Since community policing has evolved significantly during this period, however, some of its elements have been more carefully evaluated than others. In addition, programmatic complexity, multiple effects, variations in scope, and research design limitations have hampered many of the community policing evaluations conducted thus far. Nevertheless, the tactical elements of community policing do seem to produce several beneficial outcomes for citizens and officers, and have the potential to impact crime and disorder. Whether the more philosophical, strategic, and organizational elements of community policing will become firmly rooted, and whether they will ultimately have beneficial effects, is yet to be seen.

References

Bennett, Trevor. 1994. "Community Policing on the Ground: Developments in Britain." In Dennis P. Rosenbaum, ed., *The Challenge of Community Policing: Testing the Promises*. Thousand Oaks, CA: Sage, pp. 224–46.

Bureau of Justice Assistance. 1994a. *A Police Guide to Surveying Citizens and Their Environment*. Washington, DC: Bureau of Justice Assistance.

_____. 1994b. *Neighborhood-Oriented Policing in Rural Communities: A Program Planning Guide*. Washington, DC: Bureau of Justice Assistance.

_____. 1994c. *Understanding Community Policing: A Framework for Action*. Washington, DC: Bureau of Justice Assistance.

Cordner, Gary W. and Robert C. Trojanowicz. 1992. "Patrol." In Gary W. Cordner and Donna C. Hale, eds., *What Works in Policing? Operations and Administration Examined*. Cincinnati, OH: Anderson, pp. 3–18.

Eck, John E. 1992. "Criminal Investigation." In Gary W. Cordner and Donna C. Hale, eds., *What Works in Policing? Operations and Administration Examined*. Cincinnati, OH: Anderson, pp. 19–34.

Eck, John E. and William Spelman. 1987. *Problem Solving: Problem-Oriented Policing in Newport News*. Washington, DC: Police Executive Research Forum.

Goldstein, Herman. 1977. *Policing A Free Society*. Cambridge, MA: Ballinger.
_____. 1987. "Toward Community-Oriented Policing: Potential, Basic Requirements, and Threshold Questions," *Crime & Delinquency* 25:236–58.
_____. 1990. *Problem-Oriented Policing*. New York: McGraw-Hill.
Greene, Jack R. and Stephen D. Mastrofski, eds. 1988. *Community Policing: Rhetoric or Reality?* New York: Praeger.
Greenwood, Peter W. and Joan Petersilia. 1975. *The Criminal Investigation Process, Volume I: Summary and Implications*. Santa Monica: Rand Corporation.
Kelling, George L., Tony Pate, Duane Dieckman, and Charles E. Brown. 1974. *The Kansas City Preventive Patrol Experiment: A Summary Report*. Washington, DC: Police Foundation.
Kelling, George L. and Mark H. Moore. 1988. "The Evolving Strategy of Policing." *Perspectives on Policing* No. 4. Washington, DC: National Institute of Justice.
Klockars, Carl B. 1988. "The Rhetoric of Community Policing." In Jack R. Greene and Stephen D. Mastrofski, eds., *Community Policing: Rhetoric or Reality?* New York: Praeger, pp. 239–58.
Leighton, Barry N. 1994. "Community Policing in Canada: An Overview of Experience and Evaluations." In Dennis P. Rosenbaum, ed., *The Challenge of Community Policing: Testing the Promises*. Thousand Oaks, CA: Sage, pp. 209–23.
Manning, Peter K. 1988. "Community Policing as a Drama of Control." In Jack R. Greene and Stephen D. Mastrofski, eds., *Community Policing: Rhetoric or Reality?* New York: Praeger, pp. 27–46.
Mastrofski, Stephen D., Robert E. Worden, and Jeffrey B. Snipes. 1995. "Law Enforcement in a Time of Community Policing." *Criminology* 33, 4:539–63.
McEwen, J. Thomas, Edward F. Connors III, and Marcia I. Cohen. 1986. *Evaluation of the Differential Police Responses Field Test*. Washington, DC: National Institute of Justice.
Moore, Mark H. and Robert C. Trojanowicz. 1988. "Corporate Strategies for Policing." *Perspectives on Policing* No. 6. Washington, DC: National Institute of Justice.
Normandeau, Andre. 1993. "Community Policing in Canada: A Review of Some Recent Studies," *American Journal of Police* 12,1:57–73.
Skogan, Wesley G. 1994. "The Impact of Community Policing on Neighborhood Residents: A Cross-Site Analysis." In Dennis P. Rosenbaum, ed., *The Challenge of Community Policing: Testing the Promises*. Thousand Oaks, CA: Sage, pp. 167–81.
Spelman, William and Dale K. Brown. 1982. *Calling the Police: Citizen Reporting of Serious Crime*. Washington, DC: Police Executive Research Forum.
Trojanowicz, Robert and Bonnie Bucqueroux. 1990. *Community Policing: A Contemporary Perspective*. Cincinnati, OH: Anderson.
Weatheritt, Mollie. 1988. "Community Policing: Rhetoric or Reality?" In Jack R. Greene and Stephen D. Mastrofski, eds., *Community Policing: Rhetoric or Reality?* New York: Praeger, pp. 153–76.
Wilson, James Q. and George L. Kelling. 1982. "Police and Neighborhood Safety: Broken Windows," *The Atlantic Monthly* (March): 29–38.
Wycoff, Mary Ann and Wesley K. Skogan. 1993. *Community Policing in Madison: Quality From the Inside Out*. Washington, DC: National Institute of Justice.

5

Problem-Solving
Problem-Oriented Policing in Newport News

John E. Eck and *William Spelman*

Every Friday and Saturday night, residents of a suburban neighborhood complain to the police about teenagers who come in from another part of town. The youths make noise, drink, and commit minor acts of vandalism.

The parking lots around a large manufacturing plant are a haven for thieves. Thefts from autos parked in these lots account for 10 percent of all crimes reported in the city.

An apartment complex is notorious for its high burglary rates. One of every four residents are burglarized each year; follow-up investigations—and occasional arrests—seem to do no good at all.

Patrol officers and detectives spend millions of hours each year responding to incidents like these. Despite their efforts—and despite the arrests, convictions, and incarcerations that sometimes result—the incidents persist.

Research results spanning two decades have converged on a new approach for delivering police services, aimed at solving persistent problems like these. It is called *problem-oriented policing*. Using this approach, police go beyond individual crimes and calls for service, and take on the underlying problems that create them. To understand problems, police collect facts from a wide variety of sources, from outside as well as from inside police agencies. To develop and implement solutions, police enlist the support of other public and private agencies and individuals.

> *Problem-oriented policing is a department-wide strategy aimed at solving persistent community problems. Police identify, analyze, and respond to the underlying circumstances that create incidents.*

Source: National Institute of Justice. Research in Brief, January, 1987.

The Problem-Oriented Policing Project was conducted by the Newport News (Virginia) Police Department and the Police Executive Research Forum, with guidance and funding from the National Institute of Justice. In this summary, we describe the origins of problem-oriented policing, the approach that was designed and implemented in Newport News, and some of the problems officers have addressed. But first, in order to show why this approach is new, let us review current police practice.

Incident-Driven Policing

Current police practice is primarily incident-driven. That is, most police activities are aimed at resolving individual incidents, rather than groups of incidents or problems. The incident-driven police department has four characteristics.

First, it is *reactive*. Most of the workload of patrol officers and detectives consists of handling crimes that have already been committed, disturbances in progress, traffic violations, and the like. The exceptions—crime prevention and narcotics investigations, for example—make up but a small portion of police work.

Incident-driven police work relies on *limited information*, gathered mostly from victims, witnesses, and suspects. Only limited information is needed because the police objectives are limited: patrol officers and detectives are only trying to resolve the incident at hand.

The primary means of resolving incidents is to invoke the *criminal justice process*. Even when an officer manages to resolve an incident without arresting or citing anyone, it is often the threat of enforcing the law that is the key to resolution. Alternative means of resolution are seldom invoked.

Finally, incident-driven police departments use *aggregate statistics* to measure performance. The department is doing a good job when the city-wide crime rate is low, or the city-wide arrest rate is high. The best officers are those who make many arrests, or service many calls.

No department is purely incident-driven; but this is what all agencies do, almost all of the time. Appropriately responding to incidents can be effective: victims are aided, serious offenders are caught, and citizens are helped every day. But too often it fails. Handling calls for service is time-consuming, and rarely produces a tangible result. Officers become frustrated after they handle similar calls time and again, with no sign of progress. Citizens become frustrated when the difficulties that provoked their calls remain unresolved. The constant repetition of similar calls indicates that the incident-driven police department has been unable to do anything about the underlying conditions.

Problem-Oriented Policing

An alternative to incident-driven policing was described by Herman Goldstein in 1979. Goldstein contended that reacting to calls for service was only the first step. Police should go further, and attempt to find a permanent resolution of the problem which created the call. Goldstein called his alternative the "problem-oriented approach." Problem-oriented policing, as it has developed in Newport News, is a direct extension of Goldstein's approach.

The theory behind problem-oriented policing is simple. Underlying conditions create problems. These conditions might include the characteristics of the people involved (offenders, potential victims, and others), the social setting in which these people interact, the physical environment, and the way the public deals with these conditions.

A problem created by these conditions may generate one or more incidents. These incidents, while stemming from a common source, may appear to be different. For example, social and physical conditions in a deteriorated apartment complex may generate burglaries, acts of vandalism, intimidation of pedestrians by rowdy teenagers, and other incidents. These incidents, some of which come to police attention, are symptoms of the problem. The incidents will continue so long as the problem that creates them persists.

As described by figure A, the incident-driven police agency responds by dealing with each incident. Like aspirin, this symptomatic relief is valuable but limited. Because police typically leave untouched the condition which created the incidents, the incidents are very likely to recur.

A problem-oriented police agency would respond as described in figure B. Officers continue to handle calls, but they do much more. They use the information gathered in their responses to incidents, together with information obtained from other sources, to get a clearer picture of the problem. They then address the underlying conditions. If they are successful in ameliorating these conditions, fewer

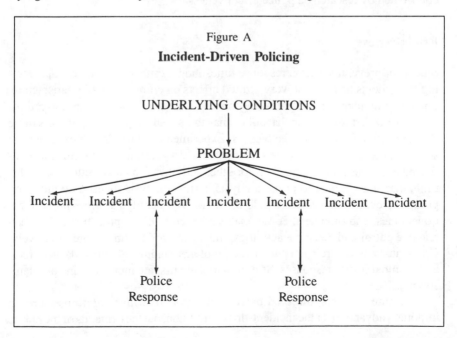

Figure A

Incident-Driven Policing

UNDERLYING CONDITIONS

PROBLEM

Incident   Incident   Incident   Incident   Incident   Incident   Incident

Police Response   Police Response

incidents may occur; those that do occur may be less serious. The incidents may even cease. At the very least, information about the problem can help police to design more effective ways of responding to each incident.

Problem-solving is not new. Police officers have always tried to solve problems. But officers have received little guidance and support from police administrators. In fact, supervisors and other officers have often discouraged problem-solving; the more time officers spent dealing with problems, the less time was available for reacting to incidents.

Problem-oriented policing—the routine application of problem-solving techniques—is new. It is based on two premises. The first premise is that problem-solving can be applied by officers throughout the agency as part of their daily work. Previous problem-solving efforts have been confined to special projects or units. The second premise is that routine problem-solving efforts can be effective in reducing or resolving problems. The National Institute of Justice, the Forum, and the Newport News Police Department undertook this project to test these premises.

Although problem-oriented policing is new, it relies on twenty years of research on incident-driven policing.

The Research Basis of Problem-Oriented Policing

Five areas of research contributed to the development of problem-oriented policing. The initial impetus for an alternative to incident-driven policing was contributed by research on police effectiveness.

Effectiveness

Studies of preventive patrol, response time, and investigations showed that reacting to incidents had, at best, very limited effects on crime and public satisfaction. For many incidents, rapid patrol responses or lengthy follow-up investigations were not needed, suggesting that police managers could deploy their officers more flexibly without reducing effectiveness. Experiments in flexible deployment such as split force, investigative case screening, and differential response to calls confirmed that time could be freed up for other activities. To make better use of this time, managers turned to crime analysis. Crime analysis focused attention on groups of events, rather than single incidents. By identifying crime-prone locations, times, and offenders, crime analysts hoped to direct proactive rather than reactive patrol and detective activities, thus using officer time more effectively. Crime analysis was restricted to crime problems, traditional police data sources, and criminal justice responses. Still, it marks the first attempt at routine problem-solving.

Crime analysis, directed patrol, and proactive investigations were an important advance over the incident-driven tradition, but the demands of the public

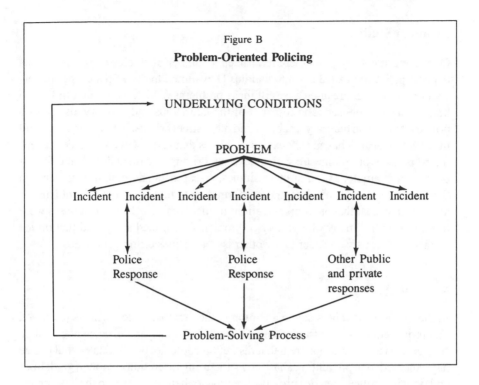

Figure B
Problem-Oriented Policing

and of officers themselves suggested that even bigger changes were needed. Community policing experiments and in-depth studies of public problems were influencing police to adopt a broader concept of their role; studies of police discretion and management were showing that changes in the police bureaucracy were needed, as well.

Community

The riots of the 1960s made police aware of their strained relation with minority communities. Community relations units, stringent shooting policies, and civilian review boards were all attempts to reduce dissatisfaction with police among minorities. By the mid-1970s, police were going further, providing storefront police stations and foot patrols in an effort to improve public attitudes through increased personal contact with police officers. These programs increased communication between police and citizens. And as police began to recognize the vital role of citizen action in controlling crime and disorder, some agencies began to work closely with citizens to reduce crime and fear. Problem-oriented policing draws on experience showing that joint police/community activities are often the best methods for solving problems.

Problem Studies

Over the last twenty years there have been a number of studies of problem areas that the police are called upon to handle. They aimed to develop a deeper understanding of the nature and causes of these problems, which would in turn lead to better police responses. The research of the late 1960s and early 1970s focused police attention on burglary, robbery, and other street crimes. In the later 1970s and the 1980s, research began to focus on problems that had not been considered central to police work: domestic violence, drunk driving, the mentally ill, and fear of crime, for example. Through these studies, researchers and practitioners learned that they would have to collect more information to understand these problems. It also became clear that other organizations needed to be involved if responses were to be effective. Finally, the variety of problems examined suggested that police needed to seriously consider many other issues besides crime.

Discretion

In the 1960s, researchers called attention to the fact that police officers exercised much discretion. This raised questions about the equity and efficiency of police service delivery. It was apparent that discretion could not be eliminated; but police have succeeded in preventing abuses by structuring discretion. Through guidelines and policies, police agencies provide direction to their officers as to the best means of handling sensitive situations. But where do the guidelines and policies come from? In 1979, Herman Goldstein described what he called the "problem-oriented approach" as a means of developing these guidelines. Goldstein's approach is the core of problem-oriented policing.

Management

While these studies were being conducted, the characteristics of American police officers were changing. More and more officers were getting college degrees and thinking of themselves as professionals. Like workers in private industry, officers began to demand a greater decision-making role in their agencies. Many police managers, recognizing that satisfaction and participation influence job performance, began to make better use of the skills and talents of their officers. Through job enrichment, managers gave their officers more interesting and challenging work, and made working conditions more flexible. Many departments made decision making more participative, by establishing task forces, quality circles, or management-by-objectives programs. Problem-oriented policing incorporates job enrichment, flexibility, and participative management, to make the fullest possible use of the skills and talents of street-level officers.

Problem-oriented policing applies findings from these five streams of research. As suggested by the effectiveness research, problem-oriented policing uses time management and thorough analysis to address groups of similar incidents, or problems. But it recognizes a broader role for police than just crime control, focusing on problems besides crime, and involving police with citizens, businesses, and other agencies to identify and resolve citizens' concerns. Finally, problem-oriented policing involves substantial changes in the police organization. It is a means for structuring discretion; it draws on the expertise of police officers and applies their desire to have decision-making roles.

Designing Problem-Oriented Policing

This was the research background when the Problem-Oriented Policing Project began in Newport News. Some departments had implemented problem-solving approaches as part of special units or projects, but no department had implemented a problem-oriented approach agencywide. An operational system had to be designed and tested. The National Institute of Justice required that the problem-solving system follow five basic principles:

- Officers of all ranks and from all units should be able to use the system as part of their daily routine.

- The system must encourage the use of a broad range of information, including but not limited to conventional police data.

- The system should encourage a broad range of solutions, including but not limited to the criminal justice process.

- The system should require no additional resources and no special units.

- Finally, any large police agency must be able to apply it.

Newport News was chosen to design and implement the system for several reasons. It is a moderately sized agency, with 280 employees serving a population of 155,000. It was small enough that changes could be made in a reasonably short time, but served an urban population with many of the crime problems of big cities. Because Newport News was close to Washington, D.C., Forum staff could conveniently spend a great deal of time in the field. Its chief of police, Darrell Stephens, was well-versed in the background research, felt the project would be worthwhile, and was committed to its success.

To design the system, the Newport News Police Department assembled a task force of twelve department members, representing all ranks and units. As this group had no experience at solving problems, they decided to test the system they were designing on two, persistent problems: burglaries from an apartment complex, and thefts from vehicles. It was understood, however, that all subsequent problems would be handled by officers in their normal assignments.

As shown in figure C, the Task Force designed a four-stage Problem Solving Process. During the *Scanning* stage, an officer identifies an issue and determines whether it is really a problem. In the *Analysis* stage, officers collect information, from sources inside and outside their agency. The goal is to understand the scope, nature, and causes of the problem. In the *Response* stage, this information is used to develop and implement solutions. Officers seek the assistance of other police units, other public and private organizations, and anyone else who can help. Finally, in the *Assessment* stage, officers evaluate the effectiveness of the response. Officers may use the results to revise the response, collect more data, or even to redefine the problem.

The heart of this process is the Analysis stage. To help officers analyze problems, the task force designed a *Problem Analysis Guide*. This guide (summarized in table A) breaks the events that comprise a problem into three components:

1. *Actors*—victims, offenders, and others involved in the events;
2. *Incidents*—the social context, physical setting, and actions taken before, during, and after the events; and,
3. *Responses*—the perceptions and responses of citizens and private and public institutions to the problem.

The guide is a checklist of issues that officers should consider when they study a problem.

All officers of the rank of sergeant and above were trained in the use of the process and the guide, as well as on the research background of problem-oriented policing. The training also emphasized the need to encourage officer initiative in finding problems, collecting information, and developing responses. Officers throughout the department then began to apply the process and the guide.

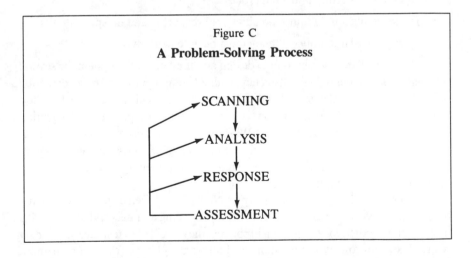

Figure C

A Problem-Solving Process

SCANNING

ANALYSIS

RESPONSE

ASSESSMENT

Table A

The Problem Analysis Guide
(List of topic headings)

Actors
Victims
  Life-style
  Security measures taken
  Victimization history
Offenders
  Identity and physical description
  Life-style, education, employment history
  Criminal history
Third parties
  Personal data
  Connection to victimization
Incidents
Sequence of events
  Events preceding act
  Event itself
  Events following criminal act
Physical context
  Time
  Location
  Access control and surveillance
Social context
  Likelihood and probable actions of witnesses
  Apparent attitude of residents toward neighborhood
Immediate results of incidents
  Harm done to victim
  Gain to offender
  Legal issues
Responses
Community
  Neighborhood affected by problem
  City as a whole
  People outside the city
Institutional
  Criminal justice system
  Other public agencies
  Mass media
  Business sector
Seriousness
  Public perceptions
  Perception of others

Problem-Oriented Policing at Work

There were two basic questions about this process that needed to be answered:

- Can officers use it routinely to solve problems?
- Are these problem-solving efforts effective?

To answer them, the Forum staff undertook an evaluation of problem-oriented policing in Newport News.

By June 1986, some two dozen problems had been identified and were in various stages of analysis, response, and assessment. As table B shows, officers considered a wide range of problems. Some problems affect citizens throughout the city; others are confined to neighborhoods. Some problems are criminal; others are related to the order maintenance, regulatory, or service roles of the police. Officers and their supervisors identified, analyzed, and responded to these problems during the course of their normal work by applying the process and guide. The number and diversity of problems tackled by department members shows that *police officers can solve problems routinely.*

The second test of the problem-solving process is the effectiveness of the responses. Three efforts have advanced far enough for us to judge their effectiveness. The results are encouraging:

- Burglaries in the New Briarfield Apartment complex were reduced by 35 percent;
- Robberies in the central business district were reduced by 40 percent;
- Thefts from vehicles parked outside Newport News Shipbuilding were reduced by 55 percent.

These results show that problem-solving efforts can be effective. To illustrate how problem-solving works, let us examine the first of these efforts below.

Burglaries in the New Briarfield Apartments

Briarfield Apartments, a complex of 450 wood-frame units, was built in 1942 as temporary housing for shipyard workers. After World War II the postwar housing shortage was acute, so it remained standing. By 1984, the complex was generally regarded as the worst housing in the city. It also had the highest crime rate in the city: 23 percent of the occupied units were broken into each year. The Task Force decided to use Briarfield as a test of problem-oriented policing. Detective Tony Duke of the Crime Analysis Unit was assigned to study the problem.

To find out how residents felt, Duke arranged for patrol and auxiliary officers to survey a random sample of one-third of the households in January 1985. The residents confirmed that burglary was a serious problem. However, they were equally concerned about the physical deterioration of the complex.

Table B

Newport News Officers are Considering a Range of Problems

	Citywide	Neighborhood
Crime problems	Domestic homicides	Personal robberies (Central business district)
	Gas station driveoffs	
	Assaults on police officers	Commercial burglaries (Jefferson Avenue business district)
		Vacant buildings (Central business district)
		Residential burglaries (New Briarfield Apts)
		Residential burglaries (Glenn Gardens Apts)
		Larcenies (Beechmont Gardens Apts)
		Thefts from autos (Newport News Shipbuilding)
		Drug dealing (32d and Chestnut)
Disorder problems	Runaway youths	Rowdy youths (Peninsula Skating Rink)
	Driving under the influence	Shot houses (Aqua Vista Apts)
	Disturbances at convenience stores	Disturbances (Marshall Avenue 7-Eleven)
		Dirt bikes (Newmarket Creek)
		Disturbances (Village Square Shopping Center

Indeed, as Detective Duke interviewed employees of city departments, he found that the burglary problem was related to the general deterioration of the complex. The fire department considered New Briarfield to be a firetrap. Public works was concerned about flooding because the complex had no storm sewers. Standing water rotted the floors, a cause for concern to the codes compliance department. Cracks around the door and window frames let in the cold and rain, and made break-ins easy. And many units were vacant and uninhabitable, providing hiding places for burglars and drug users.

Immediately after the survey, the patrol officer responsible for the area around New Briarfield, Barry Haddix, decided to clean up the grounds of the complex. By working with the apartment manager and city agencies he was able to fix a variety of unsanitary and unsafe conditions. Trash and abandoned appliances were removed; abandoned cars were towed; the potholes were filled and the streets were swept.

Meanwhile, Detective Duke found that the owners of the complex were in default on a loan from the U.S. Department of Housing and Urban Development and that HUD was about to foreclose. This presented the city with a possible solution. Duke wrote a report on New Briarfield, describing the crime problems, the views of the tenants, and the concerns of other city agencies. Chief Stephens used this report to mobilize other city agencies to make a joint recommendation to the city manager: help the tenants find better housing and demolish New Briarfield. The city manager accepted the recommendation. In June 1986, the city proposed that Briarfield be replaced with a new 220-unit apartment complex, a middle school, and a small shopping center. Negotiations are pending with HUD.

This long-run solution will take many months to implement. To hold the line until then, the police department assigned Officer Vernon Lyons to the full-time job of organizing residents of Briarfield and the surrounding neighborhood. Since January 1986, the New Briarfield Community Association has influenced residents to take better care of their neighborhood, and lobbied the resident manager and city agencies to ensure that the complex is properly maintained.

The activities of the police department and the community association have resulted in visibly better living conditions and in a 35 percent drop in the burglary rate since the police began work.

New Information, New Responses

One reason these efforts have been successful is that police managers have used the process and guide to encourage officers to gather more information, from a wider variety of sources than before. The survey of New Briarfield residents, and the extensive discussions with the apartment manager and public officials are examples. While studying other problems, officers have conducted literature reviews, interviewed prostitutes and thieves, surveyed businesses, held conferences with local public and private officials, photographed problem sites, and searched title and tax records.

As a result, the responses are more comprehensive than standard incident-driven reactions. This, too, is strongly encouraged by the department's managers. Some of the responses are improvements on standard tactics. For example, the department responded to the problems of downtown robberies and parking lot thefts by identifying, arresting, and incarcerating the most frequent offenders. But even in these examples, the involvement of people outside the criminal justice system was important. Other responses, such as the actions taken in New Briarfield, hardly involve the criminal justice process at all. While responding to other problems, officers have worked with businesses, the military, citizens' groups, state and federal agencies, and non-profit organizations. So the resources used are as diverse as the problems themselves.

Implementing Problem-Oriented Policing

Problem-oriented policing involves a substantial change from current practice. The fully problem-oriented police agency will be different from present agencies in several ways.

- Problem-solving will be the standard method of policing, not just an occasionally useful tactic.
- Problem-solving efforts will focus on problems of the public, not police administration.
- When problems are taken on, police will establish precise, measurable objectives.
- Police managers will constantly look for ways to get all members of the department involved in solving problems.

These characteristics will be true of all agencies that have committed themselves to problem-oriented policing. As these agencies gain experience with problem-oriented policing, they should develop three additional characteristics:

- Officers will consistently undertake thorough analyses, using data from many sources.
- Officers will engage in an uninhibited search for solutions to all problems they take on.
- All members of the department will be involved in problem-solving.

Developing these characteristics will take time; police executives should plan to implement problem-oriented policing over a period of many years, rather than weeks or months.

As a result, there are no police departments with all seven of these characteristics yet. Newport News has the first four characteristics; several other departments will be initiating or increasing problem-oriented efforts over the next year.

Nevertheless, problem-oriented policing represents an enormous change in the way officers think about their jobs, and in the way the entire department does business. While it will take a long time to develop, the Newport News experience has demonstrated that police executives interested in pursuing the problem-oriented approach can make their agencies more effective in a short time.

Problem-solving will be most successful if the department sets the stage by changing practices that may pose barriers to success. For example, many Newport News officers reported that time was a major constraint to their problem-solving activities. The police manager should consider such tactics as differential police response and case screening. Use of crime analysis and proactive patrol and investigation tactics can also help the department get ready for less conventional activities. Constantly changing assignments and rotating shifts can make problem-solving activities inconvenient and difficult; police executives should consider stable assignments and shift schedules to remove these obstacles. A tough line on incidents of police corruption will show officers that the discretionary management style problem-oriented policing requires is not an invitation to illegal or inappropriate behavior. Changes in promotion and reward procedures, implementation of management-by-objectives, and explicit training in effective problem-solving techniques can both motivate officers to solve problems and show them that the administration is serious about its efforts.

Getting support from institutions outside the police department is critical, since they provide information about problems and assistance in solving them. However, the problem-oriented approach may be difficult to sell to those outside policing: there is no unit, equipment, or other physical evidence to which the police can point; some will assume the police department has been solving problems all along. This puts a burden on police executives to begin teaching local government officials, members of civic organizations, the press, and others about the nature of the changes as soon as they decide to make them.

This process of educating the department and the public will continue once the police executive has committed the department to problem-oriented policing. Aside from education, the most important task for the police executive will then be to provide leadership and direction to street-level supervisors. Sergeants and lieutenants are especially important to the success of problem-oriented policing, because problem-solving efforts will rarely be cut-and-dried. Supervisors must be prepared to give their officers lots of discretion, assistance, and support, but they must also ensure that officers are putting in their best efforts. Supervisors must be patient and emphasize performance, but they must also insist that officers keep at their work until they do what can reasonably be done. Under problem-oriented policing, the first-line supervisor's job becomes one of continually balancing conflicting objectives.

In the beginning, police managers at all levels will face a tension between the quantity of problems solved and the quality of problem-solving efforts. If they set standards too high or encourage officers to take on very large problems, they may scare others off; but if standards are set too low, problem-solving may appear trivial. Police executives will have to manage this tension carefully, although both quality and quantity are possible in the long run.

Conclusions

The Problem-Oriented Policing Project was undertaken to test two premises: that officers throughout a police agency could apply problem-solving techniques as part of their daily routine, and that their problem-solving efforts could be effective. The Newport News experience suggests that these premises are correct. Many officers were able to get involved; their efforts were effective at reducing the size and seriousness of the problems they attacked.

This does not imply that all problem-solving efforts will be successful, of course, or even that all departments will be able to implement the problem-oriented approach. It does demonstrate that problem-oriented policing can be successful and that it deserves further experimentation. As other departments begin to adopt the approach, they will need to develop it further, fitting it to local conditions. If many departments adopt and develop the approach—if problem-oriented policing eventually replaces incident-driven policing as the basic organizing principle of American police work—its present stage of development will look primitive, indeed.

At base, however, it will remain the same. Problem-oriented policing emphasizes cooperation between the police, the public, and other agencies. It helps to ensure that police consider and respond to a wide variety of problems affecting the quality of life, not just crime. It gives line officers a chance to use their knowledge and experience to improve the communities they serve.

But it is much more than that. Problem-oriented policing represents a fundamental change from incident-driven policing. The Newport News Police Department—and other departments that adopt this approach—will continue to respond to incidents. But they will go beyond this first step, becoming much more than a crime control and emergency services agency. Instead, the Newport News experience suggests that the police department will become the front line in a comprehensive, human services system that includes the criminal justice system, other government agencies, private institutions, and private citizens themselves. The result will be more effective responses to crime and other troubling conditions.

6

Precipitating Factors of Paradigmatic Shift in Policing
The Origin of the Community Policing Era

William V. Pelfrey, Jr.

When Thomas Kuhn wrote *The Structure of Scientific Revolution* in 1962 he created a framework through which the evolution of science could be analyzed and conceptualized objectively. He discussed paradigms, the development of anomalies, and the necessary conditions for paradigmatic shifts which could be applied to information from any number of disciplines but has only recently been applied to policing (Sykes, 1992; Alpert & Moore, 1993). This article begins with a discussion of Kuhn's principles, then considers the paradigm of the reform era of policing and some of the anomalies which precipitated its demise and led to the era of community policing. Examples of anomalies that are suggested as precursors of the paradigmatic shift include Supreme Court decisions contrary to traditional policing, the changing image of policing, research casting doubt on the principles of the reform era, questions of improper discretion, and innovative research on new styles of policing. The purpose of this paper is to highlight the paradigm approach in an effort to explain the emergence of community policing.

The Structure of Scientific Revolution

According to Kuhn (1962), science tends to progress in a linear fashion and maintains status quo if left undisturbed. Kuhn cites such theories as Ptolemy's computations of planetary location, Aristotle's analysis of motion, and Newtonian

Source: Prepared especially for *Community Policing: Contemporary Readings.*

law as examples. These theories do not necessarily answer all possible questions, or resolve all possible situations; rather, they imply success at a higher rate than opposing theories, and they eventually supplant existing ideology. Scientific research is the process of actualizing this implication. A paradigm, like these scientific theories, exists because it is more successful than its other alternatives at explaining or resolving dilemmas.

Kuhn describes three important or critical foci for scientific investigation which have been adopted as necessary criteria for defining a paradigm. First, a paradigm must reveal the nature of the things it targets. Second, a set of facts must exist which may be posed against the predictions of the paradigm. Finally, there must exist an opportunity for empirical work to be conducted, and data generated, which supports the paradigm. Since this tenet implies that research must exist *and* data should be produced to complement the paradigm's theme, it may be the most important of all of a paradigm's characteristics. If research is not possible or not conducted, the paradigm will not succeed.

The emergence of new theories, such as the famous example of Copernican astronomy, may instigate a paradigm shift. Ptolemaic theory was widely supported and used until scientists noted that it failed to explain some of the questions to which Copernican theory responded. This theoretical crisis demanded paradigmatic shift, and a new theory (Copernican) emerged. Thus, both anomalies and crisis situations may be catalysts for paradigmatic shift.

The final issue in paradigm shift is timing. The simple emergence of a new theory is an insufficient cause for the abandonment of an old theory. A theoretical crisis must surface which creates a crevice the new theory fills. Copernican theory had been widely viewed as no better than Ptolemaic theory until Keppler's Rudolphine tables were published, which vastly improved the predictive powers of Copernican theory over Ptolemaic theory. Until this quantitative difference arose, astronomers were not prepared to change their philosophy.

In sum, paradigms are those theoretical frameworks under which science operates until events occur which require practitioners or researchers to seek a new paradigm. These events are either anomalies, which show inconsistencies or errors of the theory, or theoretical crises, which occur when a new theory explains things more successfully or fills in the gaps of the old theory. Paradigmatic shifts are influenced by issues of timing and the support of prominent members of the field. The following section describes the different eras of policing and then discusses factors which contributed to the shift to the community policing paradigm.

The Eras of Policing

Policing in America has moved through several distinct paradigm shifts over the past century. The current paradigm of community policing is a volatile concept, and numerous scholars have voiced a variety of concerns about it. For example, will the principles of community policing actually progress from "rhetoric" to reality (Mastrofski, 1991)? Is community policing actually a move forward (Bayley, 1991)? Will the development of community policing principles create an unrealistic set of goals for the police, eventually undermining their existence (Klockars, 1991)? Does the unusual nature of community policing preclude effective research on its effectiveness (Cordner, 1997)? Is community policing actually a new concept, or is it a reification of past practices (Fyfe, 1996)?

While the debate concerning community policing continues on a variety of fronts, most researchers admit that many of the practices of policing are different now than they were between 1940 and 1970. Until the late 1970s there were only two major periods of policing, so there was little need to describe them in stages. However, by the time community policing was a recognized concept, it became apparent that a classification scheme was necessary to better describe these stages of policing. Kelling and Moore (1988) recognized this and subsequently provided a classification scheme, defining the eras as the political era and the reform era.

Political Era

As urbanization became a growing phenomenon and organized public safety agencies were needed, the political machinery in most major cities created a police force. Police were the enforcers and enablers of the political machinery (Fogelson, 1977). Officer positions were generally appointed based not on qualifications but on bribes, nepotism and political appointments. The "Tammany Hall" concept of patriarchy was the driving influence behind politics, and this philosophy was evident in law enforcement ideology. In a review of some of the problems with this system, Fosdick (1920) stated police helped arrange votes for politicians and/or scared off their competitors. They helped in regulating business and development by turning a blind eye toward crime in areas of insurrection against the political machinery. As could be expected, corruption was rampant in most police organizations due to the intimate relationship with the community and the high levels of discretion the officers wielded (Kelling & Moore, 1988).

What impact did this have on crime? Low legitimacy

Reform Era

In an effort to temper the politicalization of the police, August Vollmer attempted reform by creating a professional force based on training and strong communication skills (Douthit, 1975). Vollmer was the first to send police through a "police school," which had classes on law, police procedures, fingerprinting, first aid, and a variety of academic topics. Other practitioners recognized the value of his ideas and followed his lead in personnel and administrative changes. O. W. Wilson, a student of Vollmer and former chief of police in Chicago, emphasized the importance of departmental organization and militarization.

This era was characterized by an emphasis on organization and structure, efficiency, and organizational autonomy. Technology played a tremendous role as police found themselves off the streets and riding their beats in cars. They were a response-oriented force who reacted to calls coming into an impersonal 9-1-1 number (Sykes, 1992). The distance which developed among police, police agencies, and their constituents as a result of this bureaucratic isolation eventually contributed to the downfall of the reform era.

Community Policing Era

The community policing/problem-solving era developed in response to the reform era. It recognized and sought to compensate for the deficiencies of the reform era. Many of the principles of community policing are not original (i.e., accessibility to the community, foot beats). However, during this era they were emphasized, in contrast to the reform era, during which they were suppressed.

This era is characterized by an emphasis on relationships with the community, foot beats or other highly accessible patrol tactics, programs which incorporate residents in crime solving, and other practices (Sykes, 1992). The overriding theme of community policing, however, is to foster working partnerships between the police and the community. The autonomous generalist is the core to community policing as opposed to the specialized units of the reform era. Decentralization and familiarity with the constituents are key ingredients to community policing (Greene & Pelfrey, 1997). Strong discussions of the tenets, practices, and goals of community policing are discussed in a variety of works (see Greene & Mastrofski, 1988; Rosenbaum, 1994).

Although Kelling and Moore's framework has been criticized as incomplete (Strecher, 1991) and lacking in sensitivity to minority perspectives (Williams & Murphy, 1990), it is generally recognized by researchers as an accurate division of the three principle stages of policing in this century. Some argue that a problem-oriented stage immediately preceded the advent of community policing (Goldstein, 1990) but this period is frequently grouped into the community policing era (Moore, 1992; Alpert & Moore, 1993). Accepting the descriptions and labels of the three paradigms may be sufficient for a cursory assessment, but a rigorous assessment demands that an investigation of the factors which coincided with the shift to community policing be examined.

Precipitating Factors of a Paradigm Shift

As discussed earlier, a paradigm shift can be the result of either anomalies or a theoretical crisis. A number of anomalies may be used to explain the paradigmatic shift away from the reform era to the community policing era. Lacking is a comprehensive review of these anomalies relative to the changing eras within the police paradigm framework. Although many factors could be considered, this article provides a brief outline of some key examples in the principle areas where anomalies have developed, including: anomalous research, Supreme Court decisions, discretion problems, police response to social discord, commissions, and the research paving the way for community policing.

Anomalous Research

In the past twenty years of policing, there has been a wealth of research in a wide array of areas. However, few studies have disturbed the principles of policing as much as the research conducted in Kansas City in the 1970s (Petersilia, 1993). This research questioned the most basic assumptions of police administrators and represented anomalies to the reform era ideology.

The research on the importance of preventive patrol cast significant doubt on the current practices of policing. One of the principle tenets of Vollmer's reform strategy was that officers should drive in brightly marked cars to produce a deterrent effect (Walker, 1995). Research was conducted to test this assumption by Kelling and his colleagues (1974) in Kansas City, Missouri. The city was divided into a number of smaller sectors, and three different patrol approaches were assigned to these areas: no patrol, regular patrol, and increased preventive patrol. Residents had been interviewed prior to the experiment, which continued for a year. After the year, the residents were again surveyed on a number of areas including their perceived fear of crime. Essentially, preventive patrol appeared to have no influence on crime or on resident perceptions. Some criticisms of this experimental design include the issue of random assignment of the sectors and the possible lack of zero presence, since patrol cars may have been seen responding to calls in other areas (Petersilia, 1993). Nonetheless, this study drew national attention and seriously undermined the assumptions regarding police patrol and its effectiveness.

A second study which forced police and researchers to question practices of the reform era was the rapid response time research. This research attempted to assess the need for rapid response to calls for service, a critical aspect of O.W. Wilson's efficiency model (Walker, 1995). After observing a number of cases, the researchers determined response time made virtually no difference in most cases (KCPD, 1978). Although citizens' satisfaction tended to drop greatly after 15 minutes, immediate physical presence was rarely necessary. Since the majority of crimes are discovery (discovering a crime has occurred) rather than involvement (between police/civilians and offender), rapid response is unnecessary (Walker, 1992).

These two key examples and other important studies indicated to many that the strategies of the reform paradigm were not entirely accurate. Chaiken (1978) advanced the question of the deterrent effects of police activity. Furstenberg and Wellford (1973) contributed to the scrutiny of the importance of response time. A number of other studies further questioned the efficiency and effectiveness principles (LEAA, 1978; Skogan, 1976; Rengert, 1979). While these studies had several other important impacts (police research was held to a higher standard, greater emphasis was placed on the importance of crime data, etc.), they demonstrated some of the distinct failings of the existing paradigm, suggesting a new paradigm was necessary.

Supreme Court Decisions

A number of important case rulings were handed down during the late 1960s and early 1970s, especially under the liberal Warren Court. These rulings indicated that many accepted police practices of the reform era were inappropriate, and a variety of Supreme Court rulings required the police to alter their behavior. The militaristic style of the time encouraged police behavior that was questionable, the neglect of civil rights, and the concentration on order maintenance rather than protection of rights (Walker, 1992). These cases cover a range of activities, but all placed substantial limitations on police.

The Fourth Amendment protection against unreasonable search and seizure was much neglected until *Katz v. United States* (1967). With *Katz*, the Court made one of the first major steps in securing an individual's right against warrantless searches or seizures. The case of *Chimel v. California* (1969) was critical in establishing the parameters of an officer's search. This case required that valid reasons to conduct a search be articulated, who and where an officer may search was limited, and the legal limits to a search were all addressed. This case represented the first severe limitation on police search since *Mapp* and was supported by a number of later cases.

While *Chimel* addressed the area of exceptions to the warrant requirement for searches, *Terry v. Ohio* (1968) considered the field interrogation and acceptable range of search in these stops. Both are areas of high officer discretion and thus have a high potential for abuse, necessitating the placing of limits by the Supreme Court. *Terry* was critically important to police procedure as it "distinguished between frisks and searches, creating an exception for the former" (Fyfe, 1996).

An important case in defining police interrogation was *Brown v. Mississippi* (1936). In this case, the Court concluded that a confession made under torture was not acceptable. As a result, police were forced to devise other, less obvious means of coercion. The third degree was no longer the primary means of obtaining a confession (Fyfe & Skolnick, 1993). A later case, *Spano v. New York* (1959), further limited the use of coercion; however in this case it was psychological manipulation. Coercion by an officer friend of Spano's improperly influenced his confession, which was questioned as to its "voluntariness" (ibid, 53).

A number of Fifth and Sixth Amendment protections were extended during this expansion of civil liberties. The landmark *Escobedo v. Illinois* (1964) case addressed the question of whether an individual can be denied his Sixth

Amendment right to counsel and then be held accountable for incriminating statements. The Supreme Court recognized the merits of Escobedo's case and reversed the decisions of lower courts, extending the right of protection to those held prior to seeing their attorneys. This was followed with *Miranda v. Arizona* (1966), which mandated suspects be informed of their rights prior to providing confessions. (For a more complete review of these cases see texts such as Zalman and Seigel [1996]).

Some of these cases clearly predated the shift from the reform era but, since anomalies are cumulative, it can be argued that they were part and parcel of the reform era's deterioration. These cases illustrate the Court's opinion that the police possessed extreme levels of discretion that were often abused. The militaristic, distanced police officer felt little compunction about making impositions on the suspect's constitutional rights as long as order maintenance was served. The Supreme Court therefore felt obligated to impose limits on police action, thereby serving as an agent of change. Whether these laws significantly changed police behavior or created a force of creative excuse engineers is questionable, but also secondary. The anomaly generated from the Court's involvement was that the police no longer had sweeping powers. They could not be both judge and jury, and justice was not conducted in the "gatehouse" but in the open, under the eye of the community (Fyfe & Skolnick, 1993).

Incorporate into running paper Law shifts

Discretion Problems

The most obvious example referring to problems with police discretion concerns the use of deadly force (Walker, 1993). Until 1962, there were few limits on police shootings. By then, the American Law Institute had posted the Model Penal Code, which encouraged limiting police use of deadly force. This was a relatively ambiguous rule; it was not extremely restrictive and it was not binding unless states elected to adopt it. It did not alter the image of the police in which force was a common tool used to maintain order (Bittner, 1970). The scope of the police shooting problem was not recognized until Fyfe's research in the early 1970s on deadly force usage. The 1972 New York City Police Department policy restricting the use of deadly force was a landmark event in this area. Commissioner Patrick Murphy's policy was a result of the 1967 President's Commission on Law Enforcement, which found that few cities had any policies on deadly force and those that did were neither restrictive nor effective (Fyfe, 1988). The minimal laws on deadly force were similarly not effective in defining when deadly force was appropriate. For example, in some cases offenders were essentially being executed prior to conviction simply because they fled from police (Sherman, 1980). As Sherman (1980) pointed out, offenders were being fired on simply because they fled from officers. This was a clear violation of offenders' constitutional protection against illegal seizure.

The problems of deadly force usage peaked in *Tennessee v. Garner* (1985). In this case a 15-year-old boy was shot while fleeing from police. He was unarmed, minimally dangerous, and had only stolen a purse. This elective shooting was perfectly legal, but it was clear that policies and law needed to be changed as a response to this case. The Court determined police could not use deadly force simply because a suspect was fleeing, sending the message that offenders were no longer open game.

The anomaly generated from this research, the Court's decisions, and the ensuing policies suggested that the police militaristic model, which granted far too much latitude for usage of force, needed to be changed. The policies and laws which implemented this change further altered policing and necessitated a paradigmatic shift.

Police Response to Social Discord

Throughout the reform era, following the influence of O. W. Wilson, the police were widely viewed as products of a militaristic model (Walker, 1995). This was further exacerbated by the removal of the police from the streets to their isolation within patrol vehicles. The order maintenance emphasis was all important at this time. The police cultivated an impersonal image by having individuals call an unknown voice for service through a generic, city wide number (9-1-1). This widening rift between the police and the public peaked with the riots of the 1960s. The Watts riots (1965), the student riots in Ohio (1970), and a number of social uprisings throughout the nation placed police squarely at odds with a large segment of the population.

The activities of the police at this critical time, sparking many of the riots through police shootings, created a great deal of concern regarding the police (Fyfe, 1988). On the last day of one of the bloodiest riots in history (Detroit, 1967), President Johnson appointed the Kerner Commission to consider responses to civil unrest. The militaristic approach to problem solving and the series of civil uprisings focused direct attention on the police, and the public was generally displeased.

Cohort effects

Commissions

Due to a range of instigating factors, including riots, corruption and presidential discretion, several important commissions were formed in the late 1960s and early 1970s that questioned the role and actions of the police. The Knapp Commission, the 1967 President's Crime Commission, and the Kerner Commission targeted policing problems and sought to provide solutions. Their creation, however, served as a formal indicator of the anomalies growing within the police force.

The 1967 President's Crime Commission Report, requested by L. B. Johnson, produced mixed results and varied opinions as to its significance (Reiss, 1994). The recommendations and their impact were reviewed by Walker (1994) in a 25-year follow-up. He noted that the commission had encouraged a new view of policing, especially relating to minorities. For example, police agencies were increasingly encouraged to draw from applicant pools of women and minorities.

Several recommendations regarding police-community relations were made, including improved means of handling complaints, the creation of programs which targeted community relations, and alternative approaches to policing. A careful analysis of police discretion was encouraged, especially in limiting police use of deadly force. Walker (1994:33) points out that the seeds of community policing were evident in this report, especially in the area of the changing role of police: "The commission set into motion an intellectual revolution that undermined the traditional agenda," planting the seeds for a new, yet unidentified paradigm.

The Kerner Commission was formed after the Detroit riots to consider the problems of police race relations. The commission concluded that the "traditional approach to police professionalism often aggravated community relations" (Walker, 1992:22). Recommendations included increased hiring of minorities and improved community relations through concerted efforts to involve the community (i.e., committees comprised of both citizens and police). Rather than maintain the alienated police presence of the reform era, the commission encouraged a new approach to police work.

The often-cited Knapp Commission reviewed corruption and graft within the New York City Police Department in the late 1960s. They considered everything from gambling and narcotics payoffs to the bribery of officers to overlooking the Sabbath law (Knapp Commission Report on Police Corruption, 1973). They found that corruption was widespread but generally occurred on a small scale. The "grass-eaters" made up the bulk of the problem, even though the sums they took in were modest. They concluded that the department needed significant overhaul and sweeping attitude and training changes. The highly public nature of this commission and the Serpico case that preceded it brought further public attention to the problems of law enforcement. Ironically, one of the principle tenets of the reform era was to separate the police from the community, thereby reducing opportunities for corruption. Unfortunately, the corruption problem held fast in New York and contributed to the poor image of the police.

Collectively, these commissions targeted different aspects of policing, but all concluded that there were significant policing problems and each encouraged significant change. The paradigm of the reform era was losing support, and a new paradigm would soon emerge.

Research that Set the Stage for Community Policing

For a paradigm shift to occur, anomalies must exist which call the current paradigm into question and a better conceptual explanation must be made available. As Kuhn (1962) suggested, nature abhors a vacuum—and so does science. Paradigms are not rejected, but replaced. During the late 1970s and early 1980s, just as the ideas and practices of the reform era were under scrutiny, several studies were published which provided law enforcement administrators and researchers with another conceptual framework. This section considers several of these important publications which set the stage for community policing to become the current paradigm.

In 1974, the San Diego Police Department instituted a little-known concept of community policing within a section of their department. The Community Profile Development Project sought to incorporate the community in problem identification and resolution efforts, link police patrol to specific beat issues, and develop the concept of officer accountability, where a beat cop was responsible for the problems on his or her beat (Boydstun & Sherry, 1975). After ten months of service, officers in the experimental group (the community profile officers) indicated a higher level of interaction with the community, a decrease in the perceived importance of standard motorized patrol, greater confidence in the community, and a stronger sense of beat responsibility.

A second key study in the expansion of the new concept for law enforcement occurred in Newark, New Jersey from 1978–1979 (Police Foundation, 1981). Foot patrol officers were assigned patrol beats in one of eight neighborhoods. Residents on these beats perceived a decline in public disorder problems and an increase in safety. This police patrol approach had embraced the "broken windows" approach by attempting to cope with disorder and the perceptions of crime (Greene & Pelfrey, 1997). While no change in the reporting of crime or victimization rates occurred, the program catalyzed the formation of other community policing programs. This new style of policing was emphasized in Flint, Michigan (Trojanowicz, 1983), Oakland, California (Reiss, 1985), a second study in Newark (Pate, et al., 1985), and other cities. Although each of these studies was in fact a case study of community policing, collectively they provided the framework and the principles for other departments to institute community policing.

The proliferation of these case studies on community policing, coupled with the two principal theoretical works—Goldstein's (1977) *Problem Oriented Policing* and Wilson and Kelling's (1982) "broken windows" philosophy—gave police departments a new option. They had both the research and the conceptual basis to create the new style of policing and replace the reform paradigm. Those departments which held fast to the tenets of the reform era, such as the militaristic style of the Los Angeles Police Department under Chief Darryl Gates, continued to experience the same problems which led to the shift in paradigms.

[handwritten marginalia: What about Reiss?]

Importance of Timing

One of the subtleties of Kuhn's system points out the importance of proper timing for a paradigm to successfully replace its predecessor. Several examples in policing explain why the shift from the reform era to the community policing era failed to occur earlier.

Strecher (1991) refers to Louis Radelet, a Detroit police chief in the mid 1950s, as the real pioneer of community policing. Radelet employed ideas such as mini-stations, community relations programs and store-front centers, all of which are now common community policing practices. These efforts, however, predated much of the research questioning the assumptions of the reform era. Had Radelet's innovations occurred twenty years later, he might be more widely recognized as the founder of community policing. However, insufficient anomalies were present at that time to support this new method of policing.

Former chief Lee Brown's efforts also serve as an example of the importance of timing. As the sheriff in Multnomah County, Oregon, Brown initiated programs which today would be reflective of community policing. At the time, they were not well received, and he gave them up to continue measuring response time. Several years later as chief in Houston, Brown reapplied similar programs that incorporated the community in crime solving and encouraged his officers to interact with the community. By then the reform paradigm was in question, Brown's programs were very successful, and he was heralded as a visionary. Although it is distinctly possible that Houston officers are different than Oregon officers, the principal difference is probably the timing. In Houston, both public expectations and officer cooperation had changed. Having heard of other successful community policing programs, the officers were more willing to adopt Brown's strategies. Brown and his ideas existed at the cusp of the paradigm shift and eventually benefited from the change.

Perhaps the best example of how important timing is in fitting into the right paradigm is the concept of team policing. Team policing emphasized decentralization and inclusion of the community in solving crime (Sherman, 1973). Inclusion of community residents in policy formation was encouraged, and several other ideas are similar to those of community policing (Walker, 1995). Supported by the LEAA, team policing was advocated in the early 1970s. Although similar to many of the community policing techniques in practice today, it died a sudden death in the mid-1970s due to the resistance of some officers to change their practice and philosophy (Walker, 1994).

These examples indicate that being different is insufficient to overcome a paradigm. Although these examples were all consistent with the era that eventually supplanted the reform era, they failed to occur at the proper time. When these ideas were posed, insufficient anomalies existed which called the current paradigm into question. Thus they drifted into relative obscurity.

Conclusion

Kuhn's model of scientific revolutions describes a unique strategy through which paradigms may be defined and analyzed. A paradigm will remain in existence unless it is called into question through a theoretical crisis, an accumulation of anomalies, or a series of inconsistencies within the current paradigm. Policing has not been considered from this perspective, at least not overtly. This article has attempted to highlight a number of anomalies which produced a paradigmatic shift from the reform era to the community policing paradigm. Problems with police discretion and interaction with the public, the scrutiny of commissions, research which was inconsistent with the tenets of the reform era, and important Supreme Court rulings are all anomalies which necessitated a paradigmatic shift. These factors all formed a matrix which has influenced most major police departments to adopt a community policing philosophy (at least nominally). This article does not suggest that policing has evolved in a linear fashion. There is much discussion concerning the factors which propagated the shift to community policing. Each of the sections in this article offers a partial glimpse of some factors which precipitated paradigmatic shift and should spark further exploration of those issues.

As in any research endeavor, the past experiences arguably may be maps for future occurrences. Delineating the legal, philosophical, and research anomalies which coincided with and were precipitating factors for the shift in paradigms of policing may help alert the discipline to the next impending shift. While Kuhn's (1962:52) admonition, "Normal science does not aim at novelties of fact or theory and, when successful, finds none," provides guidance for researchers, we continue to test propositions, and to support and reject hypotheses. The current paradigm, community policing, will be refined by this process and may eventually be replaced by a different paradigm.

References

Alpert, G. P. & Moore, M. H. (1993). Measuring Police Performance in the New Paradigm of Policing. In J. J. DiLulio (Ed.), *Performance Measures for the Criminal Justice System*. Princeton University: Bureau of Justice Statistics.

American Law Institute. (1962). *Model Penal Code*, 3.07.

Bayley, D. H. (1991). Community Policing: A Report from the Devil's Advocate. In J. R. Greene & S. D. Mastrofski (Eds.), *Community Policing: Rhetoric or Reality*. New York: Praeger.

Bittner, E. (1970). *The Functions of the Police in Modern Society*. Rockville, MD: National Institute of Mental Health.

Boydstun, J. E. & Sherry, M. E. (1975). *San Diego Community Profile: Final Report*. Washington DC: Police Foundation.

Brown v. Mississippi, 297 U.S. 278 (1936).

Chaiken, J. M. (1978). What is Known about Deterrent Effects of Police Activities? In J. A. Cramer (Ed.), *Preventing Crime*, (pp.109–136). Thousand Oaks, CA: Sage.

Chimel v. California, 395 U.S. 752 (1969).

Cordner, G. W. (1997). Community Policing: Elements and Effects. In R. G. Dunham & G. P. Alpert (Eds.) *Critical Issues in Policing: Contemporary Readings*, 3rd ed. Prospect Heights, IL: Waveland Press.

Douthit, N. (1975). August Vollmer. In C. Klockars & S. Mastrofski (Eds.), *Thinking about Police: Contemporary Readings*. New York: McGraw-Hill.

Escobedo v. Illinois, 378 U.S. 478 (1964).

Fogelson, R. M. (1977). *Big City Police*. Cambridge: Harvard University Press.

Fosdick, R. (1920). *American Police Systems*. Montclair, NJ: Patterson Smith.

Furstenberg, Jr., F. F. & Wellford, C. F. (1973, Spring). Calling the Police: The Evaluation of Police Service. *Law and Society Review,* 393–406.

Fyfe, J. J. (1978). *Shots Fired: An Analysis of New York City Police Firearms Discharge.* Ph.D. Dissertation, State University of New York at Albany. Ann Arbor: University Microfilms.

Fyfe, J. J. (1988). Police Use of Deadly Force: Research and Reform. *Justice Quarterly, 5,* 166–205.

Fyfe, J. J. (1996). Personal communication.

Fyfe J. J. & Skolnick, J. H. (1993). *Above the Law: Police and the Excessive Use of Force.* New York: The Free Press.

Goldstein, H. (1977). *Policing a Free Society*. Cambridge: Ballinger.

Goldstein, H. (1990). *Problem Oriented Policing*. New York: McGraw Hill.

Greene, J. R. & Mastrofski, S. D. (1988). *Community Policing: Rhetoric or Reality*. New York: Praeger.

Greene, J. R. & Pelfrey, W. V., Jr. (1997). Shifting the Balance of Power between Police and Community: Responsibility for Crime Control. In R. G. Dunham & G. P. Alpert (Eds.), *Critical Issues in Policing: Contemporary Readings*, 3rd ed. Prospect Heights, IL: Waveland Press.

Kansas City Police Department. (1978). *Response Time Analysis: Executive Summary.* Washington, DC: U.S. Dept. Of Justice.

Katz v. United States, 389 U.S. 347 (1967).

Kelling, G. L., Pate, T., Dieckman, D., & Brown, C. E. (1974). *The Kansas City Preventive Patrol Experiment: A Summary Report.* Washington DC: Police Foundation.

Kelling, G. L. & Moore, M. H. (1988). The Evolving Strategy of Policing. *Perspectives on Policing, No.4.* Washington, DC: U.S. Government Printing Office.

Klockars, C. B. (1991). The Rhetoric of Community Policing. In J. R. Greene & S. D. Mastrofski (Eds.), *Community Policing: Rhetoric or Reality.* New York: Praeger.

Knapp Commission Report on Police Corruption. (1973). New York: George Braziller.

Kuhn, T. S. (1962). *The Structure of Scientific Revolutions,* 2nd ed. Chicago: University of Chicago Press.

Law Enforcement Assistance Administration. (1978). *Response Time Analysis: Synopsis.* Washington DC: U.S. Department of Justice.

Mapp v. Ohio, 37 U.S. 643 (1961).

Mastrofski, S. (1991). Community Policing as Reform: A Cautionary Tale. In J. R. Greene & S. D. Mastrofski (Eds.), *Community Policing: Rhetoric or Reality.* New York: Praeger.

Miranda v. Arizona, 384 U.S. 436 (1966).

Moore, M. (1992). Modern Policing. *Crime and Justice, 15,* 99–158.

Pate, A. M., Skogan, W. G., Wycoff, M. A., & Sherman, L. W. (1985). *Reducing the Signs of Crime: The Newark Experience Executive Summary.* Washington DC: Police Foundation.

Petersilia, J. (1993). The Influence of Research on Policing. In R. G. Dunham & G. P. Alpert (Eds.), *Critical Issues in Policing: Contemporary Readings*, 2nd ed. Prospect Heights, IL: Waveland Press.

Police Foundation. (1981). *The Newark Foot Patrol Experiment.* Washington DC: Police Foundation.

Reiss, A. J. (1985). *Policing a City's Central District: The Oakland Story.* Washington DC: Police Foundation.

Reiss, A. J. (1994). An Evaluation and Assessment of the Impact of the Task Force Report: Crime and Its Impact—An Assessment. In J. A. Conley (Ed.), *The 1967 President's Crime Commission Report: Its Impact 25 Years Later.* Cincinnati: Anderson.

Rengert, G. F. (1979). Spatial Distribution of Police Personnel: Efficiency and Equality Considerations. In D. M. Petersen (Ed.), *Police Work.* Newbury Park, CA: Sage.

Rosenbaum, D. P. (1994). *The Challenge of Community Policing: Testing the Promises.* Thousand Oaks, CA: Sage Publications.

Sherman, L. W. (1973). *Team Policing: Seven Case Studies.* Washington DC: The Police Foundation.

Sherman, L. (1980). Execution without Trial: Police Homicide and the Constitution. *Vanderbilt Law Review, 33,* 71–100.

Skogan, W. G. (1976). Efficiency and Effectiveness in Big-city Police Departments. *Public Administration Review, 3,* 278–286.

Spano v. New York, 360 U.S. 315 (1959).

Strecher, V. (1991). Revising the Histories and Futures of Policing. *Police Forum, 1,* 1–9.

Sykes, G. W. (1992). Stability amid Change. In L. Hoover (Ed.), *Police Management: Issues and Perspectives.* Washington DC: Police Executive Research Forum.

Tennessee v. Garner, 471 U.S. 1, 105 S. Ct. 1694, 85 L. Ed. 1 (1985).

Terry v. Ohio, 392 U.S. 1 (1968).

Trojanowicz, R. T. (1983). An Evaluation of the Neighborhood Foot Patrol Program: The Flint, Michigan Project. *Journal of Police Science and Administration, 11,* 410–419.

Uchida, C. D. (1993). The Development of the American Police: An Historical Overview. In R. G. Dunham & G. P. Alpert (Eds.), *Critical Issues in Policing: Contemporary Readings,* 3rd ed. Prospect Heights, IL: Waveland Press.

Walker, S. (1992). *The Police in America: An Introduction.* New York: McGraw-Hill.

Walker, S. (1993). *Taming the System: The Control of Discretion in Criminal Justice, 1950–1990.* New York: Oxford UP.

Walker, S. (1994). Between Two Worlds: The President's Crime Commission and the Police, 1967–1992. In J. A. Conley (Ed.), *The 1967 President's Crime Commission Report: Its Impact 25 Years Later.* Cincinnati: Anderson.

Walker, S. (1995). "Broken Windows" and Fractured History: The Use and Misuse of History in Recent Police Patrol Analysis. In V. Kappeler (Ed.), *The Police and Society.* Prospect Heights, IL: Waveland Press.

Williams, H. & Murphy, P. V. (1990). The Evolving Strategy of Policing: A Minority View. *Perspectives on Policing, No. 13.* Washington DC: National Institute of Justice.

Wilson, J. Q. & Kelling, G. L. (1982). Broken Windows: The Police and Neighborhood Safety. *The Atlantic Monthly,* 249, 29–38.

Zalman, M. & Siegel, L. (1996). *Key Cases and Comments on Criminal Procedure.* Minneapolis/St. Paul: West Publishing.

Part II

Current Research

The next two sections of this book review a number of current practices and research findings from two points of view: the researchers and the practitioners. Part II offers six selections from academia, while Part III offers four selections from the practitioners.

Researchers have a unique view of the topics they study. Community policing presents an opportunity for the research community to report observations on how police officers and agencies are responding to this challenge. The first selection from the academic community is from a team of researchers from Temple University. Professors Piquero, Greene, and Fyfe, and Robert Kane and Patricia Collins discuss the impact of a community policing approach in a public housing setting. In particular, they review some of the early findings from a program in Philadelphia which experimentally evaluated the impact of community policing in four experimental sites while holding constant the treatment from five other control sites.

The second selection is contributed by Professor Jack Greene. Amidst the backdrop of the Rodney King incident, Greene reviews the historical roots of the Los Angeles Police Department (LAPD), and offers suggestions for building public confidence and trust in the LAPD. In so doing, Professor Greene grounds his case study in the organizational context of the police department, the external environment, and the larger political dynamics of the city.

In the third selection, Professor Skogan presents a review and analysis of one of the most ambitious programs designed to implement community policing. Professor Skogan, who was one of the architects of the program, presents the elements of the program and their impact on quality of life in Chicago.

In the fourth selection, Professors Brame and Piquero review the evidence on the effect of the police on the control of crime and disorder. Their review consists largely of research which has attempted to curb the tide of crime and disorder in large urban cities. The authors conclude their article by offering promising strategies for policing crime and disorder, as well as discussing the importance of strong evaluation assessments of such programs.

In the fifth selection, Professors Rosenbaum and Lurigio provide an inside look at the community policing reform movement by discussing the definitional and organizational changes, and evaluation findings of some early community policing programs. They conclude by suggesting that the existing evaluations of community policing have favorable impacts on the perceptions of police officers and neighborhood residents.

In the final selection, Professors Alpert and Moore discuss the need to change performance measures in the community policing context. These researchers argue that traditional measures of success are not appropriate for the evaluation of officers' efforts to police the community. They suggest a new approach to the ways the police view their work and how officers are rewarded for their effort and results.

7

Implementing Community Policing in Public Housing Developments in Philadelphia
Some Early Results

Alex Piquero, Jack Greene, James Fyfe,
Robert J. Kane, and *Patricia Collins*

Public housing has had a tumultuous history in the United States. From their origins in the 1930s, public housing developments were designed to assist the poor and working poor in an effort to create inexpensive housing. Throughout the following twenty years, however, public housing developments were built to house families displaced by slum clearance (President's Commission on Housing 1982). During this period, these developments included large clusters of high-rise towers, and significant crime, drug, and disorder problems began to plague individuals living within them.

These developments have become symbols for many Americans such that the reference to them is virtually synonymous with the danger of inner-city, urban life. Moreover, popular culture has produced documents that support such perceptions (e.g., Kotlowitz 1991; Vergera 1989). This portrayal, however, is based on very little empirical information (Holzman 1996:361). In fact, oftentimes, the extent to which problems in public housing developments become known are largely the result of one-shot case studies that are highly selective.

Largely emanating from a dissatisfaction of call-driven policing on many fronts, including citizen distrust of the police as well as research showing a lack of deterrent effect of police in routine patrol (e.g., Alpert and Dunham 1988; Kelling

Source: Prepared especially for *Community Policing: Contemporary Readings*.

et al. 1974), police organizations in the mid to late 1970s realized that a different form of policing was needed. The answer to their concern was community policing. This sort of policing involves a basic change in the police role, function, and organization (e.g., Skolnick and Bayley 1988). But perhaps most importantly, this approach to policing seeks to build a bridge between the police and the communities (and people) they service, a problem which was perhaps first recognized by police and other public officials during the turmoil-laden 1960s. Manifested through a number of programs and deployments such as foot patrol, bike patrol, mini-stations, and other outreach attempts, community policing is often considered to be the savior of the estranged relationship between community members and police officers.

The breadth of this approach to policing has wide appeal and has received a significant amount of attention from virtually every criminal justice occupation in the United States including academia, police departments and professionals, and public policy makers. Nowhere is the application of community policing more appropriate than in public housing developments. While many communities and neighborhoods within inner-cities have problems that include poverty, single-parent families, crime, drugs, and disorder, these social ills tend to be more severe in public housing communities (Rainwater 1970). It is these problems that begin to create a sense of despair and lack of commitment to community social control. Further, because public housing developments are discrete communities, it is relatively easy to study the effects upon them of changes in policing philosophies and operations.

The purpose of this paper is three-fold. First, we briefly review the literature on crime, disorder, and drugs in public housing communities, as well as the general community policing approach being taken by many police departments across the country. Second, we highlight the implementation of a community policing program in five distressed public housing communities along the 11th Street Corridor in north Philadelphia. Third, we present some early results from an evaluation of the effectiveness of this community policing approach in the five communities relative to four similar public housing communities which did not receive any form of community policing. In this section, we present results from a two-wave panel study designed to measure perceptions of crime and disorder among citizens residing in the public housing developments, as well as the police officers participating in the community policing program. We close by offering suggestions for future research directions with regard to the community policing of public housing communities.

Crime, Disorder, and Drugs in Public Housing

Crime

Amidst public perceptions that crime, disorder, and drugs are present to a much higher degree in public housing communities relative to other neighborhoods or sections of inner-cities, both Roncek et al. (1981) and Farley (1982) found that public housing developments were located in communities marked by generally high crime rates, both within and beyond the boundaries of the developments. At the same time, however, Roncek and his colleagues reported that, within such areas, crime was higher in blocks with housing developments than on those without developments (see also Brill and Associates 1977). In other research, Harrell and Gouvis (1994) discovered that the presence of public housing in some areas of Washington, DC did not appear to contribute to crime rates in those census tracts.

Drugs

The research on drugs in public housing is a bit more conclusive, generally suggesting that drugs are a significant problem in public housing communities (Popkin et al. 1995; Skogan and Annan 1994; Weisburd and Green 1995). In their review of drugs in public housing communities in Los Angeles, Phoenix, and Washington, DC, Dunworth and Saiger (1994) found that rates of both drug and non-drug crimes were considerably higher in public housing than in other areas. In addition, the rates in the public housing communities were higher than rates in neighborhoods directly adjacent to the housing complexes. In a similar vein, Webster and Connors (1992) noted that open drug markets also attract nonresident buyers and sellers. The areas in which drug transactions take place, then, become hubs for other criminal activities.

Disorder

The problems associated with physical and social factors in public housing communities also contribute to residents' fear. Early research by Rainwater (1966) characterized high-rise public housing as an inferior and unsafe environment because of its lack of security and amenities. Similarly, Hunter (1978) has suggested that aspects of the physical environment, such as litter, abandoned units, and graffiti and other signs of disorder, are associated with fear of crime. For example, in Boston, Brill and Associates (1975) found that 75 percent of the residents considered it very dangerous to wait for a bus alone at night, while 60 percent felt that it was too dangerous to use the elevators alone at night. In recent research, Rohe and Burby (1988:712–713) have largely confirmed that the effects of physical and social incivilities have strong impacts on the fear of crime (for a contrasting viewpoint, see Taylor 1997). Fears such as these contribute to a climate of social alienation often characteristic of public housing communities (Huth 1981). This social alienation, then, creates difficulties for effective community social control, at both formal and informal levels (e.g., Bursik and Grasmick 1993; Taylor 1997). Physical and social disorder, then, is a problematic aspect of life in many public housing communities (e.g., Kelling and Coles 1996; Skogan 1990; Wilson and Kelling 1982).

A Word of Caution

In doing research on public housing, some cautions must be kept in mind (Holzman 1996). For example, researchers must be cognizant of the fact that there is considerable variation in the distribution of crime problems across public housing sites as well as within public housing sites such that a "hot spot" label universalistically applied to public housing sites may be ill-advised (Green-Mazerolle and Terrill 1997). Nevertheless, crime, disorder, and drugs, and the fear associated with victimization, are to some degree problematic in many public housing developments. This is not meant to suggest that public housing communities lack social cohesion. In fact, some public housing developments may be more socially cohesive than their external communities. One approach that has been suggested in an attempt to alleviate these social problems in public housing communities has been the application of community policing (Matthews 1993). Before we discuss this application, however, we turn to a brief review of community policing.

Community Policing

During the 1960s, the police occupation came under criticism for the distance it had put between itself and minority and inner-city communities (Gaines et al., 1997:61; President's Commission on Law Enforcement and Administration, 1967). In the 1970s, researchers provided empirical bases for criticizing the traditional police methods of random patrol and automatic response to calls for service (Kelling et al. 1974). Largely in response to this critique, the police have turned to community and problem-oriented policing as a means for demonstrating their effectiveness.

While the term community policing oftentimes means very different things to different people, no police department in the United States is entirely community policing oriented (Bayley 1995), though most have some type of program that is characteristic of this approach to policing. Early community policing approaches to crime included fear reduction programs (Pate et al. 1985), as well as foot patrol programs (Bowers and Hirsch 1986; Reiss 1985; Trojanowicz 1986) while new foci have centered on targeting crime prevention and crime suppression (Sherman 1995) and reducing calls-for-service (Eck and Spelman 1987; Goldstein 1990), especially calls to repeat locations (Sherman et al. 1989).

In addition to improving police effectiveness, community policing highlights a concern about the accountability of the local police that has been around for quite some time. Most recently, advocates of community policing have suggested that closer police and citizen interaction can actually increase police accountability (see Mastrofski and Greene 1994). This line of reasoning suggests that police accountability will be enhanced to the extent that the police see themselves engaged in a "partnership" with the community, a partnership built on mutual trust, disclosure, shared values, and reinforced through regular interaction, critique, and discussion. Such close and enduring interaction, it is presumed, will serve as a hedge against police misuse of their public trust. The normative power of the community, while not always consistent with the law, should strengthen police accountability to the law.[1]

Our review generally supports the fact that the goals of community policing could service the residents of public housing developments, and early work on the implementation of some examples of community policing programs in public housing settings have generally been met with some success. Uchida et al. (1992) examined the influence of a police mini-station in an apartment complex in Birmingham, Alabama. They found that residents perceived their neighborhood as a significantly improved place to live because of the police mini-station. Residents also perceived that the police were more responsive to their concerns, aided more victims, worked together with residents to solve local problems, spent more time in the neighborhood, and did a better job of keeping order.

In an evaluation in Chicago, Popkin and her colleagues (1995) found that residents generally perceived that police sweeps of drugs and other public housing department services have had an overall positive impact on resident's views of the Chicago Housing Authority. At the same time, the program seemed to work better in organized communities that had a stake in the outcome. This finding is similar to a recent evaluation of drug enforcement in public housing communities in New Orleans and Denver. In those two sites, Skogan and Annan (1994) found that it was very difficult to keep the communities and the local public housing authorities in a working partnership.

The community policing of public housing, and community policing in general, has received a significant amount of research attention and program implementation in recent years. Some of these implementations have been met with success, while others have not. Nevertheless, improvements in the training of police officers and community residents, as well as increased resource distribution to public housing developments, have made for improved abilities to conduct formal evaluations of the effectiveness of community policing in a public housing context. With these issues in hand, we now turn to the main portion of this paper: a description of a community policing program in public housing settings in Philadelphia.

Strengthening the Public Safety Role of Public Housing Police in Philadelphia

An important capability of housing authority police departments, as compared to municipal police departments, is their ability to more directly coordinate their efforts with the social and physical services within the public housing authority. Since many housing authorities are charged with both social service provision and safety in concentrated areas of cities, an opportunity is created for linking safety and other social services within and across public housing communities. Such a linkage of services might ultimately strengthen the capacity of public housing police to provide a more secure environment for public housing residents.

As a matter of policy, such coordinated services within public housing communities have several implications. First, a more secured and orderly environment within public housing communities can lead to less fear and greater civic participation among residents. Second, linking safety and other services within public housing systems can support individual and collective ethics emphasizing personal and community responsibility. Third, such linking of services can support people in their transition from public support to self sufficiency.

This paper presents a preliminary report on a program that seeks to become a "new beginning" for the relations between the Philadelphia Housing Authority Police Department (PHAPD) and residents of several public housing developments in the city of Philadelphia. The goal of the community policing program of the Philadelphia Housing Authority (PHA) is to promote greater resident safety. This goal is to be achieved through a two pronged effort focusing on community policing and development of channels empowering PHA residents to assume a proactive role in reducing sources of disorder in their environment. This effort requires substantial modifications in standard police practices, as well as the linkage between PHA police and other PHA service providers. This program also requires an expanded role for community residents in their own and their community's protection. Such modifications revolve around the concept of community policing.

This program emphasizes the need for the development of "partnerships" both within and outside the PHAPD. Inside the department, this emphasis takes the form of strengthening basic patrol service delivery. Outside the department, this emphasis takes the form of building bridges with the Philadelphia public housing community and other PHA service providers—bridges that will strengthen community-based policing, thereby improving neighborhood safety and resident acceptance of the police.

In broad terms, the PHA provides the basis for community involvement in the policing and "ownership" of their residential communities. The police focus shifts from operating independently of the community to one in which the police are actively involved with the resident community in providing responsive and effective safe services. This is accomplished by implementing "The 11th Street Corridor Program."

Philadelphia's 11th Street Corridor Program

The PHA Community Policing Program is being conducted on the 11th Street Corridor in north Philadelphia. This north/south zone runs from Lehigh Avenue to the north to Spring Garden Street to the south. It is an area just over two miles in length and about one half mile in width. This area is centrally located in lower north Philadelphia. It is the area with the city's highest density of public housing, the highest rate of family and individual poverty, as well as the highest frequency of female headed households. A comparison area—the West of Broad Street Area—has a similar population base within and surrounding its public housing communities. Both the treatment site (the 11th Street Corridor, four blocks east of Broad Street) and the control site (west of Broad Street) are within the same region of lower north Philadelphia.

The four sites to the west of Broad Street, the main thoroughfare in Philadelphia, serve as controls for the evaluation, while five sites to the east of Broad Street serve as the experimental sites. There were no differences among key demographic and crime data measures except for the percentage of occupied rental units which was higher in the experimental sites. This difference is a reflection of the greater concentration of non-residential buildings east of Broad Street. Figure 1 portrays the sites in the city.

Conventional policing methods, including intensive and aggressive police presence, highly publicized drug busts, and extensive surveillance operations, have had little enduring effect in public housing environments (Weisel, 1990). While such efforts may be a vital part of a crime reduction program, attempts to implement them in isolation from the dynamics of the community have demonstrated only short term effectiveness. The PHA effort is, in contrast to traditional crime reduction programs, a systematic program dedicated to re-shaping police services and allowing for greater community involvement in safety policy and decision making. The PHA anticipates that such efforts will help promote and create better relationships between residents and PHA police, increase crime reduction and prevention activities, reduce resident victimization, and increase community cohesion.

An evaluation of community policing in a public housing context has several potential advantages over a comparable analysis in a typical neighborhood context. Public housing developments are discrete units possessing distinct resident organizations. Their relatively high level of internal organization makes them an ideal subject for a study of community policing. Moreover, public housing communities typically have a universally understood boundary with a resident population for which the development provides a clear identification. This condition provides a basis for authentic community mobilization. The 11th Street Corridor Program of the Philadelphia Public Housing Authority Police seeks to create a public/police collaboration toward increased safety within these communities.

Two major strategies to be pursued in the PHA Community Policing Program are (1) to build a problem-solving, proactive, community-involved police response to the provision of safety services in the five public housing complexes lining the 11th Street corridor, and (2) to strengthen resident associations as a source of input into police decision-making and in the provision of police services.

Figure 1
MAP of PHA Developments Included in
the 11th Street Corridor Program

North Philadelphia
1990 Census Tracts and Census Block Groups

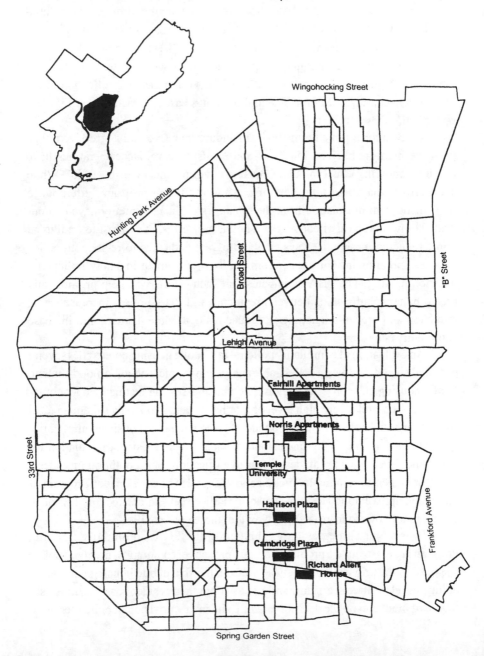

Elaborating upon the first strategy, a central element of the 11th Street Corridor Program is to establish a greater visible police presence. This presence, and the manner in which it is achieved, should accomplish four objectives:

1. Ensure that housing developments get consistent police services that are linked with other social services being provided to the residents of these communities;
2. Assign police to permanent geographical areas to produce "police owner-ship" and familiarity with community needs and concerns;
3. Utilize technology and sophisticated analysis for deployment of personnel at times and in places where there is a demand for service and a potential to impact community quality of life issues; and
4. Emphasize problem-solving and continuity of service until a problem is addressed.

In order to strengthen relationships between the PHA Police Department and the communities it serves, a process by which officers and residents become involved in close interaction and discussion of safety concerns will be initiated. This process involves the initiation of open discussions between the residents and police, while including the creation of a Police Advisory Council for the 11th Street Corridor. Three primary objectives are sought in this approach:

1. Such discussion is meant to create an ongoing dialogue among "policy equals" where the input and advice of the community is actively sought and used in local decision-making;
2. Such dialogue creates the linkage necessary for immediate accountability for police services in any particular area by redirecting police services to focus on the needs of clients; and
3. Such a process builds joint understanding (police and community) of the dynamics of social, political, and economic issues which have a direct impact on public safety.

These two strategies are hypothesized to result in the creation of a strategic emphasis within the PHA Police Department. The department will be engaged with the community in a process of determining the aims and objectives of the police. This will become the mission of the police, and ultimately a "contract" with the "citizens" of Philadelphia public housing for better police service.

Program Efforts/Activities

The first component of the PHA initiative involves redeployment of existing police personnel. The process entails reassigning officers currently in static guard duty to mobile policing units along the 11th Street Corridor. Even though the PHA Police Department has hired additional police, it also uses existing officers for this pro-gram as opposed to new recruits. These officers have completed a specialized training program in community policing.

As part of the process of improving police mobility and presence, the PHA has moved away from static fixed stations. The PHAPD acquired a mobile police mini-station for the 11th Street Corridor. The department has also doubled the size of the Bicycle Patrol Unit from seven to fourteen officers. This unit has already shown to be an effective policing strategy and has begun the process of interacting and working within the community. Officers in this unit have been drawn from the Drug Enforcement Task Force, a unit which has played a significant role in participating in drug crime reduction efforts at one of the public housing development sites. A mobile police unit allows officers to familiarize themselves with the residents, and the various conditions which contribute to problems in that particular community.

Emphasis will be on problem solving through innovation and the increased use of available technologies. In addition, a mobile mini-station has proved invaluable as a device for implementing practical, affordable community policing in a public housing setting. The mobile mini-station provides access for discussions with community members, school retention services in cooperation with the PHA's youth drug prevention program, and for other neighborhood school functions.

The station also provides residents with the community workstation info-window program which is a pilot computer application program that assists social service agencies and/or referral agents with services for individuals and families with multiple problems through a single point of entry. With the community policing initiative, the PHAPD is using the workstation info-window unit as a referral point from which it can act with greater speed and efficiency to resident requests for service.

There are four components to the larger evaluation: (1) communities, (2) institutions, (3) public housing residents, and (4) community and institutional leaders in terms of policy formulation. In this article, we focus on the first and third of these components. In particular, the two main questions driving this investigation are: (1) Is a community policing approach appropriate in a public housing setting, and (2) Can community policing work in a public housing setting? To help address the first question, we report on data regarding crimes and calls for service for all of the public housing developments. Two additional constructs identified as being salient in measuring the success of a community policing strategy include: (1) the building of relationships, and (2) increasing levels of trust among police and community residents. In order to capture the effects of these initiatives, we administered surveys to all PHA officers as well as community residents participating in the project at two different time periods, prior to the implementation of the community policing program and shortly after the program commenced. Questions for the police officers were designed to capture changes in police perceptions of the citizens and the community, levels of job satisfaction, perceived adequacy of new roles for the police, perceptions of physical and social incivilities, and nature of daily police work. Survey administration for the citizens included: resident attachment/satisfaction with the area, perceptions of community problems, fear of crime, fear of victimization, contact with police officers, perceptions of police, knowledge of public housing authority services, and involvement in the co-production of safety which includes the quality of the police-resident contact, and trust of police personnel. For the sake of brevity, this article reports on a limited number of these perceptions.

Police Officer Surveys. In the experimental site, there was a total of 44 officers at wave one (September 1996), 34 of whom completed the survey instrument at wave two (April 1997). In the control sites, 26 officers completed the first survey administration while 25 completed the second survey administration. In all, there were 129 total surveys completed for both groups at both time periods.

Over 82 percent of the officers are males. Of the officers in the study, almost 66 percent are African-American and about 34 percent are White. Most officers have about seven years of service with the Public Housing Authority Police Department and most spent a little over two and half years with another police department. Most of the officers have some college level experiences, but most have not completed a college degree.

Resident Surveys. In the experimental site, there was a total of 230 residents at wave one (September 1996), of whom 229 completed the survey instrument at wave two (June 1997). In the control sites, 156 residents completed the first survey administration while 158 completed the second survey administration. In all, there were 386 total surveys completed for both groups at both time periods.

Over 92 percent of the heads of households are female with an average of almost two children under the age of 17 per household. Slightly over half of the residents are single and have never been married. A little over 93 percent of the residents are African-American and a majority (over 60 percent) have either (a) some high school experience or (b) completed high school. In addition, almost half of the residents (45 percent) define their working life as "homemakers." The mean number of years the residents have lived at their current address surpasses 13 years.

Analytic Strategy

The analysis proceeds in the following ways. First, we provide some descriptive information on the calls for service across the control and experimental sites, as well as an aggregation of both sites. Next, we present some results based on a between-group analysis at waves one and two (i.e., experimental vs. control at waves one and two). Third, we present the results of a within-group analysis for waves one and two (i.e., experimental at wave one vs. experimental at wave two). Finally, we conduct site-specific mean level comparisons between waves one and two for the experimental group. A number of scales were constructed that were designed to measure certain aspects of community policing within a public housing context. For the officers, these include:

- perception of community problems (where low scores suggest a high perception of social and physical problems),
- the nature of daily work (where low scores reflect highly active officers),

- job satisfaction (where low scores indicate high job satisfaction),
- nature of police work (where a high score is indicative of a positive outlook on an officer's work assignment),
- perception of community "A" (where a high score suggests a high degree of community partners),
- perception of community "B" (where a low score indicates a high perception of crime),
- prognosis of success (where a high score reflects a high prognosis of success for the 11th Street Program), and
- perception of police officer role (where higher scores indicate a higher community-oriented/proactive perception of the police role).

For the residents, the measures included perceptions of community problems, perceptions of the fear of crime, and perceptions of the view of police. Appendix A contains the items used to measure the police constructs, the mean and standard deviation for each of the scales, and the alpha reliability coefficient, while Appendix B does the same for the resident scales.

Police Survey Results

Prior to discussing the results of the police and resident surveys, we would like to highlight the calls for service data. Figure 2 contains the calls for service data for both the control and experimental groups combined. Figures 3 and 4 contain the calls for service data for the control and experimental groups respectively. Two things are worth pointing out. First, as can be seen from figure 2, there appears to be no real trend in the time series for calls for service for both sites combined. Second, from figures 3 and 4, it can be seen that the trend in calls for service is pretty much the same for both the control and experimental sites.

Figure 2
Time Series Plot Showing PHAPD Calls for Service to All Sites

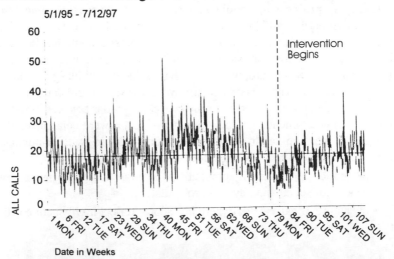

Date in Weeks

Figure 3
Time Series Plot Showing PHAPD Calls for Service to Control Sites

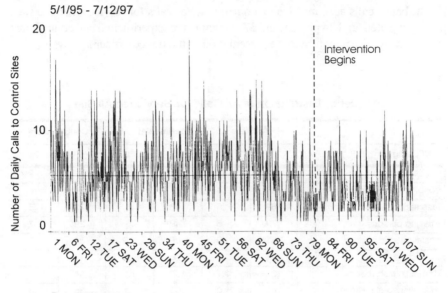

Date in Weeks

Figure 4
Time Series Plot Showing PHAPD Calls for Service to Exp. Sites

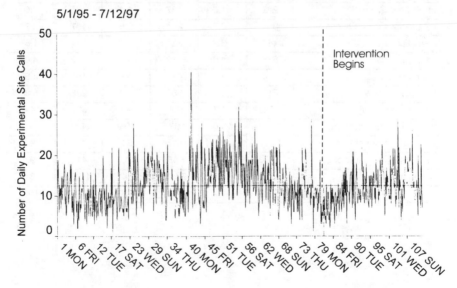

Date in Weeks

108   Part II—Current Research

In addition, table 1 presents the frequency distribution for the calls for service data for the control, experimental, and aggregated sites. As can be seen, the most common call for service across all three categories of calls for service is disturbance. Disturbance calls account for about one quarter of calls for service when the sites are aggregated, and 24 percent and 27 percent in the experimental and control sites respectively. We now turn to the presentation of the police officer surveys.

Table 1
Frequency Distribution of All Calls for Service to All Sites

Call Category	All Sites		Experimental Sites		Control Sites	
	f	%	*f*	%	*f*	%
assist officer	15	.1	7	.1	8	.2
suspicious person	60	.4	44	.4	16	.4
less serious personal crime	69	.5	46	.5	23	.5
missing person	79	.6	49	.5	29	.7
assist outside agency	131	.9	99	1.0	31	.7
pursuit	121	.9	78	.8	43	.1
domestic disturbance	151	1.1	107	1.1	44	1.0
miscellaneous juvenile	141	1.0	106	1.1	35	.8
serious property crime	161	1.1	109	1.1	54	1.2
serious personal crime	158	1.1	110	1.1	48	1.1
weapons call	254	1.8	167	1.7	86	2.0
shots fired	222	1.6	137	1.4	85	2.0
less serious property crime	381	2.7	244	2.5	137	3.2
narcotics	448	3.2	384	3.9	64	1.5
medical detail	655	4.6	482	4.9	173	4.0
maintenance	646	4.5	481	4.9	165	3.8
meet complainant	817	5.8	589	6.0	228	5.3
hazard and safety	1,523	10.7	900	9.1	621	14.4
investigate auto/property	1,512	10.6	1074	10.9	438	10.1
contact another officer	1,227	8.7	815	8.3	413	9.5
pedestrian investigation	1,860	13.1	1,450	14.7	414	9.6
disturbance	3,543	24.9	2,376	24.1	1,165	26.9
Totals	14,174	100	9,854	100	4,320	100

Table 2
Police Officers' Between-Group Comparisons
on Constructs for Waves One and Two.
(Numbers displayed are mean levels.)

Construct	Wave One		Wave Two	
	Experimental	Control	Experiemental	Control
Nature of Daily Police Work	2.798	2.789	2.649	2.998*
Job Satisfaction	3.461	3.665	3.503	3.512
Nature of Work	3.371	3.435	3.377	3.320
Perceptions of Community "A"	3.332	3.438	3.256	3.280
Perceptions of Community "B"	3.170	2.720	3.168	3.280
Community Problems	1.500	1.520	1.517	1.431
Role Expectations	4.410	4.400	4.440	4.600
Prognosis of Success**	N/A		N/A	

* $p < .05$
**Note: The prognosis of success survey question was not asked of the control group because they
were not participants in the program. Therefore, there was no analysis done on this scale for the
between-group mean comparisons.

The first column of table 2 presents the results for tests of significance between groups at wave one. One of the most important things to notice is that the experimental and control groups did not differ significantly ($p < .05$) on any of the constructs outlined above. This is important since it provides us with evidence that the groups are fairly equally matched thus diminishing the possibility that there was some *a priori* difference in the selection of officers that could bias the results. Therefore, while we did not find any significant differences between the groups at the first wave, for our purposes, this is actually encouraging evidence that the police officers in both the experimental and control sites are fairly comparable on a number of constructs.

We also undertook the same analysis between-groups for the second wave. The results for this may be found in the second column of table 2. The results for the second wave are almost the same as wave one; that is, there were not that many differences between groups at wave two. However, there was one exception. For the nature of daily work, officers in the experimental site had a lower mean ($\bar{x}=2.649$) than their control site counterparts ($\bar{x}=2.998$). Recall that higher scores on this scale represent more inactivity among officers, whereas lower scores are indicative of more highly active officers. As can be seen, the experimental officers, who were receiving community-oriented training, had lower scores on the scale reflective of more activity on patrol. This result is consistent with expectations from community-oriented policing philosophy. Officers assigned to the 11th Street Program became more proactive in their policing activities at wave two than the officers in the control group. This is an encouraging finding because the treatment dosage between the two waves was minimal; that is, the treatment portion of the program for the officers was just commencing at the beginning of the second wave of survey administration. It may be reasonable to presume that while not much was done between waves one and two to change the way officers "view" their working environments, the data, in part, suggest that the training of the treatment group officers may be having the intended effect.

Turning to the within-group analyses, we present the results in the following manner. First, we examine the within-group analysis for the experimental group on the constructs mentioned earlier. Then, we highlight the results for the control site officers. Table 3 presents a summary of the results.

The first column of table 3 provides the results of the within-group comparison between waves one and two for the experimental sites. Since most of the results are evident from the table, we only highlight a few of them here. For the nature of daily work scale, there was no significant difference for the experimental group between waves one and two (t=1.12). However, the mean value of the scale at wave two ($\bar{x}$=2.649) is lower than the mean at wave one ($\bar{x}$=2.798) which suggests that officers are becoming more active in their daily work. For all of the other scales, the results were insignificant as well. That is, mean levels did not change significantly between survey administrations on any of the scales for the experimental group.

Table 3
Police Officers' Within-Group Comparisons
on Constructs for Waves One and Two.
(Numbers displayed are mean levels.)

	Experimental		Control	
	Wave One	Wave Two	Wave One	Wave Two
Construct				
Nature of Daily Police Work	2.798	2.649	2.789	2.998*
Job Satisfaction	3.461	3.503	3.670	3.510
Nature of Work	3.371	3.377	3.436	3.320
Perceptions of Community "A"	3.332	3.256	3.438	3.280*
Perceptions of Community "B"	3.218	3.168	3.096	3.280*
Community Problems	1.500	1.510	1.520	1.510
Role Expectations	4.410	4.400	4.400	4.600
Prognosis of Success**	2.690	2.680	N/A	
* p<.05				

In the second column of table 3, the results for the control group are displayed. The story for the control group is pretty much the same as it was for the experimental group, with two minor exceptions. A couple of the mean level comparisons were marginally significant. First, for the perception of communities "A" scale, the mean score on the scale decreased between the first and second wave ($\bar{x}$'s=3.438 and 3.280 respectively; t=1.65). Since high scores on this scale are reflective of a higher number of community partners, it appears that the control officer's perceptions of community partners decreased between waves. In a related manner, for the perceptions of communities "B" scale, the mean level increased between waves one and two ($\bar{x}$'s=3.096 and 3.280 respectively; t=1.68). Since low scores on this scale reflects a higher perception of crime, this result suggests that control officers in the second wave perceived less crime than they did during the first wave.

Although it is encouraging that the means between waves did not significantly change for the comparison group, it was not encouraging to see the same pattern for the experimental group. While we did not find favorable evidence concerning a change in officer attitudes between waves one and two, we think that this has more to do with the dosage of treatment rather than the treatment itself. The officers began to receive community policing skills around the beginning of the second wave of data collection and this could be the reason why their perceptions were little changed from wave one. We now turn to the resident survey results.

Residents' Survey Results

Table 4 contains a between-group comparison for the three constructs under investigation in this analysis: perceptions of the residents' view of the police, perceptions of community problems, and perceptions of the fear of crime. The first column of table 4 presents the comparison results for wave one between the experimental and control sites, while the second column displays the results for the wave two comparison.

Table 4
Residents' Between-Group Comparisons
on Constructs for Waves One and Two
(Numbers displayed are mean levels.)

	Wave One		Wave Two	
	Experimental	Control	Experimental	Control
Construct				
Perception of View of Police	2.801	2.866	2.817	2.956*
Perception of Community Problems	2.146	2.017*	1.975	1.937
Perception of Fear of Crime	2.794	2.913	2.941	2.994
* p<.05				

In terms of the perceptions of the view of police scale, the experimental and control groups did not differ significantly on mean levels at wave one ($\bar{x}$'s 2.801 and 2.866 respectively), but at wave two the means were significantly different.

The experimental sites view the police less positively than the residents in the control group ($\bar{x}$'s 2.817 and 2.956 respectively). Recall that the survey administration at wave two was conducted after the police officers had received their training in community policing. We infer from this that the citizens in the experimental sites may be witnessing the police doing more proactive work in the community and as a result, they may feel a sense of intrusion at the outset, and may be more sensitized and critical because of their exposure to the program. While we do not have data on the third wave of survey administration, our expectation is that the mean level in the experimental group in terms of positive views on the police will increase from their responses on the second wave of survey administration.

Turning to the perceptions of community problems scale, it can be seen that the experimental sites report a significantly higher number of community problems at wave one than the residents in the control group ($\bar{x}$'s 2.146 and 2.017 respectively). At wave two, however, the mean level of community problems in both groups stabilize such that they are not significantly different from one another ($\bar{x}$'s 1.975 and 1.937 respectively).

In terms of the fear of crime scale, none of the mean comparison tests were statistically significant for either waves when comparing the experimental and control groups. At wave one, the means for the perceptions of fear of crime scale for the experimental and control groups were not significantly different ($\bar{x}$'s 2.794 and 2.913 respectively); similarly there was not a significant difference at wave two ($\bar{x}$'s 2.941 and 2.994 respectively).

In table 5 we present the results of a within-group comparison for both the experimental and control sites at waves one and two. The first column of table 5 contains the wave one-wave two comparisons for the experimental sites. As can be seen, the means for the perceptions of the view of police ($\bar{x}$'s= 2.801 and 2.817 respectively) and fear of crime ($\bar{x}$'s=2.794 and 2.941 respectively) did not differ significantly between survey administrations. However, for the perception of community problems, the mean level decreased significantly between survey administrations ($\bar{x}$'s=2.146 and 1.975 respectively).

Table 5
Residents' Within-Group Comparisons
on Constructs for Waves One and Two
(Numbers displayed are mean levels.)

	Experimental		Control	
	Wave One	Wave Two	Wave One	Wave Two
Construct				
Perception of View of Police	2.801	2.817	2.866	2.956
Perception of Community Problems	2.146	1.975*	2.017	1.937*
Perception of Fear of Crime	2.794	2.941	2.913	2.994

* $p<.05$

While at first glance this may be indicative that the police/community policing program may be having its intended effect at reducing community problems, we find essentially the same results for the control group on all three scales. For both the perceptions of the view of the police ($\bar{x}$'s=2.866 and 2.956 respectively) and the fear of crime ($\bar{x}$'s=2.913 and 2.994 respectively), the mean levels did not decrease significantly between waves one and two. However, the perception of community problems also decreased significantly in the control group between waves one and two ($\bar{x}$'s=2.107 and 1.937 respectively).

In table 6 we report mean level comparisons for the three constructs for site-specific units in the experimental sites. The units include: Richard Allen, Fairhill, Cambridge, Harrison, and Norris. Essentially, the results mimic those we found for the within-group comparisons. As can be seen, there were no significant differences between waves one and two for any of the individual sites on both the perceptions of the view of police and perceptions of the fear of crime scales. However, for the perceptions of community problems scale, four of the five experimental sites reported significant reductions in community problems. At Richard Allen ($\bar{x}$'s=2.231 and 2.055 respectively), Cambridge ($\bar{x}$'s=2.166 and 1.961 respectively), Harrison ($\bar{x}$'s=1.995 and 1.788 respectively), and Norris ($\bar{x}$'s=2.141 and 1.935 respectively), mean levels of community problems decreased from wave one to wave two. Only in Fairhill was the decrease not observed ($\bar{x}$'s=2.146 and 2.190 respectively).

Table 6
Residents' Site-Specific Comparisons
between Wave 1 and Wave 2 in Experimental Sites only

Construct	Richard Allen		Fairhill		Cambridge		Harrison		Norris	
	Wave 1	Wave 2	Wave 1	Wave 2	Wave 1	Wave 2	Wave 1	Wave 2	Wave 1	Wave 2
Perception of View of Police	2.703	2.668	3.133	3.204	2.785	2.822	2.788	2.966	2.839	2.716
Perception of Community Problems	2.231	2.055*	2.146	2.190	2.166	1.961*	1.995	1.788*	2.141	1.935*
Perception of Fear of Crime	2.754	2.822	2.668	2.706	2.628	2.706	3.104	3.386	2.756	3.032

* $p<.05$

Discussion and Conclusion

In this article, we have attempted to review the issues associated with public housing and community policing, describe the response to the intersection of these two in the city of Philadelphia, as well as provide some preliminary evidence on an on-going longitudinal evaluation of the 11th Street Corridor Program. While our results are preliminary, we found evidence that the program appeared to have some influence on officer behavior in a direction consistent with program goals. We found that between waves one and two, officers in the experimental sites were more proactive in their policing activities compared to their control site colleagues. Further, this higher level of activity seems to have been noticed by the residents, since those who live in the experimental sites reported a higher level of perception of community problems, as well as a somewhat more negative attitude about the police. From this, we draw the inference that, in the absence of contradictory evidence, the police seem to have responded to the training and the residents have not only noticed, but have become somewhat "annoyed" as a group at the intervention, at least initially. This finding is somewhat encouraging since the treatment dosage was of some concern between the wave one and two comparisons.

At the same time, differences between the control and experimental sites were not observed for many of the constructs. We must note that the training of the officers for this study occurred around the time of the second wave of questionnaire administration for both the officers and the residents, and this could be influencing our results since we are not allowing enough of a time difference to observe differences in perceptions. The third wave of data collection is to commence during the fall of 1997 and we expect to see more of a change in perceptions given that the treatment will have been underway for a significant amount of time. Future analytic plans include estimating the impact of the community policing program on crime rates and calls for service, as well as the continuation of perception changes among police officers and residents in public housing.

There is much concern about the crime and disorder problems that are plaguing public housing developments in the United States. In attempts to reduce the incidence of these problems, both citizens and public officials have called for the police to take action. With a community policing philosophy in hand, the city of Philadelphia is one of the first cities in the United States to undertake a systematic evaluation of the effect of community policing on reducing crime and disorder problems in several public housing developments along a section of north Philadelphia known as the 11th Street Corridor. Knowledge of the impact of such a program can go a long way toward developing comprehensive changes in management and controlling problem behavior in public housing developments (Feins et al. 1997; Newman 1996).

Appendix A

Police Officer Survey Constructs with Item Indicators

Construct	Indicators
	Vacant lots filled with trash
	Burglaries of homes and businesses
	Public drinking
	Groups of people hanging around causing problems
	Open-air drug dealing
	Gun shots fired
	Absence of recreation facilities for kids
Perception of Community	Cars being vandalized
Problems	Muggings, purse snatches and other forcible stealing
	Domestic violence
	Loud radios
	Urinating in public
	Outsiders coming in and causing problems
	Youth disruption—young people causing problems
$\bar{x} = 1.49$ SD = 0.29 Alpha = 0.81	

	How often do you . . .
	Patrol your beat on foot
	Patrol your beat in a marked/unmarked squad car
	Investigate minor crimes (i.e., misdemeanors)
	Attend meetings with the residents present
	Talk to residents one-on-one
	Handle maintenance calls
Nature of Daily Work	Make court appearances
	Investigate serious crimes (i.e., felonies)
	Settle domestic disputes
	Respond to intrusion alarms
	Disperse crowds
	Contact other PHA agencies
	Deal with juveniles in the developments
$\bar{x} = 0.80$ SD = 0.30 Alpha = 0.82	

	PHAPD is a good department to work for
	I like the kind of work I do very much
	I generally like the employees I work with
	My supervisor seeks my opinion when a problem arises
Job Satisfaction	I am not at all involved personally with my job
	Our management generally treats its employees quite well
	Staying with PHAPD is as much a necessity as it is a desire

Promotions are based on "who" you know, not "what" you know

The equipment supplied by the department is very good

$\bar{x} = 3.52$ SD = 0.672   Alpha = 0.68

Perception of Community: Crime and Dangerousness

Juveniles commit most of the crimes in the developments

In order to do my job effectively, I often have to use force

PHA developments are generally pretty dangerous places

When patrolling my beat, I'm concerned about my own safety

Most crime is committed by adults living illegally in public housing

When contacting people, I generally treat them as if they're dangerous

Most people on my beat are up to no good

Most crime is committed by adults living legally in public housing

There's no sense of community in public housing

In most arrests I normally have to use force

Most crime is committed by people living outside public housing

$\bar{x} = 3.19$ SD = 0.439   Alpha = 0.61

Prognosis of Success of 11th St. Program

The 11th Street Program will likely lead to . . .

More arrests

Better police/community relations

Better responses to calls for police service

Increased presence of officers in the developments

More effective use of crime information

Greater solution of community problems

Reduction in crime rate

Greater officer discretion

Fewer citizen complains about police

Greater citizen demands on police resources

Greater willingness of residents to cooperate with PHA police

$\bar{x} = 3.22$ SD = 0.744   Alpha = 0.76

Nature of Work

My job assignment allows me to use a variety of my skills and talents

My job is arranged so that I have the chance to do an entire task

My supervisors let me know how well I am doing on the job

My co-workers let me know how well I am doing on the job

My job gives me considerable opportunity for independence

My work alone provides me with clues about my performance

$\bar{x} = 3.38$ SD = 0.672   Alpha = 0.71

Please indicate the importance you place on the following activities . . .
Performing foot patrol in public housing
Helping settle domestic disputes
Investigating suspicious conditions
Getting to know juveniles
Getting to know residents
Responding to radio calls
Perception of the   Identifying potential community problems
Police Role   Solving community problems
Sharing information with the Philadelphia Police Department
Sharing information with housing site managers
Letting residents get to know you
Working with resident councils to solve community problems
Coordinating with other PHA agencies to improve quality-of-life issues

$\bar{x} = 4.30$ SD = .521   Alpha = 0.90

PHA officers know better than residents which police services are required
Most PHA residents respect the PHA police
PHA police officers should make frequent informal contact with residents
An officer in a patrol car learns more about the community than on foot
PHA officers should try to solve non-crime related problems on their beat
Residents understand the problems that face the PHAPD
I have friends who live in the developments
Perception of Communities I desire more social contact with PHA residents
Crime is the worst problem facing the residents today
PHA residents should work harder to help themselves
The use of foot patrol is a waste of personnel
Patrol cars reduce citizens' fear of crime more effectively than foot patrols
Crime prevention is a joint responsibility of the community and police

$\bar{x} = 3.32$ SD = .346   Alpha = 0.53

Appendix B

Resident Survey Constructs with Item Indicators

Construct	Indicators
	Abandoned cars
	Abandoned apartments and buildings
	Graffiti
	Public drinking
	Garbage or litter
	Groups of people hanging around causing problems
	Drug selling
	Crack vials or other evidence of drug use on streets, sidewalks, etc.
	Cars being vandalized
	Muggings, purse/jewelry snatches and other forcible stealing
Perception of Community	Burglaries and forcible entries into homes and businesses
Problems	Fights
	Assaults
	Domestic violence
	Urinating in public
	Outsiders coming in the development causing problems
	Youth disruption—young people causing problems
	Rapes or other sexual assaults
	People vandalizing vacant apartments
	Fires

$\bar{x} = 2.094$ SD = 0.43   Alpha = 0.83

Construct	Indicators
	Housing Police . . .
	Respond promptly when they are needed
	Do a good job keeping order on the streets and sidewalks
	Are polite and courteous
	Encourage residents to do their part in preventing/solving crime
	Are honest and trustworthy
	Are concerned with residents' problems
	Are excellent role models for the kids
	Are less sensitive than city police
Perception of the Police	Work closely with the community to solve problems
	Are helpful to people who have been victims of crime
	Do a lot to prevent crime
	Are known by name
	Cooperate with the community
	Are very helpful to residents
	Are eager to get crime information from residents

Are professional and helpful
Are friendly and try to get to know people

x̄ = 2.83   SD = 0.58   Alpha = 0.85

Prevented from doing things due to worry about crime
Think about being robbed or physically assaulted
Think about your unit being burglarized or vandalized

Fear of Crime   Feel afraid of being attacked/assaulted while home
Fearful of being a victim of violent crime

x̄ = 2.84   SD = 0.82   Alpha = 0.70

Note

[1] The effectiveness of community policing is difficult to measure and since the purpose of this article is somewhat different from this particular issue, suffice it to say that the overall research does not speak with one voice on this front. Measuring effectiveness, or what matters, is largely dependent on what researchers define as the barometer of effectiveness. For example, are crime rates, calls-for-service, improved police-community relationships, or all three the criteria for judging whether or not community policing works? The point is that before program effectiveness can be measured, the goals of the program must be clearly defined. Such issues are in need of immediate research attention.

References

Alpert, G., and R. Dunham. 1988. *Policing Multi-Ethnic Neighborhoods*. New York: Greenwood Press.

Bayley, D. 1995. *Police for the Future*. New York: Cambridge University Press.

Bowers, W., and J. Hirsch. 1986. *The Impact of Foot Patrol Staffing on Crime and Disorder in Boston: An Unmet Promise*. Boston, MA: Center for Applied Social Research-Northeastern University.

Brill, W. and Associates. 1975. *Victimization, Fear of Crime, and Altered Behavior: A Profile of the Crime Problem in Four Housing Projects in Boston*. Washington, DC: U.S. Department of Housing and Urban Development.

_____. 1977. *Victimization, Fear of Crime, and Altered Behavior: A Profile of the Crime Problem in Murphy Homes, Baltimore, Maryland*. Washington, DC: U.S. Department of Housing and Urban Development.

Bursik, R., and H. Grasmick. 1993. *Neighborhoods and Crime: The Dimensions of Effective Community Control*. New York: Lexington Books.

Dunworth, T., and A. Saiger. 1994. *Drugs and Crime in Public Housing: A Three City Analysis*. Washington, DC: National Institute of Justice.

Eck, J., and W. Spelman. 1987. *Problem-Solving: Problem-Oriented Policing in Newport News*. Washington, DC: National Institute of Justice.

Farley, J. 1982. Has public housing gotten a bum rap? The incidence of crime in St. Louis public housing developments. *Environment and Behavior*, 14(4): 443–77.

Feins, J., J. Epstein, and R. Widom. 1997. *Solving Crime Problems in Residential Neighborhoods: Comprehensive Changes in Design, Management, and Use*. Washington, DC: U.S. Department of Justice.

Gaines, L., V. Kappeler, and J. Vaughn. 1997. *Policing*. Cincinnati, OH: Anderson Publishing.

Goldstein, H. 1990. *Problem-Oriented Policing*. New York: McGraw-Hill.

Green-Mazerolle, L., and W. Terrill. 1997. Problem-oriented policing in public housing: Identifying the distribution of problem places. *Policing*, 20(2): 235–55.

Harrell, A., and C. Gouvis. 1994. *Predicting Neighborhood Risk of Crime*. Washington, DC: The Urban Institute.

Holzman, H. 1996. Criminological research on public housing: Toward a better understanding of people, places, and spaces. *Crime and Delinquency*, 42(3): 361–78.

Hunter, A. 1978. Symbols of incivility: Social disorder and fear of crime in urban neighborhoods. Paper Presented at the Annual Meeting of the American Society of Criminology, November. Dallas, TX.

Huth, M. 1981. Strategies for crime reduction in public housing. *Journal of Sociology and Social Welfare*, 8(3): 587–600.

Kelling, G., and C. Coles. 1996. *Fixing Broken Windows*. New York: Free Press.

Kelling, G., T. Pate, D. Dieckman, and C. Brown. 1974. *The Kansas City Preventive Patrol Experiment*. Washington, DC: Police Foundation.

Kotlowitz, A. 1991. *There are No Children Here*. New York: Doubleday.

Mastrofski, S., and J. Greene. 1994. Community policing and the rule of law. In *The Changing Focus of Police Innovation: Problems of Law, Order, and Community*, edited by D. Weisburd and C. Uchida. New York: Springer-Verlag.

Matthews, W. 1993. Policing distressed public housing developments. *Police Management*, 2–8.

Newman, O. 1996. *Creating Defensible Space*. Washington, DC: U.S. Department of Housing and Urban Development.

Pate, A., W. Skogan, M. Wycoff, and L. Sherman. 1985. *Reducing the 'Signs of Crime': The Newark Experience*. Washington, DC: The Police Foundation.

Popkin, S., L. Olson, A. Lurigio, V. Gwiasda, and R. Carter. 1995. Sweeping out drugs and crime: Residents' views of the Chicago housing authority's public housing drug elimination program. *Crime and Delinquency*, 41(1): 73–99.

President's Commission on Housing. 1982. *The Report of the President's Commission on Housing*. Washington, DC: U.S. Government Printing Office.

President's Commission on Law Enforcement and Administration. 1967. *Task Force Report: The Police*. Washington, DC: U.S. Government Printing Office.

Rainwater, L. 1966. Fear and the house-as-haven in the lower classes. *Journal of the American Institute of Planners*, 32:23–37.

_____. 1970. *Behind Ghetto Walls: Black Family Life in a Federal Slum*. Chicago: Aldine.

Reiss, A. 1985. *Policing a City's Central District: The Oakland Story*. Washington, DC: National Institute of Justice.

Rohe, W., and R. Burby. 1988. Fear of crime in public housing. *Environment and Behavior*, 20:700–720.

Roncek, D., R. Bell, and J. Francik. 1981. Housing projects and crime. *Social Problems*, 29(2): 151–66.

Sherman, L. 1995. The police. In *Crime*, edited by J. Q. Wilson and J. Petersilia. San Francisco: ICS Press.

Sherman, L., P. Gartin, and M. Buerger. 1989. Hot spots of predatory crime: Routine activities and the criminology of place. *Criminology*, 27:27–56.

Skogan, W. 1990. *Disorder and Decline: Crime and the Spiral of Decay in American Neighborhoods*. New York: Free Press.

Skogan, W., and S. Annan. 1994. Drugs in public housing: Toward an effective police response. In *Drugs and Crime: Evaluating Public Policy Initiatives*, edited by C. Uchida and D. MacKenzie. Thousand Oaks, CA: Sage.

Skolnick, J., and D. Bayley. 1988. Theme and variation in community policing. In *Crime and Justice: An Annual Review of Research*, edited by M. Tonry and N. Morris. Chicago: University of Chicago Press.

Taylor, R. 1997. Social order and disorder of street blocks and neighborhoods: Ecology, microecology, and the systemic model of social disorganization. *Journal of Research in Crime and Delinquency*, 34(1): 113–55.

Trojanowicz, R. 1986. Evaluating the neighborhood foot patrol program: The Flint,

Michigan project. In *Community Crime Prevention: Does it Work?*, edited by D. Rosenbaum. Beverly Hills: Sage Publications.

Uchida, C., B. Forst, and S. Annan. 1992. *Modern Policing and the Control of Illegal Drugs: Testing New Strategies in Two American Cities*. Washington, DC: National Institute of Justice.

Vergera, C. 1989. Hell in a very tall place. *Atlantic Monthly*, September: 72–78.

Webster, B., and E. Connors. 1992. *The Police, Drugs, and Public Housing*. Washington, DC: National Institute of Justice.

Weisburd, D., and L. Green. 1995. Policing drug hot spots: The Jersey City DMA experiment. *Justice Quarterly*, 12(4): 711–36.

Weisel, D. 1990. *Tackling Drug Problems in Public Housing*. Washington, DC: Police Executive Research Forum.

Wilson, J. Q., and G. Kelling. 1982. The police and neighborhood safety. *Atlantic Monthly*, March: 29–38.

8

The Road to Community Policing in Los Angeles
A Case Study

Jack R. Greene

The Beating Heard Around the World

The early morning hours of March 3, 1991, were not much different than most Sunday mornings in Los Angeles, although the events that would transpire this evening would forever change the Los Angeles Police Department (LAPD). It was after midnight when Rodney King and his buddies Pooh and Freddie G. cruised onto the Foothill Freeway driving a white Hyundai—music playing, perhaps looking for a little action.

The two California Highway Patrol officers who initially encountered King estimated his car to be traveling over 100 miles an hour, while it weaved in and out of traffic on the freeway. They gave chase and, as they entered the corporate limits of Los Angeles, notified the LAPD.

At some point, the pursuit of the white Hyundai left the freeway and took to the surface streets of a section of Los Angeles known as the Foothill precinct. Joining the California Highway Patrol chase of King were several Los Angeles Police Department patrol cars, as well as a car from the Los Angeles Unified School District Police. Police estimate that the chase continued for several miles at speeds ranging from 55 to 80 miles an hour. The caravan of police cars, lights flashing and sirens wailing, pursuing the white Hyundai, all came to rest in a

Source: Prepared especially for *Community Policing: Contemporary Readings* by Jack R. Greene. Excerpted from Jack R. Greene (1997) *Partnerships for Community Policing: Building Public Safety Confidence in Los Angeles: A Monograph.* Washington DC: National Institute of Justice.

middle class section of the San Fernando Valley called Lake View Terrace. There King pulled over and stopped; his car was immediately surrounded by Los Angeles and California Highway Patrol police cars.

Residents of the Mountain-Back Apartments came to their balconies, drawn by the noise and spectacle of the events that were unfolding. More than twenty residents watched the beating of Rodney King. One, George Holiday, also awakened by the commotion of the night, reached for his new video camera and, from his balcony in the Mountain-Back Apartments, filmed an event which would become the unraveling of the LAPD.

The King incident opened the less-than-healed wounds of many across America; wounds accumulated in the face of years of perceived police intolerance and abuse. Many, if not most, of these wounds were sustained in minority communities. The communities of south central Los Angeles had complained about police practices for many years. The Holiday tape was, for them, a vindication of the extent to which the LAPD was apart from, not a part of, these neighborhoods.

In the aftermath of the trials of the LAPD officers charged with beating King, the riots which ensued from the initial Simi Valley verdict, the trial of Rodney King, and the subsequent federal trial and conviction of the police officers accused of beating King; the LAPD had been exposed as a rather aloof, impatient and highly defensive organization. Once the symbol of professional policing in America, the LAPD by 1991 was seen as something to be distanced from; no longer the symbol of perfection, but rather the object of disdain and derision. The LAPD had fallen from the mountain; it was revealed as duplicitous and as having betrayed the very professional ideals it had come to embody.

Placed in historical context, however, the Rodney King incident and its subsequent impact on the LAPD must be understood as the effect of a long history and practice of the Los Angeles police—a history which distanced the LAPD from the very democratic principles they sought to "protect and serve." "Getting back to the basics," then, for the Los Angeles Police Department, meant overcoming a long and internally treasured tradition of policing; a tradition emphasizing the LAPD as in control of itself and the city of Los Angeles, and a tradition emphasizing the social and political independence of the LAPD from its constituents.

The Police, Legitimacy and Change

Policing in the United States has gone through several transformations since its inception. Throughout these transformations, American policing has been continually concerned with establishing civic legitimacy. As Walker (1977:14) indicated:

> To carry out effectively any of their various assignments, the authority of the police must be generally accepted by the public as legitimate. The crux of the American police problem has long been the fact that the legitimacy of the po-

lice is so often challenged rather than accepted. From this issue alone stems some of the most serious and long-standing problems in American policing.

Generally speaking, three factors must be present for the police to establish legitimacy. First, the police and policing must be seen as tied to overarching constitutional processes. The police must be seen as "of the law." Second, police and policing must at least maintain the pretext that they are independent of local politics. Third, the police and policing must be seen as one of the central means of producing order in society.

In Los Angeles for many years, the police and policing lacked one or more of these essential features necessary to establish police legitimacy. Prior to the 1940s, the LAPD was seen as no less politically influenced as other police departments. The source of the politics was perhaps different, but the idea that the Los Angeles Police Department was intimately caught up in the political leadership of the city was generally undisputed.

The LAPD was also shaped by the political eras the city of Los Angeles went through, as well as the personalities of several "strong willed" chiefs of police that governed the LAPD. Each of these chiefs, interacting with the LAPD political environment, greatly shaped the department and its "openness" to outside criticism, often interpreted as "political interference."

The Polis, Police and Politics

Policing is intimately tied to the political structure and process within any given community (Wilson, 1978). Whether the police distribute or redistribute values in society, they are seen as a major force shaping local communities. At the same time, these communities, directly and indirectly through the political process, shape the police service. In a reciprocal relationship with the political process, the police also shape local political structures, institutions and processes.

For years, the leadership of the LAPD sought to de-couple the political process from the administration of the department. This was primarily accomplished through the enforcement of a strict "hands-off" policy that emphasized that anyone (politician or civic leader) who wanted to review or otherwise oversee the department did so with great peril. This posture was facilitated by the fact that the chiefs of the Los Angeles Police Department enjoyed essentially "lifetime" tenure in their position. With such protection in place, L.A.'s chiefs were often outspokenly defiant of the local Los Angeles political process. Such actions served to further distance the police department from the governance of the city (see Skolnick and Fyfe, 1993).

The chiefs of the LAPD had established a fiction that they and their department were above reproach and apolitical. As Tony Bouza, former police chief in Minneapolis suggests, "the chief's selection is a political act, and virtually everything the chief undertakes can have political implications" (1990:42). To suggest that policing and local politics are not intimately intertwined is to ignore the history of American policing. Much of that history has been centered upon "taking the politics" out of policing, as if this is actually possible. What can perhaps be accomplished is limiting the effect of partisan politics in police policy and decision making. But as Wilson notes:

> . . . police work is carried out under the influence of a political culture though not necessarily under day-to-day political direction. By political culture is meant those widely shared expectations as to how issues will be raised, governmental objectives determined, and power for their attainment assembled; it is an understanding of what makes a government legitimate. (1978:233)

While the central theme of distancing the LAPD from local politics was originally aimed at professionalizing the police, its long term effects ironically made the police chiefs of Los Angeles important political power brokers. Depoliticizing the LAPD had the major consequence of casting chiefs such as William Parker, Ed Davis, and Daryl Gates as political figures within Los Angeles. Politics was alive and well in Los Angeles, but the direction of influence was more from the police department to the political system rather than from the political system to the department. This shaped both the political independence and political arrogance of the LAPD, and it significantly reduced political oversight over the LAPD. The LAPD was accountable to itself, not necessarily to the city of Los Angeles.

Ultimately, the city of Los Angeles passed a referendum to put term limits on the office of the chief of police. Willie L. Williams was the first chief of the LAPD in modern times to serve under such an arrangement. Unlike his predecessors who had no external "bosses," Williams was quick to find that he had many, including the mayor, the police commission, the public safety committee of the city council, as well as each city council member in Los Angeles. Ironically, Williams was the only person within the LAPD without lifetime tenure, as his subordinate command officers all had civil service protection. Where Williams' reforms were resisted, there were few tools available to him to restructure the internal politics of the LAPD.

The Environment as a Catalyst for Change

Built on a conservative foundation, policing is continually stressed by the external environment in ways which actually reshape police services and police organizations. As part of the change process, these environments play an important role in continuing to pressure the central police organization for change. The Los Angeles community (social and business), while having opinions and beliefs about the LAPD, was not prepared for the King incident and the subsequent riots after the first trial of the officers charged with beating King.

The environment within Los Angeles in the 1992 post-riot period called for sweeping changes within the LAPD. The Christopher Commission Report suggested that the LAPD had historically mistreated minority group residents, that the internal culture of the LAPD was racist and sexist, and that supervision of the police was lax and poorly exercised. Moreover, the Christopher Commission reported that the LAPD had a "siege mentality," had distanced itself from the public who the department saw as hostile, and had created a system of policing that was detached and brutal. This report and the subsequent attention paid to the LAPD in the national, and indeed, international media, placed the city and the LAPD under extreme pressure to adopt a differing style of policing—one emphasizing greater police and community cooperation.

Policing as Symbolic Communication

Policing is intensely value laden. The police see themselves as the "good guys" who often must wrestle power from the "bad guys" who would ultimately destroy the community if left to their own devices. This fundamental value struggle has produced great symbolism within police agencies and these symbols, in turn, greatly shape the culture of the police.

The Los Angeles Police Department, even at the height of its strength, numbered only about 8,000 police officers who were responsible for policing nearly 3.5 million people over an area of approximately 450 square miles. In comparison to many eastern cities the police to population ratio in Los Angeles was considerably smaller. In addition, the LAPD had long pursued a policy of specialization within the patrol force, such that the actual number of police officers who were actually assigned to patrol was only about 25 percent of the uniformed force within the LAPD. The relatively small size of the department in relation to the population and area for which it was attempting to provide police services, coupled with an overreliance on specialization, resulted in the reality and perception that the department was under siege in terms of workload.

Symbolism within the LAPD emphasized the "crime fighter" or "warrior" values upon which the department had been built. Internal belief systems emphasized that the department was "outgunned" and "out-manned," and that to keep any semblance of order in the city, the LAPD had to adopt an aggressive, "in your face" style of policing. Proactive policing in Los Angeles meant the continuation of practices that had been in the culture of the LAPD since James Davis was chief. Aggressive street tactics, chokeholds, and other violence prone activities were seen as modus operandi of the LAPD.

The department's symbols also called for group loyalty and honor. The Rodney King video tapes caused great strain in loyalty systems, and further fueled the "siege" mentality ascribed to the department. Perhaps more importantly, the LAPD's culture was inwardly directed; the city and the community had little to tell the LAPD. This deeply seated cultural value was directly challenged in the aftermath of the King incident and the 1992 South Central riot.

Enter Reform

In 1992 Willie L. Williams was appointed as chief of police in Los Angeles. Williams, the former police commissioner in Philadelphia, was selected from among several internal and external candidates for the position. Prior to Williams appointment there was a very public and rather acrimonious fight between then Chief Daryl Gates, the mayor and city council of Los Angeles, and advocates for Gates' ouster from the Christopher Commission (1991) which had issued a report on the Rodney King incident. At issue was the tenure of the chief of police in Los Angeles. Gates' public position was that by appointing the chief for a number of years, and then reviewing the department and its performance, the Los Angeles Police Department would be captured and manipulated by the political environment—a situation that Gates, and many chiefs before him, publicly resisted. The LAPD had seen itself as "apolitical" and the arrangement proposed for any successor to Gates was seen as "re-politicizing" the LAPD.

The opposite view, that offered by the mayor, the city council, the Christopher Commission, and many national police leaders, was that the LAPD needed to become accountable for its actions and the level and kinds of police services it provided to Angelenos. To be accountable, it was argued, meant that the head of the LAPD—its chief—should be appointed and confirmed by those within Los Angeles who were elected to pursue the "public's will." While it was recognized that the chief of the LAPD needed some job security (ultimately determined to be a five year contract, renewable for two terms), the chief and the department could no longer distance themselves from political oversight. Much of this discussion was aired in the local media, with many outside of the department calling for Gates' resignation, while many within the department were concerned that such an action would effectively throw the LAPD to the "political wolves." In the end, Gates resigned and the city of Los Angeles adopted policies for the review of its chief of police and the LAPD.

Williams, of course, arrived in Los Angeles in both the best and worst of times. It was the best of times to the extent that the LAPD had nowhere to go but up in the eyes of the public. Angelenos were shocked by the actions of the LAPD in 1991 and in the public struggle for the chief of police position. Moreover, they were quite anxious about the fate of their city. In the aftermath of the 1992 L.A. riots, many feared they had lost control of the city. They looked to Williams to return the peace and stability to a Los Angeles that was fearful of renewed civil strife.

It was the worse of times to the extent that Williams found himself in a politically conflicted organization with a history of internal division, politicking among command officers, and having a rather demoralized workforce which had been tainted with the broad brush of public criticism stemming from the Rodney King incident. Many command officers resented the idea that it took someone from the outside, and from an east-coast city long known for its politicism of the police, to lead the LAPD out of its problems. These resentments also stemmed from the fact that Williams' presence also cast some doubt on the ability of the LAPD to reform itself from the inside, necessitating this external appointment. Some resentments, no doubt, stemmed from the belief among some that this outsider chief was essentially imposed on them by the local politicians—thereby confirming their worst expectations, that the LAPD would be thrust into the center of the political process.

Nonetheless, Willie L. Williams became the first African American to head the Los Angeles Police Department, perhaps in its time of greatest need. Not representing the philosophy or history of the LAPD, Williams was to struggle with the department for nearly five years. Ultimately, Williams was forced from office; the LAPD and several political leaders within Los Angeles ultimately reasserted control over the department. Nonetheless, several important reforms were implemented, moving the LAPD along the road to community policing.

The LAPD-NIJ Partnership in Reform

In October of 1992, the Los Angeles Police Department received a "Partnerships for Community Policing" grant from the National Institute of Justice (NIJ). The grant concentrated on three objectives; first, the creation of a long-range strategic plan to provide a strategic vision and organizational value system to support community and problem-oriented policing; second, the revitalization of the department's Basic Car Plan, the central mechanism for police service delivery in Los Angeles; and third, the strengthening of the department's capacity to interact with the communities it serves, thereby creating a civic link between the LAPD and its many and varied constituents.

A series of processes were designed and implemented within the Los Angeles Police Department to accomplish the broad goals of the NIJ sponsored effort. These processes required that the Los Angeles Police Department examine closely its values and ethical premises, craft a mission statement, integrate the mission statement and values into tangible training and operational programs, build and reinforce the need for internal trust and team-centered behavior, craft a strategic vision and plan for the Los Angeles Police Department as it moves into the twenty-first century, and create and sustain an ongoing, collaborative and trusting relationship with the residents and businesses of the city of Los Angeles. All of this effort had the central objective of providing high quality, effective police services in Los Angeles, a police service emphasizing community-oriented policing.

Strategic Planning in the LAPD

Leadership patterns within the Los Angeles Police Department often relegated strategic planning as unnecessary. For nearly fifty years, the LAPD had been managed by strong, individualistic leaders—leaders who took charge of their department, cast it in their own image, and vigorously defended it from outside intrusion. While the LAPD had instituted all types of operational and contingency plans—some of which were called "battle plans"—by 1993 it had never published and disseminated a strategic plan to the Los Angeles community.

The leadership of the Los Angeles Police Department generally guided the department over the years by adhering to several commonly held principles within the LAPD. Among these principles was:

- a rather tough departmental stance on police corruption, but not on issues of police use of force;

- the conduct of a police agency that saw itself out-gunned and out-manned, necessitating an aggressive, "in-your face," policing style;

- the creation of a system of police management that actively distanced itself from its public and from political actors;

- the creation of an internal "power" system based on loyalty and to a certain extent "fear of reprisal"; and

- the maintenance of the LAPD's image as a "professional" police department.

These values shaped police activities and responses in Los Angeles and ultimately produced the "crisis of confidence" exhibited toward the LAPD after the Rodney King incident. The "veneer of professionalism" had worn thin for the LAPD, and many "publics" demanded a more accountable police management. Perhaps more importantly, those within the LAPD, particularly rank-and-file police officers, were demanding more from their leaders. Many, for example, felt that in the aftermath of the riots of 1992 their departmental leadership had let them down by not being present to better direct the actions of the police in the field. Obviously the community felt let down by the LAPD for its general inability to control the riot situation and for producing some of the circumstances which led to the riots.

Another part of the reason for an absence of strategic thinking within the LAPD is related to the general absence of such activities within most American police departments prior to the mid-1980s (Williams et al. 1993). As line-focused institutions, police agencies throughout America have been almost singularly concerned with tactical matters. Moreover, police leaders were not seen as policy makers as much as they were viewed as managers and administrators. The old adage, "we don't make the law, we just enforce it" gave police managers, including those within the LAPD, a way of distancing themselves from policy making. Their job was to administer their departments; policy making was often deferred to legislatures, city councils, mayors and the like. Such a focus often obviated the perceived need for long-range planning. In fact, the basic mission of the LAPD, as well as other police agencies, seems invariant—to serve and protect. Who to serve and who to protect, of course, is much less clear. The existence of a general policy "orthodoxy" demanded little from police managers in the way of policy making. As Moore and Stephens (1991:3) suggest:

What the traditional orthodoxy does not expect, much less demand, from police executives is any reconsideration of the basic mission of the organization,
or proposals of new ways of using the organization to meet challenges currently facing society. These are matters of policy—not administration or
management.

Yet another part of the reason for the absence of formalized strategic
planning within the LAPD prior to 1993 is no doubt related to the leadership
patterns that characterized the LAPD for a half century. Beginning with August
Vollmer and continuing through to Daryl Gates, the chiefs of the Los Angeles
Police Department were, for the most part, singularly focused on distancing the
police department from its political and social environments (see Domanick,
1995). The "thin blue line" mentality, coupled with a suspiciousness of external
"interference" with the LAPD proved to be useful tools in separating the department from municipal oversight. They were also tools that made strategic planning
unnecessary as well.

Creating a Mission Statement and Core Values
for the Los Angeles Police Department

All organizations, but perhaps most particularly service-oriented organizations
like police departments, pursue tangible and intangible goals and objectives. The
police produce arrests, car and pedestrian stops, and crimes solved, among other
things, as part of their tangible products to the public. They also produce a sense
of order, safety and fairness within communities; services that are considerably
symbolic and value laden. In some instances the symbols the police produce can
be negative and socially damaging as well. For example, if communities come to
see the police as an "occupying force," then meaningful interaction between the
police and the community is likely inhibited by the negative symbols the police
may project. Because of the mix of tangible and intangible products produced by
the police, their objectives and internal values need to be made explicit. Making
organizational missions and values explicit is important for several reasons.

Statements of organizational missions and values provide community and
political leaders with a clearer picture of where their police department is going,
its goals and objectives and its attachment to the wider political and social structure. By making missions and goals clear, police agencies can help to condition
external expectations and increase their accountability to local constituents, while
at the same time providing a point of access for input in defining the direction and
future of the local police agency.

As one of the first steps in organizational renewal, the Los Angeles Police
Department put into place several emphases which examined organizational
values and missions. For many years, the department's motto, "to serve and
protect," had been supported by a set of management principles that had been
created under the administration of Chief Ed Davis. These management principles

outlined the more generalized goals and objectives of the LAPD. They were created in the mid-1970s and had not been re-evaluated for a considerable period of time. Perhaps more importantly, while the management principles outlined in the Davis administration may have been appropriate at the time they were written, they were not very salient in the day-to-day management of the LAPD by 1991. Simply put, the LAPD had gone for years without an internal examination of its values and missions, being driven by the more centralized command process that had grown over the years within the LAPD.

During the fall of 1992 each command officer within the LAPD was surveyed about organizational values and missions. These surveys focused on the command officers' personal ratings of organizational values in comparison to those values identified in the larger sample of employees. This process was extended to involve the immediate subordinates of each command officer, pushing the discussion of core values downward throughout the LAPD. Of particular concern in all of these surveys was the commitment of the individual to the core value presented.

Finally, feedback was provided in the form of individual discussions with LAPD command officers, as well as a two-day values clarification workshop for the entire command staff in June of 1993. At this workshop the command staff began the process of adopting a series of core values which were later printed by the LAPD and distributed throughout the department. Beginning in the summer of 1993 and continuing throughout 1994 command officers were expected to continue the process of transmitting the core values throughout the department by hosting staff and community meetings to build more consensus for the LAPD values statement.

Implementing LAPD Strategic Planning Committees

As part of the process of increasing both familiarity with and use of strategic planning concepts within the Los Angeles Police Department, eight ad hoc strategic planning committees were created. These groups focused on strategic issues identified by the LAPD senior command staff at a three-day retreat in November of 1993.

The purpose of these strategic planning groups was to identify strategic issues, prioritize these issues and then make recommendations about how the LAPD should address the prioritized issues. Groups were composed of command personnel and senior civilian managers within the LAPD. They also included rank-and-file police officers and civilian employees. They were augmented by staff support from various units across the department as well. These groups began their deliberations in November, 1993 and continued until their presentation of strategic issues and recommendations in November, 1994.

Each ad hoc strategic initiative committee had from twenty-five to forty members; in all, eighty-four of the LAPD's senior leadership participated in this strategic planning and development process and a total of approximately three hundred LAPD employees participated on these committees or their sub-committees. Participants were provided information about the interviews with community members and employees, as well as key stakeholder interviews that were also conducted (see below). As this information became available, it was used as a source of input and feedback for these groups. Further, considerable time was focused within the strategic planning seminar on the product(s) to be achieved from this effort. A timetable for committee deliberations and reporting was also created to ensure that the strategic planning process actually came to a conclusion. The results of these deliberations were presented by each group at a two-day retreat held in November, 1994. This information became the basis of forming the LAPD's first strategic plan.

Collecting Information Through Focus Groups

In addition to building internal Los Angeles Police Department consensus about the goals and objectives of the department among senior commanders, the strategic planning process also needed considerable information from two important groups—the community and the rank-and-file police and civilian employees within the LAPD. Perhaps for too long, neither of these groups had been consulted much about the direction of the department, its services and the value (or lack thereof) of internal decision making and external service delivery. To overcome this information shortage, two types of focus groups were conducted—one on community needs and concerns, and the other on LAPD employee concerns. For the LAPD to become community and problem-oriented, it was clear that information from the consumers and producers of police services in Los Angeles was a necessary condition preceding any significant organizational revision.

Community Focus Groups. To facilitate community input, a total of eighteen community focus group meetings were conducted; one at each of the department's eighteen area commands. A total of 390 community members, including youth, participated in the eighteen community focus group meetings, for an average meeting attendance of approximately twenty-two people. The community focus groups were generally representative of the communities each area served. They included community residents, business leaders, civic and religious leaders, and youth.

While there was variation across the eighteen geographic areas in terms of community concerns for crime, safety and LAPD performance, four topics were consistently ranked as having a high level of community concern. They included: increased numbers and visibility of officers on the street; fast response time to radio calls; increased emphasis on gang problems; and increased emphasis on drug problems. Other highly ranked expectations made by these community focus groups included the need for the LAPD and the media to work more closely together, the need for greater curfew enforcement, the need for more consistent enforcement of the law across the city of Los Angeles, increased enforcement of alcohol related laws, and the need to keep police officers within communities for a longer period of time so that they might get to "know" the community and its problems. Community evaluation of the LAPD's level of performance on these issues characterized performance as below average. Perhaps most telling in this community assessment was the fact that in only four of the ratings made across the eighteen areas did the Los Angeles Police Department receive a rating of above average.

What is interesting in the responses provided through these community focus groups is the degree to which the community had learned what might be considered preferred police responses to external criticism—such as, we need more police, high visibility and faster police responses. And, indeed, the patterns of responses obtained from these community focus groups potentially reflect such biases. Prior to the King incident and its aftermath in Los Angeles, the city of Los Angeles had negotiated with the police department a formula for police deployment that is linked to these community perceptions. The "7/40 Plan" as it had become known, was aimed at getting an average of seven minutes in police response to calls for service, while maintaining approximately 40 percent of the officers' time as available for preventive activities. This plan had received wide attention within the Los Angeles community.

Unfortunately, the actual deployment of Los Angeles police officers fell considerably short of the staffing plan that the department had determined as minimal. As a result, L.A. residents were concerned that they were being underserved by their police department. In addition to this generalized perception about police services in Los Angeles, the Rodney King incident and the South Central riots had indeed heightened public concern with civil disorder. Some of the community responses were no doubt related to this heightened anxiety about crime and public order in Los Angeles. Finally, preceding these community focus groups had been at least a year of public discussion about the LAPD and its new chief, Willie L. Williams, an outsider to the department who promised to make the department kinder and gentler, and who was also seen as bringing some civility back to the LAPD.

Employee Focus Groups. As part of the Los Angeles Police Department's strategic planning efforts to create and adopt a strategic planning process, focus groups were also conducted with employees throughout the LAPD. Over a period of two weeks, a total of nine employee focus groups were conducted within the department. Department-wide representation was assured by selecting both police and civilian employees to participate in these focus groups. Group participation was voluntary, although individuals included within groups were randomly selected, reflecting the LAPD's workforce, both civilian and police officers.

Across all nine groups, five employee concerns were consistently identified as in need of LAPD attention. They were: better equipment and facilities; increased personnel strength; promotional consideration—merit and ability; improved morale; and modified work schedules. Other important expectations raised by these employee focus groups included the need to streamline/improve administrative procedures and practices (e.g., consolidate forms and paperwork, revamp the rating system, standardize employee evaluation), allow participative management (e.g., give greater employee input, create an internal organizational climate of commitment, be honest in where the department is heading), treat discipline between line officers and management in a similar manner, and increase opportunities for training and career development.

Generally speaking, the employees participating in these focus groups were not impressed with the LAPD's performance on these and related issues. In all of the comparisons and evaluations made by LAPD employees, the department was evaluated as average in only two cases, with the remainder of employee evaluations characterizing the department as having below average performance on most of the employee concerns.

The employee focus groups directed their attention almost entirely to the internal matters within the LAPD. In fact the top five needs as perceived by the employees participating in this process were focused on improvements to their sense of morale and to what might be termed "conditions of work," e.g., better equipment, modified work schedules and the like. Such responses might be expected from persons who saw themselves as being part of a neglected workforce. That is to say, throughout the process of conducting employee focus groups it was clear that many in the LAPD felt rather disenfranchised from their own organization. The department's rather oppressive management system had virtually left most of its employees "out of the loop." Moreover, while the LAPD enjoyed a national reputation for being "America's Finest," inside the LAPD the veneer of being a professional police department was worn thin.

Interviews with Key Stakeholders

As part of the process of assessing the LAPD, a series of interviews were conducted with several "key" stakeholders—persons external to the LAPD who were community and political opinion leaders, elected officials, and persons who had an oversight role in regard to the department itself (e.g., the mayor, city council, and the police commission). The intent of these interviews was to garner information about the department through the eyes of persons who shape policy and opinion about the department.

These interviews produced information similar to the community focus groups. Key decision makers saw the LAPD as in need of significant internal and public relations revision. The department's credibility had been significantly damaged in the wake of the Rodney King incident and the South Central riot, and the department needed to make significant improvements in its external relations with the civic and business communities. Further, the city of Los Angeles had considerable "fear" of future civil disturbance and associated disruptive behavior. Over this period of time, the federal trial of the officers accused of the King beating was taking place, as was the trial of the men accused of assaulting Reginald Denny, the truck driver whose beating was captured "live" as it happened shortly after the Simi Valley decision regarding the accused LAPD officers was announced. These ongoing remembrances of the possibility of future civil unrest, coupled with a more generalized concern with violent, gang-related crime in Los Angeles, called for the department to balance the community's need for a "sense of order" with "working within the law."

For the most part, these external key stakeholders also felt the LAPD was understaffed and needed to recruit and retain more police officers. Most agreed that the model of "community-based policing" emerging in the department was the appropriate way for the department to be heading, although some were impatient with the progress of the department in making significant changes.

Leadership Development within the Los Angeles Police Department

A central need in the strategic revision of the Los Angeles Police Department was the creation of a leadership ethic within the department that was less structured around rank differences. Of particular concern in 1993 was the idea that, for all purposes, the command staff of the LAPD received little advanced management training as part of their professional development. While several members of the LAPD command staff have participated in the California Police Officers Standards and Training (POST) Command College, there was little concerted effort to build a senior management development capacity within the LAPD until early 1992.

In its review of leadership issues within the Los Angeles Police Department, representatives of the West Point Leadership Institute reported that the LAPD was in need of significant organizational overhaul if they were to realize their goal of implementing community oriented and problem-solving policing throughout the department:

> Our initial assessment suggests community-based/problem-oriented policing will demand real changes in the way police officers at all levels perform their jobs. These changes, in turn, have definite implications for leadership. Furthermore, such human resource subsystems as recruitment and selection, performance appraisal, promotion, education and development, etc., must be modified to support these critical operational changes. Simply designing and implementing a leadership education and development plan will accomplish little unless supported by concomitant organizational changes. . . .To design and implement a comprehensive leadership education and development program that supports community-based/problem-solving policing in the absence of a coordinated, systemic change plan will not be in the best interests of the LAPD. The consequence would be a high cost, low impact endeavor.[1]

The West Point Leadership Institute Report outlined a comprehensive plan for such organizational conversion by suggesting, among other things, that the LAPD precede its program development with a full-scale leadership analysis, analyze its existing organizational culture, design programs to modify that culture, and implement a system of leadership education and development as part of a broader human resource development program. Aspects of the recommendations made by the West Point Leadership Institute have formed the basis of a Command Officers Training Program developed and implemented through the office of the director of organizational development.

The Strategic Plan

Entitled "Commitment to Action,"[2] the LAPD's first publicly announced strategic plan outlined a future for the department and for the public safety needs of the city of Los Angeles. The strategic plan outlines not only the goals and objectives of the LAPD over the period, 1994 through 1999, but also describes in some detail the process the LAPD employed to involve the community, LAPD employees, key stakeholders, and the LAPD command staff. Further, a brief accounting of the department's accomplishments in moving toward a more open and accessible style of policing in Los Angeles is provided. The strategic plan is divided into three major strategic directions: serving the community, serving our employees, and ensuring adequate resources, within which goals and subgoals are determined. In all, a total of thirty-two goals are identified within the strategic plan. These goals are accompanied by statements of the department's strategic vision—the mission and values statements are reviewed, as was the process of strategic planning identified by the LAPD. These goals are accompanied by twenty-six first-year objectives; ways the LAPD and its constituents can identify the department's movement and progress.

Revitalization of the Basic Car Plan

The Basic Car Plan was organized as a police response system based primarily on calls for police service, mediated in part by the need to assure the continuity of police services in any particular area of Los Angeles. The Basic Car Plan was implemented in 1969, by Police Chief Ed Davis. As Davis suggested, "The objective of the plan was to help society prevent crime by improving community attitudes towards the police, providing stability of assignment in the deployment of street policemen, and instilling in each team of officers a proprietary interest in their assigned area and a better knowledge of the police role in the community" (Davis, 1978).

Basic Cars were staffed by nine police officers. The plan was seen as a primary vehicle for fixing responsibility for police services with the Basic Car. The

Basic Car was the primary response unit in the area. Patrol officers assigned to a Basic Car, generally coordinated by a senior lead officer, would patrol their area and develop relationships with the public that would lead to better police and citizen "co-production" of police services. The senior lead officer (SLO) was seen as the "team leader," the person who coordinated the activities of the other officers assigned to the Basic Car. This program was intended to increase police responsiveness within the Basic Car area by making the assigned officers more accountable for their area. Over time, it was expected that the officers would come to develop a sense of "ownership" for the communities they policed. Similarly, it was anticipated that the community, too, would develop a sense of "ownership" for the police in the Basic Car.

In many respects, the Basic Car Plan of the LAPD in the late 1960s and early 1970s had most, if not all, the elements of today's community and problem-oriented policing. There was fixed responsibility in police assignment to communities, a mechanism for the police to communicate with the public, and a "method" to solve community problems, all bundled up within the LAPD's Basic Car. Unfortunately, the rhetoric and reality of the Basic Car were quite different. In an assessment of the LAPD's "team policing efforts," Sherman and his colleagues (1973) found that the concept was poorly implemented in Los Angeles as well as in other cities. The result was that much of the effort was not seen as particularly successful.

Over the years, the idea of the Basic Car being central to the Los Angeles Police Department's patrol response got lost along the way. For many years, the LAPD expanded patrol specializations to the point where it was difficult to actually staff the Basic Cars as they were intended. Moreover, shifts in population and a phenomenal growth in the greater southern California area between 1970 and 1980 resulted in Basic Cars attempting to service populations for which they were ill-equipped. Computer-aided dispatch (CAD) systems introduced into the LAPD also greatly contributed to the lack of integrity of the Basic Car Plan. CAD's central goal was to dispose of calls for service. To do so officers were often sent across Basic Car Areas thereby defeating the purpose of maintaining beat integrity. In the face of increased patrol specialization within the LAPD, the number of persons actually assigned to the Basic Car Plan had itself diminished. This often resulted in an inability to actually staff the current Basic Car Plan, adding to the dilution of the idea that there was indeed a Basic Car. Such circumstances made the revision of the LAPD's Basic Car Plan a strategic and operational necessity. This was particularly the case if any form of community and problem-oriented policing was to be re-introduced into the Los Angeles Police Department.

Redesigning the Basic Car Plan. During the ongoing research, three major strategies were employed in the revitalization of basic police services in the city of Los Angeles. The three strategies involved: (1) creating a vision of the LAPD that emphasized a style of policing focused on community-based problem solving approaches to public safety; (2) improving police services through a major revision of the Basic Car Plan itself; and (3) improved problem-solving training and support for Basic Cars in the city of Los Angeles. These three strategies assisted the transition of the Los Angeles Police Department from a "professional"and rather detached police agency to a "community-oriented" police agency, one focused on working with communities to resolve persistent community crime and disorder problems.

Adopting a Community-Oriented Style of Policing in Los Angeles. In January, 1993, the chief of police of the LAPD created a committee on community-based policing. The committee was chaired by an area commanding officer who had distinguished himself as being community oriented, and who was a strong community-oriented policing advocate within the LAPD. The Community-Based Policing Committee was tasked with among other things, the development of an LAPD definition of community policing—a definition that would serve the ends of the department well as it made its transition toward a more open system of policing. The committee held meetings for about three months and involved several LAPD personnel from both the command and rank-and-file levels of the organization.

The committee's work received considerable discussion at implementation meetings. There were command officers who wanted more clarity in the definition and those who saw the definition as either too broadly or narrowly stated. Another line of concern in this discussion was with the idea of community policing itself. Some felt that the idea had "too much baggage" in that it had become both a rallying point for those who would support and those who would oppose change within the Los Angeles Police Department. There were also strong alliances to the prior definition of community policing advanced in the Gates administration. That definition was caught up in the language and symbolism of "total quality management" (TQM) and there were several commanders who were particularly enamored with this approach. They, of course, wanted the language of TQM and "service excellence" continued in the discussion of L.A.'s version of community policing. There was also some ideological conflict in the department's consideration of competing definitions of community policing. One group saw the general ideas of "community" driving this model, while others were more focused on how the organization "managed" its services (the TQM approach). Still others were concerned that many community policing programs across the country had "left crime out of the mix" in defining the relationship between the police and the public. These concerns had been discussed in the Community-Based Policing Committee's deliberations, and to some extent they were reflected in the "working definition" that emerged from the committee.

It was not until late summer of 1993 that a more generalized definition of community policing emerged from the Los Angeles Police Department.

> Community Policing is a partnership between the police and the community.
> It is a partnership in which the police and the community share responsibility
> for identifying, reducing, eliminating and preventing problems which impact

the community. By working together, the police and the community can reduce the fear and incidence of crime and improve the quality of life in the
community. In this effort the community and police, as partners, identify and
prioritize problems of crime and disorder and share responsibility for development and implementation of proactive problem-solving strategies to address the identified issues. The strategies used combine the efforts and
resources of the police, the community and local government.[3]

This definition of community policing was accompanied by a discussion of four
key elements that further operationalized community policing in the city of Los
Angeles. Those four key community policing[4] elements were:

Problem Solving: Problem solving challenges officers and community members
to think creatively and supports the use of innovative, non-traditional methods
of policing. It employs effective law enforcement tactics, yet also relies upon
increased cooperation and commitment of the community and other government resources. The department's model of problem solving is community-
police problem solving (C-PPS).

Partnership with the Community: Community policing recognizes the importance of including community members in the decision-making processes that
identify problems, develop solutions to these problems and that involve the
community in responsibly solving these problems. Neighborhood organizations and community-police advisory boards (C-PABs) provide the vehicle
for this interaction with the Los Angeles Police Department.

Community Identified Problems: The traditional model of policing took on a role
where the police determined the policing priorities for their communities.
Community policing recognizes that the community must have input into that
process. Often, the problems identified by the police do not coincide with the
visible quality of life problems which cause the decay of neighborhoods.
Community policing ensures the police serve the specific needs of the community.

Department-Wide Orientation: Community policing is a philosophy that tran-
scends the entire organization. All department entities act to support our
community policing efforts. Decision making is pushed down to the service
level. The organization becomes more decentralized, flexible and supportive
as we encourage risk taking, and empower our sworn and civilian employees
to make decisions. Everyone has "ownership" in community policing's
success.

Perhaps the significance of this definition and operationalization of community
policing within the Los Angeles Police Department is its challenge for police officers and other LAPD employees to "take risks" and to make decisions. In an
organization that prided itself on following the chain of command and where stories of punishment for not obeying orders abounded, the shift to community
policing as outlined in the department's definitions directly competed with more

latent control struggles that were continually underway throughout the two and one-half years of this planned change effort.

Rebuilding the Basic Car Plan

Patrol has always been described as the "backbone" of policing. That is, there is general agreement that the quality of patrol services either makes or breaks the reputation of any police service. This recognition, however, has not always found its application in policing. All too often, patrol is the last place where resources are invested, and the first place from which they are taken. This is true in Los Angeles as it is in other cities. This is probably more true of Los Angeles which has very closely adhered to Wilson's (1978) "legalistic" style of policing, complete with a great emphasis on operational specialization and "attacking" crime. This was supported by internal promotional and pay schedules that actually rewarded specialized and not "street level" police officers. The philosophy and the day-to-day operational and administrative practices of the LAPD had the practical implication of actually reducing the number of persons assigned to basic patrol services in Los Angeles.

In 1992, the Los Angeles Police Department provided services to a population of over three and one-half million people, dispersed over 467 square miles lined by 6,491 miles of streets and freeways. The LAPD received over 5 million calls for police service or other forms of assistance, of which 938,066 received one or more dispatched police vehicles. Of all dispatches, 338,542 were determined to be serious Part 1 crimes.[5] The LAPD, during this same time period, made 50,355 adult arrests for Part 1 offenses and 124,215 adult arrests for other offenses. The department in 1992 also made 11,291 juvenile arrests for Part 1 offenses and 12,642 juvenile arrests for juvenile lesser serious offenses. The sheer volume of calls for service and serious crime by 1992 were overwhelming those assigned to patrol within the LAPD.

To better understand the shift of the LAPD from a "professional" to a "community-oriented" police department, the command staff of the department had to confront the issue of how basic patrol services were to be provided across Los Angeles. For years, the LAPD had become an organization of specialists, inventing one acronym after another in refining organizational specialization. The consequence of this pattern of specialization within the Los Angeles Police Department was a slow but gradual movement away from the Basic Car as the central police service delivery mechanism.

By the early 1990s, Basic Cars were seen as overworked and understaffed. For over twenty years, the Basic Car system in Los Angeles had gone unanalyzed and by 1993 was in need of significant revision. In a review of police deployment, Public Administration Service (PAS), a consultant to the LAPD on matters of police deployment, indicated that compared to a prior analysis of calls for service and field deployment, the LAPD's field strength, as measured by number of response units fielded, actually declined between 1988 and 1992.[6]

In 1993, the eighteen geographic patrol areas began a process to re-examine patrol deployment throughout the city of Los Angeles. The Basic Car Realignment Project, as this effort became known, involved several important analytic and policy shifts within the Los Angeles Police Department. First, commanders at all levels were required to "map" their patrol areas on several dimensions. Of primary concern was the identification of "natural communities and neighborhoods," that is, communities and neighborhoods defined on the basis of "common characteristics or interests . . . These common characteristics and interests included: culture, ethnicity, race, age, language, religion, economic status and life style."[7] Area commanders were also instructed to include input from several local sources such as community groups, as well as their senior lead officers, who are charged with community liaison responsibilities under the Basic Car Plan.

The identification of "natural communities" was charted for all area commands. This afforded the opportunity to examine increases and shifts in population characteristics that occurred within and across area boundaries. This proved to be extremely important in several areas of Los Angeles. Los Angeles, like most major American cities, had experienced significant growth since the original Basic Car Plan had been adopted in 1969. Over the ensuing twenty-five years, Los Angeles became home to thousands of immigrants from Latin America and the Pacific Rim. The city of Los Angeles is one of the most ethnically diverse cities in the United States, and indeed, in the world. There are presently within the city of Los Angeles large enclaves of people from Central and South America, China, Korea, Viet Nam, Cambodia, Laos and Indonesia, to name a few groupings. Areas of Los Angeles are so ethnically diverse that multiple dialects and languages are commonplace. Communities also have ethnically identified local names such as Koreatown, Chinatown and Little Tokyo. Building a better understanding of these community dynamics was a central feature of the process to review and realign Basic Car services within the city of Los Angeles.

What was perhaps most important about this aspect of the realignment exercise was that a more "qualitative" assessment of what constituted communities was used to develop some understanding of the ways in which Angelenos saw their city. It would have been more convenient, perhaps, to have begun this assessment with more statistical data. But in concluding the first assessment of what constituted Los Angeles' communities in a qualitative fashion, the department maximized the potential that "communities" in their social-psychological sense would be better represented in this reapportionment of police resources. Once "natural communities" were identified by each area commander, they were directed to "validate" community boundaries with civic leaders in these communities to assure that the boundaries they had identified were consistent with the boundaries with which communities were familiar and endorsed.

Finally, area commanders were also provided area demographic information based on the 1990 Census. Data were broken down by census tract, police reporting district and bureau. These data included general population information (e.g., total families, total household, persons in group quarters, occupied housing, vacant housing, and owner/renter occupied housing), household information (e.g., married with children, male/female households not related by birth), persons in households (number, and persons per household), housing unit information (e.g., housing type—single family, duplex, multiple units, mobile homes and the like), measures of homelessness (emergency shelter populations and street visibility), person per room (measure of density in living arrangements), real estate values, individual data (e.g., age, sex and ethnicity). These data were provided on computer disk so that area commanders could examine and manipulate data relative to the communities they had identified on the basis of more commonly accepted definitions of community boundaries.

In addition to the data provided and the area command assessments of "natural neighborhoods and communities," several Basic Car "business rules"[8] were developed to assure consistency in the definition of communities and in the construction of Basic Car areas. These "business rules" guided the determination of shifts in Basic Car areas and in the resulting shifts of the number of Basic Cars in any of the LAPD's eighteen geographic area commands. Five of these "business rules" helped to ensure the integrity of the local analysis of communities and neighborhoods. First, communities were not to be split between Basic Cars. While it was acknowledged that based on workload, a community might be serviced by more than one Basic Car, the design was intent on preserving the "community" character of all Basic Car areas. Second, neighborhoods within communities were also not to be divided, using the same reasoning as for the entire Basic Car area. Third, where communities and/or neighborhoods were not identifiable, Basic Car areas were to be defined on the basis of common land use (e.g., residential, light industrial, commercial and the like). This "business rule" also required that Basic Cars not cross or split natural boundaries such as mountains or rivers, and that artificial boundaries (e.g., school yards, parks, shopping centers and the like) should also be preserved. A fourth rule required that where communities and/or neighborhoods were not identifiable, the service needs of the area would be used to help define the Basic Car area by "leveling" service demands across Basic Car areas. This included the idea that special service areas would remain intact in this assessment.

Finally, the revised "community-based cars" were to be examined in relation to the 1993 total calls for service (CFS) hours for that area. Here the concern was to balance the workload across Basic Cars so as to afford police officers in these realigned Basic Car areas enough time to practice problem-solving and other forms of proactive policing. This "balancing" of effort also considered population distribution within and across Basic Car areas. A decision rule was adopted that Basic Car areas should have an average population of 25,000 persons. Given the physical configuration of the city of Los Angeles, this resulted in several quite large areas with small population bases and a reduction in size of several inner-city areas with high density populations. Workload and crime analysis information was aggregated by reporting district and then to community. Where reporting districts were beyond community boundaries, analysis apportioned workload and calls for service between reporting districts and identified communities.

Taking the information learned from the comparison, calls for service, land use and officer safety issues into consideration, a complete remapping of all eighteen geographic areas was completed in the fall of 1994. As a result, new Basic Car boundaries consistent with natural community boundaries were established. This caused not only Basic Car boundaries to change, but also caused area boundaries to change in some areas. City-wide, sixteen additional Basic Cars were created. This amounted to an increase of some 144 additional personnel assigned to the LAPD's Basic Car system and the leveling of workload across Basic Car areas, which had grown or changed significantly over the years.

Increasing the Problem-Solving Capacity of the LAPD through Senior Lead Officers

As previously indicated, the senior lead officer was seen as a vanguard position in the adoption of a community and problem-oriented style of policing in Los Angeles. Senior lead officers were in a rather natural position for such a role, given their intended relationship to the Basic Car. Yet, an initial analysis of the role of senior lead officers across the 123 Basic Cars revealed a high degree of role confusion and dissent regarding the SLO's role within the Basic Car and the LAPD.

A review of SLOs concluded that "few of the [SLOs] are also expected to address neighborhood crime problems. Many SLOs reported that they are frequently used to support special details and other tactical operations at the cost of postponing or canceling community meetings."[9] This study concluded that few of the area commanders actually used the senior lead officers as they were originally intended; these officers were typically managed "outside of the structure of field operations"; many were not prepared or so inclined toward community and problem-oriented policing; and many felt rather estranged from the department, given their perception that they were not well connected to the rest of the patrol force. Perhaps as damaging to the relationship of the SLOs to the Basic Car was a generalized perception that "non-apprehension/suppression oriented activities are often denigrated by peers and supervisors within the LAPD so newer officers typically do not see the SLOs work as important or valuable. SLOs often feel that they have to periodically make some arrests and 'roll in the dirt' so as to maintain credibility as police officers . . . SLOs report instances of patrol supervisors denying them available time and equipment as well as inhibiting their 'communication' with other officers and members of the community."[10]

The analysis of SLO functioning within the LAPD was accompanied by an assessment of organizational readiness to engage in problem-solving activities. This assessment, targeted to watch commanders, assistant watch commanders, field supervisors and other sergeants, asked respondents about such issues as their access to and the level of community-based information in their assignment, the current relationships between the police and the public in their work group, the level and usefulness of community contacts employed by themselves and their subordinates. Cumulatively, these measures were used to assess the current capacity of the organization at the field level to engage in problem-solving activities.[11] Based on this assessment, it was deemed important to involve supervisory personnel within area commands more directly in the community-policing, problem-solving training than had originally been planned.

The initial plan called for training of command-level personnel as well as field personnel (eight persons from each area) to form the nucleus of the problem-solving vanguard within the Los Angeles Police Department. The final design for problem-solving training was modified to include a two day problem-solving workshop for area command personnel; a one day seminar for 100 of the LAPD's senior command staff; and a one-week training program for approximately 150 line-level personnel within the Los Angeles Police Department. These training sessions were designed to provide senior and area-level commanders with an overview and appreciation for problem-solving, while at the same time developing local expertise with a cadre of Basic Car police officers and supervisors. In addition to this initial problem-solving training, the LAPD's Training Group was also tasked to design curricula to be incorporated in a broader community-policing and problem-solving training effort being conducted by the LAPD.

Rebuilding Relations Between the Police and Community

The third strategy that was integrated into the revision of police services in Los Angeles involved strengthening the relationships between the Los Angeles Police Department and the varied communities it serves. This was approached on several levels, some of which overlap with our prior consideration of rebuilding the Basic Car. The primary issues confronted in rebuilding police and community relationships were: (1) changing the "internal culture" of the LAPD through improved training and communications at both the line and command levels; and (2) creating more positive police and community contacts, primarily by structuring community input into police decision and policy-making.

Improving Communications and Culture Inside the LAPD

An important aspect of the change process within the Los Angeles Police Department was associated with how the department communicated with various audiences—internal and external. Operating as it did for many years, the Los Angeles Police Department did not communicate well, either internally with its employees, or externally with its constituents. In external matters, most of the department's communication came only from the office of the chief or persons officially charged with speaking for the department. Internally, communications were handled in a hierarchical way, with policies, procedures and the like communicated downward, and lateral communications taking the form of employee use of departmental information systems.

The LAPD's inability to communicate with its employees was found to be complicated by several factors. The ad hoc strategic committee reviewing this topic found that "Within the Los Angeles Police Department there is no universal acceptance or understanding of the department's policy as it relates to communicating with persons outside the organization. The message is frequently clouded or altered based on the personal agenda of the individual delivering the message."[12] Perhaps more importantly, the committee suggested that the department's communications with the media were "negatively affected by a deep seated anti-media bias which is cemented in the culture of the Los Angeles Police Department."[13] The committee also questioned the reliability of technical and "informational materials" produced by the department.

The committee developed a list of desired communications outcomes for both internal and external organizational communications. Among other things, these outcomes were intended to support an improved capacity of the LAPD to communicate its vision and practices of community and problem-oriented policing. Of particular interest to this process was the creation of an organization that creatively solved problems by being open in its communications within the department and outside of it.

The culture of any organization greatly affects how and what it communicates. The culture of the LAPD, as noted above, has been closed and non-communicative. Moreover, the culture of the LAPD came under sharp criticism in the Christopher Commission Report in 1991.

> The LAPD has an organizational culture that emphasizes crime control over crime prevention and that isolates the police from the communities and the people they serve. With the full support of many, the LAPD insists on aggressive detection of major crimes and a rapid, seven-minute response time to calls for service. Patrol officers are evaluated by statistical measures (for example, the number of calls handled and arrests made) and are rewarded for being "hard nosed." This style of policing produces results, but it does so at the risk of creating a siege mentality that alienates the officer from the community. . . . it is apparent that too many LAPD patrol officers view citizens with resentment and hostility; too many treat the public with rudeness and disrespect.[14]

In its review of the dominant themes in the culture of the LAPD, the Committee on Organizational Communications identified four significant cultural patterns which needed to be changed if community and problem-oriented policing were to be successfully implemented.

One of the most persistent cultural values within the Los Angeles Police Department speaks directly to its conversion from "professional" to "community-oriented" policing. In the past, the LAPD had made its considerable reputation as a "crime fighting" organization. While the change process underway within the

LAPD sought to preserve the police role in fighting crime, like the comments from the Christopher Commission, such a role did not have to come at the expense of crime prevention and better police and community relations. But the central element in the LAPD's culture was its "kick-ass" orientation toward crime fighting and crime suppression. As the Committee on Organizational Communications suggested:

> [T]he status accorded "crime fighters" is still our most revered cultural value and can be readily seen in the respect accorded SWAT and the Medal of Valor awards. Service to the community is not a strong cultural value. If good service happens to occur during crime fighting, that's acceptable, so long as it does not detract from the adventure/entertainment value of the job. It is the same cultural value that ensures officers will take a bullet for a comrade if they have to, but will also lie to protect fellow officers from the consequences of their own misdeeds.[15]

Another powerful cultural theme identified by the committee relates to the unyielding organizational structure and command system that had become the LAPD. "The department culture is based on a military authoritarian style structure. The entire organization reports up the chain of command to one officer and one boss. There is very little employee input in the basic direction and overall policies of the department."[16] Absent a "stake" in the LAPD, most internal observers suggested that there was little opportunity to adopt a new style of policing in Los Angeles. The power-centric organization of the LAPD had effectively preempted employee involvement. Even throughout the strategic planning process, the struggle to participate in the change process was offset by a watchful eye on what the "boss" wanted. This conflict was quite observable and speaks to the longstanding tradition of "taking orders" with the LAPD.

A third, and related, cultural value within the hierarchy of the LAPD is associated with the perception that most employees, but particularly field commanders, middle managers and the rank-and-file of the LAPD had little authority or power to make decisions and to take independent action. Years of "breeding out" these skills and attitudes had resulted in an organization that desperately needed, but at the same time resented, leadership. As the committee observed:

> The idea of status and prestige is ingrained throughout the department. Rank and assignment reflect this. Although very little power actually resides below the rank of Deputy Chief, every aspect of our culture reflects the status accorded rank and assignment, right down to parking spots, size of offices and chairs, new cars, who works which cases, etc. The patrol officer is perceived by many to be on the absolute bottom. The sergeants and lieutenants working patrol are either the newly promoted or the old and unpromotable.[17]

The resentment of such a control-oriented culture was also reflected in the committee's description of how LAPD's police chiefs, including senior chiefs currently in the department, had treated not only the general workforce, but other commanders within the department. Of significance in this process is the extent to which such treatment has created a culture of suspicion, inaction and resentment at all levels of the hierarchy in the Los Angeles Police Department.

> Decisions below that level [Deputy Chief] are not really decisions, they are recommendations only. The Department's top management violates their own culture when they offer possibilities of pushing down decision making and asking for input from employees, and then ignoring it. Vertical staff meetings and officer empowerment are viewed by many line officers as corporate buzz words and lip service. The opening meeting of this committee began with two hours of "Why do we have to write this report? We have done this so many times before. Top management will do what it wants anyway. It's just another lip service ploy to provide a list of ideas for top management to choose from or to add to the facade that employees actually have a say."[18]

The upshot of these "competing messages" within the LAPD's cultural system is the perception among many within the department that what the organization says is significantly different from what it does. These messages also create a leadership void, as there is always a large distance between preachment and practice. This gap between what is said and what is done contributes to a sense that the LAPD is a "mock bureaucracy" (Gouldner, 1954) in that its cultural values support the use of rules and regulations for the purpose of punishing people rather than establishing organizational routines. Organizational incumbents, having learned these values, are less willing to embrace the "new" values the organization is attempting to instill in the workplace. As the committee concluded, "Given this view of Department culture, communicating professional values and attempting to lead instead of manage are very difficult tasks, if not impossible. It is also easy to see why the current attempt to communicate the department mission statement is being resisted by some officers."[19]

Building Command Confidence and Competence in Working with the Community

Prior to 1992, the command staff within the LAPD had little formal responsibility or experience in working directly with the community. While each geographic area had community relations and crime prevention officers who oversaw such programs as Town Watch, the level of interaction between the area captain and the community at-large was rather ad hoc and sporadic. More often than not the personality of the area captain greatly conditioned the level of community interaction. While every commander invariably attended awards ceremonies and other "rubber chicken" events, the level of police command/community interaction was moderate to low and clearly in the direction of the police telling the community what it would do. In point of fact, as several assessments of the LAPD suggest, the command staff was rather distanced from and, at times, disinterested in community needs, concerns or priorities. Patrol officers too had little systematic contact with the public prior to 1992. While patrol officers patrolled their Basic Car areas, often responding to calls for service outside of these areas, they did not have any formal requirement to engage the community in any meaningful sense. The senior lead officer had this responsibility, but as we have seen this responsibility was exercised by the choice of the SLO, not by departmental policy. As a result meaningful contact between the LAPD and its most basic constituent—the community—was minimal at best in 1992. Moreover, in some areas of Los Angeles these contacts were antagonistic.

On December 3, 1993, Administrative Order #10[20] required each area commander to form a community-police advisory board (C-PAB). The purpose of the C-PAB was to provide community input into policy and decision-making at the area level of organization within the LAPD. The creation of community-police advisory boards posed a new problem within the LAPD. How should police commanders work with these boards? Who should be on them? Who will shape the board's agenda? How will the board provide input and review? Is this a standardized or flexible program? These and other questions made it clear that area commanders would need some preparation in advance of C-PAB implementation.

In anticipation of the new issues created by implementing C-PABs throughout Los Angeles, the department designed a process to assist area commanders and the C-PABs in getting started. From the perspective of area commanders, several "skills" were in need of refinement and development. They were grouped under the idea of "people management skills." Of particular concern was the need to create an "organizational perspective" on the C-PAB process and to provide area captains with the context within which their C-PAB might function. Also of importance were the refinement of communications, groups management and development, negotiation and conflict management/resolution skills, as well as the design and implementation of intervention strategies in the area commands. As these newly formed C-PABs were likely to struggle in gaining an identity and footing within the area, it was important to provide area captains with some of the skills to manage this process to a successful conclusion—that is, to build a community-police advisory board capable of articulating community interests and evaluating police service.

Working with the Communities of Los Angeles

Prior to 1993, the Los Angeles Police Department had no formal mechanism for community input into police policy-making, outside of the elective process. In Los Angeles, the chief of police reports to a police commission which is appointed by the mayor. The commission is expected to review policy-making within the LAPD, while the chief is expected to manage the department's day-to-day affairs. In addition to the police commission, the city council created a public safety committee to review, among other things, activities and actions undertaken within the Los Angeles Police Department. City council members and the mayor can, and do, contact the department for information, to raise questions, and to question and/or receive clarification on policy and operational matters. In point of fact, the LAPD has many supervisors, but few were directly from the community prior to 1993.

Since community interest in the LAPD was extremely high after the Rodney King incident, the LAPD, as part of its organizational change effort, sought to create a mechanism for the community to work with the department on matters of neighborhood crime, disorder and quality of life. But implementing community-police advisory boards was complicated in part by the way in which L.A.'s city council had come to oversee police issues. The initial announcement of the formation of C-PABs included language that separated these community-based sources of input from the larger political systems in the city. C-PAB members were expected to be representative organizations so that as much as possible a cross-section of community (residential and business) interests could be reflected in their membership. There was also a conscious effort made to "balance" membership on the C-PAB by ethnicity, gender and age. C-PAB membership was to reflect ongoing indigenous community representation by including persons from existing social and community organizations within the geographic area.

To assure that area C-PABs reflected as broad a cross section of the community within that area, the department, through its monitoring process, profiled each C-PAB across the city. In all, 371 community members and business leaders participated in the newly created C-PABs across all eighteen area commands. Fifty-four percent of the participants were male, and 46 percent were female. The boards were composed of people from a wide range of ethnic backgrounds. Whites comprised about 56 percent of total C-PAB participation, Blacks accounted for about 19 percent, Latinos represented 13 percent and Asians accounted for approximately 8 percent of C-PAB members. Of course, the patterns of representation varied across areas and within bureaus. The majority of C-PAB members resided in the area, although several representatives, typically business people from the area, actually lived outside of the C-PAB's area.[21]

The community-police advisory boards were designed to have a focal role in shaping enforcement and other police policies at the area command level of organization within the LAPD. While each board member was ultimately selected by the captain of the area, the department had made a provision for civic leadership on the board. In the creation of all boards, the first task of the board members was to recommend a co-chair from among the board. The area captain and that board member were then to oversee and help manage the board as it provided input and critique to the LAPD.

To accomplish the objectives of this program element, the Los Angeles Police Department designed and implemented community training to bring together civic and police leaders, and police officers and citizens, and provide them with substantive information and a methodology for addressing community public safety problems. This training was provided each of the eighteen geographic areas. Prior to training, an assessment was made of initial "group dynamics" of the C-PAB to ascertain the level at which groups had already formed. This was done in conjunction with providing the area captain training and assessment of the C-PAB formation in his/her area.

Consultants assisted each of the area C-PABs in developing their own mission statement and placing their efforts in the larger framework of organizational reform underway in Los Angeles. These psychological and group dynamics consultants attended C-PAB meetings, and designed a training program for members tailored to the level of group development evident. Eighteen one-day workshops were held with an attendance of about four hundred people. These workshops were primarily focused on helping the C-PAB set its agenda and congeal as group. Ongoing technical assistance was then provided over the first six to eight months of the C-PAB's development. On December 3, 1994, board members city-wide attended a C-PAB summit meeting in downtown Los Angeles. The meeting allowed C-PAB members to meet and become acquainted, discuss success stories, attend workshops, and receive additional training. This meeting was so successful that a decision was made to hold a community summit annually.

The Process of Change and its Continuation in Los Angeles

The process of implementing the changes discussed throughout this article required a significant effort within the Los Angeles Police Department. It required that the LAPD look at itself not as the "best police department in the country," but rather as a police department in need of significant internal reorganization and service delivery revision. This change process required that chiefs and other senior LAPD command personnel work in collaborative ways to define, implement and assess their interventions. This was easier said than done. Consultative decision-making was not a usual practice within the department. Heretofore, the LAPD was a "top down" control-centered management system, augmented by political intrigue and a system of protected fiefdoms.

Moreover, command personnel, including those at the senior most levels of the LAPD's hierarchy, had been conditioned in a way so as to avoid direct conflict; consequently, it was perhaps easier to "pass decisions upward" rather than suffer the consequences of potentially making a wrong decision. Passing the buck or finessing the decisional system had become an art form within the LAPD. As a control-centered organization, there was always sufficient paperwork to delay, defer, or otherwise ignore a decision. What cut through this maze of inaction was "fear." The chiefs of the LAPD had exercised their authority in straightforward ways. A key element of the exercise of the chief's role in L.A. was that dissension was not tolerated. Chiefs within the LAPD, particularly those with tenure, typically managed the department in a "hands-on" way. This, in part, conditioned many less senior commanders to expect that they would be "micro-managed."

Throughout this planned change effort command staff struggled with accepting: (1) that the LAPD needed to change in any dramatic way; and (2) that they were "in charge" of these changes. For many years, command staff within the

LAPD had accepted the omnipotent power of the chief of police. In doing so, many followed the "party line" and made few waves within the administrative apparatus of the LAPD. Command personnel reported that historically they were often given assignments and then summarily dismissed in the recommendations they made at meetings conducted by the chief. Others reported that the command staff on the sixth floor of Parker Center were "$700.00 empty suits," they looked good and spoke well, but rarely solved any problems. By 1992, few would initiate change either by conditioning or by inclination. While most paid lip service to the need to reform the LAPD, there was considerable resentment that the department had been put under such scrutiny during and after the Rodney King incident. There were competing messages within the LAPD at that time; some voices arguing for change, while others sought to return to the status quo. Resolving these conflicting messages would be the most significant obstacle faced by the LAPD in attempting to implement the changes previously described.

Learning From the Los Angeles Experience

As this article has attempted to describe the change process in Los Angeles, perhaps there are some "learning points" that can be taken from this effort and used by police managers and others interested in making the police more accountable and effective. These "learning points" can be subsumed under three major headings: (1) those relating to the importance of police departments' histories as they affect organizational change initiatives; (2) those relating to the importance of the internal culture of the department within which change is sought, and (3) the nature of the tools that are available to police administrators who seek to change police organizations.

On the Importance of Organizational Histories

Bureaucracies, formal organizations created for specific purposes, are perhaps the most stable of all social institutions. Their stability stems largely from their ability to "routinize" work, structure internal authority, and "manage" and "negotiate" with their external environment (Weber, 1947). The stability of formal bureaucracies insures that these organizations will continue long after individual leaders have left these organizations. Without such stability, formal organizations would likely experience considerable turmoil in the pursuit of their objectives. A central focus, then, in formal organizations is with creating and maintaining organizational stability.

    The very stability of formal organizations, like police departments, can also be seen as their central weakness. Focused as many police departments are on organizational maintenance issues, they may lose sight of what they were intended to produce. So it was with the Los Angeles Police Department up through 1991. The LAPD, like most police agencies, had a history and set of traditions that created some form or sense of organizational stability, but which over time actually weakened the department in its ability to respond to a changing environment.

Introducing change into an organization as steeped in tradition as the LAPD was a complex venture for many reasons. First, seeing itself as a "professional" police department, defined in Los Angeles as independent from political and community review, created a major obstacle for the department to embrace a style of community policing that would, of necessity, open the department to community input and review. Second, absent a strong internal voice for such changes, the department was left to "interpret" the changes sought of it in many ways. In fact, clear division in understandings and agreements with the need for change were evident in nearly every implementation committee meeting.[22] At the onset of the process, several commanders were blatantly indifferent to the need for change or for establishing a process through which change could be accomplished.

Understanding the Change Context

The context or motivation for change is perhaps the strongest predictor of whether changes within police departments will occur, and consequently the speed (or lack of) of change within these organizations. Generally speaking, changes designed and developed within the police department, and having normative sponsorship within the department, are the most likely and the quickest to occur. In contrast, changes imposed from the outside of the department and over matters in dispute within the department are the least likely and certainly the slowest to occur. In the parlance of change management, getting the organization ready for change is as important as sustaining momentum once changes have begun (see, for example, Daft, 1992:249–282).

When there is some agreement that the focal organization needs to re-organize, re-engineer, or otherwise change itself, the change process is made somewhat easier. Conversely, when those within the organization see little value in changing, or see the change emphasis as a statement about their own failure, change is bogged down. At the onset of this process, a significant portion of the senior leadership of the LAPD saw little utility in changing itself, and were likely oversensitive to the events that had put the LAPD in the spotlight of public assessment.

Independent of individuals' support for the changes proposed in this undertaking, the LAPD had few mechanisms for involving those within the department in strategic decision making. In a power-centric organization, such as the LAPD, decisions had always flowed downward through the organization. If decisions were made at all they were made at the top of the organizational hierarchy. Group process in decision making was nearly absent within the LAPD; decisions made by ranking officers, typically the chief of police, were the general mode of day-to-day operations. Broadening the decisional base within the department was a major contextual issue confronting this program. As senior command officers exercised considerable oversight over commanders in the field through the chain-of-command system, the chief's ability to "mobilize" others within the LAPD who were more consonant with the need for change was severely circumscribed.

Initially battered by public condemnation of the Rodney King incident and seen as ineffective in stopping the South Central riots, many within the LAPD were searching for a clearer direction than the context would allow. Absent such a clear direction and caught in the noise of conflicting command officer actions and statements, including those of Chief Williams, the LAPD was adrift. Such drift continued to reinforce those within the department who resisted these change initiatives, and detracted from the accomplishments of this process.

Changing Police Departments with Limited Tools

Many police chiefs attempting organizational change have come to realize the limited tools they have to accomplish such changes. While the change literature is replete with admonitions to develop "idea champions," restructure authority, and build a training basis for the new directions sought through the reform process, police agencies have, perhaps, seen fewer of the change tools available to assist this process. In many respects chiefs acting as "political leaders" within their departments have generally attempted to appeal to some normative values around which the changes can be packaged, or restructure power, rewards and authority within the department to accomplish the intended changes, or to do both. But unlike their corporate counterparts, chiefs of police often lack several important tools to further and expedite the change agenda.

Skolnick and Fyfe (1993:172–192), in a consideration of successful police reform, suggest that chiefs who were considered "insiders," and those who were able to pick their administrative teams, have a greater chance of success, than do those who come from outside the organization or have limited ability to reshape the administrative core of the target organization. When Willie L. Williams came to the LAPD he did so with at least two major liabilities. First, he was an outsider to the department. In a department that prided itself on internal relationships, Williams was generally without allies. Most of his allies were outside the LAPD. While Williams may have had allies within the LAPD, they were not conspicuous allies.

The second major limitation to Williams' success in implementing a change agenda in Los Angeles is associated with his inability to pick his "management team." When Williams took office as chief of police, he had virtually no appointments to assist him with a change-focused agenda. Unlike his predecessor, Daryl Gates, Willie Williams was perhaps the only person within the LAPD without tenure or the security of civil service. While younger, newly appointed captains and others within the LAPD actually supported Williams' efforts, they too were in an impotent position to affect change. The major obstacle to this process were high ranking, senior command officers within the LAPD who could systematically delay and/or block the reform agenda.

Building Momentum for Change

In physics it is generally accepted that the amount of force necessary to move an object from a state of rest exceeds the amount necessary to keep the object in motion. Overcoming organizational inertia requires considerable force, but so too does sustaining momentum for change once the organization has begun down the change path. As described above, the LAPD can be seen as an organization with considerable inertia that had to be overcome if community and problem-oriented policing was to "replace" the legalistic and crime fighter image the department had enjoyed for many years. But moving the LAPD from a "state of rest" to motion required rather extraordinary forces. These included the revelations of the Rodney King tapes, the subsequent trials of the police officers charged with King's beating, the riot that ensued after the Simi Valley verdict, and the trial of Rodney King himself. Such events created considerable external force to change the Los Angeles charter to put term limits on the office of chief of police, force the resignation of the current chief of police, Daryl Gates, and appoint an outsider to head the LAPD, Willie Williams. Such forces sought to increase the accountability of the LAPD.

Once these forces were put into motion, the opportunity for "reforming" the LAPD to make it more publicly accountable was created. The work of the Christopher and Webster-Williams Commissions had placed the source of the problem of police accountability at the feet of the LAPD, and in 1992 the city of Los Angeles passed a referendum to end a system of police management that essentially provided lifetime tenure to the chief of police. While the inertia of the LAPD was being countered with strong public opinion about the need to make the department more accountable, translating that "public will" into meaningful programs and actions that would sustain organizational change over the long term proved to be less certain than was anticipated, either by the public or by "change-minded" police administrators within the LAPD.

Momentum for change, while often viewed as an internal organizational issue, has an important attachment to the external environment as well. As previously discussed, the external forces that were mustered in pushing the LAPD toward more civic accountability created an opportunity for these reforms to occur. But, left to their own devices, many within the LAPD would have returned to the earlier days of LAPD independence from politicians and the community. Police chiefs often must use the natural forces in the external environment to help sustain change, if that change is ultimately to occur.

In Los Angeles one of the major obstacles to achieving meaningful reform was the inability of the chief to select a "management team" to oversee and push the change agenda. While L.A.'s referendum had effectively made the office of the chief of police more accountable to elected officials and the community at-large, it had not made the department necessarily more accountable. Immediately below the office of the chief of police are deputy and assistant chiefs who have significant policy making authority within the LAPD. These persons have civil service protection such that they are potentially independent actors within the department, each having significant alliances both within and outside of the department.

James Q. Wilson (1978), writing about forces shaping police departments in the late 1960s, suggested that communities indirectly help to shape the style of policing in that locale in two fundamental ways. First, the appointment of the chief of police, a person ultimately screened by the community prior to appointment, represents the opportunity to set a tone for that police department. Second, the interactions of the street-level police officers who are in constant interaction with the community also help condition the policing style on any particular locale. Here it is presumed that these officers learn the values and mores of the community and incorporate these into the style of policing evidenced on the street.

The LAPD had effectively divorced itself from the political culture of the greater Los Angeles community. Internally, loyalties were to the organization and to its often powerful chiefs. Such a system afforded the LAPD with considerable political muscle, such that it was able to effectively resist external review and oversight. Once the King incident occurred and the department was being pushed toward a more balanced relationship with its external environment, change was possible but not certain. For change to be long-lasting the LAPD had to adopt a new set of organizational values, modify its culture and focus its efforts on first building and then strengthening its external relationships with the Los Angeles community. While the L.A. community perhaps spoke with one voice in the selection of a new chief and in the dilution of the authority L.A. chiefs would exercise in the future, little was done to create a management system that was capable of visibly and consistently supporting such a "sea change" for the LAPD. The struggle for power within the LAPD that accompanied Williams' administration underscores the importance of having the appropriate tools to affect change in organizations as steeped in tradition and complex as the Los Angeles Police Department.

Beginning in 1992 and continuing long into the future, the LAPD will likely struggle with its change. Old images are indeed hard to push into the background and the new ideals of "community and problem-oriented" policing remain contested issues within the department. Change has, nonetheless, occurred. Los Angeles is, perhaps, one of the most volatile communities in America. In addition to what seem to be annual earthquakes, significant fires and mud slides, Los Angeles is a growing international community—indeed a city of the world. As such, the city of Los Angeles will continue to pose significant challenges to the LAPD. In the turbulent climate that the city of Los Angeles can often be, the Los Angeles Police Department will need to change and adjust its system of policing in light of the aggressive environment that surrounds the department. Moreover, the internal climate of the LAPD will need to shift significantly if such changes are likely to actually embed the values and work routines of the department.

Notes

[1] West Point Leadership Institute, Internal Report to the LAPD, May 10, 1993, p. 3.

[2] *Commitment to Action*, Los Angeles Police Department, 1994.

[3] LAPD, Office of the Chief of Police, Management Paper No. 2, Community Policing, ND, p.1.

[4] Ibid., p. 2.

[5] LAPD, *Statistical Digest*, Information Resources Division, Statistical Unit, 1992.

[6] Public Administration Service. (1992) *Review of Patrol Deployment of the Los Angeles Police Department*. September. McLean, VA: Public Administration Service.

[7] These definitions were created by an internal LAPD committee charged with establishing common criteria and a "template" for the remapping effort. As part of the creation of this "community template" members of this committee interviewed area captains, as well as knowledgeable academics who have studied aspects of community and neighborhood development. Finally, this committee also contacted police agencies across the country who had implemented community-based policing, and who had implemented some type of mapping and/ or geographic analysis based on community and neighborhood dynamics.

[8] These business rules were created by an internal LAPD committee composed of senior commanders who were overseeing the analysis of call workload as part of this effort.

[9] Sullivan, George J., and Peter Bellmio, Los Angeles Police Department Concept Paper. Geographic Assignment of Patrol Personnel. McLean, VA: Public Administration Service, June, 1994, p. 8.

[10] Ibid.

[11] This instrument was designed by a consulting firm, Police Management Advisors, and administered in the Fall of 1993.

[12] APD, *Strategic Planning Committee, Final Report—Organizational Communications*, August 15, 1994, p. 8.

[13] Ibid.

[14] *Report of the Independent Commission on the Los Angeles Police Department*, July, 1991. p. xiv.

[15] Op. Cit., *Strategic Planning Committee, Final Report—Organizational Communications*, p. 24.

[16] Ibid., p. 23.

[17] Ibid., p. 24.

[18] Ibid.

[19] LAPD, Intra-departmental Correspondence, National Institute of Justice Grant, Acting Director, Behavioral and Social Science Section, ND.

[20] LAPD, Office of the Chief of Police, *Administrative Order# 10*, December 3, 1993.

[21] This information was monitored within the LAPD by the community policing group, an administrative unit created to oversee community policing implementation in Los Angeles. In the post-Williams' era this unit has been eliminated.

[22] The implementation committee for this grant and planned change process was composed of the senior managers within the Los Angeles Police Department. The committee was envisioned as a means for this effort to "cut through" the bureaucracy and administrative apparatus of the department. In reality the committee itself reflected considerable variance in the definition of community policing, as well as in individual members' support of Willie Williams, the Chief of Police.

References

Bouza, A. 1990. *The Police Mystique: An Insider's Look at Cops, Crime and the Criminal Justice System*. New York: Plenum.

Christopher Commission. 1991. *Report of the Independent Commission on the Los Angeles Police Department*. Los Angeles, July.

Daft, R. L. 1992. *Organization Theory and Design*. 4th ed. St. Paul: West Publishing Co.

Davis, E. M. 1978. *Staff One: A Perspective on Police Management*. Englewood Cliffs, NJ: Prentice-Hall.

Domanick, J. 1995. *To Protect and Serve*. New York: Pocket Books.

Gouldner, A. 1954. *Patterns of Industrial Bureaucracy*. New York: The Free Press.

Moore, M. H., and D. E. Stephens. 1991. *Beyond Command and Control: The Strategic Management of Police Departments*. Washington, DC: Police Executive Research Forum.

Sherman, L. W., C. Milton, and T. Kelly. 1973. *Team Policing—Seven Case Studies*. Washington, DC: Police Foundation.

Skolnick, J. H. and J. J. Fyfe. 1993. *Above the Law: Police and the Excessive Use of Force*. New York: The Free Press.

Walker, S. 1977. *A Critical History of Police Reform: The Emergence of Professionalism*. Lexington, MA: Lexington Books.

Weber, M. 1947. *The Theory of Social and Economic Organization*. Cambridge: Oxford University Press.

Williams, W. L., J. R. Greene, and W. T. Bergman. 1993. "Strategic Leadership in a Big-City Police Department: The Philadelphia Story," *Leadership*. Greensboro, NC: Center for Creative Leadership.

Wilson, J. Q. 1978. *Varieties of Police Behavior*. Cambridge: Harvard University Press.

9

Community Policing in Chicago

Wesley G. Skogan

Chicago's experiment with community policing began in April 1993. For more than a year the police department had worked on a plan for Chicago's Alternative Policing Strategy (CAPS) and laid the groundwork for implementing it in selected districts. At the heart of the plan lay the reorganization of policing around the city's 279 police beats. Officers assigned to beat teams were expected to engage in identifying and dealing with a broad range of neighborhood problems in partnership with neighborhood residents and community organizations. To give the officers time to identify such problems, some of the burden of responding to 911 calls was shifted to rapid response teams, and in addition tactical units, youth officers, and detectives were expected to work more closely with beat officers. All of these officers shared responsibility for meeting and working with members of the community on a regular basis at beat meetings. At the district level, advisory committees were formed to review issues of wider scope and to discuss strategic issues with district commanders. A prioritizing system was developed for coordinating the delivery of municipal services to support local problem-solving efforts, and new computer technology began to be introduced that would support the analysis of local crime problems.

In the sections that follow, this article evaluates this ambitious program. First, the article examines some general principles of community policing, and then key elements of the city's program are described and analyzed in the context of how well they fit the community policing model. Furthermore, this article briefly describes the findings of an evaluation that examined the impact of community policing on the quality of life in the five pilot districts of Chicago. (Further details about the project can be found in Skogan and Hartnett, 1997.)

Source: Prepared especially for *Community Policing: Contemporary Readings.*

What is Community Policing?

Community policing is not something that is easy to pin down. However, it is evident to this author that it involves reforming decision-making processes and creating new cultures within police departments; it is not a packet of specific tactical plans. It is an organizational strategy that redefines the goals of policing, but leaves the means of achieving them to practitioners in the field. It is a process rather than a product.

One advantage of this view of community policing is that it encourages departments and even individual districts or precincts to develop tactics that are tailored to local issues. Under the rubric of community policing, departments are:

- opening small neighborhood substations,
- conducting surveys to measure community satisfaction,
- organizing meetings and crime prevention seminars,
- publishing newsletters,
- forming neighborhood watch groups,
- establishing advisory panels,
- organizing youth activities,
- conducting drug education projects and media campaigns,
- patrolling on horses and bicycles, and
- working with municipal agencies to enforce health and safety regulations.

These activities often are backed up by organizational goals that are spelled out in "mission statements," and departments all over the country are rewriting their missions to conform to new ideas about the values that should guide policing and the relationship between the police and the community.

However, behind these tactics lie four general principles that need to be recognized, principles that differentiate community policing from other organizational strategies. These four principles will be described at length in the following sections.

Decentralization

Principle 1   Community policing relies upon organizational decentralization and a reorientation of patrol in order to facilitate communication between police and the public.

Police departments traditionally were organized on the assumption that policies and practices are determined at the top, and flow down in the form of rules and orders. The job of management was to see that these rules and orders were carried out. Of course, this organizational chart did not reflect the reality of policing, which is that operational decision making is radically decentralized and highly discretionary, and that most police work takes place outside the direct control of supervisors. But departments maintained this elaborate paramilitary structure because it helped sustain the illusion that police were under control. Police were also amazingly successful at keeping information about themselves and crime proprietary; they released what was useful to them and were secretive about the rest.

The community policing model is more in accord with the way in which departments actually work. It involves *formally* granting neighborhood officers the decision-making authority they need to function effectively. Line officers are expected to work more autonomously at investigating situations, resolving problems, and educating the public. They are asked to discover and set their own goals, and sometimes to manage their work schedule.

This decentralization facilitates the development of local solutions to local problems and discourages the automatic application of central-office policies. The police are not unlike the rest of society, in which large organizations have learned that decentralization often allows flexibility in decision making at the customer contact level.

To increase responsiveness, police are also emulating the general trend in large organizations toward shedding layers of bureaucracy; most departments that adopt a serious community policing stance strip a layer or two from their rank structures to shorten lines of communication within the agency. Police are also reorganizing to provide opportunities for citizens to come into contact with them under circumstances that encourage an information exchange, the development of mutual trust, and engaging in joint or coordinated action. An improvement in relationships between police and the community is a central goal of these programs.

Problem-Oriented Policing

Principle 2   Community policing assumes a commitment to broadly focused, problem-oriented policing.

On its own, problem-oriented policing is a minor revolution in police work. It signifies a reversal of the long-standing disdain that police held for tasks that were not, in their view, "real police work." It represents a shift away from the crime-fighting orientation that police departments have professed since the 1920s. Adopting that stance was useful at the time. It provided a rationale for disconnecting police from politicians and insulating police management from narrow political concerns. Rigid discipline was imposed to combat internal corruption, and officers were shifted rapidly from assignment to assignment so that they would not get too close to the communities they served. Controlling their work from downtown via centralized radio dispatching was a way to ensure that they stuck to the organization's agenda. Later, when big city riots threatened, focusing on "serious crime" at the expense of order maintenance, and adopting a detached professional manner was a way to keep out of trouble. "Just the facts, ma'am," was all they wanted.

But police departments now are experiencing the liabilities of having disconnected themselves from any close attachment to the communities they serve. Problem-oriented policing encourages officers to respond creatively to problems that they encounter, or to refer them to public and private agencies that can help. More importantly, it stresses the importance of discovering the situations that produce calls for police assistance, identifying the causes which lie behind them, and designing tactics to deal with these causes. This involves training officers in methods of identifying and analyzing problems; police work traditionally consisted of responding sequentially to individual events, while problem solving involves recognizing patterns of incidents that help identify their causes and suggesting how to deal with them. Police facilitate this with computer analyses of "hot spots" that concentrate large volumes of complaints and calls for service. Problem-oriented policing also recognizes that the solutions to those patterns may involve other agencies and may be "non-police" in character; in traditional departments, this would be cause for ignoring these problems.

Responsive to Community

Principle 3   Community policing requires that police are responsive to the public when they set priorities and develop their tactics.

Effective community policing requires responsiveness to citizen input concerning both the needs of the community and the best ways by which the police can help meet those needs. It takes seriously the public's definition of its own problems. Following a trend that is at work throughout American society, this is often known as "listening to the customer." This is one reason why community policing is an organizational strategy but not a set of specific programs—how it looks in practice *should* vary considerably from place to place, in response to unique local situations and circumstances.

Better "listening" to the community can produce different policing priorities. In our experience, officers involved in neighborhood policing quickly learn that many residents are deeply concerned about problems that previously did not come to police attention. The public often focuses on threatening and fear-provoking *conditions* rather than discrete and legally defined *incidents*. They often are concerned about casual social disorder and the physical decay of their community rather than traditionally defined "serious crimes," but the police are organized to respond to the latter. Community residents are unsure that they could (or even should) rely on the police to help them deal with these problems. These concerns thus do not generate complaints or calls for service, and as a result, the police know surprisingly little about them. Accordingly, community policing requires that departments develop new channels for learning about neighborhood problems.

Partners in Prevention

Principle 4 Community policing implies a commitment to helping neighborhoods solve crime problems on their own, through community organizations
and crime prevention programs.

The idea that the police and the public are "co-producers" of safety predates
the current rhetoric of community policing. In fact, the community crime prevention movement of the 1970s was an important precursor to community policing.
It promulgated widely the idea that crime was not solely the responsibility of the
police. The police were quick to endorse the claim that they could not solve crime
problems without community support and assistance (in this way the public shared
the blame for rising crime rates), and now they find that they are expected to be
the catalyst for this effort. They are being called upon to take the lead in mobilizing
individuals and organizations around crime prevention. These efforts include
neighborhood watch, citizen patrols, and education programs stressing household
target-hardening and the rapid reporting of crime.

Chicago's Mission

While some operational planning took place in advance, an important step in the
development of Chicago's program was the formulation of an official "mission
statement" that set the tone for what was to follow. The statement was featured in
a thirty-page document that described, step by step, many of the key components
of change needed for the program to succeed in Chicago. The department's mission statement read as follows:

> The Chicago Police Department, as part of, and empowered by the commu-
> nity, is committed to protect the lives, property and rights of all people, to
> maintain order, and to enforce the law impartially. We will provide quality
> police service in partnership with other members of the community. To fulfill
> our mission, we will strive to attain the highest degree of ethical behavior and
> professional conduct at all times (Chicago Police Department, 1994:2).

The overall report, titled *Together We Can*, opened with a "rationale for
change" that reviewed the limits of the traditional model of policing that characterized the department. Drawing on research on policing and a depiction of a crime
rate that was soaring despite the department's best efforts, the report argued for a
"smarter" approach to policing that capitalized on the strength of the city's neighborhoods. It argued that the department had to be "reinvented" so it could form a
partnership with the community that stressed crime prevention, customer service,
and honest and ethical conduct. Almost half of the document focused on what had
to be reinvented, ranging from officer selection to department management,
training, performance evaluation, call dispatching, technology, and budgeting. The

document was mailed to every member of the department, and to help ensure that it was read, it was included on the reading list from which questions would be drawn for the next promotion exam. Its concreteness helped it become the basis for planning the eventual citywide implementation of Chicago's Alternative Policing Strategy.

The Program

While a myriad of practical details were involved in setting change in motion among the department's fifteen thousand employees, the program that emerged had six key elements.

Departmental Involvement

The entire department (eventually) was to be involved. Rather than forming special units, the department was committed to changing its entire organization. Community policing roles were to be developed for all of the units in the organization, including detectives, tactical units, officers working with gangs, and narcotics officers, rather than just uniformed patrol officers working in the districts. Most of this had to wait until the program had proven itself in the patrol division, however. During the first year a few units were decentralized, so that district commanders had control over plain-clothes tactical units and youth officers, and they could integrate the efforts of those special units with plans being developed at the grassroots level.

The commitment to citywide involvement was reflected in the decision to test the new program in diverse pilot districts, several of which were very high crime areas, using existing personnel and leadership. In the words of one department executive, they did not "stack the deck in favor of success." The department's managers knew that once the program encompassed the entire city, it had to continue to work with the talent that the department already had. While in some cities community policing is confined to selected districts, or utilizes volunteer officers (often being paid overtime through special federal programs), eventually Chicago was going to have to make the program work using its existing personnel, and within its budget.

Permanent Assignments

Officers were given permanent beat assignments. To give careful attention to the residents and specific problems of various neighborhoods required officers to know their beats, including the problems, trends, hot spots, resources, and relationships there. In order to develop partnerships with the community they had to stay in one place long enough for residents to know and learn to trust them, and officers had to have enough free time to engage in community work. However, the experience of other cities made clear the importance of continuing to maintain acceptable levels of response to 911 calls at the same time.

The fundamental geographical building block of the new program was the beat. The city's 25 police districts are divided into 279 beats, which average 10,000 residents and 4,100 households. The districts each have between nine and fifteen beats, staffed with officers that were assigned to the district partly by a "weighted workload" formula that took into account calls for service from the area. To resolve conflicts between the dual priorities of working with the public and responding promptly to calls for service, officers in each district were divided into beat teams and rapid response units. Beat teams were to be dispatched less frequently so that they had time to work on neighborhood projects. Whenever possible they were to be sent only to calls that originated in their beat, and even then they were to be exempted from certain classes of calls to which their turf specialization did not seem to make any contribution. The goal was to keep beat teams on their turf—thus maintaining "beat integrity"—at least 70 percent of the time. Other calls were to be assigned to rapid response units, tactical officers and other teams that ranged throughout the district.

Which officers served in which roles was a complicated matter that was closely regulated by the city's contract with the police union. In Chicago, officers choose their district and shift through a bidding system based on seniority. (There were tradeoffs; we knew officers with almost 20 years of seniority who had to work the midnight shift to get the district assignment of their choice.) Only within those parameters could district commanders decide which officers would serve in beat or rapid response units.

In the pilot districts they generally relied on their lieutenants and sergeants to negotiate the matter shift by shift, which was further complicated by the desire of most officers to remain attached to their partners. However, in general, officers seemed to get the assignment they wanted. Those who craved the excitement of responding to a succession of hot 911 calls jockeyed to get into a rapid response car, while those who were interested in community-oriented work gravitated to beat teams. But the yearly re-bidding process meant that they could be bumped from their position, or that they could try to improve their lot as they accumulated a bit more seniority, so that there was a steady circulation of officers through various assignments over time. The union contract thus mitigated against the creation of a force split permanently between community and traditional policing, something that CAPS' managers wanted to avoid in any event. It also meant that there was somewhat more turnover in beat assignments than some community groups thought was optimal.

Training

There was a serious commitment to training. The department invested an immense amount of effort, at a critical time, in training officers and their supervisors in the skills required to identify and solve problems in conjunction with the community. Training was considered absolutely essential to promoting officer understanding and commitment to the program, as well as providing direction to officers and supervisors in their new roles. Without adequate training they would inevitably fall back on what they knew best, which was the tried and true routines of traditional policing.

Several cities that have tried to implement community policing ignored the importance of training and, in effect, merely instructed their officers to "go out and do it." Not surprisingly, they failed to mount serious programs. Chicago believed that by putting a strong emphasis on training they also would send the message to the rank-and-file officers that community policing was real and that downtown was committed to the program. The training program that was developed was co-taught by civilian trainers. It included officers of all ranks who were about to serve in the pilot districts, and everyone received several days of training before the program began.

Community Involvement

The community is to play a significant role. At the core of CAPS lay the formation of police-community partnerships focused on identifying and solving problems at the neighborhood level. Community policing assumes that police cannot solve neighborhood problems on their own; it depends on the cooperation of the community and public and private agencies to achieve success. In Chicago, one problem-solving role for police was to engage community resources and draw other city agencies into identifying and responding to local concerns. *Together We Can* noted, ". . . the Department and the rest of the community must establish new ways of actually working together. New methods must be put in place to jointly identify problems, propose solutions, and implement changes. The Department's ultimate goal should be community empowerment" (Chicago Police Department, 1994:16).

This commitment to community involvement was operationalized in two ways. Beat meetings began in every beat. They were regular—usually monthly—gatherings of small groups of residents and officers who actually worked the beat. These meetings were held in church basements and park buildings all over the city. In addition, advisory committees were formed at the district level to meet with commanders and district staff. They were composed of community leaders, school council members, ministers, business operators, and representatives of institutions of significance in the district. Beat meetings and district advisory committee gatherings were the principal forums for the development of joint police-citizen plans to tackle neighborhood issues.

Social Service

Policing was linked to the delivery of city services. Community policing inevitably involved the expansion of the police mandate to include a broad range of concerns that previously lay outside their competence. In other words, as the program's detractors put it, they were expected to be "social workers." The expansion of the police mandate was a response to several factors.

Senior managers understood that police could put a temporary lid on many crime-related problems, but they could never fix them. They wanted to create problem-solving systems that could keep the lid on even after they had moved on. The involvement of the police in coordinating services also reflected city hall's plan to use CAPS to inject more discipline into the city's service delivery system. Service standards and accountability mechanisms were put in place that advanced the mayor's municipal efficiency agenda as well as supporting problem solving.

The expansion of the mandate also reflected consumer demand—when beat officers met with neighborhood residents, the concerns that were voiced included all types of problems, and the kinds of crimes that police traditionally are organized to tackle often were fairly low on the priority list. CAPS' managers knew that if the response of officers to community concerns was, "that's not a police matter," residents would not show up for another meeting.

Therefore, from the beginning, the delivery of city services in the pilot districts was linked to community policing via special service request forms. They were to be generated by everyone, but were the special domain of beat teams. Officers' service requests triggered a prioritizing and case-tracking process that greatly increased the responsiveness of other city agencies. The successful integration of CAPS with a broad range of city services was one of the most important organizational successes of the first year of the program.

Crime Analysis

There was an emphasis on crime analysis. From the outset, geographic crime analysis was considered a key component of community policing in Chicago. It was to form the "knowledge base" that would drive the beat problem-solving process and the tactical operations of special squads. Computer technology was to speed the collection and analysis of data to identify crime patterns and target areas that demand police attention. An easy-to-use crime mapping system was to be developed to run on computers at each district station. Overnight data entry ensured that the results were timely.

Crime maps were to be routinely distributed at beat meetings and accessible to the public at each station. Other analytic tools included "beat planners," which were notebooks of local information maintained by beat officers. Also, new roll call procedures were to be developed to encourage officers to share information across watches about beat-level events and community resources. All of this was intended to foster problem solving at the beat level.

The Pilot Districts

The police districts in which the program was developed are illustrated in figure 1. They broadly represented the city's neighborhoods. They ranged from fairly

Figure 1
Chicago's Pilot Police Districts

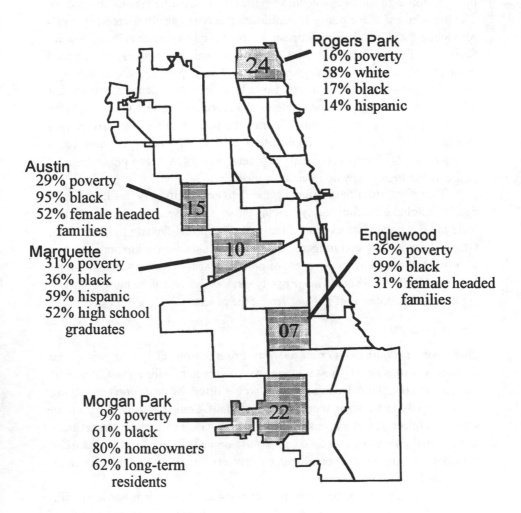

Rogers Park
16% poverty
58% white
17% black
14% hispanic

Austin
29% poverty
95% black
52% female headed
families

Marquette
31% poverty
36% black
59% hispanic
52% high school
graduates

Englewood
36% poverty
99% black
31% female headed
families

Morgan Park
9% poverty
61% black
80% homeowners
62% long-term
residents

affluent to desperately poor, and from racially heterogeneous to solidly segregated by race.

Rogers Park was the most ethnically diverse; 17 percent of its residents were black, 14 percent Hispanic, and 58 percent white, with many other ethnic groups comprising the remaining 11 percent. Almost all residents of Austin and Englewood, on the other hand, were African American. Marquette was divided among blacks (to the north) and Hispanics (to the south), with the latter making up almost 60 percent of the total. Only slightly more than half the adults in Marquette had graduated from high school. On the other hand, in Morgan Park middle-class whites constituted a 40 percent minority, while about 60 percent of the district's residents were African Americans. Morgan Park residents were easily the most affluent; 80 percent were home owners. Rogers Park residents were significantly better off than those of the remaining districts, but they were the most transient; only 24 percent had lived there for a decade, while the comparable figure for Morgan Park was 62 percent. In Austin and Englewood, about 30 percent of households were headed by females and almost an equal number of residents were living below the poverty line.

The Impact of the CAPS Program

This section summarizes what we found concerning the impact of CAPS in the pilot districts. While a great deal of data collection took place, this article reports on the findings of surveys that were conducted before the program began, and again fourteen to eighteen months later.

Census data were used to select sections of the city which closely matched the demography of the five pilot areas. These "comparison areas" were used to represent (roughly) what *would* have happened in the pilot districts *if* there had been no CAPS program, for it was not put in motion in other parts of the city until the end of the development period.

All of the interviews were conducted by telephone in English and Spanish. An average of 180 residents were interviewed twice in each of the pilot districts and 150 in their comparison areas. The analysis of the data compared the results of the two waves of surveys in pairs, contrasting any "before-and-after" changes in each pilot district with what happened over the same time span in its comparison area. When there is a change in a pilot district but no comparable shift in the comparison area—or vice versa—it could be evidence that the program made a difference.

Assessments of Trends in Policing

There was evidence that CAPS had some impact on people's *optimism* about trends in policing in Chicago. To gauge this, respondents were asked if the police in their neighborhood had gotten better, worse, or stayed about the same during the past year. Figure 2 indicates that in four out of five pilot districts there were significant increases in optimism after the first year or more of the program.

Figure 2 presents Wave 1 and Wave 2 survey results (labeled "W1" and "W2") for the pilot districts and their comparison areas, to facilitate comparisons between any over-time changes in those results. (This format will be repeated in the next figure as well.) The values in parentheses near the bottom of the figure present the statistical significance of the W1–W2 changes within an area; a figure of 0.05 or less is generally accepted as a reliable change, although we will also pay attention to patterns of results that lie within the 0.05-to-0.10 range as well.

Figure 2 depicts visible increases in optimism in Englewood, Marquette, Austin and Morgan Park. The percentage of residents who thought policing had gotten better over the first year or more of CAPS was up by about one-third in each case. For Englewood and Austin there were also no parallel changes in the comparison areas, and the differences between the two were statistically significant. However, for Morgan Park and Marquette optimism was also up in the comparison area, and the comparison area for Rogers Park was the only area of that pair that changed significantly. In these three cases it is not clear that CAPS had as much impact on this aspect of public opinion. Analysis of the data for population groups indicated that optimism was generally up among African Americans, but not much among whites or Hispanics.

Impact on Neighborhood Problems

The surveys also gathered data on the extent of neighborhood problems, as viewed through the eyes of the people who lived there. In the interviews, respondents were quizzed about 18 specific issues that the evaluators thought—before the program began—might be problems in various parts of the city. Neighborhood residents were asked to rate each of them as "a big problem," "some problem," or "no problem." The analysis focused on the *four biggest problems* that residents of each area nominated in the first interview, and tracked the ratings given these issues a year or more later when they were interviewed again. This analysis lets residents "set the agenda" for the evaluation, through their expressions of concern about neighborhood conditions.

Two problems on the list were of virtually universal concern. "Street drug dealing" was one of the top-ranked problems in every area we studied, and "shooting and violence by gangs" was one of the leading problems in four of the five pilot districts (with only the exception of Rogers Park). These are both challenging issues that lie near the core of the city's crime problems in the 1990s.

Otherwise, a wide range of problems were identified as particularly vexing. In two areas car vandalism was near the top of the list, and in two others household vandalism ranked highly. Problems with "people being attacked or robbed" were also rated highly in two areas. Auto theft, burglary, disruptions around schools,

Figure 2
Trend in Policing Last Year

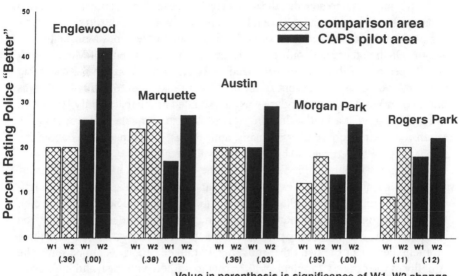

Value in parenthesis is significance of W1–W2 change

Figure 3
Neighborhood Problems in Englewood

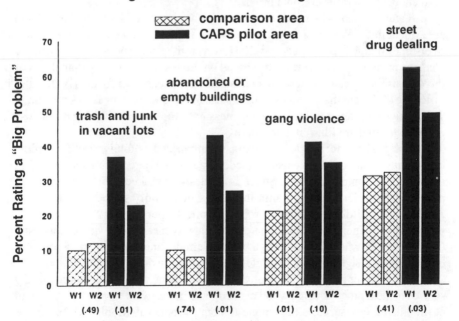

Value in parenthesis is significance of W1–W2 change

abandoned buildings, and "vacant lots filled with trash and junk" each stood near the top of the list in one district.

It is important to note that the initial level of these "biggest problems" varied considerably from district to district. For example, street drug dealing was rated a big problem by 60 percent or more of residents of Englewood, Marquette, and Austin. On the other hand, only about 13 percent of the residents of Morgan Park and 20 percent of those we interviewed in Rogers Park thought this was a big problem, even though it was one of the areas' top-ranked issues before CAPS was initiated. In Morgan Park, burglary was a top-ranked problem, but only 10 percent of residents gave it a high rating. In Morgan Park in particular, there was not as much room for improvement on many dimensions, and expectations about the impact of CAPS there should be tempered by this reality.

Figure 3 illustrates the findings for one of Chicago's experimental areas, Englewood. Englewood is an extremely poor and largely African-American neighborhood. During the early 1990s it had one of the highest homicide rates in the city. Before the program began more than 60 percent of the residents of Englewood rated street drug dealing a big problem, and gang violence was the number three problem there. But the two other most highly-ranked problems turned out to be "quality of life" issues. Problems with vacant lots filled with trash and junk stood near the top of the list, and so did the large number (600, by one estimate) of abandoned buildings which plagued the district. In fact, in four of the five experimental areas, two of the top four problems were quality of life concerns rather than conventionally serious criminal offenses.

Figure 3 also presents problem ratings for Englewood and its comparison area, for both the Wave 1 and Wave 2 surveys. The statistical significance of each over-time change is presented as well. However, the conclusions about over-time changes presented in this article are based on the results of statistical analyses of the data using repeated measures analysis of variance, which focuses on the significance of differential changes in the means of the outcome measures over time. This analysis used the full range of the measures, and not just the "big problems" percentages that are illustrated in figure 3.

The findings for Englewood can be summarized as follows: all four of the community's biggest problems declined, while none went down significantly in Englewood's comparison area. Street drug sales was ranked a big problem by 62 percent of Englewood residents in 1993, but by only 49 percent in 1994. Abandoned building problems dropped from 43 percent to 27 percent, and problems with litter from 37 to 23 percent. Gang violence was down only modestly (the percentage who thought it was a big problem declined from 41 to 35 percent), but it increased significantly in Englewood's comparison area.

These findings reflect the relative vigor with which Englewood used the city service request process. Englewood residents and police were extremely successful at mobilizing city services to respond to both of its decay problems. During the sixteen months ending in August 1994, they generated 1,314 service requests to attend to abandoned buildings, and 2,379 requests for special service from the

Department of Streets and Sanitation. In both cases Englewood's service request count ranked number one among the five experimental areas, both absolutely and relative to the size of their populations. There was a request to deal with an abandoned building for every eighty-five Englewood residents. As figure 3 illustrates, perceptions of the extent of both problems went down significantly in Englewood during that period. In addition, gang and drug problems were the focus of marches by community members, organized by a coalition of local churches. The district's commander was easily the most charismatic and energetic of the group.

Based on this kind of analysis, the findings for the other districts were:

Marquette: graffiti, the area's second biggest problem, went down; a decline in street drug dealing was not significant.

Austin: gang violence, drug dealing, and assault and robbery went down; a decline in school disruption was not significant.

Rogers Park: assault and robbery went down; declines in the area's other problems (drugs, graffiti, and car vandalism) were not significant.

Morgan Park: every problem in this area declined at least slightly, but none of the declines can be clearly attributed to CAPS: problems in Morgan Park were already lower than anywhere else, and reductions in several problems were paralleled by declines in the comparison area.

Discussion

Did Chicago's program speak to all of the core elements of community policing? As noted at the outset, the first requirement was decentralization and reorientation of patrol. In Chicago, district commanders were empowered to experiment with locally-arrived-at solutions to local problems. The roles of patrol officers were drastically altered, as many of them were "cut loose" from the 911 system to devote time to community outreach and problem solving on their own new turf.

The second requirement was that police assume a commitment to broadly focused problem solving. In Chicago, one of the biggest early successes of the program was its link to the delivery of a broad range of city services, from auto towing to street sign replacement and building code inspections. The Marquette district, where graffiti problems went down significantly, was the single greatest user of the city's graffiti-removal services.

The third requirement was that the police be responsive to the public when they set priorities. The arenas for this in Chicago were the new district advisory committees and the small-area beat meetings, places where residents could describe their problems and discuss how to solve them.

Finally, community policing implies a commitment to crime prevention and neighborhood self help. Chicago's model of problem solving stressed the role played by neighborhood residents in resolving their *own* problems, backstopped by the police where necessary. The beat meetings were to be the locus for dividing up those tasks, while at the district level the advisory committees were to focus more on finding the resources required to address larger-scale, area-wide problems.

Not only did Chicago's CAPS program seem to incorporate all of the elements of community policing, it also seemed to work. Residents of the pilot districts reported that they saw less social disorder and physical decay, and serious crime went down in several areas, due to the program. They thought they were getting better police service, and that belief grew the most among African Americans. Chicago still had a great deal left to accomplish after the experimental period, including finding ways to expand the program to encompass the entire city, but the months spent in developing and testing the program seem to have paid off.

References

Chicago Police Department. 1994. *Together We Can*. Chicago, IL.
Skogan, Wesley G. and Susan M. Hartnett. 1997. *Community Policing, Chicago Style*. New York: Oxford University Press.

10

The Police and the Control of Crime and Disorder

Robert Brame and *Alex Piquero*

How have the police been going about the business of policing? In this essay, we consider the results of research on the more traditional policing strategies and how these findings have created a social and political environment that is enthusiastic about new approaches to police work. In addition, we explore the analytical foundations of community and problem-solving approaches to policing and review the extant research on these efforts. We conclude the essay by outlining future research directions in assessing the effectiveness of police on crime and disorder.

Problem- and Community-Oriented Policing

At the heart of shifting emphasis away from the professional model to a more prevention-oriented approach is an optimism that the police are capable of preventing *some* crime and disorder by intentionally altering *some* of the underlying factors that cause or increase the risk of crime and disorder (Moore 1992; Sherman 1995). There is some evidence that law enforcement authorities have begun to use prevention-oriented strategies in their efforts to control crime and disorder (Sherman 1995). Most notable among these efforts has been the increasing prominence of community-oriented and problem-solving policing (Moore 1992). Contemplating the meaning of these concepts is not easy because they apparently mean different things to different people (Bayley 1994).

Community policing efforts tend to have a common goal of reducing crime and disorder by enlisting the active participation of the communities that are being

Source: Prepared especially for *Community Policing: Contemporary Readings.*

policed (Moore 1992; Bayley 1994). Sherman (1995:339) suggests that community policing involves policing of public property "the way a security guard treats a client property." Moore (1992) takes a different approach, arguing that community policing emphasizes a transition in not only the means of policing but the ends that police should achieve. According to this view, police legitimacy is rooted in "its ability to meet the needs and desires of the community" (p. 123) which include but are not limited to the reduction of serious crime.

Indeed, the needs and desires of the community are often broader than a focused crime-reduction strategy anticipates. Commonly expressed concerns of the public include fear of crime, minor incivilities, and community disorder; all of which may or may not be directly linked to serious crime itself (see, e.g., Wilson and Kelling 1982; Moore 1992; Bayley 1994; Kelling and Coles 1996). On the other hand, Sherman (1995) contends that community policing efforts are generally geared toward the control of short-term risk factors that are associated with higher rates of crime such as the control of guns, known offenders, and juveniles. Sherman's community policing prevention strategy can probably best be described as tertiary in nature, although one can easily imagine that policies like those targeting criminogenic commodities (e.g., guns) or aggressive patrolling of potential targets (e.g., checking doors at night) might be of a secondary or even primary variety.

Wilson and Kelling (1982) offer an alternative view, contending that community policing efforts should revolve around the elimination of factors that cause people to withdraw from and lose interest in their community, thus leading to an increase in community disorganization and its primary consequence: heightened levels of crime and disorder (e.g., Kornhauser 1978; Skogan 1986; Sampson and Groves 1989; Kelling and Coles 1996; but see Walker 1984). If interventions target communities that currently exhibit high levels of crime, disorder, and disorganization, efforts to confront those problems may be viewed as tertiary prevention—the minimization of future harm and reversal of the underlying problems to improve conditions (Skogan 1986). Should those interventions be targeted at communities that are showing signs of breakdown but have not yet reached the point where the consequences of disorganization and disorder are fully realized, they might best be described as secondary prevention efforts. Finally, efforts to strengthen communities in general could best be described as primary prevention. The importance of communities and informal control mechanisms, then, is, for the most part, without much question, especially with regard to disorder (Taylor and Harrell 1996; Taylor 1997).

Police agencies, their chiefs, politicians, and the public alike have been greatly attracted to the concept of community policing in recent years. At its most basic level, the phrase connotes a heightened level of involvement between the police and the communities in which they are responsible for law enforcement. In particular, community policing efforts generally appear to pay attention to the notion of actively involving or enlisting members of the civilian community in the effort to reduce crime and disorder in communities. Beyond this common core, however, community policing often means very different things to different people. Indeed, the diffuse nature of this concept has likely hindered efforts in developing concrete goals and evaluating whether objectives have been achieved (Skolnick and Bayley 1988).

For some, the phrase "community policing" is merely redundant, since communities are obviously a major object of police efforts (Moore 1992). Others contend that the phrase is useful, because it rectifies the tendency of professional policing to forget its need to integrate with and join the community in the policing enterprise (Goldstein 1990; Moore 1992). Still others think that community policing is basically an "umbrella term" for whatever new program the police wish to deploy that can plausibly be linked to the community (Goldstein 1987). Manning (1984:205–6) argues that "[c]ommunity policing can be seen as a metaphor based on yearning and the wish for personalization of service which contrasts with bureaucratic/professional policing."

In contrast to community policing, problem-solving policing seems to have a more widely agreed-upon meaning. Spelman and Eck (1987), for example, argue that a coherent problem-solving strategy involves four elements: (1) scanning the environment for problems that persistently demand the time and attention of the police and detract from the quality of life in the community; (2) analyzing or assessing the problem to identify possible solutions to it; (3) using problem-assessment data to formulate and implement a reaction to the problem; and (4) formally assessing the success or failure of the intervention (see also Goldstein 1990). By solving whatever problem exists, one prevents the recurrence of consequences stemming from that problem. Thus, problem-solving policies are very close to the concept of tertiary prevention described above.

Problem-solving strategies are grounded in the hypothesis that repeated calls for police service, persistent demands on police time and resources, and major sources of community concern can often be traced to solvable problems. If these problems are resolved satisfactorily, demands on police time and resources should be reduced and the effectiveness of the police should be enhanced as well. As Goldstein (1990:35) argues, police need to "extend their concern to dealing effectively with the problems that justify creating a police agency in the first instance."

To Goldstein, the resolution of problems demanding police attention is a key factor in maintaining and enhancing police legitimacy. To police departments, an emphasis on problem solving is an entirely new way of organizing and executing what they do and how they do it. If implemented as its proponents suggest, it replaces a focus on internal operations and organizational efficiency with a focus on effectiveness at doing what people expect the police to do: reduce crime and disorder in their communities (what Goldstein [1990:35–36] calls "deviance management") (see also Spelman and Eck 1987).

Notwithstanding the difference in emphasis between community and problem-solving policing, it may be difficult to distinguish them in practice (Moore, Trojanowicz, and Kelling 1988). As Moore (1992:126) contends,

[i]f both occur as a routine matter, then problem-solving policing becomes virtually indistinguishable from community policing. Community policing is designed to let the community nominate problems and focuses on what the police can do in partnership with the community to deal with the nominated problems. That generally requires thought and imagination and is therefore often indistinguishable from problem-solving policing.

The essential difference between the two approaches, then, appears to be one of emphasis rather than fundamental direction: the direction of harm minimization and prevention. Taken to the extreme, however, problem-solving strategies could exclude community concerns and insights while community-oriented strategies could result in subordination of problem-solving strategies as well as law enforcement and order maintenance (Moore 1992). While there is much overlap between the two concepts, they are, therefore, not entirely the same thing.

With these new strategies on the policy table, one might well ask whether they have been effective at achieving reductions in crime and disorder as well as other goals and what their impact on policing in the future might be. When we consider the contents and the effectiveness of the community and problem-solving tactics, it is useful to recognize at the outset that the two approaches are not mutually exclusive strategies. What they have in common is, for our purposes, more important than how they differ. The principal similarity we wish to emphasize is their common focus on prevention rather than reaction.

In this article, we discuss the relevant research on the effectiveness of police on crime and disorder. In particular, we consider the evidence within eight areas: (1) high-profile police activity, (2) aggressive enforcement, (3) high-risk persons and places, (4) police effect on guns and drugs, (5) problem-solving case studies, (6) police response to domestic violence, (7) police and communities, and (8) neighborhood crime watch programs. We discuss each of these in turn.

High-Profile Police Activity

Although evidence on high-profile, random patrol suggests that it has limited utility for crime control (see, e.g., Kelling et al. 1974), other studies of high-visibility police activity suggest that *what* the police do during patrol may make a difference (see Sherman 1992a:192; Larson 1976; Fienberg, Larntz and Reiss 1976). The primary evidence in support of this proposition comes from studies on the effectiveness of police crackdowns (both geographically- and activity-based), aggressive policing of suspicious persons, and diligent enforcement of minor disorder and incivilities in addition to serious criminal law violations (Sherman 1992a; Sherman 1990). As noted earlier, evidence on the impact of these tactics appears to be in contention, with some arguing that their effect on crime is minimal (Bayley 1994; Pfuhl 1983) and others contending that their effects are substantial (Sherman 1995).

Saturation patrol and massive police crackdowns on illegal behavior appear to have some deterrent effects while and where they are underway (Sherman 1990; Bayley 1994; Skolnick and Bayley 1988), although Sherman notes that such efforts may have negative results as well. A crackdown is marked by an abrupt and dramatic increase in propensity of police to apprehend individuals for law violations or to at least communicate the threat of apprehension (Sherman 1990). The Lynn, Massachusetts, open-air drug-market crackdown, for example, apparently reduced robbery and burglary rates for two years (Sherman 1992), but all crackdowns may not produce the intended result (see, e.g., Walker 1994:137–38). Citing Lawrence, Massachusetts and Washington, D.C. drug crackdowns as evidence, Sherman (1990) reported that the former was associated with higher robbery rates and the latter was associated with greater levels of drug homicide. Crackdowns have been used within a specified target area to combat general crime and disorder as well as specific offenses, such as drug selling, prostitution, robberies, traffic offenses, and disorderly conduct (Sherman 1990; Bayley 1994). Drunk-driving crackdowns have received fairly extensive study by Ross (1992a), who contends that these crackdowns have immediate, although short-lived, suppression effects. Legge (1991) studied the impact of new drunk driving laws in New York and California during the early 1980s and found that their suppression effect was both abrupt and lasting (see also Ross 1992b:221–22). Legge's interrupted time-series study is particularly interesting because he relied on measures like single-vehicle nighttime crashes which arguably proxy for drunk driving incidence, and he used daytime crashes as a control time series.

Evidence on whether such efforts displace crime to other areas while they are underway is mixed (see, e.g., Barr and Pease 1990:288–90; Skolnick and Bayley 1988:3; Sherman 1990:35). Summarizing results of a 1974 Rand study on a police crackdown on New York subway robberies, Barr and Pease (1990) report that street robberies increased even though subway crime decreased (see also Sherman 1990:30–31; Chaiken 1978). According to Sherman's evidence, drunk driving crackdowns did not appear to result in displacement (perhaps because of jurisdiction-wide publicity), but measurement of displacement in other categories was intractable. He concluded that displacement was probable for geographically confined crackdowns on all kinds of law violation, although one can only speculate about the extent to which such displacement still leads to a net reduction in quantity or seriousness of crime and disorder, or what Barr and Pease call "benign displacement" (Sherman 1990:284–85; see also Clarke 1995:122–32).

One interesting possibility is Sherman's residual deterrence hypothesis, which suggests that deterrent effects of short-term crackdowns, in some instances, may extend beyond the life of the crackdowns themselves. Where initial deterrence was achieved for offenses such as drunk driving, parking violations, and minor disorder, residual deterrence was likely. Sherman (1990:25, 36) concedes, however, that "there is no evidence of any residual deterrent effect from drug crackdowns," and "[w]hether residual deterrence can be found with more serious offenders remains an open question." Evidence summarized in Sherman suggests that decay in deterrent effects of long-term crackdowns is common (although not inevitable) and that policy makers may achieve more cost-effective policing by reducing the duration of long-term crackdowns and using finite resources in a pattern of place-rotating short-term crackdowns (see also Sherman 1995:332–33). This notwithstanding, the objective of such efforts is to keep offenders guessing and off balance (see also Bayley 1994:81).

Aggressive Enforcement

Research suggests that aggressive traffic and disorderly conduct enforcement and field interrogation of "suspicious persons" may yield valuable information for solving crimes and apprehending criminals. What these measures have in common is that they are both manifestations of diligent efforts by the police to *watch* the communities they are policing (Sherman 1983). In their study of police actions and robbery rates in thirty-five American cities, Wilson and Boland (1978) contend that intensive police monitoring of communities should objectively increase the probability of apprehending more criminals and should generate a perception in those communities that apprehension for criminal behavior was a high-probability event. They observe that the former function simply increases the probability of clearing prior crimes, while the latter function directly affects crime rates by modifying public perceptions of punishment certainty (e.g., general deterrence).

Wilson and Boland (1978) found that their measure of "aggressive enforcement," the number of citations for traffic violations issued per officer, exerted a positive effect on certainty of arrest for robbery which, in turn, was associated with decreased robbery rates. In a longitudinally-based nine-city replication of the Wilson and Boland study, Jacob and Rich (1980) used the number of traffic arrests as a measure of aggressive enforcement but found no relationship between it and the number of robbery arrests. Jacob and Rich also concluded that increased numbers of robbery arrests did not reduce, and in some cases increased, the robbery rate. Wilson and Boland (1981) criticized these results, arguing that they were not derived from a plausible theoretical model and that measures of key constructs such as aggressive enforcement (i.e., the number of traffic arrests rather than a standardized measure per officer on patrol) were flawed. In their 171-city study, Sampson and Cohen (1988) found that (1) aggressive enforcement, defined as the number of drunk driving and disorderly conduct arrests per officer, increased the certainty of arrest for both robbery and burglary; and (2) heightened police aggressiveness was associated with lower robbery rates (effects on burglary rates were only statistically significant at the $p < .16$ level), thereby replicating the basic claims of Wilson and Boland.

Aggressive enforcement in the way of field interrogations or interviews also appears to have crime reduction effects. The San Diego Field Interrogation Experiment studied the effect of field interviews (i.e., stopping and questioning suspicious persons) on the incidence of suppressible crimes (Sherman 1992a, summarizing Boydstun 1975). Suppressible crimes included robbery, burglary, theft, auto theft, assault, sex crimes, malicious mischief, and disturbances.[1] Three areas were included in the study: (1) an area in which field interrogations were suspended for nine months, followed by resumption of normal practices; (2) an area in which field interrogations were conducted with normal frequency, but only by "officers specially trained to reduce friction with citizens they stop"; and (3) a control site in which field interrogation practices remained the same as usual (Sherman 1992a).

The analysis results indicated that suppressible crimes increased during the suspension of field interrogation, followed by a decrease when field stops were resumed. Crime rates remained the same in the two areas where frequency of field interrogation practices remained the same (Sherman 1992a). Sherman also indicated that attitudes of citizens toward the police were unaffected by the intervention. Interrogation subjects had more favorable attitudes toward those officers who had received special training than toward those who had not, even though there was no evidence that the two groups of officers behaved differently. Even though field interviews apparently have some crime-reduction effects, sticky questions remain about who will be defined as "suspicious" and what the guidelines for such definitions will be. Sherman expresses optimism that proper training and the development of guidelines may overcome these difficulties, although he observes that efforts to write guidelines on what constitutes "suspicious" activity or appearance will have to consider how to structure a police officer's "judgment about persons in relation to the places where they are found" (p. 189).

A recent evaluation on aggressive gun confiscation by the police in Kansas City also suggested that individuals who live in high gun crime areas notice and value intensive efforts to root out guns in those areas (Shaw 1995). Another popular target of community-oriented policing efforts is the control of juveniles, particularly through the use of curfew laws and enforcement of truancy laws. Sherman (1995) reports that there is no strong evidence of whether such laws (whose enforcement apparently varies widely between jurisdictions) actually reduce crime and disorder. A 1991 San Antonio curfew law, for example, might have led to a 77 percent drop in crimes against juveniles and a 5 percent drop in juvenile arrests by 1993, but these changes cannot be conclusively linked to the law. More empirical work on interventions such as these will be necessary to establish their level of effectiveness.

High-Risk Persons and Places

Police have long known that crimes tend not to occur randomly over space and time (Bayley 1994; Sherman 1992a; Roncek and Maier 1991). For example, Sherman, Gartin, and Buerger (1989) found that half of the calls for police service during a one-year period in Minneapolis, Minnesota, were generated by about 3 percent of the addresses in that city. Among that 3 percent, the most active 5 percent of addresses were responsible for an average of twenty-four calls for service during the one-year period. Sherman and his associates (1989) described such areas as "hot spots" for police service calls. They argued that disproportionate policing in such areas might reduce the level of criminal activity in them (albeit with the possibility of displacement for certain types of crime; see e.g., Barr and Pease 1990).

Sherman and his colleagues (1989) argued that an experimental study, randomly assigning hot spots to treatment (more aggressive policing) and control (normal levels of police activity) conditions, would be the best way to test the hot spot hypothesis and examine the potential problem of displacement. Sherman and Weisburd (1995) described the results of such a test in Minneapolis for a 6.5 month period beginning in late 1988 and continuing through the summer of 1989. Randomly dividing 110 hot spots into high and regular "patrol dosage" areas, they found that high-dosage areas received about twice the level of patrol presence as the regular dosage areas.[2] Study outcomes included calls for police service about crimes and disorder.

Comparison of changes in call frequency from the year before the experiment to the year of the experiment were tallied for hard crimes, soft crimes, and total crime for both the experimental and the control areas. Hard crime calls decreased in both types of areas, but the difference in the magnitude of decrease between the experimental and control areas was not statistically significant. Soft and total crime calls both increased for the experimental and control areas but the increase was significantly greater for the control areas than for the experimental areas (Sherman and Weisburd 1995). Koper (1995) argues further that it may be possible to optimize the amount of time that patrol officers spend in a hot spot. He found that duration of police presence in hot spots was curvilinearly related to the waiting time between police departure and a new call for service. In addition, Koper discovered that for a one-minute increase in police presence at a hot spot, the length of time until the next crime or disorder occurred became significantly longer. It appears that the most effective stops were 13–15 minutes long; however, after 15 minutes, the benefits of police presence seems to decline. Sherman and Weisburd (1995) contend that some departments may wish to use heightened hot spot police patrol as a means to increase police contact with troubled communities; others may elect to initiate a strategy of roving "crackdown-backoff" patrol patterns where the crackdowns and backoffs occur in hot spot areas.

Sherman and his colleagues (1989, cited in Sherman 1992a) studied another approach to the problem of policing high-risk places. After identifying 125 commercial addresses with "highly predictable crime problems," a five-officer Repeat Call Address Policing (RECAP) squad attempted to formulate methods for reducing the calls for service at those locations. Sherman and his colleagues reported that several high crime/disorder locations were either closed down or physically modified to reduce their attractiveness to criminals. Comparison with control sites, however, revealed that the special squad was ineffective at reducing repeat calls for service (Sherman 1992a).[3]

In addition to focusing on high-risk places, research has also examined the utility of focusing on high risk-persons. One class of high-risk persons that researchers and practitioners alike have emphasized are repeat offenders, otherwise known as career criminals and habitual offenders (Blumstein et al. 1986; Wolfgang, Figlio and Selin 1972). Interest in constraining the criminal activities of repeat offenders is grounded in the persistent finding that a relatively small number of individuals contribute disproportionately to the total number of arrests within a particular cohort. The elimination of criminal behavior within this group via preventive, deterrent, or incapacitative strategies would ostensibly cause a significant reduction in crime rates (Blumstein et al. 1986).

In an application of this line of thought, Martin and Sherman (1986a, 1986b) examined the effectiveness of a specialized "repeat offender" unit in Washington, D.C. They concluded that repeat offender unit efforts were significantly more likely than routine reactive patrol efforts to arrest targeted offenders and that the repeat offender unit arrestees had significantly longer and more serious prior arrest records and faced a significantly higher probability of prosecution, conviction, and receiving a longer prison sentence. Nevertheless, officers in the repeat offender unit made fewer arrests than their counterparts in a control unit, and costs to implement the unit were high.

In a similar evaluation in Phoenix, Arizona, Abrahamse and his colleagues (1991) studied the effect of more intense investigative efforts by police officers and prosecutors on repeat offenders. After randomly assigning repeat offenders to experimental and control groups and following them for a six- to eighteen-month period, the investigators found no difference in conviction rates between subjects who were randomly assigned to experimental and control groups. Despite these similarities, however, their analysis did reveal higher likelihoods of imprisonment and longer average sentence lengths for the experimental group (among the subsample of individuals who were convicted).

Another example of high-profile police activity was the Kansas City randomized experiment on crack house raids that took place from November 1991 to May 1992. The primary theoretical proposition underlying the experiment predicted that high-profile crack house raids would "produce a short-term general deterrent effect on block-level crime and disorder" (Sherman and Rogan 1995b:762). Outcomes included calls for service and offense reports in the street block where crack houses were located. The experimental group was comprised of 98 locations where raids were carried out while a control group of 109 locations were "left alone" for at least 30 days. Analysis results revealed reductions in both outcome measures after the raids occurred, but the effects were relatively small and they decayed rapidly (within about 12 days). The results also revealed that the effect of raids accompanied by arrest did not differ from the effect of raids in general.

Police Effect on Guns and Drugs

One prominent component of contemporary problem-solving efforts includes attempts to reduce the availability of some criminogenic commodities such as guns and drugs (Moore et al. 1993). Moore and his colleagues argued that "the widespread availability of guns seems to facilitate violence by providing criminal offenders with a plentiful supply of weaponry" (p. 190). Sherman and Rogan (1995a) contended that aggressive police seizures of illegal guns or any guns from suspicious persons could result in reduced crime by one or more of three mechanisms. First, those who carry guns illegally might be deterred from carrying a gun if the certainty and severity of punishment associated with illegal carrying were increased. Second, for those who carry guns and have them confiscated, incapacitative effects for the time required to acquire a new gun might lead to net reductions in their levels of crime and violence. Third, more aggressive police monitoring of individuals for guns could increase deterrence for all crimes among all persons.

Sherman and Rogan (1995a) specifically subjected the hypothesis that increased gun seizures would be negatively associated with gun-related crimes. Using a quasi-experimental design comprised of a treatment area (increased gun-seizure activity) and a control area (regular levels of activity), they found that gun seizures increased significantly near gun-crime hot spots and that gun crimes fell significantly during the time of the intervention. The authors also reported that there was little evidence of local displacement (to contiguous areas), even though they could not rule out broader displacement patterns.

Similar approaches designed to control drug crimes and drug hot spots have been undertaken in two separate experiments. The first evaluation was conducted in Oakland, California and Birmingham, Alabama. In an effort to control street drug trafficking, the Oakland police employed a corps of specially trained officers who engaged in undercover buy-and-bust operations, aggressive patrol, and motor vehicle stops. In Birmingham, the narcotics division targeted buyers and sellers through buy-busts and sting operations and operated a minor community-oriented policing program. Both programs involved the use of "directed police-citizen contacts" in which citizens were surveyed regarding major problems in their neighborhoods. In both cities, the evaluation consisted of a pretest-posttest quasi-experimental design.

In their evaluation of the Oakland-Birmingham experiment, Uchida and his colleagues (1992) found some interesting results across the two cities. In Oakland, notable declines took place in reported crimes of violence in the beats that received door-to-door contact. In a finding that replicates much of the previous work in the foot patrol area, perceptions that drug trafficking was a problem declined and residents felt safer than before. In Birmingham, the evaluation suggested a possible reduction in property crime, and surveys of residents indicated a favorable response to police visits and police presence in the neighborhood. Uchida and his colleagues concluded that (1) police substations should be established to bring the police closer to neighborhoods with high levels of drug activity, and (2) door-to-door contacts should be conducted in areas with high levels of crime and disorder.

In the Jersey City drug market experiment, Weisburd and Green (1995) conducted a randomized experimental evaluation of an innovative drug-enforcement strategy. After identifying fifty-six hot spots of drug activity, Weisburd and Green randomized them into experimental and control conditions. The treatment involved engaging business owners and citizens in crime control efforts and applying pressure to reduce drug- and drug-related activity through police crackdowns. Comparison of seven-month pre- and post-intervention periods show evidence that the experimental strategy reduced calls for service. Furthermore, there was little evidence of displacement to study areas near the experimental hot spots.

Evidence failing to support the idea that police-community partnerships will strengthen the fight against crime and disorder comes from the Kansas City gun confiscation program (Sherman 1995). Going door-to-door in the affected communities, the police visited with homeowners, disseminated information, found that they were largely supportive of the program, and attempted to solicit tips and information that would lead to more gun confiscations and reduced crime. Evaluation of these efforts, however, revealed that they resulted in few tips and little actionable information for the police to use. As Sherman (1995) notes, such programs "may have many benefits, but reduced gun violence does not appear to be among them—at least not when attempted this way" (p. 340).

Problem-Solving Case Studies

There have been several major efforts to investigate the effectiveness of problem-solving approaches in different cities. It is worth pointing out, however, that no large U.S. city has successfully achieved full implementation of the principles of problem-solving policing throughout its entire police force, although efforts in Newport News, Virginia, suggest that it may be possible to achieve such a broad implementation (Goldstein 1990; Spelman and Eck 1987; Eck and Spelman 1987).

Three prominent examples of problem-solving case studies have been those in Madison, Wisconsin, Baltimore County, Maryland, and Newport News, Virginia (Goldstein 1990). The Madison police problem-solving efforts documented by Goldstein include attention to known sex offenders (and, more recently, other specialized groups of offenders) in the community, panhandling, prostitution, mentally ill persons in the community, and an annual hot rodder convention. At the time of the study, the department was also embarking on structural shifts toward a decentralized police force where officers were encouraged to identify problems in a proactive way.

Spelman and Eck (1987) provided detailed information on the Newport News implementation of a department-wide, problem-solving strategy. They concluded, on the basis of interrupted time-series studies of three problems, that the problem-solving strategy was a promising approach. Problem-solving efforts considered by the authors included burglaries in a lower-class apartment complex, larcenies from vehicles in Newport News shipyard parking lots, and personal robberies related to prostitution traffic in the downtown area.

The robbery problem was addressed by increasing judges' awareness of the problem and securing their cooperation in enhancing sentences and length of probation terms for convicted robbers, and increasing aggressive police enforcement of laws forbidding prostitution (especially probation violations of known prostitutes) in order to reduce the availability of targets (and the prostitution problem) in downtown Newport News. Key components to solving the problem included securing cooperation with rooming houses, bar owners, and the Alcohol Beverage Control Board to get prostitutes out of their places of business and into the street where the police could more easily intervene in transactions. The police also held liaisons with incoming Navy sailors to warn them of the consequences of participating in prostitution transactions (Spelman and Eck 1987).

Burglaries were a major problem in a particular apartment complex due in large part to the poor quality of the structure, which increased target vulnerability, and the lack of attention to basic upkeep of the facilities and grounds. Investigation of the problem led to efforts to improve these conditions, and significant burglary reductions were reported after improvements were made (Spelman and Eck 1987). On the other hand, larcenies from automobiles in a group of Newport News shipyards were a continuing source of calls and work for the police department, but officers were unsuccessful at making many arrests. After identifying an informant larcenist and interviewing officers and security guards who worked in the area, the police determined that most of the larcenies in the north end of town were drug-related while southern larcenies were more likely to be focused on stereo equipment and auto parts. Cars fitting certain "profiles" were targeted by the thieves as being likely to contain drugs and other desired commodities (Eck and Spelman 1987). The police used this information to begin aggressive monitoring of the area and of high-probability suspects, with the apparent result that arrests increased. The increases in arrests were accompanied by decreases in the number of automobile break-ins (Spelman and Eck 1987).

The problem-solving effort in Baltimore County, Maryland, involved the establishment of a forty-five-officer specialized problem-solving police unit known as COPE (Citizen-Oriented Police Enforcement) designed to confront public fear of crime. The basic operating procedure of the COPE unit was to (1) identify and assess problems that came to its attention, (2) survey households and businesses in the affected area as well as appropriate government agencies and officials (including other police officers), (3) formulate and implement a solution, and (4) conduct a follow-up survey to assess intervention effectiveness (Eck and Spelman 1987).

Eck and Spelman detailed two problems that were "solved" by the Baltimore COPE unit. Street robberies and burglaries in an apartment complex were responsible for generating a great deal of fear among residents in the complex. By surveying residents of the complex, the police found that individuals were greatly concerned about its poor physical conditions, which made them feel vulnerable to attacks. In response, the police organized the efforts of a number of agencies as well as the residents themselves in order to improve living conditions in the apartment complex. The outcome was a significant reduction in the rate of both burglaries and robberies in the community (Eck and Spelman 1987).

In another Baltimore community, residents feared using an area park because a makeshift shed on an adjacent property was a magnet for teenagers using alcohol and drugs. The highly visible, disorderly behavior of these youngsters deterred much of the public from going near the area. In response to the problem, the police tried, without much success, to get both the property owner and several city agencies to demolish the building. The police then decided to destroy the building themselves. Eck and Spelman (1987) report that the teenagers continued to engage in problem behavior, but the demolition of their meeting place forced them into less visible areas to do so. As a result of these efforts the park became much more frequently used by the neighborhood children.

Other examples of problem-solving efforts that are not rooted in a departmentally developed problem-solving strategy are described by Goldstein (1990). He gives two such initiatives prominent attention in a discussion of problem analysis: the Gainesville, Florida, police response to a rash of convenience store robberies and the Philadelphia police response to chronic disturbance calls at a local bar. In the wake of a surge in convenience store robberies during the spring of 1985, the Gainesville police department hypothesized that an ordinance requiring two clerks to be on duty at certain times of the day in convenience stores would lead to a reduction in convenience store robberies. The Gainesville city council, acting on the recommendation of the police, enacted an ordinance with this requirement, and one evaluator concluded that convenience store robberies dropped by 65 percent as a result (Clifton 1987, cited in Goldstein 1990).

Other researchers have challenged this conclusion, arguing that the recorded drop in convenience store robberies could have occurred for a number of alternative reasons (Wilson 1990, cited in Sherman 1991), including the apprehension of three known convenience store robbers and the imposition of other mandatory convenience store security laws at about the same time as the two-clerk ordinance took effect. Moreover, the steep increase in robberies immediately prior to the law's imposition implies that post-intervention robberies may have simply regressed to the mean (Sherman 1990). The problem of ruling out alternative causes would also seem applicable to the case studies reported by Eck and Spelman (1987).

The Philadelphia police response to a chronic "noisy bar problem" was, as Sherman (1990:694) notes, "an archetype of common sense." The bar in question had been responsible for 505 disturbance calls during a six-month period. Careful examination of the conditions in the bar revealed that the problem was not noise, *per se*, but the vibrations emanating from the bar's jukebox disturbed a neighbor who shared a common wall with the bar. The police successfully persuaded the bar to move the jukebox to another wall in the bar, and disturbance calls to the police about the bar stopped (Goldstein 1990). Other measures which largely remain unevaluated include steps such as access control to and locations of automated teller machines, controls on opportunities by restricting hours of operation for merchants, and restrictions on taverns that continually generate work for police as well as crime and disorder for the communities in which they are located (Sherman 1995). Unfortunately, the effects of such interventions remain largely undocumented.

In sum, the evidence on effectiveness of problem-solving strategies seems to have an optimistic tone. Unfortunately, much of it is anecdotal and not scientifically rigorous (Sherman 1991). Although anecdotal evidence of the sort typically invoked in discussions of problem-solving strategies is not inherently problematic, Moore (1992) contends that exclusive reliance on example cases to make inferences is a hazardous exercise for at least three reasons: (1) they may not accurately communicate what actually occurred; (2) the magnitude of the effect may not be substantively important even though it achieves some subjective level of importance; and (3) they do not demonstrate the ability of the strategy to operate at a general level (it may be that the tactics of problem-solving are only applicable to particular, restrictive contexts). Thus, a critical issue in the area of problem-solving is the need for more rigorous research designs and multiple-site studies to evaluate the effectiveness of various measures.

Police Response to Domestic Violence

An archetypal problem faced by police throughout the United States is determining the "optimal" response to misdemeanor domestic violence calls (those cases where officers have traditionally exercised their own discretion about whether to arrest suspects). During the past two decades, police have become increasingly concerned about the problem of domestic violence. In their Minneapolis experiment comparing arrest responses to nonarrest responses, Sherman and Berk (1984) found that suspects who were arrested were significantly less likely to recidivate. Replications of this experiment in other cities around the United States, however, produced a bewildering array of findings. In some cities (Omaha, Charlotte, and Milwaukee), arrest actually appeared to exert a criminogenic effect on future spousal assault, while arrest warrants served when offenders were absent from the scene in Omaha appeared to exert a deterrent effect; results were mixed in two additional cities (Colorado Springs and Miami), depending on the operational definition of outcomes (see, e.g., Sherman 1992b; Garner, Fagan and Maxwell 1995). Some evidence (Milwaukee, Colorado Springs, and Omaha) even suggests that characteristics of persons such as their unemployment and marital status (Sherman and Smith 1992) as well as the communities in which they live (Marciniak 1994) can condition the effects of arrest on future domestic violence.

In response to the Minneapolis results and already well-organized political movements, many police departments implemented mandatory-arrest policies in cases of misdemeanor domestic violence. The more recent replication findings have given these same police departments reason for pause. An important dilemma facing police departments and other criminal justice agencies in the future concerns the question of how research results are to be obtained and used to guide the formulation of policy. Sherman (1992b) argues that policy should be formulated on the basis of the best available evidence about expected outcomes and that police departments and researchers should continuously be engaged in the business of conducting research to improve our understanding of the likely effects of various policy alternatives.

Police and Communities

Arguing that community policing involves aggressive "watching" of communities and neighborhoods, Sherman (1995) views community policing as analogous to security guard policing of client properties. Wilson and Kelling (1982; see also Kelling and Coles 1996) take a similar position, emphasizing the value of policing that corrects the minor incivilities and disorders that detract from the ability of the community to regulate itself and achieve its common goals. Although such problems seem minor compared to serious crime, this model assumes that seemingly minor community deterioration increases fear of crime and social disorganization, which ultimately cause people to withdraw from their communities and create environments conducive to criminal behavior (Skogan 1986). To others, community policing implies relatively simple adjustments to the current professional strategy, such as increased foot patrol or heightened police strength (for criticisms, see Walker 1994).

Several attempts have been made to incorporate more aggressive community-police interaction than was traditionally the case in the professional policing model. During the early 1970s (in the wake of the 1967 Crime Commission critique of contemporary policing practices), for example, many police departments began to experiment with a concept called "team policing" that provided for numerous, small-scale police sub-departments tied to specific geographic sectors of metropolitan areas. These sub-departments had responsibility for all police activity in their assigned area, including patrol, response to service calls, and investigation.

Descriptions of team policing evaluation work vary widely. Indeed, depending on what description one reads, the evidence on team policing is read as generally positive (Moore 1992), generally a failure (Rosenbaum and Lurigio 1994), and generally unknown because of inconclusive implementation and evaluation of team policing efforts (Sherman 1986). Thus, there is no consensus on what the few evaluations of team policing actually show about its effectiveness. Despite promising early results, team policing disappeared from the landscape by the end of the 1970s, apparently because of organizational resistance to the approach and increased constraints on resources (Moore 1992; Sherman 1986). One particularly important organizational obstacle appeared to lie in the shift of power from central bureaucracies to officers and sergeants in the field (Sherman 1986).

Another prominent strategy of community-intensive policing is the use of police foot patrol. Historically, foot patrols occupied a central position in the implementation of public policing (Kelling 1988). With the emergence of motorized patrol in the early and middle years of the twentieth century, foot patrol was de-emphasized as inefficient and inadequate for the demands of modern professional policing (Kelling and Moore 1988). During the late 1970s and early 1980s, however, citizen demands for foot patrol by police intensified and police departments in a number of cities around the United States implemented them.

Two major evaluations of the effects of foot patrol were conducted during the early 1980s in Newark, New Jersey and Flint, Michigan (Moore 1992). The results of these evaluations suggested that increased foot patrol by police was not associated with reduced levels of crime, but it was noticed by citizens and it also appeared to be associated with reduced fear of crime and increased public satisfaction with the police (Moore 1992).[4] This result contrasts starkly with earlier analysis of random preventive patrol which suggested that increased motorized patrols were not noticed by citizens and did not affect their perceptions of safety (Kelling et al. 1974; see also Krahn and Kennedy 1985:706).

Elaborations of these studies assessing foot patrol in conjunction with the establishment of neighborhood ministations, the publication of newsletters, and crackdowns on disorderly conditions in Houston and Newark suggested that the package of community-oriented measures had modest (if any) direct effects on crime, but their effect on fear of crime was apparently robust (Moore 1992).[5] For example, Sherman (1992a:197) observes that such measures "produced a decline in recorded crime (but not surveyed victimization) in an experimental area in Newark." As Skogan (1986) has argued, the results of fear reduction/neighborhood stabilization efforts may also have long-term effects on criminal behavior that are not apparent from observing short-term fluctuations in crime rates. An important future task for researchers and practitioners is to put this hypothesis to a systematic test. To date much of the evidence is either inconclusive or negative (Hope 1995).

The Chicago Alternative Policing Strategy (CAPS) was designed to provide such a test (Skogan 1995). The ongoing evaluation is being conducted in five prototype police districts in Chicago, Illinois. Several tactics have been implemented in these areas in order to carry out this strategy. They have included aggressive policing of disorder and crime, active monitoring of citizen and police opinions about the effort, the implementation of district advisory committees, beat meetings, community-police partnerships, and the enlistment of community organizations in efforts to reduce disorder and crime. In the second year of the ongoing evaluation, Skogan reports that crime and disorder have both declined in the prototype areas, white and black citizen evaluations of police have improved (although Hispanic evaluations have not changed), and police involved in the program were more optimistic than their non-CAPS counterparts about the potential impact of the program in multiple areas.

Skogan (1995) also reports some obstacles, noting that (1) district advisory committees that took on short-term manageable tasks and set realistic goals were more successful than committees that emphasized broad concerns or advocated major public policy changes; (2) beat meetings were predominantly conducted by police, "hindering the development of police-citizen partnerships" (p. 2); and (3) citizen involvement in problem solving tended to diminish once the citizens had alerted public officials to the existence of a problem.

Neighborhood Crime Watch Programs

Community crime prevention programs initiated by members of the community, occasionally with police involvement, engage in a broad array of activities designed to reduce the opportunities and modify the neighborhood environment to make it less conducive to crime and disorder (Moore 1992). Crime prevention activities, as Rosenbaum (1986:19) notes, take on a variety of forms "including resident patrols, citizen crime reporting systems, block watch programs, home security surveys, property marking projects, police community councils, and a variety of plans for changing the physical environment" (see also Moore 1992:136).

Rosenbaum (1986) considered the effects of community crime prevention programs in several cities. In Seattle and Portland, programs were burglary oriented and achieved reductions in burglary incidence in the communities where they were implemented. The Hartford program emphasized community mobilization and physical arrangements and had beneficial effects on the incidence of robbery, burglary, and on citizen fear of crime. The Chicago program was a broad community organization effort and apparently had no effect on the major outcomes under study.

Specialized efforts to target fear of crime have been evaluated in Baltimore, Houston, and Newark (Rosenbaum and Lurigio 1994). The Houston program involved door-to-door surveys, community meetings, and collaborative involvement in problem solving by citizens and police officials. These programs did not reduce fear of crime but apparently did impact citizens' perceptions of neighborhood disorder and their view of the police. The Baltimore program also intensified contact between communities and the police through the use of specialized fifteen-member squads designed to confront existing crime problems and the fear that accompanied them. Evaluation of this effort revealed "reductions in fear of crime, but the evaluation had several methodological problems, including the absence of a control group and the use of police officers as interviewers" (pp. 308–9). The Newark program was successful in achieving its goals but the unique contribution of different community policing tactics could not be identified.

Evaluations of police-initiated community relations efforts, including community outreach, DARE interventions in the public schools, "Officer Friendly" programs, various crime prevention programs such as property marking and security surveys, door-to-door neighborhood visits, and special "community relations squads," have had mixed results. Indeed, most of these efforts have not been subjected to rigorous evaluation. Those that have, such as DARE interventions, have not been found to reduce problem behavior although they continue to be popular (see, e.g., Walker 1994:268; Bureau of Justice Statistics 1992:106; Reiss and Roth 1993:207). Further, Moore (1992) contends that specialized community outreach units within police departments actually impede efforts to bring the police and the community closer together because they insulate most of the department from being concerned about the issues that concern the community relations unit.

Skogan (1990) reports on the effectiveness of two neighborhood crime watch programs in Chicago and Minneapolis. Comprised of block watch groups and other crime prevention efforts, the focus in Chicago was on disorder reduction. Results from this program suggested that it operated less for the people who needed it the most (i.e., those lowest on the social ladder). Moreover, results obtained from citizens after the program was implemented revealed that both physical and social disorders, as well as fear of crime, increased rather than decreased.

In Minneapolis, the neighborhood watch program was comprised of professional organizers working for the city who attempted to create block clubs for the purpose of organizing neighborhoods. However, after general meetings between the citizens and the professional organizers, it was left up to the residents to undertake crime prevention measures. As was true for the Chicago program, those individuals who had higher incomes, owned homes, were long-term residents of single-family homes, and those higher on the social ladder were more likely to hear about the program as well as participate in it (Skogan 1990). Moreover, there was no evidence of any program impact on such factors as residents' watchfulness or reporting to the police. In addition, a two-year follow-up revealed that the residents of the program area did not differ in any significant way on measure of perceived social disorder, physical deterioration, crime problems, and fear of crime.

A question arising from these two studies concerns whether or not community approaches to crime control are viable. Perhaps the most significant barrier in both of these programs concerns the lack of official police officer involvement. In Minneapolis, not only were the residents left to fend for themselves, they could not get the police involved in their program; while in Chicago, the project chose not to have the police involved. This component is very important, since research has suggested that crime prevention groups start up and persist more easily when they operate in conjunction with the police (see Garofalo and McLeod 1986). Moreover, this problem is magnified when efforts to have solid police-community partnerships occur in neighborhoods (i.e., poor, minority) which already have strained police-community relationships (see Skogan 1990).

The most important element of community crime prevention appears to be creating social interaction, whereby residents of the community maintain a degree of familiarity with each other (Mukherjee and Wilson 1987; Skogan 1990). The model (i.e., community informal social control) that Shaw and McKay envisioned some time ago should be quite relevant to accomplishing this task (see also Bursik and Grasmick 1993). Recent work by Taylor (1997) has attempted to explicate the process surrounding the parochial (i.e., nearby acquaintances) level of informal social control in three ways by: (a) recognizing within-neighborhood variations in informal social control and responses to disorder; (b) acknowledging the central importance of street blocks as durable features of the everyday environment connecting residents to broader ecological dynamics in their neighborhoods; and (c) developing microecological principles, analogous to human ecological principles, to help clarify the connection between street block and community-level ecological dynamics.

Taken as a whole, some evidence suggests that even when police efforts are found to have relatively modest effects on the behavior of offenders, those efforts can go a long way toward helping citizens feel safer in the communities in which they live. Moreover, Moore (1992:137) contends that "these studies suggest that narrowly targeted, well-designed and executed programs that seek to mobilize citizens to produce crime preventive effects can reduce the incidence of important crimes such as robbery and burglary." This point, however, clearly continues to be controversial. Future research will be required to evaluate the success of these efforts in creating lasting change in public perceptions and their potential for indirect but important effects on crime and disorder.

Discussion and Conclusion

The critical question facing policy makers and the public is as basic as determining the very mission of the police. In short, what do we want the police to do? Everyone seems agreed that the police should control crime and disorder. Informed opinion diverges, however, on the question of whether the control of crime and disorder should be *all* that the police do (Gottfredson and Hirschi 1990; Sherman 1995). Ultimately, this is a philosophical question to be resolved by the public and their legislative representatives. Bayley (1994:220) contends, for example, that:

> If communities can define police work, a new center of political power has been established. Community policing represents a renegotiation of the social contract between the police and society.

Whether Bayley's vision should come to be is not an empirical question, although parties to the debate may well ground their opinions in empirical research (Sherman 1992b). The empirical question is whether and to what degree the police have achieved the goals that have been set for them. Research on what the police can do to prevent crime and disorder must be interpreted carefully. The field will undoubtedly benefit from the articulation of theoretical frameworks from which testable hypotheses can be deduced. Currently, the "broken windows" thesis of Wilson and Kelling is receiving a great deal of attention (see also Kelling and Coles 1996).

Much attention has been paid within the past year to the efforts of the New York City police department. By now, it is common knowledge that crime decreased dramatically in New York City under former police commissioner William Bratton. For example, homicides decreased by 25 percent between 1994 and 1995, and total felonies are down by 27 percent, a level not seen since the early 1970s (Pooley 1996).

So, what has led to this dramatic reduction in New York City? Many argue that the imposition of more aggressive policing, following the "broken windows" thesis, has had some effect. Police practices in this area include cracking down on incivilities and minor disorder, such as panhandling, public drunkenness, and loitering. In addition, the NYCPD is using crime statistics and weekly meetings of key police personnel to direct its enforcement efforts and better allocate its resources. New York City officials attribute the reductions in crime to a combination of these approaches. For example, former NYCPD commissioner William Bratton (1996) credits the dramatic crime reductions as a result of police efforts which include sustained and tactical enforcement of quality-of-life misdemeanor offenses, vigorous enforcement of "serious" felony crimes, and the concomitant incapacitation of "career criminals." Nevertheless, a key question, to which the answer is currently unknown, is whether these practices have merely been associated with or have actually caused crime reductions in New York City. Only through rigorous research designs targeted to test specific hypotheses can questions such as these be answered.

How might such a design be executed in cities like New York City? One possibility is the interrupted time-series model. The basic objective is to examine changes in the incidence of crime before and after the implementation of a new policy. For example, daily crime counts can be computed both before and after the initiation of a new patrol pattern. By developing an appropriate statistical model for the pre- and post-intervention time series, it is possible to get consistent estimates of the effect of the intervention. The problem of estimating the effect of police attacks on crime is particularly amenable to this methodology. To date, there has been much discussion in the literature about the effects of police attacks on crime without much corresponding attention to the rigorous estimation of the magnitude of those effects.

Research on the relationship between police practices and criminal behavior will also profit from the use of experimental designs to estimate the effects of variations in those practices on crime. With the notable exception of studies of police response to misdemeanor domestic violence incidents, there has been little purely experimental research in the policing literature. The effects of police patrol practices, gun and drug enforcement, and community policing initiatives can all be evaluated with completely randomized experimental designs. Moreover, while these designs maximize internal validity of cstimatcd effects, attention must be paid to replicating initial study results in different places and at different times.

This review of the research suggests that unqualified conclusions about any police intervention in any area are premature. Among the most consistent findings are the following: (1) efforts to achieve a strong police presence in communities are likely to result in some fear reduction but not necessarily crime reduction itself; and (2) efforts to aggressively police communities, through enforcement of minor disorder and incivilities as well as through interrogations of persons that appear to be "suspicious," seem to be associated with lower rates of crime. These results suggest that there are interesting possibilities for efficacious and proactive prevention-oriented policing. Whether they point the way to sound policy awaits more rigorous research and resolution of debate about the proper role of the police in American life.

Notes

[1] Sherman notes that suppressible crimes are described as such because they are "in theory most sensitive to field stops" (1992a:188).

[2] Sherman and Weisburd (1995:635) reported that only the 50 most active of the 55 experimental and control hot spots were included in the analysis for a total analysis sample of 100 hot spots. They stated that "the five 'coolest' spots in each treatment [*sic*] group were eliminated from the observations to maximize measurement of the places producing the largest volume of crime."

[3] Sherman (1992a) reports that two of the places closed down were taverns where disorderly conduct was a consistent problem due to liquor sales to intoxicated customers and drug sales. The RECAP unit had their liquor licenses suspended and both taverns were later torn down for "urban renewal."

[4] As Kelling (1988:3) notes, "[t]he Flint experiment yielded two additional important findings. First, in areas where there was aggressive foot patrol, calls for service via telephone were reduced by more than 40 percent. Second, there was a modest reduction in crime. (There were no changes in crime levels in Newark as a result of use of foot patrols)."

[5] But see Hope (1995:60), who contends that "police crackdowns on street disorder in Newark, New Jersey, seem to have bordered on the infringement of civil liberties without noticeable effect on residents' levels of fear."

References

Abrahamse, A. F., P. A. Ebener, P. W. Greenwood, N. Fitzgerald, and T. E. Kosin (1991). An Experimental Evaluation of the Phoenix Repeat Offender Program. *Justice Quarterly*, 8(2): 141–68.

Barr, R. and K. Pease (1990). Crime Placement, Displacement, and Deflection. In M. Tonry and N. Morris (eds.), *Crime and Justice: A Review of Research*, vol. 12, pp. 277–318. Chicago: University of Chicago Press.

Bayley, D. H. (1994). *Police For The Future*. New York: Oxford.

Blumstein, A., J. Cohen, J. A. Roth, and C. A. Visher (eds.) (1986). *Criminal Careers and "Career Criminals"* (vol. 1). Washington, DC: National Academy Press.

Boydstun, J. (1975). San Diego Field Interrogation: Final Report. Washington, DC: Police Foundation.

Bratton, W. (1996). *Great Expectations: How Higher Expectations for Police Departments Can Lead to a Decrease in Crime.* Discussion Paper. Washington, DC: National Institute of Justice.

Bureau of Justice Statistics (1992). *Drugs, Crime and the Justice System.* Washington, DC: U.S. Government Printing Office.

Bursik, R., and H. Grasmick (1993). *Neighborhoods and Crime.* New York: Lexington.

Chaiken, J. (1978). What is Known about Deterrent Effects of Police Activities. In J. Cramer (ed.), *Preventing Crime.* Beverly Hills: Sage.

Clarke, R. (1995). Situational Crime Prevention. In M. Tonry and D. Farrington (eds.), *Crime and Justice: A Review of Research*, vol. 19, pp. 91–150. Chicago: University of Chicago Press.

Clifton, W., Jr. (1987). *Convenience Store Robberies in Gainesville, Florida: An Intervention Strategy by the Gainesville Police Department.* Gainesville, Florida Police Department.

Eck, J. E. and W. Spelman (1987). Who Ya Gonna Call? The Police As Problem-Busters. *Crime and Delinquency*, 33(1): 31–52.

Fienberg, S., K. Larntz, and A. Reiss (1976). Redesigning the Kansas City Preventive Patrol Experiment. *Evaluation*, 3:124–31.

Garner, J., J. Fagan, and C. Maxwell (1995). Published Findings from the Spousal Assault Replication Program: A Critical Review. *Journal of Quantitative Criminology*, 11:3–28.

Garofalo, J. and M. McLeod (1986). *Improving the Effectiveness and Utilization of Neighborhood Watch Programs. Research in Action.* Washington, DC: National Institute of Justice.

Goldstein, H. (1987). Toward Community-Oriented Policing: Potential, Basic Requirements, and Threshold Questions. *Crime and Delinquency,* 33(1): 6–30.

_____. 1990. *Problem-Oriented Policing.* New York: McGraw-Hill.

Gottfredson, M. R. and T. Hirschi (1990). *A General Theory of Crime.* Stanford: Stanford University Press.

Hope, T. (1995). Community Crime Prevention. In M. Tonry and D. Farrington (eds.), *Crime and Justice: An Annual Review of Research,* vol. 19, pp. 21–89. Chicago: University of Chicago Press.

Jacob, H. and M. J. Rich (1980). The Effects of the Police on Crime: A Second Look. *Law and Society Review*, 15(1): 109–22.

Kelling, G. (1988). *Police and Communities: The Quiet Revolution.* Washington, DC: National Institute of Justice.

Kelling, G., and C. Coles (1996). *Fixing Broken Windows.* New York: Free Press.

Kelling, G. L. and M. H. Moore (1988). The Evolving Strategy of Policing. In *Perspectives on Policing*, no. 4. Washington, DC: National Institute of Justice.

Kelling, G., T. Pate, D. Dieckman, and C. Brown (1974). *The Kansas City Preventive Patrol Experiment.* Washington, DC: The Police Foundation.

Koper, C. (1995). Just Enough Police Presence: Reducing Crime and Disorderly Behavior by Optimizing Patrol Time in Crime Hot Spots. *Justice Quarterly*, 12:649–72.

Kornhauser, R. (1978). *Social Sources of Delinquency: An Appraisal of Analytic Methods.* Chicago: University of Chicago Press.

Krahn, H. and L. W. Kennedy (1985). Producing Personal Safety: The Effects of Crime Rates, Police Force Size, and Fear of Crime. *Criminology*, 23(4): 697–710.

Larson, R. (1976). What Happened to Patrol Operations in Kansas City. *Evaluation,* 3:117–23.

Legge, J. S., Jr. (1991). *Traffic Safety Reform in the United States and Great Britain.* Pittsburgh: University of Pittsburgh Press.

Manning, P. (1984). Community Policing. *American Journal of Police,* 3:205–27.

Marciniak, E. (1994). Community Policing of Domestic Violence: Neighborhood Differences in the Effect of Arrest. Unpublished Ph.D. Dissertation. College Park: University of Maryland.

Martin, S. and L. Sherman (1986a). Catching Career Criminals: Proactive Policing and Selective Apprehension. *Justice Quarterly,* 3:171–92.

_____. (1986b). Selective Apprehension: A Police Strategy for Repeat Offenders. *Criminology,* 24:155–73.

Moore, M. H. (1992). Problem-Solving and Community Policing. In M. Tonry and N. Morris (eds.), *Crime and Justice: A Review of Research,* vol. 15, pp. 99–158. Chicago: University of Chicago Press.

Moore, M. H., D. Prothrow-Smith, B. Guyer, and H. Spivak (1993). Violence and Intentional Injuries: Criminal Justice and Public Health Perspectives On An Urgent National Problem. In A. J. Reiss, Jr. and J. A. Roth (eds.), *Understanding and Preventing Violence,* vol. 4, pp. 167–216. Washington, DC: National Academy Press.

Moore, M., R. Trojanowicz, and G. Kelling (1988). *Crime and Policing.* Washington, DC: National Institute of Justice.

Mukherjee, S. and P. Wilson (1987). Neighborhood Watch: Issues and Policy Implications. In P. Wilson (ed.), *Trends and Issues in Criminology and Criminal Justice,* vol. 8. Canberra: Australian Institute of Criminology.

Pfuhl, E., Jr. (1983). Police Strikes and Conventional Crime. *Criminology,* 21:489–503.

Pooley, E. (1996). One Good Apple. *Time,* January 15:54–56.

Reiss, A, J., Jr. and J. A. Roth (eds.) (1993). *Understanding and Preventing Violence.* Washington, DC: National Academy Press.

Roncek, D. and P. Marier (1991). Bars, Blocks, and Crimes Revisited: Linking the Theory of Routine Activities to the Empiricism of "Hot Spots." *Criminology,* 29(4): 725–53.

Rosenbaum, D. P. (1986). *Community Crime Prevention: Does It Work?* Beverly Hills: Sage.

Rosenbaum, D. P. and A. Lurigio (1994). An Inside Look at Community Policing Reform: Definitions, Organizational Changes, and Evaluation Findings. *Crime and Delinquency,* 40:299–314.

Ross, H. L. (1992a). *Confronting Drunk Driving: Social Policy for Saving Lives.* New Haven: Yale University Press.

_____. (1992b). The Law and Drunk Driving. *Law and Society Review,* 26(1): 219–30.

Sampson, R. J. and J. Cohen (1988). Deterrent Effects of the Police on Crime: A Replication and Theoretical Extension. *Law and Society Review,* 22(1): 163–89.

Sampson, R. J. and W. Groves (1989). Community Structure and Crime: Testing Social-Disorganization Theory. *American Journal of Sociology,* 94:774–802.

Shaw, J. W. (1995). Community Policing Against Guns: Pubic Opinion of the Kansas City Gun Experiment. *Justice Quarterly,* 12:695–710.

Sherman, L. W. (1983). Patrol Strategies for Police. In J. Wilson (ed.), *Crime and Public Policy,* pp. 145–63. San Francisco, CA: ICS Press.

_____. (1986). Policing Communities: What Works? In M. Tonry and A. J. Reiss (eds.), *Crime and Justice: A Review of Research,* vol. 8, pp. 343–86. Chicago: University of Chicago Press.

_____. (1990). Police Crackdowns. In M. Tonry and N. Morris. *Crime and Justice: A Review of Research,* vol. 12, pp. 1–48. Chicago: University of Chicago Press.

Sherman, L. W. (1991). Book Review. *Journal of Criminal Law and Criminology*, 82:690–707.

_____. (1992a). Attacking Crime: Police and Crime Control. In M. Tonry and N. Morris (eds.), *Crime and Justice: A Review of Research*, vol. 15, pp. 159–230. Chicago: University of Chicago Press.

_____. (1992b). *Policing Domestic Violence: Experiments and Dilemmas*. New York: Free Press.

_____. (1995). The Police. In J. Q. Wilson and J. Petersilia (eds.), *Crime*, pp. 327–48. San Francisco: ICS Press.

Sherman, L. and R. Berk (1984). The Specific Deterrent Effects of Arrest for Domestic Assault. *American Sociological Review*, 49:261–72.

Sherman, L., P. Gartin, and M. Buerger (1989). Hot Spots of Predatory Crime: Routine Activities and the Criminology of Place. *Criminology*, 27:27–55.

Sherman, L. and D. Rogan (1995a). Effects of Gun Seizures on Gun Violence: "Hot Spots" Patrols in Kansas City. *Justice Quarterly,* 12:673–93.

_____. (1995b). Deterrent Effects of Police Raids on Crack Houses: A Randomized Controlled Experiment. *Justice Quarterly*, 12:755–81.

Sherman, L. and D. Smith (1992). Crime, Punishment and Stake in Conformity: Legal, Extralegal Control of Domestic Violence. *American Sociological Review*, 57:680–90.

Sherman, L. and D. Weisburd (1995). General Deterrent Effects of Police in Crime "Hot Spots": A Randomized Controlled Trial. *Justice Quarterly*, 12:625–48.

Skogan, W. (1986). Fear of Crime and Neighborhood Change. In M. Tonry and A. J. Reiss (eds.), *Crime and Justice: A Review of Research*, vol. 8, pp. 203–30. Chicago: University of Chicago Press.

_____. (1990). *Disorder and Decline: Crime and the Spiral of Decay in American Neighborhoods*. New York: Free Press

_____. (1995). *Community Policing in Chicago: Year Two*. Washington, DC: National Institute of Justice.

Skolnick, J. and D. Bayley (1988). Theme and Variation in Community Policing. In M. Tonry and N. Morris (eds.), *Crime and Justice: A Review of Research,* vol. 10, pp. 1–37. Chicago: University of Chicago Press.

Spelman, W. and J. Eck (1987). *Problem-Oriented Policing*. Washington, DC: National Institute of Justice.

Taylor, R. (1997). Social Order and Disorder of Street Blocks and Neighborhoods: Ecology, Microecology, and the Systemic Model of Social Disorganization. *Journal of Research in Crime and Delinquency*, 34(1): 113–55.

Taylor, R. and A. Harrell (1996). *Physical Environment and Crime. A Final Summary Report Presented to the National Institute of Justice*. Washington, DC: National Institute of Justice.

Uchida, C., B. Forst, and S. Annan (1992). *Modern Policing and the Control of Illegal Drugs: Testing New Strategies in Two American Cities*. Washington, DC: National Institute of Justice.

Walker, S. (1984). "Broken Windows" and Fractured History: The Use and Misuse of History in Recent Police Patrol Analysis. *Justice Quarterly*, 1:75–90.

_____. (1994). *Sense and Nonsense About Crime and Drugs: A Policy Guide* (3d ed). Belmont, CA: Wadsworth.

Weisburd, D. and L. Green (1995). Policing Drug Hot Spots: The Jersey City Drug Market Analysis Experiment. *Justice Quarterly*, 12(4): 711–35.

Wilson, J. Q. and B. Boland (1978). The Effect of the Police on Crime. *Law and Society Review*, 12:367–90.

_____. (1981). The Effects of the Police on Crime: A Response To Jacob and Rich. *Law and Society Review*, 16(1): 163–72.

Wilson, J. Q. and G. Kelling (1982). Broken Windows: The Police and Neighborhood Safety. *Atlantic Monthly*, (March): 29–38.

Wilson, J. (1990). Gainesville Convenience Store Ordinance: Findings of Fact, Conclusions and Recommendations. Unpublished Report. Crime Control Research Corporation.

Wolfgang, M., R. Figlio, and T. Sellin (1972). *Delinquency in a Birth Cohort*. Chicago: University of Chicago Press.

11

An Inside Look at Community Policing Reform
Definitions, Organizational Changes, and Evaluation Findings

Dennis P. Rosenbaum and *Arthur J. Lurigio*

Community policing is currently the watchword for law enforcement in America. Across the country, departments are experimenting with this latest reform in policing, which is designed to respond to increasing demands for a model of policing that can alleviate crime, drug trafficking, disorder, and public dissatisfaction with police services. To say that community policing is overwhelmingly popular among police managers, citizens, and politicians is a gross understatement. It is the centerpiece of the Clinton administration's anti-crime policy and the topic of numerous books and conferences, and it is touted as the "only form of policing available for anyone who seeks to improve police operations, management, or relations with the public" (Eck and Rosenbaum 1994, p. 4).

Despite a wealth of ringing endorsements, community policing leaves unanswered many basic questions about its structure and impact. What exactly is community policing? Can it be implemented as planned? Will it be a panacea or a passing fad? Should it become the prevailing paradigm for policing in the United States? This article attempts to address some of these questions. (Interested readers should consult Greene and Mastrofski [1988]; Rosenbaum [1994]; Skolnick and Bayley [1988]; Trojanowicz and Bucqueroux [1989] for fuller treatments of the area.) In this article, we discuss some of the basic issues surrounding community policing and provide a brief, selective survey of research in the field.

Source: Reprinted by permission of Sage Publications from *Crime & Delinquency*, Vol. 40., No. 3 (July), pp. 299–314. Copyright 1994 Sage Publications, Inc.

Background

During the past twenty years, numerous demonstration projects and evaluations have highlighted the limitations of traditional police practices. Specifically, evaluators have challenged the effectiveness of random motorized patrols (Kelling et al. 1974), rapid response strategies (Kelling et al. 1974; Spelman and Brown 1984), routine criminal investigations (Eck 1982; Greenwood, Chaiken, and Petersilia 1977), and traditional crime analyses (Gay, Beall, and Bowers 1984).

In the 1970s and 1980s, police research also amplified the role of citizens in solving crime. Information from the public forms the basis for the majority of arrests (Skogan and Antunes 1979). In most police departments, clearance rates are low because officers do not receive useful tips about crime (Eck 1982; Spelman et al. 1985). Moreover, local residents are the primary source of information concerning neighborhood problems; police asking citizens for their input about the community is considered a significant innovation in law enforcement (Pate et al. 1986). In short, the realization that the police are very dependent on the cooperation of private citizens to reduce crime and to improve public safety was a major impetus behind community policing.

Modern police reform has been characterized by false starts and implementation failures. However, there is growing evidence that the situation is changing. More police departments in America are now modifying their philosophies and practices and are initiating their activities with more careful planning. Many are testing new policies, programs, and organizational structures that have been variously described as community policing, neighborhood-oriented policing, and problem-oriented policing.

What Is Community Policing?

Team policing. Team policing was one of the earliest efforts to redefine police practices in terms of a community orientation. In 1967 the police task force of the President's Commission on Law Enforcement and Administration of Justice proposed team policing as a vehicle to bring together the beat officer and the community. This recommendation was followed by a series of demonstration programs and evaluations in many U.S. cities (see Anderson 1978; Bloch and Specht 1972; Schwartz and Clarren 1977; Sherman, Milton, and Kelly 1973). Team policing called for long-term beat assignments that would allow officers to become familiar with the neighborhood, to interact with other officers for the purpose of exchanging information and planning activities, and to have greater contact with the community through meetings and "walk-and-talk" foot patrols.

Although the notion of team policing was appealing, attempts to implement it generally failed. By the end of the 1970s, team policing had been discredited in most police circles. As with many reform efforts, the concept was repudiated along with the failed demonstration programs; that is, researchers and practitioners did not differentiate theory failure from implementation failure (cf. Rosenbaum 1987). Consequently, it has taken some time to restore the more useful aspects of team policing.

Overall, evaluations of team policing, including the large-scale evaluation in Cincinnati, did not produce favorable results (Schwartz and Clarren 1977). However, the majority of police officers involved with these programs believed that team policing was discarded not because its community orientation was undesirable but because the organizational problems associated with decentralized decision making became insurmountable.

The concept of community policing. In the 1980s, when team policing had been mostly forgotten, plans for narrowing the schism between the police and the community were repackaged under the rubric of community policing. The proper definition of community policing has been the source of much debate in police and academic circles during the past few years (Eck and Spelman 1987, Goldstein 1990; Rosenbaum 1988; Skolnick and Bayley 1988). The distinction between community and problem-oriented policing was a focal point of that discussion. By the 1990s the focus on differences faded and the commonality of these various approaches is now being underscored. There are numerous definitions of the theory and practice of community policing, although they have common themes, which include "an emphasis on improving the number and quality of police-citizen contacts, a broader definition of 'legitimate' police work, decentralization of the police bureaucracy, and a greater emphasis on proactive problem-solving strategies" (Rosenbaum 1988, p. 334). Skogan's (1990) notion of community policing focused on these same dimensions. The guiding principles that he articulated also emphasized that the police be "responsive to citizen demands" and committed to "helping neighborhoods help themselves" (p. 92).

Although some common threads run through many of the definitions of community policing, concerns about the ambiguity of the concept were expressed as early as 1985 (Murphy and Muir). Recently, Moore (1994) has observed that "the concept of community policing is a complex one. At the moment, it is more a set of challenging, general ideas pointing to new frontiers to explore than it is an operational and administrative blueprint for a newly designed police department" (p. 287). Perhaps Bayley (1988) best expressed the nebulousness of community policing when he wrote,

> Despite the benefits claimed for community policing, programmatic implementation of it has been very uneven. Although widely, almost universally, said to be important, it means different things to different people. . . . Community policing on the ground often seems less a program than a set of aspirations wrapped in a slogan. (p. 225)

Academics and practitioners alike will continue to struggle with the definition of community policing. Although some police chiefs see this ambiguity as an opportunity to define anything and everything as community policing for political gain, others see it as corollary of the fact that community policing is not a single police tactic or program, but a collection of strategies that share a common philosophy or set of principles about the desired role of police in society.

Practice of community policing. The practice of community policing often diverges from the expectations of criminal justice scholars and progressive police chiefs. By the late 1980s, a large number of police departments in the United States claimed to have community policing, when their actual programs had little in common with the philosophies and changes described above. This widespread endorsement of community policing concerns those who support its continued development; they fear that the concept will be redefined beyond recognition and that it will consequently suffer the same ultimate demise of previous police reform efforts.

In the field, community policing assumes many forms, with police departments

> opening small neighborhood substations, conducting surveys to identify local problems, organizing meetings and crime prevention seminars, publishing newsletters, helping form Neighborhood Watch groups, establishing advisory panels to inform police commanders, organizing youth activities, conducting drug education projects and media campaigns, patrolling on horses and bicycles, and working with municipal agencies to enforce health and safety regulations. (Skogan 1994, pp. 167–68)

Foot patrol is probably the most popular and widely implemented component of community policing; thousands of police departments across the country are now involved in this activity. Foot patrol was the central feature of federally funded demonstration programs that focused on increasing citizen-police contacts through community meetings, door-to-door visits, ministations, and other efforts.

One of the basic problems with community policing practices in the 1980s was their focus on community contact for the sake of community contact, rather than as a means to solve specific community problems. According to Goldstein (1990), such programs ran the risk of being no more effective than traditional policing practices. In his pioneering work on problem-oriented policing, Goldstein (1979) argued that police are ineffective because they suffer from the means over ends syndrome; that is, they have been too concerned with the means of responding to citizen complaints (e.g., rapid response and personnel allocations) and not concerned enough with the ends, which are the problems that lead to the citizen complaints. As a response to this criticism, Goldstein proposed problem-oriented policing, which represented a move away from the reactive "incident-driven" approach that has dominated American policing for many years. The Police Executive Research Forum, with support from the National Institute of Justice, has adapted Goldstein's approach in assisting police departments to initiate problem-solving practices in several cities (see Spelman and Eck [1986] for an elaboration of the four stages of problem solving).

The feasibility of instituting community policing reform and the best methods for achieving its purported objectives remain uncertain. What is clear from the evaluation literature is that the task of planning and implementing new approaches to policing is formidable. For this reason, community policing is almost always attempted with specialized units and within individual police districts. To date, department-wide implementation of a community policing philosophy has not been achieved within large organizations. Certainly successes have been observed on a smaller scale, but the longevity of these reforms will depend on their ability to become institutionalized and to change the status quo in police agencies.

A wide range of internal factors have limited the reported success with implementation. These factors range from rigid bureaucratic procedures to the fear of change among employees. Experience suggests that resistance to change could be minimized by making more officers aware of the program (e.g., specific objectives and activities) and by seeking their involvement in the change process, but all too often reform is undertaken without adequate education, training, and "buy-in" from the rank and file. As a consequence, officers can feel threatened by possible changes in their job, and without sufficient information they will assume that management is imposing (again) something that is not in their best interests.

Similarly, external factors can undermine the implementation of community policing. At present, police agencies often assume that after community residents and groups are invited to participate in community policing, everyone will come forth and get involved. This assumption is generally false and is especially fallacious when applied to inner-city minority neighborhoods, where participation levels are historically low and where police-community relations are poor at best. Police departments are again discovering that public awareness and education are indispensable first steps on the road to successful implementation.

To create cooperative partnerships with the community, the police need a better understanding of the social forces that influence citizen participation in community life. Although public education is important, research suggests that it is not sufficient to engender high levels of citizen involvement in community policing. There are numerous reasons for citizen nonparticipation, including fear of retaliation by drug dealers and gang members and distrust of the police and other service agencies. Hence, to build a lasting partnership, the police need significant outreach efforts, consistent contact with community leaders, and a demonstrated desire to improve neighborhood conditions over an extended period. Whether these objectives can be achieved remains to be seen.

The development of partnerships with other city agencies is viewed as increasingly important to the implementation of effective solutions to neighborhood problems. Notwithstanding this growing recognition among police agencies, often such partnerships have not materialized in the United States. The process of working together and the barriers to cooperative relationships are essential topics for future research.

Community Policing Evaluations

Early community policing evaluations focused on community-related outcomes, and their results were encouraging. The reductions in fear of crime and crime rates, and improvement in other quality-of-life indicators have been reported in a few sites, and valuable lessons in implementation have been learned from their experiences. A few central programs and activities have emerged in this area as alternative ways of operationalizing community policing. Each has produced its own kinds of effects on critical outcome variables related to crime and resident perceptions.

Foot patrol. Walking the beat has returned as a very popular form of community policing; this time around, more is expected from officers on foot patrol. In addition to the traditional surveillance and arrest functions, they are expected to assume a number of nontraditional police functions, including attending community meetings, identifying community problems and needs, organizing citizen initiatives, resolving neighborhood disputes, and making referrals to appropriate social services agencies (Trojanowicz 1986). Even so, surveys of police departments have indicated that foot patrol is often limited to the walk-and-talk approach, and historically, the talking has been primarily with merchants (Trojanowicz and Harden 1985). The rationale for foot patrol is that the highly visible presence of uniformed officers gives residents and businesspeople a feeling of security, and indeed, evaluation research generally supports this contention. Nonetheless, there is little evidence that foot patrols can diminish criminal activity in a target area.

The Police Foundation's original Newark foot patrol experiment reported significant reductions in fear of crime and changes in perceptions of disorder. The fear-reduction effect was replicated in the 1983–1984 Newark-Houston project (Pate et al. 1986), but the latter project involved strategies other than foot patrol. Victimization rates were not affected in either study; however, the more recent study did show reductions in reported index offenses. In an evaluation of the foot program in Flint, Michigan, Trojanowicz (1986) reported significant reductions in crime in a number of target areas. However, this evaluation did not include comparison groups and relied exclusively on police data.

Neighborhood ministations and community centers. Another manifestation of community policing is the effort to decentralize police services and to bring police officers closer to the communities that they serve. One of the most ambitious of these efforts was implemented in Detroit, Michigan; it involved the development of fifty-two ministations in neighborhoods across the city, which are staffed by permanently assigned police officers who are relieved of responsibility for handling radio calls. Their primary job is community crime prevention: They assist walk-in clients, offer crime prevention information at community meetings, patrol the streets both on foot and in cars, and provide police services to meet the needs of local residents. The support of local volunteers is critical in keeping the ministations running.

In 1983 and 1984, storefront community centers were field-tested as part of the Houston-Newark project described earlier (see Pate et al.1986; Skogan 1990). The results were quite promising. The introduction of the centers in Houston was associated with a decrease in residents' fear of personal crime and changes in their perceptions of the amount of crime in the area. The effects of the Newark stations could not be isolated from the other program components. Nonetheless, the overall strategy there was also quite successful at reducing fear and changing other crime-related perceptions.

Ministations can be used in various ways to help lessen the physical and psychological distance between police officers and neighborhood residents. In addition to housing standard police business, the facilities can be used to distribute newsletters, organize and hold meetings, coordinate door-to-door activities, and make referrals to service agencies. The functions of any particular community station can be modified to meet the needs and concerns of the surrounding neighborhood.

Our current knowledge of the impact of ministations is limited. Although the Detroit initiative was never formally evaluated, anecdotal evidence suggested that it experienced some organizational problems (Skolnick and Bayley 1988). The stations were disconnected from the main police structure, and therefore, the department's command personnel considered them an administrative problem. Apparently, police staff who were not associated with the ministations expressed unfavorable opinions about the assignment, labeling it *social work* rather than real police work.

In Houston, the beneficial effects of the ministations were not shared by all members of the community. Younger residents, members of minority groups, those with lower income and less education, renters, and younger and more transient residents were less likely to know about the storefront stations, to have contact with them, or to report the beneficial effects we cited earlier (Skogan and Wycoff 1986). This is a very important finding. As we have seen with other police attempts at community outreach, residents most in need of services are often the least likely to receive them.

Police organizing and outreach strategies. Organizing community residents is one of the most important aspects of community policing. The term *organizing,* however, has a variety of connotations. For many police departments, organizing means getting local residents to attend one Neighborhood Watch meeting. For others, it involves the empowerment of local residents, especially with regard to decisions that affect the quality of life in their neighborhoods. In the 1980s, numerous police departments started Block Watch programs but did not provide a structure or set of activities for sustaining citizen involvement (see Rosenbaum 1986). Many police agencies did not realize that organizing is an ongoing process that requires continual attention.

The question of whether community organizing is within the scope of police responsibility has been debated. Nonetheless, a growing number of police departments have started programs that emphasize community organizing activities. What makes these activities unique is that they go beyond the typical Block Watch objectives of surveillance and reporting and concentrate on problem identification and fear reduction.

In the Asylum Hill community of Hartford, Connecticut, police and citizens started two community organizations and a police advisory committee to help plan and implement a comprehensive community crime prevention program (Fowler and Mangione 1986). Input from the police, city agencies, community organizations, business owners, academic experts, as well as staff at the National Institute of Justice led to changes in local policing, the physical environment, and the crime prevention practices of local residents. The Hartford program was associated initially with reductions in crime and later with reductions in fear of crime.

As part of the Fear Reduction Project, the Houston Police Department started a community organization in an attempt to "create a sense of community in the area, and to identify a group of residents who would work regularly with the police to define and solve neighborhood problems" (Pate et al. 1986, p. 8). Officers on the Community Organizing Response Team (CORT) conducted a door-to-door survey of residents in the target area to seek their input in defining local problems and to locate persons who would be willing to host meetings of residents and police. From these meetings, residents formed a neighborhood task force that met each month with the district captain to discuss local problems and to develop solutions to those problems. A variety of programs emerged from this process (e.g., neighborhood clean-up campaign, "safe houses," drug information seminar, and property marking). Although the CORT initiatives did not influence fear of crime after they were implemented, residents did perceive that the frequency of social disorders had declined, and they reported more positive evaluations of the police.

Door-to-door contacts by police have been successful at gaining valuable information about local problems, improving public attitudes about the police, and reducing fear of crime. Demonstration programs in Newark and Houston were partially modeled after the popular Citizen-Oriented Police Enforcement (COPE) teams in the Baltimore Police Department (Cordner 1988). Deployed in areas with existing crime problems, the fifteen-member COPE squads worked primarily as fear-reduction programs. In addition to seeking a highly visible presence in the community, the COPE teams tried to pinpoint the sources of resident fear through police-citizen contacts. The COPE officers used input from community residents and patrol officers to develop action plans that were responsive to fear-related problems.

The Houston-Newark door-to-door demonstration project had significant effects on several outcomes. In Houston, where the impact of door-to-door visits could be isolated, researchers reported reductions in crime, changes in residents' perceptions of physical and social disorders, and increases in residents' satisfaction with the neighborhood and with the police. Fear of crime, however, was not affected. In Newark, the project also was very successful, but the door-to-door component was supported by several other programs. The Houston program's effects were dependent on the race and social class of residents. Similar to the impact of the city's ministations, the most disadvantaged residents in Houston were the least likely to hear about or to have participated in the program (Skogan 1990).

Problem-oriented policing demonstrations. Problem-oriented policing provides a process for identifying and responding to problems that are often beyond the purview of traditional police resources and activities. The problem-solving process, derived from the crime analysis model, can be highly useful to police administrators and planners. The role of the community is a key element in the model (as with all community policing strategies). The promise of this approach rests with the assumption that city leaders can more effectively address neighborhood problems by recognizing that the agencies and institutions involved in the education, health care, and general welfare of citizens all share responsibility in ensuring public safety.

Police departments have widely implemented problem-solving strategies during the past few years; nonetheless, researchers have conducted only a few controlled evaluations to assess their effects on the police or the community. Goldstein (1990) described a number of police departments that systematically approach neighborhood problems. (For another excellent discussion of problem-oriented policing, see Eck and Spelman [1987].) The early evaluations of problem-oriented policing, which were mostly case studies (e.g., Goldstein and Susmilch 1982), documented some of the difficulties with program implementation. Similarly, in their assessment of New York City's Community Patrol Officers Program, Weisburd and McElroy (1988) also found implementation problems. In particular, their findings underscored the importance of police leadership at different levels in getting patrol officers to engage routinely in problem identification and problem solving.

Impact evaluations of problem-oriented policing have been conducted on the Baltimore COPE project (Cordner 1988) and on the program in Newport News, Virginia (Eck and Spelman 1987). In Baltimore, community surveys found reductions in fear of crime, but the evaluation had several methodological problems, including the absence of a control group and the use of police officers as interviewers.

In Newport News, the Police Executive Research Forum collected some impact data to examine the efforts of problem-oriented policing (Eck and Spelman 1987). Following program implementation, time series analysis showed significant reductions in robberies and in larcenies to autos as well as a drop in household burglaries in the target area. However, this evaluation included only reported crime statistics.

Most of the evaluations of problem-oriented policing have not involved quasi-experimental or experimental designs. Furthermore, they rarely have measured a program's effects on police or local residents. An example of a study that used an experimental design to study problem-solving policing involved the Repeat Call Address Policing (RECAP) program in Minneapolis (Sherman et al. 1989). The evaluators randomly assigned officers to work on the busiest 250 addresses in terms of police dispatches. Those officers received several days of special training in problem analysis. At the end of one year, findings indicated that the number of calls received from these target addresses were not significantly reduced compared to a control group of another 250 high-call addresses.

In summary, because community policing programs are rarely implemented as planned and are almost never implemented on a large scale, our ability to answer the question, "Does it work?" has been sorely restricted. Furthermore, because community policing demands an expanded conception of the police function, evaluators no longer consider it appropriate to judge police performance simply by counting the number of dispatches, arrests, or tickets written. Indeed, greater attention is being given to quality-of-life indicators, such as fear of crime and levels of neighborhood disorder. This new emphasis implies that police will be evaluated primarily on their ability to create and maintain partnerships with the community, which are directed toward effective problem solving.

Despite these difficulties with performance measurement, the available research does provide a tentative answer to the question, "Does community policing work?" In terms of community effects, the literature suggests that community policing-type programs can have some positive effects on the community's perceptions and feelings about crime, disorder, and the police. Skogan (1994) reported that in fourteen areas targeted by community policing in six cities, nine showed positive changes in residents' attitudes about the police, seven showed reductions in fear of crime, six showed declines in perceived neighborhood disorder, and three showed reductions in victimization rates.

Research on the impact of police reform on police personnel has also produced favorable results. Reviewing twelve major studies of police officers, Lurigio and Rosenbaum (1994) reported a number of positive effects in the areas of increased job satisfaction, perceived broadening of the police role, improved relations with coworkers and citizens, and greater expectations for community involvement in crime prevention. However, the variation in methodological soundness across these studies makes it difficult to draw general conclusions about the effectiveness of police reform programs in changing police officers' attitudes and behaviors.

To conclude, most of the scientifically conducted evaluations have examined community engagement or community contact programs such as foot patrols, door-to-door contacts, and storefront stations. Although problem solving has since emerged as the dominant strategy for operationalizing community policing concepts, a paucity of rigorous evaluations have been designed to estimate the effects of these programs on either community residents or the police. In addition, few process studies have focused on the types of methods employed during problem-solving activities or the outcomes associated with those efforts. An encouraging trend in the literature is the use of the case study methodology to analyze and describe problem-solving strategies and outcomes (Capowich and Roehl 1994; Eck and Spelman 1987; Hope 1994; Wilkinson et al. 1994). For small-scale, geographically restricted projects, this is a sound evaluation model and should eventually lead to the accumulation of trustworthy knowledge about the individual, social, and organizational factors that either facilitate or impede problem-solving and community-engagement initiatives.

References

Anderson, David C. 1978. "Getting Down With the People." *Police Management* 8:240–56.
Bayley, David H. 1988. "Community Policing: A Report From the Devil's Advocate." Pp. 225–38 in *Community Policing: Rhetoric or Reality,* edited by J. R. Greene and S. D. Mastrofski. New York: Praeger.
Bloch, P. and D. Specht. 1972. *Evaluation Report on Operation Neighborhood.* Washington, DC: Urban Institute.
Buerger, Michael E. 1994. "A Tale of Two Targets: Limitations of Community Anticrime Action." *Crime & Delinquency* 40:411–36.
Capowich, G. E. and J. A. Roehl. 1994. "Problem-Oriented Policing: Actions and Effectiveness in San Diego." Pp. 127–46 in *The Challenge of Community Policing: Testing the Promises*, edited by D. P. Rosenbaum. Thousand Oaks, CA: Sage.
Cordner, Gary W. 1988. "A Problem-Oriented Approach to Community-Oriented Policing." Pp. 135–52 in *Community Policing: Rhetoric or Reality*, edited by J. R. Greene and S. D. Mastrofski. New York: Praeger.
Eck, John E. 1982. *Solving Crimes: The Investigation of Burglary and Robbery.* Washington, DC: Police Executive Research Forum.
Eck, John E. and Dennis P. Rosenbaum. 1994. "The New Police Order: Effectiveness, Equity, and Efficiency in Community Policing." Pp. 3–23 in *The Challenge of Community Policing: Testing the Promises*, edited by D. P. Rosenbaum. Thousand Oaks, CA: Sage.
Eck, John E. and William Spelman. 1987. *Problem-Solving.* Washington, DC: Police Foundation.
Fowler, Floyd J. and Thomas Mangione. 1986. "A Three-Pronged Effort to Reduce Crime and Fear: The Hartford Experiment." Pp. 87–108 in *Community Crime Prevention: Does It Work?* edited by D. P. Rosenbaum. Beverly Hills: Sage.
Gay, William, Thomas Beall, and Robert Bowers. 1984. *A Four-Site Assessment of the Integrated Criminal Apprehension Program.* Washington, DC: University City Science Center.
Goldstein, Herman. 1979. "Improving Policing: A Problem-Oriented Approach." *Crime & Delinquency* 25:236–58.
_____. 1990. *Problem-Oriented Policing.* New York: McGraw-Hill.
Goldstein, Herman and C. E. Susmilch. 1982. *Experimenting With the Problem-Oriented Approach to Improving Police Service: A Report and Some Reflections on Two Case Studies.* Madison: University of Wisconsin Law School.
Greene, Jack R. and Stephen D. Mastrofski, eds. 1988. *Community Policing: Rhetoric or Reality.* New York: Praeger.

Greenwood, Peter J., Jan Chaiken, and Joan Petersilia. 1977. *The Criminal Investigation Process.* Lexington, MA: Heath.

Grinc, Randolph M. 1994. "'Angels in Marble': Problems in Simulating Community Involvement in Community Policing." *Crime & Delinquency* 40:437–68.

Hope, Timothy J. 1994. "Problem-Oriented Policing and Drug Market Locations: Three Case Studies." Pp. 5–31 in *Crime Prevention Studies,* edited by R. V. Clarke. Monsey, New York: Criminal Justice Press.

Kelling, George L., Tony Pate, Duane Dieckman, and Charles Brown. 1974. *The Kansas City Preventive Patrol Experiment: A Technical Report.* Washington, DC: Police Foundation.

Lurigio, Arthur J. and Dennis P. Rosenbaum. 1994. "The Impact of Community Policing on Police Personnel: A Review of the Literature." Pp. 147–63 in *The Challenge of Community Policing: Testing the Promises,* edited by D. P. Rosenbaum. Thousand Oaks, CA: Sage.

Lurigio, Arthur J. and Wesley G. Skogan. 1994. "Winning the Hearts and Minds of Police Officers: An Assessment of Staff Perceptions of Community Policing in Chicago." *Crime & Delinquency* 40:315–30.

Moore, Mark H. 1994. "Research Synthesis and Policy Implications." Pp. 285–99 in *The Challenge of Community Policing: Testing the Promises,* edited by D. P. Rosenbaum. Thousand Oaks, CA: Sage.

Murphy, C. and G. Muir. 1985. *Community-Based Policing: A Review of the Critical Issues.* Ottawa, Canada: Solicitor General of Canada.

Pate, Antony M. and Penny Shtull. 1994. "Community Policing Grows in Brooklyn: An Inside View of the New York Police Department's Model Precinct." *Crime & Delinquency* 40:384–410.

Pate, Antony M., Mary Ann Wycoff, Wesley G. Skogan, and Lawrence W. Sherman. 1986. *Reducing Fear of Crime in Houston and Newark: A Summary Report.* Washington, DC: Police Foundation.

Rosenbaum, Dennis P., ed. 1986. *Community Crime Prevention: Does It Work?* Beverly Hills: Sage.

_____. 1987. "The Theory and Research Behind Neighborhood Watch: Is It a Sound Fear and Crime Reduction Strategy?" *Crime & Delinquency* 33:103–34.

_____. 1988. "Community Crime Prevention: A Review and Synthesis of the Literature." *Justice Quarterly* 5:323–95.

_____, ed. 1994. *The Challenge of Community Policing: Testing the Promises.* Thousand Oaks, CA: Sage.

Rosenbaum, Dennis P., Sandy Yeh, and Deanna L. Wilkinson. 1994. "Impact of Community Policing on Police Personnel: A Quasi-Experimental Test." *Crime & Delinquency* 40:331–53.

Schwartz, Alfred I. and Sumner N. Clarren. 1977. *The Cincinnati Team Policing Experiment: A Summary Report.* Washington, DC: Police Foundation.

Sherman, Lawrence, Michael E. Buerger, Patrick R. Gartin, Robert Dell'Erba, and Kinley Larntz. 1989. *Beyond Dial-A-Cop: Repeat Call Address Policing.* Washington, DC: Crime Control Institute.

Sherman, Lawrence, C. H. Milton, and T. V. Kelly. 1973. *Team Policing: Seven Cities Case Studies.* Washington, DC: Police Foundation.

Skogan, Wesley G. 1990. *Disorder and Community Decline: Crime and the Spiral of Decay in American Neighborhoods.* New York: Free Press.

———. 1994. "The Impact of Community Policing on Neighborhood Residents: A Cross-Site Analysis." Pp. 167–81 in *The Challenge of Community Policing: Testing the Promises*, edited by D. P. Rosenbaum. Thousand Oaks, CA: Sage.

Skogan, Wesley G. and George Antunes. 1979. "Information, Apprehension, and Deterrence: Exploring the Limits of Police Productivity." *Journal of Criminal Justice* 7:217–42.

Skogan, Wesley G. and Mary Ann Wycoff. 1986. "Storefront Police Offices: The Houston Field Test." Pp. 179–201 in *Community Crime Prevention: Does It Work?* edited by D. P. Rosenbaum. Beverly Hills: Sage.

Skolnick, Jerome H. and David H. Bayley. 1988. *The New Blue Line: Police Innovation in Six American Cities.* New York: Free Press.

Spelman, William and Charles Brown. 1984. *Calling the Police: Citizen Reporting of Serious Crime.* Washington, DC: U.S. Government Printing Office.

Spelman, William and John Eck. 1986. "Sitting Ducks, Ravenous Wolves, and Helping Hands: New Approaches to Urban Policing." *Public Affairs Comment* 1:1–19.

Spelman, William et al. 1985. *Crime Suppression and Traditional Police Tactics.* Cambridge: Harvard University, Program in Criminal Justice Policy and Management.

Trojanowicz, Robert C. 1986. "Evaluating a Neighborhood Foot Patrol Program: The Flint Michigan Project." Pp. 157–79 in *Community Crime Prevention: Does It Work?* edited by D. P. Rosenbaum. Beverly Hills: Sage.

Trojanowicz, Robert and Bonnie Bucqueroux. 1989. *Community Policing: A Contemporary Perspective.* Cincinnati, OH: Anderson.

Trojanowicz, Robert C. and H. Harden. 1985. *Job Satisfaction: A Comparison of Foot Patrol versus Motor Patrol Officers.* East Lansing: Michigan State University, National Neighborhood Foot Patrol Center.

Weisburd, David and Jerome E. McElroy. 1988. "Enacting the CPO Role: Findings From the New York City Pilot Program in Community Policing." Pp. 89–102 in *Community Policing: Rhetoric or Reality,* edited by J. R. Greene and S. D. Mastrofski. New York: Praeger.

Wilkinson, Deanna, Dennis P. Rosenbaum, M. Bruni, and S. Yeh. 1994. *Community Policing in Joliet: Year 2 Process Evaluation* (Vol. 1, Final Report submitted to the Illinois Criminal Justice Information Authority). Chicago: University of Illinois at Chicago, Center for Research in Law and Justice.

Wilson, Deborah G. and Susan F. Bennett. 1994. "Officers' Response to Community Policing: Variations on a Theme." *Crime & Delinquency* 40:354–70.

Wycoff, Mary Ann and Wesley G. Skogan. 1994. "The Effect of a Community Policing Management Style on Officers' Attitudes." *Crime & Delinquency* 40:371–83.

12

Measuring Police Performance in the New Paradigm of Policing

Geoffrey P. Alpert and Mark H. Moore

During the 1980s and 1990s there has been a resurgence of interest in community policing. As an outgrowth of police-community relations, the concept of community policing has become the goal, method, and guiding principle for police. Unfortunately, community policing remains a concept and philosophy in search of a process without proper ways to document or evaluate its efforts. This article focuses on community-oriented policing and takes a new approach to the measurement and evaluation of police performance. Before outlining our paradigm of police performance measures we will review the conventional measures and why we believe a new way of thinking must direct our attention to new performance measures.

Citizens and their elected representatives have long sought a bottom line to measure police performance. The goals have been to reassure the public that hard-earned tax dollars were being spent to achieve important results and to hold police managers accountable for improving organizational performance. As police agencies matured, four generally accepted accounting practices became enshrined as the key measures to evaluate police performance. These include (1) reported crime rates, (2) overall arrests, (3) clearance rates, and (4) response times.

As these measures became institutionalized over the years, investments were made in developing information systems to record police performance consistent with these measures. Statistical reports using these measures were routinely issued. Further, the media, overseers in city councils, and auditors in city managers' offices have all been primed to acknowledge and use these measures to compare police performance from year to year and to compare local accomplishments with

Source: Reprinted from *Performance Measures for the Criminal Justice System* (October 1993), pp. 109–40. U.S. Department of Justice: BJS–Princeton University Study Group.

those of other cities. For most practical purposes, these are the statistics by which police departments throughout the United States are now held accountable.

These measures remain critical as part of an overall system for measuring police performance. As currently used, however, these measures reflect an increasingly outmoded model of police tasks and fail to capture many important contributions that police make to the quality of life. More important, these measures may misguide police managers and lead them and their organizations toward purposes and activities that are less valuable than others that can be achieved with limited and diminishing resources.

Police performance measures should focus on a new model of policing that emphasizes their charge to do justice, promote secure communities, restore crime victims, and promote noncriminal options—the elements of an emerging paradigm of criminal justice (DiIulio, 1992:10–12). The purpose of this article is to describe how policing fits in with this new paradigm, including implications for restructuring the overall objectives and measuring the accomplishments of policing through police agency performance measures (Kelling, 1992).

The Evolving Strategy of Policing

Historically, policing in America has been inspired and guided by a vision of professional law enforcement. This vision is a coherent strategy of policing defining the principal ends, means, and legitimating principles of the police enterprise (Wilson and McLaren, 1977).

Professional Law Enforcement: The Dominant Strategy of Policing

In this vision, the primary, perhaps exclusive goals of the police are to reduce crime and criminal victimization. Police seek to achieve this goal by arresting and threatening to arrest those who violate the criminal law. They organize themselves to produce this result by: (1) patrolling city streets hoping to detect and deter crime, (2) responding rapidly to calls for service, and (3) conducting investigations after crimes have been committed to identify criminal offenders and develop evidence to be used in prosecutions.

In essence, in the vision of professional law enforcement, the police are seen as the all-important entry point to the criminal justice system—the gatekeeper managing the first step in bringing the force of the criminal law to bear on offenders.

To deal effectively with serious crime and dangerous criminal offenders, specialized skills are required. The police have had to learn how to use legitimate force with skill and confidence. They have had to improve their ability to investigate and solve crimes to reduce the chance that serious offenders could escape accountability. Thus, in search of increased effectiveness in dealing with an increasingly challenging and urgent problem, the police consciously narrowed their focus and refined their skills in responding to serious crime and dangerous offenders. By relying on the techniques of patrol, rapid response, and retrospective investigation, the police have been kept at the forefront of community life and have been made available to anyone who needed them when a crime occurred.

Limitations of Professional Law Enforcement

Recently, enthusiasm for this strategy of professional policing has waned. The professional policing model has been ineffective in reducing crime, reducing citizens' fears, and satisfying victims that justice is being done. Indeed, recent research indicates that a majority of the population believes that the crime problem has become progressively worse during the past decade (Gallup, 1992, cited in Bureau of Justice Statistics, 1992:185). Similarly, citizens have lost confidence in the criminal justice system to protect them (Cole, 1992:23).

Such charges are, in many respects, unfair to the police. It is unreasonable to expect the police to reduce crime all by themselves. Crime rates are affected by vast social, economic, and political forces. No matter how professional, police cannot solve the "root causes" of crime. They cannot be blamed for increasing unemployment, increasing inequality, or eroding family structures (Bazelon, 1988). In addition, police are dependent on the rest of the criminal justice system to give significance to arrests.

Toward a New Paradigm of Policing

Many police executives are beginning to think about and experiment with a strategy of policing that differs from the professional model and emphasizes the development of a strong relationship with the community. *The essence of this new paradigm is that police must engage in community-based processes related to the production and maintenance of local human and social capital. The means by which these lofty goals are to be achieved are through the development of strong relationships with institutions and individuals in the community.* While the specific elements of this new strategy of policing have not been agreed upon or clearly delineated, the broad characteristics are reasonably clear.

The major theme of *building a strong relationship with the community* has two justifications. First, it is an important way to make enforcement more effective. Second, it is a way to prevent crime and make the community co-producers of justice (Skogan and Antunes, 1979).

One excellent example comes from the Metro-Dade Police Department (MDPD) in Miami, Florida. In June 1992 the staff of the Northside Station of the MDPD conducted a survey of local residents (mostly African-American) to determine if any public personalities or activities could serve as common ground between the police and young males (Metro-Dade Police Department, 1992). What emerged was a fascinating finding. The young respondents identified local rap radio disc jockeys and rap music as personalities and activities that interested them.

In March 1993 the police turned these empirical findings into action. They created a series of "Jammin' with the Man" concerts. Local disc jockeys were invited to hold concerts in local parks sponsored by the police. While the youths enjoyed the music and festivities, the police were there, talking with the youths and encouraging them to talk and work with the police to understand each other. Although more than 5,000 people attended the first event, there were no negative incidents. The MDPD report concluded by noting:

> While *Jammin' with the Man* was originally intended to be a single step in a process to improve police-community relations, a step aimed particularly at young men, [it] seems to have become part or all of the answer. It has also become an educational experience for the community as they see police as agents of peace rather than enforcers of law. More importantly, it has demonstrated that the mere act of the police engaged in active listening has the effect of empowering them and perhaps alleviating some of their sense of alienation (Metro-Dade Police Department, 1993:6).

In other words, this project provided an excellent vehicle for the police to create and maintain positive contacts with members of the community they serve and to be seen in a positive light. Further, by initiating and participating in activities the youths enjoyed, the police had an opportunity to see youth in a positive light.

Dr. Trevor Bennett has classified the various ways to consider community policing and has reduced them to three categories. First, he notes that there are arguments which refer to the intrinsic "goodness" of the general relationship between police and the community. Second, he recognizes relationships in which the police and the public work together to achieve common and specified goals, including the shared responsibility for crime control. Third, he acknowledges the need for police to take into consideration the wishes and concerns of the community. In Bennett's words:

> . . . [A] workable definition of a community policing philosophy might include the following basic elements: a belief or intention that the police should work with the public whenever possible in solving local problems and a belief that they should take account of the wishes of the public in defining and evaluating operational police policy (Bennett, 1992:7).

A second theme emphasizes *attacking the communities' problems on a broader front*—in effect, rejecting the exclusive focus on serious crime. The theme emerging from research is that much fear of crime is independent of victimization and that there are things the police can do to deal with fear (Bureau of Justice Statistics, 1988, 1992). Research findings and practice make clear that citizens use the police for many purposes other than crime control and that things other than crime are principal concerns (Alpert and Dunham, 1992:2–3). Certainly, goals other than the reduction of serious crime should be emphasized when it is realized that crime control is not the principal or only objective of the police. In any case, the police cannot achieve the reduction of fear or crime by themselves. What the police can achieve is the independent goal of public or customer satisfaction.

A third theme emphasizes some important *changes in the way the police visualize their work and their methods.* In the traditional strategy of policing, the key unit of work is the "incident." That is, patrol officers respond to a specific incident, and it is the incident that becomes the focus of a criminal investigation. What we have recently learned, however, is that a large proportion of incidents emerge from a relatively small number of situations and locations. Moreover, analysis of the problems underlying many incidents reported to the police suggests that the police might be able to imagine and mount different kinds of intervention (Goldstein, 1990).

The concept known as problem-oriented policing emphasizes involvement of the police in community life. This strategy has police serve as community agents rather than adversaries with the community. Study group member Professor James F. Short suggests that police should not maintain their gatekeeper function and solve problems *for* the community but should be involved in solving problems *with* community support and assistance. In this way, police can help develop and promote a sense of community (Short, 1990:225–226). Professor Short makes a critical link from the 1990s problem-oriented policing to the role of police in the Chicago Area Project during the 1940s. As he informs us, there are many similarities in police functioning then and what we are suggesting for the future. The vision was—

> . . . [T]he police as a resource for the community, aiding local residents and working with indigenous leaders to solve community problems, with special focus on the problems of young people. The goal in each of these programs is to promote the achievement of "functional communities," that is, communities in which family life, work, religion, education, law enforcement, and other institutional areas reflect and reinforce common values (Short, 1990: 226).

Although arrests of offenders remains an important tactic, the police repertoire must be widened to include a variety of civil actions, mobilization of citizens and other government agencies to change the conditions that generate crime or that will likely escalate deteriorating conditions. For example, the strategy of "Weed and Seed" is to eliminate drug-related crime and to restore economic vitality to inner cities through multi-agency cooperation and the use of community empowerment and resident involvement (Department of Justice, 1991). An important aspect of this third theme is that the police should become pro-active, interactive, and preventative in their orientation rather than rely solely on reacting and control.

A fourth theme focuses on *changes in internal working relationships.* That is, police agencies need to examine the potential strengths and weaknesses of decentralization of authority by seeking ways to guide discretion and police behavior generally through increasing reliance on values rather than rules and strict methods of accountability (Alpert and Smith, 1993). These ideas are central to the concepts of community policing, problem-solving policing and smarter policing. Incorporating these ideas into strategies of policing, we believe, would truly professionalize police rather than treat them as blue-collar workers. In addition to making police work more effective, these four strategies may increase job satisfaction—and most importantly—community satisfaction (Greene, Alpert and Styles, 1992).

These four themes combine to form the overarching principle of changed police-community relationships. Current police work revolves around serious crimes. The community participates by becoming the eyes and ears of the police; however, this strategy keeps the police outside and above the community. Police are summoned by the community through individual requests for service, and those requests are evaluated primarily in terms of whether an offense has been committed and a crime has been solved.

Creative, problem-oriented policing strategies place the community in a much different position than they have been in the recent past. Under this new paradigm, police work is oriented toward community satisfaction and the increase in human and social capital in the community. Satisfaction is determined not only by the police response to individual calls, but also by community members banding together to advise and consult with the police. Further, community institutions play the most important roles in changing community conditions that generate crime and in shaping police activities related to crime and other community conditions. Placing police and the citizens in communication with community leaders creates a dialogue and interaction. This removes the police from a hierarchical position and has the effect of increasing the accountability of the police to the community.

One of the crucial issues that must be faced by all concerned with community policing is the assumption that there is a community to organize. Some cities and suburbs have developed rapidly and have not formed what sociologists refer to as communities or neighborhoods. Similarly, some precincts or reporting areas may not be contiguous with natural neighborhoods or communities. Finally, some areas that have deteriorated or are in the process of deteriorating may be difficult to organize. Areas needing organization the least will be the easiest to assist, while less well-organized communities, particularly underclass areas of the inner city, will be the hardest to organize (Alpert and Dunham, 1988). However, examples of difficult and complicated organization are available.

One example of this community-building comes from Judge Thomas Petersen in Dade County, Florida. Judge Petersen was able to create a sense of community in several areas known for their lack of community spirit or allegiance. Judge Petersen, with assistance from the housing authority, law enforcement officials, and private industry, established three community stores that sold essential items in housing projects. In each, the housing authority found sufficient space and turned the space into grocery stores with supplies donated by private industry. The shelves were stocked with no up-front costs. Further, training for the people necessary to run the business was procured from professionals in the grocery business. Those who were hired to run the store were in need of child care, and the space and training for that service was provided by the housing authority.

After a short period of time, a group of people were working in the store, others were working in the child care center, and all were removed from public assistance. More important, however, was the sense of community created by the stores and child care centers. The stores became a focal point of the projects, and residents, police, and others involved in their establishment gained a mutual respect and trust for each other. Residents who had been scared to talk to other residents began to realize the importance of community spirit and the benefits of mutual assistance. The workers and residents began to identify with the operation of the store, and when anyone began to cause trouble or tried to sell drugs, the police were called immediately, and residents would point out the offender and work with the police to do justice. After a short period, the stores earned the reputation as establishments that would not only sell goods but also as the heart of the housing projects, serving as a rumor control center, a place to get assistance from others, and a place with respect for the police function.

This new-found respect for police spread very quickly through the projects and neighborhoods. Residents who once despised the police were now working with them to solve crimes and create an atmosphere where street criminals would not be tolerated. In many respects, Judge Petersen had *created* a community spirit that fit neatly into the community-oriented policing strategy (Petersen, 1993).

Implications for Police Performance Measurement

As society and the police approach a new understanding of how each can contribute to the other, it is critical to develop new measures to determine how well the police perform. Measures of performance rely on the definition of what the police are expected to do and how they are expected to do it. The measures must not only reflect but also help to shape community expectations of the police. For example, consider how neatly the current enshrined measures of police performance fit the dominant current strategy of policing.

Current Performance Measures as a
Reflection of Professional Law Enforcement

Recall that the current strategy of policing emphasizes crime control through arrests and that arrests are produced by patrol, rapid response to calls for service, and retrospective investigation. Current police performance measures are linked directly to these tasks. First, the overall objective of police has traditionally been perceived to reduce crime. It follows that the traditional measure of police performance is the level of reported crime measured by the Uniform Crime Reports. Another police task is apprehending offenders. This task is measured by arrests. Other traditional measures related to the crime rate include the ability to solve crimes (clearance rates—a very subjective measure) and the ability to get to crime scenes quickly (response times). These existing measures fit the traditional policing strategy perfectly, and they have become recognized as the important measures.

What Is Missing from These Measures

Limitations of the traditional policing strategy are also represented by the current performance measures. It is important that crime is measured in terms of reported crime, rather than through victimization surveys. Indeed, the police long resisted the development of criminal victimization surveys, concerned that they would reveal differential reporting and would be too subjective. This emphasis on reported crime left invisible many crimes such as domestic assault, child abuse, extortion by armed robbers and drug gangs, and other crimes in communities that did not trust or have confidence in the police (Bureau of Justice Statistics, 1992; Federal Bureau of Investigation, 1992).

It is also important that the measures that could have revealed the fairness and economy within which the authority of the police was deployed got less attention than the question of police effectiveness. There was no routine expectation that the police would publish data on patrol allocations, response times, or crime solution rates across neighborhoods.

Similarly, no serious efforts were made to develop statistical evidence on the incidence of brutality, excessive use of force, discourtesy, or corruption. In principle, one could have collected information about these things by soliciting civilian complaints and taking them as indicators of problems, if not probative of individual officer misconduct (U.S. Civil Rights Commission, 1981). Again, the argument, albeit flawed, was that unlike official crime statistics, such information was suspect and too subjective. Thus, in this area as elsewhere, the commitment to fairness and discipline in the use of authority was less important than the claim of crime control effectiveness.

Further, there was no real way to capture the quality of the response that the police made to citizen calls other than those involving criminal offenses for which an arrest could be made. In fact, most of the operational indicators implicitly viewed responding to non-crime complaints as something to be avoided and resisted rather than taken seriously. Measures included a comparison between time out of service and time in-service. In-service meant being on patrol, while out-of-service included meal breaks but also included meeting citizens and responding to their calls for service. Similarly, time spent on high-priority calls was compared with time spent on "nuisance calls." The purpose was to reduce time on nuisance calls, despite the fact that it was these calls that could be used to build the relationship with the community that was necessary to make their current tactics effective in dealing with crime (Sparrow, Moore, and Kennedy, 1990).

Finally, there was no real way to account for or measure pro-active operations. The only way to do this was through monitoring specialized squads or units.

Units were created to deal with particular problems, often on a temporary basis, without the establishment of a method to capture the nature or extent of the units' activities. Similarly, there was no attempt to determine how much of the organization's resources was being committed to such pro-active operations (Bureau of Justice Statistics, 1992).

Reforming Police Performance Measures

Orienting the agency to the community. Several options exist to reform police performance measures. First, existing measures could be improved to live up to the challenge of professionalism. This would include audited clearance and arrest rates and the development of statistical evidence on the use of force and the incidence of brutality, discourtesy, and corruption, among others. Second, performance measures could be linked more closely to action in the community, including the level of centralization and community-level programs. Under this structure, programs must be established that encourage calls to the police and evaluate calls to the police for service as well as concerns regarding criminal behavior. Measures should also include—

- police-related and inter-governmental activities that improve the social fabric of the community
- projects with the assistance of private industry that improve informal and formal social control in the community
- fear of crime
- victimization and police service programs that help promote community spirit in those neighborhoods where none existed.

Further, measures of the form and level of self-defense efforts by citizens and measures of trust and confidence in the police should be routinely taken and evaluated. Measures of the quality of service delivery by the police should be taken to improve departmental functioning and reveal the quality of individual officers as reported by the citizens with whom they come in contact (Furstenberg and Wellford, 1973; U.S. Civil Rights Commission, 1981).

Encouraging pro-active problem solving. One of the biggest problems in accounting for the performance of police departments is to capture what is accomplished during pro-active and problem-solving activities. One way to measure this concept is to view each problem-solving initiative as a particular program to be evaluated for its immediate impact. A second way to measure the impact is to view each as equivalent to a criminal investigation or special operation. In this way, a file is created, activities are monitored, and results recorded and evaluated.

The problem, of course, is that the problems come in different sizes. Size can be measured in terms of (1) total resources committed to the problem, (2) amount of time taken to solve, (3) the number of specialized resources required, (4) the extent to which higher-ranking officers must mobilize and coordinate efforts within and outside the department to deal with the problem, and (5) its importance and scale within the community.

One way to deal with these concerns is to develop a tailored program for individual areas. In other words, do not assume that each community has the same concerns or problems or that each community should respond similarly to certain problems. One product that would result from the effort to create, deliver, and measure these community-oriented programs and surveys is a database on which a department or a division within a large department could customize a pro-active or interactive problem-solving approach. Pressure to build a portfolio of problems solved successfully and improved attitudes toward the police could become as intense as current pressures to maintain low crime rates and quick response times.

Managing the transition to the new strategy. One of the most difficult problems faced by police managers in the short run is the awkward period of transition to the new strategy. The new programs will not be up and operating, and the new measurement systems will not be working and widely accepted. Yet the police will still be accountable to the public. Thus, they will have to develop measures that can keep them accountable during the transition.

One method is to identify the particular investments and efforts that are required to implement the new strategy of policing and report progress on these activities. If new training is required, they can report on the development of the new curriculum and the number of participating officers. If the formation of community groups is identified as important, that progress can be monitored and recorded. If the development of a new call management system or a new scheduling system is required, that too, can be monitored. The point is simply to identify and monitor the key organizational investments that are required. Unfortunately, no data sets exist on which to begin an analysis. The Bureau of Justice Statistics has compiled the most comprehensive data set (Law Enforcement Management and Administration Statistics—LEMAS) but its elements do not include many of the critical measures discussed in this article (Reaves, 1992).

Toward a New Strategy

The urgent need today in measuring police performance is to move away from a sterile conversation about performance measurement as an abstract technical problem and to understand it as a device that can be used managerially to shape the future of policing. This is neither a question of the essential unchanging measures that finally capture the value of policing nor a discussion of outcomes versus outputs nor a discussion of single versus multiple measures of performance. Instead, it is a discussion about a strategy of policing that will work in the future and how to measure its effects. Current measures of policing are holding police departments in their current mold and are keeping them mired in the past. These current measures need to be supplemented by innovative policing and new ways to measure their successes.

Our suggestion has several organizational elements that must be added to the traditional components already existing in many police departments. The police initiative must stress the need to learn about the residents and business people in their neighborhoods and to see them in situations that are not always defined as negative or at best neutral. This increased role for the police must include two basic approaches. First, a method must be devised to solicit information from members of the community. This method can incorporate meetings or citizens' advisory and focus groups with the police and can be enhanced by community surveys to determine attitudes and suggestions concerning the police and the police role. Another important dimension of this information gathering is the analysis of what Skogan has found to be measures of neighborhood decline and disorder (Skogan, 1990). Second, the police must use this information to reduce isolation between police and the citizens. The strategy is to assign officers for an extended period, supervised by command staff and advised by community groups. This move toward stability will increase the identification of an officer with the residents, geography, politics, and other issues in a given neighborhood.

These operational elements require proper training, feedback mechanisms, and an institutionalized reward system. Additionally, it is important that these efforts are measured, analyzed, and evaluated by the police officers, command staff, and members of the public.

Neighborhood Training

Neighborhood training involves two basic questions the police must answer according to the needs of each community or neighborhood: what to do and how to do it. In other words, the priority of police resources, whether fighting crime or providing social services, changes from neighborhood to neighborhood. Police officers must identify these needs from their own experiences and expectations, from the perspective of the consumers, and from that of the police administration. Neighborhood training can effectively inform the officer as to what he or she can expect from the residents, physical surroundings, or other influences. This in-service training can introduce officers to community characteristics while they are working the streets under a supervisor (in a way similar to a field training officer). What to do can be determined by problem-solving techniques. How to do it is the all-important style of policing that needs to be developed and supervised by command staff.

Distinct differences may exist among officers, administrators, and citizens concerning style. Matching the style of policing to community needs and requirements will improve both the police and the community. This can be achieved through training based upon knowledge of community values and beliefs as well as the attitudes and priorities of police officers. A necessary aspect of this is the continuous dialogue between residents and the police. Research on attitudes, expectations and evaluation of services of both the police and the members of the community is critical.

Monitoring

The final component of this strategy includes institutionalized monitoring and a formal reward system. This requires an ongoing system to monitor both the community and the police. The needs of the community can be determined by periodic social surveys, which, if linked to census data and local planning information, can inform officials of the changing nature of a given neighborhood. While it is relatively easy to identify what constitutes negative behavior, it is difficult to specify exemplary behavior. The proper use of good research, including appropriate sampling and a panel design, could provide a clear snapshot of the needs expressed by a given community. Police officers and administrators can work together to identify critical questions and a research design that can answer them. A Blue-Ribbon Committee studying the Miami Police Department concluded that while crime fighting activities are important, service activities are equally as important in terms of the new paradigm. In the final report, the committee noted:

> It is our conclusion that a minor organizational change can have a major impact on community relations and on the interrelationships between citizens and police. We believe that confidence in the police will be enhanced if the police measure and make more visible the activities they perform. Moreover, police work is usually rewarded by the gratitude an officer receives from those whom he or she helps. Status in the department, promotions, raises, commendations, etc., rest largely on his or her crime-fighting activities, the number of arrests, crimes he or she solves, etc. As a result, the patrol officer may regard service calls as a necessary evil (Overtown Blue Ribbon Committee, 1984:199).

These creative data, together with traditional law enforcement information, will permit the development and maintenance of neighborhood profiles. Analyzing and monitoring these profiles can assist the police in improving their training, tactical decisions, effectiveness and efficiency.

Rewarding the Officers

Most police departments provide incentives for their officers. These include traditional promotions, merit increases, and "officer-of-the-month" recognition. Many departments offer several opportunities for their officers to receive or earn rewards. Traditionally, these rewards have been based upon aggressive actions that led to arrest(s), the capture of a dangerous felon, or some other heroic activity. These criteria for rewarding police officers are important and serve to encourage similar actions from others. Yet other types of police behavior deserve recognition but remain lost and hidden behind the visible, aggressive activities of police officers. Activities that should receive more attention include exemplary service to the community and the reduction or diffusion of violence. Those who provide meritorious service may be recognized but often their actions are lost behind the brave shooting incident or heroic rescue. The local community needs to recognize officers who serve their "beat" or neighborhood in an exemplary fashion. A "Best Cop on the Block" recognition would be an important reward, if provided by local residents or merchants. When an officer avoids a shooting or talks a suspect into custody, his or her superiors may not find out; if they do, the officer may be labeled as a "chicken" or one who cannot provide needed back-up to his [or her] fellow officers. Nonaggressive behavior that reduces violence needs to be reinforced, rewarded, and established as the model for other officers to copy.

An institutional reward system should be established for officers who avoid or reduce violent situations and who avoid the use of force, especially deadly force, when avoidance is justifiable. When command officers, from the chief to the sergeants, support and reward violence reduction, private business and service groups can be enlisted to provide symbolic and monetary rewards for such behavior. The institutional support for the effective policing of a neighborhood can only encourage others to consider a change in priorities and style. While this is only one aspect of a neighborhood intervention and community evaluation model, it could serve as a successful step toward meeting the joint needs of the citizens and the police.

Data on these activities should be collected, assessed and evaluated to help determine police departments' performance to do justice and promote secure communities.

Summary and Conclusion

Police departments around the country have instituted one or more of the foregoing organizational components into community policing programs, but we are not aware of any agency that has incorporated them all or that uses many of these nontraditional performance measures. The components of the suggested program need coordination and individual assessment as well as analysis as a total effect.

Effective neighborhood policing requires that police administrators acquire adequate information on the specific neighborhood, including knowledge of the informal control structure of the neighborhood, attitudes about the police, and policing strategies and styles. This information can be obtained from citizen surveys, census data, community advisory groups, and community leaders. After accumulating the information, police administrators can decide how to deal with any incongruence between the neighborhood context and police policies, strategies, and styles. Some of these differences can be reduced by campaigns to educate

Table 1

The mission of the police consists of many diverse activities, not objectives in themselves but which are directed toward the protection of life. Goals include doing justice, promoting secure communities, restoring crime victims, and promoting non-criminal options.

Police: Goals, Methods, and Performance Indicators

Goals	Methods/Activities	Performance indicators
1. *Doing Justice*, treating citizens in an appropriate manner based upon their conduct.	Balancing formal and informal social controls, responding to calls for service, patrolling tactics, issuing traffic tickets, conducting investigations, writing reports, making arrests, and assisting in criminal prosecutions.	Nature and type of patrolling strategy, number of traffic tickets issued, known crimes that are cleared by audit or arrest, quality of reports, analysis of who calls the police, evaluation of policies emphasizing values over rules, time invested and quality of investigations, number of known crimes cleared by conviction, arrests and arrests cleared by conviction, cases released because of police misconduct, citizen complaints, lawsuits filed, and results of dispositions and officer-initiated encounters.
2. *Promoting secure communities*, enabling citizens to enjoy a life without fear of crime or victimization.	Preventing/deterring criminal behavior and victimization, problem-solving initiatives, training for community differences, assisting citizens by reducing fear of crime and victimization.	Programs and resources allocated to crime prevention programs, inter-governmental programs, resources, both time and dollars dedicated to problem-solving, rewards and monitoring of police, public trust and confidence in police performance, public attitudes toward police actions and public fear of crime, and home and business security checks.

3. *Restoring crime victims*, by restoring victims' lives and welfare as much as possible.

Assisting crime victims to understand the criminal justice system, assisting crime victims with their difficulties created by the victimization, assisting crime victims to put their lives back together.

Number of contacts with victims after initial call for assistance, types of assistance provided to victims, including information, comfort, transportation, and referrals to other agencies.

4. *Promoting noncriminal options*, by developing strong relationships with individuals in the community.

Develop and assist with programs that strengthen relationships between police and members of the community and among community members, increase human and social capital in the community and linkages with private industry.

Programs and resources allocated to strengthening relationships between police and the community and among community members, including traditional community relations programs, school programs and resources spent to meet with the public in a positive alliance. Innovative programs to develop a sense of community, organizational measures of de-centralization, community storefront operations and officer contacts with citizens for positive relations and feedback on performance are aspects of developing strong relationships with members of the community.

the citizens and change public opinion and attitudes. In other cases, discrepancies can be reduced by training programs for officers who are assigned to the areas. The training can focus on neighborhood-specific strategies, appropriate styles for the specific neighborhood, and placing priorities on tasks consistent with the neighborhood's expectations. Subsequent to appropriate neighborhood-based training, police administrators need to create and institutionalize a system of monitoring and rewarding police officers' behavior. The police officers assigned to the neighborhood provide the final link integrating the formal control system of the police with the informal system in the neighborhood. Officers must apply the training principles appropriately through their use of discretion.

From data collected from the neighborhoods, a good plan for neighborhood intervention and community evaluation can bring modern police work in line with our modern world. Moore and Kelling (1983:65) have previously summarized these ideas quite well:

> Police strategies do not exist in a vacuum. They are shaped by important legal, political, and attitudinal factors, as well as by local resources and capabilities, all factors which now sustain the modern conception of policing. So there may be little leeway for modern police executives. But the modern conception of policing is in serious trouble, and a review of the nature of that trouble against the background of the American history of policing gives a clear direction to police forces that wish to improve their performance as crime fighters and public servants.

> The two fundamental features of a new police strategy must be these: that the role of private citizens in the control of crime and maintenance of public order be established and encouraged, not derided and thwarted, and that the police become more active, accessible participants in community affairs. The police will have to do little to encourage citizens to participate in community policing, for Americans are well practiced at undertaking private, voluntary efforts; all they need to know is that the police force welcomes and supports such activity. Being more visible and accessible is slightly more difficult, but hiring more "community relations" specialists is surely not the answer. Instead, the police must get out of their cars, and spend more time in public spaces such as parks and plazas, confronting and assisting citizens with their private troubles. This is mundane, prosaic work but it probably beats driving around in cars waiting for a radio call. Citizens would surely feel safer and, perhaps, might even be safer.

Private citizens working together and through community institutions can have a profound impact on policing. Those community organizations and police agencies that have developed reciprocal relationships will enjoy more success than those attempting to work without the benefit of the others' knowledge and information.

The maintenance and analysis of administrative statistics can provide community members and police supervisors with performance outcomes that promote justice. Patrol officers can be in the best position to understand the varied and changing needs of the community, and with input from research and training, appropriate activities can be devised to do justice and promote safe communities and develop a new meaning for the phrase "professional policing."

References

Alpert, Geoffrey, and Roger Dunham. *Policing Urban America*. Prospect Heights, IL: Waveland Press. 1992.

Alpert, Geoffrey, and Roger Dunham. *Policing Multi-Ethnic Neighborhoods*. New York: Greenwood Press. 1988.

Alpert, Geoffrey, and William Smith. "Developing Police Policy: Evaluating the Control Principle." *American Journal of Police*. 1993.

Bazelon, David. *Questioning Authority*. New York: Knopf. 1988.

Bennett, Trevor. *Community Policing in Britain*. Paper presented to the International Conference on Community Policing. Institute of Criminology, University of Heidelberg, Heidelberg, Germany. September 1992.

Bureau of Justice Statistics. *Crime and the Nation's Households, 1991*. Washington, DC: Bureau of Justice Statistics. 1992.

Bureau of Justice Statistics. *Sourcebook of Criminal Justice Statistics, 1991*. Washington, DC: Bureau of Justice Statistics. 1992.

Bureau of Justice Statistics. *Report to the Nation on Crime and Justice*, 2nd. ed. Washington, DC: Bureau of Justice Statistics. 1988.

Cole, George. *The American System of Criminal Justice*. Pacific Grove, CA: Brooks/Cole Publishing Co. 1992.

Department of Justice. *Operation Weed and Seed: Reclaiming America's Neighborhoods*. Washington, DC: U.S. Department of Justice. 1991.

DiIulio, John. *Rethinking the Criminal Justice System: Toward a New Paradigm*. Washington, DC: Bureau of Justice Statistics. December 1992.

Federal Bureau of Investigation. *Crime in the United States 1991*. Washington, DC: United States Department of Justice. 1992.

Furstenberg, Frank, and Charles Wellford. "Calling the Police: The Evaluation of Police Service." *Law and Society Review* 7:393–406 (1973).

Gallup, George. *The Gallup Poll Monthly,* Report No. 318. Princeton, NJ: The Gallup Poll. 1992.

Goldstein, Herman. *Problem-Oriented Policing*. New York: McGraw-Hill. 1990.

Greene, Jack, Geoffrey Alpert, and Paul Styles. "Values and Culture in Two American Police Departments: Lessons from King Arthur." *Journal of Contemporary Criminal Justice* 8:183–207 (1992).

Kelling, George. "Measuring What Matters: A New Way of Thinking About Crime and Public Order." *The City Journal* Spring 2:21–34 (1992).

Metro-Dade Police Department. *Survey of African-American Males 15–30 Years of Age*. Miami: Metro-Dade Police Department. 1992.

Metro-Dade Police Department. *"Jammin' with the Man" Project Summary*. Miami: Metro-Dade Police Department. 1993.

Moore, Mark, and George Kelling. "To Serve and to Protect: Learning from Police History," *The Public Interest* 70:49–65. (1983).

Overtown Blue Ribbon Committee. *Final Report.* City of Miami, 1984.

Petersen, Thomas. Personal communication. February 1993.

Reaves, Brian. *Law Enforcement Management and Administrative Statistics, 1990: Data for Individual State and Local Agencies with 100 or More Officers.* Washington, DC: Bureau of Justice Statistics. 1992.

Short, James F. *Delinquency in Society.* Englewood Cliffs, NJ: Prentice-Hall. 1990.

Skogan, Wesley. *Disorder and Decline: Crime and the Spiral of Decay in American Neighborhoods.* New York: Free Press. 1990.

Skogan, Wesley, and George Antunes. "Information, Apprehension and Deterrence: Exploring the Limits of Police Productivity." *Journal of Criminal Justice* 7 (1979).

Sparrow, M., M. Moore, and D. Kennedy. *Beyond 911: A New Era for Policing.* New York: Basic Books. 1990.

U.S. Civil Rights Commission. *Who's Guarding the Guardians?* Washington, DC: USGPO. 1981.

Walker, Samuel. *The Police In America.* New York: McGraw-Hill. 1992.

Whitaker, Catherine. *Crime Prevention Measures.* Washington, DC: Bureau of Justice Statistics. 1986.

Wilson, O. W., and Roy McClaren. *Police Administration,* 4th ed. New York: McGraw-Hill. 1977.

Part III

Current Practices

In the previous section six selections were offered that covered current research findings and practices from the point of view of academia. This section is from the point of view of the practitioners. Practitioners have different experiences than researchers. A sample of these experiences is presented in this section. The first selection, by Carl Hawkins, is an overview of the Edmonton, Alberta, experience. This article traces the changes from traditional law enforcement to the current effort to work with the community and problem solve.

The second selection, by Jeff Young, reports the community-oriented policing experiences of Savannah, Georgia. This article also provides an overview of the changes made from traditional to community-oriented policing but emphasizes the added dimension of the political reality of this transition. The various elements of this successful program are presented and discussed.

The third selection is a speech given at the annual meeting of the Police Executive Research Forum by one of America's most dynamic and thoughtful police chiefs, Dennis Nowicki. Chief Nowicki's comments focus on the role of the administrator in making successful an agency's effort to provide community policing. He points out that administrators must provide officers with the appropriate tools to be successful in implementing community-oriented and problem-solving policing.

The final selection in this section by Lieutenant Tim Oettmeier and Mary Ann Wycoff, discusses the need for organizational change and the change in performance evaluations as agencies move to community-oriented policing. Oettmeier and Wycoff have conceptually and strategically identified an innovative approach to performance evaluations.

13

Ready, Fire, Aim
A Look at Community Policing in Edmonton, Alberta, Canada

Carl W. Hawkins, Jr.

Downtown Edmonton business owners and office workers were complaining to Constable[1] Patricia Murray about the panhandlers in the area. According to Murray, "The complaints included that these people smelled bad, asked for money and were alcoholic or drug dependent." The business owners and office workers wanted the police to do something.

Murray looked into the problem. She found that the panhandlers were concentrated in five areas, and based on her research, she concluded there were three viable courses of action the police department could take. One option was to arrest the panhandlers, another was to move them out by any means, and the third was to have the business owners create a paper voucher system for basic necessities. She knew the first two options had been tried in many cities, with limited success. "The problem was one of perception; most citizens wanted to help the panhandlers by giving them money," she said. This only escalated the problem, she concluded, by drawing even more panhandlers to the area. Murray recommended that a paper voucher system be established.

The system allowed downtown business owners to print paper vouchers that they then sold to customers. These vouchers could be redeemed only for food, non-alcoholic drinks or bus transportation. The panhandlers received the paper vouchers from citizens who would normally have given them money. Murray said, "A lot of education had to be done to have the public use the voucher system," but she believed this approach would reduce the problem.

This is an example of community policing in Edmonton in 1993. It had not always been that way; historically, the department policed the city in a more traditional way. A quick look back shows how community policing has evolved in Edmonton from its traditional roots.

The History of Edmonton, Alberta, Canada

The capital of Alberta, Canada, Edmonton owes its existence to an abundant supply of natural resources. These resources prompted each of its three major growth periods. In 1795, the Hudson Bay Company founded Fort Edmonton on the banks of the North Saskatchewan River. Traders bartered with native Indians for mink and fox pelts. A trading settlement developed and became the main stopping point for routes to the north and west.

During the 1800s, Edmonton also became a starting point for gold prospectors rushing to the Klondike region. Gold diggers stocked up on supplies in Edmonton for the harsh trip north. When the gold failed to materialize for some, they headed back to Edmonton to settle for a slower but surer way of life. The city grew to six times its previous size, making it a prime choice for the provincial capital when Alberta was formed in 1905.

In the years that followed, Edmonton earned the nickname "Gateway to the North" because of its status as a transportation hub and gateway to regions beyond. In 1915, the city became a major link to the Canadian Pacific Transcontinental Railroad and emerged as an important crossroads for travel.

Edmonton's reputation as a gateway city was reinforced during the 1930s, when pilots transported vital medical supplies, food and mail to the north. When construction began on the Alaska Highway in 1942, the city again found itself in the role of major transportation and supply center.

Just as the last big growth period was fading from memory, the Leduc Number One Well, approximately 25 miles southeast of Edmonton, gushed forth black crude oil in 1947. This was just the beginning. Since then, more than 2,250 wells have been drilled around the city. Enormous industrial growth resulted, and the city's population quadrupled. Today, over 600,000 people live in Edmonton.

The History of Law Enforcement in Edmonton

In the early 1870s, the new Dominion government established law enforcement in Edmonton by providing it a contingent of officers known as the North West Mounted Police. As a result of "stirred up political trouble" in 1892 between this agency and the Edmonton City Council, the city began hiring a group of officers who later became the Edmonton City Police. Although the origins of the Edmonton City Police were rooted in the conflict between the city council and the mounted police, the agency's early history was shaped by chief constables who came from the Royal Canadian Mounted Police (RCMP).

In the early 1900s, the police focused primarily on liquor violations, prostitution and gambling. Several chief constables were fired for not addressing these problems. During World War I, Edmonton police leaders placed an extreme emphasis on discipline and the use of the military model for command and control. In the 1930s and 1940s, the advent of the automobile, radio communications and other developing technologies moved the Edmonton City Police into a new era of policing.

On Sept. 27, 1954, the Edmonton City Council chose M. F. E. Anthony, who had worked as an assistant RCMP commissioner, as the new chief constable. Anthony instituted many changes in the city police, including the establishment of new sections or units such as central registry, case supervisors, crime index, communications, garage, drawing office, and personnel. For greater efficiency, existing divisions were broken down into smaller squads. The first-ever recruit training class graduated in 1955. Also during Anthony's tenure, the police moved into newly renovated police headquarters. During this period, Edmonton annexed several surrounding towns, and the city population began to rise again.

In the mid-1960s, the city council created and appointed the Edmonton Board of Police Commissioners. This board was formed to serve as a buffer between the city government, the police department and the public. Shortly thereafter, Anthony died and was succeeded by two other chief constables who had also worked for the RCMP.

Ready: The Lunney Years

In 1974, the city council appointed yet another RCMP member, Robert F. Lunney, to head the Edmonton City Police. Lunney, who had been the superintendent in charge of classification and compensation, had received two national awards for his contributions to policing prior to his appointment. These awards and Lunney's high ethical standards brought a new sense of pride and professionalism to the office. Staff Sgt.[2] Keith "P.J." Duggan reflected, "Prior to Bob Lunney becoming chief, officers were hired by the pound [i.e., the bigger, the better], and the police were seen as [engaged] in a war."

Lunney also brought to the department a general concern for the constables and a sense of openness. "Lunney would walk around the department and know each officer's name, spouse's name and children's names," added Duggan. Once, Lunney walked into a parade (roll call) and noticed that the cross straps over the constables' handguns could easily come off, which could be dangerous. The constables had been concerned about this for some time. Lunney asked whether the cross straps were necessary, and when shown how easily they came off, he ordered that their use be discontinued. Duggan stated, "Lunney, by that one act, demonstrated his concern for the constable on the street."

During Lunney's tenure, another growth period for Edmonton was under way, due to an oil boom. As the population rapidly grew, so did the police department. Recruit training classes graduated every fifteen weeks, one after another.

The average amount of police experience per officer declined from thirteen years to eighteen months, according to Duggan. Also, Edmonton was attracting single males "without high life skills" from all over North America to work in the oil fields. The period from the late 1970s to the early 1980s was one of the most unstable times for the police department, but it also provided an opportunity for Lunney to change the department's culture.

Monthly meetings were held at which the constables could provide input about issues facing the department. Safety, job functions, weapons, holsters, uniforms, and beards were discussed at these meetings. Other changes were implemented: school resource officers were stationed in schools; the victim services, street crimes and child abuse units were established; and community service officer positions were created. The departmental changes reflected a sense of social consciousness regarding the policing of Edmonton. The agency's name was changed from the Edmonton City Police to the Edmonton Police Department, and the title of chief constable was changed to chief of police.

In 1984, Lunney approved a sabbatical for Inspector Chris Braiden, so he could work for the Solicitor General's Office in Ottawa, Canada. During his tenure as a special advisor to the solicitor general on policing, Braiden focused his efforts on reading, traveling and collecting information that sharpened his views of community policing and problem solving. Braiden found support compatible with his view of how police services should be delivered. The experience also gave him ideas, knowledge and access to people who would be helpful to him later in further refining his vision of community policing. The seeds of change—young officers, openness, a new chief, community consciousness, research on community policing—were planted during Lunney's tenure. The Edmonton Police Department became "used to change" and was poised and ready for a new style of policing.

Fire: Neighborhood Foot Patrol

During the 1980s, the Edmonton oil boom began to slow down. For economic reasons, the police department stopped hiring new constables; in fact, there was a call to start laying off constables. In 1983, the entire department elected not to accept a pay raise to preserve eighty-six constables' jobs.

Braiden returned from his sabbatical and was promoted to superintendent in 1987. Upon his return, Braiden was full of new ideas for policing and insisted that the Edmonton Police Department look into community-based approaches to policing. However, Lunney was not in a position to make such a decision, as he was planning to retire soon from the department.

The selection of a new police chief provided Braiden with a unique opportunity. He applied for the position so he could argue his case for neighborhood foot patrols before the police commission. Commission members asked Braiden many questions about community policing during his interview, but they ultimately appointed Leroy Chahley to be the new chief. Chahley was concerned with managing internal departmental problems; he did not become active in the neighborhood foot patrol movement.

In April 1987, Chahley agreed to let neighborhood foot patrols be implemented in twenty-one of Edmonton's most problematic areas. Braiden sought out and obtained additional monies from Canada's solicitor general and the Mott Foundation to help fund the program and pay for an evaluator. Twenty-one neighborhood foot patrol constables with forty hours of training were assigned to the city's hottest areas, as identified through an examination of 153,000 calls for service. (Significantly, 81 percent of the calls in these areas were repeat calls.) Braiden issued beepers to the foot patrol constables and helped them set up neighborhood offices equipped with telephones and answering machines. The constables' objectives were to work with the community in solving problems and to decentralize operations by answering calls for service from their beat offices. Braiden told them, "I want people contact, not pavement contact." He added: "You must go to where the people are. If they are inside, you must go inside." As the problem areas changed, Braiden directed the neighborhood foot patrols to new problem areas.

One of the new foot patrol constables was Dave Hut. He found he was getting a high number of repeat calls regarding public drunkenness and general disturbances from a neighborhood near the downtown area. Traditionally, the Edmonton Police Department responded to this problem by arresting inebriated people and keeping them in jail until they sobered up. Hut studied the problem and discovered that the offenders' drink of choice was Chinese cooking wine. This substance was 38 percent alcohol, easy to obtain and very inexpensive. The wine's salt content was so high that ingesting it was sometimes fatal.

Hut contacted the Alberta Liquor Control Board and found that because the cooking wine contained so much salt, it was not classified as an alcoholic beverage and could not be regulated under the Liquor Control Act. The constable approached Canadian Customs and tried to limit importation of the wine. This tactic proved unsuccessful because the wine was not considered alcoholic, and therefore, it was not taxable or under Customs' control.

Hut organized a meeting with the police commission, Solicitor General's Office representatives, Liquor Control Board, and Edmonton Police Department members. The Liquor Control Board agreed to change its policy to include the cooking wine in its definition of alcoholic substances.

The wine could then be regulated under the Liquor Control Act, which prohibited the sale of any alcohol-based product that was over 20 percent alcohol per volume. Also, because the wine would be considered alcohol, it consequently would be subject to an importation tax. Eventually, the importation of the wine was banned under the Liquor Control Act. Although the area still had its share of alcoholics, they no longer succumbed to the effects of the deadly cooking wine.

Joe Hornick, executive director of the Canadian Research Institute for Law and the Family at the University of Calgary, evaluated the neighborhood foot patrol program and found that its objectives were met: repeat calls for service decreased, reporting of information to the police increased, community problems were solved, job satisfaction among constables increased, and citizens were more satisfied with the police. Hornick recommended that the program be expanded to other high-calls-for-service areas so other constables would have the autonomy to deal with problems in their communities.

Aim: Looking at the Structure Within

Even with the success of the neighborhood foot patrol program, Chahley was pre-occupied with the internal problems facing the Edmonton Police Department. Several constables were arrested for crimes, and the press began to pressure Chahley about the department's problems; at times, it seemed as though every day brought a new encounter with the press over internal problems. During this time, Chahley strengthened the department's unity of command and created platoons and squads.

In 1988, the department received accreditation through the Commission on Accreditation for Law Enforcement Agencies. Inspector Roger Simms, the accreditation manager, felt community policing and accreditation were mutually reinforcing. According to Simms, accreditation helped the police elicit community support and fostered interaction. "Many of the concepts of community policing are built into the standards," said Simms. For example, standard 54.2.10 required the police agency to seek input from the community so that the agency's policies would reflect the community's needs. Standard 45.2.3 required the agency to conduct drug-related crime prevention programs in schools, as well as conduct security surveys and encourage citizens to properly mark their property so it could be recovered if stolen. These and many other standards convinced Simms that accreditation provided the department with a foundation to address problems and community needs.

During this period, additional technology became available to the department. The identification section obtained an automated fingerprint and identification system, and mobile digital terminals were installed in police vehicles.

During the city's economic decline in the 1980s, the population increased significantly, which led to more calls for police service and more reported crime. Because of the city's economic difficulties, the Edmonton Police Department did not hire any additional constables during that decade. Even with these mounting concerns, the neighborhood foot patrol program continued to operate and brought some problems under control.

Constable Lew Evans-Davies patrolled a neighborhood with a large number of apartment buildings. The majority of the apartment residents received social assistance. Because the apartment mailboxes were located outside the security doors, anyone could access them. Thieves began stealing government checks from the mailboxes, frequently cashing them with phony identification. Evans-Davies felt new tactics were necessary to address this problem, as the traditional law enforcement approach was not working. Evans-Davies contacted the city newspaper, which published an article titled "Operation Bank It." This article led to a television story. The media coverage informed the public about the problem and introduced them to the concept of direct deposit.

The direct deposit program allowed the social service agency to electronically transfer a check into a recipient's bank account. Evans-Davies also circulated information pamphlets and questionnaires to the apartment residents to both educate them about the problem and elicit additional information about the thefts. The building managers cooperated by moving the mailboxes behind the security doors.

These tactics eliminated mailbox damage and check theft. The amount of money lost by the companies that cashed the checks was also reduced.

Ready: A Mandate for Change

From 1980 to 1990, Edmonton's population increased by 19 percent, and reported crime increased by 44 percent. With the economic downturn creating budget shortfalls, the police department was faced with the prospect of having no new constables to handle the increase in calls for service. In 1991, the city council cut $1.7 million from the police department budget. As a result, the department was unable to hire additional constables for the ninth straight year, despite a population increase of 100,000 since 1983. Norm Koch, of the Edmonton Police Association, stated, "If the public [were] aware of how [few] officers there are out there, it would be alarmed." Inspector Hugh Richards added, "We're finding guys who joined in 1987 saying, 'I'm drained; I can't take any more of this.'" Adding to the stress was an angry public complaining about being kept waiting. Emergency calls still received a quick response, but other calls did not.

Koch told of a complaint that was held for seven hours because no constables were available to respond. "I'm not sure about neighborhood foot patrol walking up and down the street holding hands with businessmen. It's great policing within a three-block area, and the rest of the area gets only standard policing," he said.

Braiden continued speaking to various police groups, the community and the police commission about his vision of a new style of policing, which he called community-based policing. "Policing must get back to its roots—policing of the people, by the people, for the people," said Braiden, paraphrasing Abraham Lincoln and Sir Robert Peel. "I get exasperated when people say community-based policing is new. Who in the hell were the police ever intended to police but the community?" added Braiden. The former chair of the police commission, Zaheer Lakhani, said he heard Braiden speak about community-based policing several times. He added, "We also read many of the publications about this type of policing, and it made sense." Hornick's evaluation also gave the police commission some assurance that the Edmonton Police Department was on the right track and that, perhaps, community-based policing was the answer to the city's crime and disorder problems.

In 1992, the new chair of the police commission, Wayne Drewry, stated that "Chris Braiden got us all revved up about community-based policing [as] being the way to police smarter." A variety of factors contributed to the police commission's decision that the Edmonton Police Department would embrace community-based policing. They included Edmonton's economic difficulties, Braiden's leadership, police commission members' exposure to community-based policing concepts, and public support for neighborhood foot patrol constables.

On New Year's Day, 1990, the name of the Edmonton Police Department was changed to the Edmonton Police Service. Chahley retired later that year, and the search was on for a new police chief. After many interviews, the police commission selected Doug McNally. A career officer who had risen through the ranks, McNally knew of the problems facing the city and the department. When he was hired, the police commission told him they wanted the city to practice community-based policing. McNally stated, "We must be careful and not use labels; we should police the way it was meant to be." He added, "We should empower the community to solve their own problems, while providing them with a better product." McNally also knew from his prior experience that to keep policing the city in the traditional way, he would need two hundred new constables and $12 million in additional funding—and there was little chance the city council would give him either. Regardless, McNally knew changes had to be made.

McNally asked Braiden to take on the job of expanding community-based policing across one of four divisions. Braiden agreed, on two conditions: he wanted community-based policing to occur across the board, and he wanted to formulate a plan for making this happen. McNally agreed, and Braiden started working on a blueprint for change.

Braiden's blueprint was called "A Process for Change." In it, Braiden proposed five steps:

- an organizational review;
- an in-depth analysis of workload;
- a decentralization through the addition of neighborhood foot patrols, satellite police offices and wheeled trailers that could be used for problems of a transient nature;
- a reevaluation of specialization; and
- a stratification of the service delivery system around a four-tiered level of delivery: high-priority units, complaint units, satellite police offices, and neighborhood foot patrols.

Braiden next proposed a team retreat for the department's executive officers to "tell us where everybody stands and enable us to get a consensus on the core components of the overall project." Braiden also asked that all six superintendents be full-time members of the proposed project team. "Each must have a piece of the action so that they each have a vested interest in its success or failure," stated Braiden.

Braiden called for the establishment of a community-based policing project team to conduct an organizational review, and he looked for volunteers throughout the department. In May 1990, Braiden selected four members to serve on the team, based on their knowledge of departmental operations. Braiden told them there were two basic rules he wanted them to follow: "I would rather you ask for forgiveness than permission," and "Don't ask a question if you can live without the answer."

Within a few months, the executive officer's team retreat was held, and the process of change Braiden proposed was adopted. At the retreat, the team adopted the phrase "Committed to Community Needs" as the Edmonton Police Service's core value. They also vowed to implement community-based policing throughout the department.

In March 1991, the community-based policing project team conducted a complete organizational review of the Edmonton Police Service. They did so with an eye toward limiting specialization and centralization, as Braiden did not like either. He often said, "Generalize whenever possible, specialize when necessary, decentralize whenever possible, centralize when necessary." Braiden felt specialization and centralization added to the bureaucracy that hindered the agency's community-based policing efforts. "What happened to the Edmonton Police Service is what happens to all bureaucracies on the public dollar that have a monopoly on their product," he said. "Over time, the product becomes what those on the inside want it to be. The only way the police can get back to being a real part of the community they are charged with serving is by dismantling the bureaucratic structure that isolates them from the community." Braiden insisted that the Edmonton Police Service needed a "bureaucratic garage sale."

The organizational review achieved two things: it eliminated parts of the old system that were contrary to the department's new core value, and it freed up resources to build a new organization. The organizational review looked at the department from two perspectives: the "big picture," or a bird's-eye view of the agency, and the unit analysis, or a review of the details of the organization.

The "big picture" review documented that the department was in its tenth year of "cutback management" and employed twenty-eight fewer constables than it had a decade before—despite the fact that the population had increased by 105,000 and that calls for service had increased proportionately over the same period. The unit analysis showed that, due to increased specialization, the number of organizational units increased from 64 to 120 between 1974 and 1988. The number of constables assigned to calls for service dropped from 545 to 468. As part of the analysis, review team members also visited each unit to determine its role within the organization and see whether its activities were aligned with its original purpose.

An eleven-member evaluation team made up of department leaders from many sections and ranks examined the organizational review findings and made 164 recommendations. After five intense days of review, the group approved 132 of the recommendations for inclusion in the final recommendation package. As a result of this process, sixty-eight department members were moved to front-end positions, which helped improve the response to community needs. Additional recommendations were delayed until approval of the 1992 budget.

In December 1991, the community-based policing project team concentrated on completing a workload analysis to determine how to redesign the districts and where to place new facilities. From this analysis, the team decided that some city areas needed closer attention than others. This in-depth analysis provided the rationale for new beat boundaries.

Also in December 1991, the project team started working on the department's new service delivery model. The model proposed the following:

- the opening of 12 community stations throughout the city where citizens could report nonemergency incidents in person,
- a "red page" insert in the telephone directory to encourage citizens to call or go to a community station for service,
- a new call path chart to enable complaint evaluators and station members to determine the most effective way to resolve calls for service,
- a first-contact reporting concept to reduce repetitive information-gathering,
- a mobile digital terminal reporting system to reduce paperwork and processing time, and
- a delayed response procedure for nonemergency incidents to allow for a later response at a mutually agreed-on time.

The new service delivery model was designed to divert as many reports as possible to community stations and, at the same time, to reduce the number of fraudulent reports by requiring citizens to report incidents in person. Detective David Veitch, who worked on developing the model, said the Edmonton Police Service predicted over 100,000 calls for service would be routed to community stations rather than to central police headquarters as a result of the changes.

The model also established a four-tiered response: priority 1—immediate, priority 2—urgent, priority 3—service, and priority 4—delayed. The model further established four types of constables for delivering police services: neighborhood foot patrol constables, ownership constables, community station constables, and response constables. Any constable in an area, regardless of type, would respond to priority 1 and priority 2 calls. Ownership and response constables would respond to priority 3 calls. Priority 4 calls that were not picked up voluntarily through call stopping would be assigned at parade (roll call) and monitored by area supervisors. Many of the priority 3 calls would end up being handled at the community stations. Also, many additional calls would go directly to the neighborhood foot patrol and ownership constables through their answering machines, beepers or cellular phones, thereby bypassing centralized police operations. This layered process was designed to increase face-to-face contacts and free constables to do more problem solving, while continuing to handle true emergencies.

The concept of constables' "ownership" of specific geographical areas was integrated into many of the design functions of community-based policing in

Edmonton. "The only way to motivate anyone in the workplace is to give them meaningful work and control over that work," claimed Braiden, adding that "all attempts at external motivation have failed, whether they are better salaries, fringe benefits, less hours, human relations training, sensitivity training, or communications training." The establishment of ownership and neighborhood foot patrol constables was designed to give the constables meaningful work and control over that work.

One of the areas that was most affected by decentralization and despecialization in the department was the criminal investigations division. After the changes, most detectives worked out of district stations and reported to the station commanders. A few detectives, for the most part specialists in violent crime, worked out of headquarters. Criminal investigations division Superintendent Al Buerger said Edmonton detectives saw many benefits from community-based policing. He stated: "In the past, we had everybody to talk to and nobody to talk to. Now we know who works a geographic area and can pass information back and forth to the constables." He added that not all problems were geographically based, and therefore, detectives could see problems that occurred in other communities. This enabled detectives to solve problems they may have missed by concentrating on neighborhoods alone. Buerger claimed that decentralization and despecialization alone did nothing to change investigations work, because many communities do not have geographical boundaries, but rather, are spread throughout the city. Similar interests bring members of nongeographical communities, such as a city's business community, together. A centralized group of investigators can address their concerns more directly than a neighborhood constable or detective can.

During this time, detectives became involved in many problem-solving initiatives. Detective Ken Montgomery told of an Edmonton service station chain that was open 24 hours a day and accounted for 27 percent of all city robberies. Some of the robberies were internal. Montgomery stated: "One of the biggest problems was that the service stations had very little security. Cigarettes were out in the open for anyone to steal, most of the money was kept in the registers, and employees were not screened before they were hired." Montgomery went to the service stations and put basic crime prevention measures in place. He also set up a security check system under which any person whom the service stations were to hire had to be cleared by the Edmonton Police Service. He also asked the owner to contact him any time there was a robbery or theft at the stations. After these measures were instituted, the robbery rate at this chain dropped to levels comparable to those of other city service stations.

Fire: Community-Based Policing in Edmonton

On Jan. 6, 1992, at a special meeting of the Edmonton Board of Police Commissioners, McNally presented all the proposed changes relating to the implementation of community-based policing in the city. The police commission adopted the proposals.

The Edmonton Police Service began the implementation process with a media blitz informing citizens of how they could request police services at their community stations. Radio and television spots, as well as newspaper advertisements and articles regarding the new process, were run. The ads dramatized the old way Edmonton police provided services. They showed citizens waiting on the phone for a call-taker, and then waiting even longer for an officer to arrive. The ads also explained how convenient the community stations were to where citizens lived, and how easy it was to report complaints to uniformed constables at the stations. The telephone company provided a red, one-page directory insert that explained where to go to make nonemergency requests for service. All utility customers were sent a flier with a label they could place by their phone with directions on how to report nonemergency problems.

When opened, community stations were staffed 12 hours a day, every day except Sunday, on which they were open from 10 A.M. to 6 P.M. Uniformed constables and volunteers were available to assist the public. The stations were equipped with telephones, copiers, fax machines, mobile digital terminals, and other office equipment. The stations handled motor vehicle accidents in which the cars could be moved, vehicle thefts, general thefts, mischief and vandalism, lost and found property, minor assaults, and ongoing problems.

Within one month, the department's organizational studies unit began to evaluate the media campaign's impact. A random-sample survey of Edmonton residents revealed that

• over 97 percent knew there were community stations in their areas;
• 51 percent learned about the community stations from the media, with newspapers being the most frequently cited source of information; and
• before the media campaign, only 15 percent would likely go to their community stations for police services, but after the media campaign, 22 percent would.

The training of all employees in problem solving, community policing concepts and the new service delivery model began in October 1991. McNally spoke at most sessions and provided statistics demonstrating why community-based policing was necessary for the city. Braiden and Buerger delivered portions of the training, as well. The number of neighborhood foot patrol constables increased to twenty-seven, and the new ownership constables started working their assignments.

A new performance evaluation system was developed during this time. The performance evaluation covered aspects of community-based policing and problem solving. One section evaluated constables on their conflict resolution skills and proactive project work, as well as their efforts to target disorder, network with the private sector and interact with the public. Superintendent John LaFlamme stated, "We recognize success, with a tolerance for failure." LaFlamme added that the police service was working to develop constable I and II ranks to recognize officers with a minimum number of years of experience who passed the required promotional tests.

By the end of 1992, several results of the community-based policing effort were evident. According to Veitch, complaints and total calls decreased by about 30 percent, indicating that many calls were being handled at the community stations. "We've had 200,000 people walk into our community police stations in 1992 to report problems or ask for advice," added McNally. The number rose to 235,000 in 1993. Veitch also related that "abandoned calls" decreased by 36 percent, indicating that fewer people were hanging up after being put on hold, and that telephone calls for service were answered 40 percent quicker than before. Nonemergency calls that were dispatched were also handled quicker than before; there was almost a one-hour reduction in response time to these calls, according to Veitch.

But not everyone was so optimistic. One researcher was concerned that community-based policing in Edmonton might be in some trouble. The only department personnel who interacted with the community were the constables on the street and the executive officers. The middle managers interacted only with each other. The researcher believed a flattening of the organization was in order. He also felt that during tough economic times, the community-based policing plan might be streamlined. For example, in one area, neighborhood foot patrol offices were closed and constables were told to work out of the community stations.

Another area of concern was the ownership constables' role. Ownership Constable Jerry Vercammen stated, "I spend about 80 percent of my time on calls for service and about 20 percent of my time on problems in my ownership area." He felt the department should look at ways to better define the ownership constable's role and free up more time for addressing problems.

Some of the neighborhood foot patrol constables were concerned about the lack of training for this new assignment. When the first constables were assigned to the new program in 1988, they received 40 hours of training. Due to attrition over the next three years, new neighborhood foot patrol constables were assigned to the program, but many received no training. One neighborhood foot patrol constable said, "All I received in the way of training was that I walked with another constable for two days and was told to take ownership of the area."

Aim: The Future

McNally viewed further stratification of the constables' roles as one of the last steps to be taken to fully implement community-based policing in Edmonton. His plan included assigning new recruit graduates as response constables. As constables gained more experience and improved their job skills, they could progress from handling calls to working at community stations. With more experience and improvement, they could be assigned as ownership constables, and their last assignment would be as neighborhood foot patrol constables.

The Operational Support Communications and Records System was being developed to provide constables with the latest information on repeat calls in their neighborhoods. This system is designed to encode data on previous calls and dispositions and integrate this information into future calls for service. Mike Derbyshire, who was working on the system, said, "The system will provide information by geographic area, address or community league." According to Derbyshire, this should enable constables to have the latest information on problems in their areas.

In February 1993, Braiden retired from the Edmonton Police Service to devote more time to lecturing and sharing his vision of policing. He noted that some officers do not easily form the bonds with the public that are needed for a police-citizen partnership, which he believes is at the heart of community-based policing. "When the police work alone, without public help, they solve less than 10 percent of criminal cases. With a lead, a kick-start from somebody in the public, there is more than an 85 percent success rate," he estimated.

With Braiden's retirement, Inspector Hugh Richards took over the community-based policing project. Richards believed that the Edmonton Police Service was well on its way in the implementation process, and that there was no turning back. Other project team members concurred. Sgt. Tony Harder felt that the patrol force bought into the change the most, and that other divisions were moving in the same direction. Staff Sgt. P.J. Duggan agreed, adding, "Most change is generational." He thought the change would be complete once most of the old guard retired.

At the end of February 1993, all north division constables and supervisors met at a luncheon to discuss ownership. The issue of ownership was creating some problems in the stratification process, and the north division was trying to work through these concerns with input from everyone in the division. Many questions were asked at the meeting, and they continue to frame the evolution of community policing: Should the number of ownership constables be increased or decreased? Should the geographic areas be enlarged or reduced? Should the ownership constables be on day shift or be rotated through the shifts? The meeting also sparked many heated discussions between constables who were not convinced that there was much difference between the ownership and response constables, except for some flexibility. The ownership issue remains to be resolved, and experimentation continues. McNally stated: "There are no models out there. We are trying things, fixing them and making things work. When I leave this service, I want to go back and speak to the ownership constables. If they understand the concept of ownership, then we will have fully reached community-based policing in Edmonton."

Notes

[1] A constable is the equivalent of an American police officer.

[2] A staff sergeant is the equivalent of an American lieutenant.

14

Community Policing in Savannah, Georgia

Jeff Young

The 1991 mayoral race in Savannah, Georgia, was a heated campaign. The incumbent mayor, Democrat John P. Rousakis, had served for over twenty years. Until 1991, he had not faced a serious challenge to his reelection bids. His opponent was an unlikely adversary. Republican Susan Weiner was a former resident of New York and had lived in Savannah for only five years. She was the type of candidate who would not ordinarily get voters' support in this Deep South, traditionally democratic city.

Crime, especially violent crime, was a major campaign issue. In 1991, violent crime was up by 17 percent over the previous year and had risen by over 66 percent since 1989. The city had experienced a large increase in homicides: there were 59 in 1991, compared with 35 in 1990 and 20 in 1989. Much of the violence was attributed to narcotics.

The media focus on the crime problem was significant during the election period. Crime had been cited as the reason for cancellation of a large convention, which greatly concerned local chamber of commerce members. Crime was also a major issue in the city council race.

During the bitter campaign, Weiner contended that the city manager should be replaced along with the mayor. Like Rousakis, the city manager had served for many years, and although the position had civil service protection and was not subject to mayoral action, Weiner's call to "clean house" resonated with local voters.

As November drew near, the campaign grew increasingly heated, generating public interest and focusing attention on the police department. Weiner's focus on violent crime provided an incentive for the incumbent mayor and city manager to increase the police department's effectiveness. The police chief recalled: "The city manager told me to do something creative. Community policing seemed like the best bet because of our [previous] successes [using this approach] in public housing."

In October, the police department officially "flipped a switch" and formally launched its community-oriented policing (COP) and problem-oriented policing (POP) initiatives. However, these responses to the crime problem, aimed at improving police service to the community, did not improve the mayor's chances for reelection. With a large voter turnout of 58 percent, Rousakis lost the general election by 2,698 votes; five new aldermen were also elected.

Despite the election-related focus on crime and police service, the first steps in the process of improving police services were already under way by early 1991. The city manager had commissioned a study, known as the Comprehensive Community Crime Control Strategy, which was completed in August 1991. The stated purpose of the study was to develop a comprehensive set of strategies for addressing the city's crime problem. The 350-page study was an extensive assessment of the city's needs, analyzing the distribution and composition of crime among the various neighborhoods, as well as the social and physical characteristics of those neighborhoods. For example, the study mapped the distribution of poverty, physical deterioration, unemployment, child abuse and neglect, teenage pregnancy, and teenage mothers, along with various crime problems.

Proposed strategies addressed not only crime, but also the conditions that foster it. This study became the foundation for the implementation of COP in the Savannah Police Department.

This new, politically motivated emphasis on community policing was not the first example of the department's efforts to develop a cooperative relationship with the community. The department had several earlier programs that were community-based.

Early Community-Based Programs

The Savannah Police Department had experience with community programs before 1991. In 1987, the department participated in the "Showcase Neighborhood Program," which the city manager established as part of the new Neighborhood Services Program to improve the quality of life in troubled neighborhoods. A variety of sources funded the program, including city, state and federal agencies and private foundations. The police department played a major role in the program by working with residents and other city departments to identify needs and establish community priorities. The program philosophy was that city government was a partner with community residents, not a provider for them. In 1990, Savannah received the City Livability Award from the U.S. Conference of Mayors for this program.

In 1988, the police department established four ministations in the city's most troubled public housing developments. Each station had one officer permanently assigned to provide needed police services and develop community links. These officers established relationships with the area residents, especially youths and the elderly. Ministation officers also served as DARE officers in nearby schools and as Boy Scout leaders. Many of these officers organized and coached recreational sports teams.

Before the ministations were established, criminals controlled these neighborhoods. Lt. James Barnwell, who was in charge of the ministations, recalled that fire and paramedic crews had to have a police escort into and out of the areas when responding to calls for service. Patrol officers did not enter these areas without backup from assisting officers. By 1993, officers walked alone in the developments on foot patrols. Children played freely throughout the area, without fear of getting caught in drug dealers' cross fire. Elderly residents were no longer isolated inside due to fear.

The department made other efforts to interact with the community. The department had experimented with bicycle patrols since 1989. Formal implementation began in 1990, and bicycle patrols were used extensively in the downtown and waterfront areas. As a result of public interest, a horse patrol was established in 1987. The horse patrol was also used mainly in the downtown area. The department was working with the community long before it had a formalized COP program. Previous initiatives were, however, solitary efforts that had no relationship to a department-wide philosophy. These programs are still in operation and are important parts of the department's current community policing program.

The City of Savannah

Savannah is located in the northeastern corner of Georgia. It is a beautiful coastal city, close to the famous Hilton Head, South Carolina, resort area. The Spanish moss that cascades from the trees and the numerous rows of magnificent old homes evoke memories of Southern splendor. The city boasts one of the nation's largest urban historic districts. Many narrow streets and public squares are still laid out as originally designed by Georgia's founder, James Oglethorpe. Blocks of reclaimed waterfront warehouses have been converted into shops and restaurants that are now major tourist attractions.

The main industries are manufacturing and transportation (port and airport). While not the largest industry, tourism is the fastest-growing industry in Savannah. About 5.1 million people visit Savannah each year. Tourism generates $580 million annually and 16,000 jobs.

The city's current economic status is promising. While not immune, Savannah was resistant to the last recession due to the diversity of its economic base. While the national average for unemployment increased by 4 percent, Savannah experienced a 2 percent increase. The city had a reputation for being financially sound.

Savannah also has its share of problems. Besides the crime problem in the early 1990s, there have been serious problems with urban blight. Many old Victorian homes stand in decay, providing a visual contrast to those homes that have been restored to their previous grandeur. These blighted areas are also the locations for a significant portion of the city's crimes.

Savannah's corporate boundaries encompass 62.6 square miles. According to the 1990 census, the city has a population of 137,560. This population is 51 percent black, 47 percent white and 2 percent other. These percentages have changed gradually over the past ten years. In 1980, 49 percent of the population was white, and 48 percent was black. From the 1960s to the mid-1970s, there were a number of civil disorders related to racial tensions, but there has been significantly less racial tension over the past fifteen years. Instead, there is a high degree of interaction between the black and white populations. Racial tension was not a dominant issue in the implementation of community-based policing.

Savannah operates under a council-manager form of government. The city council, consisting of the mayor and eight other aldermen, is the governing board. The council appoints the chief executive, the city manager, who serves at the pleasure of the board.

The City Manager

City Manager Arthur A. Mendonsa has served in the position since 1962. His office is decorated with numerous awards he and the city have received during his tenure. When he joined the city, Savannah's infrastructure was deteriorated. The personnel director had a fourth-grade education, a fact Mendonsa offered as an example of the quality of the city's management employees. Mendonsa's prior experience included eight years as a planner.

Mendonsa has taken an active role in managing the police department, which accounts for 29 percent of the city's budget. Mendonsa describes his input as making "suggestions" for planning by frequently asking, "What are we trying to accomplish?" Mendonsa's office is about one-half mile from police headquarters, and the police chief frequently made the short trip to meet with him.

The Reshaping of the Savannah Police Department

The Comprehensive Community Crime Control Strategy study is an example of the influence Mendonsa's prior planning experience had on his management style. He gathered staff from the city's police, research and budget, and planning and community development departments to conduct the study. The study made recommendations in five strategy areas. The police strategies called for significant changes in the police department and were implemented immediately (in October 1991). All other strategy recommendations were implemented throughout the next year.

The report recommended that the police department decentralize by distributing command accountability on a geographical basis. Previously, patrol captains were assigned to an eight-hour shift and were responsible for all the crimes committed in the city during that time. All line personnel were deployed from the central station, a historic police barracks built in 1870. Based on the report's recommendation, four precincts were designed that grouped crime problems and service areas into manageable sections. Each of the department's four patrol captains was assigned to one of these geographical zones and was responsible for the police activities in that area on a twenty-four-hour basis. They also had authority to schedule and deploy personnel according to precinct and community needs. Precinct stations were established in each defined area, but only for line personnel.

The report's second recommendation was that the department deploy manpower to equally distribute patrol time and increase interaction with the community. Even though the patrol workload was analyzed twice a year and reconfigured as needed, the report described an uneven distribution of patrol resources. As a result of the shift scheduling, some officers had very little uncommitted time, while others had large blocks of uncommitted time. Deployment is now based on the report's recommendation that no more than 40 percent of an officer's time be devoted to handling calls for service. Officers were previously assigned to the same general service area; however, these assignments were not permanent. In its revamping, the department ensured that officers could more readily interact with residents by remaining in permanent geographical assignments.

The report's third recommendation was that the department institute COP, as related to the recommendation for permanent area assignments. The report stated that there was no well-established interaction or communication between the police and citizens. COP was intended to directly address the need for officers to interact more with the residents in the areas they patrolled. This department-wide philosophy emphasized that the police and citizens are coproducers of safety and order, and that they must mutually identify and resolve community problems.

The report's fourth recommendation was that the department institute POP. The report stated that the department was an incident-driven, reactive service provider. POP was described as a department-wide, proactive approach to patrol operations in which officers identify, analyze and respond to specific community problems. This problem-solving approach was intended to address the underlying circumstances that caused crime, whereas COP was intended to create programs and an environment that increases interaction, communication and understanding between police and citizens.

The report's fifth recommendation was that the department establish a differential response system. The report highlighted a problem with the way calls for service were handled. Officers were sent immediately to every call received, even though only 19 percent could be classified as emergencies requiring immediate mobile response. There was no prioritization or management of the service workload. The recommended police response was a deliberate stacking of non-emergency calls so as not to occupy too many officers at once. A telephone reporting unit was also established to handle many reports by telephone, such as those regarding lost property, missing persons and threatening telephone calls. The department initiated a media campaign to explain telephone reporting. The department stressed that this program would keep more officers available for emergency response and give the officers larger blocks of time to conduct proactive patrol. By 1993, the telephone reporting unit was handling between 9 and 17 percent of calls for service.

The report's final recommendation was that the department improve its analytical capabilities. This was seen as necessary for basing deployment and tactics on accurate and timely information. Response times and dispatch services were also targets for improvement. The study revealed that the computer-aided dispatch (CAD) system and the records management system (RMS) were not compatible. The department subsequently hired a planning and research director to oversee data management efforts, and by 1993, integration of the CAD/RMS system was under way.

The Savannah Police Department implemented these six recommendations immediately. As a result of the recommendations, $2.6 million was budgeted to the department to fund 34 new sworn positions, vehicles and equipment, and five telephone report-takers. The department's structure was decentralized into a precinct system. Fixed geographical beats were designed to increase officers' familiarity with citizens and community problems. Using a differential police response balanced the workload and freed up officers' time.

The Savannah Police Department

The Savannah Police Department employs 517 people, including 386 sworn personnel. The department is striving to be demographically balanced and had made progress in achieving racial balance in most ranks. The number of women had increased throughout the ranks, but they are still underrepresented.

At the time of this writing, there were 154 officers, including 71 white men, 62 black men, 10 white women, and 7 black women. There were 136 corporals, including 77 white men, 41 black men, 8 white women, and 6 black women. Sergeants were predominantly white men. Of the 44 sergeants, 30 were white men, 11 were black men, 1 was a white woman, and 1 was a black woman. There were 16 lieutenants: 8 white men, 5 black men, 2 white women, and 1 black woman.

There were no women above the rank of lieutenant. There were 6 captains: 3 white men and 3 black men. Of the 4 majors, 2 were white men and 2 were black men.

Each major commands one of four department bureaus: patrol, investigations, special operations, or management services. Captains are assigned as precinct commanders in the patrol bureau or as assistant bureau commanders in investigations and management services. Command, management services, investigations, and special operations personnel are all deployed from a central police headquarters. All other personnel are assigned and deployed from their precincts.

Patrol officers are assigned to one of three eight-hour shifts. The first and third shifts rotate each month. The second shift is a permanent assignment. Officers are rarely moved from one precinct to another, and they are assigned to the same geographical service areas within precincts as much as possible.

Two units work directly for the police chief: media relations and internal affairs. The media relations unit is staffed with a civilian public information officer who informs the local media about special programs under way and is also the contact for special events or cases of interest. The internal affairs unit is supervised by a lieutenant, who reports that the police chief "takes [complaints] very seriously. The chief will set up a hearing board in a minute."

Departmental Leadership

The police department's top administrator is the chief, David M. Gellatly. He has held this position for over thirteen years. Gellatly had some ten years of experience as chief at other police departments before joining Savannah's force. Before becoming chief in Savannah, Gellatly was chief in Addison, Illinois, for six years. His resume lists several accomplishments since he became Savannah's chief, including getting the department national accreditation in 1989 and reaccreditation in 1993, implementing COP/POP and updating promotional procedures by using assessment centers at all levels. His subordinates describe him as a strong, decisive leader who makes it clear where he stands on issues. He is quick to point out that he hires and fires all employees. He personally interviews all new officers, and he also controls all promotions. Such an active role with these administrative responsibilities provides him with a unique opportunity to reward and punish employees for their behavior.

"The advantage of being chief in Savannah [as opposed to other cities] is that you can say, 'We're going to do this,' and there aren't too many hurdles," said Gellatly. There is no labor union to consider, and he reports that the city manager effectively shields the police department from the vagaries of local politics.

Gellatly has a reputation as a hands-on manager. "While I can be a dictator if I want to, I know where the talent is in the department," he said. He feels he provides autonomy to his personnel but also holds them accountable for results.

Gellatly says the implementation of COP/POP played a big part in the 11 percent decrease in violent crime during 1992. He is very supportive of all the community-based programs and makes his support known. Personnel throughout the agency were extremely aware of his commitment to the COP/POP initiatives and of the importance he attached to these efforts.

A key figure in the implementation of COP/POP has been Maj. Dan Reynolds, who commanded the management services division. He is the coordinator of the COP/POP initiatives and was appointed by the chief as the COP/POP "czar." In the Savannah Police Department, the czar position is an informal but recognizable position the chief creates to focus attention on certain programs or coordinate the department's efforts in solving problems, such as a pattern of street robberies. The czar designation effectively assures department personnel that the person is serving as the chief's emissary and has his full support.

Under Reynolds' guidance, the department developed a comprehensive training program in COP/POP and established processes to review and track POP projects. Reynolds heads a steering committee that discusses projects and distributes information throughout the department. As head of the department's management services, Reynolds also coordinated several aspects of COP, such as the development of standard operating procedures. Many in the department describe Reynolds as the driving force behind COP/POP and its biggest "cheerleader."

Problem-Oriented Policing in Savannah

Problem-oriented policing or problem solving is a cornerstone of COP in Savannah. Although structured as separate approaches to policing, *COP* and *POP* are terms used interchangeably by many officers, police managers and citizens. Some view the efforts as a single approach, while others see distinct differences.

The department's 1991 annual report states the following:

> Problem-Oriented Policing (POP) is so closely related to COP that, in order for either to be successful, the two must be considered effectively inseparable. POP strategies employ law enforcement as well as community resources to attack the problems [that] not only breed crime, but [also] contribute to other common annoyances [that] generate dissatisfaction in the community. This "proactive" police stance eliminates, or at least mitigates, these conditions before they develop into incidents requiring police response. . . .

> Community-Oriented Policing removes the barriers that have traditionally existed between law enforcement and the public. By acquainting the police with the people they serve and, as a result, acquainting the public with individual officers, citizens no longer view police as nameless blue uniforms.

The department's patrol bureau commander, Maj. William L. D. Lyght Jr., summed up the different views: "COP is the philosophy; POP is a strategy. This strategy is used throughout the department and starts with the initiation of a POP project."

POP projects are documented problem-solving efforts. A formal process for addressing a problem is set forth in a standard operating procedure. A project starts with the submission of a project proposal, through the chain of command, by an officer or other employee who has identified a problem. Personnel follow the chain of command to eliminate duplication of effort, facilitate cooperation between involved units, and ensure that projects are not started for minor matters that can be resolved by other means.

Reynolds serves as the chairman of a POP steering committee composed of representatives from all ranks and from all bureaus and precincts. Monthly meetings are held to discuss active or pending POP projects. Information shared at the meetings is later shared with other department personnel; similarly, published meeting minutes are used to distribute information about POP throughout the department. POP projects are also discussed at weekly staff meetings, attended by all command and management personnel. Officers and detectives are given the opportunity to present their projects to staff to provide information and receive recognition. Gellatly acknowledges the officers for their efforts. Periodic status reports are required from the officers or special unit working on a project. These status reports are incorporated into the monthly and quarterly reports the precinct or division commanders submit to the bureau commanders and chief. Some of this information may also be periodically provided to the city manager.

Project proposals and procedures follow a standardized problem-solving process of identifying and analyzing specific problems, developing tailored responses and measuring the effectiveness of results. Any employee can initiate a POP project. Usually, an officer or detective who has noted a continuing or recurring problem initiates a project. The problem need not be a specific crime. For example, several projects have involved neighborhood conditions that affect residents' quality of life. Other problems have involved procedures that need improvement, such as the development of a medical protocol for handling child abuse victims. Officers who initiate projects are encouraged to make the contacts with other agencies or resources necessary to complete the project. The supervisors' role is to facilitate this process, if necessary.

Community-Oriented Policing in Savannah

Community-oriented policing was implemented in Savannah to address the need for the police department and community to frequently interact and work closely together to solve mutual problems. COP was intended to establish an underlying philosophy and value system that emphasize the importance of the community. The community policing values echoed the ministations' and assigned personnel's stated goals—to place police in closer proximity to the community and maximize police visibility, communications and interaction.

The most significant organizational change the department made when implementing community policing was the establishment of the precinct system. Each precinct has a substation. Any type of fixed beat or service area system would probably have addressed the geographical accountability problem the crime control study highlighted. According to Capt. Stephen Smith, the department's accreditation manager, the precinct system was developed to put the police and community together and to give the captains "ownership" of their part of the city.

Each precinct is commanded by a captain, who has a great deal of latitude to deploy resources according to identified needs. Maj. Lyght, patrol commander, pointed out that there is a great deal of responsibility along with this freedom. He and the chief hold each captain accountable for results. Captains report that the precinct system truly made them police managers. They have to be more actively involved in long-range planning and in developing support systems in the community.

Within each precinct, operational practices varied and were adapted to meet the area's specific needs. A few custom forms, such as daily activity reports, were used, and some precincts produced analysis and statistical reports specific to their areas. Each precinct had an administrative officer who compiled crime information for patrol officers to review. The precinct lieutenants and sergeants also used this information to determine deployment needs and special tactics. Any information on trends was shared at shift briefings and posted on bulletin boards.

The 1st Precinct was commanded by Capt. Ralph M. Bashlor Jr. and was a prototype for the department's COP/POP effort. This precinct is responsible for providing police services to the historical and downtown district, where the majority of the tourist attractions are located. Bashlor was very supportive of COP/POP. This support was evident in an article he wrote for a local newspaper in December 1992, describing COP as "something exciting happening at the Savannah Police Department" and reporting "a level of energy being generated by both the new officers and the seasoned veterans, a level of excitement unequaled in years past."

The 1st Precinct has a full-time bicycle patrol unit. The unit is used extensively to patrol the historic and waterfront areas that are the city's main tourist attractions. Many daytime workers also shop and dine in the area.

Citizens most frequently complained about panhandling and public drinking by homeless men, who were often aggressive and belligerent. Recently, one corporal started a POP project to address this ongoing problem. The entire bicycle unit worked on the project, which began when officers conducted a survey of citizens who worked in the area and of their customers. The survey asked what the most serious problems were and how the police could be most effective. The bicycle unit was deployed on a split shift that covered the times suggested in the survey responses.

The project had an immediate impact. The bicycle officers made frequent contacts with the transients and arrested several of them, quickly reducing the number of transients who loitered in the area. The officers then conducted a second survey to measure the project's impact. Citizens reported that conditions had improved significantly since the project had begun, although they also requested the continued presence of the bicycle unit. The officers also held a public meeting to share the results of the high-visibility project and of the follow-up survey. This ensured that area citizens were aware of the police's responsiveness and of the tactics' effectiveness. The officers took this opportunity to exchange information with citizens and to explain the operation, reflecting the overall community-based policing philosophy.

Another example of COP in the 1st Precinct was its "Park, Walk and Talk" initiative. To carry out COP, officers are required to get out of their patrol cars and conduct 30-minute foot patrols at least twice a shift. These foot patrols are not directed patrols intended to address specific crime problems. Rather, they are intended to establish a relationship between officers and the people who live and work in the area. Officers are encouraged to make as many citizen contacts as possible, especially with business owners and residents, to get to know them on a personal, cooperative level. Officers are also required to attend any community meetings that are held during their shift. The precinct maintains a monthly schedule of all such meetings. The department planned to expand the "Park, Walk and Talk" program to all precincts as a core part of its COP effort.

In contrast to the 1st Precinct, the 2nd Precinct is still in the early stages of implementing COP/POP. The precinct experimented with using a POP team to address community problems. One officer from each shift was assigned to work on a group approach. According to the precinct's lieutenant, the team approach prevented many officers from gaining experience in problem solving. To correct this problem, there were tentative plans to rotate the POP team assignment every three months to expose more officers to problem solving; however, during 1993, the POP team was temporarily suspended due to an unusually heavy workload. The lieutenant said many officers did not really understand the program, were unaware of available resources and were too busy on calls for service to work on POP projects.

The 2nd Precinct is the busiest area of the city in terms of calls for service and crime problems, and officers spend much of their time handling calls for service. A bicycle unit is infrequently deployed on an as-needed basis. The 2nd Precinct also has "Park, Walk and Talk," but, according to the lieutenant, "this fizzles out when calls increase." He reported that officers try to spend a little extra time on their calls and "get to know the people."

Thus, there are distinctions in the level of problem solving that occurs in patrol. However, captains' monthly reports to the patrol major highlight POP projects undertaken and progress made, as well as community organization efforts (such as Neighborhood Watch) and crime prevention initiatives. It is noteworthy that these reports also detail time lost due to injuries on duty, sick leave taken, overtime and compensatory time used, personnel and vehicle inspections made, numbers of specific types of arrests made, and crimes that occurred in the precinct.

Despite the emphasis on proactive approaches, the Savannah Police Department is still highly traditional. For example, there was much excitement in early 1993 about the department's acquisition and distribution of Glock .45-caliber pistols. Most daily activity reports still track standard law enforcement measures such as arrests.

How much problem solving has occurred in the department? Although much of the problem solving may in fact occur informally, without officers' using forms or the formal process, during 1992, the department logged forty-three POP projects. These projects addressed such problems as drug dealing, false alarms, prostitution, and Sunday liquor sales. By 1993, many of the 1992 projects were reported as completed. However, a number of projects—fourteen—were canceled for various reasons.

Organizational Support for Community Policing

Despite what might seem to be an uneven implementation of COP/POP in the Savannah Police Department, the agency has been heavily involved in developing organizational support structures to systematically expand the concept. For example, the department has emphasized integrating the COP/POP concept into other units, ranging from communications to crime prevention, from tactical to traffic.

In its decentralized delivery of police service, each precinct has a crime prevention officer assigned by the special operations division. These officers analyze all crime reports as they are processed through the precinct. They produce spot maps for officers to use, and they also produce a report that recaps crimes for the past three days. This effort ensures that useful and timely information is available to the patrol officers.

The special operations bureau is heavily involved in COP/POP. This bureau includes the traffic unit and the tactical reaction and prevention (TRAP) unit, a special-mission and antidrug unit. Both these units routinely use POP techniques. This is especially true in the traffic unit's work on reducing accidents. The traffic and TRAP units are often involved in helping the precincts with problem areas. The TRAP unit may be used for any POP project that involves a large commitment of personnel or a plainclothes, tactical approach.

Training

The department has developed an extensive training program for COP/POP that is much more than simply an introduction to the philosophy and procedures. In the planning stages of the COP/POP implementation, a comprehensive review of the two initiatives was conducted to determine what skills and knowledge officers would need to perform well in COP and to carry out POP projects. Based on the review, eight independent training modules were developed and personnel training was initiated. All sworn and nonsworn personnel were included in the training. The training was launched in a developmental manner so that modules may be changed as additional training needs are identified.

In addition to the main concepts of COP and problem solving, a variety of other topics are presented. For personal and professional development, there is training in participatory decision making and leadership. To improve officers' ability to better relate with citizens, there is training in improving communications skills and organizing citizens groups. Officers are informed of resources in the community and in other public agencies during training in referral systems. A POP training manual guides instruction.

The total training program lasts about four days for supervisors and three days for officers. Modules usually last four hours. One module for supervisors lasts six hours. Each precinct schedules its own training, but personnel are required to complete at least one module quarterly. Training was well under way in 1993.

Evaluation

In 1993, Savannah police officers were being evaluated on their problem-solving activities, although there was still significant consideration of more traditional performance indicators, such as arrest statistics. An officer productive in traditional performance areas would still receive excellent evaluations. However, supervisors were beginning to place more emphasis on involvement in COP/POP. Supervisors were also beginning to recognize that officers heavily involved in these efforts would not produce easily quantifiable work products.

Promotion and Recognition

Involvement in COP/POP, while not a prerequisite, may improve officers' chances for promotion. A recently promoted sergeant, Richard Zapal of the 2nd Precinct, was sure his work on POP projects and interaction with the community helped earn him his promotion. As a patrol officer, he personally delivered to residents in his assigned area a letter in which he introduced himself and provided his work schedule and phone number.

According to Reynolds, the emphasis on COP/POP involvement in evaluation and promotion is intended to help institutionalize community policing and problem solving within the department. This consideration and the extensive training program are important steps toward this goal.

Officers who develop projects are recognized at staff meetings and in department publications such as the training and information bulletin, published bimonthly.

Forms

The department had developed and used a number of standardized forms to track COP/POP efforts. For example, there is a form that formalizes a request to open a POP file. This form establishes a problem identification number and provides guidance regarding agencies from which to obtain information or assistance.

The department also uses a POP tracking form, which tracks the start and completion dates of the phases of the problem-solving model. Patrol captains' monthly reports to the patrol major include the status of COP strategies, status of POP, information about community interactions, and other related information.

Planning

Consistent with the city manager's background in planning, the police department routinely engages in strategic planning for the future. The department develops formal goals as part of the city's planning process. For 1993, many of these goals were related to COP/POP—some were broadly related, while others were related to specific crime problems. These were developed department-wide, by bureaus, units and patrol precincts. Many of the patrol goals related to reducing serious community problems in specific service areas (for example, reducing commercial robberies and false alarms in Service Area 1). The horse patrol wanted to reduce thefts from vehicles, street robberies and purse snatches in the historic district by 10 percent during on-duty hours. Despite the department's commitment to COP/POP, however, many of the standards relate to achieving the ends of problem solving (for example, "increasing the number of arrests for prostitution" instead of the incidence of prostitution).

Community Outreach and Collaboration

In addition to developing internal mechanisms to support COP/POP, the police department has invested time and effort to build a supportive external environment for its proactive response. One example of this external investment has been the agency's launching of a citizens academy.

Citizens Academy

The department started a citizens academy to give citizens an inside look at the practices of law enforcement in general and of the Savannah Police Department in particular. The academy meets for three hours a week for ten weeks. All of the department's functional areas, such as patrol, communications and investigations, are discussed and explained through lectures or demonstrations. Other topics include high-liability areas and COP. The academy also includes a ride-along of at least four hours.

The first class was held in February 1993 and included a cross-section of the community, men and women of all ages, business owners and those interested in a law enforcement career. Although any citizen can attend, the police department has targeted community leaders. Over time, the academy is expected to help citizens develop a greater understanding of police resources and limitations and improve the department's relationship with the community.

Volunteer Program

The Savannah Police Department has an extensive volunteer program that was established in 1992 as a means to improve service delivery without increasing costs, using citizen volunteers to supplement police resources. In 1993, the department had forty-two volunteers, ranging from young adults to the elderly. Volunteers engage in a variety of assignments, such as taking vehicles to and from service stations, answering questions at the information desk or helping detectives with call-back work. As they have gained experience and acceptance, their duties have been expanded.

Volunteers receive training and also learn about the basic philosophy of COP and POP. Most of the volunteers have developed a good understanding of COP and have learned much about the department. "They know that the police want to improve the overall quality of life in Savannah—not alone, but as partners with the community," said the volunteer coordinator.

The department's outreach efforts create an opportunity for department members to interact and communicate with a wide spectrum of the community. In addition, there are many other means by which this involvement takes place. Department members are involved in a variety of committees and task forces throughout the city. The chief encourages this involvement. These groups deal with issues ranging from dilapidated housing to artwork for the city.

One important group in which police have been active is the Savannah Crime Control Collaborative (known as the Collaborative). The Collaborative's mandate is to effect changes in the policies, procedures and funding patterns of community institutions in Savannah and Chatham County to free the area of crime, juvenile delinquency and drug abuse and addiction.

The Collaborative addresses crime from a multidisciplinary perspective. Its thirty-eight members come from local law enforcement, criminal justice, social services, education, health services, and religious organizations, as well as other civic and professional organizations. The Collaborative has a special law enforcement committee that addresses issues specific to the police. The Collaborative monitors programs and funding and makes recommendations to coordinate efforts and increase interagency problem solving. Savannah Police Department members, including the chief, are actively involved in the Collaborative. Though many citizens want more police officers or at least more police visibility, the Collaborative tries to determine whether the police department is using its officers in the best possible way.

The Future of COP/POP

The department has several goals for expanding COP/POP in the future. One goal is to have all precincts involved in the programs at a relatively equal level. While it is acknowledged that there will always be differences between precincts, a more consistent approach is desired.

Perhaps this growth of COP/POP throughout the department will make the distinctions between the two programs clearer to officers and other staff. Many could not articulate a difference between COP and POP.

It is clear that the Savannah Police Department is working hard to have a successful community-based policing program. The department has demonstrated concern for the community through the community-based programs already in place, and it has experienced some success. With progressive leadership, the department was already involved in some community-oriented programs. With the completion of the department's restructuring and with the initiation of POP training and other implementation activities, the department has completed its first experimental stage and "learned a lot." Although the department had conducted no formal evaluation of the COP/POP efforts at the time of this writing, it planned to reevaluate its implementation and make any needed modification.

Regardless of the political nature of the original motivation to implement COP/POP, the Savannah Police Department has seized the opportunity. Additional funding and staff have enabled the department to make progress in becoming a community-oriented agency and to move forward in its problem-solving efforts.

15

Mixed Messages

Dennis E. Nowicki

For most officers, the advent of community policing and its problem-solving activities is the most promising sign of change that our profession has seen in some time. Community policing neither accepts the thought that there are some crimes that police cannot impact, nor does it allow the officer to use his patrol car as a shield from the public. Instead, community policing demands that the officer establish trust, communication, and ultimately, a problem-solving partnership with the citizens he or she serves. The officer's goal is to make a lasting difference in the community.

We, as officers, no longer want to diffuse a problem, we want to solve it. We no longer want to claim success because we've made a lot of arrests, rather we want to make a difference in the level of harm suffered in our communities, preferably before the harm occurs. As one of my officers just recently said to me: "The only limit to community policing is the imagination."

On the one hand, we have given officers many of the tools they need to function in a community policing, problem-solving environment. These tools include enhanced problem-solving skills, new technology and access to unprecedented amounts of information about crime and demographics. However, I fear that we, as police administrators, have failed to give our officers appropriate guidelines on how to do the right thing in a policing environment that confronts the officer with a mass of contradictions.

Many of these contradictions are the result of the nature of community policing, public policy makers, and community activists. Others spring from laws, public expectation, and the unique nature of the police culture. These contradictions or, as I call them, mixed messages, are perplexing to me as a police administrator. If I am puzzled, with thirty plus years experience, I can only guess at the

Source: Speech presented at Police Executive Research Forum Annual Meeting, Gary Hayes Luncheon, May 2, 1997.

level of confusion these mixed messages create for the young officer who is armed with a shiny new badge, a couple months of training, and a rules and regulations manual that can be easily lifted only by the most physically fit officers.

Officers are bombarded with these mixed messages every day and are not always able to ask "what should I do?" For that reason, I believe that every police organization must have clearly articulated and operationalized values to guide the officer, and that we as administrators must reinforce those values at every opportunity, including through the example that we personally set for our officers. When all else fails, organizational values can serve as a road map leading to the "right thing." The officer who functions effectively in today's police environment will consider the department's values to be a crucial lifeline.

One mixed message that is sent to police officers these days has to do with the issue of empowerment. Let's try to imagine that we are community problem-solving police officers in today's police environment. If we are like those at many police departments, including my own, we are young and don't have a lot of life experience to draw on, but we are eager to serve and idealistic enough to believe that we can make a difference. We are told that in a community policing environment we are *empowered*, a word that neither we as police administrators nor other city leaders and public policy makers have been able to successfully define in a law enforcement context. We tell the officer that he should be a creative problem solver and use whatever resources he feels are appropriate to solve a problem. The officer, trying to define the limits of empowerment, looks around the organization. He has been told that empowerment starts from the top of the organization but he gets a mixed message when he sees the chief of that organization being micromanaged by the city's elected officials and city management.

An illustration of this mixed message is occurring in Charlotte, where we are in the process of trying to meet citizen demands for expanded civilian review of police, fueled by two recent shooting incidents in which white police officers shot and killed unarmed black citizens. One of the issues being debated by elected officials is whether final disciplinary authority over police officers, especially in cases involving deadly force, should remain with the police chief or be given to the city manager or even the city council. Imagine the mixed message that officers receive on empowerment if they feel that the person hired to lead and set the tone for the organization is not empowered to make the disciplinary decisions which reinforce the organization's values. It is one thing to provide an appeal process from a chief's decision, but it is quite another thing to prevent the chief from reinforcing the organization's values. That is what would happen if we refused to let the chief decide how those values will apply to questionable decisions in police work.

To continue my previous scenario, the typical community problem-solving police officer also looks around the organization and gets the message from his peers and middle managers that "yes, you are empowered, go forth and make the world a better place. If you succeed, you may receive faint praise; if you fail or make a mistake, you will most assuredly be hung out to dry." The law enforcement culture is very comfortable with the absolutes of the law. What we have not made our peace with is a policing environment that asks the officer, in the name of the department, to take risks and to try problem-solving techniques that have no guarantee of success. Police departments are inherently afraid of failure and do not know how to handle it. Granted, much of this fear comes from the public criticism we receive when we make a mistake. Nevertheless, the result is that we tend to create an environment where officers feel that failure will not be tolerated. They fear that they will be punished, if not overtly through the discipline system, then more subtly through denial of a transfer or training opportunity, an undesirable shift assignment or through some type of social sanction. They hear horror stories from their peers, many of which are nothing more than unsubstantiated rumors.

The officer listens to the mixed messages from the many subcultures that establish themselves in large diverse organizations and he reaches the conclusion that empowerment is a trap he had best avoid. How does he do that? He suppresses his creativity and uses only narrowly defined enforcement techniques, withdraws into the security of the police car and the 911 call, and builds no effective relationships with the citizens he serves. That is his loss, the organization's loss and the community's loss and it adversely impacts the great potential of community problem-oriented policing.

The concept of empowerment clearly runs counter to the paramilitary structure of police agencies and the chain of command's sense that their accountability is directly tied to their access to information; information is seen as power. Yet, in an organization where officers truly feel empowered, they are more frequently involved in activities that members of their chain of command know nothing about. They are not necessarily doing anything wrong; they are just doing what they feel they need to do to get the job done.

The chain of command from the chief to the first line supervisor must be willing to relinquish some of the power that comes with information if empowerment is truly going to be effective. As police administrators, we must be able to deal with the elected official who gleefully plays the "gotcha" game with information that he has that the chief does not. Even if the information is about a positive initiative that an officer has undertaken in a neighborhood, the elected official may make much of the fact that the chief was not aware of it.

From a practical standpoint it is virtually impossible for a chief to know everything that is going on in a department, although some of us may try. We must learn to be comfortable with not having every piece of information at our fingertips and we must understand that, in a community policing environment, the good intentions of empowered officers may sometimes lead to mistakes or situations where you wince and wish the officer had chosen some other course of action. We must learn to give credit for effort and initiative even when the results fall short.

When we, as administrators, are caught unknowing, we must not take out our discomfort and embarrassment on everyone down the chain, especially the officer whose actions are the subject of the discussion. If officers and their supervisors feel that the chief cannot accept not knowing everything that is going on in the organization, the end result will be reams of documentation, and the loss of the energy that is generated by officers who feel empowered to take a problem and run with it. A police chief who truly believes in empowerment will be pleased, not upset or shocked, when another city department head telephones to say that "some lowly police officers have been telling community groups how to organize to get better services from the rest of municipal government." A police chief who truly believes in empowerment will graciously accept an invitation to a barbecue hosted by some of his officers where the food is prepared on a $2,000 smoker that was a "gift" from a local businessman and is now the property of one of his patrol districts. He will complement the food and ask questions later.

Community policing clearly raises some potential conflicts between the traditional police role of enforcer and the problem-solving philosophy under which the answer to every crime problem is not arrest. We tell officers and citizens that one of the basic principles of community policing is that the officer approaches each problem he confronts with the attitude that the problem has a long-term solution which may require the officer to utilize resources outside the police department. One of the rationales behind this is that prosecutors, courts, and corrections institutions are so lacking in resources that they can deal effectively with only a fraction of the offenders that officers funnel into the system.

Under community policing, it may ultimately be more effective to deal with the neighborhood winos who loiter on the corner by working to take the liquor license of the convenience store where they purchase their wine than it is to haul the offenders to jail. It is a longer term solution to the problem than the arrests which must be made repeatedly, and it frees the criminal justice system to deal more effectively with the serious offender.

Into this mix, we sometimes see injected the idea that, in the name of community policing, a police leader demands that officers take a zero tolerance attitude toward crime in a certain neighborhood. While there are times when a strict enforcement strategy may be an effective and necessary short term tactic to restore order to the streets, zero tolerance by itself will not have a long-term effect on crime and disorder. Zero tolerance is a move away from empowerment. It is counter to creative problem solving, use of discretion, and community involvement that are crucial to the success of community policing.

Once officers begin exclusively using their arrest powers to make the very arrests that problem solving should minimize, they are once again in a situation where they deal with the same offender day after day. The arrests they generate, especially those for quality of life offenses, receive no meaningful sanctions from an overburdened court system. In many cases, the officers are perceived as hassling certain segments of the community. The officers often end up using improper levels of force, all in the name of zero tolerance and, often, with the long-term solutions to the problem left unaddressed.

This mixed message often leaves the officer not knowing what to think. It occurs to some of them, in the quiet recesses of their minds, that zero tolerance really means zero thinking but they dare not offend the chain of command or the mayor by asking impertinent questions. The officer is told that the department embraces the community policing philosophy which espouses communication and partnerships with the community, long-term problem solving, and the use of discretion. Then suddenly he is told to take a zero tolerance attitude which removes his discretion and places him in the role of the traditional enforcer. The end result is an officer who is confused as to what his role in the community should be. Such an officer is more likely to do the wrong thing or nothing at all.

As police leaders we must provide a value-driven environment wherein the officer has clear and consistent organizational values to guide him in achieving the department's goals. As administrators, we must make it clear to our officers under what circumstances we want them to apply strict enforcement tactics as a problem-solving tool and where that strategy fits with the broader community policing philosophy.

The transition to community policing has been difficult for both officers and citizens. Traditionally, police have placed distance between themselves and the community, as if their authority were somehow linked to their aloofness. We have also enjoyed the mystique of police work. Many officers like the idea that the public image of the police officer comes from television. They secretly like being perceived as action heroes who crack the case, win a just and fair fight, and get the girl in an hour. Now they are told they should no longer hold themselves aloof from the community. Now they should get to know the people they serve, communicate openly and share much of the information that they guarded so zealously in the past; the officers must take ownership of the problems in the neighborhood where they are assigned.

For example, in many cities, including Charlotte, officers are being offered financial incentives to live in the neighborhoods where they are assigned, a concept diametrically opposed to the old safety tenet that an officer's home should never be in the same area as his beat. As officers forge these new relationships with the community, they are confused about what the limits should be. Officers are told to avoid conflicts of interest or take any action that may look as if they are using their position to gain something.

In the past, officers have been cautioned about taking free or discount meals or soliciting funds or goods from a citizen or business. Now the officer is told that it is acceptable to break bread with people within the community and to request help from citizens for community projects. The officers get vendors to donate food for community meetings and festivals, playground equipment for inner city neighborhoods, tickets to sporting events as rewards for at-risk youth who perform well in school, and paint and furniture for police district offices. As an example, in Charlotte, our NBA basketball team provides the salaries, benefits, and vehicles for two community policing officers as well as money for the patrol districts to use for community policing projects.

Where do you draw the line between an officer being resourceful and being beholden to some special interest in the community? When does the citizen feel intimidated by the police officer's inherent authority and donate goods or a service out of fear? At what point does the vendor have the expectation that his contribution will somehow get him a higher level of police service, and when does the officer believe that it should? Again, the officer should be guided by the values of his or her organization. If clearly articulated and consistently practiced at all levels, these values should serve as a moral compass when the officer is exercising his discretion. The answers will not always be crystal clear, because at times there is a need to balance competing values and to apply those values to a wide variety of circumstances. In other words, the officer's need is fidelity to a reasoning process that sincerely and openly strives to honor the organization's fundamental operating values.

The chief must clearly lead by example, avoiding mixed messages, to be sure that the appropriate course of action is clear. For example, officers must not perceive that the chief is using his position for preferential treatment or to intimidate community movers or shakers into partnerships, particularly of a financial nature, with the police department. Under community policing, there will be more offers of assistance and financial aid to worthwhile projects.

The organization's values must guide the officers at all levels of the organization in dealing with this new wrinkle in police work. Do not underestimate the confusion that this aspect of community policing creates for the officer. A veteran officer in my department told me that he is uncomfortable accepting a cup of coffee in the home of a citizen because officers were traditionally taught not to accept anything that could be perceived as a gratuity. The organizational values of community policing, if consistently practiced, will teach that officer that a simple cup of coffee, freely offered, may be the cornerstone of that officer-citizen relationship.

It is not just police chiefs who send the officer a mixed message about what tactics they want the officer to use. Most citizens want violent crime eradicated from their neighborhoods but they send mixed messages about how that should be done. If it is somebody else's children who are creating disorder, "throw the book at them." But if it is their own children, "wait a while—boys will be boys—no need to be so heavy handed." Community policing, as Ray Davis once said, "cannot be a blind pilgrimage to the temples of community control." In addition, we must remember what Dr. Wilson says, that the "constitution's protection of individual rights still must trump the anti-democratic proclivities of the vocal majority."

Regardless of what enforcement action a police department takes, there will almost always be someone whose goals are counter to those of the police. Recently, one of our third shift officers realized that there were an unusually high number of DWI arrests in his response area. He requested permission from his captain to run periodic DWI checkpoints to determine the scope of the problem and attempt to reduce the number of DWIs in the area. The officer would ask anyone arrested for DWI where he or she had been drinking prior to getting in his or her vehicle. On the Monday after the first of these checkpoints was conducted, the mayor got a call from the owner of a bar in the area, claiming that the police officer was attempting to ruin his business by establishing the checkpoint at what he described as across the street from his bar. When the mayor inquired about the checkpoint, it was discovered that the checkpoint was actually a half mile from the bar and that two of the nine people arrested for DWI within a two-hour period said they had been drinking at this particular bar. The officer had contacted the bar manager about insuring that all of his employees try to keep patrons from drinking and driving. This officer tried to apply the problem-solving techniques that he had been told to adopt and, for his trouble, became the subject of an inquiry from the mayor.

Indeed, elected officials are among the worst offenders in sending police officers mixed messages. They claim to embrace the concept of community policing and its emphasis on long-term problem solving and accountability; however, their knees jerk as soon as one citizen says that his problem is not being solved fast enough. One of our citizens recently appeared before the city council to complain about the noise generated by a business that tests race car engines. The community police officer for the area where this citizen lives had been working with both the citizen and the business in an attempt to find a solution that would satisfy everyone involved. The business had modified its testing times and had agreed to spend money for baffling material and a computerized sound cancellation system that would reduce the noise level. The officer had spent hours of time addressing the problem, had worked overtime, and had responded to countless questions from the citizen, all of which he had documented.

When the citizen appeared before council, he said that the police officer had not done his job and indeed lied about the efforts that the officer had made. As the officer stood in front of the city council attempting to respond, he was caught in a barrage of rhetoric from council members. Why didn't he write a ticket or arrest someone every time there was any noise? Why did the citizen even have to take the responsibility of calling the police when the noise started? If the officer knew there was a problem, why was he not out there? The officer was stunned to hear the council essentially repudiate the problem-solving policing philosophy that they claim to wholeheartedly support. In addition, the city council also negated the concept of problem-solving partnerships by absolving the citizen of any responsibility for calling the police. The officer was given the message that his time and effort were for nothing and that he should have used those traditional enforcement methods that would have ended up in the criminal justice system where no one's needs were met. This officer is, however, committed to community policing. He still believes that this problem can be solved.

As administrators, we send our officers mixed messages every day. As I have tried to make the community problem-oriented policing philosophy the method of service delivery for our entire department, I have talked about my desire to promote officers who are clear proponents of community policing. Clearly one of the best ways to build an effective police department is to place personnel who exemplify the department's values in supervisory positions. However, court decisions, the fear of litigation, and officer perceptions of bias have forced many departments, including mine, to develop promotional processes that leave little room to consider an officer's past performance, the relationships he has built in the community, or any of the intangible qualities that we know an effective supervisor must possess. An officer who can test well and who can parrot the information that he knows the department wants to hear can get promoted. Every time we set in motion a promotional process that results in a rank ordered list, derived only from written tests and assessment centers, we end up forced to promote some officers who less than enthusiastically support or practice the values of the organization. It is hard to tell officers that the organization's values are all important and then be forced to promote those people who negate them. It matters very little to these officers that we wish we did not have to send this mixed message—they see it as our message and within our control.

Another thing that most of us do is tell officers that patrol is the backbone of the police department. I genuinely believe that, but I know that actions speak louder then words so the officer must really be confused about whether being assigned to the department's backbone is a good thing or not. As soon as a vacancy occurs in a specialized unit it gets filled, at the expense of a patrol district. Patrol is often a punitive assignment for those officers who have incurred our displeasure. You rarely see an officer who gets into trouble and is taken off patrol and put into investigations or administration, but you often see the reverse.

Patrol officers rarely get to attend specialized schools, they work terrible hours, and they do not get the recognition that is automatic for the investigator who cracks a big case. If we really believe that patrol is the backbone of a police department, we must find a better and more tangible way of delivering that message to our officers. The same point is true of our claiming we want teamwork but then leaving in place performance recognition systems that honor highly individual actions and encourage hoarding of information and stealing credit. A starting place, even if we lack truly developed solutions, is being honest with our officers in recognizing such inconsistencies and welcoming their suggestions for remedies.

I think that the most serious mixed messages that our officers get are on the use of force. We expend a considerable amount of time, energy, and money training our officers to protect themselves. However, we live in a society where an officer who uses that training and follows it to the letter can be subjected to unbelievable second guessing, especially if he takes a life. As I mentioned earlier, our department has been involved in two shooting incidents in the last six months, both of which resulted in white officers taking the lives of unarmed black citizens. In one incident, the shooting was ruled justified by the district attorney. The department and the officer faced no criminal charges or departmental discipline. The second incident is still under investigation. A small but vocal segment of the community argues that these shootings have strong racial implications and they have demanded that the city council increase the level of civilian review of police in Charlotte.

Obviously, conflicting opinions are inevitable in an open society but they send a potentially fatal mixed message to the officer. We train officers to protect themselves and other innocent citizens within strictly defined departmental policies and procedures. If, however, the officer's actions result in public threats to seek justice in the streets, the officer may, in a split second, attempt to assess the political ramifications of any potential action he or she may take. That assessment may result in death or serious injury to the officer or the innocent citizen whom the officer has sworn to protect.

The potential use of force creates a major dilemma for our officers. Joe McNamara was quoted in Bill Geller's recent book on police use of force as saying, "It ain't easy out there. You don't want an officer getting killed because he's afraid of the chief and hesitated too long, and you don't want jumpy officers shooting someone when they go to scratch themselves." Clearly, it is difficult to train officers to make the appropriate judgments on when to use force. If you add into the mix a politically charged atmosphere where every act is judged, not by the situation, but by the characteristics of the other party involved, you leave officers potentially afraid to act. In some cases these officers are less aggressive in the performance of their duties because they do not want to expose themselves to situations where the potential use of deadly force is an issue. The officers learn by example that, while much of the community silently supports them, a small but vocal minority can subject even those officers whose actions are justified to trial by the media and political rhetoric.

At the same time we can send a mixed message to the officer and our community resulting in the use of needless force. We properly emphasize in our training and supervision that officers should exhibit restraint where possible and seek nonviolent conflict-reducing resolutions to police-citizen encounters. Yet we undermine our message if the only officers who receive the big awards and shiny medals are those who have engaged in daring shootouts or some other traditional police action which attracts the attention of tabloid television cop shows.

In a potentially violent encounter, there is no way that the chief can be there in that split second to lean over the officer's shoulder and tell him what to do in that particular situation. For the officer, there is probably no other moment when he or she feels so alone. However, I would like to believe that those officers who have a clear understanding of the mission, goals, and values of their departments have a better framework in which to make those split-second decisions in which their lives and the integrity of the department are on the line. The hypocrisy that I am concerned about is that, after the officer has faithfully tried to apply our values to the circumstances he has encountered on the streets, too many of us are willing to throw the officer to the wolves if it suits our political expediency.

All of us know how tough it is to be a police administrator in today's environment. What I hope I have done is remind you how tough it is to be that young officer trying to do the right thing in performing a job where public trust and confidence are crucial to his or her success. I truly believe that one way of helping that officer to succeed is by providing an organizational environment where values guide officers' decisions in the range of situations they confront, from deadly force to accepting a cup of coffee. How do we do that?

First of all, I believe that we, as professional police administrators, should turn our attention to how to help officers understand and interpret the mixed messages they receive. Groups such as PERF (Police Executive Research Forum), are the think tanks of urban policing in this country. However, too many times we let our research and our conference agendas be governed by the hot issue of the moment, whether it is pursuit driving, video cameras for patrol cars, or the merits of adopting 311 in our communities.

Perhaps we should commit some of our collective time, energy, and talent to addressing these mixed messages, especially if we are in agreement that community problem-solving policing is the way that we want to do business in the twenty-first century. These are tough issues because they are not based on absolutes. If we can create an environment where empowered police officers can make appropriate value-driven decisions, we will make life a little easier for the next generation of police administrators. As an organization, PERF should commit to identifying those community policing initiatives that have made a genuine difference in their communities and educate police departments across the country on how those successful initiatives were planned, implemented, and evaluated. We should commit to making our annual problem-oriented policing conference a showcase for the best that community problem-oriented policing has to offer. Our conference should emphasize quality over quantity. If we are to make PERF a vital force in shaping police work in the twenty-first century, we must critically examine the mission and values of this organization and insure that our resources are focused on accomplishing that mission.

Second, we must clearly articulate the values of our organizations and then find effective ways to relate our policies, training, operations, and every decision to those values. Our values can sound good and look impressive in print but they are meaningless unless the officer understands their practical application. Again, this is a tough task but one that we cannot shy away from if we are to be comfortable in a policing environment that is based on empowerment. For the officer, the department's values must be more than what he says, they must be what he does. The same applies to all of us concerning the statement of principles on racial issues which PERF's board adopted at this conference. As Bob Lunney says, "the real challenge is what we do because of the statement."

Finally, we must avoid what some have noted existing in many police departments, two police cultures: one a street cop culture and the other a management cop culture. We must involve the officers in all we do, lead by example, and be aware that our officers constantly have us under the microscope. At the first hint that we do not practice what we preach, our credibility will be at risk and our ability to set the tone for the organization will be diminished. We are often so caught up in responding directly to the community, the city administrators, and elected officials, that we do not have the time or patience to think about the message that our actions and words send to our officers. Far too often, the officer becomes the forgotten man or woman in our decision making. We can not afford to let that happen. We must let our conduct and every decision be a primary illustration of our department's values in action. As Albert Schweitzer said, "In trying to influence others, example is not the main thing; it's the only thing."

16

Personnel Performance Evaluations in the Community Policing Context

Timothy N. Oettmeier and *Mary Ann Wycoff*

The Context of Community Policing

Community policing is an approach to the delivery of police service that recognizes the varying characteristics and needs of different parts of a community. Rather than being seen as an undifferentiated entity, a city—viewed from a community policing perspective—is seen as consisting of many neighborhoods, each of which may represent a particular combination of qualities and service needs. In adopting community policing, police agencies commit to tailor service to meet the specific needs of individual areas of the community.[1]

As defined by the Community Policing Consortium (1994), community policing consists of two complementary core components: community partnership and problem solving. Community partnership is the means of knowing the community; problem solving is the tool for addressing the conditions that threaten the welfare of the community. To attack crime and disorder problems at their roots, police officers and managers need to be fully familiar with the nature of the problem in a given area; the cause of a crime pattern in one area may be quite different from the cause of a similar crime pattern in another area. Effective problem solving is dependent on knowing the territory and the people who reside and work there. They are the ones who can best inform officers about the nature of the neighborhood and its problems and resources, and their involvement is essential to creating effective and enduring responses to problems.

Community policing is full-service policing. It is a way of more effectively delivering all of the services citizens have always needed from police. It can be seen conceptually as consisting of three functions (Oettmeier 1992) (see figure 1).

Source: Community Policing Consortium, Washington, D.C., July 1997.

Figure 1 Functional Continuum of Policing

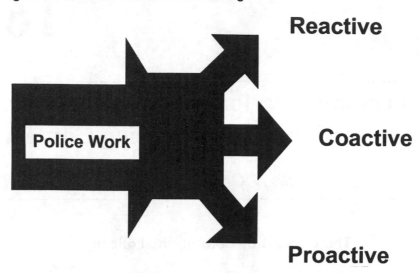

The elements of this model represent an evolution in thinking about the police role. The *reactive* function is the traditional response mode to a cry for help or other requests for service from citizens. Citizens initiate and police respond. In the 1990s, the most common response is the rapid dispatch of an officer to a 911 call.

The *proactive* function includes activities initiated by police, examples of which are directed patrol, crime prevention programs, repeat offender programs, police-initiated investigations, etc. The expansion of proactive efforts was characteristic of policing in the 1970s and 1980s.

From the early 1980s to the present, the profession has broadly embraced the idea that effective policing is the result of *coactive* citizen and police partnerships. Either party can identify conditions that need to be addressed to increase the safety of a neighborhood, but citizens and police will work together to define and design the response to threatening conditions. The coactive element does not replace the reactive or proactive elements; these first two remain critical to the police role. The third element expands the role of the police by expanding the capacity to address causes of crime and disorder. This expanded definition of the police role means that officers will continue to handle calls for service, write traffic citations, conduct investigations and respond to citizens' needs for service. Officers will continue their proactive efforts to catch burglars, robbers, murderers, dopers and rapists. When criminals prey on their victims, the public expects the police to take quick and decisive action. These functions remain the same, but community policing further requires officers to form active partnerships with citizens residing and working in neighborhoods for the purpose of developing coactive strategies to address short- and long-term neighborhood crime and disorder problems.

In an effort to incorporate the coactive function, many police chiefs and sheriffs have used specialization to implement new efforts that are labeled as community policing programs. Despite the fact that, in a national random sample of police and sheriffs' agencies, 73 percent of executives said that community policing ought to be the responsibility of all personnel (Wycoff 1994), agencies commonly relieve officers of patrol duty and place them in community policing squads or designate them as community police officers. In some cases, this specialization results from executives not perceiving community policing as full-service policing. In some others, specialization is a beginning effort to implement community policing, although the agency may have a long-term goal of department-wide implementation. And, in some cases, it may be a "quick fix" response to federal funding initiatives. In any case, the intent of this specialization is to equip people to address neighborhood problems that may require more time to handle than is available to a "regular" patrol officer.

While the newly appointed community police officers may enjoy perks (e.g., special equipment, flexible work schedules, unusual autonomy), the "real" police officers are left struggling in the trenches with fewer personnel and resources. Confusion, frustration and animosity among personnel are common results of this specialization, and frequently there is a lack of coordination of service delivery at the local level.

Such specialization may be the quickest, easiest and most familiar way of organizing a department in response to a particular goal. However, when the focus is on a local area or neighborhood rather than on distinct role functions, specialization is not so obvious an answer. Communities or neighborhoods have complex service needs that citizens do not categorize as reactive, proactive or coactive. They see themselves as needing an officer—preferably, their officer. The local-area focus of community policing is important because different communities have different mixes of service needs. Every area will have needs for reactive, proactive and coactive police responses, but the nature and magnitude of each will vary across neighborhoods, by time of day in any given neighborhood and across time. The needs on the north side of town differ from those on the south side. In either area the needs are different at 9 P.M. than at 9 A.M. As a general rule, evening shift officers spend the bulk of their time responding to calls for service. Night shift officers have more time to implement directed patrol strategies, while day shift officers are in the best position to implement community engagement strategies. Finally, needs in any area may be different in 2006 than in 1996.

Theoretically, the most efficient and effective way to meet these varying demands is for the officers who serve these areas to be capable of interpreting the needs and delivering the appropriate type of response. One style of policing cannot effectively address diverse service demands. In any neighborhood, handling a call effectively is as important as handling a problem-solving project. Catching a thief is as important as working with community members to close down an abandoned house that is a front for illegal activity. Officers need to deploy a variety of responses.

While it may seem relatively easy to create special units along functional lines, it would be almost impossible for a manager to oversee several geographic areas and effectively distribute special units in appropriate response to ever-changing needs in each area. When community policing is viewed as full-service policing, the management challenge is to prepare officers to accurately identify and respond appropriately to the needs of the areas they serve. The management challenge is to determine how officers can use existing resources more effectively and efficiently in working with citizens to develop innovative or unique approaches—both to attack crime and disorder and to prevent it from occurring in the first place.

If management can enhance and improve the knowledge, skills and attitudes (KSAs) of officers, these officers will be able to provide a wider array of quality services within neighborhoods. A most effective, but largely untapped, resource for facilitating the professional development of personnel is performance evaluations. Research has demonstrated that well-designed performance evaluations can be used as a catalyst to shape behavioral responses and facilitate organizational change (Wycoff and Oettmeier 1993). Performance evaluations can be used to alter the service expectations, policing styles and responsibilities of patrol officers.

The trick is to develop evaluations that accurately reflect the work officers are expected to do. The need to develop such evaluations is neither new nor unique to community policing. Probably the majority of police agencies have needed for years to revise performance evaluations in order to reflect the reality of police work, regardless of the philosophic context in which that work is done.

The advent of community policing has simply re-raised consciousness about this need and has focused fresh attention on both the potential substance and methodology of the evaluation process.

Evaluation Perspectives For Policing

Most performance evaluations currently used by police agencies do not reflect the work officers do. Evaluations typically consist of compliance audits, statistical comparisons or descriptive summaries of events. Mastrofski (1996) notes that:

> A contemporary police department's system of performance measurement remains substantively rooted in the perspective of the reform wave that was gathering force in the 1930s under the leadership of August Vollmer, J. Edgar Hoover, the Wickersham Commission, and others. More effort is put into recording UCR data (e.g., arrests, clearances, reported crime, etc.) than any other indicators (pp. 209–210).

According to Whitaker et al. (1982), these measures have a number of well-documented technical weaknesses and an even more compelling limitation at the policy level. Because they do not reflect the work officers do and are seldom used for the purpose of making individual career decisions, it is not surprising that police personnel tend to perceive evaluations as academic exercises that have neither relevance for them nor utility for their departments.

There is nothing simple about constructing a valid and reliable evaluation process, and few agencies are staffed for the task. Many agencies lack basic planning and research units and those that do have such units seldom have the resources to hire staff with evaluation expertise. And these units are not typically expected to do this kind of work; they more commonly function as an administrative arm of the executive. They may be used to develop new programs and initiatives, conduct phone or mail surveys, or generate statistical reports. They seldom serve as a repository of significant police-related research findings that could influence managerial decision making, and they seldom conduct empirical evaluations that could guide policy decisions. While the thinking about performance evaluations will be advanced by some individual agencies, the largest gains are likely to result from the combined efforts—through national agents such as the Community Policing Consortium—of departments to trade ideas and information. That exchange can be enhanced by a common framework for thinking and talking about evaluation and related issues. One such framework is presented in figure 2 in which individual performance measurement is viewed in the larger context of organizational assessment.

Figure 2 contains three categories of variables, represented by the three dimensions of the cube, that probably can include the universe of evaluation measures of police effectiveness. The top face of the cube represents the "Actor"

Figure 2

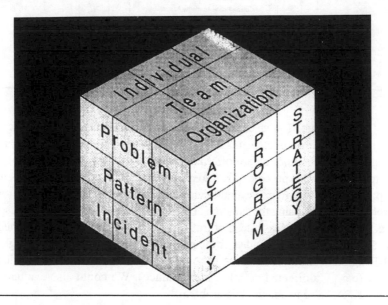

variable; the actor can be the individual member of the organization, a team (or division unit) or the entire organization. The horizontal face represents "Service Demands," which can analyzed and treated as incidents, patterns or problems. The vertical face reflects "Responses," which may be in the form of activities, programs or strategies. The entire cube should be nested in the context of organizational goals, so that measurement related to any of the twenty-seven separate cubes will also reflect those goals. The result will be that performance measurement at all levels will consistently reinforce organizational philosophy and goals. Evaluations can be designed to assess the effect of activity within any of the smaller cubes (see figure 3).

Figure 3

Evaluation Perspectives for Policing

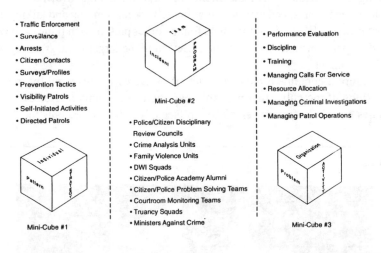

• Traffic Enforcement
• Surveillance
• Arrests
• Citizen Contacts
• Surveys/Profiles
• Prevention Tactics
• Visibility Patrols
• Self-Initiated Activities
• Directed Patrols

Mini-Cube #2

• Police/Citizen Disciplinary
  Review Councils
• Crime Analysis Units
• Family Violence Units
• DWI Squads
• Citizen/Police Academy Alumni
• Citizen/Police Problem Solving Teams
• Courtroom Monitoring Teams
• Truancy Squads
• Ministers Against Crime

• Performance Evaluation
• Discipline
• Training
• Managing Calls For Service
• Resource Allocation
• Managing Criminal Investigations
• Managing Patrol Operations

Mini-Cube #1

Mini-Cube #3

Take mini-cube 1 as an example. In this instance, we are interested in evaluating how an individual implements a strategy to address a crime or disorder pattern. Once an officer becomes aware of a pattern of traffic accidents occurring at a specific location, we expect the officer to properly analyze the problem, implement an appropriate strategy (e.g. prevention via increased ticket writing, erecting traffic control signs or discussing the situation at local civic club meetings) and assess the results of those efforts. Or, instead of traffic problems, officers may be alerted by crime analysts to a series of other crime patterns occurring within their neighborhood. Evaluation efforts could focus on how well officers implement an interdiction strategy (e.g., via directed patrol or surveillance). We could also evaluate the officer's KSAs used to address this problem.

For mini-cube 2, evaluation efforts could focus on how well a team implements a program aimed at addressing a series of incidents. Groups such as Ministers Against Crime are working across the country with the police to prevent additional churches from being burned. Truancy squads are working with school officials to help keep children in school and off the streets where they are apt to cause trouble. DWI teams work with local media outlets to apprise the public of where they will be working during holidays and weekends to keep people from leaving drinking establishments in an inebriated state. In each of these instances, criteria can be developed to monitor and assess the effects of team efforts.

Mini-cube 3 represents yet another evaluation perspective in which the organization revamps internal activities (i.e., procedures) to address certain problems. For example, departments may find their disciplinary system is inadequate as it neither prevents illicit behavior from recurring nor offers adequate discretion to handle a wide range of violations. The chief may authorize a task force to examine the issue and develop a new disciplinary system with procedures that provide administrators with ample flexibility to respond to different types of behavioral problems. Or the chief may be dissatisfied with the processing of calls for service in the emergency communication center. The agency might then take steps to develop differential response procedures that alleviate the bottleneck and increase the efficiency of police response. In these situations, process evaluations are used to assess organizational efficiency and effectiveness at addressing specific administrative or operational problems.

For the purpose of this article, we will focus on redesigning performance measurement systems to more effectively evaluate officer performance. The evaluation should center on measuring differences in individual knowledge, skills and attitudes; the nature of the effort; and/or the attainment of results.

A Model of Performance Analysis

An evaluation process requires an initial definition of concepts and a model that links them. For the purpose of this article, the term "performance analysis" refers to the collection of activities or analyses that identify and evaluate purposive work. Purposive work assumes an objective to be accomplished. In the case of policing, that purpose might be to have an officer available to respond to calls in a specified area for a specified period of time, to close a drug house, to reduce the probability that citizens will become victims, to increase community structure in a given neighborhood, etc. For any objective, performance can be analyzed in terms of the components presented in figure 4.

Figure 4

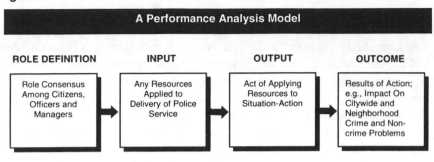

Role definition involves identifying types of tasks to be undertaken by the police. Before any evaluation instrument is designed, consensus must be attained among citizens, officers, supervisors and managers as to the scope of work responsibilities. Failure to attain consensus will lead to confusion over who is responsible for which work assignments. This complicates the ability to conduct valid and reliable performance evaluations.

Inputs are any resources that contribute to the delivery of police service. In most instances, inputs include support mechanisms within the organization or community that facilitate the attainment of results through work efforts. Examples of this support include identifying crime patterns through crime analysis; modifying standard operating procedures; training and education; availability of personnel to implement an action plan, strategy or tactic; time; equipment, etc.

Outputs are the activities or strategies used, and can be analyzed in terms of content, quantity, quality and motivation. The content (what is done) is the act or set of acts performed or strategies implemented. Quantity (how much is done) refers to the number of specified acts within a given period of time. Quality (how well the act is done) is a function of the competence with which actions are performed and the style in which they are performed. Competence depends on knowing what needs to be done and how to do it. The style refers to the personal manner of the person(s) conducting the act.[2] Motivation refers to the reason why the act is performed.

Outcomes are the results, effects or consequences of the work that is done. The outcome that is assessed will be determined by the purpose of the work. For the examples given above, appropriate outcomes could include the number of calls for service answered during the shift, the fact that the targeted drug house was closed, a reduction in the victimization rate in a neighborhood, or action taken by neighborhood residents who worked with the police through organized community meetings.

At each stage of the model, the process of analysis requires both documentation or enumeration and evaluation. For role definition, the question is whether a decision has been made about how to address an issue. In the case of inputs, one asks what the inputs were (enumeration) and whether they were the right ones and in sufficient quantity (evaluation). For outputs, the questions are what actions were taken (enumeration) and what the quality of the actions was (evaluation). For outcomes, the question is whether the actions taken accomplished the objective (evaluation) and whether the nature and magnitude of the results merited the combination of inputs and outputs required to achieve them (cost/benefit analysis).

The model can be applied to any unit of organizational analysis; it can be used to conceptualize the performance of an organization, a unit or team, and (as most commonly applied) individual employees. An organization committed to

- accountability to a governing body,

- meeting the needs of customers,

- meeting the needs of employees,

- efficient management of resources, and

- the continual improvement of the organization's ability to keep the first four commitments

will create and regularly employ performance analysis of each type outlined above for all divisions and levels within a respective system.

The Challenge of Performance Measurement

Creating a valid and reliable means of measuring performance in the workplace is a continuing challenge in the life of any organization (Gabor 1992) involving issues of timing, unit of analysis, purpose, content and requirements for performance evaluation systems.

Timing

Scholtes (1987) notes that an employee's work, including the work of managers, is tied to many systems and processes that have a direct effect on individual performance. For example, patrol officers cannot perform their job effectively without appropriate input from dispatch, training, information or technological support systems. In some departments, a rush to implement community policing has led to the development of new roles for patrol officers without concomitant changes in the support systems available to them. This makes the timing of the development of new performance measurement systems a significant issue, since it would be both unfair and counterproductive to hold employees accountable for performances that are not adequately supported by the organization.

Unit of Analysis

An early management decision will need to involve the unit of analysis or the target of the performance evaluation. Most performance measurement systems are based on the premise that individuals work alone. In reality, most work is the product of a group of people. Scholtes (1987) argues that performance evaluation encourages "lone rangers" and is a divisive influence keeping individuals from working together consistently over time. The manager who is implementing community policing will need to decide whether a performance evaluation should emphasize individual or team work, whether the individual should be evaluated at all, and if so, whether separate criteria need to be developed for individuals and teams. Organizations that retain individual evaluations may abandon them as a means of differentiating among employees for the purpose of rewards and, instead, use them to help individual employees identify and meet their own career goals (Gabor 1992).

Rather than being used to "grade" employees, individual evaluations might still

- inform governing bodies about the work of the organization—accountability that will become ever more critical in the face of shrinking resources;
- determine the nature of problems in various neighborhoods and the strategies that are more and less effective in dealing with them;
- permit officers to record and "exhibit" the work they are doing; and
- determine career objectives and progress for individual employees.

Purpose of the Evaluation

What is measured and how it is measured should depend on the reasons for collecting the data. Mastrofski and Wadman (1991) identify three principal reasons for measuring employee performance:

1. **Administration**—to help managers make decisions about promotion, demotion, reward, discipline, training needs, salary, job assignment, retention and termination.

2. **Guidance and counseling**—to help supervisors provide feedback to subordinates and assist them in career planning and preparation, and to improve employee motivation.

3. **Research**—to validate selection and screening tests and training evaluations, and to assess the effectiveness of interventions designed to improve individual performance (p. 364).

From research conducted within the Houston Police Department on performance evaluation in the context of community policing, three more reasons are added:

1. **Socialization**—to convey expectations to personnel about both the content and style of their performance, and to reinforce other means of organizational communication about the mission and values of the department.

2. **Documentation**—to record the types of problems and situations officers are addressing in their neighborhoods and the approaches they take to them.

Such documentation provides for data-based analysis of the types of resources and other managerial support needed to address problems and allows officers the opportunity to have their efforts recognized.

3. **System improvement**—to identify organizational conditions that may impede improved performance and to solicit ideas for changing the conditions (Wycoff and Oettmeier 1993a).

In an organization that is undertaking a shift in its service-delivery philosophy, these last three functions of performance measurement are especially important. A philosophy that is articulated and reinforced through the types of activities or performances that are measured should be more readily understood by personnel than one simply espoused by sometimes remote managers.

This operational articulation is needed not only by officers but by their supervisors as well. Sergeants and lieutenants who are the first to be introduced to community policing will have less familiarity with the operational implications of the philosophy than will the officers they supervise and manage. As much or more than their subordinates, supervisors may need a new performance assessment system as a guide to, or validation of, appropriate role behaviors for the employees they supervise.[3]

When the new service philosophy calls on officers to identify problems in areas they serve, the systematic documentation of these problems will be the best data available for the guidance of management decisions about resources and other types of support officers may need.

The ability to identify impediments to improved performance is important at any stage in the life of an organization. Conditions, both internal and external, that can affect quality of performance can change constantly (if imperceptibly) and must be regularly monitored. But this need is perhaps never greater than when the organization is in the midst of a shift in its service philosophy that will require deliberate realignment of organizational policies and practices. Management must be able to determine what, if anything, is preventing employees from doing what is expected of them.

A department may be interested in designing a new performance measurement system to accomplish any or all of these purposes. Multiple purposes are not always easy to accommodate with the same process. For example, it is not easy to design a system that meets administrative needs while providing guidance for the officer, and the conflict between these two objectives can be stressful for the evaluator. McGregor (1957) believes that managers are uncomfortable with the performance appraisal processes not because they dislike change or the techniques they must use, or because they lack skills, but because they are put in a position of "playing God." He feels the modern emphasis on the manager as a leader who strives to help his subordinates achieve both their own and the company's objectives is inconsistent with the judicial role demanded by most appraisal plans. A manager's role, he claims, is to help the person analyze performance in terms of targets, and plan future work that is related to organizational objectives and realities. Rather than focusing on weaknesses, the employee needs to better identify strengths and accomplishments.

Since the purpose will determine the nature of the evaluation, it will be essential for managers to identify the organizational purposes of the evaluation before beginning the redesign process.

Content of the Evaluation

Decisions also must be made about what is to be measured. Traditional assessments frequently report what might be called officers' administrative behaviors (punctuality, accuracy and completeness of reports, etc.). Most, however, have relatively little to say about the nature of the officer's work behaviors, a fact that Levinson (1976) argues causes most performance appraisal systems to be unrealistic. An analysis of behavior could include documentation and evaluation of the content of work done, the amount of work done, its appropriateness, the style with which it is done and the results of the effort. The issue of style or the way in which the work is done concerns Levinson (1976), who claims that a crucial part of any manager's job, and the source of most failures, is informing subordinates "how" work is to be done.

Consideration of content raises the question of whether all employees should be evaluated with the same criteria and, specifically, whether a given employee should be evaluated with the same criteria across the span of his or her career. It is reasonable that as an employee's tenure lengthens, individual competency should increase (see figure 5).

Early in a career, it is important to determine whether the employee has the requisite knowledge, skills and attitudes (KSAs), the ability, and willingness to do the job. In other words, we want to determine if the employee has the capacity to do police work. Once this is established, performance assessment might more reasonably focus on whether the employee effectively uses these KSAs in the field. Evaluation is used to determine whether the officer is consistently doing things correctly. At some advanced stage of the career, assessment could focus on whether the officer does the right thing—in other words, whether the officer is able to select the correct response to fit the service needs of the area for which he or she is responsible (see figure 6).

Over the course of a career, assessment moves from an initial focus on ability to a focus on effort and, finally, to a focus on judgment and the results of an officer's efforts. Each of these stages would require using different performance criteria, instrumentation and assessment processes.

Requirements for Performance Evaluations

In addition to this wide range of decisions managers need to make about performance evaluations, there are at least five standards that an employee performance measurement process should meet: validity, reliability, equity, legality and utility (Mastrofski and Wadman 1991).

Figure 5

Individual Competence Compared to Employee Tenure and Evaluation Complexity

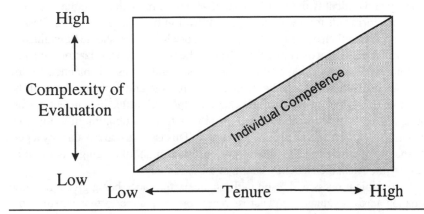

Figure 6

Performance Evaluation System

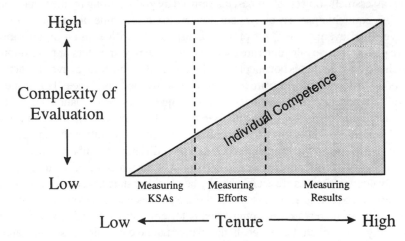

If the process is valid, it accurately reflects the content of the job an employee is expected to perform, as well as the expected quality of the job performance. The validity of an evaluation process is tied to job task analyses for the positions in question. The purpose of a job task analysis is to determine what specific tasks are performed by employees. Employees are asked to provide feedback regarding the frequency and criticality of tasks associated with their respective assignments. The tasks are prioritized, followed by the identification of associated KSAs. Performance criteria are then developed to represent those KSAs that should be evaluated.

The Achilles heel of a job task analysis in the context of organizational change is that it describes a position as it currently exists, and not as it is planned for the future. An evaluation process that is meant to promote and sustain change of the police role has to reflect the desired behavior while still reflecting current performance. As organizations modify responsibilities to reflect community policing, new performance criteria need to be developed. This issue is one reason why a performance evaluation process should not be fixed; it should change as often as necessary to reflect the changing nature of the job.

A reliable process will result in the same performance being given the same evaluation across evaluators and across repetitions of that performance. Any time one person is designated to evaluate the performance of another, subjectivity will be a factor. The challenge, irrespective of the type of evaluation used, is to minimize the subjectivity. According to Lawler (1971), the more subjective the rating system, the higher the degree of trust is required to make it work. Oberg (1972) suggests that management identify appraisal techniques designed to achieve a particular organizational objective; such "results-focused" appraisals will be less vulnerable to subjective influences. There is probably no way to guarantee full objectivity of performance assessment; objectivity is best maximized by good training for the evaluators.

An equitable process allows employees doing the same or similar work to receive equal evaluations. This process is especially critical in an organization where performance evaluations are used to determine pay, transfers or promotions. In such organizations, it is not uncommon for one evaluation point or even a fraction of a point to separate the rewarded from the unrewarded employee. This issue is difficult for policing because the nature and frequency of performance occur, to a large degree, in response to external conditions that vary by temporal and geographic variables. This element is accentuated under community policing because of the need to provide customized services within different neighborhoods.

Legality is a significant issue in departments for which certain requirements of the evaluation process are established by law—either state law, city ordinance or civil service code. It is also an issue for those agencies using performance evaluations to determine rewards and punishments for employees. Legality and validity are usually interwoven. People challenge performance evaluation systems that are invalid because they result in management decisions that are inherently unfair to employees deserving equal treatment and consideration.

Utility refers simply to the purpose for the evaluation. If nothing is done with it, and if employees see no benefit from the evaluation for either the organization or themselves, the process will not only be useless, but it will also breed contempt for management among employees.

It is beyond the scope of this article to instruct the reader in the various ways of meeting each of these standards. These issues are discussed extensively in Whitaker et al. (1982) and by Mastrofski and Wadman (1991) whose works provide technical reference of value to agencies struggling with these topics.

The need for assessment procedures to be valid, reliable, equitable, legal and useful exists regardless of an organization's philosophy. Meeting these requirements is a difficult task given the high probability of conflicts among them. The goal of equity, for example, may conflict with the goal of validity. When patrol jobs are dissimilar because of geographic assignment or duty time, the need for equity may reduce the evaluated job dimensions to the most common elements of the role. This situation could result in an evaluation that fails to reflect any officer's actual job responsibilities.

Concerns for both legality and reliability have pushed departments toward quantifiable performance indicators. The increased emphasis administrators placed on crime-fighting aspects of the police role in previous decades (Kelling and Moore 1988) also created pressure for quantifiable measures. The indicators most readily available were those associated (even if spuriously) with crime fighting (e.g., rapid response, numbers of arrests, etc.) and with administrative regulations (e.g., tardiness, sick time taken, accidents, etc.; see Kelling 1992). When important behaviors or activities cannot be counted, then the ones that are counted tend to become those that are considered important (Wycoff 1982b).[4]

Performance Measurement in the Community Policing Context

Revision of performance measurement systems to reflect the diverse responsibilities of an ever-broadening police role is something many executives still need to accomplish in the 1990s, regardless of whether they have any interest in changing their organization's current approach to policing. Changes in policing philosophies only make more apparent the need for managers to acknowledge and support activities that effective officers have conducted but that have gone officially unrecognized. As Trojanowicz and Bucqueroux (1992) note, the challenge is (as it always has been) one of

> finding ways to express a quality as quantity, in other words, to make quality a countable commodity. . . . The challenge is to identify quantifiable outcomes that truly relate to the job and to ensure that this does not corrupt "community policing" [or any other orientation to policing] into policing by the numbers.

Community policing draws attention to other issues about employee performance evaluation, including

1. the means by which supervisors and managers can hold officers accountable for the greater discretion they are permitted;

2. the inclusion of the community in the evaluation process; and

3. the evaluation of team, unit or organization as distinct from the evaluation of the individual officer.[5]

Weisburd, McElroy and Hardyman (1989) suggest that the paramilitary model of policing facilitates close supervision of the officer's traditional role but is inappropriate for the broader, more discretionary role associated with com-munity policing (see also Goldstein 1979 and Bittner 1972).[6] While it is debatable how many sergeants effectively "supervise" their officers in departments that restrict what officers are allowed to do, it is clear that community policing will require a reformulation of the sergeant's role that corresponds with changes in officers' roles.

Official expansion of the officer's role will require sergeants, for example, to support the use of, and to hold officers accountable for, the greater discretion they are permitted. To support the work of officers, sergeants will need to become more efficient managers, team builders and group facilitators. Sergeants should develop the capacity to build resource capabilities for their officers. They should be active participants in devising more global approaches to addressing problems of crime and disorder. Of critical importance is their ability to sense and interpret local oppor-tunities for, and hindrances to, officers' actions.

To accomplish this, sergeants, like officers, will need to seek more effective means of getting information from the community. Generally, the only significant form of citizen feedback has been in the form of complaints about improper police activity. Notwithstanding the importance of attending to citizen complaints, depart-ments need to collect data about services citizens want and about whether citizens believe their service needs are being met. A number of strategies have been advocated for accomplishing this. Numerous departments have used community meetings as a forum for eliciting service needs and preferences (e.g., Houston's Positive Interaction Program). Some have employed door-to-door surveys conducted by officers (e.g., Grand Rapids, Michigan, and Newark, New Jersey). A few departments with substantial resources have conducted scientific community surveys. The Madison, Wisconsin, Police Department has surveyed by mail a sample of all citizens who have received service from the department in an effort to measure satisfaction and collect information about ways of improving service.

In addition to recognizing the value of community feedback, community policing has also caused some administrators to question the appropriateness of individual employee evaluations. Some departments are emphasizing focus teams or workgroups rather than individuals. Those retaining individual evaluations may abandon them as a means of differentiating among employees for the purpose of rewards and, instead, use them as a means of helping individual employees identify and meet their own career goals (Gabor 1992).

The appropriate role of employee performance evaluations in a community policing context (or perhaps any policing context) is being explored. The answers for each department may depend ultimately on the uses the agency wishes to make of the evaluations. Perhaps, as agencies embracing Deming's philosophy of management argue (Scholtes 1987), there is no reason to "grade" individuals relative to each other. Individual evaluations may still be used for other purposes, however, as discussed in the previous section of this article titled "Unit of Analysis."

Some organizations may improve individual evaluations to better serve other purposes, and other agencies may design alternative means of accomplishing these ends. One of the valuable consequences of the current interest in community policing should be the creation of a variety of new approaches to performance measurement.

Redesigning the Evaluation System

There are many ways for an organization to approach the redesign of their performance evaluation system. For illustration, this section describes briefly the process used in Houston in the late 1980s; this section also examines issues that will be germane to any agency undertaking redesign, regardless of the specific process used.

The Houston Experience[7]

The redesign of performance measurement in Houston was undertaken in conjunction with the development of neighborhood-oriented policing (NOP) and its implementation at Westside—Houston's first decentralized police facility. The project was directed by an Internal Advisory Committee, which consisted of a project director, a representative from the chief's office, the deputy chief from Westside and the Westside Operations Captain.

An early meeting with Westside sergeants led the committee to conclude that patrol officer activities under the NOP concept were still not sufficiently articulated to support the redesign.[8] Consequently, a task force of eleven patrol officers, one investigator and two sergeants was created. The group met eight times over a six-month period to discuss the nature of activities being conducted by patrol officers who were attempting to implement the NOP philosophy, and the challenges of measuring these activities. Representatives of the committee visited four other agencies in (New York City; Baltimore County, Maryland; Newport News, Virginia; and Madison, Wisconsin) to observe and discuss other approaches to performance measurement.

The committee developed a list of tasks, roles and skills they felt would be essential to the role of officers working in the NOP context. The project manager developed a data collection instrument designed to capture detailed information about the actions of police officers, sergeants and lieutenants at Westside. Eight members of the task force were trained as facilitators, each of whom was to identify six other officers to complete the instrument. Data from these forms was then analyzed to identify attitudes and activities that were considered important for officers implementing NOP.

This process was supported by a two-day meeting with an External Advisory Committee. Eight individuals representing other police departments, police professional organizations, the National Institute of Justice and private corporations spent two days in a seminar setting with the task force, the project's Internal Advisory Committee and other selected department personnel, discussing the nature of performance evaluation, its purposes, and the various forms it could take. Following this meeting, the task force designed performance evaluation instruments that were then field tested and revised based on the feedback from the test.

Some aspects of this process (the trips to other cities and the work of the External Advisory Committee) were financially feasible because of a grant from the National Institute of Justice to support the redesign effort. The other parts of the process, however, should be possible for most agencies, without additional funding. It may be necessary to provide overtime pay for task force members, and it should be anticipated this is not an undertaking that can be accomplished quickly. It is estimated that in Houston, each task force member contributed approximately two months of time (spread out over a six-month time period) and the role of the project director was also critical.

The project director did a great deal of work between task force meetings that would be difficult for a task force of officers to accomplish without this type of organizational support. The amount of time the process takes will concern managers who are watching budgets and implementation time tables, but this is a process that will undergird other implementation efforts and should not be rushed. This assignment is difficult and discussion about it will lead task force members into critical discussions about other systems in the organization that are related to (or should be related to) the performance evaluation system. An effort should be made to capture and utilize information from these discussions for the sake of redesigning other systems.

Observations and evaluation of the Houston experience and of similar experiences in other departments have led to the identification of several issues that need to be addressed in any redesign of performance evaluations.

Adopt New Assumptions

Management has an obligation to provide structure and guidance in developing the performance capabilities of employees. Typically, this structure is provided using multiple formats: training, education, job enrichment, disciplinary action, rewards, incentives and performance evaluation. To be effective, each of these management tools must be flexible in design and application, and each should be governed by a set of assumptions. In the case of performance evaluations, many of the baseline assumptions governing how it should be done have not been changed in years, if not decades. Common assumptions include the following:

- All personnel performance will be assessed at least once (or twice) a year.
- All personnel will be assessed using the same performance criteria.
- All personnel will use the same performance evaluation instrumentation.

• The results of one's performance evaluation may (or may not) be used to help determine promotability, etc.

These assumptions are not necessarily improper or incorrect. In many agencies, they are legal requirements set forth by state statutes, local ordinances or civil service codes. These requirements, however, do not preclude executives from re-examining them to determine what flexibility, if any, they have to make adjustments.

The manner in which performance is assessed should be dynamic. As performance expectations change, the methodology and criteria used to measure effectiveness should also change. The following assumptions may be appropriate under a new evaluation system:

1. Employee competency is expected to improve as a result of experience.

2. Performance evaluation criteria should vary in accordance with an employee's assignment, tenure and competency.

3. The relationship between the number and type of performance criteria and individual competency is *not* linear. People learn at different rates.

4. Performance can be assessed in phases, consistent with individual development.

5. Employees should be allowed to voluntarily progress through an evaluation system at varying speeds.

Define Purposes of Evaluations

In many organizations, performance evaluation is an annual ritual people try to administer routinely and consistently.[9] Executives and employees alike view it as an administrative duty. As this paper suggests, however, performance evaluations can have much more meaningful objectives.

In organizations seeking to become community-based, performance measurement systems can be used as a management tool to accomplish the following:

1. enhance officers' and supervisors' knowledge of community policing;

2. clarify officers' and supervisors' perceptions of their respective behavior under community policing;

3. redefine productivity requirements to include changes in the type, amount and quality of work to be performed;

4. build consensus between and among officers and supervisors regarding each other's work responsibilities;

5. improve officers' levels of job satisfaction with department operations; and

6. measure citizens' perceptions of the way in which police deliver service to the community.

These objectives allow executives to recast performance evaluation systems, but require them to think differently about the nature of performance criteria, the design of evaluation instruments, and the participants in the process.

Performance evaluation must be more than just a means of obtaining information about how well employees improve their KSAs. It should help management gauge, from different perspectives, how well employees are *using* their KSAs, what results they are attaining, and how susceptible they are to accepting and implementing other organizational changes. This information is critical because it helps management decide the pace at which organizational change can occur. Without this knowledge, managers will develop inaccurate expectations of what is occurring in the workplace.

These inaccurate expectations will cause decisions to be made that will heighten resistance among employees. This resistance will be based on the employees' perception that management is out of touch with reality. When this happens, managers will have more difficulty gaining support from employees for any initiatives, let alone those associated with improving the overall performance of the organization.

Identify New Performance Criteria

Determining what should be measured is heavily dependent on the work demands associated with an officer's work assignment and management's expectations regarding results. Earlier in this paper, the various functions performed by an officer in a community policing context were classified as reactive, proactive or coactive. Adding the coactive function requires criteria to be developed that reflect this function. And, as suggested previously, many departments still need to develop criteria that accurately reflect reactive and proactive work.

Even within these three functional categories, the "career model" of performance evaluation that this article proposes argues that different criteria need to be applied at different times in an officer's career. Again, this does not mean completely abandoning traditional criteria. It will still be important, for example, to measure the attainment of knowledge, skills and attitudes in the early stages of an officer's career; such information will provide officers with information about their self-development, but it can tell us little about what an officer does to impact crime and problems in a neighborhood. At some point, criteria must be developed that tell us what is being done to improve the neighborhood in addition to those that tell us what is done (or needs to be done) to improve the officer.

In response to this concern, Stephens (1996) identified the following performance inputs and outcomes for which executives who are implementing community policing and problem solving are attempting to develop indicators:

• problem solving,
• citizen satisfaction,
• repeat business,

• displacement, and

• neighborhood indicants (e.g., truancy rates, traffic patterns, occupancy rates, presence and actions taken by neighborhood groups, etc.)

The Houston task force (Wycoff and Oettmeier 1993a) based the creation of new performance criteria on tasks and activities officers performed within their neighborhoods (see figure 7). This information was collected from a representative sample of officers who kept record of their actual work during their shifts.

Other examples of "new" performance criteria include the following:

• having a sense of personal responsibility for an area and its people,

• believing in the importance of improving conditions in an area,

• accessing worthwhile information from citizens,

• collaborating with citizens to address crime and disorder problems,

• working with other agencies or community groups,

• using crime analysis data,

• strategic neighborhood planning,

• managing uncommitted time, and

• developing/implementing/assessing neighborhood action plans.

Measure the Effects of Officer Performance

Goldstein (1990) has contended that traditional evaluation criteria have required officers to emphasize means over ends. For example, traffic enforcement is measured by the number of tickets issued for moving violations (e.g., improper turns, running red lights, speeding, etc.). The association is seldom made between the need to issue speeding tickets and the need to reduce minor accidents or fatalities at a particular location. Police managers are only beginning to address the need to evaluate performance in relation to specific problems.

According to Goldstein (1990), evaluating police response to any problem requires the following:

• a clear understanding of the problem;

• agreement on the specific interest(s) to be served in dealing with the problem, and their order of importance;

• agreement on the method to be used to determine the extent to which these interests (or goals) are reached;

• a realistic assessment of what might be expected of the police (e.g., solving the problem vs. improving the quality of the police management of it);

• determination of the relative importance of short-term vs. long-term impact; and

Figure 7 Tasks/Activities

Activities are listed beneath the tasks they are intended to accomplish. Several activities could be used to accomplish a number of different tasks.

1. **Learn characteristics of area, residents, businesses**
   a. Study beat books
   b. Analyze crime and calls-for-assistance data
   c. Drive, walk area and make notes
   d. Talk with community representatives
   e. Conduct area surveys
   f. Maintain area/suspect logs
   g. Read area papers (e.g., "shopper" papers)
   h. Discuss area with citizens when answering calls
   i. Talk with private security personnel in area
   j. Talk with area business owners/managers

2. **Become acquainted with leaders in area**
   a. Attend community meetings, including service club meetings
   b. Ask questions in survey about who formal and informal area leaders are
   c. Ask area leaders for names of other leaders

3. **Make residents aware of who officer is and what s/he is trying to accomplish in area**
   a. Initiate citizen contacts
   b. Distribute business cards
   c. Discuss purpose at community meeting
   d. Discuss purpose when answering calls
   e. Write article for local paper
   f. Contact home-bound elderly
   g. Encourage citizens to contact officer directly

4. **Identify area problems**
   a. Attend community meetings
   b. Analyze crime and calls-for-service data
   c. Contact citizens and businesses
   d. Conduct business and residential surveys
   e. Ask about other problems when answering calls

5. **Communicate with supervisors, other officers and citizens about the nature of the area and its problems**
   a. Maintain beat bulletin board in station
   b. Leave notes in boxes of other officers
   c. Discuss area with supervisor

6. **Investigate/do research to determine sources of problems**
   a. Talk to people involved
   b. Analyze crime data
   c. Observe situation if possible (stakeout)

7. **Plan ways of dealing with problem**
   a. Analyze resources
   b. Discuss with supervisor, other officers
   c. Write Patrol Management Plan, review with supervisor

8. **Provide citizens information about ways they can handle problems (educate/empower)**
   a. Distribute crime prevention information
   b. Provide names and number of other responsible agencies; tell citizens how to approach these agencies

9. **Help citizens develop appropriate expectations about what police can do and teach them how to interact effectively with police**
   a. Attend community meetings/make presentations
   b. Present school programs
   c. Write article for area paper
   d. Hold discussions with community leaders

10. **Develop resources for responding to problem**
    a. Talk with other officers, detectives, supervisors
    b. Talk with other agencies or individuals who could help

11. **Implement problem solution**
    a. Take whatever actions are called for

12. **Assess effectiveness of solution**
    a. Use data, feedback from persons who experienced the problem, and/or personal observation to determine whether problem has been solved

13. **Keep citizens informed**
    a. Officers tell citizens what steps have been taken to address a problem and with what results
    b. Detectives tell citizens what is happening with their cases

• a clear understanding of the legality and fairness of the response (recognizing that reducing a problem through improper use of authority is not only wrong, but likely to be counterproductive because of its effects on other aspects of police operations).

Goldstein cautions against defining success as problem eradication since many problems by their very nature are intractable or unmanageable because of their magnitude. Despite this limitation, there are a sufficient number of problems within the boundaries of police control that merit attention.

To differentiate types of outcomes officers might achieve in problem solving, Spelman and Eck (1987) developed five degrees of effectiveness:

• total elimination of the problem,

• reducing the number of incidents it creates,

• reducing the seriousness of the incidents it creates,

• designing methods for better handling of the incidents, and

• removing the problem from police consideration (assuming it is dealt with more effectively by some other entity than the police).

In this context, Goldstein claims that for much of police business, the most realistic goal is to reduce the number of incidents a problem creates and to reduce the seriousness of these incidents.

Correspondingly, he suggests it is helpful to characterize the police role more realistically as "managing deviance" and then concentrate on equipping the police to carry out this role with greater effectiveness. Officers should be involved in identifying the measurable conditions they would expect to see change before they undertake a problem-solving effort, and they should be allowed to identify factors not under an officer's control that can affect outcomes.

Strengthen Verification Process

One of the most difficult aspects for supervisors conducting evaluations is verification of performance. Technically, the assessment of officer performance is dependent on the ability of supervisors to observe what occurred.[10] Unfortunately, the verification of performance doesn't always occur for a number of legitimate reasons. For example, the span of control can make it difficult for a supervisor to consistently view officer performance. Supervising many officers going in many directions makes it hard to observe performance. Another variable is the type and amount of work officers perform. Officers who constantly respond to calls for service, write numerous reports or patrol indiscriminately do not provide their supervisor with a wide array of settings from which different types of performances can be observed.

Supervisors may not be motivated to observe officer behavior. It is not surprising that supervisors don't always hold performance evaluation as a priority duty.

Many are apt to say it requires too much work and it interferes with "my other responsibilities." "Besides," they go on to say, "officers don't really care and it doesn't mean that much to them anyway." In actuality, it means a lot to them. Many officers want feedback, they want their performance to be noticed and they want to be recognized for what they have accomplished. If anything, officers are inclined to feel they don't receive enough credit for all the things they do during their tours of duty.

One way of addressing this conflict is to alter one of the traditional assumptions governing who participates in the evaluation process. Should performance evaluations be limited to the observations of an officer's immediate supervisor? Not necessarily. Granted, the supervisor should have a major impact on determining how well an officer has performed, but not to the extent of ignoring input from citizens, investigators or officers themselves.

As officers increase the amount of time that they work directly with citizens on neighborhood crime and disorder problems, citizens will form certain opinions about different aspects of their performance. Community leaders, civic club or association personnel, business association personnel and even apartment managers are all capable of providing input to a sergeant about an officer's performance. They can provide comments on communication skills, the nature of their relationship and collaborative problem-solving efforts.

Investigators provide another potential source of verification for supervisors. Investigators working in the same neighborhoods as officers often end up conducting follow-up investigations based on an officer's preliminary investigation. Investigators can provide information regarding the officer's written communication skills, procedural knowledge, legal knowledge, and in instances when they are actually working together on a case, feedback on their ability to get along and their initiative in pursuing a case to its logical conclusion.

Officers should have the opportunity to contribute to their own evaluations. Their input should not be limited to just agreeing or disagreeing with the supervisor's observations. In addition to providing their supervisors with examples of successful work products, officers should be invited to identify efforts that may not have been known by the supervisor. They should be encouraged to discuss any perceived failure, including why it occurred and what was learned from the experience.

Should officers be allowed to assess each other's performance? Many Houston officers said "no" for a number of reasons, including the following:

• officers will use it to "snitch off" other officers,

• it will cause conflicts among officers,

• officers are not competent to evaluate KSAs, and

• it will create role confusion.

Verification of officer performance is difficult. One rule of thumb is to ensure that the source of feedback provides current, reliable and practical information about an officer's performance. If there is any doubt about the integrity of the information, it should not be used.

Develop New Instrumentation

The nature of a new evaluation form should be determined by the expectations of officer performance. It should be purposeful and consistent with supporting an officer's career development throughout his or her tenure with the agency.

Management should be concerned about a number of instrumentation questions. For instance, should one form be used by all officers, or should forms be developed to support an officer's assignment (e.g., patrol vs. investigative vs. support assignments)? How many copies of the form are needed? Will the supervisors be required to complete them by hand or will they be automated? If additional forms are created, where will each copy and/or form be filed and for how long? Will it be necessary to provide each supervisor with an instructional booklet? Is training necessary to acquaint supervisors with the new form(s), and if so, how long will the sessions last and who will do the training?

A rule of thumb to follow when developing new instruments is to make sure the forms capture information that adequately reflects what officers are capable of doing and what management expects them to accomplish within their respective neighborhoods.

Solicit Officer Feedback about the Sergeant

Officers cannot perform a full evaluation of their supervisors because they are familiar with only one part of a supervisor's responsibilities. They can, however, provide significant feedback in a number of areas including the nature of officer/supervisor relationships, how well officers and supervisors get along, how responsive supervisors are, whether they act as a leader or coach, the clarity of communications, etc.[11] The process should be designed so that the feedback is couched in constructive terms; otherwise sergeants may have difficulty hearing it. And the process could be designed to be anonymous; otherwise officers may not be inclined to provide this information for fear of retaliation.

Revise Rating Scales

Most performance measurement systems contain rating scales.[12] The criteria used to describe scale points can become dated and should be re-examined periodically.

Determining the type of scale to be used depends on the distinction one wants to make regarding a person's performance. If the interest is in distinguishing between acceptable vs. unacceptable behavior, a pass/fail scale is appropriate. In most cases, supervisors want more discretion in determining how well their officers are performing. The Likert scaling technique, involving a five- or seven-point scale, is a popular format used by many agencies. Seven-point scales tend to include detailed descriptions of a few anchor points (e.g., 1, 4 and 7), while five-point scales are apt to describe each point in detail.

The fewer descriptions of anchor points, the greater the discretion for supervisors and hence, the higher the probability for subjectivity and error. The greater the number of scale points, the less subjectivity there is, but the more difficult it becomes to describe behavioral differences between them.[13]

All scale points for each performance criterion should be clearly defined. Definitions should be specific and not global. The reason most definitions are global is because departments use one form for all personnel regardless of rank or assignment. In constructing scale-point definitions, make sure the descriptive criteria are consistent from one scale point to the next. For example, if five different descriptive criteria are used to define what "unacceptable" means, make sure those criteria are addressed in each of the succeeding scale-point descriptions. Do not use different descriptive criteria from one scale point to the next. This will skew the reliability of the evaluation tremendously.

If possible, develop instrumentation unique to both assignment and rank. Even if legally mandated to use a generic evaluation form, agencies can customize evaluations by developing "worksheets" that feed into the primary instrument.

Conclusion

A performance measurement system is an important management and leadership tool for police agencies. It should be designed to support individual professional development and behavioral changes. If the decision is made to revise an organization's current performance measurement system, these points are worth bearing in mind:

1. Performance evaluations are not bad in and of themselves. Frustration comes from how the process is administered and the lack of suitable performance criteria.

2. Officers want feedback and a permanent record of their accomplishments and performance.

3. Officers often feel they are doing more than they are receiving credit for given the typical narrow design of their evaluation instruments and performance criteria.

4. The goals and structure of the organization should be decided before new performance measurement is developed. Form follows function.

5. There should be separate forms for different assignments (unless law prohibits).

6. Administrative convenience should not be a primary criterion in the redesign. The goal of the performance evaluation should dictate the way in which it is conducted.

7. Any significant alteration of past practices is likely to cause some dissatisfaction among supervisors. It is likely that this, too, shall pass as the new process becomes familiar.

8. Performance evaluation should be reprioritized as a critical supervisory responsibility. Without overreacting to sergeants' concerns, managers should be responsive. Removing meaningless administrative duties from sergeants allows them to spend more time verifying officer performance. In time, what was once considered drastic will become routine, provided it is perceived as having practical value to the supervisor.

9. Citizen involvement is central to performance evaluation. Citizens can be a good source of information about an officer's style and adequacy of effort, and community satisfaction with results. They also can provide valuable feedback about the status of neighborhood conditions. They should not, however, be put in a position of judging the appropriateness of an officer's decisions.

10. The process should be as simple as reasonably possible. This will increase both acceptance and the probability that the information will actually be utilized.

Finally, performance measurement systems are critical to facilitating change within personnel and throughout the organization. Executives who accept the challenge of modifying their system will discover an effective management tool to attain results in neighborhoods and their organizations.

Appendix

Assumptions Associated with Community Policing

1. Continued reliance on random, preventive patrol should be minimized. Random, preventive patrol should only be used as a strategy when police visibility is an issue.

2. Citizens will accept a range of response times for different types of calls.

3. Differential police response strategies should be implemented to improve the effective management of the dispatch function.

4. Effective management of the patrol function is dependent on intelligent management of the dispatch function.

5. Effective management of criminal investigations is indirectly dependent on intelligent management of the dispatch function and directly related to management of the patrol function.

6. Case management systems must be developed and implemented to fit the needs of various investigative functions.

7. Work demands and resource allocation studies are necessary to ensure equitable deployment of personnel.

8. The development of crime and operational analysis procedures is vital in managing patrol and investigative functions.

9. The use of directed and self-directed patrol activities for officers should increase when and where appropriate.

10. Officers assigned to the patrol function must be actively involved in criminal investigations (e.g., conducting follow-up investigations, recommending early case closures).

11. Patrol officers need enhanced status and enriched job responsibilities.

12. Attention must be devoted to reassessing the purpose and function of existing beat configurations.

13. Initiatives must be taken by the police to identify citizen service expectations and to work with citizens in addressing and resolving neighborhood crime and disorder problems.

14. To facilitate the development of stronger ties with the community, policies requiring frequent rotation of officers across shifts must be seriously reconsidered.

15. Regular public forums should be established so frequent exchanges of information can occur between the police and public, preferably between patrol officers and neighborhood residents.

16. Performance measurement systems should serve as a management tool that guides personnel development and facilitates organizational change.

17. More meaningful performance evaluation criteria must be developed to reflect the change in officer roles and responsibilities.

18. Training curricula must be redesigned so they are more relevant and supportive of patrol and investigative operations.

19. Disciplinary processes must become part of a behavioral system that incorporates education, training and counseling as strategies designed to assist officers experiencing behavioral problems.

20. Management styles must be more adaptive to varying situations and personalities.

21. Managers must begin directing their attention toward the qualitative aspects of service delivery processes and outcomes.

22. Police agencies must cultivate leaders who are comfortable and effective working in an environment characterized by constant demands for change.

Notes

[1] What separates departments striving to become community-based from the "pretenders" is management's conviction to pursue a different set of assumptions that guide the implementation of operational and managerial initiatives. Many of these assumptions are grounded in police research conducted over the past twenty years. Evaluation efforts should measure the effectiveness of changes in processes, programs and strategies linked to these assumptions (see Appendix).

[2] In the case of a police officer, for example, an act might be conducted competently by an officer who does everything required by the department and yet be conducted in either a positive or negative style, depending on whether the officer is civil and polite or uncivil and rude (Wycoff 1982, p. 11).

[3] A patrol officer in Houston suggested that his peers exercised patience with sergeants who initially did not know what was needed from them as supervisors working in the context of neighborhood-oriented policing. He pointed out that existing sergeants had never performed the roles they were now expected to supervise. As an unavoidable result, they knew less than the officers who were only now in the process of recreating and redefining the roles (Wycoff and Oettmeier 1993b, p. 3).

[4] The record of researchers is no better in this respect than the record of police managers. Despite their disclaimers about the validity and reliability of such indicators, researchers continue to use recorded crime data, arrest data and administrative data as indicators of performance and outcome because other indicators are unavailable or are too costly or time consuming to create. This fact led to Kelling's (1978) call for "a modest moratorium on the application of crime related productivity measures" until the full range of the police role could be documented and decisions about how to measure a much wider range of police activity (and results).

[5] There is also the issue addressed by Trojanowicz and Bucqueroux (1992), Wadman and Olson (1990) and others of the need to develop outcome or impact measures that correspond to the problems officers are trying to solve in communities. We do not deal with that issue in this discussion, since it is beyond the scope of this article.

[6] Discretion and the greater flexibility it gives an officer for how, when and where to work is not a new issue for supervisors. It has always been an issue for rural police departments and sheriffs' agencies in which officers and supervisors may never have occasion to meet after roll call (and sometimes not even at roll call). Researchers need to develop information about supervision in these types of agencies.

[7] This summary of the process used to redesign performance evaluation in Houston is taken from Wycoff and Oettmeier (1993), where a more detailed discussion is available (pp. 25–32).

[8] The Westside Command Station represented Houston's first effort to define NOP operationally, and new role definitions were being explored at every level. There were no models of community-oriented policing at the time Houston undertook this effort. Today, departments can undertake redesign with a more broadly shared understanding of the job requirements of community-oriented policing than existed in Houston in 1986.

[9] Some departments have abandoned using performance evaluations because of legal liabilities associated with not taking corrective action for poorly performing employees. The rationale for this decision is that if you don't know the problem exists, you cannot be held accountable for not correcting it. Other departments do not use evaluations because they are perceived to have no value to recipients, are not valid or have become an administrative nightmare to complete.

[10] The St. Petersburg, Florida Police Department (1994) identified a number of different sources to verify officer performance, among them: reviewing reports, responding to crime scenes, reading complimentary letters from citizens, reviewing internal affairs files, reviewing productivity statistics, monitoring radio communications, monitoring rumors, conducting street inspections, reviewing training records, monitoring community involvement, monitoring sick time, etc.

[11] See Wycoff and Oettmeier (1993a) for additional examples of supervisory criteria.

[12] Departments using open ended narrations to describe accomplishments may not feel the need to use a rating scale.

[13] For a point-counterpoint discussion on seven- versus five-point Likert scales as it applies to the Field Training programs, see Oettmeier (1995).

References

Bittner, Egon. 1972. *The Functions of the Police in Modern Society*. Rockville, Md.: National Institute of Mental Health.

Community Policing Consortium. 1994. *Understanding Community Policing: A Framework For Action*. Washington, DC: Bureau of Justice Assistance.

Gabor, Andrea. 1992. Take This Job and Love It. *New York Times*. 26 January.

Goldstein, Herman. 1979. Improving Policing: A Problem-Oriented Approach. *Crime and Delinquency* 25.

Goldstein, Herman. 1990. *Problem Oriented Policing*. New York: McGraw Hill.

Kelling, George L. 1978. The Role of Research in Maximizing Productivity. In *Report of the Proceedings, Workshop on Police Productivity and Performance,* edited by Peter Engstad and Michele Lioy. Ottawa, Canada: Ministry of the Solicitor General of Canada.

Kelling, George L. 1992. Measuring What Matters: A New Way of Thinking About Crime and Public Order. *The City Journal*. Spring.

Kelling, George L. and Mark H. Moore. 1988. *The Evolving Strategy of Policing*. Washington, DC: National Institute of Justice and J. F. Kennedy School, Harvard University.

Lawler, E. III. 1971. *Pay and Organizational Effectiveness: A Psychological View*. New York: McGraw Hill.

Levinson, Harry. 1976. Appraisal of What Performance. *Harvard Business Review,* July–Aug.

Mastrofski, Stephen D. 1996. Measuring Police Performance in Public Encounters. In *Quantifying Quality in Policing,* edited by Larry T. Hoover. Washington, DC: Police Executive Research Forum.

Mastrofski, Stephen D. and Robert C. Wadman. 1991. Personnel and Agency Performance Measurement. In *Local Government Police Management,* edited by William A. Geller. Washington, DC: International City Management Association.

McGregor, Douglas. 1957. An Uneasy Look At Performance Appraisal. *Harvard Business Review*. May–June.

Meyer, Christopher. 1993. How the Right Measures Help Teams Excel. *Harvard Business Review*. May–June.

Oberg, Winston. 1972. Make Performance Appraisal Relevant. *Harvard Business Review*. Jan–Feb.

Oettmeier, Timothy N. 1992. Matching Structure to Objectives. In *Police Management:*

Issues and Perspectives, edited by Larry T. Hoover. Washington, DC: Police Executive Research Forum.

Oettmeier, Timothy N. and Mary Ann Wycoff. 1994. Police Performance in the Nineties: Practitioner Perspectives. *American Journal of Police* 8:2.

Schay, Brigitte W. 1993. In Search of the Holy Grail: Lessons In Performance Management. *Public Personnel Management* 22:4 (Winter).

Scholtes, Peter R. 1987. *A New View of Performance Evaluation.* Paper presented to William G. Hunter Conference on Quality. Available from Joiner Associates, Inc., Madison, Wis.

Spelman, William, and John E. Eck. 1987. Newport News Tests Problem-Oriented Policing. *NIJ Reports.* Jan–Feb.

St. Petersburg Police Department, 1994. *St. Petersburg Police Department Performance Evaluation Workshop: Summary of Workgroup Comments.* October.

Stephens, Darrel W. 1996. Community Problem-Oriented Policing: Measuring Impacts. In *Quantifying Quality in Policing,* edited by Larry T. Hoover. Washington, DC: Police Executive Research Forum.

Trojanowicz, Robert and Bonnie Bucqueroux. 1992. *Toward Development of Meaningful and Effective Performance Evaluations.* East Lansing, Mich.: National Center for Community Policing, Michigan State University.

Wadman, Robert C. and Robert K. Olson. 1990. *Community Wellness:* A *New Theory of Policing.* Washington, DC: Police Executive Research Forum.

Weisburd, David, Jerome McElroy, and Patricia Hardyman. 1989. Maintaining Control in Community-Oriented Policing. In *Police and Policing: Contemporary Issues,* edited by Dennis Jay Kenney. New York: Praeger.

Whitaker, Gordon P., Stephen Mastrofski, Elinor Ostrom, Roger B. Parks, and Stephen L. Percy. 1982. *Basic Issues In Police Performance.* Washington, DC: U.S. Department of Justice.

Wycoff, Mary Ann. 1982a. Improving Police Performance Measurement: One More Voice. *The Urban Interest.* Spring.

Wycoff, Mary Ann. 1982b. *The Role of Municipal Police: Research as Prelude to Changing It.* Washington, DC: Police Foundation.

Wycoff, Mary Ann and Timothy N. Oettmeier. 1993a. *Evaluating Patrol Officer Performance Under Community Policing: The Houston Experience.* Technical Report. Washington, DC: Police Foundation.

Wycoff, Mary Ann and Timothy N. Oettmeier. 1993b. *Evaluating Patrol Officer Performance Under Community Policing: The Houston Experience.* Research in Brief. Washington, DC: Police Foundation.

Wycoff, Mary Ann. 1994. *Community Policing Strategies.* Washington, DC: Police Foundation.

Part IV

Future Directions in Community Policing

A great deal has been learned from theoretical and empirical research on community and problem-oriented policing. At the same time, many challenges await researchers, practitioners, policy-makers, and citizens as they attempt to implement the innovative approach to policing to reduce the effects of crime and disorder. Several scholars have had important influences on ideas and approaches to the development and implementation of community policing. The final section of this book includes six articles which are likely to shape the future directions of community policing.

In the first selection, Professors Alpert, Dunham, and Piquero review the literature surrounding neighborhoods and crime, and introduce the importance of neighborhood variation on the role of policing. They develop the critical need for law enforcement to understand the neighborhood characteristics and the infrastructure of informal social control before strategies of policing are developed.

In the second selection, Professor Mark Moore discusses the theories underlying both problem solving and community-oriented policing. His article develops potential risks and benefits of community-oriented policing for law enforcement and the community.

In the third selection, (the late) Professor Shaw reviews the findings of a program whose purpose was to target the reduction of guns in Kansas City. In particular, Shaw focuses on public opinion of the police and the program. He reports public support for intensive police efforts which target guns.

The fourth selection in this section is written by Professors Bayley and Shearing. These authors examine the risks and rewards associated with the restructuring of policing in democratic society. They conclude that the future of policing will include a transition based on the fear about security. They also look to the private sector to supplement the efforts of government.

In the fifth selection, Professors Zhao, Thurman, and Lovrich investigate the extent of organizational change and community-oriented policing. In particular, the authors pay due attention to the reciprocal relationship between individual employee values and organizational reform.

In the final selection, Professors Webb and Katz present findings from a community survey of citizens who rated the importance of police practices commonly associated with community policing. Their work is critical as it is one of the few studies that has looked at the factors that influence citizens' opinions of the importance of community-policing activities.

17

On the Study of Neighborhoods and the Police

Geoffrey Alpert, Roger Dunham and *Alex Piquero*

The study of neighborhoods in criminology and criminal justice traces its heritage back to the pioneering work of Shaw and McKay (1942). Repeatedly finding that delinquents came from certain areas within major urban cities, Shaw and McKay developed their version of social disorganization theory. In this approach, crime is essentially the result of a breakdown of informal controls which include the norms and values of the neighborhood culture. This breakdown, in part, is caused by the growth and urbanization of large cities. While growth can yield certain benefits, the growth that accompanied such cities in the late nineteenth and early twentieth centuries, however, came at a price. Poverty, homelessness, crime, and other social problems directly affected the viability and quality of life in large urban centers (e.g., Jacobs 1961; Skogan 1988).

Throughout this growth, one of the early functions of developing urban police forces was to establish social regulation to supplement their law-enforcement duties. This need was created as police effectiveness declined, as urbanization increased, and as communities became more cosmopolitan (Black 1980; Kelling 1985). In the most disorderly parts of American cities, the traditional police officer became an "institution" who responded to a "moral mandate" for informal social control in situations where individuals violated community or neighborhood norms and impinged on the personal and property rights of others. This role, often referred to as the "street justice" function (Sykes 1986), or "order maintenance," refers to police behavior that is responsive to situational and organizational factors which reflect the interpretations of community needs and expectations by the police. "Street justice," then, is a response to a community or neighborhood man-

Source: Prepared especially for *Community Policing: Contemporary Readings.*

date that something be done about situations where formal institutions cannot or will not respond for a variety of reasons.

The purpose of this article is to suggest that an understanding of neighborhood characteristics and the infrastructure of informal social control networks are necessary prior to the establishment of tailored policing strategies, particularly those centered around community policing. In other words, policing strategies, particularly those which attempt to instill a sense of informal social control, must be linked with existing neighborhood dynamics. If the dynamics of particular neighborhoods are not well understood, then police approaches to crime may be ill-founded.

The first part of this article presents a brief overview of neighborhoods. The second part of the article reviews the literature on models of informal social control. The third part of the article examines police behavior and strategies within neighborhood contexts. The final part of the article discusses how the integrated study of neighborhoods and police strategies is important in understanding the strengths and weaknesses of implementing community policing, particularly in the neighborhoods that require it the most.

Neighborhoods

The neighborhood is frequently described as though it were a continuation of small-town America, a place where a true community spirit exists. When police focus on these smaller units, it allows them the opportunity to move closer to the people, and to respond more fully to their unique needs. A decentralization of police administration and an increased awareness of neighborhood differences should turn the focus of policing to meet the needs of those who share a common fate and a common style of life. It can be argued that the smaller geographical area is critical for many other social processes as well as generating strong neighborly relationships, mutual aid through volunteer organizations, and other social support networks.[1]

The study of neighborhoods has preoccupied scholars since the turn of the century (see Olson 1982; Bursik and Grasmick 1993). Cooley (1909) conceptualized the neighborhood as one of the three principal forms of social organization exemplifying the "primary group" (other than the family and children's play groups). In essence, neighborhoods may be seen as a transactional setting that influences individual behavior and development both directly and indirectly (Elliott et al. 1996:391). Park's (1915:579–580) definition of a neighborhood inspired a research agenda that has continued to this day:

> In the course of time every section and quarter of the city takes on something of the character and qualities of its inhabitants. Each separate part of the city is inevitably stained with the peculiar sentiments of its population. The effect of this is to convert what was at first a mere geographical expression into a neighborhood, that is to say, a locality with sentiments, traditions, and a history of its own . . . In the social and political organization of the city it is the smallest local unit.

Beginning in the 1950s, however, the neighborhood concept came under strong attack. Critics of the concept claimed that the role of the residential community had weakened (Keller 1968; Stein 1960; Webber 1970). They argued that the neighborhood was no longer important to the identity and sense of belonging of its inhabitants, and that local units of population were no longer able to establish and maintain a stable moral order. Even though other criticisms of the concept exist (Janowitz 1967; Greer 1962), there has persisted for many, a sense of local sentiment, close-knit networks, and a stable moral order, especially in working-class, culturally homogenous neighborhoods (Greenberg and Rohe 1986; see also Suttles 1972). Rather than spending too much time on defining and conceptualizing the functional form of a neighborhood, perhaps it would be beneficial to examine how and under what conditions the local community is related to social integration at the different levels of society (see also Olson 1982:508).

Our use of the neighborhood focuses on the social unit, rather than the ecological unit. This distinction between ecological factors and dimensions of social organization is important in clarifying the difference between the urban community and the urban neighborhood as Olson (1982:495) notes:

> Whereas the urban community represents ecological considerations of human life, particularly the social space involved in the daily transactions of sustenance, the urban neighborhood represents the patterns of social organization (located in residential areas) focused on day-to-day activities.

Therefore, our conceptualization, like that of Park, Burgess and McKenzie (1925) is to categorize sections of the city as "natural areas" where residents share common lifestyles, are of the same cultural types, are a relatively social group, and have identifiable boundaries (see also Greenberg and Rohe 1986:85). The definition used here incorporates the idea that residents of different neighborhoods are marked by a particular pattern of life, and perhaps even a subculture of their own with social traditions. At the very least, within its physical and symbolic boundaries, a neighborhood contains inhabitants having something in common. Even if this commonality is only the current sharing of an environment, it gives the residents a certain collective character and alternatives for adapting to the larger society (Keller 1968:90). The importance of the neighborhood as the unit of analysis lies in its dual characteristic of combining both ecological and interpersonal aspects of human interaction (Caplow and Foreman 1950:357).[2]

Neighborhoods will differ in the types of characteristics shared by their members as well as the level of intensity to which these residents adhere to the characteristics. Some neighborhoods will include members who share many common goals and values, while others will have members who share relatively few characteristics. There is no set rule for what constitutes a common goal, as often commonalities change and the intensity to which one believes in them fluctuate. What is important is the sense of security one has with his or her neighbors. Integration at the neighborhood level, then, can be defined as the tendencies within the small and relatively homogenous residential area that give its residents a common orientation, a sense of belonging and participation that they find absent in the larger society. This sense of integration at the neighborhood level, so long as it exists, makes them feel a part of the larger society by providing them with ways of adapting to an interfacing with the larger system. In sum, a cohesive neighborhood structure provides a way for residents to identify with and relate to the larger society, and therefore is a component of social integration.

Social Control within Neighborhoods

Cohesive neighborhoods are an important source of informal social control. Park and his colleagues (1925:23) contrast the potential for social control between face-to-face primary relations (such as those found in cohesive neighborhoods) and indirect or secondary relations characteristic of larger urban areas:

> The interactions which take place among the members of a community so constituted (such as a cohesive neighborhood) are immediate and unreflecting. Intercourse is carried on largely within the region of instinct and feeling. Social control arises, for the most part spontaneously, and in direct response to personal influences and public sentiment. It is the result of personal accommodation, rather than the formulation of a rational and abstract principle.

When these intimate relationships of the primary groups are weakened, social control is gradually dissolved. According to Park et al. (1925:26), the resulting indirect or secondary relationships have a much different effect on social control:

> It is characteristic of city life (in the absence of neighborhood cohesion) that all sorts of people meet and mingle together who never fully comprehend one another. The anarchist and the club men, the priest and the Levite, the actor and the missionary who touch elbows on the street still live in totally different worlds. So complete is the segregation of vocational classes that it is possible within the limits of the city to live in an isolation almost as complete as that of some remote rural community.

Park and his colleagues observed differences between social control based upon mores and neighborhood cohesion, and social control based upon indirect and secondary relationships and positive law. The latter is much weaker and less capable of establishing order.

In 1986, Greenberg and Rohe reviewed the empirical research on the relationship between informal control and crime. They concluded that emotional attachment to the neighborhood, perceived responsibility for the control over the neighborhood, and the expectation that onself or one's neighbors would intervene in a criminal event, are associated with low crime rates. This evidence suggests a relationship between informal control of a cohesive neighborhood and crime. Greenberg and Rohe suggest that more research should be conducted on the process by which norms for public behavior develop in neighborhoods and are communicated to residents.

Informal social control in the residential context refers to the development, observance, and enforcement of local norms for appropriate public behavior (Greenberg and Rohe 1986:80). It is the process by which individual behavior is influenced by a group, and usually functions to maintain a minimum level of predictability in the behavior of group members, and to promote the well-being of the group as a whole. Formal social control, on the other hand, is based on written rules or laws and prescribed punishments for violating these rules and laws. The police and the courts are the institutions most directly charged with maintaining order under formal social controls. The means of formal social control are not very effective without the direct support of the informal means of control. While the intersection of the two are particularly important for effective control of crime, much of the recent research has been centered around informal control models. We now turn to a brief review of two of the most prominent models of informal social control: the systemic model of Bursik and Grasmick (1993) and Taylor's (1997) expansion of Bursik and Grasmick's model.

Models of Informal Social Control

Informal control may take the form of close surveillance or questioning, or verbal correction of behavior seen as inappropriate in the local context (Greenberg and Rohe 1986). Within this notion, Bursik and Grasmick differentiate three levels of resident-based control. They separate informal social control into the primary level (i.e., family members and close friends), the parochial level (i.e., acquaintances within a neighborhood), and the public level (i.e., links between neighborhoods and outside actors). While the control processes operating at each level are qualitatively different, the primary level of control is "grounded in the intimate informal primary group that exist in the area" (Bursik and Grasmick 1993:16).

In essence, Bursik and Grasmick's systemic model of neighborhood crime contains four key characteristics. First, systemic approaches emphasize ongoing patterns of information exchange as reflected in the networks and ties among the components of a system. There is a complex set of affiliations between members of friendship groups, kinship groups, and associations in a community. The function of these networks is to regulate behavior. The second component of their model suggests that social disorganization is characterized by varying degrees of "systemness" (see Buckley 1967:42). This refers to the notion that an organized neighborhood may be reflected in a variety of social structures.

The third part of the systemic model suggests that aspects of a system's structure may change from time to time or even continuously without the dissolution of the system itself (Buckley 1967:43). Relational networks are embedded in a larger system of relationships. Therefore, just as networks bind the residents of particular neighborhoods into a systemic structure, the individual neighborhoods also have ties among themselves that bind them into the broader ecological structure of the city (Bursik and Grasmick 1993:177). Finally, Bursik and Grasmick (p. 118) suggest that systems not only engage in interchanges with the environment, but that this interchange is an essential factor underlying the system's viability, its reproductive ability or continuity, and its ability to change (e.g., Buckley 1967:52).

Taylor (1997) expands Bursik and Grasmick's notion of control at the parochial level in three ways. First, Taylor recognizes within-neighborhood variations in informal social control and responses to disorder. Second, he acknowledges the central importance of street blocks as durable features of the everyday environment connecting residents to broader ecological dynamics in their neighborhoods. Finally, Taylor develops microecological principles, analogous to human ecological principles to better understand the connections between street block and community-level ecological dynamics.

A general theme evident throughout Taylor's (1997:116) expansion of the systemic model suggests that street blocks need to be considered within the context of the overall neighborhood and its position within the broader urban landscape. This is a significant contribution to the systemic model because Taylor acknowledges that there can be different responses to crime and disorder within one neighborhood at the street-block level. Consider the following example. In a neighborhood in an inner-city, there is a four-by-four-block radius which is known as "Coventry City." Within this four-by-four-block neighborhood, crime may be concentrated in a certain area (perhaps one of the blocks where an open-air drug market resides). The residents of that block are likely to have perceptions of fear, disorder, and crime that are significantly higher than those individuals who live three blocks away with little, if any, criminal activity. Therefore, by only conceptualizing the entire neighborhood as the unit of analysis, researchers may be missing the important dynamics that operate at the block level. By reducing the unit of analysis from the neighborhood to the street-block level, then, Taylor sets up a framework within which one could make use of hierarchical modeling (i.e., neighborhoods impact street blocks which in turn, affect individuals) (Bryk and Raudenbush 1992).

These models notwithstanding, informal social control is not present in every neighborhood; rather it is a variable that differs both in form and degree among neighborhoods. In other words, not all neighborhoods have a substantial degree of cohesion with regard to norms and values specifying appropriate public behavior. Many lack any degree of fundamental integration, and thereby the means for an effective informal social control system (Greenberg and Rohe 1986:81). It is this that creates a serious problem for effective policing.

The Neighborhood Context, Crime, and the Police

The results of research on neighborhoods indicate that shared norms are less likely to develop in low-income neighborhoods that are heterogeneous with regard to ethnic composition, family type, or lifestyle, than they are in low-income, culturally homogenous neighborhoods or in middle-class neighborhoods (e.g., Greenberg and Rohe 1986; Merry 1981). Residents of low-income heterogeneous neighborhoods tend to be more suspicious of each other, to perceive less commonality with other residents, and tend to feel less control over their neighborhoods than do the residents of more homogenous neighborhoods.

Low-income neighborhoods which develop strong informal control tend to be characterized by the dominance of one group. As Merry (1981:230–31) emphasizes, "the social order in a neighborhood depends on the presence of a dominant group that perceives itself as responsible for public order." When this influence is absent in low-income neighborhoods, distrust and hostility tend to prevail, leaving only the formal means of social control (police and courts) to control crime and maintain order.

For example, many inner-city black neighborhoods lack this dominant cultural group. Even though the residents are all black, housing discrimination, and other factors result in neighborhoods which vary considerably in the social values, lifestyle and family type characteristic of its residents (Erbe 1975; see also W. J. Wilson 1991). As a result of this diversity, residents have little consensus on conceptions of appropriate public behavior, and informal social control within the neighborhood tends to be weak. In extreme cases, the conceptions of appropriate public behavior are in conflict among neighborhood residents.

The situation in many predominantly white, middle-class neighborhoods is much different. These neighborhoods tend to be more homogenous due to self-selection resulting from the greater freedom of choice in locating a residence. Residents tend to self-select their location based upon similarities of other residents of family type, lifestyle, and values. This process tends to group residents according to their basic underlying assumptions of appropriate public behavior and values. Therefore, informal social controls tend to be much more developed in these types of neighborhoods, when compared to low-income neighborhoods.

It is this and other types of neighborhood differentiation that requires the police to fully understand the social milieu within which they are operating. A substantive knowledge of neighborhood differences must be developed, and police must respond to those different characteristics in controlling crime and protecting residents. A failure to do this often results in the formal system of social control attempting to operate alone or even in opposition to the more powerful informal system of social control. There is, then, an important place for the police function within this informal control structure in all types of neighborhoods. As Wilson and Kelling (1982:34) point out:

> The essence of the police role in maintaining order is to reinforce the informal control mechanisms of the community itself. The police cannot, without committing extraordinary resources, provide a substitute for that informal control. On the other hand, to reinforce those natural forces the police must accommodate them.

A considerable amount of research suggests that neighborhood contextual factors are important to the related aspect of the overall crime problem (Simcha-Fagan and Schwartz 1986). In addition, the influence of neighborhood factors on police behavior has also been of interest to police researchers. A great deal of this interest concerns the issue of neighborhood stigma and the police response to residents in a discriminatory manner consistent with a specific neighborhood identity.

Moreover, in many neighborhoods, there is a perception of the police as "outsiders" who have little understanding of or sympathy for the residents of the communities they are patrolling (McConville and Sheperd 1992). This perception, oftentimes, is a function of neighborhood cultures that vary along racial and class differences (Jacob 1971). As Podolefsky (1983) and Skogan (1988) suggest, even when neighborhood community-based crime prevention programs have been established through the initiatives of the police, the efforts oftentimes face a significant degree of resentment from local residents who feel that law enforcement officers have a limited understanding of the problems the residents face on a daily basis. Even with an increasing emphasis on the development of police-community partnerships, unfortunately the communities that need help the most, more often than not, cannot sustain the existence of programs with or without police involvement due to their inability to effectively mobilize (Walker 1992:190). The result of this, of course, is that extremely impoverished communities have very little potential for the establishment of the necessary relationships to create informal social control networks.

Research examining the link between neighborhood characteristics and crime began with the work of Shaw and McKay (1942). The majority of the work conducted since their pioneering research has been devoted to aggregate-level analysis and to examining and elaborating their propositions (e.g., Cohen and Land 1984; Sampson 1985; Bursik and Webb 1982). In summarizing this research, Sampson (1995:201) suggests that communities characterized by (a) anonymity and sparse acquaintanceship networks among residents, (b) unsupervised teenage peer groups and attenuated control of public space, and (c) a weak organizational base and low social participation face an increased risk of crime and violence. Add to this the fact that crime is concentrated in a relatively small number of locations within a city (e.g., Sherman, Gartin and Buerger 1989), the implications for formal level enforcement by the police are substantial.

Police Behavior and Strategies within a Neighborhood Context

In terms of neighborhood context and police behavior, early work by Banton (1964:181) suggested that the police departments provide different services in different neighborhoods (see also Bordua 1958). Police research in the past forty years has helped develop the theme that to understand police behavior, one must consider the neighborhood context in which the police operate (Werthman and Piliavin 1967; Sherman 1986; Smith 1986; Skolnick and Bayley 1986; Taub, Taylor and Dunham 1984; Decker 1981; Cao, Frank and Cullen 1996; Webb and Marshall

1995). The primary focus of this line of research has been to assess the degree to which discretionary police behavior, such as making arrests, filing reports of crimes, and exercising coercive authority toward citizens are influenced by the type of neighborhood in which the encounters between the police and the citizens occur.

Early work in this area by Schuman and Gruenberg (1972:386) found that the primary factor explaining satisfaction and dissatisfaction with police services was the neighborhood. They found race to be an important factor as well, but the within-race variation was largely accounted for by neighborhood. Walker and his colleagues (1972) also found neighborhood context to be an important factor in attitudes toward the police and more specifically, in the amount of support residents gave to the police. The general finding from this study was that involuntary contacts with the police contributed to the more negative attitudes exhibited by blacks than by others toward the police. However, they found that it was the nature of the contact and the cumulative contextual effect within the neighborhood that best accounted for the low level of support for the police shown among blacks.

Sherman (1986:347) argues that there is considerable variation among neighborhoods in the ways the police manage resources, exercise discretion, and decide when to respond to problems. Yet, he concludes, there is little relativity in basic police strategy. Because of this, he argues for a mixed-strategy model to policing particular communities based upon their unique characteristics (see also Whyte 1943). Unfortunately, there is little empirical research assessing the assumption that residents of neighborhoods or communities have distinct preferences or dislikes for specific police strategies or practices. Indeed, it is unclear whether these preferences or dislikes vary from one type of neighborhood to another.

In an attempt to shed light on this issue, Smith (1986) used data from 5,688 police-citizen contacts in three metropolitan areas and observed that police act differently in different neighborhood contexts. From this, Smith (1986:314) identified two specific questions: (1) To what extent do characteristics of neighborhoods directly influence police behavior after controlling for the influence of encounter-specific or situational factors on police behavior?; and (2) To what degree do police respond differently to cues in encounters in different types of neighborhoods?[3] Both of these questions concern the degree to which police actions are influenced by the neighborhood context in which the encounters with citizens occur.

In much the same way that people select which places to go at night based on perceptions of safety, a substantial portion of research has focused on how the police categorize the "good" and "bad" neighborhoods. This process has been called "ecological contamination" (Smith 1986). In other words, police react as if everyone in the "bad" areas is suspect, and treat them harshly, as though they possess the moral liability of the particular area. Smith found that suspects encountered by police in lower-status neighborhoods were three times more likely to be arrested compared to offenders encountered in higher-status neighborhoods, regardless of type of crime, race of offender, offender demeanor, and victim preference for arrest.

Alpert and Dunham (1988) examined attitudinal differences in five culturally distinct neighborhoods in Miami. Neighborhood comparisons revealed a number of differences. For example, Hispanic groups, who displayed support for the police in general, also reported high levels of agreement with specific forms of policing, but did not support the use of ethnic distinctions in directing police activities. Also, there existed a general agreement among all of the groups (i.e., whites, blacks, and Hispanics) that, to be effective, police must use discretion in following police procedures, a finding which appears to indicate considerable citizen support for individualized policing styles. Another finding from their study suggested that, overall, blacks were much more negative and suspicious toward the police than Hispanics. Perhaps, the most important findings from Alpert and Dunham's study of Miami neighborhoods suggested that residence in a specific neighborhood was a more influential factor than gender or ethnicity in explaining variation in attitudes towards policing.[4]

While this line of research has shown that police action varies systematically across neighborhood context, no research has attempted to develop a systematic theory linking police behavior to the context in which it occurs. Klinger (1997), however, has attempted to fill this void. Specifically, four properties that are part and parcel of patrol work—normal crime, victim deservedness, officer cynicism, and workload—are hypothesized to lead to variation in comportment rules across police districts (p. 293). In addition, Klinger's theory of the ecology of police behavior attempts to explain why officers who patrol districts with higher levels of crime and other forms of social deviance tend to police in a more lenient fashion than officers who patrol lower crime districts in the same neighborhood (p. 279). In other words, as district crime rates increase, deviant acts must be more serious to prompt a given label of police vigor. Similarly, officers in a low-crime district, for example, are less cynical, view less crime as normal, view victims as more deserving, and have more time on their hands than their peers working in a high-crime district. Such perceptions lead these officers to handle situations with greater vigor. By paying attention to police districts and their boundaries, Klinger (p. 299) draws attention to the fact that similar neighborhoods can experience different levels of policing depending upon the level of deviance in the police district in which they are situated.

Having shown the importance of neighborhood context, we now discuss the implications of this context with regard to the philosophy of community policing.

The Community Policing of Neighborhoods

Perhaps emanating from a failure of the professional model of policing, many police departments around the country have returned to a more "order-maintenance" model of policing otherwise referred to as community policing. In general, the community policing model refers to police behavior which is responsive to situational and organizational factors that reflect the interpretations of community needs and expectations by the police (see generally Sykes 1986; Skolnick and Bayley 1988; Moore 1992).[5] The major theme of the community policing model is increased interaction between the police and the community, or between the informal control system of the neighborhood and the formal control system of the police. The most common elements of this model include: increased involvement of the community in getting the police job done; increased nomination of problems by the community for police to address; the permanent assignment of police officers to a neighborhood in order to cultivate better relationships with citizens; setting police priorities consistent with the specific needs and desires of the community; and meeting these needs by the allocation of police resources and personnel otherwise assigned to responding to calls for police assistance.

The purpose of the community policing model is to achieve a greater emphasis on non-adversarial problem solving in lieu of traditional strategies which conflict with normative structures in the neighborhood. Non-adversarial policing is achieved through the development of specific tasks and policing strategies which should be based upon a combination of law enforcement requirements, community needs, and techniques of crime prevention. Similarly, Greene (1987:1) emphasizes that community policing is an attempt to clarify the relationship between the formal and informal systems of social control.

Perhaps the first major attempt in the 1980s to implement aspects of community-oriented policing was New Jersey's "Safe and Clean Neighborhoods Program" (Wilson and Kelling 1982). This program instituted foot patrols in twenty-eight New Jersey cities. Evaluations of the effectiveness of these foot patrols indicated that they did not reduce crime or victimization, but they did make citizens feel safer and they did maintain order in the communities they patrolled. Further, the officers involved in the program reported higher levels of job satisfaction than other officers.

Since then, a number of programs that have implemented community policing in one form or another have been developed. In their review of eight community policing strategies implemented in several cities, Greene and Taylor (1988:36–37) conclude that there was not much consistency in findings across the studies; the results of the studies disagree on the effectiveness of foot patrols in reducing crime. Similar inconsistencies are reported in the findings regarding the reduction of the fear of crime. Nevertheless, evaluations designed to measure officer attitudes regarding community policing suggest that more often than not, officers generally have a positive view of the philosophy and their role in it (Rosenbaum, Yeh and Wilkinson 1994). Moreover, officers designated as community policing officers do yield arrest and enforcement patterns that differ from their more traditional, law-enforcement oriented officers (Mastrofski, Snipes and Supina 1996).

On a related topic, community policing is very much concerned with disorder and its effects in neighborhoods (Wilson and Kelling 1982; Kelling and Coles 1996). Disorder and its relationship to crime and the decay of America's neighborhoods has received a considerable amount of research attention in recent years. Skogan's (1990) examination of crime, community policing, and disorder in

Houston and Newark evaluated the effectiveness of many attempts made by police to alleviate those problems.

The Houston phase of the program focused on two problems: (a) lack of contact between citizens and police and (b) a nonexistent neighborhood life. To help address these problems, the Houston police set up a community station, created a community organizing response team, and a citizen contact patrol. The results indicated that disorder of all kinds decreased, and satisfaction with the area and police service increased, though the evidence on fear of crime was mixed (Skogan 1990:107). Perhaps the most important finding, however, suggested that those at the lower end of the status ladder were severely underrepresented in terms of awareness and contact with the programs, and were unaffected by them.

In Newark, police set up an intensive enforcement program that included: street sweeps to reduce loitering and disruptive behavior; foot patrol to enforce laws and maintain order; radar checks to enforce traffic regulations; bus checks to enforce ordinances and maintain order aboard the buses; and roadblocks to identify drivers without proper licenses or under the influence of alcohol. In addition, the city of Newark intensified city services that would improve garbage collection, as well as setting up a sentencing program that put youths to work in community service. The community policing part of the program addressed several causes of fear identified by the planning force in Newark including a lack of information on what to do about crime, a lack of communication between citizens and the police, and a high level of disorder in the city's neighborhoods. This phase of the program included the opening of a community station, the initiation of a citizen contact patrol, the establishment of a neighborhood police newsletter, and a neighborhood clean-up program.

The results in Newark suggested that the intensive enforcement program, as well as the community policing program, appeared to reduce the level of social disorder problems in the area, though the intensive enforcement program did not appear to reduce the fear of crime. In addition, the community policing program reduced physical and social disorder as well as the fear of crime, while increasing area satisfaction and police performance. The difference between Houston and Newark could have been due to the fact that Newark's program was much more visible (Skogan 1990:123).

In sum, it appears that certain police strategies, tailored to the needs of the community, can have some impact in reducing crime, fear of crime, disorder, and also on increasing citizen satisfaction with police services. We now discuss the implications of the relationship among neighborhoods, crime, and the police for police practice and police research.

Discussion and Conclusion

The duties and expectations of the police are extremely complex. Not only are the police charged with the duty of protecting lives, but they are charged with maintaining order, enforcing the law, and providing a variety of social services. In a society as diverse as ours, there are bound to be different priorities placed on these demands by different people who live in different geographic areas and perhaps within these same jurisdictions. In addition, police officers are not all the same, do not have similar opinions or expectations, do not have the same style and do not perform at the same level. In fact, police departments may operate under a number of separate philosophies and these differences influence the policies which allocate resources and ultimately determine how a police department and its officers operate in the neighborhoods they serve. This is important since no currently existing police department in the United States is entirely community policing oriented (Bayley 1995).

Given the different character of cities and neighborhoods, police administrators must decide how to allocate their scarce resources. In other words, administrators have to make policies concerning how well-trained the officers are going to be, in what they will be trained, how they will be deployed, what their enforcement priorities will be, and what tactics they will use. This requires administrators to place priorities on police officers' use of time, choice of activities, and overall style of dealing with the public.

A strategic factor in the administration of resources is the style of law enforcement desired by the community that is served by the police department. Citizen leaders can set reasonable boundaries on police actions, and these usually depend upon the social, economic, and political characteristics of the community. Police chiefs must respond to the differences among communities and should balance the tasks their officers perform to include the conceptual categories outlined by J. Q. Wilson (1968) some time ago.

Effective neighborhood policing requires that police administrators acquire adequate information of the specific neighborhood. This includes a knowledge of the informal social control structure of the neighborhood, attitudes about the police, policing strategies, and styles. This information can be obtained from citizen surveys, census data, community advisory groups, and from neighborhood leaders. After accumulating the information, police administrators can decide how to deal with any incongruence between the neighborhood context and police policies, strategies, and styles. Some of these differences can be reduced with campaigns to educate the citizens and change public opinion and attitudes. In other cases, discrepancies can be reduced with training programs for officers who are assigned to the areas. The training can focus on neighborhood-specific strategies, appropriate styles for the specific neighborhood, and placing priorities on tasks consistent with the neighborhood's expectations.

From data collected from the neighborhoods, police strategies for community policing will be grounded in empirical data. With this in mind, the two fundamental features of a new police strategy include (a) the role of private citizens in the control of crime and maintenance of public order and (b) the role of police in being active, accessible participants in community affairs (Moore and Kelling 1983:65). After all, police patrol both places and people, and research suggests that police do act differently in different neighborhood contexts (Smith 1986:337).

Our model will work most effectively in homogenous neighborhoods, and in areas where police administrators have strong control of their officers. It is important that police officers work for the community, not merely to impress their supervisors. That is why it is so important for community members to provide information to police administrators. Some cities will find it quite reasonable to split police jurisdictions to use our model, as many geographic locations attract or limit certain groups of people. Other cities may find their demographic mixture just too complex to divide a police jurisdiction for this type of policing.

Regardless of the administrative level of commitment, patrol officers can be in the best position to understand the varied and changing needs of the community, and with input from research and training, appropriate activities can be devised to control crime and provide service. The model elaborated upon here utilizes the individual officer's talents and experiences to provide expert assistance to the neighborhood. It is they who can provide a sense of balance to community relations within the context of law enforcement.

Further, the structure of the police administration determines how much influence the police officer has in his or her patrol area. Smith (1984), for example, argued that organizational and supervisory structures of police agencies influence police decision making in encounters with offenders. To some extent, aggregating police behavior within neighborhoods may be measuring processes that operate at a higher level of aggregation (Smith 1986:340). Higher levels of aggregation may include the department and its leaders, or perhaps even local political bodies, and their respective leaders. Regardless, examination of neighborhood context and police practices cannot exist in a vacuum. Examination of these levels is necessary for a better understanding of how neighborhood context influences police behavior.

In addition, it is our suggestion that a police department incorporate a total commitment to neighborhood intervention and community evaluation. There is a price to pay for such enhanced community involvement in policing. This price tag includes chipping away at some traditional police activities and perhaps adding or changing administrative controls. In addition, research shows that citizens who have confidence and trust in the police will take a more active role in reporting crime than those citizens who do not have confidence or trust in the police. This is likely to lead to a higher reported crime rate and the corresponding need for more officers and a greater capacity to process criminals through the justice system (Dukes and Alpert 1980). There is also an economic price to pay for data collection, data analysis, and the special police training that is entailed in community policing, but policing in America can take this information and integrate it into its operating procedure.

Unfortunately, there is no guarantee that this model or any other reform will be an acceptable answer to a yet unsolved problem. It is, however, a move toward something Sir Robert Peel would have been proud to see.

Notes

[1] We choose not to use the concept of community because it has been used by sociologists and others with so many different shades of meaning that it is difficult to understand and discuss with any degree of precision (e.g., Poplin 1979:4).

[2] Taylor (1997) has further reduced the unit of analysis to street blocks within neighborhoods.

[3] Recently, there have been numerous discussions in the literature concerning the impact of offender characteristics, particularly the demeanor of a suspect, and how it influences police decisions to arrest. Since this issue is not of central importance to the task at hand, interested readers should consult (Klinger 1994, 1996; Lundman 1994; Mastrofski, Snipes and Supina 1996; Worden and Shepard 1996).

[4] Our concentration on the relationship between neighborhoods, crime, and police should not preclude the fact that neighborhood contexts also influence a number of other social problems. For example, neighborhood effects, particularly within inner-city neighborhoods, exist for joblessness, welfare receipt, school dropout, rate and years of schooling, teenage childbearing, single parenthood, the level of annual earnings, and political participation among others (W. J. Wilson 1996:265). Similarly, Elliott and his colleagues (1996) evaluated the argument that the effect of poverty on individual development is mediated by the organizational structure and culture of the neighborhood. They found that the effect of ecological disadvantage was mediated by specific organizational and cultural features of the neighborhood, however the unique influence of the neighborhood effects was relatively small. Nevertheless, the authors found that the higher the level of neighborhood disadvantage, the lower the level of informal control.

[5] To be sure, the problem solving model is very similar to the community policing model and oftentimes, the two are hard to distinguish in practice. For reviews of problem-oriented policing, readers should consult Goldstein (1990).

References

Alpert, G., and R. Dunham. 1988. *Policing Multi-Ethnic Neighborhoods*. New York: Greenwood Press.

Banton, M. 1964. *The Police and the Community*. New York: Basic Books.

Bayley, D. 1995. *Police for the Future*. New York: Oxford University Press.

Black, D. 1980. *The Manners and Customs of the Police*. New York: Academic Press.

Bordua, D. 1958. Juvenile delinquency and anomie: An attempt at replication. *Social Problems,* 6:230–38.

Bryk, A. S., and S. W. Raudenbush. 1992. *Hierarchical Linear Models: Applications and Data Analysis Methods*. Newbury Park, CA: Sage.

Buckley, W. 1967. *Sociology and Modern Systems Theory*. Englewood Cliffs, NJ: Prentice Hall.

Bursik, R., and H. Grasmick. 1993. *Neighborhoods and Crime: The Dimensions of Effective Community Control*. New York: Lexington Books.

Bursik, R., and J. Webb. 1982. Community change and patterns of delinquency. *American Journal of Sociology*, 88:24–42.

Cao, L., J. Frank, and F. Cullen. 1996. Race, community context, and confidence in the police. *American Journal of Police*, 15:3–22.

Caplow, T., and R. Foreman. 1950. Neighborhood interaction in a homogeneous community. *American Sociological Review*, 15:357–66.

Cohen, L., and K. Land. 1984. Discrepancies between crime reports and crime surveys: Urban and structural determinants. *Criminology*, 22:499–530.

Cooley, C. 1909. *Social Organization*. New York: Scribner.

Decker, S. 1981. Citizen attitudes toward the police. *Journal of Police Science Administration*, 9(1): 80–87.

Dukes, R., and G. Alpert. 1980. Criminal victimization from a police perspective. *Journal of Police Science Administration*, 8:21–30.

Elliott, D., W. J. Wilson, D. Huizinga, R. Sampson, A. Elliott, and B. Rankin. 1996. The effects of neighborhood disadvantage on adolescent development. *Journal of Research in Crime and Delinquency*, 33(4): 389–426.

Erbe, B. 1975. Race and socioeconomic segregation. *American Sociological Review*, 40:801–12.

Greenberg, S., and W. Rohe. 1986. Informal social control and crime prevention in modern neighborhoods. In R. Taylor (ed.), *Urban Neighborhoods: Research and Policy*. New York: Praeger.

Greene, J. 1987. Foot patrol and community policing: Past practices and future prospects. *American Journal of Police*, 4:1–16.

Greene, J., and R. Taylor. 1988. Community-based policing and foot patrol: Issues of theory and evaluation. In J. Greene and S. Mastrofski (eds.), *Community Policing: Rhetoric or Reality?* New York: Praeger.

Greer, S. 1962. *The Emerging City: Myth and Reality*. New York: Free Press.

Jacob, H. 1971. Black and white perceptions of justice in the city. *Law and Society Review*, 6:69–89.

Jacobs, J. 1961. *The Death and Life of the American City*. New York: Vintage.

Janowitz, M. 1967. *The Community Press in an Urban Setting*. Chicago: University of Chicago Press.

Kelling, G. 1985. Order maintenance, the quality of urban life, and police: A different line of argument. In W. Geller (ed.), *Police Leadership in America: Crisis and Opportunity*. New York: Praeger.

Kelling, G., and C. Coles. 1996. *Fixing Broken Windows*. New York: Free Press.

Keller, S. 1968. *The Urban Neighborhood: A Sociological Perspective*. New York: Random House.

Klinger, D. 1994. Demeanor or crime? An inquiry into why 'hostile' citizens are more likely to be arrested. *Criminology*, 32:475–93.

_____. 1996. More on demeanor and arrest in Dade county. *Criminology*, 34:61–82.

_____. 1997. Negotiating order in patrol work: An ecological theory of police response to deviance. *Criminology*, 35(2): 277–306.

Lundman, R. 1994. Demeanor or crime? The midwest city police-citizen encounters study. *Criminology*, 32:631–56.

Mastrofski, S., J. Snipes, and A. Supina. 1996. Compliance on demand: The public's response to specific police requests. *Journal of Research in Crime and Delinquency*, 33(3): 269–305.

McConville, M. and D. Sheperd 1992. *Watching Police Watching Communities*. London: Routledge.

Merry, S. 1981. *Urban Danger: Life in a Neighborhood of Strangers*. Philadelphia: Temple University Press.

Moore, M., and G. Kelling. 1983. To serve and protect: Learning from police history. *Public Interest*, 70:49–65.

Olson, P. 1982. Urban neighborhood research: Its development and current focus. *Urban Affairs Quarterly*, 17:491–518.

Park, R. 1915. The city: Suggestions for the investigation of human behavior. *American Journal of Sociology*, 20:577–611.

Park, R., E. W. Burgess, and B. McKenzie. 1925. *The City*. Chicago: University of Chicago Press.

Podolefsky, A. 1983. Community response to crime prevention: The mission district. *Journal of Community Action*, 1:43–48.

Poplin, D. 1979. *Communities: A Survey of Theories and Methods of Research*. New York: Macmillan.

Rosenbaum, D., S. Yeh, and D. Wilkinson. 1994. Impact of community policing on police personnel: A quasi-experimental test. *Crime and Delinquency*, 40(3): 331–53.

Sampson, R. 1985. Neighborhood and crime: The structural determinants of personal victimization. *Journal of Research in Crime and Delinquency*, 22:7–40.

_____. 1995. The community. In J. Q. Wilson and J. Petersilia (eds.), *Crime*. San Francisco: ICS Press.

Schuman, H., and B. Gruenberg. 1972. Dissatisfaction with city services: Is race an important factor? In H. Huhn (ed.), *People and Politics in Urban Society*. Beverly Hills: Sage.

Shaw, J., and H. McKay. 1942. *Juvenile Delinquency and Urban Areas*. Chicago: University of Chicago Press.

Sherman, L. 1986. Policing communities: What works? In A. Reiss and M. Tonry (eds.), *Crime and Justice: An Annual Review of Research*. Chicago: University of Chicago Press.

Sherman, L., P. Gartin, and M. Buerger. 1989. Hot spots of predatory crime: Routine activities and the criminology of place. *Criminology*, 27:27–56.

Simcha-Fagan, O., and J. Schwartz. 1986. Neighborhood and delinquency: An assessment of contextual effects. *Criminology*, 24:667–703.

Skogan, W. 1988. Community organizations and crime. In M. Tonry and N. Morris. (eds.), *Crime and Justice: An Annual Review of Research*. Chicago, University of Chicago Press.

_____. 1990. *Disorder and Decline: Crime and the Spiral of Decay in American Neighborhoods*. New York: Free Press.

Skogan, W., and D. Bayley. 1986. Theme and variation in community policing. In M. Tonry and N. Morris (eds.), *Crime and Justice: An Annual Review of Research*. Chicago: University of Chicago Press.

Smith, D. 1984. The organizational context of legal control. *Criminology*, 22:19–38.

_____. 1986. The neighborhood context of police behavior. In A. Reiss and M. Tonry (eds.), *Crime and Justice: An Annual Review of Research*. Chicago: University of Chicago Press.

Stein, M. 1960. *The Eclipse of Community: An Interpretation of American Studies*. Princeton: University of Princeton Press.

Suttles, G. 1972. *The Social Construction of Communities*. Chicago: University of Chicago Press.

Sykes, G. 1986. Street justice: A moral defense of order maintenance policing. *Justice Quarterly*, 3:497–512.

Taub, R., D. G. Taylor, and J. Dunham. 1984. *Paths of Neighborhood Change*. Chicago: University of Chicago Press.

Taylor, R. 1997. Social order and disorder of street blocks and neighborhoods: Ecology, microecology, and the systemic model of social disorganization. *Journal of Research in Crime and Delinquency*, 34(1): 113–55.

Walker, S. 1992. *The Police in America*. New York: McGraw-Hill.

Walker, D., et al. 1972. Contact and support: An empirical assessment of public attitudes toward the police and the courts. *North Carolina Law Review*, 51:43–79.

Webb, V., and C. Marshall. 1995. The relative importance of race and ethnicity on citizen attitudes toward the police. *American Journal of Police*, 14:45–66.

Webber, D. 1970. Order in diversity: Community without propinquity. In R. Gutman and D. Popnoe (eds.), *Neighborhood, City, and Metropolis: An Integrated Reader in Urban Sociology*. New York: Random House.

Werthman, C., and I. Piliavin. 1967. Gang members and the police. In D. Bordua (ed.), *The Police: Six Sociological Essays*. New York: Wiley.

Whyte, W. 1943. *Street Corner Society*. Chicago: University of Chicago Press.

Wilson, J. Q. 1968. *Varieties of Police Behavior*. Cambridge: Harvard University Press.

Wilson, J. Q., and G. Kelling. 1982. The police and neighborhoods safety. *Atlantic Monthly* (March): 29–38.

Wilson, W. J. 1991. Studying inner-city social dislocations: The challenge of public agenda research. *American Sociological Review*, 56:1–14.

_____. 1996. *When Work Disappears: The World of the New Urban Poor*. New York: Albert A. Knopf.

Worden, R., and R. Shepard. 1996. Demeanor, crime, and police behavior: A reexamination of the police services study data. *Criminology*, 34(1): 83–105.

18

Problem Solving and
Community Policing

Mark H. Moore

Recently, much fuss has been made about "problem-solving policing" and "community policing." Proponents herald them as important new concepts that bid to replace "professional law enforcement" as the dominant paradigm of modern policing (Kelling 1988). Critics are more skeptical (Greene and Mastrofski 1988). To some, the ideas are nothing but empty slogans—the most recent public relations gimmicks in policing, devoid of substantive content, and lacking in operational utility (Klockars 1988). Others find attractive content to the ideas but judge them utopian—their popularity rooted in nostalgia. Still others see these new conceptions as distractions from the most urgent challenges now facing policing; against the urgent need to control a rising tide of violence, the interest in problem solving and community relations seems a dangerous avoidance of the real business at hand (Bayley 1988).

This article explores what is known or might reasonably be surmised about the value of problem-solving and community policing. It is necessary, first, to understand what these concepts mean and how they intend to change the practice of policing. These concepts are best understood not as new programmatic ideas or administrative arrangements but as ideas that seek to redefine the overall goals and methods of policing. In the literature on business management, these concepts would be characterized as "organizational strategies" (Andrews 1971). As such, the strengths and weaknesses of the concepts must be considered not only in achieving the traditional operational objectives of police forces such as reducing crime but also

Source: Reprinted by permission of The University of Chicago Press from *Crime and Justice*, edited by M. Tonry and N. Morris, Vol. 15, pp. 99–158. Copyright 1992 by The University of Chicago.

in guiding the future development of police departments and enhancing their public support and legitimacy.

My basic claim is that these ideas usefully challenge police departments by focusing departmental attention on different purposes to be achieved by them and different values to be realized through police operations. These ideas also encourage police to be more imaginative about the operational methods that might be used to achieve police department goals and the administrative arrangements through which these departments are guided and controlled. More particularly, the ideas emphasize the utility of widening police perception of their goals beyond the objectives of crime fighting and professional law enforcement to include the objectives of crime prevention, fear reduction, and improved responses to the variety of human emergencies that mark modern urban life. They also suggest the importance of bringing careful analysis and creative thought to bear on the problems citizens nominate for police attention and to find the solutions to those problems, not only in police-initiated arrests, but instead in a variety of responses by police, communities, and other municipal agencies. They suggest the wisdom of shifting from very centralized command-and-control bureaucracies to decentralized professional organizations.

This article examines the promise of problem-solving and community policing as a means to reduce and prevent crime, to protect and enhance the quality of life in urban America, to secure and strengthen police acceptance of legal and constitutional values, and to achieve heightened accountability of the police to the communities they serve. Section I introduces problem-solving and community policing by describing and distinguishing them, by contrasting them with "professional law enforcement," and by discussing well-documented efforts of individual police departments to adopt them as organizational strategies.

Section II presents the findings of evaluations of early applications of problem-solving and community policing approaches. Of the former, only a handful of evaluations are available. A sizable number of evaluations of recent innovations are pertinent to community policing; these include work on team policing, community relations units, community crime-prevention programs, and various patrol and fear-reduction experiments.

Section III introduces and assesses a variety of objections that have been raised to adoption of these new organizational strategies for policing. These include claims that new policing strategies will unwarrantedly distract police from the core responsibilities of crime prevention and law enforcement, that weakened central authority threatens to politicize the police in bringing them into closer contact with partisan and community political pressures, and that the police will become too powerful and intrusive, to the detriment of both their commitment to constitutional values and their accountability to the public.

Section IV examines problems of implementation. These include problems of limited financial resources, the inherent uncertainties and potential lack of support that discourage innovation, and the police culture's resistance to change. Section V, the conclusion, argues that the promise of these new strategies is bright, even with respect to seemingly intransigent crime problems such as drug dealing and related widespread violence.

I. Defining Problem-Solving and Community Policing

Scholars approach new ideas about policing from three different perspectives. The oldest tradition and, in many ways, the richest, tries to explain why the police behave as they do (Wilson 1968; Bittner 1970; Reiss 1971; Rubenstein 1973; Black 1980). These studies seek to give as accurate and general an account of police behavior as is practically possible and then to lay bare the historical, social, political, and organizational factors that give shape to that behavior.

A second, more recent, tradition relies on scientific methods to assess the impact of police operations on particular objectives—usually reduced crime (Skogan 1977). Some of the most important of these studies have looked generally at the effectiveness of such widely used police methods as random patrol (Kelling et al. 1974), directed patrol (Pate, Bowers, and Parks 1976), rapid response to calls for service (Spelman and Brown 1984), and retrospective investigation (Greenwood, Chaiken, and Petersilia 1977; Eck 1983). Others have looked more narrowly at programs devised to deal with particular problems the police encountered such as domestic assaults (Sherman and Berk 1984), armed robberies (Wycoff, Brown, and Peterson 1980), or burglaries (Clarke 1983).

A third tradition has sought to offer advice to police executives and leaders about how police departments ought to be organized and administered (Wilson 1950; Goldstein 1979; Geller 1985). The goal of such studies has been to define the functions of the police and to recommend particular administrative arrangements for ensuring that the police perform their mandated functions efficiently and effectively.

How problem-solving and community policing are evaluated depends a little on the intellectual tradition within which evaluation is attempted. Scholars from the first tradition might imagine that these concepts were intended as descriptions of how police now behave and measure their worth in terms of the accuracy of that portrayal. Scholars from the second tradition might think of these concepts as new operational programs whose worth could be assessed by gauging their impact on crime or rates of apprehension. Scholars from the third tradition might view these concepts as new ideas about how to manage police forces whose value could be weighed by considering whether the implied structures and managerial processes could be relied on to produce a professional, law-abiding, and law-enforcing organization.

The problem is that the concepts of problem-solving and community policing do not fit neatly into any of these traditions. They are certainly not offered as descriptions of how the police now behave. Indeed, no police departments in the United States can today be accurately characterized as community policing or problem-oriented policing departments.

These ideas could be considered more plausibly as ideas in the second tradition: that is, as new operational approaches to the tasks of policing that may be evaluated in terms of their operational results. This seems reasonable because particular operational programs have been closely identified with community or problem-oriented policing.

For example, foot patrol and the establishment of neighborhood ministations have been linked closely to the concept of community policing, while directed patrol operations, dispute resolution, and the use of other agencies of city government to help eliminate conditions that give rise to crime have sometimes been associated with problem-solving policing. These operational programs become "signature programs" of community or problem-solving policing because they reflect the particular influence of some of the important ideas that are contained in these concepts.

Still, the ways that proponents talk about community and problem-solving policing and the ways that practitioners put them into action do not suggest that the concepts are fully captured by any particular operations program. The ideas suggest a far more general approach to policing than can be captured by reference to any particular operational program.

Perhaps the concepts come closest to being managerial ideas that seek to instruct police executives about the best ways to define their purposes or structure their organizations. They are, after all, offered as advice to executives. Moreover, they seem to entail some important organizational and administrative changes in police departments. For example, community policing seems closely associated with shifts by police organization from centralized, functional, organizational structures to decentralized geographic structures that encourage closer ties with local communities (Moore and Stephens 1991). Problem-solving policing is associated with the decentralization of responsibility to the lowest possible level in the organization, with the encouragement of lateral rather than vertical communications, not only across the department, but also outside the department to other agencies of government (Eck and Spelman 1987).

But, again, these ideas seem quite different from the usual kinds of managerial devices that are studied by police researchers partly because they seem large and fundamental and partly because they do not entirely exhaust the set of managerial ideas that could be associated with problem-solving or community policing.

A. Community and Problem-Solving Policing as "Organizational Strategies"

If the concepts of community and problem-solving policing are not accounts of police behavior or tests of operational programs or managerial recommendations to police executives, what are they? The answer is that they are best understood as new organizational strategies that seek to redefine the mission, the principal operating methods, and the key administrative arrangements of police departments. In this respect, they are ideas more akin to ideas that have emerged from the private-sector management literature than to any of the traditions of police scholarship outlined above.

An important part of that literature is concerned with defining (and redefining) an organization's goals and developing suitable organizational capabilities in the light of environmental demands and opportunities (Andrews 1971). The completion of that task is signaled by the development of something called an "organizational strategy."

An organizational strategy is a declaration of goals to be achieved by a given organization along with detailed plans for achieving them. It is also an account of the principal values that animate the organization's efforts and that regulate the organization's internal administrative relationships and external client relationships. The strategy is justified as a whole by explaining why the particular course of action chosen is a beneficial and feasible one in the light of current environmental challenges and opportunities.

Sometimes the concept is used retrospectively and descriptively to give a coherent account of a past set of actions taken by an organization. For example, the concept might be used to explore the past behavior of an organization and to discover that the organization had an *implicit* strategy that guided its operations and determined its success even if that strategy was never fully articulated by its leaders. Often these historical analyses of the implicit strategies of organizations resemble sociological analyses of the factors that shape the development of particular social institutions.

More often, though, the concept is used prospectively and prescriptively as a device that leaders of organizations might use as an instrument of leadership and organizational development. An organizational strategy is offered as a vision of what the leader of the organization would like the organization to achieve or become. The visions contained in organizational strategies are often cast in terms of "new" purposes that the organization is asked to achieve, or "new" values that the organization is asked to express. For example, a police department might be challenged to assume responsibility for the quality of its responses to calls for service as well as its crime-fighting effectiveness or to embrace the values of promoting tolerance and protecting individual rights as well as ensuring that those who commit crimes are brought to justice.

Commonly, as the example suggests, the new purposes or values being advanced are not really new. They have long been part of the organization's conception of its purposes and goals or an important constraint on its performance. What is new is usually the weight or significance that the old values are given in the new regime. In this respect, the value statements contained in organizational strategies are usually declarations of the direction in which the organization's values should now begin to change *at the margin*. They are not necessarily complete accounts of the whole set of values being advanced by the organization. As statements about how the values should change at the margin, the descriptions of organizational strategies can often be understood only against the backdrop of the organization's past history. Without that perspective, it is difficult to understand in what directions the organization is being encouraged to adjust.

It should be clear by now that there is nearly always some discrepancy between the rhetoric that leaders use to explain and justify their organization's performance and the performance of the organization, but the discrepancy can be viewed in two different lights. Sometimes these discrepancies exist because the leader is using the rhetoric of his organizational strategy cynically to deceive and mystify those whose task it is to oversee the organization's performance. He thereby preserves some continuing scope for the organization to misbehave without penalty and allows a subculture of deceit to arise in the organization. This use of rhetoric is hardly foreign to police departments and leaders.

At other times, leaders use the rhetoric of an organizational strategy to challenge and guide their organization toward new purposes. The rhetoric that goes into defining an organizational strategy is potentially useful in this endeavor because it can expose organizations to increased accountability by openly defining the terms by which the organization is prepared to be held accountable. In this view, a leader's rhetoric about organizational purposes and values establishes an implicit contract with the organization's overseers, clients, and employees to which the organization can be held accountable.

What use leaders make of the rhetoric associated with a particular organizational strategy can ultimately be discovered only by observing the extent to which they establish their accountability to overseers, clients, and employees in terms that are consistent with their avowed aims and by whether they use their administrative tools to nudge the organization toward the purposes and kinds of performances envisioned in their strategy.

Obviously, leaders of organizations can be more or less bold in defining their organizational strategies. A conservative approach defines an organizational strategy in terms of familiar purposes and values that the organization is already organized and trained to achieve. A more radical approach defines a strategy in terms of some new and unfamiliar values and purposes that the organization does not now know how to achieve. This is radical because it exposes the leader to criticism from within and outside the organization and to the possibility of operational failure (Moore 1990).

In principle, even the most radical organizational strategy must encompass an explanation not only of its value but also of its feasibility; otherwise it is disqualified as an appropriate organizational strategy. Indeed, that is what is required of the analyses that go into developing an organizational strategy. A strategy is developed by searching for and finding a "fit" between the organization's capabilities and its environmental opportunities. That, in turn, depends on a simultaneous analysis of two key factors: the challenges and opportunities that are present in the firm's market environment and an assessment of the firm's distinctive capabilities for producing particular products or services that can be used to establish its market niche and identity.

The concept of organizational strategy needs to be modified to some degree to be of use to public sector executives. The environment that concerns them is not only the task environment they encounter (e.g., the level and nature of crime in the society) but also the political and legal environment that supplies them with money and resources to accomplish their goals (e.g., the willingness of budget authorities to provide increased automobiles and equipment and the tolerance of the courts for particular police tactics). Moreover, the "value" they create is not profits to be distributed among shareholders, but the achievement of a set of collectively valued purposes, such as reduced victimization or enhanced security, that justify the public investment in their activities.

The challenge of developing an organizational strategy in the public sector, then, is to find some characterization of the organization's overall mission that will be more or less enthusiastically supported by the political and legal authorizing environment; that, if accomplished, is plausibly of value to the community; and that can be accomplished by the organization's existing (or properly enhanced) operational capabilities.

The concepts of community and problem-solving policing are best understood as proposed new organizational strategies of policing because they seek to redefine the overall purposes of policing, to alter the principal operating programs and technologies on which the police have relied, and to found the legitimacy and popularity of policing on new grounds (Andrews 1971; Moore and Stephens 1991). They aim to do this not only in the minds of police leaders and executives but also in the minds and actions of police officers on the street and in the expectations and evaluations of political leaders and the broader citizenry.

B. The Current Strategy of Policing: Professional Law Enforcement

There is great variety in American policing (Wilson 1968). With 17,000 individual departments, each with different histories, operational challenges, and leadership, a great deal of variation is inevitable (Bayley, 1992). Yet, the surprising fact is that, despite these conditions that favor variety, the basic strategy of policing is remarkably similar from one city to the next. Viewed at a sufficiently high level of abstraction, many things that are significantly different can be made to appear similar. There is, however, a way to describe modern American policing that is sufficiently general to capture much of what currently occurs and yet sufficiently particular to reveal choices not taken in organizing and using police departments. And it is against the backdrop of what has been the dominant strategy of modern American policing—the concept of "professional law enforcement"—that the claims of these new concepts of problem-solving and community policing can be most easily seen, understood, and evaluated.

The essential uniformity of American policing is most immediately obvious in organizational structures. Typically, American police departments are divided into a patrol force that constitutes 60 to 70 percent of the department's personnel, and a detective bureau that makes up another 8 to 15 percent (Farmer 1978). Police departments also often have special squads devoted to specialized activities such as narcotics investigations, juvenile offenses, traffic, and special weapons and tactics. An administrative bureau is responsible for ensuring that the organization is supplied with automobiles, police stations, operational funds, and manpower and accounts for the use of such resources to municipal authorities.

The administrative style of the organization is formally hierarchical, and quasi-military (Bittner 1970). Each officer has a rank and is obliged to take orders from those who outrank him. Elaborate policies and procedures are encoded as standing orders and regulate the conduct of officers. One of the most important jobs of superior officers is to see to it that junior officers' conduct accords with the standing orders. Policies typically flow from the top down, and obedience is expected. The person in command is the person who is responsible for the performance of the unit.

This formal structure guides activity in a working environment quite different from the military organizations and classic production lines for which it was originally created (Wilson 1989). Actual working conditions involve one or two officers working alone without close supervision (Rubinstein 1973). The situations they encounter fall into patterns but it is difficult to describe them as routine. Unusual aspects of the situations that arise often require initiative and invention. In short, the work more closely resembles a hospital emergency room than a military organization at war or a manufacturing production line.

What really determines how police departments operate is not the formal organizational structure or chain of command but the principal operational tactics or programs on which the police rely (Wilson 1989). There are essentially three such tactics: patrol (both random and directed), rapid response to calls for service, and retrospective investigation of crimes. By and large, the patrol division is responsible for the first two, the detectives for the third. Patrol units may differ in how much of their time is committed to directed patrol operations and in what they do when they are not responding to calls for service, but all are connected to the citizenry through telephones, radios, and automobiles that allow police to reach a serious crime call from anywhere in the jurisdiction in under five minutes. Similarly, detective bureaus may differ in their degree of reliance on informants, intelligence files, undercover operatives, and other active methods of investigation, but for the most part, they go to work after a crime has been committed and reported. Their job is to identify the likely culprit and develop evidence to be used at trial.

In most departments, it is taken for granted that the most important responsibility of the police is to control crime and that the most powerful instrument for achieving that objective is to make arrests under the criminal law. Police believe in the power of deterrence and incapacitation to control criminal offenders and keep crime rates low. They also believe strongly in the justice of holding criminal offenders to account for their crimes. They understand that they will be called on by citizens to perform other duties, but the heart of their enterprise is simply "putting bad guys in jail." That is what counts when promotions are handed out and in the locker rooms where "high fives" are given for achievements.

The police also understand that they are creatures of municipal governments, and are, to some degree, accountable to them and through them to the citizenry at large. But police cling to a strong sense of their own independence. They know from their past history that close political ties risk corruption (Fogelson 1977). Moreover, they feel strongly a need for aloofness and authority to do their job. They resist close oversight of their conduct both in individual cases and overall (Geller 1985). They establish popular support in the communities they police by stressing the importance of crime control as an important social objective and by claiming a substantial and distinctive professional competence in achieving that objective. They maintain their legitimacy to use force and the authority of the state by rooting their actions in the obligations of the law.

This can be described as a coherent organizational strategy because it does successfully find a fit between the organization's purposes, its operational capabilities, and its external support. The objective is the successful control of serious crime. Its principal operational capabilities consist of patrol, rapid response, and retrospective investigation. And it finds its support and legitimacy in the popularity of crime control as a purpose and in its commitment to lawfulness in arrests and investigations.

Of course, among police there has always been a certain ambivalence about the role of the law and of legal (as opposed to instrumental) values in controlling the operations of police departments. That ambivalence is reflected to some degree in the distinction between "professional law enforcement" and "crime fighting." When the police take the high road in search of professional autonomy and status, they tend to talk in terms of professional law enforcement rather than crime-fighting, thereby rooting police legitimacy in the law rather than in its instrumental purposes or in politics. Consistency requires that this strategy commit the police to enforcing not only the criminal laws but also those laws that protect citizens from arbitrary action by government agencies—including the police.

At other times, when the police pursue political popularity, they are more apt to talk about themselves as crime fighters, which implies subtly different values that guide the legitimate police departments. The instrumental value of controlling crime and punishing offenders is emphasized; the importance of the law as a constraint on police operations is diminished. The professionalism the police claim changes from a professionalism rooted in legal values and knowledge to one rooted in the technical skills and values associated with putting bad guys in jail.

Police ambivalence about these matters has long been sustained by a similar ambivalence among citizens about the kind of police force they want. The Philadelphia Police Study Task Force (1987) discovered that the citizens of Philadelphia approved strongly of their police force despite believing that officers slept on the job, were rude to citizens, took bribes, and physically abused defendants. One interpretation of these puzzling findings is that the citizens of Philadelphia agreed with the attitude expressed by one police officer who explained: "Look, if we're going to do the hard work of shoveling society's shit and keeping the good folks safe from the bad guys, we ought to be indulged a little bit."

In many American cities, two different deals may have been struck between police departments and their political and legal communities: the public deal—the one that is discussed at Rotary Club meetings—is the commitment to professional law enforcement. The subterranean, implicit deal—the one that is discussed informally and covertly—is the commitment to crime fighting. Insofar as that is true, the distinction between professional law enforcement and crime fighting signals the incompletion of the reform project that sought to internalize legal norms within police departments as important values to be pursued in their operations rather than as constraints on crime-fighting operations. These values remain largely outside the culture of the police.

Still, with the exception of this continuing contradiction, professional law enforcement has been embraced and developed as a coherent strategy of policing. It is often hard for those within and outside the profession to imagine any other style of policing. If, however, one stands back from this dominant strategy of policing, important limitations become apparent—even when evaluated against the announced objectives of controlling serious crime (Neustadt and May 1986; Kelling and Moore 1988). The strategy seems even more limited when one asks the broader question of how municipal police departments might best be used to enhance the quality of life in today's cities. That necessarily involves dealing effectively with crime and violence. But it also means finding ways to deal with drugs, fear, and the unraveling of family and community networks of obligation. Such purposes may not now be defined as police business. They are close enough to current police objectives, however, and the capabilities of the police are sufficiently valuable in addressing them, to make it valuable for the police to redefine their operations to create a greater contribution to their solution.

C. The Limitations of Professional Law Enforcement

An assessment of professional law enforcement as a strategy of policing should begin by observing that it has not so far had a great record in controlling crime. That observation has often been made, and (quite properly) seems to the police to be a cheap shot. They argue that they have done their part well but that they have been let down by the rest of the criminal justice system that has been unable or unwilling to prosecute, convict, and jail those whom police have convincingly accused of crimes. Some, in policing and elsewhere, also argue that adverse changes in society—increasing poverty and unemployment, continuing racism, an increase in the size of crime-prone age groups, the collapse of families, the decay of moral values— tend to increase levels of crime, and that the police and the criminal justice system have done well to keep crime at current levels.

Such finger pointing may well be appropriate and accurate. But if the police are but one factor (and apparently not a very important one) in controlling crime, then that should undermine claims by police that their funding and authority should be increased when crime increases. It should also suggest to police executives the wisdom of founding the popularity and legitimacy of their institutions on some grounds other than effective crime control. Yet these implications have not been widely accepted in policing. The police would like to have it both ways: to be thought to be important, even fundamental, in the nation's attack on crime, and yet not to be held accountable for increasing crime rates.

1. Weakness in Operational Methods. But there is worse news for the strategy of professional law enforcement. Two decades of research have cast doubt on the operational effectiveness of the principal tactics on which the police now rely. We can no longer be confident that patrol deters crime (Kelling et al. 1974), that detectives, working only from evidence at the scene of the crime, can often solve crimes (Greenwood, Chaiken, and Petersilia 1977), or that rapid response results in the apprehension of offenders (Kansas City Police Department 1977–79; Scott 1981; Spelman and Brown 1984; for an alternative view, see Larson and Cahn 1985). Nor can we be sure that arrests, even when followed by successful prosecutions, convictions, and jail terms, produce general deterrence, specific deterrence, or rehabilitation (Blumstein, Cohen, and Nagin 1978). We can still rely on incapacitation to control some crimes by some offenders (Cohen 1978; Greenwood with Abrahamse 1982). And it is certainly too much to claim that these tactics have no effect on levels of crime. Nonetheless, the confidence we had a decade ago in the professional strategy of policing as a set of operational crime-controlling programs has now eroded.

2. The Limits of Reactiveness. Strategists now recognize that the reactive nature of current police strategy sharply limits its crime control potential. Reliance on patrol, rapid response to calls for service, and retrospective investigation virtually guarantees that police efforts to control crime will be largely reactive. Police on patrol cannot see enough to intervene very often in the life of the community. If they wait to be called, they are, by definition, waiting until an offense has occurred. That is particularly true if they view the calls as discrete incidents to be examined for serious law breaking rather than as signs of an underlying problem that has a past and a future (Goldstein 1979).

Being largely reactive has some important virtues. It insures that the police operate at the surface of social life and do not intrude too deeply; vast spaces of privacy are maintained. When the police do intrude, they have clear reason to do so and at least one citizen who supports their intervention—the person who called. In these respects a reactive strategy of policing protects privacy and liberty and economizes on the use of state authority by keeping the state's agents at a distance.

The vices of the reactive strategy have been more apparent than its virtues. To many, it is simply common sense that preventing crimes is better than waiting for them to occur. What this position ignores, however, is that, in waiting, privacy and liberty are protected; and further, that insofar as specific deterrence and incapacitation discourage current offenders from committing future crimes, the current strategy produces future crime prevention. But there are two better arguments about the weakness of the reactive approach than the argument that it is not sufficiently preventive.

First, the reactive strategy is systematically unable to deal with crimes that do not produce victims and witnesses. This has long been obvious in trying to deal with so-called victimless crimes such as prostitution, gambling, and drug dealing. It has recently become clear, however, that many other crimes do not produce victims and witnesses ready to come forward (Moore 1983a). Sometimes people have been victimized and know it but are reluctant to come forward because they are afraid or they are closely related to the offender and reluctant to see him or her arrested, or some combination of the two. It is hard for the reactive strategy to reach systematic extortion or wife battering or child abuse, for the victims do not give the alarm. It may even be hard to get at robbery in housing projects where the victims and witnesses fear retaliation.

It is also difficult for the reactive strategy to reach criminal offenses that produce victims who do not know they have been victimized. Many white-collar crimes ranging from insurance frauds to dumping of toxic waste fall into this category of producing delayed harms. Because such offenses are essentially invisible to a strategy that depends on victims or witnesses raising alarms, such crimes cannot be handled well by a purely reactive strategy.

Second, the reactive strategy weakens the sense of police presence in a community and makes citizens unsure that they can rely on the police to come when they call or to handle the situations that bother them with any kind of responsiveness to their objectives and concerns. Police operating reactively rarely have time to visit victims and witnesses in the days or weeks following their involvement in criminal offenses. Detectives may show up to obtain statements, and prosecutors may call to notify of court appearances, but patrol officers will seldom call again to offer comfort and reassurance.

Similarly, the police for the most part will not get out of their cars to talk to citizens (Sherman 1986, p. 356). And, if called, police will often cut short the encounter if there is no legal action to be taken. Indeed, George Kelling has pointed to the irony that the abrupt end of many encounters with citizens is justified by the desire of the officers to get back "in service"—in service to a dispatcher who may need a car to be dispatched (Moore and Kelling 1983). Finally, the police know little about the people or situations they encounter. In Sherman's words, reactive policing becomes historical, and without a context (1986, p. 356). Taken together, this means that the police feel distant from a neighborhood's citizens: being distant, they seem both unreliable and uncontrollable. The price is that citizens, and particularly those who are afraid, do not call the police and, instead, absorb their losses and live with their fears.

3. Insufficient Preventiveness. Closely related to the charge that professional law enforcement is too reactive is the claim that the current strategy is not sufficiently preventive. Indeed, to some critics, and particularly those who emphasize the failure of the reactive strategy to prevent the crime to which the reactive strategy reacts, the criticisms are identical (Brown 1989). But the argument goes beyond the simple claim that police must wait until a crime occurs before swinging into action to arrest the offender. It emphasizes that there may be factors other than offenders' evil intentions that occasion crimes and that these might be the focus of police interventions. Some commodities (such as guns, alcohol, and drugs) may be criminogenic (Moore 1983b). Some situations (such as festering domestic disputes or dark exits from subway stations or crowded streets with many check-cashing facilities) may facilitate the commission of crimes (Clarke 1983). Perhaps the police could more effectively control crime by reducing the availability of criminogenic commodities or by ameliorating criminogenic conditions than by waiting to apprehend criminals when crimes occur.

A focus on preventive action eventually leads to a concern that police pursuing the strategy of professional law enforcement ignore the potential contributions of many individuals and organizations outside the police department who could contribute to crime-prevention and control objectives. This has long been obvious to police chiefs who urged citizens to support their local police by calling, and many departments have made an effort to enlist citizens in efforts to prevent burglaries through devices such as property marking and security surveys. But the critics argue that the police do not think often enough or carefully enough about how to mobilize individual and collective efforts of citizens or the capabilities of other government agencies such as schools, licensing boards, and recreation departments to take actions that would eliminate some criminogenic conditions (Goldstein 1979).

4. Citizens' Demands for Police Services. Note that these criticisms of professional law enforcement are made within a conception of policing that establishes crime control as the most important, perhaps the only, objective of policing. In essence, these criticisms seek more effective and more far-reaching methods of controlling crime. But other criticisms of the current strategy of policing begin to break out of this frame (Moore and Trojanowicz 1988). They are rooted in observations of what actually happens in police departments and raise troubling questions about whether the police *should* be single-mindedly focused on reacting to serious crimes.

Most calls for police service do not report serious crimes; even fewer report serious crimes in progress (Wycoff 1982). Instead, they request a variety of services. A large portion of them involve emergencies that could deteriorate rapidly and lead to bad consequences unless someone responds quickly with help. But these are rarely crime emergencies. More often, they are social emergencies such as domestic disputes that have not yet become knife fights or children on the street alone at night or the sudden fears of an elderly woman who hears noises or health emergencies like drug overdoses or miscarriages.

To a great degree, a police department pursuing the strategy of professional crime fighting is inclined to see these calls as "garbage calls" that waste their resources and special capabilities and distract them from the main job of being ready to deal with serious crime whenever and wherever it occurs. The only reason the police get these calls is that they work twenty-four hours a day, seven days a week, and are linked to citizens through phones and radios. They must work that way to be able to deal with crime. But police who are committed to professional law enforcement believe it is wrong for them to waste much time with these nonmission-related calls.

There is a different way to look at such calls. Some might be harbingers of future crimes and, if taken seriously now, would prevent a crime later. That is certainly true for domestic assault cases (Wilt et al. 1977). Alternatively, responses to such calls might be important ways for the police to establish a trustworthy presence in the community. That, in turn, might lead to an enhanced flow of information from the community and greater crime deterrence (Skogan and Antunes 1979). In both respects, an improved response to garbage calls might actually improve police crime-control capabilities.

An even more radical way to view such calls is to see them as appropriate claims on the police, and as clues to how *citizens* (as opposed to the police themselves) think the police might best be used. Perhaps the garbage calls should be regarded as falling well within the police mission. If citizens call because they are afraid or because they need help dealing with health and social emergencies, perhaps the police should think of such calls as central to their mission rather than peripheral.

The point becomes sharper when police arrange meetings with citizens to mobilize their assistance; police often discover that citizens are less interested in talking about robbery and burglary than the police expected (Sparrow, Moore, and Kennedy 1990). Instead, they seem to focus on "quality of life" problems such as noisy kids, visible drug dealing, graffiti, and dangerous-looking, rotted-out buildings. In short, citizens keep nominating problems for police attention different from those the police have taken for themselves as their principal purposes. This raises questions about the continuing viability and value of a strategy that assigns these citizens' concerns to the periphery of police consciousness and operational attention.

5. Incomplete Professionalization. The existing strategy of policing has also disappointed citizens and police by failing to establish the legitimacy of the police or to elevate its professional status. Policing continues to be rocked by intermittent scandals and is the continuing object of mistrust and suspicion. While pay has increased and educational standards have been raised, policing remains largely a blue-collar occupation. This is disappointing because enhanced legitimacy and professional status were among the principal objectives of the recent wave of police reform that sustained professional law enforcement as a concept of policing. In retrospect, two factors seem to have thwarted the reformers' purposes.

One is the continuing inability of the police to establish appropriate mechanisms of accountability linking them to the overall structure of city governance and to the citizens. A central idea in professional law enforcement is that the police should be independent of political influence and should take their guidance strictly from the law and the standards of their profession. As noted above, their commitment to the law as a basis of legitimacy has been undermined to some degree by their continued criticism of constitutional restrictions and by the evidence of ongoing (but diminishing) corruption and brutality. They have preferred to base their legitimacy on their own professional standards—hence the popularity of higher educational standards, more training, even the movement to accredit law enforcement agencies (Williams 1989).

The effort to base police legitimacy on their own professionalism (rather than on lawfulness or political responsiveness or a combination of all three) was intrinsically problematic. It makes the police responsible only to themselves and to no one else—always a suspect position in democratic governance. But the police compounded that strategic error by invoking the principle of professional autonomy and independence to defeat all mechanisms of external control, even in situations where strong evidence indicated that the police had failed in their professional duties. Civilian review boards were, for the most part, defeated and probably for good reason (*Civilian Review of the Police* 1980). They were flawed mechanisms of accountability since they focused far too much attention on individual incidents of brutality or corruption, gave far too much power to individual complainants against the police, and failed to hold police departments accountable for improvements in their overall performance. But having defeated these initiatives, the police offered no satisfactory alternatives.

The absence of continuing external accountability may have seemed a real advantage to the police since it spared them the daily pressures of responding to the oversight and criticism of outsiders. It also made them feel in control of their own destiny. But the reality was that, over time, the absence of ongoing accountability weakened police departments. Without any continuing, formal dialogue between the police, their political overseers, and the community about the overall goals and performance of the police, the police lacked any way of advancing their status. They could avoid criticism, but it was hard for them to win praise. As a result, their standing tended to stagnate.

Without ongoing aggregate measurements of their performance, police became extremely vulnerable to the damaging effect of individual incidents that became the focus of intensive news coverage. A shooting or instance of negligence loomed large in the public mind when the public lacked a larger context in which to understand and evaluate an individual incident.

The police gradually became cut off from the aspirations, desires, and concerns of citizens. Increasingly, the important work to be done was defined by the police rather than by the taxpayers who paid their salaries and bought them their equipment. True, the police remained responsive to the citizenry by responding to their calls for service. But in each case, whether a call was important was subjected to police judgments about its urgency. By tying themselves operationally to citizens only through 911 systems, police could neither see nor hear from citizens about problems that were not embodied in particular incidents. Since there were many such problems, the police were increasingly seen as irrelevant to the concerns of citizens.

Finally, from the vantage point of police executives and leaders, insulation from external accountability made it harder for them to challenge their own organizations to perform. In the traditional imagery of professional independence and strong leadership, the insulation of a police chief from political pressures was supposed to enhance his stature and control over the department and to give him the freedom to chart the organization's future. In reality, however, the effect was to make him more vulnerable to the demands of his own troops. That was particularly true in a world in which many chiefs came from inside their departments, already mired in ongoing obligations to departmental friends, and in which police leaders felt obligated to support their own troops, lest morale decline. These powerful informal influences often made chiefs defenders of their own organizations and personnel rather than managers of the organization for the benefit of the public at large. Stronger external accountability would, it seems, have strengthened their hands vis-à-vis their own organizations and made it more likely that the values pursued through the organization's operations actually reflected the values that citizens would have liked to see reflected.

The second major impediment to legitimacy and enhanced professional standing for policing was that the police never seemed fully to embrace the constitutional values that were the only sure path for accomplishing these goals. In society's hierarchy of values, crime fighting is important, but it is less important than the rule of law. As long as the police embraced the former as their principal raison d'être, some avenues of advancement were cut off. Constitutional values were lawyers' values, not police values. As long as the police failed to embrace them (and sometimes even when they did), prosecutors and judges viewed police as suspect. They were also suspect in the eyes of reporters who covered their operations. And they were vulnerable to outside attacks whenever an incident occurred in which legal values seemed to have been sacrificed to crime-control expediency or to individual officer's desires for money or revenge. In short, even with the reform strategy, the police were standing for the wrong values.

The absence of effective accountability mechanisms and police reluctance to embrace constitutional values undermined the efforts of the reform strategy to enhance the legitimacy and professional stature of the police. Attempts to base legitimacy on educational standards and professional accreditation have not filled the gap. As a result, the foundations of policing seem shaky, individual organizations quite vulnerable to scandal, and police leaders vulnerable to scapegoating.

6. The Growth of Private Self-Defense. A last criticism of the professional strategy of policing is that it has not allowed public police departments to hold onto their share of the market for security services. There has been a dramatic growth in private security that has occurred over the last two decades (Shearing and Stenning 1981; Cunningham and Taylor 1985; Shearing, 1992). Increasingly, American citizens rely on mechanisms other than public policing to protect them from criminal victimization, and allay their fears (Lavrakas and Lewis 1980; Lavrakas et al. 1981; Skogan and Maxfield 1981; Lavrakas and Skogan 1984). They buy locks, guns, and dogs in increasing quantities. They patrol their own neighborhoods in increasing numbers. And they band together to buy private security services from commercial firms—sometimes even from public agencies (Reiss 1985).

This has occurred even as the overall popularity of public policing has remained high and even risen. Although Americans seem to like public police forces, they apparently find them increasingly irrelevant to their security concerns. Insofar as one of the important tests of a corporate strategy is its ability to maintain a competitive advantage for an enterprise, professional law enforcement has not performed well.

The eroding position of public policing can be evaluated from two quite different perspectives. Viewed from the perspective of those in public policing, the loss of competitive position is unfortunate because it means less money, status, and opportunity for them and their colleagues. That may be important to police, but it is less important to the general citizenry, particularly if citizens are benefiting from lower taxes and the opportunity to buy security more neatly tailored to their individual desires.

But the decline of public policing can also be viewed from the vantage point of citizens who are interested in the overall quality of justice delivered by the society. Viewed from that perspective, the demise of public policing and the growth in private security portends several significant problems: a more unequal distribution of security; less respect for the rights of defendants; less professional competence overall to be drawn on in times of trouble (Reiss 1988). Thus the decline of public policing is a problem for society at large, not just for those who make careers in public policing.

These weaknesses in the current strategy of policing do not necessarily mean that it is wrong. It may be the best strategy available or the proper one for this stage of the development of policing in American society. Nor do the weaknesses necessarily mean that the strategy will quickly change to something else. Many forces operate to sustain commitment to any orthodoxy—including its familiarity and wide acceptance. What the weaknesses do mean is that there might be room to consider alternatives.

It is in that fertile ground that the ideas of community and problem-oriented policing have taken root. They give different answers to the questions, how might police departments best be used to confront crime, fear, drugs, and urban decay, by redefining the purposes of police departments, their principal operational methods, and even their bases of legitimacy. They have also sought to redefine the working relationships among the police, the community, and the other agencies of local government.

D. Problem-Solving and Community Policing as Alternative Organizational Strategies

To see problem-solving and community policing as alternatives to the current strategy of policing requires that they be seen as more abstract than any particular program or set of organizational arrangements. They define general approaches to policing rather than a definitive set of activities. Moreover, the particular programs that reflect a problem-solving or community-oriented style of policing in a particular locality might well differ. The problem-solving approach to domestic assault in Kansas City might be quite different than in San Francisco or Seattle. The community approach to drug dealing in Detroit might be quite different than in Phoenix (Police Executive Research Forum 1989).

Indeed, one common idea across these concepts is that there may be no one best way to deal with each of the problems facing policing. The best response will often depend on local circumstances. Thus the mark of an effective police department will not be how successful it is in implementing the most recent national model of a successful program but instead in how thoughtfully it crafts a local solution to a local problem, taking into account the local character of the problem and the local means of dealing with it.

What makes these concepts distinctive, then, is neither that they embody a particular set of activities nor that they give particular guidance to operations. Instead, they orient the thoughts and actions of police officers and managers in ways that differ characteristically from traditional ways of thinking about police work and, to a certain degree, from one another.

1. Problem-Solving Policing. Fundamental to the idea of problem solving, for example, is the activity of thought and analysis to understand the problem that lies behind the incidents to which the police are summoned (Goldstein 1979; Eck and Spelman 1987; Sparrow, Moore, and Kennedy 1990). This is not the same as seeking out the root causes of the crime problem in general. It is a much shallower, more situational approach. It takes seriously the notion that situations might be criminogenic and that crime can be prevented by changing the situations that seem to be producing calls for service (Clarke 1983). The problem-solving challenge is to imagine and design a plausibly effective response to solve the underlying problem. That can and often does include arresting troublemakers or assigning officers to patrol in certain places and times (Eck and Spelman 1987, pp. 43–44). But the important point is that the response is not necessarily limited to these traditional police responses. The challenge is to use mechanisms other than arrests to produce resolutions and to look outside the department as well as within for usable operational capacity.

Some concrete examples taken from Eck and Spelman's pioneering work will make these abstract points clearer (Eck and Spelman 1987; Spelman and Eck 1989):

In 1984, thefts from vehicles parked near the Newport News Shipyards constituted about 10 percent of all index crimes reported in Newport News. An
officer assigned to analyzing and resolving this crime problem discovered
that most of the crimes occurred in a few parking areas. By interviewing patrol officers, detectives, and officers from the Shipyards' private security
force, and those already caught and convicted of thefts in the area, the officer
was able to identify a small number of suspects for the ongoing crimes. This
information was given to patrol officers patrolling the area who became more
aggressive in interviewing suspects when they were seen in the area, and succeeded in making on-view arrests. In addition, the officer gained valuable information from the convicted offenders about what made the autos attractive
targets. That information is being used by the workers and the private security
force to develop and implement a theft prevention strategy. Thefts have decreased by 55 percent (from 51 per month to 23 per month) since the field interrogations and arrests of repeat offenders began. [Eck and Spelman 1987,
pp. 73–77]

The solution to this problem rested on traditional police methods, and relied
principally on departmental sources of information. What was unique was the
sustained effort made by the officer assigned the responsibility to deal with the
problem as a whole to tap and collate previously untapped information and use that
information to give coherence and impetus to what otherwise would have been a
fragmented effort.

Here is a second example:

In the spring of 1985, Gainesville, Florida, was hit by a rash of convenience
store robberies. The police thought the robberies were the work of one or two
repeat offenders. A review of suspect descriptions proved otherwise: many
different offenders were suddenly knocking over convenience stores. Officers assigned to analyze this problem observed that the convenience stores that
were being robbed differed from the others in that their interiors (and particularly their cash registers) were less visible from the street, tended to hold
more cash in their registers, and were staffed by only one person during the
late night hours. They then interviewed offenders who had been convicted of
convenience store robberies and learned that robbers always avoided convenience stores staffed by more than one clerk.

These findings were presented to an association of local merchants that had
been formed to help deal with the problem. The police were surprised by the
fact that the merchants rejected the police requests to change their practices
to make their stores less vulnerable. Undeterred, the police designed a local
ordinance requiring the owners to remove window advertising that blocked
the view of the store's interior from the street, to place cash registers in full
view of the street, to install security cameras in the store and outside lighting
in the parking lot, to limit the amount of cash in the registers, and to staff the
stores in late night hours with two employees trained in crime prevention
techniques. Despite continuing opposition from the merchants, the City Commission approved the ordinance. Following the implementation of the ordi-

nance, robberies fell 65 percent overall, and 75 percent at night. [Eck and Spelman 1987, pp. 5–6]

Exactly what caused the robbery rates to fall remains controversial. Some claim that the arrests of a small number of offenders who were committing these crimes was the principal explanation (Sherman 1990). From the point of view of those interested in problem solving, however, what is important is that it remains plausible that the particular features of the situation that became the focus of interventions were important causes of the robberies and that the police force was able to persuade the city government to shift some of the burden of dealing with the problem from the police to the merchants through the force of their analysis. But for that, the police would still be responding to robbery calls and explaining to everyone else in the city why they could not supply more police services for them.

2. Community Policing. The fundamental idea behind community policing, by contrast, is that effective working partnerships between the police and the community can play an important role in reducing crime and promoting security (Skolnick and Bayley 1986; Sparrow, Moore, and Kennedy 1990). Community policing emphasizes that the citizens themselves are the first line of defense in the fight against crime. Consequently, much thought must be given to how those efforts might best be mobilized. One important technique is for the police to open themselves up to community-nominated problems.

Opening the department to community-nominated problems often affects the police understanding of their ends as well as their purposes, for the communities do not always nominate serious crime problems as their most important concerns. In expressing their concerns, citizens' fears become as important as their actual victimization. The factors that trigger fears often turn out to be things other than serious crime (Skogan 1986). Thus community policing changes one's vision of the ends of policing as well as its means.

The concept of community policing also changes thinking about the bases of police legitimacy. In community policing, the justification for policing is not only its capacity to reduce crime and violence at a low cost while preserving constitutionally guaranteed rights but also its ability to meet the needs and desires of the community. Community satisfaction and harmony become important bases of legitimacy along with crime fighting competence and compliance with the law. Politics, in the sense of community responsiveness and accountability, reemerges as a virtue and an explicit basis of police legitimacy.

Thus community policing sees the community not only as a means for accomplishing crime control objectives but also as an end to be pursued. Indeed, as an overall strategy, community policing tends to view effective crime fighting as a means for allowing community institutions to flourish and do their work rather than the other way around (Stewart 1986; Tumin 1986). Community policing also seeks to make policing more responsive to neighborhood concerns.

None of this is intended to make the police entirely subservient to communities and their desires. The police must continue to stand for a set of values that communities will not always honor. For example, the police must defend the importance of fairness in the treatment of offenders and the protection of their constitutional rights against the vengeance of an angry community. The police must stand for and seek to produce fairness in the allocation of publicly financed protective services across the population of a city rather than cater to the most powerful neighborhoods. And police executives must retain control over such things as the assignment of particular personnel and the establishment of department-wide policies and procedures, lest the enterprise cease to operate as a citywide institution and become instead a mere compilation of several independent departments. Under a strategy of community policing, police departments should become more responsive and accountable to the demands of citizens.

An example of community policing in action may usefully illustrate these abstract ideas (Vera Institute of Justice 1988):

> In New York in April 1987, a representative of a tenants' association called a Community Patrol Officer with specific information about drug dealers and locations in the housing project in which he lived. The informant complained that the building was inundated with dealers and purchasers who occupied apartments and loitered in the halls making deals. The building's residents were frightened and frustrated, as were other members of the community. . . . The officer's first move was to call a meeting with the tenants' association. There was a good turnout of the residents, and the officer initiated a discussion in which conditions in the building were described clearly. He insisted that no specific details be given or accusations made, however, since some of the building's drug dealers were attending in order to observe and intimidate the others. . . . The meeting showed clearly that most of the building's residents shared a common attitude toward the problem, but that, because drug dealing is illegal, it is the responsibility of the police department to eliminate it. Their demand was clear; they wanted the police to clean up the building by more frequent patrolling and evictions or arrests of the drug dealers.

> The officer believed it essential that he convince the tenants they could not wait passively for the problem to be solved for them, but had to become active participants in the solution. He argued that the police could not possibly devote to one building as much time and attention as these tenants were requesting. He explained that the building's residents needed to act not only as reporters of the problem, but also to take some responsibility for eliminating it. The officer suggested the formation of a tenants' patrol . . . to supplement police activity and promised his support of the patrol. The tenants came around; they formed their own patrol unit.

> Within two weeks the tenants' association had been transformed from a rather limited and fragmented organization to a far more cohesive and powerful group. The association established an around-the-clock patrol of the building which monitored and recorded the presence of every person who entered it. . . . The officer conducted vertical patrols of the building five or six times

a day . . . and regularly informed special narcotics units in the Police Department about the situation. In addition, he met with representatives of the Department of Housing Preservation and Development, the local City Councilman, the Bureau of Family Services . . . these different resources collaborated in providing information to the tenants, worked on renovating apartments, and assisted in responsibly choosing future tenants in order to assure that the problem would not simply begin again with new faces when the present dealers were evicted. [Pp. 11–12]

3. Police Strategies Compared. When the concrete examples offered above are compared and contrasted in light of the abstract characterizations of police strategies, several important observations emerge. The differences between good professional policing, on the one hand, and problem-solving and community policing, on the other, seem less sharp. As one participant in a management-program class exclaimed when these illustrations were offered, "But we've always done things like that! That is not professional policing, or problem-solving policing, or community policing, that is simply *good* policing."[1]

Other members of the class pointed out, however, that while actions that were presented as problem-solving and community policing had always occurred in police departments, they were seldom acknowledged by supervisors or the managerial systems of the organization as effective policing. They remained covert and unacknowledged. Therefore they were rarer than they could or should have been.

Even though these methods and techniques had long been part of a resourceful patrol officer's operational repertoire, they were different from the standard, acknowledged methods of the organization. The scope of the problems addressed was unusual. They were larger than incidents to which the police were summoned but smaller than citywide crime problems for which the police were held accountable. The way data were used to define problems and analyze possible solutions, while not unheard of, are, nonetheless, rare in police circles. The extent to which the community and other governmental agencies were involved in identifying and resolving problems was also unusual. In these respects, then, the concrete examples do reveal a different approach to policing that is characteristic of problem-solving and community policing.

To a great extent, problem-solving and community policing are overlapping concepts (Moore and Trojanowicz 1988). A commitment to problem solving leads quite naturally to the invention of solutions that involve the broader community. Moreover, while problem solving often begins with police-nominated problems, many of the departments that have committed themselves to problem solving have also developed mechanisms to consult with local communities to discover what the problems are. If both occur as a routine matter, then problem-solving policing becomes virtually indistinguishable from community policing. Community policing is designed to let the community nominate problems and focuses on what the police can do in partnership with the community to deal with the nominated problems. That generally requires thought and imagination and is therefore often indistinguishable from problem-solving policing.

Despite the overlaps, each concept has its own distinctive thrust (Moore and Trojanowicz 1988). Problem solving emphasizes thoughtfulness and analysis over community cooperation. Community policing seeks to rivet the attention of the organization not on its own internal operations but instead on how its cooperation with the community seems to be developing. As a matter of emphasis, a problem-solving police department could err by becoming too focused on problems that the police thought were important and by not being responsive enough to community-nominated problems. A community-oriented department might become so focused on maintaining its relationships with the community that it forgot that it was supposed to mount operations that reduced crime, victimization, and fear.

So at abstract and strategic levels and at a concrete operational level, the concepts of problem-solving and community policing seem to differ both from professional law enforcement as an operational philosophy and from one another. While the concrete examples are here presented as a way of revealing the differences in approach, they also remind us that, in the end, these abstract and strategic levels are important not simply as abstractions but as devices that can be used to influence the conduct of police officers in the field.

The most important ways in which these new strategies are supposed to influence police conduct is by authorizing individual officers to gather data about the situations that lie behind incidents so that their underlying causes might be understood; to be thoughtful about the design of police operations to deal with the problem; to construct measures to determine whether one has been successful; to acknowledge the important role of the community in nominating problems for solution, in designing effective solutions and in executing the solutions; to see that the goal of crime fighting might best be pursued by establishing more trusting relations with the communities that are policed; and to acknowledge that the police have broader opportunities to prevent and control crime and to promote security and ease some of the danger and pain and frustration of living in today's cities than is acknowledged in the conception of professional law enforcement.

To accomplish these things, however—to make these abstract ideas work to provide useful guidance to operational officers—requires important changes in the ways that police departments are structured and managed as well as in the ways that their purposes and operating philosophy are understood. It is not enough to have the general idea. It is not enough even to have the general idea translated into operational realities on an intermittent basis. The organizations must be structured and operated to produce that result day in and day out. That is an organizational and managerial task as well as a conceptual task. It is in this complicated sense that problem-oriented and community policing must be evaluated as organizational or corporate strategies rather than as operational programs or even as discrete activities undertaken by officers.

II. Evaluating Problem-Solving and Community Policing

If problem-solving and community policing are viewed as strategic concepts seeking to redefine the overall mission of policing, how might they be evaluated? This
question becomes urgent as more and more police departments consider changing
their basic strategies. After all, there is far more at stake in changing the overall strategy of policing than in changing particular programs or administrative
arrangements. A much larger fraction of the organization's resources is involved.
And changes, once initiated, may be quite expensive to reverse.

Unfortunately, it is far more difficult to evaluate strategic ideas than programmatic ones. Because changes in the basic strategy of policing take years, even
decades, to implement successfully, it is difficult to say at what moment the new
strategy became operative. This makes pre- and postevaluations that compare performance before and after implementation of innovations difficult to conduct.

Even worse, because a change in strategy often involves a redefinition of
purposes as well as means, it is by no means clear what criteria should be used to
evaluate success. Obviously, it is important to know whether the new strategy is
more or less successful than the old in controlling crime. But the issue is whether,
in changing the basic strategy of policing, new criteria such as reducing fear or
restoring the quality of life also become important, and if so, how they might be
measured. It may also be important to evaluate a strategy in terms of its long-run
institutional consequences as well as its operational effectiveness: for example,
whether the police become more or less law-abiding over time; whether they
become more or less important relative to private security in supplying security
services in the nation's cities; and whether the occupational status of policing rises
or falls.

Finally, no police department in the United States has as yet fully made the
transition to these new styles of policing and operated long enough to produce a convincing record of performance. Consequently, there is little experience to rely on in
estimating the value of these new strategies, let alone their long-run institutional
consequences.

This leaves an evaluator in an awkward position. The most important claim
is that these new styles of policing represent an important shift in the overall strategy
of policing. But the available evidence is not really up to assessing this claim. What
one can do is more modest. First, lay out the principal arguments that supporters of
these styles of policing make for the value of their approach and examine empirical
evidence on the success of particular "signature programs" associated with the
different ideas. Then, because this evidence is too thin to allow a complete evaluation (and because the empirical evidence would, in any case, be insufficient for a
proper normative assessment of the long-run institutional consequences of a fundamental shift in strategy), turn to a close consideration of the principal criticisms of
these new strategies of policing.

A. The Effectiveness of Problem-Solving Policing: Empirical Evidence

The theoretical justification for problem-solving policing was set out by Herman Goldstein in a pioneering article in 1979. The fundamental notion was that much of the real knowledge about what worked in policing lay in the operating experience of police officers. Goldstein emphasized the importance of representing problems in much more specific, hence local, terms (1979, pp. 244–45). For example, arson was not a single category of offense; it included fires set by "firebugs," pranks by juvenile delinquents, and efforts to defraud insurance companies. Each element of the arson problem demands a separate solution. Similarly, in seeking out information about how problems are actually handled, it is not enough to learn the policies and procedures of the department, one had to observe how resourceful and experienced police officers dealt with individual cases. Only then would the "rich resource" represented by individual officers' practices be well used (Goldstein 1979, pp. 248–49).

The value of problem solving in practice has now been demonstrated anecdotally in operations carried out by police departments in such places as Newport News, Virginia; Santa Ana, California; Baltimore County, Maryland; and New York City, New York. The stories presented above are similar to scores of others from around the nation. Such stories are satisfying mostly because they describe a set of concrete activities that seem to produce attractive concrete results. In this, they have the persuasive power of anecdotes.

But there are at least three risks in relying on anecdotes as evidence for the success of problem solving as an overall strategy. First, the anecdotes may not be accurate descriptions of what occurred. Without outside auditing, there is no way to be sure that the successes are real or that they resulted from police operations rather than from some other factor. For example, debates continue about the real causes of the reduced number of convenience store robberies in Gainesville, Florida, described above (e.g., see Wilson 1990).

Second, the anecdotes may not be significant enough to count for much, even if they are accurate. The worst fear is that the problems are not really solved but are simply displaced to new locations. Even if that were not true, the solution of one or two small problems could hardly justify the operations of an entire police department.

Third, the success of one or two operations is not enough to demonstrate that the department as a whole can engage in this kind of activity repeatedly across the range of problems the police face. If the police cannot do this, then the claim that problem-solving efforts are doing something more than displacing local problems to new areas, or that they are producing something more valuable than what the police are now doing is substantially weakened.

The most sustained and rigorous test of problem solving as a strategy for policing a city is contained in an evaluation of the Newport News police department (Eck and Spelman 1987). The investigators identified precisely these two issues as being important to resolve: first, whether the problem-solving efforts eliminated or abated the problems attacked; and, second, whether the department was capable of carrying on such activities on a widespread, continuing basis—that is, as a routine way of operating (Eck and Spelman 1987, p. 65).

To answer the first question, the researchers examined three of eighteen problems that the organization defined as problems to be solved. One began as a police operation to reduce residential burglaries in a housing project but gradually became a multi-agency effort to improve living conditions in the project. The second was the previously described effort to reduce thefts from automobiles in the Newport News shipyards. The third was an effort to reduce prostitution and associated robberies on a particular street.

Many of these problem-solving efforts began essentially as directed patrol operations designed to identify patterns of offending or known offenders and to deploy police to catch the offenders. All gradually evolved into quite different efforts that involved activities other than arrests and agencies other than the police. The attack on burglaries in the housing project involved surveying tenants, cleaning the projects, creating a multi-agency task force to deal with particular problems in the housing project, and organizing the tenants not only to undertake block watches but also to make demands on city agencies. The attack on thefts from cars eventually involved the inclusion of police officers in the design of new parking lots to make them less vulnerable to theft. The attack on prostitution and robbery involved enhanced code enforcement against hotels and bars that provided the meeting places for prostitutes and their customers as well as decoy operations against the prostitutes.

The investigators concluded that these problem-solving efforts largely succeeded in achieving their objectives: burglaries in the housing project dropped by about 35 percent and there was no evidence of displacement (Eck and Spelman 1987, p. 72); the number of thefts from automobiles in the shipyards declined by more than 50 percent (p. 76); the number of prostitutes working the particular street dropped from twenty-eight to six, and the number of personal robberies committed in the downtown area of which this street was a part declined by 43 percent (p. 80).

With respect to the second question, the investigators looked at the overall volume and pattern of problem-solving efforts that the department had launched. There were eighteen such problems in the research period. Some were short-lived, local problems; others were local but more durable; still others had citywide significance. It would be nice to know how much of the department's overall efforts over the research period was committed to problem solving as opposed to reactive approaches to crime, what fraction of the department's personnel was engaged in such efforts, and what fraction of the city's overall crime problem came within the scope of problem-solving efforts. Unfortunately those data are not supplied. What the authors conclude, however, is that "police officers can solve problems as part of their daily routine; they enjoy problem solving; and their efforts are often successful" (Eck and Spelman 1987, p. xxv).

The evaluators also observed an important relationship between the depth of the analysis that went into the design of a problem-solving approach and the sort of response that was selected. The more extensively a problem was analyzed, the more likely it was to lead to an approach that did not rely exclusively on police resources or police methods. Changing police officers' views of the sources of the problem changed the nature of the response that seemed appropriate.

B. Evaluating Community Policing

In many respects, the concept of community policing is as old as policing itself. Indeed, many think it is redundant to add the word community to policing since policing, by definition, assumes the existence of a political community with shared norms codified in laws and enforced with day-to-day support from citizens (Cain 1973, pp. 21–25).

To others, adding the word "community" to policing serves to remind the police that the community is an important resource to tap in pursuing the goals of crime reduction and that the cultivation of community support must be an operational goal of policing, influencing decisions about the priority given to certain kinds of activities and about the overall structure of the organization.

To still others, adding the word "community" to policing redefines the ends as well as the means of policing. In this view, the goal of policing is not just to reduce crime but also to reduce fears, restore civility in public spaces, and guarantee the rights of democratic citizens; in short, it is to create secure and tolerant democratic communities. In both these latter cases, advocates of community policing think it is important to add the word to the enterprise of policing because it focuses the attention of police departments on their relationship to the communities they police, and that is an important corrective to the style of policing that had emerged under the professional model of policing.

1. Team Policing. The urgency of maintaining a close connection between the police and the community was brought home to professionally oriented police departments toward the end of the 1960s when they confronted large-scale urban unrest. Disciplined, competent, professionalized police forces found themselves unable to deal with this problem. One despairing member of the Los Angeles Police Department now recalls the experience of the Watts riot: "Everything we believed would be effective didn't work. We withdrew officers; that didn't work. We put more officers in; that didn't work. We used our black and liaison officers; that didn't work" (Kennedy 1986, p. x). On review, the Los Angeles Police Department concluded that it had failed because it had lost touch with the communities it policed, and with that, it had lost a crucial capacity to enforce the laws of the state.

Why the police had lost touch was not hard to understand. Like most professional police departments, the Los Angeles Police Department had shifted away from an organizational structure based on local neighborhoods. Geographically based precincts had given way to functional or programmatic units. And while the patrol division retained a geographical structure, centralized dispatching systems had made all the patrol cars available for dispatching throughout the city. The focus of the department had become citywide rather than local.

The solution to this problem, initiated by Chief Edward Davis in 1970, was to reestablish a sense of territorial responsibility in the basic structure of the police department's operations (Kennedy 1986). Davis divided his patrol force into two different kinds of patrol unit. One unit (called the "X car") was available to be dispatched throughout the city as needed. The other unit (called the "basic car") was to be kept in a given geographical area. The dispatchers were instructed to give the "basic car" the first crack at calls within its own service delivery area, and to refrain from dispatching it to other parts of the city except in dire emergencies. In addition, Davis established the position of "senior lead officer" to be assigned to the basic car. In return for greater rank and higher pay, this officer assumed a broader set of responsibilities for establishing and maintaining liaison with local communities.

Davis went further several years later. In 1973, he committed his organization to a concept called "team policing" to give the organization an even stronger sense of geographic accountability. The city was divided into seventy geographic units, each consisting of three to five basic patrol cars. A lieutenant was placed in charge of each area. In an important innovation, the lieutenant commanded not only patrol units but also detectives and representatives of specialist units such as traffic, narcotics, and juveniles, depending on the area's problems. In effect, the lieutenants became minichiefs of small territories. They were told that they were accountable for only one thing: "Whether conditions improved in their areas of responsibility or did not deteriorate." Here was the first modern model of what is becoming community policing.

At this stage, by the mid-1970s, many departments were experimenting with team policing. What evaluations were completed showed generally positive results: when the programs were fielded and sustained, they seemed to enjoy popularity with citizens and police and to produce some improvements in neighborhood conditions, including reductions in crime (Sherman, Milton, and Kelly 1973; Koenig, Blahna, and Petrick 1979).

Other studies, however, documented the enormous difficulty of introducing and sustaining team policing in police departments committed to professional crime fighting. In Dallas, a skilled police executive, supported by substantial outside resources, was unable to implement a reform program (Kelling and Wycoff 1978). In many other cities, successful team-policing programs were unaccountably abandoned despite their apparent success (Sherman, Milton, and Kelly 1973). Even Los Angeles eliminated team policing in 1979 (Kennedy 1986, p. 8).

Why team policing seemed to disappear despite its apparent successes remains obscure. Some blame declining police resources and the dramatic increase in calls for service that made it impossible for large city police departments to sustain the commitment to maintain geographic responsibility. Others see the culprit in the determined opposition of midlevel managers who resented the increasing independence and autonomy of the sergeants and patrol officers who worked on the teams (Sherman 1986, p. 365). Still others think that the schemes fell to the power of the police culture, which preferred professional isolation to close engagement with the community. Whatever the exact reason, it gradually became clear that team policing could not be introduced and sustained within organizations whose dominant purpose was something else and whose culture would not support it. As long as the organization's most important task was getting to calls on time, and as long as the organization remained a steep hierarchy of commanders, it would be hard to fit team policing into existing police organizations.

2. Community Relations Units. A different effort to restore strong working relationships between the police and the community lay in the creation of community relations units. These units have had a long but checkered history (Geary 1975; Walker 1980).

Some were created in the mid-fifties as part of a concerted program undertaken by chiefs to develop public support for policing and overcome "the attitudes of contempt that middle-class citizens held toward the police" (Geary 1975, pp. 373–74). These units arranged for police officers to visit schools and speak at meetings of civic associations in order to communicate the police perspective.

Other community relations units, created in response to riots in the 1940s and 1960s, were designed to help the police shore up relations with minority communities and to help prevent riots. Goldstein (1990) has described the activities and significance of these units: "The units sponsored Officer Friendly programs, maintained contacts with civil rights activists, monitored demonstrations, attended meetings of militant groups, and advised command staff on rising tensions. . . . The value of these units . . . was, in my view, a major factor alerting police chiefs to the potential of what has now emerged as community policing."

Still other community relations units sought to enlist direct citizen participation in specific crime-control efforts (Bickman et al. 1976). At first, they concentrated on encouraging citizens to call the police when suspected crimes were occurring. Later, they emphasized crime prevention. They helped citizens analyze their own vulnerabilities through security surveys. They encouraged citizens to mark their property to make it easier for the police to identify property as stolen in investigations and to facilitate its return. They sought to form citizen block watches in which citizens agreed to watch one another's homes.

Unfortunately, these latter efforts were not successfully evaluated. The exact nature and scale of police efforts in this area remains obscure, as are their effects on levels of crime and attitudes toward the police. Consequently, we do not really know whether these police initiatives reduced crime or calmed fears.

What these varied uses of community relations units reveal, however, is how confused the police are about the functions that improved community relations are supposed to serve, and how the units should organize to secure whatever benefits are associated with performing this function well. Many police continue to think that the most important purpose of improved community relations is to build support for policing: community relations units should be megaphones for the department and its purposes rather than antennae tuned into neighborhood concerns. Many police remain skeptical about the operational utility of mobilizing citizens to help them prevent and control crime—particularly when those citizens seem to have little respect or affection for the police.

Even worse, they succumb to the common police tendency to deal with particular problems by forming special squads. (As a saying in the London Metropolitan Police puts it, "When in doubt, form a squad and rush about" [Sparrow, Moore, and Kennedy 1990].) Four adverse consequences flow from concentrating the responsibility for effective community relations in a special squad.

First, by isolating the function in a specialized unit, it becomes vulnerable to organizational ridicule. This often occurred. The community relations units became known as the "grin and wave" or "rubber gun" squads.

Second, once a special squad is formed, everyone else in the department is seemingly relieved of responsibility for enhancing the quality of community relations. That has become the responsibility of the community relations unit.

Third, if the community relations unit should obtain important information about community concerns or ways in which the community might be able to help the department, it is difficult to make those observations heard inside the police department—particularly if what they have to report is bad news or imposes unwelcome demands on the rest of the organization. Goldstein (1990) described the dilemma for officers charged with maintaining liaison with racial minorities: "Officers were often caught in a double-bind, expected by department personnel to stamp out any sign of unrest and expected by minority communities to achieve changes in police practices affecting them."

Fourth, the organization no longer looks for other ways to improve community relations. It does not consider the possibility that the right way to improve community relations is to make every patrol officer a community relations officer, or to make special efforts to ensure that its organizations are representative of the best from the neighborhoods it polices.

In short, while the establishment of community relations units reveals the continuing vitality of the important idea that the police must stay close to the communities they police, it also indicates how difficult it is for that idea to begin to influence the operations of the entire department. The units operate to insulate most of the department from the continuing challenge of sustaining links to the community that can serve not only as a basis of support for policing but also as a conduit for community demands on police agencies and an opportunity to enlist community groups in operational efforts to control crime and improve the quality of life.

3. Community Crime Prevention Programs. Team policing and community relations units were largely police-initiated responses to the sense that there was an untapped potential in the community for dealing more effectively with crime problems. At the same time that the police were experimenting with these approaches, a series of field experiments was undertaken to test crime prevention programs initiated by communities themselves—sometimes in alliance with the police. In many respects, these programs resembled the activities that were being carried out by police departments through their community relations units. As one commentator described them: "The fundamental philosophy of community crime prevention is embodied in the notion that the most effective means of combating crime must involve residents in the proactive interventions and participatory projects aimed at reducing or precluding the opportunity for crime to occur in their neighborhoods. In practice, this involvement translates into a wide range of activities including resident patrols, citizen crime reporting systems, block watch programs, home security surveys, property marking projects, police community councils, and a variety of plans for changing the physical environment" (Rosenbaum 1986, p. 19). The most important difference was that these programs were usually designed, executed, and evaluated outside of police departments.

Rosenbaum (1986) summarized four significant experiments in community-based crime prevention efforts: the Seattle Community Crime Prevention Program conducted in the early 1970s; the Portland Burglary Prevention Program;[2] the Hartford Community Crime Prevention Program; and the Urban Crime Prevention Program in Chicago. These particular programs were selected because the methodology for evaluation was particularly strong; the program designs and execution apparently were also strong.

The two programs directed at burglary (the Seattle and Portland programs) seemed to achieve reductions in burglary in the impact areas. The Hartford program, which relied on community mobilization and physical arrangements, also seemed to produce short-run effects on robbery and burglary and citizens' sense of personal security. Moreover, the effort and its effects might have been extended, had the police not stopped supporting the effort. The only effort that seems to have failed is the broad community organization effort that was undertaken in Chicago. Thus these studies suggest that narrowly targeted, well-designed and executed programs that seek to mobilize citizens to produce crime preventive effects can reduce the incidence of important crimes such as robbery and burglary.

4. Fear Reduction and Foot Patrol. Beginning in the early 1980s, the concept of community policing began once again to gather momentum within the world of policing. This time, however, both the ends and the means of policing were redefined.

The initial spark came from the findings of experiments with foot patrol in Newark, New Jersey, and Flint, Michigan. These experiments concluded that added foot patrols did not reduce property and violent crime but that, unlike the use of motorized patrol, the efforts were noticed by citizens and succeeded in reducing citizens' fears (Police Foundation 1981; Trojanowicz 1982). The Flint experiment was sufficiently popular to lead to passage of a special tax to support the program; the total number of calls to central dispatching stations for service declined (Trojanowicz 1982).

In the usual course of things, these findings would have fallen on deaf ears because they did not report any significant impact on crime. But in the mid-eighties, when these reports were published, attention was shifting from preoccupation with crime to a growing concern over fear about crime as a problem in its own right. Fear began to claim this status partly because its costs were increasingly being recognized as a major, if not the single largest, component of the overall social costs of crime (Cohen, Miller, and Rossman 1990, pp. 64–79), and partly because it was becoming clearer that fear of crime was curiously disconnected from objective levels of victimization (Skogan 1987). Once fear was recognized as a problem in its own right, the foot patrol experiments became much more important because they suggested that the fear-reducing effect of foot patrol was potentially quite valuable.

This line of thought was boosted when Wilson and Kelling (1982) published "Broken Windows" in the *Atlantic Monthly,* which argued that fear was not only a problem in its own right but also a cause of both crime and neighborhood degradation. They argued that the minor events and incivilities that frightened people, far from being a distraction for police departments, should be identified as key targets of police action. The ongoing disorder, if left unattended, would lead to still more disorder, crime, and neighborhood degradation. More recently, these arguments have been supported with some empirical evidence (Skogan 1990).

Impressed by these arguments, police agencies began altering their operations to see if they could influence levels of fear in the community and, in turn, halt cycles of more fear, crime, and decline. The Los Angeles Police Department conducted fear-reducing efforts in the Wilshire District (Sparrow, Moore, and Kennedy 1990). The Baltimore County Police Department decided to respond to some frightening murders not with more police patrols but with more sustained efforts to discover and alleviate the sources of fear (Taft 1986; Kennedy 1990). The National Institute of Justice sponsored two major experiments in Houston, Texas, and Newark, New Jersey, to determine whether the police could reduce levels of fear by such activities as increasing foot patrol, establishing neighborhood ministations, publishing newsletters, or cracking down on disorderly conditions in public transportation (Pate et al. 1986).

The conclusions of the fear reduction experiments were basically encouraging—at least with respect to the police capacity to still fears. James Q. Wilson summarized the results of the two experiments: "In Houston . . . opening a neighborhood police station, contacting the citizens about their problems, and stimulating the formation of neighborhood organizations where none had existed can help reduce the fear of crime and even reduce the actual level of victimization" (1989, p. ii). As to the more complex question of whether fear reductions will stimulate neighborhood responses that reduce crime and prevent urban decline, the jury is still out (Greene and Taylor 1988).

III. Criticisms and Cautions

The basic logic of problem-solving and community policing, the anecdotal successes, and the positive evaluations of operational programs offer reasons to believe that problem-solving and community policing can be effective in dealing with crime and enhancing security in the general population. But even if the empirical evidence were more complete, the case for adopting these new strategies of policing would still be insufficient, for, in evaluating an overall strategy, other, broader considerations come into play.

To evaluate an organizational strategy in the public sector, one must consider whether the new strategy is well founded as well as effective. A well-founded strategy should honor historical experience, operate in accord with important public values, and be properly accountable to the public. Also of concern are long-run institutional effects of the change in strategy on such things as the future lawfulness of policing, its standing vis-à-vis other public agencies, and its importance relative to private security. In this domain, problem-solving and community policing encounter sharp criticisms (Greene and Mastrofski 1988).

Bayley (1988) identifies a dozen serious threats to the quality of policing that could result from a shift in strategy toward problem-solving and community policing:

1) reduced crime-control effectiveness;

2) deteriorating will to maintain order in the face of violence;

3) an unseemly escape from accountability for crime control;

4) increased grass-roots political power for police departments and their leaders that threatens to distort the proper political processes of cities;

5) increased bureaucratic power for police departments and their leaders that threatens to distort proper governmental processes;

6) increased police/governmental involvement in community affairs and private lives to the disadvantage of liberty and privacy;

7) increased risks that the law will be enforced in discriminatory, unequal ways that vary from one neighborhood to another;

8) erosion of constitutional rights through the encouragement of street-level justice and the encouragement of vigilantism by citizens;

9) increased unfairness in the allocation of police services across neighborhoods, with wealthier, more powerful communities claiming more than their fair share;

10 losses in effective managerial control as a consequence of decentralization;

11) loss of citywide accountability and control as a consequence of decentralization; and

12) diminished professionalism among officers.

A. The Power of the Values of Professional Law Enforcement

Taken individually and as a whole, this list is a serious indictment of the foundations of problem-solving and community policing. To help in addressing these objectives, however, it is worth noting that much of their power derives from the belief that any relaxation of the commitment to the fundamental values and beliefs that have guided police reformers over the past generation threatens to lead the police astray. In effect, the criticisms assume that the past strategy of policing, including the values and assumptions that guided it, was the appropriate one, and any deviation from the orthodoxy must be suspect. To see the grip that the image of professional law enforcement has on our imagination and orientations to policing, consider Bayley's particular criticisms at one higher level of abstraction than the one at which they are presented.

The first three criticisms (loss of crime-control effectiveness, loss of will to maintain order, and escape from accountability for crime control) express the continuing conviction that crime control is the primary—even exclusive—focus of the police. Given this perspective, one would quite naturally be concerned that any broadening of police responsibilities to include fear, urban disorder, and the variety of emergencies that prompt citizens' calls will weaken policing by diluting its focus on serious predatory crime.

Points 4–6 (increased political power, increased bureaucratic power, and increased governmental influence over private affairs) reflect the continuing concern of a liberal democratic society that the police might become too powerful and intrusive a governmental institution. They help to remind us that one of the reasons the sharp focus on serious crime seemed so appropriate in the strategy of professional law enforcement was not only to help the police become successful in that enterprise but also to keep them out of many other social affairs narrowly focused on that task. Since any growth in police power could be viewed as a long-term threat to freedom, it was important to keep the police narrowly focused on serious crime, and reliant primarily on reactive methods of patrol and investigation.

Points 7–9 (discriminatory enforcement, erosion of civil liberties, and unequal distribution of police resources) focus on the possibility that the determined efforts of the last generation of reformers to make the police conform to important legal values such as fairness, impartiality, and respect for the constitutional rights of suspected criminals will be undermined by bringing the police into contact once again with politics—the old enemy of these values. Politics threatens these values because the unequal distribution of private power and privilege is believed to work through politics to shape the enforcement of the law (Black 1980). To the extent that the police are once again brought into a close embrace with communities, some of the most important successes of past reforms are threatened.

The last triad of criticisms (loss of managerial control, loss of citywide accountability and control, and loss of professionalism) reflects the conviction that tight, centralized control was the only way to ensure that the police performed competently in their jobs and complied with the important legal values that should guide them. Since problem-solving and community policing encourage decentralization, both control and efficient citywide allocations are threatened by any shift in this direction.

The fears that we have about community and problem-solving policing are the natural fears associated with moving away from a powerful set of beliefs and assumptions that have guided us in the past. Arguably, such fears are characteristic of any "revolutionary" period in which powerful values and beliefs that have long lighted the path toward improvement are challenged by new ideas. To say that the criticisms are psychologically powerful because they are closely aligned with our prior beliefs and assumptions, however, is not to disparage their substantive content. Indeed, there *are* enduring social values embedded in the strategy of professional law enforcement that *do* continue to define important virtues of police organizations. It is simply to remind us that it is sometimes difficult to be fully objective about new possibilities when the grip of past commitments holds us so tightly that we can hardly find the room to imagine how things could be different.

So, to defend problem-solving or community policing against these powerful criticisms it is necessary to consider once again the arguments that are made for community and problem-solving policing in terms of the values that were so important to the strategy of professional law enforcement: namely the sharp focus on crime control as the predominant objective of the police; the interest in limiting the power of the police; the promotion of legal values such as fairness, nonintrusiveness, and constitutionalism; and the reliance on centralized control to achieve these objectives.

B. Emphasizing Crime Fighting

Initially, the sharp focus on crime fighting as the dominant objective of the police is justified on practical grounds. It is an urgent public problem. The police are uniquely qualified to meet the challenge. It makes sense that crime should be the primary focus of police attention. But, as noted above, the focus on crime fighting is also linked to concerns about keeping the police from becoming too powerful and too intrusive in society. If the police were to use all of their capabilities to help society deal with its problems, they might become too powerful a force in the community and stunt the development of other less coercive social institutions. Or if the police were to intrude in areas where the law offered little guidance or control of their activities, they might well behave badly. Thus, the concern about keeping the sharp focus on crime fighting is closely tied to concerns about controlling the police as well as using them effectively.

I consider below whether community and problem-solving policing threaten to increase the power of the police and weaken their commitment to legal values. At this stage, it is worth addressing the narrower question of whether crime control, *particularly as it is now performed*, is the most important or only valuable use of police resources.

Initially, it seems that there is a great deal of weight behind the critics' concerns that crime-control effectiveness might be diluted. After all, it is impossible to argue that crime is not now an urgent problem for urban communities. And it seems difficult to argue that effectiveness in combating crime would not be diluted if the police were asked to shoulder additional responsibilities.

What advocates of problem-solving and community policing argue, however, is not that crime control should be deemphasized. They agree that crime-control effectiveness must remain the principal touchstone against which police strategies should be evaluated. Instead, they argue that there may be better ways of controlling crime than the techniques common to professional law enforcement. In particular, they are interested in techniques that focus less on reacting to crimes and more on prevention and that rely less on the police themselves and more on the capacities of communities and other public agencies.

They also argue that many activities that do not look like direct crime-control activities may, nonetheless, help build relations with communities that will increase crime-control effectiveness in the future and are, in any case, valuable in reducing fears and improving the quality of neighborhood life. For example, dealing with instances of minor disorder may not only still fears in the community and enhance the neighborhood's morale but also increase the likelihood that citizens will help the police solve crimes (Wilson and Kelling 1982; Skogan 1990).

Thus the real target of those who advocate problem-solving and community policing is not the central focus on crime control as the dominant purpose of the police; it is, instead, the equation of an *exclusive* focus on crime control pursued through a *particular set of operational tactics* with effective crime control. In their view, a somewhat more indirect approach may hold more potential for controlling crime than the direct methods of professional law enforcement, and may, in addition, achieve other valuable benefits such as reducing fears and enhancing citizens' confidence in the police.

C. Limiting the Power of the Police as an Institution

As the police become more responsive to community concerns and more skilled in using crime-prevention and problem-solving techniques, there is the risk that they will become politically and bureaucratically more powerful, and that they will intrude more deeply into the affairs of citizens and other government agencies. As noted above, this conflicts with the desire to keep the police from becoming too powerful an institution in the society.

The desire to limit the power of the police is a patently important objective in a liberal society. Yet, advocates of community and problem-solving policing would argue that slavish adherence to this principle would prevent the police from making important contributions to the solutions of today's urban problems. Most current analyses of conditions in cities indicate a significant breakdown in the important mechanisms of informal social control including responsibilities to family and community. The collapse of these intermediate institutions allow disorder, crime, and fear to flourish.

In this situation, several scenarios are possible. If formal controls are not increased (e.g., if the police remain indifferent to drugs and violence on city streets), the quality of life may continue to deteriorate for many living in the distressed communities. If formal controls are expanded to fill the void (e.g., if police establish curfews and street sweeps), then conditions may improve, but only at the expense of further weakening informal control mechanisms and increasing the dependence and vulnerability of the local communities to state control.

Better than either of these approaches would be one in which the formal social controls were used in ways that were designed to strengthen informal social control (e.g., if the police were to engage in joint problem-solving efforts with those elements of the community that were concerned about alleviating the problems). It is precisely this latter approach that is recommended by problem-solving and community policing. So while these approaches may use the police more intensively in dealing with social problems than would be ideal, they may be appropriate in the relatively desperate circumstance in which we now find ourselves.

There is one additional reason to be interested in increasing rather than holding constant or diminishing the overall strength of policing as a community institution. That reason has to do with the ominous growth of private policing and private security efforts. The reason these are growing is that citizens are losing confidence in the police. The consequence of that growth is potentially disastrous since private policing, even more than politicized public policing, will be sure to be marked by both unfairness and contempt for the rights of the accused.

Indeed, this point reminds us that one of the main reasons public police forces were initially established was not only to increase the overall level of social control but also to produce an alternative to private vengeance and enhance the overall fairness of control efforts. In this respect, the police are a bastion of democratic values rather than a threat to them, and their enhanced standing in the community could become a celebration of these values rather than an attack.

D. Promoting Fairness, Restraint, and Other Legal Values

Critics are also right to focus attention on the possibility that important legal values might be sacrificed by shifting away from the strategy of professional law enforcement to a strategy of community or problem-solving policing. Once policing is cut loose from an obsessive focus with enforcing law and brought back in touch with community concerns, it is entirely possible that the corruption, discrimination, and brutality that once shamed policing will return with new vigor or become an even more exaggerated feature of policing than it is now.

If this were likely, it would be an important reason in itself to resist pressures to change the strategy, for no one would quarrel with the importance of promoting compliance with the legal values of fairness, impartiality, and respect for individual rights. Surely one of the proudest accomplishments of the last generation of policing has been the wider embrace of these values as defining characteristics of quality policing. The strategy of professional law enforcement had a great deal to do with this.

How the commitment to these values would be affected by a shift to problem-solving or community policing, however, remains unclear. To critics, a serious danger appears to be that both strategies seek to establish closer, more intimate connections with those being policed. Such intimacy threatens police fairness and impartiality. In individual incidents, the police might be tempted to side with those whom they have come to know well or those who are locally influential. In deploying forces across a city, the police may be tempted to provide better service to those with whom they identify or those who are politically powerful. Such fears seem particularly apt for departments that never embraced the legal values in the first place. Hence, there are reasons to be concerned.

In assessing the magnitude of the risks associated with the change, however, several things are worth noting. At best, the achievement of professional law enforcement in promoting legal values within police departments has been incomplete. In many departments, legal values are still seen as burdensome constraints rather than as important goals to be expressed in, and protected by, police operations.

Part of the reason may be that these values have been imposed from the outside rather than championed from the inside. It seems significant, then, that many of the chiefs who have committed their departments to problem-solving or community policing have spent time developing explicit value statements to guide the operations of their departments, and that the protection of constitutional values figures far more prominently in these statements than it has in the explicit statements of many other police departments (Wasserman and Moore 1988). Of course, words on paper are not the same as cultural commitment, but it is one of the ways that a culture supporting these values is created.

It may also be important that police departments that engage in problem-solving and community policing will frequently find themselves in situations in which they will be pressured to take actions by some groups that abridge the rights of others or asked to resolve disputes among citizens each of whom has reasonable claims. In dealing professionally with such situations, the police may discover for themselves the reasons why they cannot behave illegally. They may also end up communicating to citizens why they, too, must develop tolerance for the rights of others. In short, in the experience of negotiating solutions to problems among several interested parties, the police will learn to rely on legal principles. That, in turn, may encourage them to become "street-corner judges" as well as "street-corner politicians" (Muir 1977). They might also rediscover why it was once considered plausible that they should be part of the judicial branch of government rather than the executive and might thereby discover a commitment to legal values that has so far eluded them.

It would be wrong to be too optimistic about these possibilities. And it is right to be concerned about the threat that district and neighborhood politics pose for the fairness of police operations. But it can reasonably be argued that a relentless police focus on crime-control effectiveness encourages the police to view legal values as constraints rather than as goals. If police were more responsible for ordering relationships in the community, they would more often find legal values a useful guide to proper conduct than they now do.

In any case, the concerns about legal values remind us that problem-solving and community policing must be seen as strategies that build on the past successes of professional law enforcement rather than on abandonment of these principles in favor of a return to the "good old days." The accomplishments of several decades of reform efforts in creating legal culture in the police departments should be preserved and enhanced rather than overturned.

E. Maintaining Central Control

The view that centralized control is essential for making the police law abiding and competent also now seems more suspect than it once did. It has long been apparent that centralized control cannot reliably control police conduct since some amount of irreducible discretion always remained to officers (Elmore 1978). Yet police continued to develop these methods since no other ways to control discretion seemed available.

More recently, other control mechanisms have become more apparent. The threat of civil liability, for example, may be doing more to control misconduct than any amount of effective supervision (McCoy 1985). Some police departments are looking to administrative methods used by industry that rely on the promotion of organizational values, worker participation, and mutual responsibility to promote quality in products and operations rather than continuing to rely on close supervision and "defect finding" (Hatry and Greiner 1986). Others are looking to peer review and other methods of accountability common in professional organizations such as hospitals and law firms for new models of assuring responsible professionalism (Couper and Lobitz 1991). While it is not clear whether these methods will work in policing, they have helped expand current thinking about other kinds of administrative arrangements that can assure quality and integrity in police operations at least as well as even closer supervision.

F. Summary

An advocate of problem-solving and community policing could make a response to the principal criticisms of skeptics. Whether skeptics or advocates will ultimately be proven right remains unclear.

The criticisms do, however, make three key points. First, problem-solving and community policing must be seen and managed as an advance, not as a retreat.

Crime-control effectiveness remains an important goal. Lawful arrests remain an important operational tool. Commitment to the law and professionalism remain important bases of professionalism. None of these hard-won goals of the reform era should be abandoned.

Second, the important reform project of integrating the commitment to the law and to constitutional rights into the ideology and operations of the police department remains incomplete. Under community or problem-solving policing, with their emphases on officer and local discretion, the need to embrace these values fully increases rather than decreases. Exactly how to encourage police commitment to legal values remains unclear, but it may be advanced by articulating those values from inside police departments rather than by imposing them from the outside and by asking the police to undertake tasks where legal principles will help them rather than restrain them.

Third, the mechanisms of external and internal accountability need a great deal of work to ensure that the police are pursuing appropriate goals using appropriate means. One of the key ideas of both problem-solving and community policing is that external accountability to the community and to the agencies of municipal government should increase rather than decrease. Both strategies call for experiments with new methods for promoting internal and external accountability including after-the-fact peer evaluations of performance.

Fourth, standards for recruiting and training officers are both raised and changed under problem-solving and community policing. These new strategies are much more dependent on the initiative and resourcefulness of individual officers than is the current strategy that treats all patrol officers as employees who must be continuously supervised. The strategies' effectiveness depends on the officer's knowledge of his local community and government. It is not so much that commitment to professionalism is ending as that it is changing its focus and accelerating. Much more will be expected of officers in the future than was true in the past.

Nobody wants to be too Pollyannaish about the ease with which these ongoing problems of policing may be overcome. But there are so many attractive trends occurring that it is hard to resist encouraging them a little—particularly if we recall both the virtues and the shortcomings of the reform era of policing. Even David Bayley agrees that it would be advisable to continue experimenting with these new concepts, as long as we remain alert to the hazards.

IV. Problems in Implementation

For a new policing strategy to be attractive, it must be feasible for police departments to shift from their current strategy to a new one. It is not enough that there be evidence that the strategy could successfully control crime and promote security. Nor is it enough that the concept withstand skepticism about its value.

It is not easy to change the overall strategy of an organization (Sparrow 1988; Brown 1989). That no police organizations in the United States have successfully made this change is powerful evidence of how hard it is. Many police executives have begun this process, however, revealing that the foreseeable obstacles are not entirely insurmountable and providing clues to what particular methods might be useful in overcoming the problems (Sparrow, Moore, and Kennedy 1990).

A. Limited Resources

The most common practical objection is that there are simply not enough resources available in the department to meet simultaneously the demands of responding rapidly to calls for service, interrupting and solving crimes, and engaging in the crime-preventive, fear-reducing activities associated with problem-solving and community policing. Something has to give. In a world in which both citizens and police look to rapid responses to calls for service as a mark of quality police services, proactive policing methods will always be the thing to give. If this is true, problem-solving and community policing will be consigned to the status of attractive luxuries.

Such observations seem to doom prospects even for *programs* in problem-solving and community policing, let alone entire shifts in organizational strategy. Skilled police executives are discovering, however, that there are ways out of this apparently unresolvable dilemma.

First, the new strategies of policing—first introduced as add-on programs—may prove sufficiently popular to justify additional resources for police departments. It is one thing for citizens and mayors to pour money into police departments pursuing the traditional strategy of policing; it is quite another for them to pay for a strategy of policing that seems more responsive to their concerns. Citizens of Flint, Michigan, an economically distressed community, were opposed to general tax increases but were, nonetheless, willing to support a tax increase to expand foot patrols (Trojanowicz 1982). Similarly, in New York City, the Community Patrol Officers Program has been sufficiently popular to have, to some degree, insulated the police department from absorbing the full share of budget cuts that they would otherwise have been expected to take.

Second, even if resources are not available from the outside, aggressive managers can often free up additional resources inside the organization. Using civilian personnel for some functions and reorganizing shifts to fit manpower more to demands for work beckon as potential sources of additional resources. So does the elimination of special squads that have emerged as a consequence of the tendency to create new squads to solve new problems (Kennedy 1987). Dissolving such squads has the additional virtue of spreading the accumulated expertise of the special unit more widely through the force. Other reallocation possibilities include reducing the number of layers of management and thinning ranks of headquarters personnel (Philadelphia Police Study Task Force 1987). These are radical and difficult steps, but some managers have taken them.

Third, proven technologies can alleviate pressures that come from unmanaged calls for service (Farmer 1981). Calls can be ranked in order of priority, thereby eliminating a large fraction of the need for an emergency response to incoming calls. Citizens can be educated to accept a certain delay in the police response. They can be asked to fill out the reports that officers would complete if they arrived on the scene and to deliver reports to a police station. These innovations reduce pressure for emergency responses and restore some opportunities to the police for proactive methods of policing.

Fourth, strategies are available for addressing needs before incidents occur that lead to calls. There is a structure to the calls for service received by a police department (Pierce, Spaar, and Briggs 1984; Sherman et al. 1987; Spelman and Eck 1989). A small fraction of locations and people account for a very large proportion of calls. It is possible, then, that overall calls for service might go down if the police designed effective responses to the problems underlying the repeat incidents. At a minimum, the proactive police might intercept calls from citizens that would otherwise reach police dispatchers.

It is by no means clear, then, that police executives are without resources for implementing community policing. Some are finding ways to do it.

B. Uncertainty and Accountability

A second difficulty is that there will be turmoil and confusion in the process of transition. Moreover, at the end, there is no guarantee that things will be better. To many police executives, it seems irresponsible and dangerous to plunge into this process of change with uncertain payoff. Indeed, as one chief explained when asked about how he felt when he committed his organization to a strategy of community policing, "I felt like I had just jumped off a cliff" (Sparrow, Moore, and Kennedy 1990). They fear, quite reasonably, that they will be held accountable to standards and images from the past and that their performance in running the organization will look bad.

That is certainly a problem, but it has a solution. It consists of creating an outside constituency for change that will hold the commissioner and the police department accountable to new standards, not the old ones (Moore 1990). Kevin Tucker did this in beginning to turn the Philadelphia Police Department around, and that has been what has allowed Sir Kenneth Newman in London, England, and John Avery in New South Wales, Australia, to advance as far as they have in shifting the course of their organizations (Sparrow, Moore, and Kennedy 1990). Mobilizing an outside constituency for change is also consistent with the goal of attracting additional outside resources, for the outside constituency is often a route to new resources.

C. Changing the Culture of Policing

Probably the biggest obstacle facing anyone who would implement a new strategy of policing is the difficulty of changing the ongoing culture of policing (Sparrow, Moore, and Kennedy 1990). That culture is deeply entrenched in the minds and souls of people now doing the work (Manning, 1992). It is sustained by current administrative arrangements.

Three approaches are available for changing the culture. First, the organizations should be opened to many more external pressures than they now feel. This means embracing openness as a value and changing the organizational structure so that everyone in the organization is exposed to much more contact with relevant communities than they now are (Sparrow, Moore, and Kennedy 1990). This requires that police executives take steps to get officers out from behind the wheels of their cars and midlevel managers out from behind their desks and reports. Close contact with communities must be made at these levels as well as at the chief's level.

Second, the dominant values of the organization must be articulated (Wasserman and Moore 1988). Such a step is critical for establishing terms of accountability and inviting a partnership with outside groups. It is also critical for announcing to those inside the police department what is expected and what important values they must serve. It is especially critical in police organizations in which direct supervision cannot control behavior because much of the work takes place beyond the eyes of the supervisors.

Third, aspects of existing administrative systems that are inconsistent with new values must be changed. This includes changing from centralized, functional organizations to decentralized, geographic organizations. It means attracting personnel moved by the spirit of service rather than the spirit of adventure and rewarding them for maintaining peace on their beats rather than making numbers of arrests. It means changing performance evaluations from those that emphasize levels of crime, volumes of arrests, and speed of response, to those that measure victimization and fear and community satisfaction with the quality of police service. Unless these systems are lined up to communicate a message to individual officers and managers that is consistent with the overall strategy of problem-solving or community policing, the strategy will not be successfully implemented.

V. Conclusions

Problem-solving and community policing represent interesting new concepts in policing. Evaluated as alternative strategies of policing, they show both promise and hazards. These hazards, though daunting, must be compared not with some ideal but with the current operational reality of policing as it now occurs. Against that standard, the benefits begin to look a little greater and the hazards a little smaller.

Key to the successful implementation of either of these ideas as an overall strategy of policing are efforts to build an outside constituency, and broaden the terms of police accountability. Key to that is articulating a set of values that can serve as a basic contract to guide the working partnership of the police and the community as they seek together to define and resolve the problems of crime and fear.

There is one further point worth making as one thinks about community and problem-solving policing as possible future strategies of policing. That has to do with the question of how the current drug crisis and the looming threat of more wide-spread violence will affect the potential success of these strategies. To many, the urgency of these problems constitutes an important reason to stand with the tried and true and resist any experimentation.

I tend to think the opposite. If there are any areas in which the strategies of problem-solving and community policing are likely to be most needed, it is in dealing with these particular problems. Surely, an important part of dealing with drugs is learning how to mobilize communities to resist drug dealing. Surely, an important part of dealing with random violence is dealing with rational and irrational fears. Surely, an important part of controlling riots is having networks of relationships that reach deeply into ethnic communities. If anything, then, these problems give impetus to further developments in problem-solving and community policing. It is an interesting time to be a student or manager in policing.

Notes

[1] Comment made to author during Senior Managers in Policing Program sponsored by the Police Executive Research Forum. Andover, Mass.

[2] This was managed by the Portland Police Department Community Relations Unit, but the unit was staffed by civilians.

References

Andrews, Kenneth R. 1971. *The Concept of Corporate Strategy.* Homewood, Ill.: Dow Jones-Irwin.

Bayley, David H. 1988. "Community Policing: A Report from the Devil's Advocate." In *Community Policing: Rhetoric or Reality,* edited by Jack R. Greene and Stephen D. Mastrofski. New York: Praeger.

_____. 1992. "Comparative Organization of the Police in English-Speaking Countries." In *Modern Policing,* edited by Michael Tonry and Norval Morris. Chicago: University of Chigago Press.

Bickman, L., P. J. Lavrakas, S. K. Green, N. North-Walker, J. Edwards, S. Barkowski, and S. Shane-DuBow. 1976. *Citizen Crime Reporting Projects—National Evaluation Program—Phase 1: Summary Report.* Washington, D.C.: National Institute of Law Enforcement and Criminal Justice.

Bittner, Egon. 1970. *The Functions of the Police in Modern Society: Background Factors,*

Current Practices, and Possible Role Models. Chevy Chase, Md.: National Institute of Mental Health.

Black, Donald. 1980. *The Manners and Customs of the Police.* New York: Academic Press.

Blumstein, Alfred, Jacqueline Cohen, and Daniel Nagin, eds. 1978. *Deterrence and Incapacitation: Estimating the Effects of Criminal Sanctions on Crime Rates.* Washington, D.C.: National Academy of Sciences.

Brown, Lee P. 1989. "Community Policing: A Practical Guide for Police Officials." *Police Chief,* August, pp. 72–82.

Cain, Maureen E. 1973. *Society and the Policeman's Role.* London: Routledge & Kegan Paul.

Civilian Review of the Police—The Experiences of American Cities. 1980. Hartford, Conn.: Hartford Institute of Criminal and Social Justice.

Clarke, Ronald V. 1983. "Situational Crime Prevention: Its Theoretical Basis and Practical Scope." In *Crime and Justice: An Annual Review of Research,* vol. 4, edited by Michael Tonry and Norval Morris. Chicago: University of Chicago Press.

Cohen, Jacqueline. 1978. "The Incapacitative Effect of Imprisonment: A Critical Review of the Literature." In *Deterrence and Incapacitation: Estimating the Effects of Criminal Sanctions on Crime Rates,* edited by Alfred Blumstein, Jacqueline Cohen, and Daniel Nagin. Washington, D.C.: National Academy of Sciences.

Cohen, Mark A., Ted R. Miller, and Shelli B. Rossman. 1990. "The Costs and Consequences of Violent Behavior in the U.S." Paper prepared for the Panel on the Understanding and Control of Violent Behavior, National Research Council, National Academy of Sciences, Washington, D.C.

Couper, David C., and Sabine H. Lobitz. 1991. *Quality Policing: The Madison Experience.* Washington, D.C.: Police Executive Research Forum.

Cunningham, William C., and Todd H. Taylor. 1985. *The Hallcrest Report: Private Security and Police in America.* Portland, Oreg.: Chancellor.

Eck, John E. 1983. *Solving Crimes: The Investigation of Burglary and Robbery.* Washington, D.C.: Police Executive Research Forum.

Eck, John E., and William Spelman. 1987. *Problem Solving: Problem-oriented Policing in Newport News.* Washington, D.C.: Police Executive Research Forum.

Elmore, Richard F. 1978. "Organizational Models of Social Program Implementation." *Public Policy* 26:185–228.

Farmer, Michael T. 1978. *Survey of Police Operational and Administrative Practices.* Washington, D.C.: Police Executive Research Forum.

_____, ed. 1981. *Differential Police Response Strategies.* Washington, D.C.: Police Executive Research Forum.

Fogelson, Robert M. 1977. *Big-City Police.* Cambridge: Harvard University Press.

Geary, David Patrick. 1975. "The Impact of Police-Community Relations on the Police System." In *Community Relations and the Administration of Justice,* edited by David Patrick Geary. New York: Wiley.

Geller, William A., ed. 1985. *Police Leadership in America: Crisis and Opportunity.* New York: Praeger.

Goldstein, Herman. 1979. "Improving Policing: A Problem-oriented Approach." *Crime and Delinquency* 25:236–58.

_____. 1990. Personal communication with author, July 27.

Greene, Jack R., and Stephen D. Mastrofski, eds. 1988. *Community Policing: Rhetoric or Reality.* New York: Praeger.

Greene, Jack R., and Ralph B. Taylor. 1988. "Community-based Policing and Foot Patrol: Issues of Theory and Evaluation." In *Community Policing: Rhetoric or Reality,* edited by Jack R. Greene and Stephen D. Mastrofski. New York: Praeger.

Greenwood, Peter, with Allan Abrahamse. 1982. *Selective Incapacitation.* Santa Monica: Rand.

Greenwood, Peter W., Jan M. Chaiken, and Joan Petersilia. 1977. *The Criminal Investigation Process.* Lexington, Mass.: Lexington.

Hatry, Harry P., and John M. Greiner. 1986. *Improving the Use of Quality Circles in Police Departments.* Washington, D.C.: U.S. Department of Justice, National Institute of Justice.

Kansas City Police Department. 1977–79. *Response Time Analysis.* 3 vols. Kansas City, Mo.: Board of Commissioners.

Kelling, George L. 1988. "Police and Communities: The Quiet Revolution." *Perspectives on Policing,* no. 1. Washington, D.C.: National Institute of Justice and Harvard University.

Kelling, George L., and Mark H. Moore. 1988. "The Evolving Strategy of Policing." *Perspectives on Policing,* no. 4. Washington, D.C.: National Institute of Justice and Harvard University.

Kelling, George L., Anthony M. Pate, Duane Dieckman, and Charles E. Brown. 1974. "The Kansas City Preventive Patrol Experiment: A Summary Report." Washington, D.C.: Police Foundation.

Kelling, George L., and Mary Ann Wycoff. 1978. *The Dallas Experience: Vol. 1: Organizational Reform.* Washington, D.C.: Police Foundation.

Kennedy, David M. 1986. "Neighborhood Policing in Los Angeles." Case no. C16-86-717.0. Cambridge, Mass.: Harvard University, Case Program of John F. Kennedy School of Government.

_____. 1987. "Neighborhood Policing: The London Metropolitan Police Force." Case no. C15-87-770.0. Cambridge: Harvard University, Case Program of John F. Kennedy School of Government.

_____. 1990. "Fighting Fear in Baltimore County." Case no. C16-90-938.0. Cambridge, Mass.: Harvard University, Case Program of John F. Kennedy School of Government.

Klockars, Carl B. 1988. "The Rhetoric of Community Policing." In *Community Policing: Rhetoric or Reality,* edited by Jack R. Greene and Stephen D. Mastrofski. New York: Praeger.

Koenig, David J., John H. Blahna, and Richard L. Petrick. 1979. *Team Policing in St. Paul, Minnesota: An Evaluation of Two Years of Implementation.* St. Paul, Minn.: Team Police Evaluation Unit, Police Department.

Larson, Richard C., and Michael F. Cahn. 1985. "Synthesizing and Extending the Results of Police Patrol Studies." Research report. Washington, D.C.: U.S. Department of Justice, National Institute of Justice.

Lavrakas, Paul J., and Dan A. Lewis. 1980. "Conceptualization and Measurement of Citizens' Crime Prevention Behaviors." *Journal of Research in Crime and Delinquency* 17:254–72.

Lavrakas, Paul J., J. Mormoyle, W. G. Skogan, E. J. Herz, G. Salem, and D. A. Levis. 1981. *Factors Related to Citizen Involvement in Personal, Household, and Neighborhood*

Anti-crime Measures. Washington D.C.: U.S. Department of Justice, National Institute of Justice.

Lavrakas, Paul J., and Wesley J. Skogan. 1984. *Citizen Participation and Community Crime Prevention, 1979 Chicago Metropolitan Area Survey*. Evanston, Ill.: Northwestern University Center for Urban Affairs and Policy Research.

McCoy, Candace. 1985. "Lawsuits against Police: What Impact Do They Really Have?" In *Police Management Today: Issues and Case Studies,* edited by James J. Fyfe. Washington, D.C.: International City Management Association.

Manning, Peter K. 1992. "The Police and Technology." In *Modern Policing*, edited by Michael Tonry and Norval Morris. Chicago: University of Chicago Press.

Moore, Mark H. 1983a. "Invisible Offenses: A Challenge to Minimally Intrusive Law Enforcement." In *ABSCAM Ethics: Moral Issues and Deception in Law Enforcement,* edited by Gerald M. Caplan. Washington, D.C.: Police Foundation.

_____.1983b. "Controlling Criminogenic Commodities: Drugs, Guns and Alcohol." In *Crime and Public Policy*, edited by James Q. Wilson. San Francisco: ICS Press.

_____. 1990. "Police Leadership: the Impossible Dream?" In *Impossible Jobs in Public Management*, edited by Erwin C. Hargrove and John C. Glidewell. Lawrence: University Press of Kansas.

Moore, Mark H., and George L. Kelling. 1983. "'To Serve and Protect': Learning from Police History." *Public Interest* 70:265–81.

Moore, Mark H., and Darrel Stephens. 1991. *Police Organization and Management: Toward a New Managerial Orthodoxy*. Washington, D.C.: Police Executive Research Forum (forthcoming).

Moore, Mark H., and Robert C. Trojanowicz. 1988. "Corporate Strategies for Policing." Perspectives on Policing, no. 6. Washington, D.C.: National Institute of Justice and Harvard University.

Muir, W. K., Jr. 1977. *Police: Streetcorner Politicians*. Chicago: University of Chicago Press.

Neustadt, Richard E., and Ernest R. May. 1986. *Thinking in Time. The Uses of History for Decision Makers*. New York: Free Press.

Pate, Anthony M., Robert A. Bowers, and Ron Parks. 1976. "Three Approaches to Criminal Apprehension in Kansas City: An Evaluation Report." Washington, D.C.: Police Foundation.

Pate, Anthony M., Mary Ann Wycoff, Wesley G. Skogan, and Lawrence W. Sherman. 1986. "Reducing Fear of Crime in Houston and Newark: A Summary Report." Washington, D.C.: Police Foundation.

Philadelphia Police Study Task Force. 1987. *Philadelphia and Its Police: Toward a New Partnership*. Philadelphia: Police Department.

Pierce, Glen L., Susan A. Spaar, and LeBaron R. Briggs IV. 1984. "The Character of Police Work: Implications for the Delivery of Services." Report to the National Institute of Justice. Boston: Northeastern University Center for Applied Social Research.

Police Executive Research Forum. 1989. "Taking a Problem-oriented Approach to Drug Enforcement." Interim Report. Washington, D.C.: U.S. Department of Justice, Bureau of Justice Assistance.

Police Foundation. 1981. *The Newark Foot Patrol Experiment*. Washington, D.C.: Police Foundation.

Reiss, Albert J., Jr. 1971. *The Police and the Public*. New Haven: Yale University Press.

Reiss, Albert J., Jr. 1985. *Policing a City's Central District: The Oakland Story.* Washington, D.C.: U.S. Government Printing Office.

———. 1988. *Private Employment of Public Police.* Washington, D.C.: U.S. Department of Justice, National Institute of Justice.

Rosenbaum, Dennis P., ed. 1986. *Community Crime Prevention: Does It Work?* Beverly Hills: Sage.

Rubinstein, Jonathan. 1973. *City Police.* New York: Farrar, Straus & Giroux.

Scott, Eric J. 1981. *Calls for Service: Citizen Demand and Initial Police Response.* Washington, D.C.: U.S. Department of Justice, National Institute of Justice.

Shearing, Clifford D. 1992. "The Relation between Public and Private Policing." In *Modern Policing*, edited by Michael Tonry and Norval Morris. Chicago: University of Chicago Press.

Shearing, Clifford D., and Philip C. Stenning. 1981. "Modern Private Security: Its Growth and Implications." In *Crime and Justice: An Annual Review of Research*, vol. 3, edited by Michael Tonry and Norval Morris. Chicago: University of Chicago Press.

Sherman, Lawrence W. 1986. "Policing Communities: What Works?" In *Communities and Crime*, edited by Albert J. Reiss, Jr., and Michael Tonry. Vol. 8 of *Crime and Justice: A Review of Research*, edited by Michael Tonry and Norval Morris. Chicago: University of Chicago Press.

———. 1990. Personal communication with author, April 13.

Sherman, Lawrence W., and Richard A. Berk. 1984. "The Minneapolis Domestic Violence Experiment." *Police Foundation Reports.* Washington, D.C.: Police Foundation.

Sherman, Lawrence W., et al. 1987. *Repeat Calls to the Police in Minneapolis.* Washington, D.C.: Crime Control Institute.

Sherman, Lawrence W., Catherine H. Milton, and Thomas V. Kelly. 1973. *Team Policing— Seven Case Studies.* Washington, D.C.: Police Foundation.

Skogan, Wesley G. 1977. "The Promise of Policing: Evaluating the Performance, Productivity, and Potential of Local Law Enforcement." Paper presented at Workshop on Policy Analysis in State and Local Government, Stony Brook: State University of New York.

———. 1986. "Fear of Crime and Neighborhood Change." In *Communities and Crime*, edited by Albert J. Reiss, Jr., and Michael Tonry. Vol. 8 of *Crime and Justice: A Review of Research*, edited by Michael Tonry and Norval Morris. Chicago: University of Chicago Press.

———. 1987. "The Impact of Victimization on Fear." *Crime and Delinquency* 33:135–54.

———. 1990. *Disorder and Decline: Crime and the Spiral of Decay in America's Neighborhoods.* New York: Free Press.

Skogan, Wesley G., and George E. Antunes. 1979. "Information, Apprehension, and Deterrence: Exploring the Limits of Police Productivity." *Journal of Criminal Justice* 7:217–42.

Skogan, Wesley G., and Michael G. Maxfield. 1981. *Coping with Crime—Individual and Neighborhood Reactions.* Beverly Hills: Sage.

Skolnick, Jerome H., and David H. Bayley. 1986. *The New Blue Line: Police Innovation in Six American Cities.* New York: Free Press.

Sparrow, Malcolm K. 1988. "Implementing Community Policing." *Perspectives* on *Policing,* no. 9. Washington, D.C.: National Institute of Justice and Harvard University.

Sparrow, Malcolm K., Mark H. Moore, and David M. Kennedy. 1990. *Beyond 911: A New Era for Policing*. New York: Basic.

Spelman, William, and Dale K. Brown. 1984. *Calling the Police: Citizen Reporting of Serious Crime*. Washington, D.C.: U.S. Department of Justice, National Institute of Justice.

Spelman, William, and John E. Eck. 1989. "Sitting Ducks, Ravenous Wolves and Helping Hands: New Approaches to Urban Policing." *Public Affairs Comment*, pp. 1–9. Austin: University of Texas, Lyndon B. Johnson School of Public Affairs, Winter.

Stewart, James Q. 1986. "The Urban Strangler: How Crime Causes Poverty in the Inner City." *Police Review* 37:2–6.

Taft, Philip B., Jr. 1986. *Fighting Fear: The Baltimore County C.O.P.E. Project*. Washington, D.C.: Police Executive Research Forum.

Trojanowicz, Robert C. 1982. An *Evaluation of the Neighborhood Foot Patrol Program in Flint, Michigan*. East Lansing: Michigan State University.

Tumin, Zachary. 1986. "Managing Relations with the Community." Working Paper no. 86-05-06. Cambridge, Mass.: Harvard University, John F. Kennedy School of Government. Program in Criminal Justice Policy and Management.

Vera Institute of Justice. 1988. *CROP: Community Policing in Practice*. New York: Vera Institute of Justice.

Walker, Samuel E. 1980. "The Origins of the American Police-Community Relations Movement: The 1940s." In *Criminal Justice History: An International Annual*, vol. 1, edited by Henry Cohen. New York: Crime and Justice History Group, Inc., in association with John Jay Press.

Wasserman, Robert, and Mark H. Moore. 1988. "Values in Policing." *Perspectives on Policing*, no. 8. Washington, D.C.: U.S. Department of Justice, National Institute of Justice and Harvard University.

Williams, Gerald L. 1989. *Making the Grade: The Benefits of Law Enforcement Accreditation*. Washington, D.C.: Police Executive Research Forum.

Wilson, James Q. 1968. *Varieties of Police Behavior*. Cambridge, Class.: Harvard University Press.

_____. 1989. *Bureaucracy*. New York: Basic.

Wilson, James Q., and George L. Kelling. 1982. "Broken Windows: The Police and Neighborhood Safety." *Atlantic Monthly* 249(3): 29–38.

Wilson, Jerry. 1990. "Gainesville Convenience Store Ordinance: Findings of Fact, Conclusions and Recommendations." Report prepared for the National Association of Convenience Stores. Washington, D.C.: Crime Control Research Corporation.

Wilson, Orlando W. 1950. *Police Administration*. New York: McGraw Hill.

Wilt, G. Marie, James Bannon, Ronald K. Breedlove, John W. Kennish, Donald M. Sandker, and Robert K. Sawtell. 1977. *Domestic Violence and the Police: Studies In Detroit and Kansas City*. Washington D.C.: Police Foundation.

Wycoff, Mary Ann. 1982. "Role of Municipal Police—Research as a Prelude to Changing It." Technical Report. Washington, D.C.: Police Foundation.

Wycoff, Mary Ann, Charles Brown, and Robert Peterson. 1980. "Birmingham Anti-robbery Unit Evaluation Report." Washington, D.C.: Police Foundation.

19

Community Policing Against Guns
Public Opinion of the Kansas City Gun Experiment

James W. Shaw

Over the last decade, Americans have been besieged with constant reports of firearm crime wreaking havoc on their streets. These reports range from accounts such as the execution-style murder by fellow gang members of 11-year-old Robert Sandifer, who himself was wanted by Chicago police for the murder of a 14-year-old girl the previous month (*LEN* 1994:8), to reports of errant gunfire taking the lives of innocent bystanders. In Fresno, California, in late 1994, an 11-year-old girl was struck by gunfire as she took out the trash; an eight-year-old boy was shot in the head as bullets whizzed through his home; and another young child was grazed on the back as she and her family cowered on the floor trying to escape flying bullets (*LEN* 1995:1). Such incidents have led the FBI to conclude that "every American now has a realistic chance of murder victimization in view of the random nature the crime has assumed" (*LEN* 1994:18).

As a result of such tragedies, legislatures have responded by drafting new criminal offenses and imposing harsher penalties. Social scientists struggle with the causes of violence (e.g., Reiss and Roth 1993) and the relationship between guns and crime (e.g., Cook 1991; Kleck 1991; McDowall 1991; Rand 1994). Police departments around the country have begun to experiment with innovative approaches and to reexamine previously tried, but less than successful, approaches for dealing with violent and gun-related crime. One such effort, the Kansas City Gun Experiment, has attracted national attention (Butterfield 1994: Castaneda 1995; NIJ 1994; Walters 1995; Worthington 1994).

Source: Reprinted by permission of the Academy of Criminal Justice Sciences from *Justice Quarterly*, Vol. 12, No. 4, December 1995. Copyright 1995 by Academy of Criminal Justice Sciences.

The Kansas City Gun Experiment was based on the hypothesis that gun seizures and gun crime would be inversely related (Sherman, Shaw, and Rogan 1995). In testing that hypothesis, Sherman and Rogan (1995) found in a time-series analysis of the 52 weeks before and after initiation of the program that gun crime dropped significantly. This reduction coincided with more than a 65 percent increase in gun seizures resulting from proactive patrol tactics. ARIMA time-series analysis of gun crime in a control area did not show a similar significant decrease, nor was gun crime displaced significantly to patrol beats adjoining the program area (Sherman and Rogan 1995).

Regardless of the experiment's promise for reducing gun crime, the strategy it tested will have limited value if the price of success is community hostility toward the police. Such hostility harms police work in many respects—for example, by making citizens unwilling to assist the police or even report crimes to the police when victimized, by making the police reluctant to act when they should or by tending to overreact when they do act, by making police work more dangerous, or by contributing to major riots and disturbances (President's Commission 1967:144–45). Thus one critical question about Sherman and Rogan's results is whether the method was acceptable to the community.

Patrol Methods and Community Relations

Tactics targeted at recovering more guns make police more vulnerable to criticism, both for how they initiate contacts with citizens and for what they do during an encounter with a citizen. Discussing the viability of a police strategy targeting illegally carried handguns, Moore (1980:26) questioned the "basic fairness of the approach" because it "invites the police to be more intrusive." Simply by looking for people who might be carrying guns, police will undoubtedly find people who would commit crimes, or who may already have done so. At the same time, they will find people carrying guns who might never commit a crime but who feel the need to protect themselves.

A more serious question involves procedural due process. Even with the most reliable, empirically based predictors indicating who is likely to illegally carry a concealed weapon, police will stop and frisk many people who are not carrying guns. Even those who advocate greater enforcement of laws against carrying concealed weapons caution against the appearance of harassment (Kleck 1991:442): "to the majority of searched persons who were not in possession of weapons or other contraband, street searches look like police harassment, aimed largely at young men and minorities."

Modern police executives are not eager to create even the appearance of such harassment, much less the reality. Yet the recent rise in deaths due to inner-city gun crime is a staggering American problem, crying out for a solution. The key question is whether an enforcement strategy against illegally concealed weapons can be adopted so as to be acceptable to a community suffering high levels of gun violence. The Kansas City Gun Experiment was designed to work in partnership with the community and avoid the appearance of racist harassment. Whether it succeeded, one can argue, is a matter of (1) what the police did, (2) how the community residents viewed police actions, and (3) how the persons stopped by police viewed police actions.

This article addresses the first two questions, but not the third. Insufficient funding prevented the interviewing of persons stopped by police. This is unfortunate because those persons would be expected to have the most unfavorable reaction to the police methods employed. Future research on this strategy should make every effort to include interviews with suspects as well as more quantitative systematic observations of the police encounters initiated by hot spot gun patrols. This article provides qualitative data on how the program was implemented, and a door-to-door survey of the area residents' reaction to the program.

Research Design

The research employs a quasi-experimental nonequivalent control-group design (Cook and Campbell 1979) comparing pre- and postexperimental household surveys from the program area, Police Beat 144, with identical measurements taken from the comparison area, Police Beat 242. The comparison area was selected because its crime and demographic characteristics were similar to those of the 8-by-10-block area of Beat 144, where the homicide rate was 20 times higher than the national average and where a drive-by shooting occurred every two weeks in 1993 (Sherman et al. 1995).

The author observed police conduct during some 50 percent of door-to-door visits in the program area (Shaw 1993) and during 300 of the 2,256 patrol-car hours of hot spot gun patrols, spread over 50 days of the 178-day program. He also conducted all interviews of sampled community residents before and after the program patrols began in both the program and the comparison area.

Police Practices in the Kansas City Gun Experiment

Police practices in this experiment occurred in two phases. In the first phase, from March 4, through May 21, 1992, 1,410 police attempts to make home visits on regular duty time were aimed at a list of every household in the program area (Shaw 1993). Although these visits failed to produce the desired phone calls to an anonymous gun tips hotline, they provided a form of consultation with the community in advance of the proactive patrols. The visits were friendly and informational: when contact with an adult was made, the resident was given a flyer (titled "Get a Gun off the Street") bearing the phone number of the hotline. Residents were presented with a brief description and a rationale for the gun tips program, as well as a brief description of the proactive patrols that would be initiated that summer.

The second phase of the program, lasting from July 7, 1992 through January 27, 1993, consisted of overtime two-officer patrols with an emphasis on recovering firearms (Sherman and Rogan 1995). Police were instructed to stay in the target area and to concentrate on gun crime "hot spots" identified by University of Maryland computer analyses. Although the officers actually spent most of their time in neither of the two tasks, they generally were focused on finding illegal guns.

Observations revealed a mixed level of intensity in looking for guns. Assignments to this overtime-pay duty were not restricted to officers who had conducted the door-to-door visits, but were made available to all officers in the Central Patrol District who sought the opportunity (or the extra pay). For example, the signup sheet for October was posted in the station house on the morning of August 22, and almost every time slot was filled by evening. Some of these officers were focused more strongly on the hot spot patrols. Some remained parked near gun crime hot spots; others drove around constantly, looking for "action." Some stayed on patrol in the area all night; others went to calls officially assigned to other cars outside the area to see whether fellow officers needed more help. Some drove around slowly, talking to informants in the field; others spent hours in the station doing paperwork. In one instance, paperwork associated with a gun seizure early in the evening lasted for the rest of the shift, or 10 officer-hours.

Officers were required to record every pedestrian and car check and to specify the reason why the contact was initiated. Car checks were the most common citizen encounter, and frequently involved some type of traffic violation. Other checks were based on arrest warrants associated with the registered owner of the car, as detected by a computerized license check. In still other instances, officers conducted car checks when they had a reasonable suspicion or belief that criminal activity was under way—for example, when they say a car pulled up in front of a known drug house for two minutes, while one person ran to a side door and another stayed in the idling car.

No evidence of discrimination against blacks was observed in the selection of cars for further inquiry, especially because the moving autos in the area were almost always occupied by blacks. In fact, some officers gave automatic attention to any white people in the area because whites' motives for being there were considered suspect (for example, buying drugs). Some other "defiant" categories (Sherman 1993) thought to provoke special police attention, such as "low rider" cars, did not do so, partly because those cars usually had thousand-dollar paint jobs. In general, police tended to look more closely at beat-up cars with equipment violations—burned-out lights, missing license plates, cracked windshields—than at "clean" cars.

The citizen encounters resulting in gun seizures were typical of encounters generally. One car stop for a violation of the loud music ordinance, for example, resulted in the seizure of two illegal guns, crack cocaine, and $600 cash. Another gun seizure resulted from police talking to a "little gangster" who provided a tip about a 17-year-old carrying a weapon. The latter then was located and stopped. In another seizure, a computerized warrant check showed that the suspect was wanted for arrest on an assault charge; when the suspect was arrested, a gun was found on his person.

Gun seizures were not made without police discretion, even when guns were found. In one case, police stopped a man who had no criminal record, was with a woman, and answered "yes" when police asked him if he had a gun in his car. They let him go. On the same night, the same officers stopped a different man, who had a prior arrest for carrying a concealed weapon and was in a car with three other males. This one also told police he had a gun in his car. He was arrested.

[Whether officers ever made stops without reasonable suspicion is a difficult question. The author's text at his death does not contain any report on that point, but his notes reflect several instances in which it apparently occurred, at least in his judgment. Yet it is hard to say to what extent that judgment represents a reasonable difference of opinion from the officer's, or even incomplete information on the part of the author as an observer. Police do not always reveal to an observer in the back seat all the information they have at the time of a stop, and even questioning may not reveal everything the police know.

One clear fact is that the author's notes contain no record of observed beatings, insults, or profanity against persons stopped by police. Although some discretion was clearly based on suspects who conveyed a defiant attitude to police, the worst the author says about police behavior in the encounters is that one officer was "obnoxious" when using the loudspeaker to address people in cars stopped during a rainfall. In another instance an officer "jumped on" a suspect who disobeyed a command during a search. The absence of citizens' complaints or lawsuits arising from encounters made during this program tends to corroborate the author's notes on the general absence of excess in police encounters.—LWS][1]

Residents' Opinions

To measure residents' opinion of these practices, the author conducted surveys before implementing the proactive gun detection patrols (Time 1) and again approximately seven months later (Time 2) in both program and comparison areas. The goal was to survey approximately 100 adults from a randomly selected sample of residences in each of the two areas (for details see Shaw 1994, ch. 7). The Time 1 surveys were administered less than six weeks apart, respectively in Beat 144 (program) and Beat 242 (control). Approximately seven months later, the second survey was administered similarly. A panel design was used in selecting the Time 2 survey respondents, with a 36 percent rate of attrition in Beat 144 and a 27.6 percent rate in Beat 242. Such attrition is a potential threat to the internal validity of the research. To examine the extent of this threat, the author surveyed additional randomly selected respondents at Time 2.

Randomly selected residences were visited up to four or five times in order to produce a survey response (for a more detailed discussion of procedure, see Shaw 1994, ch. 7 and table 13). Time 1 surveys were conducted in Beat 144 in the period from June 27 through July 8, 1992 and in Beat 242 in the period from July 21 through August 5. The response rates in the two beats were almost identical. In Beat 144, 225 residences were visited; 58 of these were found to be unoccupied. Of the remaining 167 residences, contact could not be made at 23, and another 44 refused to participate, for a total of 100 completed surveys. The response rate is 69.4 percent when only refusals are considered, and 60 percent completion overall. In Beat 242, 194 residences were visited and only 20 were found to be unoccupied. Contact could not be made at 32 residences, and another 44 refused to participate, for a 69.0 percent response rate and a 53 percent completion rate. A total of 98 residents were surveyed in Beat 242.

Time 2 surveys were completed in Beat 144 between January 26 and February 13, 1993. Surveys were conducted in Beat 242 between February 5 and March 5. Because some people had moved, some refused to participate in the second survey, and some were simply unavailable, 64 of the 100 Time 1 survey respondents were interviewed again at Time 2. At 17 of the residences from the original sample, a different person, such as a relative, was interviewed.

In addition, a respondent at 19 of the residences originally selected (but not surveyed) at Time 1 was surveyed, for a total of 100 Time 2 surveys in Beat 144. In Beat 242, 71 of the 98 Time 1 survey respondents were interviewed again at Time 2. A relative or other person at the same address was surveyed in five residences; similarly, a respondent at 13 of the residences originally selected (but not surveyed) at Time 1 was surveyed, for a total of 89 Time 2 surveys in Beat 242. Although more respondents refused to participate at Time 2 in Beat 242 than in Beat 144 (19 versus 8; see table 2), this difference was due almost entirely to new potential respondents. Only six panel respondents in Beats 144 and seven in Beat 242 refused to participate at Time 2.

Survey Respondents' Demographic Characteristics

Survey respondents in the program and the comparison beat were similar in many ways. There was no difference in the number of males surveyed or in the median education level, although a few more nonblacks were surveyed in Beat 242 than in Beat 144. Respondents in Beat 144 were somewhat older than in 242, but the difference in median age was only 3 years (see table 1).

The survey respondents were slightly more "upscale" in Beat 242 than in the program area. A much larger percentage reported full-time employment in Beat 242 (53.91%) than in Beat 144 (28.79%). In a related finding, respondents of Beat 242 were much less likely to report an annual income of less than $10,000 (31.25%) than were respondents in Beat 144 (56.35%). Also, perhaps because the population in Beat 144 was somewhat older, respondents in that area had lived at

Table 1. Demographic Characteristics of Community Survey Respondents: Comparisions for Target Area (Beat 144) and Control Area (Beat 242) Respondents

	Beat 144			Beat 242			Test	P
	N	Mean	(SD/%)	N	Mean	(SD/%)		
Age	129	49.68	(18.97)	111	44.05	(14.90)	$t_{(236.1)}=2.58$	0.01
Median		47			44			
Male	44		(33.33)	44		(37.93)	$\chi^2_{(1)}=0.57$	0.45
Black	131		(99.24)	106		(91.38)	$\chi^2_{(1)}=9.0$	0.003
Education	132	11.42	(2.42)	115	12.63	(2.22)	$t_{(245.0)}=-4.1$	0.000
Median		12			12			
Income Under $10,000/Year	71		(56.35)	35		(31.25)	$\chi^2_{(1)}=15.22$	0.000
Employment								
Full-time	38		(28.79)	62		(53.91)		
Part-time	15		(11.36)	14		(12.17)	$\chi^2_{(2)}=18.27$	0.000
Retired	39			20				
Time Unemployed (mos.)	27	42.52	(45.76)	6	52.33	(72.10)	$t_{(31)}=-0.43$	0.67
Own Home	91		(68.42)	86		(74.14)	$\chi^2_{(1)}=0.99$	0.32
Years at Address	131	16.36	(13.21)	113	11.58	(9.52)	$t_{(234.9)}=3.27$	0.001
Median		15			10			
People at Residence	131	3.41	(2.39)	115	2.88	(1.52)	$t_{(223.4)}=2.11$	0.03
Children at Residence	132	1.33	(2.03)	113	1.01	(1.40)	$t_{(233.1)}=1.47$	0.14
Married	47		(35.88)	49		(42.61)	$\chi^2_{(1)}=1.17$	0.28
Have Religious Affil.	104		(78.79)	82		(71.30)	$\chi^2_{(1)}=1.85$	0.17
Saw Police Car	53		(39.55)	39		(33.63)	$\chi^2_{(1)}=0.94$	0.33

their present address about five years longer than had respondents in Beat 242. The author found no significant difference, however, between the proportion owning their own home (68.42% in Beat 144 and 74.14% in Beat 242).

Community Awareness and Acceptance of Police Efforts

Time 1 community surveys were conducted about six weeks after the police had completed their door-to-door visits. Thus an important question at that time was whether people were aware of the police department's door-to-door program. Seventy-nine percent of the residents surveyed in the program area responded affirmatively. At the same time, however, 30.6 percent of the comparison sample, who did not receive door-to-door visits, said they were aware of the program (see table 2). A more realistic estimate of the percentage of people who knew about the program is the proportion of program area respondents who said they remembered the police visiting and recalled receiving a flyer: that figure was 49 percent. Although this figure is much smaller than the 79 percent who reported awareness of the gun tips hotline, it still represents a substantial proportion of the sample. Only two people in the comparison area responded similarly.

Table 2. Time 1 Survey Respondents' Knowledge of the Gun Tips Program, Willingness to Help, and Opinions about Proactive Patrols

	Beat 144		Beat 242	
	N	(%)	N	(%)
Aware of Gun Tips Program	79	(79.0)	30	(30.6)
Recall Receiving "Gun Tips" Flyer from Police	49	(49.0)	2	(2.04)
Claim Willing to Call in a Gun Tip	88	(88.0)	76	(77.55)[a]
Claim to Have Called in a Gun Tip	4	(4.0)	2	(2.04)
Believe Tips Program Could Be				
Very helpful	31	(31.0)	33	(33.67)
Somewhat helpful	45	(45.0)	44	(44.90)
Would Like to See Proactive Patrols	94	(94.0)	95	(96.94)
Believe Proactive Patrol Could Be				
Very helpful	51	(51.0)	61	(62.24)[b]
Somewhat helpful	47	(47.0)	29	(29.59)

[a]$\chi^2_{(1)}=3.80; P<0.051$
[b]$\chi^2_{(2)}=8.74; P<0.013$

Whether or not they knew of this program, 88.0 percent of the respondents told the author that they would be willing to assist the police and call a hotline with information about illegal guncarrying. Survey respondents also were asked how helpful they thought the door-to-door and gun tips programs could be for residents in their neighborhood. Their answers were distributed fairly broadly: 24 percent thought it would do no good, and only 31 percent thought it would be very helpful. This distribution held even for individuals who stated that they would be willing to make a gun tip call. Of those 23 percent (20) thought the program would do no good, and only 33 percent (29) thought it would be very helpful.

Individuals who said they would not be willing to assist the police seemed fearful. The majority (5) of these persons responded that it was too dangerous. In one respondent's words, the program could be helpful if a person was "brave enough to speak up and take a chance on your life being taken." Another resident responded, "[I] don't want nobody comin' 'round here shooting at me." Only three individuals responded with lack of concern—for example, "It's not my problem" or "I don't want to meddle in other people's business."

It is important to remember that the police went to every residence in that community, and to some more than once, and spoke with residents in a friendly, nonthreatening manner. In response, the residents were generally receptive and glad to see the police going door-to-door. They frequently responded with comments such as "God bless you all, we shoulda' had a program like this before" or "Thank God! I didn't think you all would ever come. Maybe now we won't have to move."

During the Time 1 interview, respondents were asked prospective questions about the proactive patrols. Almost all were interested in seeing the patrols implemented (table 2); respondents in the program area, however, were somewhat less likely to believe that the patrols could be "very helpful" in their neighborhood (51.%) than were residents in the comparison area (62.2%).

Time 2 surveys showed a high awareness of police activities in the program area (table 3). Residents living in Beat 144 were almost three times more likely ($p<0.001$) than residents in Beat 242 to have heard about police breaking up groups of people hanging out on streets and street corners (32.0% versus 11.24%). The number of residents in Beat 144 who actually saw police breaking up such groups, although smaller, was nonetheless four times as great ($p<0.000$) as in Beat 242 (26.0% versus 6.74%). Residents in both areas were equally likely to believe that this type of enforcement activity was good for the neighborhood (88.0% and 82.02%).

Table 3. Time 2 Survey Respondents' Perceptions and Attitudes about Recent Police Proactive Patrol Activity in Their Neighborhood

	Beat 144		Beat 242		Test	*p*
	N	(%)	*N*	(%)		
Have Seen Police Walking on Foot Patrols	10	(10.0)	2	(2.25)	ns	
Police Breaking Up Groups of Youths on Streets/Corners						
Heard about	32	(32.0)	10	(11.24)	$\chi^2_{(1)}=11.7$	<0.001
Personally saw	26	(26.0)	6	(6.74)	$\chi^2_{(1)}=12.4$	<0.000
Believe good	88	(88.0)	73	(82.02)	ns	
Police Making Drug Busts in Their Neighborhood						
Heard about	42	(42.0)	28	(31.46)	$\chi^2_{(1)}=2.24$	<0.13
Personally saw	15	(15.0)	11	(12.36)	ns	
Believe good	96	(96.0)	86	(96.63)	ns	

In a final question about awareness of the proactive patrols, community residents were asked whether they believed the number of police patrolling their neighborhood had increased, stayed the same, or decreased in the past six months. Although the difference was only marginally significant ($p<0.108$), residents in Beat 144 were more likely to believe that the number of police patrols had increased (44.0%) than were residents in Beat 242 (29.21%).

Impact of Police Efforts on Quality of Life

Questions from the community survey, in which both pre- and postprogram questions were asked, are organized into the three following "quality of life" categories: (1) satisfaction with life in their neighborhood; (2) the perception of social and crime problems in the neighborhood; and (3) fear of crime and victimization.

Regarding satisfaction with life in the neighborhood, the author asked several questions about change in the previous six months (for better or worse), satisfaction with the area as a place to live, and likelihood of living in the neighborhood in the future. These were examined separately because they do not form a single dimension. For example, respondents frequently indicated that it was very likely they would be living in the same neighborhood a year later, not because they were satisfied with the neighborhood but because they could not afford to move elsewhere.

Respondents also were asked a number of questions about potential disorder and problems in the neighborhood (e.g. drug buyers and sellers on the streets, people being attacked or robbed). Skogan (1990) found that two dimensions of disorder—physical and social—were correlated fairly highly, although distinct (p. 51). Yet because the proactive patrol activities could not be expected to affect physical variables (e.g. litter, broken windows, abandoned cars), only the social variables are examined here. Three variables (congregating youths, drug buyers and sellers, and speeding or careless driving) were summed to form an indicator of social disorder.

In addition, as an indicator of respondents' perceptions of crime problems, four variables (burglaries, robberies, rape, and shootings) were summed. Finally, two variables were combined to create a measure of fear felt by residents in the community. Respondents were asked whether they were afraid to walk alone in their neighborhood during the day or at night, and whether they simply avoided certain places.

For each of these variables, the author conducted a multivariate repeated-measures analysis of variance. A univariate ANOVA using the full, increased Time 2 sample was also conducted for each variable.[2] These results are not reported here, however, because they support those of the appropriate repeated measures.

As a final measure of the impact of these programs on residents' perceptions of neighborhood crime, the survey respondents at Time 2 were asked direct questions about changes in drug selling and in gun-related crimes over the last six months, compared with the previous six months. This ad hoc measure of change is clearly less satisfactory than if respondents had been asked identical questions at Time 1 and Time 2; these questions were asked, however, to provide an additional measure of perceived change.

Even though Beat 242 would appear to be a somewhat better place to live (e.g., the median value of the homes was nearly $10,000 more in Beat 242 than in Beat 144 and the number of gun crimes per capita was lower), the Time 1 survey showed very little difference between random samples of approximately 100 residents from each neighborhood in their satisfaction with the neighborhood. Respondents in Beat 242 were slightly more likely than respondents in Beat 144 to think the neighborhood had changed for the better in the previous six months (BETTER) and to be satisfied with the neighborhood (SATISFY) (see table 4); this difference was not significant, however. Respondents were virtually identical in their estimate of whether they would be living in the neighborhood a year from the time of the survey (LIKELY).

Table 4.   Time 1 Survey Respondents' Satisfaction with the Neighborhood, Perception of Problems, and Level of Fear

Variable	Beat 144 N=100		Beat 242 N=98		Test	p
	Mean	(SD)	Mean	(SD)		
Better	1.79	(0.67)	1.89	(0.59)	$t_{(196)}=-1.09$	<0.28
Satisfy	2.62	(0.89)	2.82	(1.02)	$t_{(196)}=-1.45$	<0.15
Likely	3.39	(0.89)	3.39	(1.03)	$t_{(196)}=0.02$	<0.99
Social	5.69	(2.02)	4.91	(1.83)	$t_{(196)}=2.85$	<0.005
Crime	5.62	(1.83)	5.41	(1.79)	$t_{(196)}=0.82$	<0.41
Fear	1.41	(1.06)	1.20	(1.04)	$t_{(196)}=1.37$	<0.17

In contrast, residents perceived some difference between these areas in the measure of social disorder (table 4). As might be expected, residents of Beat 144 saw a greater problem with social disorder (SOCIAL: $t_{(196)}=2.85$, $p<0.005$) than did residents of Beat 242. Yet they perceived no difference in several types of crime (indicated by the variable CRIME). Finally, although slightly less in Beat 242, respondents' reported fear of walking alone or their avoidance of certain places did not differ significantly between the two areas.

Approximately seven months later, respondents were asked the same questions again. Consistent with the hypothesis that proactive patrols were welcomed by residents of Beat 144, the repeated measures analyses in table 5 show several interactions. Although residents of both areas perceived their neighborhood as having changed for the better in the previous six months, in comparison with their responses at Time 1, this change was marginally greater in the target area ($F_{(1,133)}$=3.08, p<0.08). During the program period respondents in Beat 144 also became more satisfied with their neighborhood as a place to live ($F_{(1,133)}$=3.48, p<0.06).

Table 5. Repeated-Measures Analyses Examining Neighborhood Questions from Time 1 and Time 2 Community Surveys in Police Beats 144 and 242

Analyses examining survey respondents' belief that their neighborhood had become a better place to live (BETTER), satisfaction with the neighborhood (SATISFY), and likelihood of living in the area in one year (LIKELY) before and after police proactive patrols began:

	N	Better Time 1	Better Time 2	Satisfy Time 1	Satisfy Time 2	Likely Time 1	Likely Time 2
Beat 144	64	1.83	2.28	2.58	2.91	3.55	3.48
Beat 242	71	1.87	2.07	2.82	2.86	3.54	3.66
Time x Beat	F(df)	3.08	(1,133)	3.48	(1,133)	1.02	(1,133)
	p	0.08		0.06		0.32	
Time	F(df)	19.91	(1,133)	5.85	(1,133)	0.12	(1,133)
	p	0.0001		0.02		0.73	
Beat	F(df)	0.95	(1,133)	0.39	(1,133)	0.49	(1,133)
	p	0.33		0.53		0.49	

Analyses examining survey respondents' perception of social problems (SOCIAL), crime problems (CRIME), and level of fear (FEAR) in their neighborhood, before and after police proactive patrols began:

	N	Social Time 1	Social Time 2	Crime Time 1	Crime Time 2	Fear Time 1	Fear Time 2
Beat 144	64	5.73	4.83	5.53	4.95	1.64	1.42
Beat 242	71	4.87	4.86	5.34	4.99	1.14	1.31
Time x Beat	F(df)	7.84	(1,133)	0.59	(1,133)	4.40	(1,133)
	p	0.006		0.44		0.04	
Time	F(df)	8.34	(1,133)	10.09	(1,133)	0.07	(1,133)
	p	0.005		0.002		0.79	
Beat	F(df)	2.28	(1,133)	0.11	(1,133)	3.71	(1,133)
	p	0.13		0.74		0.06	

Perhaps the most impressive change reported by the survey respondents pertained to the index of social disorder. Table 5 reveals a highly significant interaction ($F_{1,133}$=7.84, P<0.006): the perception of social disorder declined significantly in Beat 144. No corresponding change was observed in Beat 242. In contrast, the two beats reported similar perceived reductions in crime

$(F_{1,133}=10.09, p<0.002$, table 5). Yet in response to specific questions at Time 2 regarding drugs and shooting (data not displayed), respondents in Beat 144 reported significantly more improvement in the drug problem than did residents in Beat 242 $(t_{(185)}=3.39, p<0.0009)$, and slightly more improvement in the shooting problem $(t_{(187)}=1.61, p<0.109)$.

The survey data strongly suggest that the program had a positive effect on Beat 144 residents' fear of crime. Table 5 shows a significant beat-by-time interaction with the panel respondents $(F_{(1,133)}=4.40, p<0.04)$. Between the Time 1 and the Time 2 survey, respondents in Beat 144 became less fearful, whereas respondents in Beat 242 actually became somewhat more fearful.

Discussion and Conclusions

This article offers evidence supporting two claims. First, the Kansas City Police implemented proactive patrols in an area of high gun crime without being discriminatory in selection or aggressive in manner towards the citizens they stopped, observing a high level of legality in their basis for stopping the citizens they stopped. Second, the patrol program did not increase community tensions, and in fact was supported both in advance and in results by the majority of local households surveyed. Residents of the program area evaluated crime conditions at the end of the program more favorably than residents of the comparison area.

As a test of the broader concern about proactive policing, this article has its limitations. First, the study included no direct measures of residents' concern about police brutality, procedural fairness by police, respect shown by police to citizens, or police attitudes towards minorities. Because most of the police in this predominantly black area were white, these omissions are important. We cannot reject the hypothesis that the program would have produced Time 1–Time 2 changes for the worse on such measures.

A second, less serious limitation is the absence of interview data from persons stopped by police. The effects of this shortcoming, however, may be embedded at least partially in the community responses. Support for this claim can be found in an alternative interpretation of a key finding in the data on gun seizures: about one-third (35.5%) of the 83 persons arrested for carrying concealed weapons in all of 1992 in the program area also lived in that area (Shaw 1994:260). Two-thirds, of course, did not.

One interpretation of this finding, as residents suggested during interviews, is that most offenders in such an area may be outsiders who come there only for trouble. This suggests that the community is different from the street population that police stopped and checked, and may have very different views from those individuals.

On the other hand, the visibility of the program to the community went far beyond the arrests of community residents for carrying guns. The 1,090 traffic citations, 616 arrests, 948 car checks, and 532 pedestrian checks may have made a stronger impression on residents. The author's field notes state that police "ticketing of illegal parked cars ticked residents off." The undocumented actions, such as breaking up groups of youthful loiterers on street corners, were observable by community residents and also may have affected their own children. If the community was inclined to be angered by this program, it evidently had ample grounds—grounds of which the residents may have been well aware, and which affected persons close to them.

Although the reduction in gun crimes and actual shootings (Shaw 1994: 252–53) associated with the program is of primary concern, it is important that residents in the program area also *perceive* the reduction in offenses. Such perceptions cannot be expected to be entirely objective, but if residents perceive even somewhat accurately the actual reduction in offenses, a sense of predictability is more likely to be restored to persons living in the neighborhood, followed by a reduction in fear. Each of these developments is supported by the data.

The most important conclusion, however, is that the community supported the proactive patrols and efforts. For many proponents of community policing, the fact that the program may have reduced firearms crime is not enough. It is also vital that the community view the effort as legitimate. Although we do not know what the arrestees and the people who were stopped thought of the method, the residents showed appreciation of police efforts. Increasingly the complaints about police in some high-crime neighborhoods are less about what police do than about the need for extra police. These findings, like Skogan's (1990), further support the conclusion that residents of high-crime neighborhoods notice additional police presence when it is provided, and show measurable improvements in their assessments of local crime conditions.

Notes

[1] The final revision of this paper at the time of the author's death was completed by Amy Patterson, Jon Sorenson, and Lawrence W. Sherman.

[2] A potential disadvantage is associated with the repeated-measures analysis when the mortality or attrition rate for the panel is significant, as with these respondents (36% in Beat 144 and 27.6% in Beat 242): the reduction in the samples from which inferences are to be drawn increases the chances of a Type II error in the analyses. Because of this observed attrition, additional households randomly selected (but not surveyed) at Time 1 were surveyed at Time 2 to increase the sample N. These univariate ANOVAs were examined for the main effects of TIME (Time 1 and Time 2), SAMPLE (Beat 144 and Beat 242), and CONTACT (whether the respondent was surveyed at both Time 1 and Time 2), after all interactions were examined.

References

Butterfield, F. (1994) "Novel Way to Stop Gunmen: Simply Go after Their Guns." *New York Times,* November 20, p. A1.

Castaneda, R. (1994) One City's Attack on Handguns." *Washington Post,* January 30, p. B1.

Cook, P. J. (1991) "The Technology of Personal Violence." In M. Tonry (ed.), *Crime and Justice: A Review of Research,* Vol. 14, pp. 2–72. Chicago: University of Chicago Press.

Cook, T. D. & D. T. Campbell (1979) *Quasi-experimentation: Design and Analysis Issues for Field Settings.* Chicago: Rand McNally.

Kleck, G. (1991) *Point Blank: Guns and Violence in America.* New York: Aldine.

Law Enforcement News (LEN) (1994) "Law Enforcement around the Nation, 1994." Vol. 20 (414). New York: John Jay College of Criminal Justice.

McDowall, D. (1991) "Firearm Availability and Homicide Rates in Detroit, 1951–1986." *Social Forces* 69:1085–1101.

Moore, M. H. (1980) "The Police and Weapons Offenses." *Annals, American Academy of Political and Social Sciences* 452:22–32.

National Institute of Justice (NIJ) (1994) *The Kansas City Gun Experiment.* Washington, DC: National Institute of Justice.

President's Commission of Law Enforcement and Administration of Justice. (1967) *Task Force Report: The Police.* Washington DC: U.S. Government Printing Office.

Rand, M. (1994) *Guns and Crime.* Washington DC: Bureau of Justice Statistics.

Reiss, A. J., Jr. & J. A. Roth, eds. (1993) *Understanding and Preventing Violence.* Washington, DC: National Academy Press.

Shaw, J. W. (1993) "Community Policing to Take Guns off the Street." *Behavioral Sciences and the Law* 11:361–74.

_____ (1994) "Community Policing Against Crime: Violence and Firearms." Doctoral dissertation, University of Maryland at College Park.

Sherman, L. W. (1990) "Police Crackdowns: Initial and Residual Deterrence." In M. Tonry and N. Morris (eds.), *Crime and Justice: A Review of Research.* Vol 12, pp. 1–48. Chicago: University of Chicago Press.

_____ (1993) "Defiance, Deterrence, and Irrelevance: A Theory of the Criminal Sanction." *Journal of Research in Crime and Delinquency* 30:445–73.

Sherman, L. W. & Rogan, D. P. (1995) Effects of Gun Seizures on Gun Violence: Hot Spots Patrol in Kansas City." *Justice Quarterly,* 12:673–93.

Sherman, L. W., J. W. Shaw, & D. P. Rogan (1995) *The Kansas City Gun Experiment.* Washington, DC: National Institute of Justice.

Skogan, W. (1990) *Disorder and Decline.* New York: Free Press.

Walters, L. S. (1995) "Kansas City Police Target Crime 'Hot Spots.'" *Christian Science Monitor,* January 12, p. 1.

Worthington, R. (1994) "Trial Program Gets Aggressive about Guns." *Chicago Tribune,* December 11, p. 25.

20

The Future of Policing

David Bayley and Clifford Shearing

Modern democratic countries like the United States, Britain, and Canada have reached a watershed in the evolution of their systems of crime control and law enforcement. Future generations will look back on our era as a time when one system of policing ended and another took its place. Two developments define the change—the pluralizing of policing and the search by the public police for an appropriate role.

First, policing is no longer monopolized by the public police, that is, the police created by government. Policing is now being widely offered by institutions other than the state, most importantly by private companies on a commercial basis and by communities on a volunteer basis. Second, the public police are going through an intense period of self-questioning, indeed, a true identity crisis. No longer confident that they are either effective or efficient in controlling crime, they are anxiously examining every aspect of their performance—objectives, strategies, organization, management, discipline, and accountability. These movements, one inside and the other outside the police, amount to the restructuring of policing in contemporary democratic societies.

The restructuring of policing, which is already well advanced, has profound implications for public life, especially on the level and distribution of public safety, the vitality of civil rights, and the character of democratic government. Yet, despite the fatefulness of these changes, there has been hardly any public debate on the future of policing. If Thomas Jefferson was right that the price of liberty is eternal vigilance, then the current silence about these issues is a source of great risk for democratic societies.

In order to begin a debate that is long overdue, we first describe in greater detail the pluralizing of policing and the changing character of public policing.

Source: Reprinted by permission of the Law & Society Association from *Law & Society Review*, Vol. 30, No. 3 (1996), pp. 585–606.

Second, we examine the impact of these developments on society and government. Third, we predict the likely future of policing by pinpointing the factors shaping each movement. Finally, we specify the policies that are needed to ensure that the current restructuring of policing serves the broad interests of a developed democratic society.

It is very important to be clear about what we mean when we talk about policing. We are not concerned exclusively with "the police," that is, with people in uniforms who are hired, paid, and directed by government. We are interested in all explicit efforts to create visible agents of crime control, whether by government or by nongovernmental institutions. So we are dealing with poli*cing*, not just *police*. At the same time, we say *explicit* attempts to create policing institutions so as not to extend our discussion to all the informal agencies that societies rely on to maintain order, such as parents, churches, employers, spouses, peers, neighbors, professional associations, and so forth. The activities of such people and institutions are undoubtedly critically important in crime control, but they have not been explicitly designed for this purpose. They are rarely objects of explicit crime policy. So the scope of our discussion is bigger than the breadbox of the police but smaller than the elephant of social control. Our focus is on the self-conscious process whereby societies designate and authorize people to create public safety.

The End of a Monopoly

In the past 30 years the state's monopoly on policing has been broken by the creation of a host of private and community-based agencies that prevent crime, deter criminality, catch lawbreakers, investigate offenses, and stop conflict. The police and policing have become increasingly distinct. While the customary police are paid, the new policing agents come in both paid and unpaid forms. The former are referred to as private security; the latter as community crime prevention.

To complicate matters further, private security—the paid part of private policing—comes in two forms: people employed by commercial companies who are hired on contract by others and persons employed directly by companies to work as security specialists. Private police now outnumber the public police in most developed countries. In the United States, for example, there are three times more private security agents than public police officers (Bayley 1994).[1] There are twice as many private police as public police in Canada and in Britain (Johnston 1992). In all countries for which there is information, the private security sector is growing faster than the public. This has been true since the early 1960s, when the contemporary rebirth of private security began. Businesses and commercial firms, by the way, are not the only customers for private security. Private guards are now often used to guard many government buildings, including police stations.

The increase in the numbers of private police reflects a remarkable change in their status (Shearing 1992). Through World War II, private security was looked on as a somewhat unsavory occupation. It had the image of ill-trained bands of thugs hired by private businesses to break strikes, suppress labor, and spy on one another. The police, as well as the public, viewed private security companies as a dangerous and unauthorized intrusion by private interests into a government preserve. Since World War II, however, a more tolerant attitude has developed, with private security seen as a necessary supplement to the overburdened public police. In the past few years especially, governments have gone beyond passive acceptance to active encouragement of commercial private security. There now seems to be a general recognition that crime is too extensive and complex to be dealt with solely by the police and that the profit motive is not to be feared in policing.

In recent years private policing has also expanded under noncommercial auspices as communities have undertaken to provide security using volunteered resources and people. A generation ago community crime prevention was virtually nonexistent. Today it is everywhere—citizen automobile and foot patrols, neighborhood watches, crime-prevention associations and advisory councils, community newsletters, crime-prevention publications and presentations, protective escort services for at-risk populations, and monitors around schools, malls, and public parks. Like commercial private security, the acceptability of volunteer policing has been transformed in less than a generation. While once it was thought of as vigilantism, it is now popular with the public and actively encouraged by the police. Because these activities are uncoordinated, and sometimes ephemeral, it is hard to say how extensive they are. Impressionistically, they seem to be as common as McDonald's golden arches, especially in urban areas.

Policing has become a responsibility explicitly shared between government and its citizens, sometimes mediated through commercial markets, sometimes arising spontaneously. Policing has become pluralized. Police are no longer the primary crime-deterrent presence in society; they have been supplanted by more numerous private providers of security.

Searching for Identity

During the past decade, police throughout the developed democratic world have increasingly questioned their role, operating strategies, organization, and management. This is attributable to growing doubts about the effectiveness of their traditional strategies in safeguarding the public from crime.

The visible presence of the police seems to be stretched so thin that it fails to deter. Police devote about 60% of their resources to patrolling but complain about running from one emergency call to another, often involving noncriminal matters. The scarecrow has grown tattered in relation to the prevalence of crime. At the same time, regrettably few villains are caught in relation to crimes committed: 21% in the United States, 26% in Britain, and 16% in Canada (1992 statistics).[2]

Even fewer receive any sort of punishment through the criminal justice system. Crime pays, as scarcely more than 5% of crimes committed in the United States result in the imprisonment of the criminals involved. Because the police know all this, they are desperately searching for new approaches, responding in part to the competition they face from private security whose strategies overwhelmingly favor prevention over detection and punishment. The central question underlying police soul-searching is whether they can become more effective in truly preventing crime.

One answer to this has been community policing. Its philosophy is straightforward: the police cannot successfully prevent or investigate crime without the willing participation of the public; therefore police should transform communities from being passive consumers of police protection to active co-producers of public safety. Community policing changes the orientation of the police and represents a sharp break with the past. Community policing transforms police from being an emergency squad in the fight against crime to becoming primary diagnosticians and treatment coordinators.

Although community policing has gotten most of the publicity in recent years, many police believe that law enforcement, their traditional tool in crime fighting, can be made more efficient. This approach might be called crime-oriented policing. It involves developing smarter enforcement tactics so that crime will not pay. Some examples include the setting up of fencing operations to catch habitual thieves and burglars; harassing drug markets so as to raise the cost of doing business; monitoring the activities of career criminals and arresting them for minor infractions of the law; cracking down unpredictably on criminal activity in particular locations; installing video cameras on public streets; and analyzing financial transactions by computer to spot cheating and fraud.

Police are also discussing, and sometimes implementing, a strategy that is a hybrid of community-oriented and crime-oriented policing. It is referred to as order-maintenance policing and involves stopping the disorderly, unruly, and disturbing behavior of people in public places, whether lawful or not. This suppressive activity not only reassures the public, demonstrating the limits for unacceptable behavior, but reduces the incidence of more serious crime (Wilson & Kelling 1982; Skogan 1990). The New York City Police Department employed this strategy against the "squeegy men" who extorted money from motorists by washing the windshields of cars stopped at traffic lights and asking for donations. The New York City Transit Police reduced the incidence of robbery on the subways by undertaking an energetic campaign against fare-beaters who vaulted over turnstiles. In both cases, the police reduced menacing activity that frightened law-abiding citizens and warned off criminals who would take advantage of what seemed to be unguarded territory (Kelling & Coles 1994). Like community policing, order-maintenance policing requires diagnosis and problem solving, but like traditional policing, it emphasizes law enforcement. It might be called community policing with a hard edge.

In addition to rethinking their standard strategies, the police are themselves helping to blur the line between government and nongovernment policing. For example, some police departments now sell the protective services they used to give away. Rather than considering police protection as a public good, free to all citizens, police are increasingly taking the view that people who derive a commercial benefit from police efforts should pay for it. Accordingly, ordinances have been enacted requiring private burglar-alarm companies to be fined or charged a fee if their electronic systems summon police to false alarms more than a specified number of times. Police are also beginning to charge fees for covering rock concerts, professional sporting events, and ethnic festivals. In some cities, businesses have banded together to pay for additional police patrols in order to get the protection they think they need.

In a development that is found across northern America, police not only sell their protective services but allow their own officers to be hired as private security guards—a practice known as "moonlighting." Many American police regularly work two jobs, one public, the other private. Indeed, moonlighting is considered a valuable perquisite of police employment. What this means is that the pluralizing of policing is being directly subsidized in the United States by public funds. Private policing uses police that have been recruited, trained, and supported by government. When acting as agents of private entities, police retain their legal authority and powers.

Not only do public police work as private police but civilians—nonpolice people—increasingly share responsibilities within public policing. Special Constables in Great Britain and Cadets, Police Auxiliaries, and Reserves in the United States often work on the street alongside regular police personnel. Though they serve without pay, and often without weapons, they are virtually indistinguishable in appearance from police. Some communities in Britain have hired able-bodied unemployed persons to patrol the streets, and others have deployed partially trained police officers as community liaison officers (Johnston 1994).

Furthermore, work traditionally performed by uniformed officers has increasingly been given to civilian employees. Usually these are jobs that don't require law enforcement, such as repairing motor vehicles, programming computers, analyzing forensic evidence, and operating radio-dispatch systems. Of all police employees, 27% in the United States are now civilians; 35% in Great Britain; 20% in Canada and Australia; and 12% in Japan (Bayley 1994). A variation on this is to contract out—privatize—support functions altogether, such as publishing, maintaining criminal records, forensic analysis, auditing and disbursement, and the guarding of police premises. Police departments are also beginning to use senior citizen volunteers to provide specialized expertise as pilots, auditors, chemists, or computer programmers.

Some communities employ special support personnel, often dressed in uniforms similar to those of the police, in frontline functions as well. The most common of these are the now ubiquitous parking-meter patrols. But uniformed civilians also conduct crime-prevention classes, make security inspections of premises, provide follow-up counseling to crime victims, resolve neighborhood disputes, and advise about pending criminal matters (Skolnick & Bayley 1986).

The innovations that are being made in operational strategies as well as the increasing use of civilians in police work have important implications for the management and organization of the police. For example, police increasingly resent being used by government as an omnibus regulatory agency. So, in an effort to save money and focus on crime prevention, many departments are considering reducing the scope of regulatory activity, such as licensing bars and nightclubs, enforcing parking regulations, maintaining lost and founds, organizing neighborhood watches, conducting crime-prevention seminars, and advising property owners about protective hardware (Johnston 1994; Bayley 1985).

Police are also beginning to recognize that the traditional quasi-military management model, based on ranks and a hierarchical chain of command, may not accommodate the requirements of modern policing. Several forces have recently eliminated redundant supervisory ranks, and almost all are talking about the value of participative, collegial management. This involves decentralizing command and allowing subordinate commanders to determine the character of police operations in their areas. There is also a great deal of talk about treating the public as customers and about measuring performance by surveys of public satisfaction rather than exclusively by the number of crimes and arrests.

Finally, police are being subjected to more intense and rigorous supervision by both government and nongovernment agencies than has ever been true in the past. In Britain, Canada, and Australia civilian review boards have recently been created that can independently investigate instances of police misbehavior, especially those involving allegations of brutality. In the United States, too, 66 major police departments had civilian review by late 1994 and the number was steadily increasing (Walker & Wright 1994). From the police point of view, the unthinkable is happening: the behavior of individual officers is now subject to civilian oversight, including, in some jurisdictions, determining blame and the severity of punishment.

Moreover, great attention is now being given to developing mechanisms for the systematic evaluation of the quality of police service. Checklists of performance indicators have been developed and national data bases assembled to assist the evaluation exercise. Private management consultant firms are now regularly hired to assist local governments in evaluating police. Accrediting organizations have been set up nationally as well as in several American states and Canadian provinces to develop standards of police performance and organization.

Taken together, the pluralizing of policing and the search by the public police for a new role and methodology mean that not only has government's monopoly on policing been broken in the late twentieth century, but the police monopoly on expertise within its own sphere of activity has ended. Policing now belongs to everybody—in activity, in responsibility, and in oversight.

What's at Stake

Does it matter that policing is being reconstructed? Should we care that policing is pluralizing and that the public police are having an identity crisis? Yes, we should. These developments have fateful consequences for the level of public safety, for access to public security, for human rights, and for accountability. Let us examine restructuring's implications for each of these.

Safety

Expanding the auspices under which policing is provided increases the number of security agents. If visible policing deters, then communities should be safer if there are private uniformed security guards and designated civilian patrols and watchers to supplement the public police. If the expansion of private policing was occurring at the expense of public police, of course, then safety would not be enhanced. But that does not appear to be happening. Relative to population, there are more police in developed democracies in 1995 than in 1970 despite the growth in private security. It seems reasonable to conclude, therefore, that pluralizing has made communities safer.

Pluralizing the sources of policing affects not only the quantity of policing but its quality as well. Although both public and private police rely on visibility to deter criminality, private police emphasize the logic of security, while public police emphasize the logic of justice. The major purpose of private security is to reduce the risk of crime by taking preventive actions; the major purpose of the public police is to deter crime by catching and punishing criminals.

Arrest is the special competence and preferred tool of the public police. By using it quickly and accurately, they hope to deter criminality. Private police, on the other hand, both commercial and community based, have no greater enforcement powers than property owners and ordinary citizens. Thus, their special competence and preferred tool is anticipatory regulation and amelioration. By analyzing the circumstances that give rise to victimization and financial loss, they recommend courses of action that will reduce the opportunity for crime to occur. These recommendations are followed because they become conditions for employment or participation. For a secretary in an office, locking doors and keeping a purse in a desk drawer are conditions of employment; for a teenager in a shopping mall, wearing shoes and not playing loud music are conditions of access; for a retailer, not selling goods on the sidewalk in front of his store is a condition for acceptance by the local business community; and for airline passengers, passing through a metal detector is a condition of travel. Because such regulations are legitimized by the fiction of being self-imposed, as opposed to being mandated by government, they avoid most constitutional challenge.

There is a closer connection between the end—safety—and the means—policing—with private police, both commercial and volunteer, than with public police. Governments protect communities by providing police and then limiting their authority; private institutions and informal communities protect themselves by determining what circumstances produce crime and then finding people who know how to change them (Shearing 1996). Private police are more responsive than public police to the "bottom line" of safety. If safety is not increased, private police can be fired. For public police the bottom line is not safety but clearance rates. But even here failure has few negative consequences. Police are not fired for not achieving this objective.

The public police are beginning to recognize the inherent limitations of their justice-based approach. Through community policing and order-maintenance policing, the public police are developing strategies for reducing disorder and the opportunities for crime that are similar to the practices readily accepted by commercial and informal communities from private police.

Both quantitatively and qualitatively, then, the pluralizing of policing should increase public safety.

The gains in public safety from the soul-searching currently unsettling public policing are less predictable. It depends on which way they go: more of the same, crime-oriented law enforcement, order maintenance, or community policing. Improvements in crime prevention will require commitment to experiment with new approaches and a willingness to subject them to rigorous evaluation. What is required is a shift in the logic of policing from one that conceives of it as remedying past wrongs to one that seeks to promote security.

Equity

The pluralizing of policing promises to increase public safety and has already done so in some places. The problem is that pluralizing under market auspices at present does not improve security equally across society. It favors institutions and individuals that are well-to-do. Commercial policing not balanced either by voluntary neighborhood crime prevention or by public policing following a preventive, presumptive logic leads to the inequitable distribution of security along class lines. If public safety is considered a general responsibility of government, perhaps even a human right, then increased reliance on commercial private policing represents a growing injustice.

The effects of pluralization under commercial auspices would be even more harmful if the prosperous sectors of the community who pay most of the taxes were to withdraw resources from the public sector, objecting that they were paying twice for security—once to the government and once again to hired private security. If this were to occur, the government's ability to develop qualitatively improved policing for the poor would be undermined. It might even be difficult to maintain existing levels of police service. Sam Walker (1976) has argued that this has already occurred and explains the chronic underpolicing of lower- and middle-income neighborhoods throughout American history. It may also be happening today in the form of tax revolts, such as Proposition 13 in California. Undoubtedly the people who are most interested in reducing taxes are those who feel relatively secure and spend most of their time in privately protected places.

That people are calculating the cumulative costs of policing would be unambiguously indicated if communities began to ask for vouchers from the government to spend on policing, public or private, as has happened in public education. In such a system, communities could opt out of the public sector, or substitute an alternative public supplier of police services. The contract system of policing in Canada is like this, although communities must choose exclusively among government suppliers. Despite the popularity of the idea of privatization in the public sector, no government we know of has allowed communities to use public money to substitute private for public police. As we will argue shortly, this provides one element in a response to the injustice of the growing inequality of access to security.

Some of the efforts the public police are making to restructure themselves may help to solve the equity issue, others will not. If police concentrate on law enforcement, the dualism between rich and poor will be exacerbated. The rich will be increasingly policed preventively by commercial security while the poor will be policed reactively by enforcement-oriented public police. Moreover, since there seems to be a qualitative difference in the efficacy of these approaches—deterrence versus prevention—the poor will also be relatively less secure. There are three ways theoretically to prevent this inequitable dualism from arising, given the unavailability of market mechanisms for poor people.

First, the numbers of traditional police could be increased in poor high-crime areas. Unfortunately, this might be as unpleasant for the poor as the dualism itself, because it would lead to an intensification of traditional law enforcement.

Second, the public police could adopt the community policing model for economically poor high-crime areas. Community and order-maintenance policing incorporates many of the adaptive, consensual, ends-oriented practices of private security. Unfortunately, despite pronouncements to the contrary, police are often reluctant to adopt such policies in high-crime areas where they are already feeling hard pressed and where the efficacy of new approaches is unproven. Although community policing in theory is a powerful way to provide preventive policing for the poor, it may be distributed across cities in such a way that it reinforces rather than offsets the growing inequity in public security along class and racial lines.

Third, communities themselves might spontaneously develop their crime-preventing capacities. The chances of community-based pluralizing offsetting the defects of public policing are difficult to predict. Mobilization takes place more easily where people trust one another, possess leadership skills, have a stake in their communities, and are organized politically to achieve it. Although such efforts are growing by leaps and bounds, their efficacy, especially in high-crime areas, is unproven (Rosenbaum & Heath 1990: Skogan 1990).

The mobilizing activities of the public police through community policing are probably necessary, therefore, to offset the emerging dualism. This alone is likely to be of limited value, however, because experience so far suggests that community policing is harder to introduce in poor than in affluent neighborhoods. The irony may be that community policing compensates for the emerging dualism best where it is least needed and worst where it is most needed.

Human Rights

Because government is deeply distrusted in Anglo-American tradition, the powers of the police are circumscribed; their activities closely monitored. Private commercial policing and community-based private security, on the other hand, are apt to be more intrusive, premonitory, and presumptive than public policing. They impose the more onerous and extensive obligations of custom and public opinion. The pluralizing of policing, therefore, increases the informal regulatory control of crime. This, indeed, is the strength of policing under nonstate auspices: social pressure rather than law ensures discipline.

Seen in these terms, community policing, which is community-based crime prevention under governmental auspices, is a contradiction in terms. It requires the police, who are bound by law, to lead communities in informal surveillance, analysis, and treatment. Community policing is a license for police to intervene in the private life of individuals. It harnesses the coercive power of the state to social amelioration. This represents an expansion of police power, and is much more in keeping with the continental European than with the Anglo-American traditions of policing. Community policing may be an answer to the dualism brought by pluralizing but at the risk of encouraging the "vigilantism of the majority" (Johnston 1994).

Community policing, and its cousin community-based crime prevention, are attractive solutions to the problem of security inequity in a society where policing is being pluralized. But both impose costs. Community-based crime prevention, like commercial private policing, imposes social rather than governmental constraints. Community policing, on the other hand, couples social pressure with government direction. The mitigating factor is that community policing, as we note below, can provide for some measure of "bottom-up" accountability if it is developed in ways that encourage and permit genuine citizen participation.

Democracy

Democratic principle requires that police be accountable so that they serve the interests of the people. This is surely no less true for policing generically, which, as we have just seen, determines in a practical way the balance between freedom and order that people experience. At first glance, pluralization would not seem to pose a problem for accountability. Commercial private security is accountable to the market. If customers don't like what their security experts do, they can fire them. This alternative is not available for public police, who can only be fired by revolution. The problem with this view is that the accountability provided by markets accrues to buyers of private security and not to all the people who might be affected by it. Private security inevitably serves employers better than workers, owners better than patrons, and institutions better than individuals. The great advantage of public policing in democratic countries is that it is accountable to every citizen through the mechanisms of representative government.

Furthermore, the pluralizing of security under commercial auspices changes the social basis on which policing is organized. In democratic countries, police have been created to serve the interests of people territorially defined. Public policing is based on geographical communities. Private police, by contrast, serve primarily interest communities, that is, communities united by function rather than geography. It follows that the decentralization of policing that occurs through pluralizing is very different from the decentralization that occurs when government does it. The former is more selective in social terms; the latter includes everyone.

Voluntary community crime prevention, the other way in which pluralizing is occurring, does not suffer from the defect of social selectivity. The social basis for it is the same as under government, namely, people territorially defined. The problem with volunteer private policing, however, is its organizational informality. It may fail to represent the interests of people who are inarticulate, unorganized, and marginalized. The volunteers in private policing are likely to have interests that may differ from those of people who decline to participate. Community crime prevention is policing by the self-appointed, which is what people usually think of as vigilantism.

In sum, commercial private policing provides accountability through the formal mechanism of contracts but on the basis of social interests that may exclude many citizens. Volunteer private security provides accountability through informal mechanisms organized on the basis of citizenship that may or may not include everybody. Public policing provides accountability through formal mechanisms organized on the basis of citizenship that, in principle, cover everyone. Unless new alternatives are developed, it follows that accountability is best achieved through public policing operating according to principles of community policing. Community policing supplements the customary accountability of representative political institutions with grassroots consultation, evaluation, and feedback.

Trade-offs

What trade-offs among these qualitatively different features—safety, equity, human rights, and accountability—does the current restructuring of policing present?

Broadening the auspices under which policing is organized, especially substituting private for governmental ones, probably raises the level of public safety because it increases the number of security agents and also substitutes a preventive security paradigm for a deterrent one. However, pluralizing increases safety at the cost of equity. This can be offset if community policing is strongly implemented in disorganized poor communities afflicted by crime.

Pluralized policing, however, is less constrained by formal rules and, therefore, puts the rights of the people it polices at risk. Pluralized policing is more security conscious than rights conscious.

Pluralized policing, under both commercial and community auspices, is only fictively consensual and democratic. Although it represents and empowers new groups, it does so on the basis of social interest rather than citizenship, and it provides haphazardly for the representation of all who might be affected by it. Pluralized policing inevitably shifts power away from government, but it does not necessarily distribute it to more people. Community policing, on the other hand, combines the traditional accountability of representative government with the informal accountability of volunteer crime prevention.

The point to underscore is that the changes occurring in policing are more than technical adjustments in the way policing is delivered. They represent the restructuring of government itself and the redistribution of power over one of government's core functions. By shifting policing to new auspices through markets, community action, and police reform, the nature of governance is changing.

The Likely Future

Recognizing that fundamental changes are being made in policing that have profound consequences for the quality of civic life, is it possible to predict what the future holds? What balance among the overlapping and competing movements of pluralization and reformation will emerge? Will a new and stable equilibrium be found between state and nonstate policing? Might the state reassert itself, once again dominating policing? Could the public police become increasingly marginalized, confined to the policing of poor inner cities? And what will the character of public policing become—enforcement oriented, community based, or some new combination?

The current restructuring is driven by the public's concern about security. It is hardly an accident that the expansion of private security as well as the development of community policing coincided with rising crime rates throughout the developed world. If the threat to security were to decline significantly, the impetus to restructuring would be largely removed. This is unlikely to happen. Crime, notwithstanding the recent decline in overall rates in some countries, will continue to rise and even perhaps get worse for two reasons. First, crime is disproportionately committed by young males between the ages of 15 and 25. Twenty-nine percent of serious crime in the United States is committed by people under 19.[3] This group will rise by over 20% in the next decade. In Canada 14% of crime of violence and 25% of crimes against property are committed by people 12 to 17 years old (Statistics Canada 1993). Second, the violence of crime has been increasing. During the past 10 years the rate at which American teens are murdered has doubled (Blumstein 1994). The homicide arrest rate for white youths rose by 80% during the past decade, for black youths 125%. This rising lethality can be traced to the increased availability of sophisticated firearms that in turn is related to the penetration of drug markets into poor urban neighborhoods (Butterfield 1995). Unless circumstances change fundamentally, the violence of crime will continue to be perceived as a serious threat.

Furthermore, whatever happens to crime objectively, the public's fear of crime will certainly not decline. Because crime is fascinating, the media can be counted on to continue to exploit and exaggerate it. Only criminologists and police seem to know that crime is not randomly distributed in society; that it is not a national problem affecting everyone to the same extent. Crime is concentrated in particular localities characterized by unemployment, poverty, poor education, and single-parent homes. Crime has indeed risen and become more deadly during the last generation, but it has only marginally worsened for most of us. Unfortunately, because there seems to be no economic incentive, or political one either, for pointing this out, the public will continue to be terrorized by the exploitation of crime news (Chermak 1995).

Assuming that crime and the fear of crime are unlikely to decline, can we expect governments to adopt policies that would rectify the underlying conditions, the so-called root causes, that breed crime? If this happened, then the restructuring of policing would be less imperative. This, too, is unlikely for several reasons. The political mood, currently represented by Reagan, Thatcher, Major, and Gingrich, is certainly against large-scale social intervention by government. Rising crime rates are often considered to be evidence that Great Society programs have failed. Ironically, then, the very rise in crime that impels the restructuring of policing may have helped convince people that social programs undertaken by government are a waste of money. Conservative social theorists also argue that government doesn't know how to remedy criminogenic conditions. Social programs are as likely to be counterproductive as they are wasteful (Murray 1988; Wilson 1983). The political hostility to amelioration is also fueled by a general perception that taxes are too high. Tax revolt has become a permanent condition, and placating it an enduring political necessity. All governments seem resigned to doing less with less for the foreseeable future.

For demographic, social, and political reasons, then, the threat of crime will intensify. The search for security will not diminish but may grow in desperation. How, then, will government and the larger community provide for its intense desire for security?

First, government is unlikely to be able to respond effectively through traditional law enforcement programs. It will certainly not be able to do so through simply increasing the number of public police. Most research over the past 30 years has failed to show a connection between variations in the numbers of police and the incidence of crime.[4]

At the same time, the cost of increasing the "visible presence" of the police, that is, police on the streets, remains dauntingly high. Because of staffing and deployment rules, 10 additional officers must be hired in order to get one extra uniformed police officer on the streets around the clock throughout the year (Bayley 1985). The incremental cost of a unit of "visible presence" on American streets is, therefore, about $500,000—10 times a patrol officer's average annual salary plus benefits. Few governments are going to be willing to make such investments.

Moreover, the distributional requirements of democratic politics ensure that additional police officers will not be concentrated in high-crime neighborhoods where their marginal utility would be highest, but will parcel them out in dribs and drabs so that every politician can claim to have gotten some police for his or her constituency. The allocations made under the 1994 Crime Control Act in the United States show this clearly. Distributional politics reduces the effectiveness of public expenditures on policing in any democratic society.

Democratic governments are also limited in their ability to respond to crime by political values. In the Anglo-American tradition, government is distrusted. As a result, public pressure to "get tough" on crime invariably encounters stiff resistance from people concerned about civil liberties. Governments may sometimes enact Draconian policies, but in the long run they swing back and forth between punishment and due process. Deterrence, which will continue to dominate the efforts of modern democratic governments to control crime, clashes with the very precepts on which government has been established. Democratic societies may fear crime, but they fear authoritarianism more.

We believe, therefore, that democratic governments are unlikely to be able to allay the public's desperate need for safety through the criminal justice system. The demand for security is unlikely to be met by governmental action, whether through amelioration or deterrence.

Second, we are unsure but skeptical of the ability of Western societies to respond to the demand for order by spontaneous crime-preventive activities undertaken by communities. Our skepticism arises out of the value Western societies place on individualism. Westerners want to be free not only from government constraint but from social constraint as well. Because people in Western countries, unlike the Japanese, Chinese, and Koreans, place great importance on individual development and freedom, they do not readily submit to the informal discipline of groups (Bayley 1985, 1991). If they do so, it is for short-term instrumental ends, such as winning a game, obtaining emotional support for a particular problem, making useful contacts, or obtaining particular advantages. The capacity of families, neighborhoods, schools, churches, and employers to discipline their members and to organize against crime and disorder is weak in individualistic societies. Although the vitality of community crime prevention in Western democratic countries currently is impressive and heartening, its staying power and its effectiveness are doubtful. Experience so far indicates that efforts at community organization are difficult to sustain after initial enthusiasm wears off. Moreover, the rigorous research so far done on community crime prevention has failed to show substantial benefits.

Individualistic democratic societies are caught between a rock and a hard place with respect to crime control. On the one hand, they are limited by their political values from authoritarian controls and, on the other, they are limited by their cultural values from the discipline of informal social control.

Third, caught in this bind, it is inevitable that Western democratic societies will continue to resort to the marketplace for security solutions. Free enterprise capitalism is the mechanism the West must rely on to compensate for the deficiencies of governmental control and social cohesion in controlling crime. Market-mediated private security is the natural response of societies like ours, just as privatization generally has been to problems of health, education, research, information dissemination, and income support. Security can hardly not become "commodified" in individualistic democratic societies. There is no other place to turn.

Commodification of security has been encouraged by the rise of "mass private property" in the latter half of the 20th century—meaning facilities that are owned privately but to which the public has right of access and use (Shearing & Stenning 1983). These include shopping malls, educational campuses, residential communities, high-rise condominiums and apartments, banks, commercial facilities, and recreation complexes. The world is no longer divided simply between privately owned space used by its owners and the numerous public streets used by the public. By blurring the distinction between the public and the private, mass private property attenuates and marginalizes government's responsibility for security. It constricts government efforts at preventive policing to clearly public venues. Preventive policing in mass private property has become the responsibility of security specialists bought privately through the market.

If we are right that governments cannot provide satisfactory public safety, that neighborhoods will have only haphazard success in doing so, and that mass private property will continue to dominate urban space, then market-based private security will inevitably increase relative to public policing. It may even begin to cannibalize public policing if affluent people become more reluctant to pay twice for safety. It follows, therefore, that there will be no avoiding the emergence of dualistic policing stratified by race and class. The affluent will be protected by private security agents organized by interest groups and operating according to preventive principles backed up by the requirements of specialized membership or participation; the poor will be protected by a weakened public police operating according to principles of deterrence based on procedurally limited law enforcement. Western democratic societies are moving inexorably, we fear, into a Clockwork Orange world where both the market and the government protect the affluent from the poor—the one by barricading and excluding, the other by repressing and imprisoning—and where civil society for the poor disappears in the face of criminal victimization and governmental repression.

Fourth, there is one more factor that may powerfully influence the security trends outlined here, namely, outbreaks of collective violence, especially in large cities. The United States has already experienced serious but isolated instances of this—the "Rodney King" riots in Los Angeles, the Thompkins Park and Crown Heights riots in New York City, and the Liberty City riots in Miami. But collective violence is happening in quieter, more pervasive ways that are not so easily recognized. Gang violence in some inner-city neighborhoods has attained the dimensions of an ongoing riot. The former Mayor of Washington, DC, formally requested the deployment of the National Guard in August 1994. And Americans asked why the Army and Marines were sent to Somalia when the United States had its own gang warlords terrorizing inner-city neighborhoods. England now has "slow riots" in the summer in which unemployed youths from public housing estates regularly burn tires, cars, and sometimes buses "for fun."

Collective violence, whether in the form of short, intense riots or persistent, endemic criminality, powerfully reinforces the dualistic tendencies in the current restructuring of policing. Portrayed as unpredictable and random, such violence scares the well-to-do and demonstrates the impotence of the police. This encourages further privatization along class lines. At the same time, collective violence weakens community crime prevention impulses among the disadvantaged by polarizing communities and weakening trust among neighbors and even family members. Furthermore, in the face of collective violence, governments become less willing to allow poor communities to develop self-defense capabilities (Bayley 1975, 1985). Collective violence is inevitably perceived in political terms. The standard response of governments is, therefore, to centralize policing power rather than allow it to be decentralized among what appear to be unpredictable and politically untrustworthy communities.

Collective violence not only drives a wedge deeper between the rich and the poor; it undercuts the ability of the state to more equitably distribute security among the rich and the poor by undermining the capacity and enthusiasm among the public police for community policing. Persistent collective violence causes the police to centralize decisionmaking, adopt a military style of command, emphasize law enforcement, deploy heavier weaponry, patrol in groups rather than as individuals, take preemptive action, and distrust the public. Collective violence also makes commanders cautious about tying down officers in community-development work. They want to save resources for "the big event," which weakens their capacity for flexible adaptation and problem solving, both of which are essential elements of community policing.

Collective violence is like a bus waiting to broadside the evolution of policing in the late 20th century. If it hits, there may be nothing anyone can do to prevent the emergence of a dualistic system of policing.

Fateful Choices

The fear of crime, the absence of ameliorative social policies, the ineffectiveness of deterrence, the rise of mass private property, and the commodification of security are powerful forces shaping the future of policing. The dualistic tendencies in policing are almost certain to be strengthened, with consequent distortions of equity, human rights, and accountability. In the face of these developments, can modern democratic, individualistic societies provide humane policing equitably for all their members? We believe they can, but only if two policies are adopted.

First, it is necessary to enable poor people to participate in markets for security. For this to happen it will be necessary to develop mechanisms to provide for the reallocation of public funding for security. The objective should be to provide poorer communities with the ability to sustain self-governing initiatives.

One way of achieving this would be through block grants to poor communities so that they can participate in the commercial market for security. Not only does this level up access to security, it vests directive authority in the people most affected. If appropriate mechanisms for community self-government are created, block grants raise the likelihood that policing will be responsive to the wishes of the community. Block grants would encourage poor communities to develop security regimes that fit their problems and mores in the same way that private security adapts to the goals of businesses. In effect, communities would be given security budgets that they could spend on various mixtures of public and private policing. Distributional problems between rich and poor might still arise, of course, particularly if the rich refused to pay. All policies that have any prospect of mitigating the growing class differences in public safety depend on the affluent segments of our societies recognizing that security is indivisible. The well-to-do are paying for crime now; but they have not learned that they will save more by leveling up security than by ghettoizing it.

Second, community policing must become the organizing paradigm of public policing. Through community policing governments can develop the self-disciplining and crime-preventive capacity of poor, high-crime neighborhoods. Community policing incorporates the logic of security by forging partnership between police and public. Since safety is fundamental to the quality of life, co-production between police and public legitimates government, lessening the corrosive alienation that disorganizes communities and triggers collective violence. Community policing is the only way to achieve discriminating law enforcement supported by community consensus in high-crime neighborhoods.

Community policing faces substantial obstacles and will not be easy to achieve. Most police are still not convinced it is needed, and research so far is equivocal about its success. The latter may be attributable more to failures in implementation than defects in the program. Community policing requires substantial revision of organizational priorities within the police and is managerially demanding. It requires new styles of supervision and new methods of evaluating performance. Although community policing sounds appealing, few politicians have the nerve to force community policing on reluctant police departments. They would rather give unrestricted grants to police agencies, thereby earning credit for being tough on crime while not challenging standard operating procedures. Finally, as we have noted, community policing is hardest to achieve in the places that need it most. In terms of resources, it requires government to take the security problems of the poor as seriously as it does the security problems of the rich.

Both of these policies—community block grants and community policing—highlight a fundamental question: does government have the wisdom, even if it has the will, to guide the course of security's restructuring without making it worse? Vouchers and community policing will work to offset the socially divisive effects of restructuring only to the extent that they empower communities to take responsibility for themselves and, in some cases, to heal themselves. This requires government not only to reform the police but to redistribute political power with respect to one of the core functions of government. This is a lot to ask, because faced with shortcomings in public safety, governments will be tempted to enhance directiveness rather than encourage devolution. To avoid this, a radical rethinking of the role of government is required.

Fortunately, while the inclination of government to stipulate rather than facilitate remains strong, there is a widespread and growing movement to challenge this. Just as the past is prologue to the continued restructuring of policing, so, too, there seems to be a growing realization in democratic, individualistic societies that in order to create a more humane, safe, and civil society, government must be reinvented, specifically, that grassroots communities must be made responsible for central aspects of governance. The rethinking of security that our proposals require is consistent with this rethinking of governance. Restructuring is a problem that may contain the seeds of its own solution.

Notes

[1] In the United States there are about 2 million private security people as opposed to about 650,000 sworn police.

[2] These calculations based on clearances for U.S. Index crimes or their near equivalents in Britain and Canada—homicide, rape, aggravated assault, robbery, burglary, larceny, and auto theft. U.S. Bureau of Justice Statistics 1993; United Kingdom Home Office 1992; and Statistics Canada 1993.

[3] "After the Respite, Crime Rises," *Albany Times Union*, 14 Dec. 1994, p. 1.

[4] This conclusion has recently been challenged by Stephen Levitt who has demonstrated for the first time that hiring additional police may be cost effective (Levitt 1994a, 1994b). Levitt's analysis shows that in large American cities each additional officer prevents between 7 and 10 crimes per year, at an annual saving that is $150,000 more than the cost of the officer's hire.

References

Bayley, David H. (1975) "The Police and Political Development in Europe," in Charles Tilly, ed., *The Formation of National States in Western Europe*. Princeton: Princeton Univ. Press.

_____ (1985) *Patterns of Policing: A Comparative International Policing*. New Brunswick, NJ: Rutgers Univ. Press.

_____ (1991) *Forces of Order: Policing Modern Japan*. Berkeley: Univ. of California Press.

Bayley, David H. (1994) *Police for the Future.* New York: Oxford Univ. Press.

Blumstein, Alfred (1994) "Youth Violence, Gangs, and the Illicit-Drug Industry." Unpub., Carnegie-Mellon Univ., Pittsburgh (July 26).

Brogden, Michael, & Clifford Shearing (1993) *Policing for a New South Africa.* London: Routledge.

Butterfield, Fox (1995) "Grim Forecast on Rising Crime," *New York Times, p.* A24 (19 Feb.).

Chermak, Steven M. (1995) *Victims in the News.* Boulder, CO: Westview Press.

Johnston, Les (1992) *The Rebirth of Private Policing.* London: Routledge.

_____ (1994) "Policing in Late Modern Societies." Paper for the Workshop on Evaluating Police Service Delivery, Montreal (Nov.).

Kelling, George L., & Catherine M. Coles (1994) "Disorder and the Court," *Public Interest,* p. 57 (Summer).

Levitt, Steven D. (1994a) "Reporting Behavior of Crime Victims and the Size of the Police Force: Implications for Studies of Police Effectiveness Using Reported Crime Data." Unpub., Harvard Univ. (Aug.).

_____ (1994b) "Using Electoral Cycles of Police Hiring to Estimate the Effect of Police on Crime." Unpub., Harvard Univ. (Nov.).

Murray, Charles (1988) *In Pursuit of Happiness and Good Government.* New York: Simon & Schuster.

Rosenbaum, Dennis P., & Linda Heath (1990) "The 'Psycho-Logic' of Fear-Reduction and Crime-Prevention Programs," in John Edwards et al., eds., *Social Influence Processes and Prevention.* New York: Plenum Press.

Shearing, Clifford (1992) "The Relation between Public and Private Policing," in M. Tonry & N. Morris, eds., *Modern Policing.* Chicago: Univ. of Chicago Press.

_____ (1996) "Reinventing Policing: Policing as Governance," in O. Marenin, ed., *Policing Change: Changing Police.* New York: Garland Press.

Shearing, C. D., & Philip Stenning (1983) "Private Security: Implications for Social Control," 30 *Social Problems* 493.

Skogan, Wesley G. (1990) *Disorder and Decline.* New York: Free Press.

Skolnick, Jerome H., & David H. Bayley (1986) *The New Blue Line.* New York: Free Press.

Statistics Canada (1993) *Canadian Crime Statistics, 1993.* Ottawa: Statistics Canada.

United Kingdom Home Office (1992) *Criminal Statistics: England and Wales, 1992.* London: HMSO.

U.S. Bureau of Justice Statistics (1993) *Sourcebook of Criminal Justice Statistics, 1993.* Washington: Bureau of Justice Statistics.

Walker, Samuel (1976) "The Urban Police in American History: A Review of the Literature," *J. of Police Science & Administration*, pp. 252–60 (Sept.).

Walker, Samuel, & Betsey Wright (1994) "Civilian Review of the Police: A National Survey." Washington: Police Executive Research Forum.

Wilson, James Q. (1983) *Crime and Public Policy.* San Francisco: ICS Press.

Wilson, James Q., & George L. Kelling (1982) "Broken Windows: The Police and Neighborhood Safety," *Atlantic Monthly,* pp. 29–38 (March).

21

Community-Oriented Policing Across the U.S.
Facilitators and Impediment to Implementation

Jihong Zhao, Quint C. Thurman, and *Nicholas P. Lovrich*

Citizen demand for responsive public services has grown considerably since the end of World War II. Similarly, Walker (1977) notes that the public's appetite for police services has increased as well over this time period, although not always at pace with the abilities of departments to respond.

While police executives will decry the dilemma of having to do more without significant increases in resources, a long practiced reliance upon further police professionalization to deliver efficient services—often at the expense of effective outcomes—has set the stage for re-examining how police agencies do their jobs and how they might wish to change in the 1990s. Similarly, many police scholars (e.g., Goldstein, 1987, 1990; Osborne and Gaebler, 1992; Kelling and Moore, 1988), have identified organizational change as a more pressing issue now than ever before in the history of modern American policing.

Skolnick and Bayley (1986) and Trojanowicz and Bucqueroux (1990) have noted that policing is in the midst of a time of transition from a bureaucratic model of operation to a Community-Oriented Policing (COP) model. Broadly defined, COP represents an ideal organizational form which emphasizes a set of new values and beliefs related to the coproduction of public order (Angell, 1971; Wasserman and Moore, 1988), modified organizational structures featuring employee empowerment and risk-taking, and essential operational activities relating to bridge-building between the police and the communities they serve (Brown and Wycoff, 1987; Lurigio and Skogan, 1994; Wycoff and Skogan, 1994).

Source: Reprinted by permission of MCB University Press, Ltd., from *American Journal of Police*, Vol. 14, No. 1, copyright 1995, pp. 11–28.

However, despite considerable development of COP in the past twenty years, information regarding COP deployment and its consequences has been slow to emerge (Reiss, 1992). Most published research concerning COP falls into one of the two broad categories. The first primarily centers on the discussion of COP values and change in general (e.g., Kelling and Moore, 1988; Mastrofski, 1988; Mastrofski and Uchida, 1993). The second approach largely focuses on the impact of COP programs in a few celebrated case studies. Sadly, a key issue—COP implementation in the process of change in American policing—has essentially been neglected. Such an oversight has resulted in the tendency to focus on "successful" programs (defined as those which demonstrate efficient service delivery) rather than to acquire important knowledge about the process of COP implementation.

Pressman and Wildvsky (1973) have highlighted the importance of implementation and have noted that programs often fail due to poor implementation. In a similar vein, Walker (1993) stresses the wealth of knowledge related to American policing that might be gained from past experiences involving the implementation of police innovations such as team policing. Other examples might include recent case studies reported by the Vera Institute of Justice involving Innovative Neighborhood Oriented Policing programs (INOP) in eight cities (Sadd and Grinc, 1994; Grinc, 1994).

To date there has been little attention paid to COP implementation beyond case studies of a few selected cities. One exception in this regard is a recent study by Greene (1993). Greene's study concerning the extent of COP implementation in the State of Florida addressed the process of organizational change from a bureaucratic model to a COP model in a single American state.

The present study builds upon the important scholarship of Greene and others to extend to a national scale the investigation of the extent of organizational change and COP implementation in American policing. In so doing we both explore the extent of COP training underway in the U.S. and identify the conditions which promote or impede COP implementation. While many policing scholars have highlighted the importance of these two areas of research in studying the transition from the bureaucratic model to the COP model (e.g., Trojanowicz and Bucqueroux, 1990; Goldstein, 1990; Greene, 1993), there has been little systematic research on this subject and none that we know of which has relied upon data from a national survey of police agencies.

Literature Review

Trojanowicz and Bucqueroux (1990:3) argue that a set of values relating to the proper role of the police in contemporary society is of primary importance for organizational change to COP (cf. Goldstein, 1977). Accordingly, Kelling and Moore (1988) have identified the central feature of COP as the shared empowerment of both the police agency and the community in controlling crime and reducing disorder. They believe that coproducing order in this way will result in strengthening public support for police work.

Sparrow (1988) and Moore (1992) both summarize the change in value orientation advocated in the COP reform model. Key to their arguments is the assumption that American police agencies inherently cannot be "neutral" entities with respect to their surrounding community. On the contrary, accountability to the local community is regarded as an essential feature of COP. Furthermore, there is a close linkage between value orientation and effective operational activities (vs. "public relations" programs) which particularly reflect these new values. Consequently, COP might be conceptualized as an expansion of the police role in American society beyond a more limited and narrowly-focused "crime fighting" function.

Operationally, Lurigio and Skogan (1994:315) point out that the COP philosophy "translates into a variety of specific operations and practices" (cf. Wasserman and Moore, 1988; Weisel and Eck, 1994; see Sparrow et al., 1990, for a discussion). As such, the examination of organizational change in policing should be firmly rooted in the structure of COP programs.

A review of the literature pertaining to COP programs suggests that the dimension of *externally focused change* (Huber et al., 1993) has been more frequently discussed and investigated than *internally focused change*. A reorientation of police operations in the form of crime prevention activities is illustrative of the former and reflects a police department's conscious effort to redefine its mission within the broad community while the latter is exemplified by an internal reorganization of the agency itself.

Many "re-oriented" police operations have been highlighted in professional journals. For example, the implementation of a foot patrol program is viewed as an important reorientation of police operations because of the patrol officers' direct involvement with the community through such programs (Skolnick and Bayley, 1986). Similarly, the use of special task units to address unique local problems is viewed as another strategy for the police to respond to the needs of a community (Goldstein, 1990). Furthermore, in their summary of COP programs in Houston, Brown and Wycoff (1987) emphasized the use of storefront stations, community crime prevention newsletters, and victim contact programs as effective examples of the reorientation of police activities toward COP goals. Other studies also have identified programs such as crime prevention education and permanent assignment of officers to a neighborhood as often useful methods of organizational change (e.g., Wycoff, 1988; Moore, 1992; Thurman, Bogen and Giacomazzi, 1993).

In a broad sense, the theme of community crime prevention represents the common denominator of externally focused change. Such an emphasis upon prevention over more efficient crime fighting implies the recognition of the supreme importance of the health of the community and the acknowledgment of the limited capability of police to control crime without the help of residents at large (Kelling and Stewart, 1989; Moore, 1992).

Some facilitators of and impediments to contemporary organizational change in American policing have been identified in the research literature. For example, two variables which might contribute to successful change are education and training (see Goldstein, 1977, 1990; Bittner, 1972). It is widely believed that a better educated and more highly-trained police officer can meet the essential requirements of contemporary organizational change.

Similarly, policing scholars and practitioners also have identified a number of variables that are regarded for their negative impact on organizational change. For example, Sherman (1975) pointed out that failure to win the support of middle management was the primary contributor to the end of the team policing movement in the early 1970s (cf. Walker, 1993). Similarly, the lack of understanding of COP by line officers is another important obstacle which is highlighted in the research literature (Goldstein, 1990; Kelling and Moore, 1988; Sadd and Grinc, 1994).

Methods and Measures

The data used in this analysis are derived from a national survey of police chiefs conducted by the Division of Governmental Studies and Services (DGSS) at Washington State University. DGSS has conducted mail-out and mail-back surveys in three-year intervals since 1978. The cities in the sample are selected from among those municipalities initially included in a representative national survey of chiefs of police in cities of over 25,000 population conducted by the International City Management Association in 1969. The sample size includes 281 municipal police departments in 47 states. In addition, this sample takes into consideration the representativeness of regions and sizes of cities. Included in the data base for this study is the sixth survey of municipal police departments conducted in 1993.

After three waves of mailings sent in 1993, 228 (81%) out of 281 police departments completed and returned a survey questionnaire. The survey instrument contained a wide variety of questions pertaining to COP programs implemented in each police department. Either a police chief or an appointed representative was asked to identify from a prepared list the presence or absence of COP programs elements compiled from a review of the relevant literature. Furthermore, information regarding interest in COP training and education and perceived major obstacles also was collected in the survey.

Externally focused change was measured by the presence of twelve commonly found COP programs identified from the research literature. These COP programs comprise both reorientation of police operations and efforts in crime prevention. The extent of COP training or education is assessed by a battery of fourteen items which cover COP philosophy and operational practices. Each item was rated based on a four-point scale varying from "not interested" to "very interested." Commonly hypothesized obstacles to COP implementation are represented by thirteen items which include both external and internal barriers to COP implementation. Each item was judged based on a similar four-point scale ranging from "no obstacle" to "a serious obstacle."

Findings

The frequency distribution presented in table 1 suggests that a majority of police departments across the nation report the implementation of some types of COP programs in the past three years. For example, foot patrol (88.4%), special task units (91.6%), education of the public (98.1%), and block watch programs (97.7%) are the most commonly adopted COP programs.

Table 1   Frequency Distribution of Externally Focused Change: COP Programs

	Yes	No
1. Community newsletter	49.8%	52.2%
2. Foot, horse patrol	88.4%	11.6%
3. Storefront station	41.4%	58.6%
4. Special task unit	91.6%	8.4%
5. Victim contact program	62.8%	37.2%
6. Education of public	98.1%	1.9%
7. Fixed assignment	87.0%	13.0%
8. Citizen survey	62.3%	37.7%
9. Block watch	97.7%	2.3%
10. Business watch	65.1%	34.9%
11. Block meeting	86.5%	13.5%
12. Volunteer program	68.4%	31.6%
	n=215	

The average number of programs implemented in the survey is 9 out of a possible 12, with a standard deviation of 2.1. Furthermore, 66.7 percent of the police departments reported they have implemented new programs in the past three years; 31 percent remained at the same level as 1990, and only 2.3 percent indicated that they have reduced the number of COP programs which were in operation in 1990.

In terms of interest in COP training and education, principal component factor analysis was used to identify any underlying themes which were of concern to police administrators using the usual method for determining the number of factors present among a number of like constructs (that is, the retention of factors with Eigen values greater than one). Furthermore, a variable was selected if its factor loading correlated greater than .5 with a particular factor. Finally, the commonly used approach of varimax orthogonal rotation was adopted for presentation of these data since this approach is more appropriate than other techniques for undertaking exploratory analysis (Kim and Mueller, 1978:48–50).

Three distinctive factors were identified in the analysis. Mean ratings for these three factors are reported in table 2.

Table 2   Factor Analysis: Interest in COP Training and Education*

Factor**	Loading[1]			Mean Rating***
	I	II	III	(SD)
1. Overall Performance Skills (INT1)				
a. Quality circles: an overview	.82	.09	.14	
b. Applying quality circles	.79	.16	.08	
c. Positive risk taking	.64	.33	.26	
d. Liability awareness	.52	.34	.16	
e. Excellence in community service	.50	.35	.24	3.29
				(.66)
2. Middle Manager Skills COP Principles (INT2)				
a. Middle management				
authority delegation	.24	.75	.08	
b. Survival strategies for managers	.40	.68	.07	
c. Comprehensive overview of				
COP principles	−.10	.66	.53	
d. Principles of neighborhood				
organizations	.22	.63	.11	3.42
				(.60)
3. Police Community Relations (INT3)				
a. Minority relations	.23	.12	.82	
b. Cultural awareness	.10	.05	.82	
c. Police ethics and values	.32	.27	.54	3.75
				(.43)

*   Alpha level of all three factors > .70
**   % of variance (Eigen Value) of three factors are: 40.5 (5.7), 9.8 (1.4), and 7.4 (1.0) respectively.
***Mean Rating: 1=not interested, 2=slightly, 3=moderate, 4=very interested.

Findings from table 2 suggest that police departments across the nation tend to display similar kinds of interest in COP training and education. The underlying theme for the first factor noted reflects a broad interest in improving overall performance skills among police personnel. The second factor represents concern for the training and education of middle-level managers seeking to make the transition from a bureaucratic agency toward COP. The final factor involves the improvement in police-community relations in the process of implementing COP programs, especially in culturally diverse communities. The overall ratings of themes composing each factor show that an interest in improving police and community relations is the top priority for the police chiefs surveyed in 1993.

Table 3 identifies the obstacles that can hinder the development and implementation of COP in police organizations. Once again, principal component factor analysis with the same approach as before was used. This generated three primary types of obstacles to COP implementation as noted by police administrators nationally.

The pattern of factor loadings for thirteen items indicated three underlying factors which appear to represent internal organizational obstacles, external community barriers, and inhibition as a result of the transition from a traditional paramilitary policing approach to the COP philosophy. The mean ratings associated with each factor suggest that police agencies are more concerned with internal organizational barriers than obstacles in their community. In particular, the factor labeled the "transition obstacle" is composed of one variable relating to the balancing of COP activities versus traditional crime fighting ones. This factor had the highest mean rating of the three factors identified.

Table 3   Factor Analysis: Impediments to COP Implementation*

Factor**	Loading[1]			Mean Rating*** (SD)
	I	II	III	
1. Organizational Impediments (IMP1)				
a. Resistance from middle-management	.75	−.03	.05	
b. Line officers resistance	.75	.16	.08	
c. Departmental confusion of what COP is	.68	.15	.31	
d. Problem in line-level accountability	.66	.25	.22	
e. Officers' concern: COP is "soft" on crime	.63	.46	−.18	
f. Lack of COP training	.55	.24	.41	
g. Union resistance	.52	.51	−.18	2.41 (.76)
2. Community Impediments (IMP2)				
a. Community resistance	.07	.71	.16	
b. Community concern: COP is "soft" on crime	.11	.69	−.00	
c. Civil service rules	.13	.64	.10	
d. Pressure on chief to demonstrate COP reduces crime in short term	.23	.59	.34	
e. Lack of support from local government	.22	.56	.36	1.96 (.87)
3. Transition Impediment (IMP3)				
a. Problems in balancing increased foot patrol activities while maintaining emergency response time	.11	.15	.84	2.98 (1.10)

*   Alpha level of first two factors>.70.

**   % of variance (Eigen Value) of three factors are: 36.9 (4.8), 10.7 (1.4), and 8.0 (1.0), respectively.

***Mean Ratings: 1=no obstacle, 2=slightly, 3=moderate, 4=serious obstacles.

The findings presented in table 4 present bivariate correlations obtained among training and education concerns, perceived obstacles to COP implementation, and the presence of externally focused COP programs in each police agency surveyed. The direction of these correlations suggests that the higher a police agency's interest in training and education, the greater the number of COP programs they implement. Conversely, the perception of serious obstacles is negatively associated with the level of COP program implementation as might be expected. These findings indicate that many police departments continue to be confronted with significant impediments to COP implementation, and as a result, these obstacles evoke considerable caution on the part of many police executives facing opportunities for organizational change.

Table 4   Correlation Coefficients of Externally Focused Change, Interest in Training and Education, and Impediments (N=171)

	EXTER (No. of COP Prog.)	INT1	INT2	INT3	IMP1	IMP2
Perf. Skill (INT1)	.13[a]					
Mid-Mgmt. Skill (INT2)	.22[b]	.60[d]				
Pol.-Comm. Rel. (INT3)	.34[c]	.50[d]	.49[d]			
Org. Imped. (IMP1)	−.15[a]	−.16[b]	−.15[a]	−.14[a]		
Comm. Imped. (IMP2)	−.22[b]	.01	−.05	−.06	.56[d]	
Trans. Imped. (IMP3)	−.14[a]	−.09	−.07	−.08	.59[d]	.33[d]

[a]$p<.05$, [b]$p<.01$, [c]$p<.001$, [d]$p<.0001$

Discussion

As an exploratory study focusing on the extent of COP implementation at the national level, these findings suggest several important observations pertaining to both theoretical and practical issues. Theoretically, a key question emanating from these data is whether or not COP implementation represents (or at least is consistent with) the theme of organizational change. With respect to this issue, we think that it is important to discuss an essential concept concerning organizational change—the expansion of an organizational domain.

Meyer (1975:599) defines an organizational domain as "the technology employed, population served and services rendered by an organization." Scholars of American policing have long discussed whether or not COP represents the expansion of the police role in the society in terms of technology employed (Manning, 1992; Eck and Spelman, 1987; Eck, 1993; Goldstein, 1990), population served (Kelling and Moore, 1988; Mastrofski, 1988; Klockars, 1988), and services rendered (Skolnick and Bayley, 1986; Moore, 1992).

Based upon the number of COP programs implemented and the frequency distribution of COP development nationally, these data suggest that police departments across the U.S. have been expanding the organizational domain (or functions) in these three areas during the past three years (cf. Greene, 1993; Langworthy, 1992). In turn, such expansion in the organizational domain is consistent with organizational change in COP values that we might expect to see if police organizations indeed are moving toward the COP philosophy.

These data also indicate some disturbing trends in American policing with regard to impediments to organizational change. We speculate that many organizations are at a loss to move much further forward at this point in time beyond some incremental amount. Simply put, American police agencies do not appear to know what it is that they should be doing next.[2]

Operationally, growth is apparent in the implementation of foot patrols, special task units, and public education regarding the contemporary police mission. Similarly, we find that interest in COP training and education is positively associated with the expansion and implementation of COP programs, and that most important within the training area is line officer education with respect to police-community relations and particularly pertaining to law enforcement in racially diverse communities. All these developments reflect new requirements under the COP model for police personnel in terms of overall service skills and value orientation in a time of transition.

Sadd and Grinc's study (1994) of police agencies in eight cities identified several common problems that organizations face when implementing COP programs. These include: (1) confusion among line officers concerning what COP means, (2) lack of support from middle management, and (3) lack of support of the residents from a community (cf. Grinc, 1994).

In general, our national study of COP implementation identified similar obstacles to those previously mentioned. For example, the factor we identified as one consisting of organizational impediments was considered the most serious barrier to implementation. Key to the underlying theme of this factor identified is the perceived resistance from police employees. Furthermore, the survey results suggest the widespread appreciation of the importance of middle management in COP implementation.[3]

Factor analysis also suggested that the issue of transition from a more traditional model of policing to the COP model uniformly has attracted the attention of administrators across the nation. Such concerns are not limited to the ideological sphere (e.g., soft on crime, etc.) but also include practical concerns such as the deployment of personnel (e.g., emergency response vs. foot patrol). This implies an important issue that often is overlooked by police administrations. Goldstein (1987) has pointed out that the traditional approach of policing focuses on incidents but neglects broader issues underlying such incidents. As such, organizational effectiveness instead of efficiency should be considered the top priority.

Based upon our findings, it seems that most police departments have difficulty emphasizing organizational effectiveness on par with efficiency (cf. Weisel and Eck, 1994). One of the reasons as pointed out by Sparrow et al. (1990) is that they lack the resources to achieve both simultaneously due to constraints imposed upon them by the increased demand for citizen services.[4]

In sum, it appears from our data that after nearly two decades of efforts, police agencies across the nation still are having difficulty transforming themselves from bureaucratic agencies into community-oriented ones at both theoretical and practical levels. Pfeffer (1982:228) finds that the process of organizational change, by its very nature, is inescapably "traumatic and unsettling." This description may well depict the current state of organizational change in American policing. The traditional approach to policing still has a popular audience which has become attached to an "old, comfortable way of doing things."

Conclusion

As a first attempt to investigate COP implementation by focusing on externally focused change across the U.S., our findings highlight some policy-relevant issues which are important for both police administrators and future research. We found that organizational change in contemporary American policing has gained momentum in the past three years. It is clear, however, that this transition toward the COP model is not a matter of simple changes. This transition is affected by several dynamics present within a police organization and its surrounding environment. First, police officers' training and education is seen as an important area for successful implementation of COP innovations. Without the cooperation and support of all levels of police personnel, lasting and effective organizational change in policing is problematic. Under the present circumstances, it seems that training in ethics, police-community relations, and the principles of COP are recognized as important by police administrators nationally.

Furthermore, how to overcome impediments in the process of organizational change toward the COP model is another important area of study. We found that top priority must be afforded to the organizational problems which emerge during the change process. Particularly, the balance between the traditional approach versus a community-based orientation of policing is seen as critical: how might police organizations maintain adequate response time to calls for service while pursuing COP goals?

Findings from this study at the national level suggest several issues which might serve as foci for future studies concerning COP implementation. One issue concerns strategies of balancing the outcomes attributable to the traditional approach versus the expected benefits of the COP approach. Special attention should be given to identifying those police agencies which have been successful in striking such an effective balance. Similarly, employees' value orientation and change during a time of transition needs to be further investigated both within and across police organizations.

Successful organizational change toward the COP model should correspond with a change in values among police personnel as well. Furthermore, the relationship between facilitators and impediments involving COP implementation should be explored further in both aggregate studies as well as qualitatively on a case-by-case basis. And lastly, longitudinal data should be collected to find out whether or not the same facilitators and impediments persist over time.

Notes

[1] Two factors failed to reach the level of .5 on any of the three factors. Crime-fighters v. peace keeper: Value conflicts was loaded .27, .46, and .43 while Principles of neighborhood block organizations was .27, .46, and .43 on each factor respectively. The variable, Comprehensive overview: principles of COP, is placed in Factor II because of higher loading on the factor.

[2] Twenty-six percent of the sample is derived from the western part of the U.S., 30 percent originates from the North Central, another 30 percent from the South, and the remaining 14 percent represents the Northeast. Similarly, about 50 percent of the police agencies are located in cities with fewer than 100,000 populations (the sample also takes types of cities into consideration—e.g., rural, independent, and urban—as indicated in the *Municipal Year Book*, 1977). However, despite consistent findings regarding the variation between rural and urban law enforcement (e.g., Decker, 1979; Weisheit et al., 1994), smaller departments and larger ones, and variations by region (Warner et al., 1989; Meagher, 1985; Powell, 1990), it is interesting to note that the common obstacles identified by police agencies across the country are strikingly identical—all other differences among police departments across the nation disappear when the foci are obstacles to COP implementation.

[3] Sherman (1975) has argued that the primary cause for the failure of numerous team-policing efforts in the early 1970s was the inability of middle management to handle the role conflict elements of change (cf. Walker, 1993). Based upon results from this survey, contemporary police administrators seem to have taken Sherman's proclamation to heart and realized the critical role of middle management in the transition to COP in American policing.

[4] Kessler (1993) has refined this issue further based upon analysis of the patrol distribution in one district of the Houston Police Department. He noted a common problem is the lack of human resources to balance emergency calls with proactive COP activities. Particularly, the issue becomes one of management concerning how to prioritize calls for service and minimize patrol intervals between calls. Kessler found that a reduction from 15 to 14 officers on regular patrol duty has virtually little impact on the overall efficiency of police response time. Furthermore, by introducing other strategies such as teleserve and a combination of motorized patrol and foot patrol (e.g., response to different calls) considerable personnel resources can be reallocated to COP activities.

References

Angell, J. (1971). "Toward an Alternative to the Classic Police Organizational Arrangement: A Democratic Model." *Criminology,* 8:185–206.

Bittner, E. (1972). *The Functions of the Police in Modern Society: A Review of Background Factors, Current Practices, and Possible Role Models.* Rockville, MD: National Institute of Mental Health.

Brown, L. and M. Wycoff (1987). "Policing Houston: Reducing Fear and Improving Service." *Crime and Delinquency,* 33:201–18.

Decker, S. (1979). "The Rural County Sheriff: An Issue in Social Control." *Criminal Justice Review,* 4:97–111.

Eck, J. (1993). "Alternative Features for Policing." In D. Weisburd and C. Uchida (eds.), *Police Innovation and Control of the Police: Problems of Law, Order, and Community.* New York: Springer-Verlag.

Goldstein, H. (1977). *Policing a Free Society.* Cambridge, MA: Ballinger Publishing Company.

_____ (1987). "Toward Community-Oriented Policing: Potential, Basic Requirements and Threshold Questions." *Crime and Delinquency,* 33:6–30.

_____ (1990). *Problem-Oriented Policing.* New York: McGraw-Hill Publishing Company.

Greene, H. (1993). "Community-Oriented Policing in Florida." *American Journal of Police,* 12:141–55.

Grinc, R. (1994). "'Angels in Marble': Problems in Stimulating Community Involvement in Community Policing." *Crime and Delinquency,* 40:437–68.

Huber, G.; K. Sutcliffe; C. Miller; and W. Glick (1993). "Understanding and Predicting Organizational Change." In G. Huber and W. Glick (eds.), *Organizational Charge and Redesign: Ideas and Insights for Improving Performance.* New York: Oxford Press.

Kelling, G. and M. Moore (1988). "From Political to Reform to Community: The Evolving Strategy of Police." In J. Greene and S. Mastrofski (eds.), *Community Policing: Rhetoric or Reality?* New York: Praeger.

Kelling, G. and J. Stewart (1989). "Neighborhoods and Police: The Maintenance of Civil Authority." *Perspectives on Policing,* No. 1. Washington, DC: National Institute of Justice and Harvard University.

Kessler, D. (1993). "Integrating Calls for Service with Community- and Problem-Oriented Policing: A Case Study." *Crime and Delinquency,* 39:485–508.

Kim, J. and C. Mueller (1978). *Introduction to Factor Analysis: What It Is and How to Do It.* Beverly Hills: Sage Publications.

Klockars, C. (1988). "The Rhetoric of Community Policing." In J. Greene and S. Mastrofski (eds.), *Community Policing: Rhetoric or Reality?* New York: Praeger.

Langworthy, R. (1992). "Organizational Structure." In G. Cordner and D. Hale (eds.), *What Works in Policing? Operations and Administration Examined.* Cincinnati, OH: Anderson.

Lurigio, A. and W. Skogan (1994). "Winning the Hearts and Minds of Police Officers: An Assessment of Staff Perceptions of Community Policing in Chicago." *Crime and Delinquency,* 40:315–30.

Manning, P. (1992). "Information Technologies and the Police." In M. Tonry and N. Morris (eds.), *Criminal Justice: A Review of Research.* Chicago: University of Chicago Press.

Mastrofski, S. (1988). "Community Policing as Reform: A Cautionary Tale." In J. Greene and S. Mastrofski (eds.), *Community Policing: Rhetoric or Reality?* New York: Praeger.

Mastrofski, S. and C. Uchida (1993). "Transforming the Police." *Journal of Research in Crime and Delinquency,* 33:330–58.

Meagher, S. (1985). "Police Patrol Styles: How Pervasive is Community Variation?" *Journal of Police Science and Administration,* 13:36–45.

Meyer, M. (1975). "Organizational Domains." *American Sociological Review,* 40:599–615.

Moore, M. (1992). "Problem Solving and Community Policing." In M. Tonry and N. Morris (eds.), *Criminal Justice: A Review of Research.* Chicago: University of Chicago Press.

Osborne, D. and T. Gaebler (1992). *Reinventing Government: How the Entrepreneurial Spirit is Transforming the Public Sector from Schoolhouse, City Hall to the Pentagon.* New York: Addison-Wesley Publishing Company.

Pfeffer, J. (1982). *Organizations and Organization Theory.* Boston: Pitman.

Powell, D. (1990). "A Study of Police Discretion in Six Southern Cities." *Journal of Police Science and Administration,* 17:1–7.

Pressman, J. and A. Wildvsky (1973). *Implementation.* Berkeley: University of California Press.

Reiss, A. (1992). "Police Organization in the Twentieth Century." In M. Tonry and N. Morris (eds.), *Criminal Justice: A Review of Research.* Chicago: University of Chicago Press.

Sadd, S. and R. Grinc (1994). "Innovative Neighborhood Oriented Policing: An Evaluation of Community Policing Programs in Eight Cities." In D. Rosenbaum (ed.), *The Challenge of Community Policing.* Thousand Oaks, CA: Sage Publications.

Sherman, L. (1975). "Middle Management and Police Democratization: A Reply to John E. Angell." *Criminology,* 12:363–77.

Skolnick, J. and D. Bayley (1986). *The New Blue Line: Police Innovations in Six American Cities.* New York: The Free Press.

Sparrow, M. (1988). "Implementing Community Policing." *Perspectives on Policing,* No. 9. Washington, DC: National Institute of Justice and Harvard University.

Sparrow, M.; M. Moore; and D. Kennedy (1990). *Beyond 911· A New Era for Policing.* New York: Basic Books.

Thurman, Q.; P. Bogen; and A. Giacomazzi (1993). "Program Monitoring and Community Policing: A Process Evaluation of Community Policing in Spokane, Washington." *American Journal of Police,* 12:89–114.

Trojanowicz, R. and B. Bucqueroux (1990). *Community Policing: A Contemporary Perspective.* Cincinnati, OH: Anderson Publishing Co.

Walker, S. (1977). *A Critical History of Police Reform.* Lexington, MA: D.C. Heath.

_____ (1993). "Does Anyone Remember Team Policing? Lessons of the Team Policing Experience for Community Policing." *American Journal of Police,* 12:33–55.

Warner, R.; B. Steel; and N. Lovrich (1989). "Conditions Associated with the Advent of Representative Bureaucracy: The Case of Women in Policing." *Social Science Quarterly,* 70:562–578.

Wasserman, R. and M. Moore (1988). "Values in Policing." *Perspectives on Policing,* No. 8. Washington, DC: National Institute of Justice and Harvard University.

Weisel, D. and J. Eck (1994). "Toward a Practical Approach to Organizational Change: Community Policing Initiatives in Six Cities." In D. Rosenbaum (ed.), *The Challenge of Community Policing: Testing the Promises.* Thousand Oaks, CA: Sage

Publications.

Weisheit, R.; L. Wells; and D. Falcone (1994). "Community Policing in Small Town and Rural America." *Crime and Delinquency,* 40:549–67.

Wycoff, M. (1988). "The Benefits of Community Policing: Evidence and Conjecture." In J. Greene and S. Mastrofski (eds.), *Community Policing: Rhetoric or Reality?* New York: Praeger.

Wycoff, M. and W. Skogan (1994). "The Effects of a Community Policing Management Style on Officers' Attitudes." *Crime and Delinquency,* 40:371–83.

Citizen Ratings of the Importance of Community Policing Activities

Vincent J. Webb and *Charles M. Katz*

Community policing has become an increasingly popular alternative to what many professionals, politicians, citizens and scholars see as a failure of the traditional policing model to deal with increases in crime (Sadd and Grinc, 1994, p. 27). As of 1993, approximately 50 percent of law enforcement agencies nationwide had either implemented or were in the process of implementing community policing (National Institute of Justice, 1995). Furthermore, community policing has been endorsed and supported financially by the federal government with the passage of the 1994 Crime Act, in which 8.8 billion dollars was appropriated for the "Cops on the Beat" program. Under the program, law enforcement agencies who apply and receive federal dollars to hire new police officers are required to implement community policing. As a result, it appears that law enforcement agencies which have not already implemented community policing will do so soon (Maguire, 1995).

Ironically, given the attention and resources that community policing has received, there is limited agreement among police professionals and academics as to the definition of community policing (Bayley, 1994; Green and Mastrofski, 1988; Rosenbaum, 1994). It appears, however, that community policing models stress greater police and citizen interaction, in which the police and public act as "co-producers" of crime control and prevention (Skolnick and Bayley, 1986). Such models seek to create a working relationship between the community and the police in which the police are more fully integrated into the community structure and citizens assume an active role in crime control and prevention. Anecdotal evidence is often

Source: Reprinted by permission of MCB University Press, Ltd., from *Policing: An International Journal of Police Strategy and Management*, Vol. 20, No. 1, copyright 1997.

used to illustrate this feature of community policing. One such example is offered by Weisburd and McElroy (1988) quoting a neighborhood police officer in New York:

> People get to know you. They get to trust you a little bit, and if something's going on, they figure, if they tell you, you'll act upon it—because you'll have to answer back to them in a couple of days . . . Well basically, I have people calling me up . . . and they say "Hey, this guy, he's dealing drugs right now in front of this address"—you would never get that on regular patrol . . . They're also sending in anonymous letters, giving detailed descriptions of drug operations (p. 99).

Advocates of community policing often cite examples similar to the one above in an attempt to explain how community policing is capable of increasing the amount of communication about crime and disorder between the police and the citizenry.

This broadened view of the police recognizes that cooperation between the police and the public will give police greater access to information provided by the community, which, in turn, will lead to the police being more responsive to community needs (Bureau of Justice Assistance, 1994). Such a relationship, between the police and the public, enables the police to focus on specific concerns of the community. While this is not necessarily an easy task, it requires the police to create a consensus regarding conflicts of priorities, interests and values within the community (Bayley, 1994; Goldstein, 1990). Therefore, when evaluating a community policing program, an important measure is the perception of the community regarding different police services. Routine evaluations that include the public's opinion regarding the police may show changes in community concerns and may "show how perceptions vary by neighborhood, age, race, gender, and other characteristics" (Eck and Rosenbaum, 1994, p. 12).

Unfortunately, nearly all the scholarly literature thus far has focussed on aspects of how the *police* will facilitate and collaborate with the public on matters of crime control and crime prevention (e.g. police as consultants, police and adaptation, police as mobilizers, police as problem solvers (Bayley, 1994; Green and Mastrofski, 1988; Rosenbaum, 1994)). While this literature is rich with descriptive research and general theorizing, there has only been a minimal amount of research concerning *citizens* and their perceptions of community policing and activities associated with community policing. This is somewhat disturbing in light of the fact that the success of community policing is assumed to be highly dependent on "citizen awareness, understanding, and support of the concept and a willingness to be involved in crime prevention and crime reduction activities" (Webb et al., 1994, p. 20). At a general level, community needs assessments or surveys "are a widely used means to determine what bothers the public and what goals it sees and seeks (Marenin, 1989, p. 75). However, as Flanagan (1985) points out, consumer perspectives of the police role have largely been ignored. Although a great deal is known about the public's general attitudes toward the police, relatively little is known about their assessment of specific police activities. He suggests that researchers need to get beyond studying public support for the police and focus on consumer preferences for specific police policies and practices. In Flanagan's view, the failure to do so could lead to diminished support for the police (p. 19).

In this study, we examine citizen ratings of the importance of different community policing activities. Our primary objective is to identify patterns of variation in the rating of the importance of a number of specific community policing activities. In doing so we are interested in identifying those community policing activities rated as more or less important by citizens and factors which influence how citizens rate the importance of selected community policing activities. Very little empirical work has been done in this area, even though several scholars have emphasized the importance of such research (Green and Decker, 1989; Green and Mastrofski, 1988; Murphy, 1988; Rosenbaum, 1994).

Community Preferences for Police Role and Community Policing Activities

A fundamental assumption of the community policing approach is that the community is more likely than the police to recognize and understand its public safety needs. Advocates of community policing argue that under the traditional model, the police became alienated from the public and their needs, and became unable to reinforce local community norms and values (Wilson and Kelling, 1982). As a result, community policing proponents assert that to restore informal social control processes the police need to be responsive to citizen demands in prioritizing police services in accordance with the preferences of the consumers" of police services. Therefore, under the community-oriented approach, the "proper" role of the police is defined in terms of the public rather than the police. Accordingly, Green and Decker (1989, p. 107) argue that an implicit assumption imbedded in community policing is that a consensus exists within the community regarding such issues as crime suppression, prevention and control. Such a consensus implies that citizens within a community have similar attitudes regarding their preferences toward different police duties.

However, the research that has been done to date fails to find much community consensus on community policing activities. One of the few studies done to assess the "collective social control values of the community" was conducted by Murphy (1988) using data collected from a community policing project in Toronto. Specifically, Murphy randomly surveyed approximately 1,400 selected adults in an attempt to identify important community problems. The author reported that he was unable to find any evidence of a consensus within the community with respect to neighborhood problems. Specifically, he stated that "the opinion survey appears to better illustrate the wide variation of opinions, perceptions, and values in a local community rather than validate the community policing model assumption of value consensus" (p. 403). These findings, however, may reflect the fact that Murphy's (1988) examination did not focus on individual (e.g. ethnicity, gender, age) or contextual variables (e.g. geographic location) that may be associated with a citizen's attitudes toward community problems. In fact, recent evidence suggests that these characteristics may be associated with identifying citizen preferences for policing activities.

One of the few empirical studies to examine directly citizen preferences for various police duties was conducted by Alpert and Dunham (1986, 1988). In 1985, they randomly sampled five neighborhoods in Dade County, Florida, and conducted 200 interviews with residents. In addition to simply focussing on how the respondents ranked particular police tasks, the authors examined how respondent ethnicity, gender and neighborhood affiliation were associated with their rankings of particular police tasks. The authors concluded that living in a particular neighborhood was a more influential factor in the ranking of specific police tasks than was the respondent's ethnicity or gender (Alpert and Dunham, 1988, p. 120). They found that those residents who lived in the same neighborhood displayed similar patterns with regard to their preferences for police duties.

Another effort to examine citizen ratings of police duties was conducted by Webb and Graham (1994) in their examination of 1,000 respondents who were asked to rate the importance of nine crime control and order-maintenance police duties, ranging from the enforcement of traffic laws to the investigation of family disturbances. The authors reported that nearly all the police duties were rated as being highly important. However, they did find that for two of the duties, investigating drug violations and investigating gang related activities, all respondent characteristics, situational factors and contextual variables were found to be non-significant predictors of respondent ratings. In other words, there appeared to be a broad consensus within the community about these two police duties.

Findings such as those described above suggest that public agreement on the role of the police may vary significantly, depending on the community's characteristics. One must keep in mind, however, that the above examinations by Alpert and Dunham (1986,1988) and Webb and Graham (1994) did not take place in communities that had yet implemented community policing, nor did they examine citizens' preferences for specific community policing activities. Accordingly, all communities may not share the same level of enthusiasm, concern or consensus for order maintenance and service activities which are often emphasized in community-oriented police departments. In fact, it may be that many citizens will view community policing activities as unimportant, due to the fact that these activities are intended only to attack crime indirectly. For example, a goal of community policing is not necessarily to emphasize the arrest of street-level drug dealers but to prevent the conditions which allow drug dealing to take place. Accordingly, activities such as hauling away abandoned cars and cleaning up parks lack a sense of urgency and importance to many citizens when compared to crime control activities. Community perceptions of the potential effectiveness of community policing may determine how residents rate the importance of community policing activities carried out by the police.

Community Participation in Community Policing

This leads to the second assumption imbedded in the community policing approach: the community will support and participate in community policing (Green and Decker, 1989; Murphy, 1988). It is somewhat surprising that professionals have paid little attention to educating the public concerning the concepts underlying community policing (Grinc, 1994) and academics have neglected to link empirically the assumptions about the community's involvement in community policing to program outcomes (Murphy, 1988).

Initial feedback from the public concerning support for community policing has generally been favorable. Several examinations of community policing have concluded that the public perceives benefits resulting from community policing in their neighborhood, regardless of the specific form of community policing that was implemented. One such benefit that has been reported is the perception of an improved relationship between the police and the public (Skogan, 1994; Tien and Rich, 1994; Uchida and Forst, 1994; Uchida et al., 1992). However, the evidence on perceived benefits should not be taken as an indication that the community will rate all types of community policing activities as being equally important.

More specifically, the findings described above should be viewed with caution in that they do not take into account whether or not the respondents understand the basic concepts underlying community policing. One of the few investigations thus far to examine community involvement in community policing was performed by Sadd and Grinc (1994) (see also Grinc, 1994). Their analysis included focus groups of residents and police officers in nine sites where community policing had recently been implemented. Evidence provided by these authors suggests that many citizens may not even be aware of the fact that community policing exists in their neighborhood. They found that knowledge about community policing was closely associated with the individual's status in the community. First, community leaders were among those knowledgeable about community policing. This group was much more likely to know that community policing existed in the community and have knowledge about project goals, strategies and tactics used by the police and community. Second, residents who were involved in community groups or who were city employees were the next most knowledgeable group. These residents had an idea that community policing was being conducted in some neighborhoods but had very little knowledge about project goals, strategies and tactics used by the police and community. Finally, residents who were not members of community groups (which made up a majority of residents in the community) were the least likely to be aware that community policing existed in their neighborhood and had little if any knowledge about community policing.

Sadd and Grinc (1994) argue that the lack of support among citizens for community policing is also made evident by the lack of participation in community policing activities by community members. Their interviews revealed that there is strong resistance from community members to becoming involved in community policing efforts and two reasons were given for the lack of community support. First, there was fear of retaliation from drug dealers. Citizens at many of the study sites reported that if drug dealers and gang members saw individuals advertising Neighborhood Watch or passing out flyers for community meetings they were severely harassed. The second reason is related to the historically poor relationship between the police and the community; neighborhoods chosen for the implementation of community policing are frequently the same neighborhoods that have the poorest relationship with the police. As a result Grinc (1994) suggests that it may be difficult to involve the citizens in community policing "because community residents may not want to involve themselves in community policing" (p. 465).

On a similar note, Walker (1992) points to the fact that a community may simply be unable to participate in the community policing process because there may be no viable community to mobilize. He claims that in many "underclass" communities the residents do not identify themselves with the neighborhood or any of the local organizations within the community. He claims that this is often the result of a largely transient population with no ties to the community in which they live. Accordingly, Walker (1992) refers to this as the paradox of community policing in that, "the communities that need it most are least able to take advantage of it" (p. 190).

The Present Study

The present study has two primary purposes. The first is to identify overall patterns in citizen ratings of the importance of activities frequently associated with community policing. The goal is to begin to gauge the extent of consensus in the community about the importance of various community policing activities. The second purpose is to identify and assess the relative importance of those factors that influence the ratings of these activities by citizens. The general hypothesis is that citizen sociodemographic attributes, experience with crime, beliefs about importance of crime as a problem, and awareness and understanding of community policing influence the ratings of importance of police activities.

A survey of a random sample of citizens in Omaha, Nebraska was conducted as a means of getting direct input from citizens on their views of the importance of community policing activities. The survey also enabled us to gather data on the factors which might influence citizen assessments of the importance of these activities.

As noted, the setting for the study is Omaha, Nebraska, a Midwestern city with a population of approximately 340,000 in a metropolitan statistical area (MSA) of about 650,000. At the time of the survey (November, 1994), the Omaha Police Department (OPD) was wrapping up a year-long strategic planning process aimed at implementing jurisdiction-wide community policing. Prior to the strategic planning effort, the OPD had implemented community policing on a limited basis through the establishment of a special patrol unit that worked within the boundaries of the city's "Weed and Seed" district. The campaign for the mayoral election held in November of 1994 entailed substantial discussion of community policing philosophy that was widely reported on by the local media.

Methodology

The findings reported here are taken from a larger survey of a random sample (n = 800) of Omaha, Nebraska MSA residents 18 years of age and older and are part of an annual survey known as the Omaha Conditions Survey. This survey asks citizens to prioritize local problems and rate municipal services. In 1994, the survey included an extensive set of items related to the Omaha Police Department. Since the focus was on the Omaha police, only respondents who legally resided in the City of Omaha (n = 450) were asked to respond to Omaha police-related questions included in the present analysis. About 87 percent of the respondents in the sample were white, about 54 percent were married, and about 53 percent were female. These percentages indicate that the sample was representative of the larger Omaha community.

Independent Variables:
Citizen Characteristics and Knowledge of Community Policing

The independent variables used in this study include the respondent characteristics of race, marital status, whether or not the respondent has children, education, income, gender, employment, whether or not the respondent was a crime victim during the preceding 12 months, and his/her rating of the crime problem in the neighborhood. Whether or not a respondent had heard of community policing, the respondent's assessment of their understanding of community policing, and the respondent's beliefs about the police role and their own role in public safety are four additional independent variables included in the analysis. These four variables were measured using attitude statements with a five-point response scale ranging from "strongly agree" to "strongly disagree." Table 1 provides the metric and frequency distributions of each the independent variables used in the analysis.

Table 1. Metric and Frequency Distribution for Independent Variables

Independent variable	Metric	N	%
Race	0=White	431	87.4
	1=Non-white	62	12.6
Gender	0=Female	262	53.0
	1=Male	232	47.0
Age (years)	1=18–24	70	14.3
	2=25–34	116	23.7
	3=35–49	133	27.2
	4=50–64	80	16.4
	5=65+	90	18.4

Independent variable	Metric	N	%
Education	1=Less than HS graduate	35	7.2
	2=HS graduate/GED	134	27.5
	3=Some college/associate degree	176	36.1
	4=College graduate	106	21.8
	5=Graduate/professional school	36	7.4
Employment	0=Not in labor force	127	25.8
	1=In labor force	365	74.2
Income	1=Under $5,000	41	5.1
	2=5,000–9,999	105	13.1
	3=10,000–14,999	83	10.4
	4=15,000–19,999	90	11.2
	5=20,000–24,999	193	24.1
	6=25,000–29,999	56	7.0
	7=30,000–34,999	58	7.2
	8=35,000–39,999	46	5.7
	9=40,000–49,999	61	7.6
	10=50,000–59,999	29	3.6
	11=Over $60,000	39	4.9
Married	0=Not married	225	45.9
	1=Married	265	54.1
Child	0=No children	322	65.2
	1=Have children	172	34.8
Victim	0=Non-victim	345	69.8
	1=Victim	149	30.2
Crime problem	0=Not most important problem	458	92.7
	1=Most important problem	36	7.3
Only police can control crime	1=Strongly agree	8	1.7
	2=Agree	72	14.9
	3=Undecided	26	5.4
	4=Disagree	312	64.5
	5=Strongly disagree	66	13.6
I can make Omaha safer	1=Strongly agree	42	8.7
	2=Agree	357	73.6
	3=Undecided	35	7.2
	4=Disagree	47	9.7
	5=Strongly disagree	4	0.8
I have heard of community policing	1=Strongly agree	20	4.2
	2=Agree	294	61.9
	3=Undecided	29	6.1
	4=Disagree	129	27.2
	5=Strongly disagree	3	0.6
I have a good understanding of community policing	1=Strongly agree	18	3.8
	2=Agree	224	47.0
	3=Undecided	60	12.6
	4=Disagree	169	35.4
	5=Strongly disagree	6	1.3

Dependent Variables Rating Community Policing Activities

Survey respondents were asked to rate the importance of 11 "community policing activities," using a five-point rating scale where 1 represents a duty being rated as "unimportant" and 5 as "important." The activities included in the survey were selected as a result of being mentioned as community policing activities in various police professional, government or academic publications. The array of activities included is far from exhaustive, and the activities listed are not exclusively "community policing" activities. For example, neighborhood watch, drug sweeps in high crime areas, and road blocks targeting DWI offenders, may or may not be part of a larger community policing strategy. Certainly each of these activities has been performed by police outside the context of community policing; however, they are usually not thought of as typical police activities carried out as part of traditional police patrol.[1]

Findings

The frequency distributions for each of the 11 policing activities along with the mean ratings and standard deviations are presented in Table 2. Investigating gang activities and performing drug sweeps had the highest mean ratings (4.71 and 4.43 respectively) and the smallest standard deviations (0.64 and 0.86 respectively), which indicates substantial consensus about the importance of these two police activities.

Community policing activities, including neighborhood clean-ups ($\bar{x} = 2.07$, $s = 1.76$), removing graffiti ($\bar{x} = 2.83$, $s = 1.39$), meeting with business owners ($\bar{x} = 2.93$, $s = 1.14$) and removing abandoned cars ($\bar{x} = 2.97$, $s = 1.19$), were given ratings of importance below the mid-point of the scale (less than 3.0 on the five-point scale), and the fairly large standard deviations indicate less consensus on their importance.

Five community policing activities were given average ratings of importance between 3.62 and 3.89. These activities include: bike patrols ($\bar{x} = 3.62$, $s = 1.12$), assisting in after-school youth programs ($\bar{x} = 3.77$, $s = 1.07$), public presentations on drugs and crimes ($\bar{x} = 3.79$, $s = 1.03$), meeting with neighborhood groups ($\bar{x} = 3.83$, $s = 1.01$) and road blocks for speeders and drunk drivers ($\bar{x} = 3.89$, $s = 1.13$).

Multivariate Analysis

Ordinary least squares regression (OLS) was used to assess the effects of the independent variables on the ratings of the importance of community policing activities. A separate model was estimated for each of the 11 police activities rated by the respondents. The results of the regression analyses are presented in Table 3. Four of the independent or predictor variables were significant in the model for Remove cars. Higher ratings for this community policing duty were given when the respondent was female ($b = 0.23$), had a lower education level ($b = -0.19$), was unemployed

Table 2. Ratings of Community Policing Duties: Items and Frequency Distributions

Duty	Unimportant 1 n	%	2 n	%	Rating 3 n	%	4 n	%	Important 5 n	%	Mean	Standard deviation
Remove abandoned cars from neighborhood	53	10.9	120	24.7	173	35.0	67	13.8	73	15.0	2.97	1.19
Meet with neighborhood watch groups	10	2.1	30	6.2	141	29.3	148	30.7	153	31.7	3.83	1.01
Remove graffiti from public areas	119	24.4	81	16.6	131	26.8	75	15.4	82	16.8	2.83	1.39
Assist in neighborhood trash clean-up	229	47.0	101	20.7	89	18.3	29	6.0	39	8.0	2.07	1.26
Assist in after-school youth programs	16	3.3	37	7.7	135	28.0	145	30.1	149	30.9	3.77	1.07
Public presentations on drugs and crime	12	2.5	36	7.4	140	28.7	152	31.2	147	30.2	3.79	1.03
Meet business owners on regular basis	61	12.6	101	20.8	184	37.9	88	18.1	52	10.7	2.93	1.14
Provide bike patrols where requested	24	4.9	47	9.7	143	29.5	143	29.5	128	26.4	3.62	1.12
Investigate gang-related activities	3	0.6	4	0.8	21	4.3	76	15.5	385	78.7	4.71	0.64
Perform regular sweeps of high drug areas	7	1.4	11	2.2	44	8.9	125	25.8	297	61.4	4.43	0.86
Road blocks for speeders and drunk driving	24	4.9	30	6.2	108	22.3	135	27.8	188	38.8	3.89	1.13

(b = -0.23), did not have children (b = -0.30) and when the respondent did not report having an understanding of community policing (b = -0.13).

Only two predictors were significant for the Neighborhood watch model; respondent age (b = 0.10) and respondent education (b = -0.15). Older respondents gave higher ratings of importance than younger respondents, and the ratings of importance decreased as respondent education increased.

Three of the effects for the Remove graffiti model were significant: education (b = -0.20); employment (b = -0.43); and whether or not the respondent had heard of community policing (b = 0.09). Ratings of importance decreased as education increased and when respondents were employed. The importance of graffiti removal was rated higher when a respondent reported having heard of community policing.

The Trash clean-up model has two significant effects; ethnicity (b = 0.40) and education (b = -0.16). Non-white respondents rated having the police assisting with neighborhood trash clean-ups more importantly than white respondents, as did those respondents with less education.

In the Youth programs model, gender (b = -0.22), education (b = -0.13), and whether or not the respondent was a victim (b = -0.25) have significant effects. Compared to men, women gave higher ratings of the importance of having police assist with after-school programs. Respondents with less education rated this activity as being more important, and respondents who were crime victims rated this activity as being less important than non-victim respondents.

Three significant effects were found for the Presentations on drugs and crime model: education (b = -0.15), whether or not the respondent was a crime victim (b = -0.25), and whether or not the respondents rated crime as being the number one problem in their neighborhood. The rating of importance increases as education decreases and when the respondent is a victim. The rating of importance increases when respondents define crime as the number one problem in their neighborhood.

The pattern of significant effects is quite similar for the Meet with business owners model, with one exception. Education is non-significant, and age has a significant effect (b = 0.13). In comparison to younger respondents, older respondents rated this duty as being more important. Crime victims rated meeting with business owners as being less important than non-victims (b = -0.24) as did respondents who ranked crime as the number one problem in their neighborhood (b = -0.54).

Two significant effects were found for the Bike patrol model, income (b = -0.05) and ranking of crime problem (b = 0.47). The importance of this police duty increased as income decreased. The rating of importance increased when the respondent rated crime as being the number one problem in their neighborhood.

Only one of the predictor variables was significant for the Investigate gangs and Drug sweeps models. Female respondents rated these two activities as being more important than did their male counterparts (b = -0.24 and b = -0.23 respectively).

Table 3. OLS Regression Models for 11 Community-Oriented Policing Duties
(Unstandardized Regression Coefficients and Standard Errors)

Independent variable	Remove cars b (SE)	Neighborhood watch b (SE)	Remove graffiti b (SE)	Trash clean-up b (SE)	Youth programs b (SE)	Presentations on drugs and crime b (SE)	Meet with business owners b (SE)	Bike patrol b (SE)	Investigate gangs b (SE)	Drug sweeps b (SE)	Road blocks b (SE)
Ethnicity	0.27 (0.18)	0.16 (0.15)	0.22 (0.21)	0.40* (0.18)	0.21 (0.16)	0.16 (0.15)	-0.03 (0.17)	0.10 (0.17)	0.03 (0.08)	0.05 (0.13)	0.30 (0.17)
Gender	-0.23* (0.11)	-0.13 (0.10)	-0.13 (0.13)	-0.23 (0.12)	-0.22* (0.10)	-0.15 (0.10)	0.02 (0.11)	-0.08 (0.11)	-0.24* (0.05)	-0.23* (0.08)	-0.48* (0.11)
Age	0.06 (0.05)	0.10* (0.04)	-0.08 (0.06)	-0.03 (0.05)	0.05 (0.05)	0.08 (0.04)	0.13* (0.05)	0.02 (0.05)	-0.01 (0.02)	0.07* (0.04)	0.07 (0.05)
Education	-0.19* (0.06)	-0.15* (0.05)	-0.20* (0.06)	-0.16* (0.06)	-0.13* (0.05)	-0.15* (0.05)	-0.09 (0.05)	-0.03 (0.05)	-0.05 (0.02)	-0.07 (0.04)	-0.07 (0.05)
Employment	-0.23 (0.17)	-0.12 (0.14)	-0.43* (0.19)	-0.23 (0.17)	-0.01 (0.15)	0.00 (0.14)	-0.22 (0.16)	-0.14 (0.16)	0.02 (0.08)	-0.01 (0.12)	-0.47* (0.15)
Income	0.01 (0.02)	-0.01 (0.02)	-0.03 (0.02)	-0.02 (0.02)	-0.02 (0.02)	-0.02 (0.02)	-0.04 (0.02)	-0.05* (0.02)	0.00 (0.01)	0.01 (0.01)	0.02 (0.02)
Married	0.19 (0.14)	0.02 (0.12)	-0.16 (0.16)	-0.17 (0.14)	-0.09 (0.12)	-0.03 (0.12)	0.00 (0.13)	0.06 (0.13)	0.05 (0.06)	0.04 (0.10)	0.07 (0.13)
Child	-0.30* (0.13)	-0.08 (0.11)	-0.13 (0.15)	0.02 (0.13)	0.10 (0.12)	0.05 (0.11)	0.14 (0.13)	0.14 (0.12)	-0.06 (0.06)	0.17 (0.09)	0.16 (0.12)
Victim	-0.17 (0.12)	-0.07 (0.10)	-0.13 (0.14)	-0.03 (0.12)	-0.27* (0.11)	-0.25* (0.10)	-0.24* (0.12)	-0.13 (0.11)	0.04 (0.05)	-0.09 (0.08)	-0.02 (0.11)
Problem	0.21 (0.20)	0.23 (0.17)	-0.11 (0.23)	-0.03 (0.21)	0.28 (0.18)	0.34* (0.17)	-0.54* (0.20)	0.47* (0.19)	0.07 (0.09)	0.22 (0.14)	0.27 (0.19)
Only police can control crime	-0.09 (0.06)	0.03 (0.05)	-0.11 (0.07)	-0.10 (0.06)	-0.02 (0.05)	0.02 (0.05)	-0.00 (0.06)	-0.09 (0.06)	0.04 (0.03)	0.07 (0.04)	-0.00 (0.06)
I can make Omaha safer	0.05 (0.07)	-0.02 (0.06)	0.17 (0.09)	-0.04 (0.08)	-0.01 (0.07)	-0.04 (0.06)	-0.06 (0.07)	-0.09 (0.07)	0.03 (0.03)	0.01 (0.05)	-0.09 (0.07)
Heard of community policing	0.08 (0.07)	-0.10 (0.06)	0.09* (0.01)	0.02 (0.07)	-0.07 (0.06)	-0.01 (0.06)	-0.09 (0.07)	0.01 (0.07)	0.01 (0.03)	-0.03 (0.05)	-0.03 (0.07)
Understand community policing	-0.13* (0.07)	-0.02 (0.06)	-0.15 (0.08)	-0.09 (0.07)	-0.08 (0.06)	-0.05 (0.06)	-0.04 (0.06)	-0.11 (0.06)	-0.05 (0.03)	-0.05 (0.05)	0.01 (0.06)
R^2	0.14	0.09	0.14	0.10	0.09	0.10	0.11	0.09	0.08	0.08	0.13

Note: $p \leq 0.05$

Gender (b = -0.48) and employment (b = -0.47) had significant effects in the Road blocks model. The rating of importance of this activity increased when respondents were female and when they were not in the labor force.

Individually, each of the 11 models explains between 8 and 14 percent of the variation in respondents ratings of importance. Gender and education were the two variables that most consistently exhibited significant effects across the 11 models.

Discussion

In general, these findings show that "preventive" community policing activities, or those usually considered as having an indirect effect on crime, are regarded by the community as being less important than "enforcement " activities, or policing activities thought of as having a more direct effect on crime. Recall that mean ratings of the importance of police activities were lowest for "broken windows-like" community policing activities such as neighborhood clean-ups and graffiti removal, and highest for proactive enforcement activities such as investigating gang activities and conducting drug sweeps. Both the univariate and regression analyses indicate that there is considerable consensus about the importance of the more proactive enforcement activities. The average ratings of the importance of investigating gang activities and performing drug sweeps were 4.7 and 4.4 respectively, where the highest possible rating could have been 5.0. The magnitude of these averages, along with the fairly small standard deviations for these activities, suggests that most respondents, regardless of personal characteristics and awareness and knowledge of community policing, believe that these are important activities for the police to perform.

The most consistent exception to this pattern of consensus is reflected in the significant effects of gender and education in the 11 regression models. Gender had a significant effect in five of the 11 models: Remove cars, Youth programs, Investigate gangs, Drug sweeps and Road blocks. This indicates that female respondents differed from male respondents in that they rated a combination of "prevention" and "enforcement" policing activities as being more important. On the other hand, gender did not have a significant effect in six of the models: Neighborhood watch, Remove graffiti, Trash clean-up, Presentations on drugs and crime, and Meet with business owners.

One of the most interesting findings has to do with the educational achievement of the respondent, a variable that had a significant effect in six of the 11 regression models, each of which included a "prevention" community policing duty as the dependent variable (Remove cars, Neighborhood watch, Remove graffiti, Trash clean-up, Youth programs and Presentation on drugs and crime). The relationship between education and ratings of importance is inverse in these six models. Respondents with less education rate these activities as being more important; conversely, respondents with more education rate them as being less important.

Aside from gender and education, few significant effects of predictor variables were found. Somewhat surprising is that only one significant effect was found for the ethnicity/race variable, with non-whites giving trash clean-ups higher ratings of importance. This could reflect the actual conditions of the neighborhoods in which the respondents live. Trash may well be more of a neighborhood problem for non-whites than whites. However, the more important implication of this finding has to do with the lack of a significant effect in the other ten models: there do not appear to be major differences between non-whites and whites, in the ratings of the importance of community policing activities.

The finding that respondents without children rated the importance of removing abandoned cars as being more important than did respondents with children runs contrary to what we expected to find and is somewhat surprising. We expected that in comparison to respondents without children, those with children would be concerned about the impact of neighborhood conditions on the safety of their children and would see removing abandoned cars as an important community policing activity.

Whether or not the respondent was a crime victim had a significant effect on ratings for three of the models (Youth programs, Presentations on drugs and crime, and Meet with business owners). It is interesting that crime victims rated these three activities as being less important than did non-victims. This may provide some indication that those who experience crime as a victim do not view these activities has being efficacious in addressing crime. In other words, they may not believe that their victimization would have been prevented if the police had been engaging in these types of activities.

The findings related to perceptions of the importance of crime as a problem in the neighborhood are difficult to interpret. Rating crime as the number one problem in the neighborhood was significant for three of the models (Presentation on drugs and crime, Meet with business owners and Bike patrol), however, the pattern is inconsistent. Respondents who rated crime as the number one problem in their neighborhood tended to rate police involvement in presentations on drugs and crime, and the use of bike patrols as being important, but they rated meeting with business owners as being less important than did the other respondents.

The predictor variables related to awareness and knowledge of community policing exhibited surprisingly few significant effects. Respondents who reported understanding community policing rated police involvement in removing abandoned cars as being more important, and those respondents who reported that they had heard of community policing were more likely to rate graffiti removal as being more important.

No significant effects were found in any of the models for the two variables related to police and citizen role in controlling crime. We expected that respondents who agreed that only the police can control crime would differ significantly in their ratings of the importance of community policing activities in comparison to respondents who disagreed with such a claim. We also expected that respondents who agreed that citizens could help to make the community a safer place would also rate community policing activities as being more important. However, as the analysis indicates, respondent beliefs about who can affect crime is not related to their views about the importance of various community policing activities.

As was noted earlier, the purpose of this study was to gauge citizen consensus about the importance of community policing activities and identify factors which influence that consensus. Our findings indicate that there appears to be more consensus about the importance of activities which emphasize enforcement rather than prevention. The only respondent characteristic that had a significant effect on the rating of these types of activities was gender: women rated them as being more important than men. Overall, few of the predictor variables included in this study had significant effects on the ratings of importance of any of the community policing activities, prevention or enforcement. In sum, it appears that there is considerable consensus among citizens with differing social and demographic characteristics that some community policing activities are important and some are not.

The lack of significant effects of the knowledge and awareness of community policing variables on the ratings of importance of community policing activities may be the result of citizens' lack of understanding of the basic assumptions about the causal pathways of community policing. Even though citizens are aware of community policing, and even if they report an understanding of it, they may not see the same connections between "broken windows" and crime causation that academic and professional proponents of community policing see. Instead, community policing activities that indirectly impact on crime may not be understood or seen as efficacious. One implication of this is that promoters and implementers of community policing may need to focus more on educating the public about community policing "theory" so as to develop a better understanding of how and why community policing is supposed to affect crime. It may be easy for the public to understand how gang investigations, drugs sweeps and bike patrols can directly impact on crime, but the processes whereby neighborhood trash clean-ups and graffiti removal efforts reduce crime are probably much more difficult to understand.

The analysis reported here uses only one neighborhood specific variable, whether or not respondents rated crime as the number one problem in their neighborhood. Better measures of neighborhood variables, especially a measure that locates respondents in their immediate neighborhoods, might link location with preferences for community policing activities. It may be that respondents residing in neighborhoods most in need of community policing activities, those that reduce disorder and its consequences and promote crime prevention, have a better understanding of how it can work and its potential benefits. However, in many communities, implementing community policing is not just a matter of selling its theory and philosophy to those residing in disorderly and high-crime neighborhoods, but requires gaining support for its implementation from citizens residing in all sorts of neighborhoods. In many communities, tax payers from relatively crime-free neighborhoods will play a more important role in extracting strategic decisions by city councils and police departments to engage in community policing than citizens from those neighborhoods most directly affected by community policing.

The implication that public understanding of community policing will enhance public support for its practice is not supported by the survey data reported here. While much attention has been paid to the perceptions of the police and their attitudes toward community policing activities (Green and Decker, 1989) less attention has been given to the education and inclusion of citizens in their assessment of community policing. As a result, much of the community policing movement has been focused on police reform rather than on citizen education and involvement. Friedman (1994, p. 263) poignantly illustrates this point: that while police scholars and professionals have been busy meeting at conferences, exchanging ideas about community policing in academic journals and hiring one another as consultants, little opportunity has been afforded to citizens for participating in the local dialogue concerning which duties they would like their police to perform. However, one must keep in mind that citizens have been excluded from such a dialogue for the past 50 years, in which the only relationship between the police and the public has been one of the public being expected to be relatively passive recipients of police services (Kelling and Moore, 1988).

Future studies should continue to explore the link between the public's knowledge and understanding of community policing and their assessment of community policing tactics and strategy. However, other factors such as the impact of citizen-held political ideology on the assessment of community policing should be incorporated into these studies. Studies that permit cross-community comparisons, where the level of information about community policing that is available to citizens varies, should also help to advance our understanding of the role that citizen knowledge of community policing plays in shaping assessments of its importance and preferences for its implementation.

Note

[1] For a thoughtful discussion of the different approaches to community policing and some of the confusion surrounding policing strategies see Hoover and Caeti (1994). By their definition, the activities rated in this study would include a combination of community policing, problem-oriented policing and crime specific policing activities. The important point is that they are not usually thought of as activities carried out under the traditional professional model or incident driven policing.

References

Alpert, G. and Dunham, R. (1986). "Community policing." *Journal of Police Science and Administration*, Vol. 14, No. 3, pp. 212–22.

Alpert, G. and Dunham, R. (1988). *Policing Multi-ethnic Neighborhoods*. New York: Greenwood Press.

Bayley, D. (1994). *Police for the Future*. New York: Oxford Press.

Bureau of Justice Assistance (1994). *Understanding Community Policing: A Framework for Action.* Washington, DC: U.S. Government Printing Office.

Eck, J. and Rosenbaum, D. (1994). "The new police order: Effectiveness, equity, and efficiency in community policing." In *The Challenges of Community Policing*, edited by D. Rosenbaum. Thousand Oaks, CA: Sage.

Flanagan, T. (1985). "Consumer perspectives on police operational strategy." *Journal of Police Science and Administration*, Vol. 13, No. 1, pp. 10–21.

Friedman, W. (1994). "The community role in community policing." In *The Challenges of Community Policing: Testing the Premises*, edited by D. P. Rosenbaum, pp. 2623–69. Thousand Oaks, CA: Sage.

Goldstein, H. (1990). *Problem-oriented Policing.* New York: McGraw-Hill.

Green, J. and Decker, S. (1989). "Police and community perceptions of the community role in policing: The Philadelphia experience." *The Howard Journal*, Vol. 28, No. 2, pp. 105–23.

Green, J. and Mastrofski, S. (1988). *Community Policing: Rhetoric or Reality.* New York: Praeger.

Grinc, R. (1994). "'Angels in marble': Problems in stimulating community involvement in community policing." *Crime and Delinquency*, Vol. 40, No. 3, pp. 437–68.

Hoover, L. and Caeti, T. (1994). "Crime specific policing in Houston." *Telemasp Bulletin*, Vol. 1 No. 9, December.

Kelling, G. L. and Moore, M. H. (1988). "The evolving strategy of policing." *Perspectives on Policing*, Vol. 4.

Maguire, E. (1995). "Community policing and structural change in large municipal police organizations," unpublished manuscript, the University of Nebraska at Omaha.

Marenin, O. (1989). "The utility of community needs surveys in community policing." *Police Studies*, Vol. 12, No. 2, pp. 73–81.

Murphy, C. (1988). "Community problems, problem communities and community policing in Toronto." *Journal of Research in Crime and Delinquency*, Vol. 25, No. 4, pp. 392–410.

National Institute of Justice (1995). "Community policing strategies." *Research Preview*, Washington, DC: U.S. Government Printing Office.

Rosenbaum, D. (1994). *The Challenge of Community Policing.* Thousand Oaks, CA: Sage.

Sadd, S. and Grinc, R. (1994). "Innovative neighborhood oriented policing: An evaluation of community policing programs in eight cities." In *The Challenge of Community Policing,* edited by D. Rosenbaum. Thousand Oaks, CA: Sage.

Skogan, W. (1994). "The impact of community policing on neighborhood residents: Across-site analysis." In *The Challenge of Community Policing,* edited by D. Rosenbaum. Thousand Oaks, CA: Sage.

Skolnick, J. and Bayley, D. (1986). *The New Thin Line: Police Innovation in Six American Cities.* New York: Free Press.

Tien, J. and Rich, T. (1994). "The Hartford COMPASS program: Experiences with a weed and seed-related program." In *The Challenge of Community Policing,* edited by D. Rosenbaum. Thousand Oaks, CA: Sage.

Uchida, C. and Forst, B. (1994). "Controlling street-level drug trafficking: professional and community policing approaches." In *Drugs and Crime*, edited by D. Mackenzie and C. Uchida. Thousand Oaks, CA: Sage.

Uchida, C., Forst, B. and Annon, S. (1992). "Modern policing and the control of illegal drugs: Testing new strategies in two American cities." *Department of Justice*, Washington, DC: U.S. Government Printing Office.

Walker, S. (1992). *The Police in America*. New York: McGraw-Hill.

Webb, V. and Graham, N. (1994). "Citizen ratings of the importance of selected police duties," paper presented at the annual meeting of American Criminology Society, 7–12, November 1994, Miami, FL.

Webb, V., Gartin, P. and Katz, C. (1994). "Omahans' views on community policing and the importance of different policing activities." In *Omaha Conditions Survey: 1994*, Center for Public Affairs Research, University of Nebraska at Omaha.

Weisburd, D. and McElroy, J. (1988). "Enacting the CPO role: Findings from the New York pilot program in community policing." In *Community Policing: Rhetoric or Reality*, edited by J. Green and S. Mastrofski, pp. 89–101. New York: Praeger.

Wilson, J. and Kelling, G. (1982). "Broken windows: The police and neighborhood safety." *Atlantic Monthly*, Vol. 249, pp. 29–38.

Index